GW01271694

# Handbook of Ethical Education

The *Handbook of Ethical Educational Leadership* brings together an array of key authors to provide comprehensive coverage of the field of ethical educational leadership. This important volume describes contemporary educational issues that necessitate the practice of ethical leadership, reviews current theory and research-informed practices, and explores a coherent framework for how ethical educational leadership can be achieved. With chapters from leading authors and researchers from around the world, each author contributes to a discussion of current thinking and an analysis of the field of ethical educational leadership. Coverage includes professionalism, educational purpose, social justice, multiculturalism, sustainability, empathy and caring, organizational culture, moral development, motivation, integrity, values, and decision making. Providing practical, philosophical, and experiential insights into the field, The *Handbook of Ethical Educational Leadership* is an essential resource for the study of ethical leadership.

**Christopher M. Branson** is Professor of Educational Leadership at the University of Waikato, New Zealand. He is Executive Director of the UCEA Center for the Study of Leadership and Ethics.

**Steven Jay Gross** is Professor of Educational Administration at Temple University. He is also Founding Director of the New DEEL (Democratic Ethical Educational Leadership) Community Network.

# Handbook of Ethical Educational Leadership

Edited by
**Christopher M. Branson and
Steven Jay Gross**

Routledge
Taylor & Francis Group

NEW YORK AND LONDON

First published 2014
by Routledge
711 Third Avenue, New York, NY 10017

and by Routledge
2 Park Square, Milton Park, Abingdon, Oxon OX14 4RN

*Routledge is an imprint of the Taylor & Francis Group, an informa business*

© 2014 Taylor & Francis

*Library of Congress Cataloging-in-Publication Data*

Handbook of ethical educational leadership / edited by Christopher M. Branson, Steven Jay Gross. — First edition.
   pages cm
   Includes bibliographical references and index.
 1.  Educational leadership—Moral and ethical aspects.  2.  Education—Moral and ethical aspects.   I. Branson, Christopher M.   II. Gross, Steven Jay.
   LB2806.H3 2014
   371.2′011—dc23
   2013046862

ISBN: 978-0-415-85390-3 (hbk)
ISBN: 978-0-415-85391-0 (pbk)
ISBN: 978-0-203-74758-2 (ebk)

Typeset in Minion
by Apex CoVantage, LLC

MIX
Paper from
responsible sources
FSC
www.fsc.org   FSC® C013604

Printed and bound by CPI Group (UK) Ltd, Croydon, CR0 4YY

# CONTENTS

# FIGURES

# TABLES

# 1

## INTRODUCTION: WHY ETHICAL EDUCATIONAL LEADERSHIP?

CHRISTOPHER M. BRANSON AND STEVEN JAY GROSS

Clearly the 2008 global financial crisis brought the concept of ethical leadership into the international spotlight. Now, after 5 years, has the world really recovered from the physical and psychological devastation caused by the unethical practices of a few individuals and institutions within the banking and investment world? In reality, this incident was only one of a growing number of very serious unethical activities in the political, industrial, religious, media, and education spheres. Within the political sphere there appears to be a growing number of coalition governments as voters become disillusioned and skeptical about whom to support. On the industrial scene, shortsighted leadership decisions are thought to be behind the catastrophic oil pollution incident in the Gulf of Mexico and mining disaster in New Zealand that led to the death of 39 miners. Religious leaders can be seen as civil militia leaders in Ireland, the Middle East, and North Africa or to have concealed unacceptable behavior by some of their ministers. England has witnessed alleged phone hacking by media leaders. Educational leaders have been found to have deliberately mismanaged formal student assessment procedures, while others have misappropriated their institution's financial and/or physical resources. Unethical leadership has no boundaries. Indeed, the responsibility of leadership is a double-edged sword because it not only provides the opportunity for doing good but also simultaneously provides the opportunity and temptation for advancing one's own needs, most often at the expense of the needs of others.

### WHAT MAKES LEADERSHIP ETHICAL?

Thus, it is understandable why our more contemporary definitions of leadership include a responsibility for achieving an outcome that meets the needs of all. Rost (1993) argues that leadership is "an influence relationship among leaders and collaborators who intend real changes that reflect their mutual purposes" (p. 99). Similarly,

Burns (1978, 2010) proposes that "leaders address themselves to followers' wants, needs, and other motivations, as well as their own, and thus they serve as an *independent force in changing the makeup of the followers' motive base through gratifying their motives*" (p. 20, italics in original). Hamel (2007) extends this view by positing that "leadership is not defined by the exercise of power, but by the capacity to increase the sense of power among those who are led. The most essential work of a leader is to create more leaders" (p. 186). Together, these views draw attention to the fundamentally distinguishing feature of leadership as being leaders' concern for the best interests of those they are leading. Was this the case with the financial leaders at the heart of the global financial crisis?

Today, while the US economy appears to be recovering from the effects of the 2008 financial catastrophe, the same cannot be said for many other countries, such as Ireland, Greece, Iceland, Spain, and Italy, to name but a few. Moreover, although national economies may have recovered, the same cannot be said for the millions of individuals and families who lost their homes during this crisis. It is far too simplistic to look at the mega-picture of national or international economics and feel comfortable and pleased—but the micro-picture of individual and family financial circumstances for millions of people still looks bleak and miserable.

Even more regrettable is the knowledge that the unethical practices that caused the global financial crisis were essentially the same that were used in the downfall of Enron in 2001. However, in that case the devastation was largely restricted to the US. What this repeated experience shows, though, is that corporate compliance policies and laws do not seem to be having the desired influence on eradicating unethical leadership. The US designed new financial policies and practices following the Enron collapse, yet these new rules and laws did not prevent the same practices being used prior to the global financial crisis. Moreover, other than in Iceland, no leading financier or politician was held legally accountable for his or her unscrupulous role in causing the economic collapse that saw millions of people around the world lose their homes, employment, lifestyle, and dignity.

Thus, it is not surprising to read that public trust in organizations is now at an all-time low. Today, perhaps more so than ever before, people want leaders with ethical codes that are deep, innate, and instinctive, so that they will not lose direction in the face of uncertainty or external pressure. There is now a clear expectation that our leaders will always act justly and rightly and will promote good and not harm. Today our leaders are expected to demonstrate ethical judgment by being accountable to those they serve and to begin to restore social trust.

## THERE'S MORE TO ETHICAL LEADERSHIP THAN GOOD INTENTIONS

What is apparent also from the very limited impact of these new rules and regulations is that the desire for ethical leadership does not translate, necessarily, into actually having ethical leadership. Ethical leadership is an achievement and not a given. A leader has to strive to become an ethical leader, as it is unlikely to happen automatically. Ethical behavior is not a natural outcome, particularly for leaders, even under the threat of punitive accountabilities. Leaders need to learn how to be ethical and to become diligently committed to acting ethically. Such action emanates from the very being of the leader and not from legislation or from a role statement or from policy guidelines.

## EDUCATION AND ETHICAL LEADERSHIP

But, really, *is the practice of ethical leadership an issue for educational leaders?* Certainly, the need for educational leaders to abide by legal obligations and proper fiscal practices is unequivocal, and it is only on very few occasions that individual school principals have not met this mandatory expectation. But, is there more to the practice of ethical leadership by an educational leader than these obligatory expectations? The very thought of entertaining such a simplistic perspective emphasizes the critically important need to see the fundamental place of ethical leadership in the role of today's school principal.

As more and more is being asked of educational leaders, choosing what to attend to and what to put off or overlook is an ethical decision. Each person can be influenced by personal preferences, and our minds are very adept at defending these perspectives. Thus, any choice by an educational leader about where to concentrate his or her interests and energy must be based on common good and not self-interest—it must be an ethical choice and not for personal benefit.

Also, the learning environment within an educational setting must be in the best interests of each student's future and not what maintains, necessarily, the professional and personal interests and comfort of the teachers. This means that change is a constant companion for everyone working in an educational organization. We all know that leading change, which begins in the role of the leader, is fraught with difficult challenges. But to ignore the future needs of the students, or to ignore the need to change because of their challenges, is an unethical leadership decision.

Into these ethical dilemmas for the educational leader, add issues associated with the need for an authentic commitment to properly attending to cultural needs, family needs, and local community needs within the educational setting. There is also the need by educational leaders to lead their educational communities to appropriately respond to political initiatives that may or may not benefit the students and the organization.

Not least, of course, is the need for educational leaders to ensure that they make proper choices about their own life balance, whereby neither work nor family/leisure gain an inappropriate hold or prominence on their lifestyle.

Every choice an educational leader makes is based on values that are either known or unknown, acknowledged or unacknowledged, by them. The less known or acknowledged the values that direct a choice, the more likely is it that an unethical decision will be made, particularly in very unusual, complex, and challenging situations. More and more today, educational leaders are being regularly confronted by unusual, complex, and challenging situations, which demand that they make choices. Indeed, ethical leadership is part and parcel of educational leadership today. Perhaps the most important choice that an educational leader has to make is to answer the question *Do I want to be an ethical leader?*

## WHY A HANDBOOK FOR ETHICAL EDUCATIONAL LEADERSHIP?

Hence, this handbook is a practical and philosophical response to this crucially important situation that now confronts every educational leader. But while it is a tangible response to a very contemporary issue, it is a response that has been a long time in the making. This handbook of ethical educational leadership draws upon an array of literature from authors directly or indirectly associated with the Center for the Study of Leadership and Ethics (CSLE), which is a program center affiliated with the University Council for Educational Administration (UCEA). Consequently, it is only proper to wholeheartedly and unreservedly acknowledge that the capacity to collate this handbook and, thereby, to be able to provide a coherent and comprehensive overview of the nature and practice of ethical educational leadership is due in no small way to the work and inspiration of Dr. Paul Begley, who established the CSLE in June 1996 and served as its executive director until his retirement in June 2011.

At the time of its establishment, the CSLE was housed in the Department of Theory and Policy Studies at the Ontario Institute for Studies in Education at the University of Toronto. During the early years, the CSLE was operated in partnership with the University of Virginia. From 1996 to 2001, Paul Begley and Margaret Grogan (now dean at Claremont Graduate School in California) codirected the Center. In 2003, the CSLE was relocated to Penn State University, and the University of Virginia ceased its formal involvement as a sponsor of the center. However, Professor Eric Bredo of the University of Virginia continued on as a member of the Center's board of trustees.

Specific to the publication of this handbook was the tireless work and invaluable contribution of Paul Begley toward the ongoing development of academic research, knowledge, and practices associated with the role of ethics and values in leadership. Through building on the foundational principles of Emeritus Professor Christopher Hodgkinson, Paul Begley established a wide network of highly credible, unquestionably dedicated, and eminently enthusiastic protagonists. Together, these ethical leadership pioneers established the annual Values and Leadership International Conference, as well as the journals *Values and Ethics in Educational Administration* and the *Journal of Authentic Leadership in Education*. Each of these initiatives not only has provided a unique avenue for sharing and, thereby, advancing knowledge and understanding about ethical leadership, but has also attracted the attention of many more international researchers and writers to the study of ethical leadership.

In early 2009, a proposal was tabled at a business meeting of the board of trustees to reorganize the governance structure of the Center in anticipation of Paul Begley's return to Canada and appointment to the faculty of Nipissing University. The intent of the new governance structure was to ensure the continuation of the Center's work, reconfirm Paul Begley as executive director for a term of 3 years, and formally incorporate within the CSLE seven research centers located at universities in five countries: Australia, Canada, Hong Kong, Sweden, and the United States. Faculty and students associated with each of these institutions had been long-standing and active contributors to the CSLE for many years, and in many respects the new governance structure formally recognized their critical role as associates of the CSLE. In June 2011, upon the retirement of Paul Begley, Dr. Christopher Branson was elected by the board of trustees as executive director and took the duties of executive director to the University of Waikato in Hamilton, New Zealand.

Specific to the genesis of this handbook were the editors' experiences and perceptions during the 2011 UCEA convention in Pittsburgh. Here it was noted by both editors that there was an unexpectedly high number of presenters concerned with the issue of ethical leadership. However, many appeared unfamiliar with the range and extent of available research-informed literature that had already been generated through the CSLE. Consequently, the ethical leadership research being undertaken was not as well developed as it could otherwise have been. From these observations, the crucial need to more widely distribute the breadth of existing ethical leadership literature, as captured in this handbook, became obvious.

## AN OVERVIEW OF THE HANDBOOK

### Part I

To this end, this handbook is organized into three parts. Simply stated, the first part, "Issues and Perspectives," describes *why* ethical leadership has become a critically important component of contemporary educational leadership. Each chapter in this part focuses on comprehensively describing a specific issue inherent within educational leadership today and extends this description to show how this issue mandates a commitment to the practice of authentic ethical leadership. Moreover, these Part I writers confront foundational questions surrounding ethical educational leadership. These include explorations into the nature of our profession and its connection to leadership and to ethics (Kristinsson, Shields, Starratt), contextual questions that impact ethical educational leadership (Gross, Bottery, McNae), and dispositions needed in leadership that aims to be ethical (Walker & Qian; Kuusilehto-Awale, Holte).

### Part II

Having solidly and unequivocally established the philosophical and professional reasons that ethics must be an integral part of contemporary educational leadership, Part II, "Developing Ethical Educational Leadership," describes *how* ethical educational leadership can be developed by any leader with a willingness to learn. The prevalence of unethical leadership across diverse contexts clearly indicates that the development of ethical educational leadership is not an automatic outcome for every leader. Indeed, as you will read in this handbook, the literature suggests quite the contrary—consistent and deliberate ethical leadership is more often the exception than the norm. People, generally, struggle with trying to act ethically, and becoming a leader does not, in itself, change this natural propensity. Thus, it is nonsensical to raise the expectation that educational leaders need to be ethical without providing a clear means for helping each leader to achieve this desirable outcome. Part II addresses this essential responsibility because it turns our attention toward personal qualities and skills needed for ethical educational leadership. Overall, this essential responsibility is informed by Nancy Tuana's widely acclaimed framework for the development of ethical leadership, which is substantially described in the first chapter of Part II. Then, each subsequent chapter focuses on a particular component of Tuana's framework so as to not only deepen the reader's understanding of it but also provide research-informed practical ways for personally developing the component. Here will be found practical ways for developing ethical sensitivity by reflecting on one's values (Notman, Branson), for further refining techniques and skills in ethical decision making (Shapiro, Stefkovich, & Gutierrez; Cranston, Ehrich, & Kimber; Gross; Branson), and for examining the nature and practice of ethical motivation (Bezzina & Tuana, Branson).

## Part III

Putting the ideal into reality can be problematic and therefore off-putting when one first tries something new, and this is a likely outcome for something as challenging and demanding as striving to establish ethical educational leadership. Thus Part III, "Examples From the Field," offers readers examples of *what* has already been achieved in this regard. In this way, this part of the handbook seeks to afford both clarity and inspiration. Simply, Part III connects theory to practice. Leading with moral purpose is explored (Leonard, Schilling, & Normore; Burford & Bezzina), along with the imperative of having to understand the implications of a leader's integrity (Frick & Covaleskie). Leadership preparation and its implications in Canada (Langlois & Lapointe), Turkey (Aksu & Kasalak), and the increasingly multicultural world of Swedish schools (Johansson & Norberg) provide specific descriptions of approaches to the development of ethical leadership within very different settings. Finally we explore a direction that one group has taken when their ethical code requires them to act in opposition to current educational policy (Gross & Shapiro).

## SUMMARY

Although each chapter, and each part, provides important and unequaled theoretical and practical insight into the phenomenon of ethical educational leadership, it is the compilation of all of these chapters and parts that provides the essential learning. In a real sense, this handbook has deconstructed the totality of the phenomenon. In order to provide a never-seen-before insight into the nature and practice of ethical educational leadership, this handbook has differentiated the phenomenon into its distinguishable imperatives, components, and practicalities. But the comprehensive manner by which this has been achieved is both a benefit and a bane. Each chapter and each part can be read and treated in isolation and separated from the rest of the handbook. While such an approach may well provide some good, it won't necessarily lead to authentic ethical leadership. It is only when all imperatives, components, and practicalities provided throughout the handbook are considered and embraced that it becomes most likely that ethical educational leadership will eventuate. As you will discover as you read this handbook, ethical educational leadership is a complex, multifaceted, and demanding activity, which requires a holistic, and not a differential, commitment to be truly employed.

## REFERENCES

Burns, J. M. (1978). *Leadership.* New York: HarperCollins.
Burns, J. M. (2010). *Leadership.* New York: HarperCollins.
Hamel, G. (2007). *The future of management.* Boston: Harvard Business School Press.
Rost, J. C. (1993). *Leadership for the twenty-first century* (2nd ed.). Westport, CT: Praeger.

# I

## Issues and Perspectives

1

Issues and Perspectives

# 2

## THE ESSENCE OF PROFESSIONALISM

### SIGURÐUR KRISTINSSON

Educational leaders are faced with difficult and exciting challenges every day. They are responsible for the effective functioning of an institution or division and are accountable to a variety of stakeholders with different interests and priorities, including staff, students, parents, community, and government. They must constantly ask themselves what they ultimately hope to achieve and, relatedly, what values they hope to promote and serve.

Many educational leaders are school principals, but educational leadership is not restricted to that occupational role. According to Starratt (2005), educational leadership may be manifested in a person's conduct as a human being, citizen/public servant, educator, and administrator/manager, and all of these roles or "levels of ethical enactment" come into play when a school principal acts as an educational leader. Leadership has been defined as a form of social influence bringing people together to work toward a common goal (Chemers, 1997). Such influence may or may not be exerted through a position of formal authority and is not to be confused with the narrower role of the administrator/manager. But what are the common goals with which educational leaders should be concerned, and is there a distinct body of knowledge or expertise upon which educational leaders may draw in their leadership efforts? What ethical and epistemological grounds might we have for regarding educational leadership as a distinct profession?

These are examples of interesting conceptual and normative questions raised by the notion of educational leadership. The main objective of this chapter is to argue that educational leadership is an essentially ethical professional enterprise. The main focus will not be on the epistemological side of that coin but rather on the ethical one. More specifically, the aim is to establish that educational leadership should not be characterized as an activity with an ethical aspect but rather as an inherently ethical activity. Following a clarification of the meaning of that somewhat cryptic statement, the discussion moves on to defend two claims: first, that educational leadership is a professional activity; second, that all professional activities are essentially ethical. Together, these two claims entail that educational leadership is an essentially ethical professional activity. The chapter closes with a discussion of some consequences of this conclusion for the practice of educational leadership and the training of educational leaders.

## EXPLAINING THE CLAIM

What does it mean to say that educational leadership is an essentially ethical enterprise rather than merely an activity with an ethical aspect? To say that an activity has an ethical aspect can be explained by saying that the activity may incidentally involve circumstances where moral questions arise, even though the activity as such may be fully described and understood independently of moral concepts. A good example of an activity that can be described independently of moral concepts is that of baking a cake. When recipes tell us to pour a "good" amount of this and that, or shake something "well," or make sure the temperature is "right," these terms are certainly not used in their moral senses. No moral purposes need to be mentioned in a recipe for a cake, and no moral concepts are used; we can quite easily describe and understand this activity without such concepts. Yet, as with any other human activity, the process of actually baking a cake may incidentally confront the baker with moral questions. He might consider whether to steal some of the ingredients, share the completed cake with others, adjust the recipe to make it more healthy (or less unhealthy) for those who will be eating it, or indeed be spending time baking a cake when he had perhaps promised not to or when he could instead perhaps be making a much more positive difference in the world. In other words, the activity of baking a particular cake on a particular occasion may reasonably prompt moral deliberation and even critical reflection by the baker and be subject to moral assessment by him or others, as regards his motives, the manner in which he proceeds, and the very fact that he is baking the cake. Nevertheless, the activity of baking a cake is not as such an inherently ethical activity because it can be described and understood independently of moral terms.

By contrast, other activities are essentially ethical, because they cannot be described or understood without reference to moral purposes and moral concepts. Consider charity and deception, for example. To describe an act as either charitable or deceitful is already to use a moral term. To take a slightly more complex example, consider the activity of ensuring that a patient, or a research participant, has given informed consent to a particular treatment or participation. Although less obviously than in the cases of charity and deceit, this activity cannot be fully understood without reference to moral purposes and concepts (Kristinsson & Árnason, 2007). To describe fully what is involved in giving or receiving informed consent, we must answer questions like the following: What information must be provided? How much information is sufficient? Under what circumstances and by whom should the information be provided and consent requested? To answer such questions, we implicitly or explicitly rely on a normative context where autonomy, rational reflection, and free choice are considered morally desirable and coercion, manipulation, and deception morally undesirable. In this way, the activity of soliciting informed consent from patients or research participants is essentially ethical in a way that baking a cake is not.

My contention that educational leadership is an essentially ethical enterprise can now be expressed by saying that it is more like soliciting informed consent than it is like baking a cake. Unlike baking, educational leadership cannot be fully characterized without reference to moral purposes and moral concepts. Just like the activity of soliciting informed consent, it has an internal action-guiding logic that necessarily involves ethical evaluative terms that are used to express educational values and disvalues. Ethical evaluation is therefore necessary in order to define the boundaries of educational leadership—that is, in order to know when an activity counts as educational leadership and when it doesn't—and by implication to know what is required of a person who wishes to exercise educational leadership.

## THE ARGUMENT

My basic argument for this claim takes the form of a simple syllogism:

> All professions are essentially ethical (premise 1).
> Educational leadership is a profession (premise 2).
> Therefore, educational leadership is essentially ethical (conclusion).

This is obviously a valid argument, i.e., the conclusion follows necessarily from the premises. To accept the premises and reject the conclusion would involve a contradiction. What needs to be argued, then, is that both premises are in fact true and the argument, therefore, sound.

The second premise should be accepted without much argument. Educational leadership may reasonably be regarded as a specialized branch of the broad profession of education, a branch with a distinctive role or purpose on the one hand and a base of specialized knowledge and skills on the other. Other educational professionals include teachers, educational researchers, and specialists working within administrative government structures at municipal and state levels. It may, of course, be debated whether educational leadership involves a distinct form of professionalism, different from that of teachers, for example, or whether education as a whole should count as a single, uniform profession based on its common role and specialized knowledge. That question need not concern us here, however, because even if education were to be regarded as a single, undivided profession, educational leadership would certainly have to be seen as at least a specific instance of the profession of education, and thus a professional enterprise. Educational leaders must certainly be seen as professionals, regardless of whether their profession is regarded as independent or, instead, as a specialization within the more general profession of education.

Assuming, then, that educational leadership is a profession, let us turn to the first premise, according to which all professions are essentially ethical. Why should we agree? Aren't lawyers the stereotypical and obvious counterexample?

## PROFESSIONS AND PROFESSIONALISM

A profession consists of a collective body of professionals in an occupation for which they profess to be qualified and prepared to serve. Professions are customarily taken to have structural characteristics that include licensing, professional organization, a code of ethics, monopoly, self-regulation, and autonomy. They are also taken to have essential characteristics that include higher education, intellectual orientation, and important service or social functions (Kultgen, 1982).

The concept of a profession must be distinguished from the related concept of professionalism. Professionalism is conduct befitting a professional, as well as the personal characteristics conducive to such conduct. By "befitting a professional," I mean conduct that can be legitimately expected of the professional given a reasonable understanding of the proper role of professionals in society. Because of this essential reference to a reasonable understanding and the proper role of professionals in society, professionalism is a normative concept.

Once we recognize this often neglected distinction between profession and professionalism, we are able to acknowledge the rather obvious fact that professionalism can be found in occupations well beyond those that are professions in the narrow sense modeled on the "learned" or "liberal" professions of medicine, law, and the clergy. This narrow sense includes only occupations that satisfy all the structural and essential requirements just mentioned. But key elements of professionalism can be found in a much wider range of occupations—plumbing, carpentry, and hairdressing, for example (Kristinsson, 2013).

The distinction between profession and professionalism also helps us appreciate Englund's (1996) point that it is largely a contingent matter whether professionalism is improved when an occupational group takes deliberate measures to develop its organization, entry requirements, and practice, toward satisfying conventional conditions for being recognized as a profession. Such developments in the name of professionalization may be viewed as a sociological project, whereas teacher professionalism may be viewed as a pedagogical project. Although professionalization may increase professionalism—for example, via added requirements for formal education leading to improved service—such an effect cannot be taken for granted. Steps taken in the name of professionalization might on some occasions have no positive effect on professionalism, as for example when they include the introduction of an approach based on methodological principles that do not fit the subject matter and hence do not lead to improved service. A case in point is the effort to turn the teaching profession into a technical science; such efforts are arguably more likely to hinder than help professionalism in teaching practice (Hargreaves, 2000). The same applies to early efforts to define educational leadership as an organizational science of management, while neglecting the art of leadership. The promulgation of a technical management approach may perhaps have been instrumental in earning the occupation professional status in society and yet is unlikely to engender true professionalism in educational leaders.

## PROFESSIONALISM AS KNOWLEDGE, SKILL, AND CARE IN AN OCCUPATIONAL ROLE

What exactly is true professionalism, then? The analysis I want to suggest is that professionalism consists of *knowledge, skill,* and *care* in an occupational role (Kristinsson, 2013). This tripartite set of qualities needs to be publicly certified in order for clients and the public to be able to distinguish reliably between those who have it and others. Certification provides an assurance that service is delivered according to current standards of practice in the occupational field in question, and generally attests to the professional's requisite knowledge, skill, and care.

The knowledge component is necessary for obvious reasons: You cannot be professional if you don't know what you are doing. Some degree of insight into general principles is part of what distinguishes professionalism from mere skill or enthusiasm, even professionalism within the broad range of occupations that includes those that do not require higher education. This insight into general principles implies some ability to describe and explain underlying principles and to present customers and clients with helpful and realistic options and advice.

Skill is also a necessary component of professionalism. We would certainly and legitimately complain of lack of professionalism if a hired practitioner could merely describe and explain what needs to be done but was entirely inept at actually doing it. This component of professionalism is, of course, especially crucial in occupations that are crafts rather than professions, but there is also no profession where the element of art is entirely absent or irrelevant. Skill or art connects theory and practice, and making that connection is, of course, the constant endeavor and challenge of every profession.

Care is perhaps the most easily overlooked component of professionalism, but in the present context the most important one. We would certainly be justified in complaining of a breach of professionalism if someone we counted on for service had requisite knowledge and skill but did not care to use them unless this happened to coincide with his or her prevailing desire or self-interest at the time. Care, in this sense, implies an independent commitment to what might be called the values internal to the occupation. More specifically, the care component of professionalism may be further broken down into three elements: service, morality, and occupational standards.

First, those who care about their work in a way characteristic of professionalism take seriously the basic and foundational commitment of their occupation to a certain role, or service, to society. They are concerned to help clients and society achieve the important value around which their occupation is specifically organized. The classical professions of medicine, law, and the clergy are thus committed to the values of health, justice, and salvation, respectively, and teachers and educational leaders are committed to the value of education. However, a much wider range of occupations, far beyond those that are strictly speaking professions, have an important social function to which its practitioners are committed insofar as they approach their work in a spirit of professionalism. Carpenters are committed to the construction of houses and furniture in a safe and desired way; hairdressers to managing people's hair in a way they find comfortable, aesthetically pleasing, and socially acceptable; plumbers to installing heating and draining systems according to current standards, etc. Whatever the occupation may be, professionalism means taking its basic commitment to service seriously and being prepared to follow it even in situations where another course of action would better serve the practitioner's personal self-interest. By this I don't mean being prepared to sacrifice one's self-interest entirely, but rather to regard the commitment to service as an independent end that is not merely a means to one's self interest and should sometimes take priority over it.

This foundational commitment to service helps the practitioner not only to think about priorities between self-interest and occupational commitments but also to think about priorities internal to the work itself. Different occupational concerns are not all equally related to the occupation's underlying purpose, and it is easy to be carried away by institutional and social forces within the workplace or occupation, without reflecting on their ultimate effect on service. Increased awareness of the occupation's foundational commitment should therefore lead to a more reflective and responsible practice in the complex, and easily confusing, social and institutional contexts of work.

Second, those who care about their work in a way characteristic of professionalism take seriously their commitment to morality generally. A craftsman shows lack of professionalism if he cuts corners in order to serve too many clients, if he overcharges his customers, gives them misleading information for the sake of his own profit, or gossips and spreads personal information about his clients. Such behavior is unprofessional because it is morally irresponsible and not worthy of trust. Because moral failures of this sort undermine trust, it is fortunately often in the craftsman's own best interest to behave morally toward his clients or customers—hence the saying that honesty is the best policy. However, our trust in professionalism demands more than this; we want to be able to trust that the craftsman's honesty toward us is not contingent on his or her belief that dealing honestly with us now happens to be in her own self-interest. We want the craftsman's honesty to be based on reliable principles, and when it is, we recognize this as part of the craftsman's professionalism. This is why professionalism necessarily includes a genuine commitment to moral behavior, including honesty, integrity, and fidelity.

This commitment to morality is necessary if professions and occupations generally are to be justifiably trusted (Koehn, 1994). It does so by assuring the public and individual clients and customers not only that the practitioner will generally be honest rather than self-serving, but also that the practitioner will not be unduly enthusiastic in the quest for effective service. A zealous defense attorney might allow or even encourage a witness to commit perjury for the sake of victory in a case (Freedman, 1966). An ambitious school principal might perhaps fabricate assessment data in hopes of improving the school's comparative standing and future funding. In fact, it has been noted that such competitive concerns may lead to the fabrication of the very identity of the school as an educational institution (Keddie, Mills, & Pendergast, 2011). The public needs to be assured that professionals resist such temptations even if what tempts them is their genuine interest in effective service rather than their personal self-interest.

The third and final element in the care component of professionalism is a commitment to standards of practice. People who care about their work want to do a good job that satisfies current standards in their occupational field. Their commitment to good occupational practice carries independent weight and provides clients and the public with an assurance that irrelevant interests or external pressure will not govern the practitioner's conduct. This commitment to occupational standards underpins public trust in much the same way as the practitioner's general commitment to morality does. If we say, borrowing the language of Immanuel Kant's (1785/1959) moral theory, that the general commitment to morality means that the practitioner can be counted on to act out of respect for the moral law, we can add that her commitment to occupational standards means she can be counted on to act out of professional self-respect.

The care component of professionalism, with its threefold commitment to basic service, morality, and occupational standards, distinguishes professionalism from freelance work. Although actual freelance workers may, in fact, exhibit professionalism, they do so not in virtue of their being freelance workers but in virtue of their being also, to some extent, professional in their attitude and approach. Being a freelance worker does not, in itself, bring with it an ultimate commitment to anything except the worker's own desire or self-interest. The reward is the only thing that matters at the end of the day. This attitude of working only for the sake of the reward is contrary to professionalism, which entails an independent commitment to the internal values of the occupation. An occupational group that evinces the freelance attitude in its daily practice does not deserve or earn public trust. There is no guarantee that it will have a systematic tendency to serve the public interest, and every client must protect her own interests in dealing with such practitioners. As the commitment of the practitioners to the internal values of their occupation becomes weaker, detailed contracts about specific tasks, and austere external management and accountability requirements by public authorities, become more important as protections of the public interest.

All this helps to explain why a code of ethics is considered a necessary structural characteristic of a profession. A professional code of ethics provides members of the profession, and the general public, some assurance that each member is committed to the values internal to the occupation (Davis, 1991). To the members of the profession, the code should reduce worries about free riders and signal a collective concern for public service, moral behavior, and professional standards. To the public, the code promises that individual members of the occupation will not have the freelance attitude and can therefore be counted on to work honestly even when nobody is looking.

The general definition of professionalism we have arrived at can be put as follows: *Professionalism is certified knowledge, skill, and care in an occupational role. The component of care entails a commitment to the internal values of the occupation, the elements of which are a service to society, moral behavior, and occupational standards. This threefold commitment distinguishes professionalism from freelance work.*

## THE ETHICAL NATURE OF PROFESSIONS

With this definition, we have moved much closer to being able to assert that all professions are essentially ethical enterprises, where this means that they cannot be described or understood independently of moral purposes and concepts. Professionalism is conduct befitting a professional given a reasonable interpretation of the proper role of professionals in society. In order to characterize professionalism, we have used moral concepts and made numerous references to moral purposes. To try to describe professionalism without moral concepts or any reference to moral purpose would be rather like trying to describe charity by enumerating examples of charity and not saying what these examples have in common. In both cases the concept that enables us to identify the different cases as cases of the same sort is indeed a moral concept.

It may be objected that even if we agree that *professionalism* is an essentially ethical concept, this does not mean that the concept of *a profession* is. After all, these are distinct concepts, as previously pointed out. Perhaps we could describe and understand what it is for something to be a profession without reference to any of the normative notions we used to describe professionalism. Perhaps the concept of a profession has a descriptive meaning only, referring to what a profession *is*, even though the concept of professionalism is normative, referring to how a professional *ought* to behave.

In order for this objection to be convincing, we would have to be able, in principle, to characterize the boundary that distinguishes professionals from nonprofessionals without any recourse to moral evaluation. This has, in fact, been accepted practice among sociologists studying the professions. One advocate of this value-neutral approach states: "If lawyers are, in the words of one of the earliest American writers on legal ethics, George Sharswood, 'a hord [*sic*] of pettifogging, barratrous, custom-seeking, money-making' persons, they nonetheless constitute a profession" (Bayles, 1988, p. 29). They do so in virtue of the required licensing, professional organization, code of ethics, monopoly, self-regulation, autonomy, higher education, intellectual orientation, and the fact that society generally accepts that they provide an important service. To this descriptive list, there is no need to add that members of the profession are characterized by professionalism, according to the value-neutral approach.

This value-neutral approach is untenable, however. If professionalism, with all its normative implications, were in fact completely absent from an occupational group claimed to be a profession, the claim itself would sound fraudulent. A group of skilled freelancers who otherwise satisfied the descriptive elements of the concept of a profession would certainly be an odd and unexpected discovery. They would have a professional association, code of ethics, self-regulation and autonomy, an avowed purpose that society recognized as important, and a requirement of long training with an intellectual orientation based on scholarship and research, and yet the members of the occupation would, by and large, have the attitude and approach of a freelancer and hence not deserve public trust. This would be an odd discovery because the concept of a profession arises out of a need to make sense of, and discuss, a very different social phenomenon from that of a collection of freelancers. The social phenomenon picked out by the concept of a profession is a group of individuals sharing a collective commitment to serve society in a responsible manner through the specialized skills and knowledge they possess. To describe that social phenomenon without referring to the underlying mission and moral purpose would miss what these individuals have in common. The reference to professionalism, and thus the moral purposes and commitments of the practitioners, simply makes for a better explanation of the observed phenomena relating to professions than a value-neutral explanation. The actual phenomena, of course, include a lot of observed professionalism, and this would certainly be harder to explain based on a value-neutral explanatory framework than a framework that allows reference to moral purposes.

I want to make it clear that although I state that a lot of professionalism can actually be observed, I'm not in denial about the actual phenomenon of freelancers masquerading as professionals or, to put it conversely, professions where individual members have the attitude and approach of the freelancer. Indeed, it has been argued, and convincingly so in my view, that many professions, in fact, fail to live up to their professed moral commitments (Larson, 2003). Such arguments expose alleged professions as mere collections of freelancers who have adopted a professional ideology in order to deceive the public about their real motives and actual function in society. This is not always exclusively the profession's fault. Sometimes, the reason why the public has an unduly optimistic faith in the integrity and skill of an occupational group is the public's and politicians' own wishful thinking that professionalism exist where it doesn't, as for example in the banking world (Kanes, 2010). So, my point is not by any stretch that all claims of professionalism are true. My point is, instead, that a profession as a social phenomenon is not properly understood or explained if reference to its normative commitments is omitted.

It might be thought that the remedy for this is to allow it to be one of the defining characteristics of a profession that its members tend to agree on a common purpose, which is also considered legitimate and important by society at large. This is not my view, however. In order for something to actually be a profession, it is not enough that the professionals themselves, or even society at large, share a view about the profession's normative commitments. Instead, these commitments must actually be morally legitimate and pursued in morally legitimate ways. Imagine, for example, an occupational group that was specialized in using generalized physiological knowledge for the ultimate purpose of torturing people with maximal pain without actually killing them. This group shares the strong sentiment and belief that people ought to be tortured regularly for no particular reason, especially children. Suppose, also, that this group somehow managed to satisfy all the descriptive criteria for being a profession, including not only monopoly, self-regulation, higher education, and intellectual orientation, but also a code of ethics and being regarded by society as serving an important social function. Surely, we would hesitate to call this a profession, and rightfully so.

Admittedly, it is hard to imagine that the monstrous social movement I have just asked you to imagine would, in fact, ever satisfy all the descriptive criteria for being a profession. The reason for this is telling: In order to complete the thought experiment, we would need to do either of two things. First, we might imagine that the profession had extremely clever and effective ways of spreading dangerous and incredible propaganda, thereby manufacturing society's general assent to their twisted professional ideology despite its obvious clash with universally held core beliefs about human well-being and social justice. The second alternative would be to imagine that the society in question had a moral framework so completely different from ours that it somehow justified investing significant social resources in the arbitrary torturing of children. In either case, we would be trying to force the concept of a profession onto a phenomenon imagined to be void of the very qualities that make occupations worthy of their title, namely their commitment to serve the public by providing a particular good in morally acceptable ways. This shows that a reference to valid normative commitments is a central characteristic of the concept of a profession.

Once this is recognized, we see that a profession in need of moral reform should not be compared to a house that just needs to be painted, but rather to a house that is so structurally damaged that it can no longer function as a house. This point is highly relevant to contemporary issues confronting various professions, many of which are, in fact, regularly criticized for not living up to their professed moral ideals. The medical profession in the United States can, for example, be criticized for not only tolerating but actually promulgating a health care system where far more is spent as a percentage of GDP than in any other industrialized country, and yet access to medical care is very unequal, and consequently public health is not particularly good. What the expensive system delivers, instead of outstanding public health, is high pay for doctors and a profitable environment for the medical insurance industry and other private interests (Larson, 2003). This criticism echoes the old phrase from a play by George Bernard Shaw (1909) that "all professions are conspiracies against the laity." If my arguments are correct, professions deserving that label should be considered professions in name only, because they do not live up to the normative requirements of professionalism. A profession needs to live up to its name, and it does so by taking its normative commitments seriously.

One way to take them seriously is to ask what a profession needs to be like in order to deserve public trust. Koehn (1994) provides perhaps the best-argued response to this question in the literature on professional ethics: A profession deserves public trust only if the professionals, by and large, show in practice their will to serve their clients' interest, serve that interest as effectively as possible, demonstrate competence, command responsibility and discipline from their clients, have the authority to prioritize tasks for the sake of the overall interests of the clientele, and have a strong sense of social responsibility. This can be a complicated matter, but these are at least general guideposts for professions that want to live up to their name and function.

## PROFESSIONALISM AND VALUES RESEARCH
## IN EDUCATIONAL LEADERSHIP

My argument has been that professions and professionalism are best understood from an interpretive framework that contains normative assumptions referring to a morally legitimate foundational purpose, moral ways of pursuing it, and an independent commitment to professional standards. By arguing this, I have rejected a value-neutral understanding of the concept of a profession. What are the implications of these arguments for educational leadership, administration, and management?

There are many ways to go toward answering this question. The most obvious would be to reflect on educational leadership based on the threefold normative commitment of professionalism: (1) How should we describe the foundational commitments of educational leadership as an independent profession? (2) How can educational leaders make sure their professional conduct is true to their general commitment to moral behavior? (3) How would the professional standards for educational leadership be best described? Each of these questions opens up a large topic for another occasion. Instead of entering these topics now, I want to conclude by pointing out, as further food for thought, how an argument, similar to the one I have presented in this chapter regarding professions and professionalism, could be applied to the question of how to conceptualize values in educational leadership research.

Values are an important topic of study in the scholarly context of professional educational leadership, administration, and management (Richmon, 2003). In that context, values are sometimes studied from an exclusively descriptive point of view rather than a partly normative one. In studies that are primarily descriptive, conceptual work serves to prepare the ground for empirical studies. For example, the general phenomenon of values is described and different types of values classified in order to facilitate valid and reliable instruments for measuring the constructs arrived at in this way. Such measurements then deliver data on the basis of which behavior can be predicted and explained. The overall aim is, presumably, to understand, and ultimately manage, behavior that is determined not only by external factors but also by highly variable internal factors like values and personality traits. The perspective in such studies is the external perspective of someone trying to figure out how other people are likely to behave based on their complicated and multifaceted motivational characteristics. It is not the first-person perspective of the valuing agent.

This approach can be criticized both from an epistemological point of view and from a moral one. To start with the epistemological worry, it seems that if values were viewed from this descriptive and external perspective only, it would in fact be difficult ever to successfully predict or manage human behavior, because we would not be making use of our sophisticated and basic capacity to understand each other through something like simulation (Gordon, 2009). To complement the external perspective, we gain much from also viewing values from the first-person point of view of the agent, who interprets her options and deliberates based on the normative assumptions that constitute her values. The internal logic of a person's deliberation is understandable to other rational agents insofar as it is minimally coherent, even if they do not as agents share exactly the same normative outlook and are therefore not motivated by values in exactly the same way. This possibility of understanding another person by trying to imagine that you are that person, faced with her particular situation, is the basis on which different rational agents can come to know each other. By stepping in one another's shoes, we can understand each other's reasons for action and come closer to seeing each other's ventures as part of a reasonable project that can be understood and interpreted from the inside, as it were, rather than a curious phenomenon to be explained, predicted, and managed.

These epistemological reservations about the external perspective on values research are analogous to the previous objections to the sociological, value-free conception of a profession. In both cases, the perspective deliberately puts quotation marks around the normative assumptions of the agents they are trying to understand. That is, no stance is taken on the reasonableness or intelligibility of particular normative assumptions that agents may be making in the context of particular deliberations and actions. Instead, motivating values are taken to be subjective and arbitrary. But in both cases, the value-neutral approach runs the risk of resulting in a loss of understanding, insofar as a framework for explaining and predicting human behavior must make use of our ability to interpret behavior as an intelligible or reasonable consequence of embracing certain normative assumptions. By leaving normative assumptions out on principle, and avoiding all reflection on values *qua* normative assumptions, the researcher may have imposed an unnecessary handicap even if his or her only goal is to explain and predict. Hence the epistemological worry.

The moral worry is perhaps more fundamental than the epistemological one, however. The moral reservation about the descriptive approach to values research is that if educational leaders, administrators, and managers are trained to think about values from this perspective, they may as a result develop a questionable attitude to their coworkers, clients, and constituents, such as teachers, students, and parents. They may come to view them as vehicles of behavior to be managed rather than persons to be respected. What is worse, they may come to think that professional standards require them to take this attitude of external manipulation to other people—that such an attitude marks their professional approach and expertise, because of its aura of scientific objectivity and technical effectiveness.

There is something deeply disturbing about such an approach to other human beings. Immanuel Kant (1785/1959) argued that insofar as we view ourselves as rational agents, we must necessarily adopt the principle of never treating humanity as a mere means but always as an end in itself. When a leader, administrator, or manager adopts the external perspective, he or she must be careful not to fall into the role of a puppet master who disregards this very basic moral injunction.

It is telling that what used to be called educational administration and management is now usually referred to as educational leadership. This signals a change from the external perspective of managing people based on an alleged scientific understanding of the law-like determinants of human behavior to an internal perspective of leading fellow human beings on a meaningful quest toward shared goals that are actually worthwhile and important. If the arguments I have presented in this chapter are on the right track, this is indeed a fortunate development that needs to be continued.

## REFERENCES

Bayles, M. D. (1988). The professions. In J. C. Callahan (Ed.), *Ethical issues in professional life* (pp. 27–30). New York: Oxford University Press.

Chemers, M. (1997). *An integrative theory of leadership.* Mahwah, NJ: Lawrence Erlbaum Associates.

Davis, M. (1991). Thinking like an engineer: The place of a code of ethics in the practice of a profession. *Philosophy and Public Affairs, 20*(2), 150–167.

Englund, T. (1996). Are professional teachers a good thing? In I. Goodson and A. Hargreaves (Eds.), *Teachers' professional lives* (pp. 75–87). London: The Falmer Press.

Freedman, M. H. (1966). Professional responsibility of the criminal defense lawyer: The three hardest questions. *Michigan Law Review 64*(8), 1469–1482.

Gordon, R. M. (2009). Folk psychology as mental simulation. *Stanford encyclopedia of philosophy.* Retrieved from http://plato.stanford.edu/entries/folkpsych-simulation/

Hargreaves, A. (2000). Four ages of professionalism and professional learning. *Teachers and Teaching: History and Practice, 6*(2), 151–182. doi: 10.1080/713698714

Kanes, C. (2010). Challenging professionalism. In C. Kanes (Ed.), *Elaborating professionalism: Studies in practice and theory* (pp. 1–16). Dordrecht, Netherlands: Springer.

Kant, I. (1959). *Foundations of the metaphysics of morals. Translated with an introduction by Lewis White Beck.* New York: Macmillan. (Original work published 1785)

Keddie, A., Mills, M., & Pendergast, D. (2011). Fabricating an identity in neo-liberal times: Performing schooling as 'number one'. *Oxford Review of Education 37*(1), 75–92. doi: 10.1080/03054985.2010.538528

Koehn, D. (1994). *The ground of professional ethics.* London and New York: Routledge.

Kristinsson, S. (2013). Að verðskulda traust: Um siðferðilegan grunn fagmennsku og starf kennara [Deserving trust: The ethical foundation of professionalism and the work of teachers]. In F. Eggertsdóttir & S. Kristinsson (Eds.), *Fagmennska í skólastarfi. Skrifað til heiðurs Trausta Þorsteinssyni [Professionalism in schools. Essays in honor of Trausti Þorsteinsson].* Reykjavík, Iceland: Háskólaútgáfan.

Kristinsson, S., & Árnason, V. (2007). Informed consent and human genetic database research. In M. Hayry, K. Chadwick, V. Árnason, & G. Árnason (Eds.), *The ethics and governance of human genetic databases: European perspectives* (pp. 199–216). Cambridge, UK: Cambridge University Press.

Kultgen, J. (1982). The ideological use of professional codes. *Business and Professional Ethics Journal, 1*(3), 53–69.

Larson, M. (2003). Professionalism: The third logic. *Perspectives in Biology and Medicine, 46*(3), 458–462.

Richmon, M. J. (2003). Persistent difficulties with values in educational administration: Mapping the terrain. In P. T. Begley and O. Johannsson (Eds.), *The ethical dimensions of school leadership* (pp. 33–47). Dordrecht, Netherlands: Kluwer Academic Publishers.

Shaw, B. (1909). *The doctor's dilemma—with preface on doctors.* New York: Brentano.

Starratt, R. J. (2005). Ethical leadership. In B. Davies (Ed.), *The essentials of school leadership* (pp. 61–74). Thousand Oaks: Sage.

# 3

# ETHICAL LEADERSHIP: A CRITICAL TRANSFORMATIVE APPROACH

## CAROLYN SHIELDS

When I hear the phrase "ethical leadership," I am always reminded of a strange conversation with a senior colleague when I was still a young and untenured assistant professor. Together, we had been assigned to develop a position description for a potential new colleague, and as we thought about areas of expertise we might want to emphasize, my colleague stated bluntly in response to one of my suggestions, "Ethics has nothing to do with educational administration."

At the time, I was so taken aback, I failed to respond. But the comment festered. Perhaps his response came from adherence to the highly technical emphasis of much of the last quarter of the 20th century related to making educational administration a respected academic discipline. Perhaps his response grew out of an understanding of ethics as a set of immutable moral principles good for all times and places and a sense that this might not be an appropriate concept for educational leadership. In any case, I believed then, and still believe unequivocally, that he was wrong. Ethics is at the heart of good leadership. And yet, the topic is challenging and consensus is elusive. What do we mean when we speak about ethical leadership? In an age of increasing leadership pressures for accountability, new forms of educator evaluation, fiscal crises, concern about achievement gaps, rapidly changing demographics, and polarized political perspectives, is it possible to determine what ethical leadership might comprise? In recent years, in the United States at least, conflict over moral and ethical positions has epitomized political debate and caused gridlock in terms of decision making. In fact, taking firm and unequivocal positions led several politicians, during the 2011 presidential election, to make outlandish and erroneous claims—for example, regarding rape, pregnancy, and abortion.[1]

I want to make it clear from the outset that taking firm and ridiculous positions, sometimes in the guise of a particular religious belief, is *not* what I understand by ethical leadership. In other words, taking a firm stance to support a policy that mandates suspending any student who might swear three times or be absent without excuse four times or forget his or her homework is *not* ethical leadership. Moreover, even following rules in a more flexible fashion, taking into account a student's particular home situation (or homelessness) may come closer to being ethical but is insufficient in today's complex and diverse world where educational institutions are as often chilly, unwelcoming, and unsupportive as they are inclusive and supportive intellectual communities. Moreover, when countries throughout the world are struggling to provide equitable educational opportunities to male and female, rich and poor students, and when what is commonly called the "achievement gap" dominates much of educational discourse and policy deliberations, it is clear that more is needed than simply adhering appropriately to rules and regulations. In fact, I believe firmly that ethical intercultural leadership requires an approach to school leadership that is ethical, socially just, and indeed transformative.

However, in today's highly politicized educational climate, school leaders who wish to promote an inclusive, equitable, excellent, socially just, and transformative agenda for their educational institutions are often confronted with questions about how to ensure that their leadership praxis is ethical. My position is that despite the need for rules, regulations, and policies, there may be times when following the letter of the law (i.e., being right) is absolutely not the right course of action. Moreover, as one thinks about the diverse sociocultural mix of most classrooms and educational institutions in this century, trying to develop and adhere to "one size fits all" policies and practices may actually be unethical. A common and relatively simplistic example might relate to imposing similar sanctions for swearing on a homeless child who hears coarse words on a regular and daily basis from most of the adults in his or her life and on an affluent middle-class student who intentionally chooses illicit language to emphasize her displeasure with a teacher's disciplinary action. Although both students have committed an "offense" against school rules, applying a policy without attending to context may be "right" but concomitantly highly unethical.

With the increasing diversity of today's schools, students from various ethnic groups, differing socioeconomic conditions, religious beliefs, sexual orientations, and abilities/disabilities find themselves living and studying side by side. Further, growing diasporic populations throughout the globe bring people with conflicting beliefs and practices into daily contact, forcing school leaders to develop ways of interacting that demonstrate respect for multiple perspectives, without falling into relativistic "anything goes" attitudes and approaches. School leaders are therefore frequently faced with the need to develop some principles for ethical action in the face of conflicting values and belief systems. Thus, in this chapter, I first briefly discuss what I understand "ethical leadership" to be and provide a cursory overview of how historic approaches to thinking about administrative and leadership theories have exacerbated the challenges for today's educational leaders. Then, I propose some ways of thinking about, and developing, principles from which ethical intercultural leadership may emerge and illustrate with examples drawn from my international studies of school leadership.

## FROM ADMINISTRATION TO LEADERSHIP: A MOVE TOWARD ETHICAL PRACTICE

To begin, when we think of ethics, we may think about a branch of philosophy defined in the *Merriam-Webster* dictionary as a system or "set of moral principles," or as "the discipline dealing with what is good and bad and with moral duty and obligation." When one turns to the definition of *moral* in the same dictionary, one reads: "of or relating to principles of right and wrong in behavior" and "expressing or teaching a conception of right behavior." Although ethics and morality are often thought of by the layperson as synonymous, philosophers and ethicists have spent many hours and numerous pages attempting to distinguish between the two concepts. Although I am not convinced that educational leaders need to focus on the nuances, I am convinced that it is the focus on moral *principles* found in each definition that most appropriately and helpfully undergirds the praxis of ethical leadership. This is to say that an ethical leader does not develop a rigid set of practices and policies to which every individual must conform but that, instead, she develops a system for determining what is right or wrong in a given situation, informed but not determined entirely by the beliefs of the society in which the school is located.

Hence, if a school principal lives in a highly conservative community in the United States in a state that may have rejected any acknowledgment of domestic partners (or gay marriage), he or she will not simply uphold the position of the community to criticize or perhaps even ostracize the child of same-sex partners, but instead will uphold the democratic principle that every taxpayer's child in America has the right to the same safe, caring, and high-quality education—regardless of the child's home situation. Similarly, if a school principal in a fundamentalist Muslim community attempted to exclude female students from the processes of education, a higher principle related to the right of every individual to an education should likely override the local practice.

Upholding the rightness of the principle, instead of the community norm or practice, is what distinguishes ethical leadership; however, this is challenging because it seems to imply that educational leaders must each decide for themselves when to uphold the community moral code and when there is a different set of principles that might inform their actions. Nevertheless, there are historic antecedents for today's confusion over what constitutes ethical educational leadership that may help us to better understand current tensions.

## LONG-STANDING TENSIONS

From the time of Plato's *Republic,* written in 5th-century b.c.e. Greece, arguments have been waged about the purposes and role of education. The class of teachers known as Sophists, for example, demanded a form of education that could enhance one's opportunities for desirable employment and hence largely reflected a desire for (spurious) learning that would lead to political success. Sophists were concerned more with the *form* of an argument than with its truth. In fact, clearly demonstrating this equation of power with ethics (or justice), Thrasymacus states, "Justice is nothing else than the interest of the stronger" (Plato, Book I, http://classics.

mit.edu/Plato/republic.2.i.html). This leads Socrates, Thrasymacus, and others to a lively debate over whether the stronger and more powerful are always right, with such circuitous logic that Socrates concludes by having Thrasymacus agree with him that "the life of the unjust is more advantageous than that of the just" (Book I). The conversation continues in Book II (http://classics.mit.edu/Plato/republic.3.ii.html) between Socrates and Glaucon, with Glaucon's questioning whether Socrates really wanted to persuade them that "to be just is always better than to be unjust." Wanting to be right for the sake of being right, upholding existing rules, and being unwilling to consider nuances and meanings, as well as statutes, led ultimately to similar ridiculous conclusions.

Over 20 centuries later, in North America, with the origins of compulsory, free, public education in the early 19th century, Tyack (1974) describes schools as largely bureaucratic and instrumental institutions, whose primary purposes were to socialize, sort, and often segregate various social groups in society. He states that along with a strong police force, public education was seen as a means of maintaining social order and that "stringent legislation [was passed] to force truants to go to school" and remove them from the decadent influence of "the streets" (p. 68). Here again, we see an emphasis on conformity, on forcing everyone to uphold the same code and values, regardless of background or culture. If one came to America, one learned to conform; America had little, if anything, to learn from newcomers.

As these early compulsory schools expanded, largely to educate immigrants and the working class, a theory of administrative leadership developed as well. In those early days, various perspectives may be found—some argued that "educational organizations are not 'objective' phenomena regulated by general laws" (Payne in Culbertson, 1988, p. 3); others were influenced by the scientific norms of management theorists like Frederick Taylor and Henri Fayol and urged the development of a "science of leadership" that followed a specific set of objective principles. Hence, by the time that a group of "'more than fifty professors from twenty leading universities travelled by car, train, and plane to Chicago on November 10, 1957, to take part in a seminar' entitled *Administrative Theory in Education*" (Culbertson, p. 34), the climate was ripe for what became known as the "theory movement." Inspired by the thinking of members of the Vienna Circle, a group that strongly believed that "natural science methods can and should be applied to the study of social and human phenomena" (p. 35), the scholars agreed that "ought" questions—i.e., questions about ethics and moral purpose, right and wrong—had no place in science, and hence lay outside of the study and practice of educational administration. Halpin, author of the influential book *Administrative Behavior in Education,* explained: "Theory must be concerned with how the superintendent *does* behave, not with someone's opinion of how he *ought* to behave"(in Culbertson, 1995, p. 41).

For a quarter of a century, the theory movement was unchallenged, until T. B. Greenfield in 1975 argued for a different approach that redefined theory as "sets of meanings which people use to make sense of their world" (quoted in Culbertson, 1995, p. 77) and launched a series of often acrimonious debates between himself and Daniel Griffeths, as part of what became more widely known in social science as "the paradigm wars." The current emphasis and uncertainty about ethical leadership has its origins in these Greenfield–Griffeths debates; although with extensive writing by such authors as Starratt, Shapiro, Langlois, and Lapointe represented in this volume, as well as many others, the issue of ethical leadership has come into much clearer focus.

And, of course, the "postmodern" acknowledgment of the existence of multiple and valid views of reality offers an important counterbalance to logical positivistic, "modernist" thinking, with its emphasis on objectivity and value neutrality. Simultaneously, these new perspectives also raise the spectre of relativism, a kind of "anything goes as long as one believes it is a right or good" approach—another perspective I believe it necessary to eschew. Parker Palmer (1998) emphasizes the need to reject both approaches—absolutism and relativism, saying that if one takes an absolutist stance, there is "no need to continue in dialogue"—either to evaluate our position or to engage with one another, because our position cannot be influenced; similarly, if one takes a relativistic stance, "we cannot know anything with certainty beyond our personal point of view"; there is one truth for you and another for me, and so, again, there is no need for dialogue, as there is nothing to be decided (Palmer, p. 109).

These cursory comments capture the ethical dilemma of educational leaders in today's diverse educational contexts. As we attempt to serve students from numerous linguistic, cultural, socioeconomic, political, and religious backgrounds, we constantly encounter perspectives that are not our own, traditions and values that seem to contradict the traditional norms of the communities within which our schools are located, and hence we find ourselves challenged and often conflicted. How can one, for example, ensure a safe and challenging learning environment for all students and, at the same time, take into account the varied needs and backgrounds of different segments of the student body? To respond to this question and to develop a reasonable and workable approach to intercultural ethical leadership, we must return to the topic of *principles* that help us to determine what is right and wrong in a given situation.

## DEVELOPING SOME PRINCIPLES FOR ETHICAL INTERCULTURAL LEADERSHIP

As one thinks about developing some principles, the question of whether it is ever possible to develop universal principles or guidelines is at the forefront. Here I hasten to emphasize two points. The first is that context is always critically important in education. It does make a difference whether a school is in the middle of a bustling urban area or in a more remote rural setting, or whether it is adequately funded and resourced or struggling with basics, whether children come from advantaged or disadvantaged backgrounds, and whether immigrant or refugee children have had prior opportunities to attend school or not. At the same time, we must be able to identify some general ethical principles and guidelines that may be universally applicable— even though they may play out very differently across different contexts. Trying to develop a parental involvement program, for example, may be a laudable and important goal for every school leader, but it will be quite a different task depending on whether the school is located on the Navajo reservation of southeastern Utah, where

**Table 3.1** Two sets of principles

| Principles for Democratic and Social Justice Education | Tenets of Transformative Leadership |
| --- | --- |
| All persons in a given organization shall be treated respectfully | The mandate to effect deep and equitable change |
| The education institution will ensure equitable access for all | The need to deconstruct and reconstruct knowledge frameworks that perpetuate inequity and injustice |
| The education institution will promote equitable outcomes for all | A focus on emancipation, democracy, equity, and justice |
| The practices of the organization should emphasize mutual benefit | An emphasis on both private and public (individual and collective) good |
| The norms and practices of the organization shall be equally inclusive of all members | The need to address the inequitable distribution of power |
| All members of a designated group (society, community, school) shall have equal civil, political, and social rights as citizens | An emphasis on interdependence, interconnectedness, and global awareness |
| Competition for funds to ensure basic needs is undemocratic | The necessity of balancing critique with promise |
| | The call to exhibit moral courage |

many parents live in remote and distant dwellings; a New Zealand Marae working hard to uphold traditional Maori cultural practices; a blighted and dangerous urban center where many parents hold several jobs in their struggle to support their families; or a relatively well-to-do suburban center. In each case, the needs, timing, and approaches may differ, while the principle of the importance of parental involvement would need to be upheld.

In a chapter in the *Handbook of Educational Theories* (Shields, 2013a), in which I was asked to develop some principles related to "theorising democratic or social justice education," I identified seven principles, which I argued might be good starting points for democratic education; elsewhere, I have developed eight tenets of the theory of *transformative leadership*—a theory, I argue, that is inherently ethical and focused both on excellence and social justice. Here I attempt to unify these two sets of principles as starting points for thinking about transformative and ethical leadership. The seven principles identified on the left-hand side of Table 3.1 are those discussed in the *Handbook of Educational Theories*, while those on the right come from several publications related to transformative leadership (Shields, 2011, 2012, 2013b).

As I reflected on how the two sets of principles intersect, I reorganized them as presented in Table 3.2. I am convinced that one can behave ethically without necessarily focusing on either social justice or transformation; however, when we consider the challenges related to intercultural leadership and the ways in which most highly diverse (or multicultural) educational institutions tend to fail some of their students or groups of students, it behooves us to expand our definition of "ethical" to ensure a focus on equity and transformation. Moreover, as I reflected deeply on what it takes to engage in ethical, transformative leadership for intercultural contexts, it seemed to me that one implements the tenets of transformative leadership *in order to* promote the principles of ethical intercultural leadership, and so I reversed

**Table 3.2** Starting points for ethical transformative leadership

The call to exhibit moral courage
The mandate to effect deep and equitable change
The necessity of balancing critique with promise

| Transformative ethical intercultural leaders . . . | So that . . . |
|---|---|
| need to deconstruct and reconstruct knowledge frameworks that perpetuate inequity and injustice | all persons in a given organization shall be treated respectfully |
| | all members of a designated group (society, community, school) shall have equal civil, political, and social rights as citizens |
| focus on emancipation, democracy, equity, and justice | the education institution will ensure equitable access for all |
| emphasize both private and public (individual and collective) good | the education institution will promote equitable outcomes for all |
| address the inequitable distribution of power | the practices of the organization should emphasize mutual benefit |
| emphasize interdependence, interconnectedness, and global awareness | the norms and practices of the organization shall be equally inclusive of all members |

and reordered the items from the two columns. The final aspect of the 2011 hand-book principles, identified in Table 3.1 as relating to competition for funds, is more an illustration of a topic that requires concerted ethical leadership than an actual principle, and hence I deleted it from Table 3.2. Instead of identifying the call for a leader to exhibit moral courage as the final tenet of ethical leadership, I moved it to the beginning to signal its central importance. Similarly, the mandate to effect deep and equitable change and the necessity of balancing critique with promise are general principles that undergird all other aspects of transformative ethical inter-cultural leadership.

## EXHIBITING MORAL COURAGE

It must be said at the outset that taking a principled stand not necessarily on behalf of the majority, or based on principles that have always been accepted as the norm in a community that is rapidly changing, requires moral courage. A few years ago, as I engaged in dialogue with the staff of an elementary school in a very wealthy, highly homogeneous, and largely white and conservative Christian community, one of the teachers asked how one should treat a situation if it went against the values and beliefs of the community. The issue at hand was a discussion and recognition of Islam. A fourth-grade teacher had been reading with her class a story that happened to have, as a character, a young Muslim child. When the story prompted a number of comments and questions about Muslims, the only Muslim student in the school stepped up and said, "I am Muslim and I would like to have my father come and talk to the class about what we believe." Following the presentation, the teacher, school principal, and district superintendent were bombarded with angry phone calls, won-dering how the teacher could possibly have permitted this discussion in class. One especially distraught parent complained that the Muslim father had stated that Islam is a religion of peace, and argued that the children should have been taught, instead, that Muslims were out to "take over America."

Although this example may seem extreme, it is actually quite typical of situations facing school leaders in increasingly diverse communities. Moreover, there is little doubt that the principal needed to have thought carefully about his reasons for permitting the discussion in the face of general community opposition. In fact, he might want to claim he had done so in order to promote the first principle of equal respect for all members of the school community and the right of every parent, whose child legitimately attended that school, to have his or her beliefs understood and respected.

Whenever a situation relates to a deeply seated religious belief, it requires considerable courage to go against the majority. Here, Gutmann (2001) is helpful. She uses the example of a science curriculum teaching about evolution (one might also add the topic of human impact on global warming). Consistent with the argument for a set of basic principles that I am making here, she argues the importance of "finding a principled, rather than simply a pragmatic, way of living with the tensions" (p. 217) inherent in contentious situations. For her, the principle is that a decision should be "nonrepressive and nondiscriminatory" (p. 222). Hence, upholding a request from parents that children should not be taught a theory with which they disagree would not meet either test. Although it is every parent's right to draw a line regarding right and wrong in their home or place of worship, it is not acceptable to "stifle rational understanding and inquiry" (p. 226). She argues that repression "entails restriction of rational inquiry, not conflict with personal beliefs, however deeply held those beliefs" (p. 227); moreover, excluding "some children from [certain] educational goods for reasons unrelated to the legitimate social purposes of those goods . . . therefore is discriminatory" (ibid.).

To take such a stance—that it is in the interest of all children to learn specific information even if their parents believe it is wrong—requires a bold and courageous educational leader who has a firmly and carefully developed understanding of what is possible and what should not be permitted within the walls (or curriculum) of a public school. These examples barely scratch the surface of the situations a school leader will encounter that require moral courage.

## THE MANDATE TO EFFECT DEEP AND EQUITABLE CHANGE

Unless an educational leader is convinced that his or her school meets all of the criteria identified on the left side of Table 3.1, then the next step is to consider carefully how to attain that goal and to determine what change is necessary. Oakes, Rogers, and Lipton (2006) wrote extensively about the failure of decades of educational reform to promote educational equity—either in terms of narrowing the "achievement gap" or in terms of providing more inclusive and equitable educational environments for all children. They argue that this failure is not a surprise, given that

> [t]echnical changes by themselves, even in the hands of committed and skillful professional "change agents" or backed by court orders, are too weak to interrupt the intergenerational transmission of racial inequality.
>
> (pp. 21–22)

Moreover, they claim: "Theorists and change agents have not treated equity reforms as distinctly different from other school improvement initiatives" (p. 20). In part, this is because technical changes (changing rules, schedules, organizational structures) do not address the underlying inequitable power structures of schools and do not address the fundamentally unequal "cultural norms about race, merit, and schooling that underlie the status quo" (p. 14).

To effect deep and equitable change, therefore, requires the moral courage to take on deep-seated issues of power and privilege and to carefully consider what changes will level the playing field to permit both equitable access and equitable outcomes for all students. Hence, ethical leaders adopt criteria that promote equity for all members of the community, as opposed to simply identifying approaches that might make the organization in the aggregate seem to be more efficient or even more effective. For example, it may well be true that eliminating free or reduced-price lunch or breakfast programs would reduce expenditures and help to balance the budget, but if one's school population includes a number of students who are either homeless or live in poverty (as is so often the case today), then one must ask if it is the most ethical decision. Further, reducing nourishment may have the more costly consequences of increasing student absenteeism and illness, as well as repressing students' abilities to learn.

Similarly, it may be that a popular senior teacher has, for years, proudly required students to complete an independent study project about a state or country beyond their own and to present their research with data, charts, images, and even typical food of the chosen entity. Nevertheless, the requirement to provide food for the class may appear to make the assignment more interesting and engaging but will certainly make it less equitable for impoverished or homeless students. I once heard of a situation in which a homeless student carefully selected the state of Florida for his research project, believing he could find enough pennies to provide orange juice for the class. Imagine his dismay when the teacher informed him that juice was not a food and hence did not meet the assignment's criteria. Ethical leaders will ensure that those who are already struggling are not further disadvantaged by school practices or policies.

## BALANCING CRITIQUE WITH PROMISE

Ethical leadership also requires building capacity and providing conditions that offer hope for present and future success. It is not adequate for a school leader to simply critique current practices, whether of a legislature, governing district, or individual teacher.

Critique, for ethical, transformative leadership, may begin with an examination of schoolwide data and a dialogue about why immigrant students, whose home language is not the language of instruction, outperform indigenous minoritized[2] students who speak the language of instruction at home. In the United States, for example, one might ask why non-English speaking immigrant students so often outperform African Americans whose home language is English; in New Zealand, one might ask why students from India outperform Maori students in many schools. Obviously it is not simply an issue of language proficiency. Critique might therefore begin with an examination of current assessment practices and an in-depth discussion of the term "achievement gap" itself. An ethical leader would help others to understand the extent of the cultural bias (racial and socioeconomic) inherent in standardized tests and of the ways in which tests reward those from the dominant (test-making) culture and stigmatize many children whose backgrounds differ from that (often dominant middle-class) culture. Children from inner-city areas, for example, where fresh food is often difficult to obtain, might find it more challenging to write about a trip to the supermarket than their middle-class peers or to recognize and distinguish among pictures of various fruit on a test. Here, critique might be accompanied by recognition that the achievement gap may actually be a gap in the ability of families to access adequate nutrition and in the ability of educational institutions to offer relevant and equitable educational opportunities to all students. Promise, in this case, will not be provided by narrowing the curriculum and increasing test preparation sessions, but by working to eliminate the barriers that create "food deserts" in urban contexts and perpetuate an unequal playing field for students of some "subgroups."

These critical examinations could lead to a need to address the norms of race and class identified by Oakes and colleagues (2006) as central to inequity. But, as they rightly pointed out, acknowledging inequity and critiquing it do not automatically lead to change. They express it this way: "Merely documenting inequality will not, in and of itself, lead to more adequate and equitable schooling" (p. 13). What is needed is both political will and courageous action. Moreover, as we also teach students the art of deconstructing and critiquing political arguments, economic premises, or cultural assumptions, they will learn to understand not only that the world is full of inequities ("unfulfilled promises," Maxine Greene [1998] would say), but why they exist and how to begin to offer redress. It is not enough, for example, to document the association of high blood levels of lead in impoverished children and lower academic test scores if one does not take action to change the situation.

To engage in deep and meaningful ethical, transformative leadership, therefore, requires that a leader have the courage to examine, challenge, and, as necessary, correct situations and practices that promote inequity. But perhaps more difficult, and more important, is the need to also challenge beliefs, attitudes, and assumptions associated with the perpetuation of the status quo. Once one has reflected on the starting points—moral courage and the need for change, action, and advocacy to affect the change—several specific aspects of schooling will need to be considered.

## NEW KNOWLEDGE FRAMEWORKS

The above discussion has implied the need to deconstruct existing knowledge frameworks that promote inequity and to replace them with reconstructed knowledge frameworks with respect to a more equitable education. This reconstruction is absolutely fundamental to creating an environment in which every child, regardless of his or her home situation, is treated with respect. For example, it is common amongst overworked educators to hear discussions of particular children who are struggling to succeed, often in terms that place the locus of blame and responsibility on the child or home. One hears comments like "They are hardly ever in school; the parents just don't care; they never have their homework done"; and so on. Rarely do we stop to consider that for families living in impoverished or challenging situations relocation is rarely voluntary. While middle-class families tend to relocate for a better job or a newer, bigger, or more luxurious house, families from less fortunate situations often relocate for reasons beyond their control. Although middle-class parents sometimes also struggle with finances, they are generally much more able to take a day off of work to attend a child's musical or dramatic performance or to participate in a school event than is a single parent who is holding several jobs to put food on the table. I was recently involved in a conversation at the university about new, higher admissions standards and how the university could attract students "with more ability to learn." I was amazed. The assumption that families in poverty care less or have less intrinsic ability to learn is absolutely incorrect and leads to inaction and blaming the victim; acknowledging lesser opportunity to learn and fewer prior opportunities can lead to corrective action.

Hence, deconstructing inappropriate knowledge frameworks begins with the need to reject deficit thinking. Assumptions based on inappropriate generalizations about who cares and does not care, blaming children for their family situation, assuming students have less ability to succeed must all be rejected. Too often we still hear reports of students' aspirations being quashed, with comments like "You should not think about going to university; you should really consider being a hairdresser, a housecleaner, or a waitress." Too often, children who do not look or sound like those from the mainstream are relegated to low-level classes or streams when educators have failed to differentiate between what is often called "opportunity to learn" as opposed to "ability to learn" (Shields, 2008). A child who has never seen the ocean may find it much more challenging to write a paragraph about a summer vacation than one whose parents own a timeshare and travel extensively. A small child who is often required to fend for himself, preparing a meal from whatever is available in the cupboard, may be less likely to understand measures or even fractions than one who has spent hours baking with a parent. Similarly, it is well known that children who come to school ready to learn to read have spent hours in pre-reading activities at home—pointing to elements of pictures, learning vocabulary, distinguishing between letters and numbers, understanding that one reads from left to right (in English), and so forth. Children who come from disadvantaged homes may not have had these opportunities due to a lack of available reading material, lack of parental time, or even lack of confidence on the part of the parent. Nevertheless, taking the time to teach students these basic skills and to provide a breadth of vicarious experiences can provide the foundation for academic success and high-level achievement. Moreover, Jensen (2009) emphasizes how important it is to provide disadvantaged children with high-quality enriched learning experiences (in contrast to the more traditional, slow, and sequential remedial activities) if they are to be successful in school.

The first step is to ensure that children feel that they each belong at school, that their family and cultural traditions are accepted, and that their lived experience is valued so that their knowledge and experience base will help them to succeed. The importance of this step cannot be overestimated. Too often, a child whose parents may be in a loving homosexual relationship or whose religious or linguistic background differs from that of the majority of the community is made to feel less important and less valued than his or her peers. Too often, the child is forced to go, ashamed, to the teacher to beg for assistance, an alternative assignment, or exclusion from a requirement he or she cannot meet. I have often been asked by teachers and principals what course of action is appropriate if the community engages in fund-raising for a field trip and a child from an impoverished background does not meet the target (we find alternative tasks they *can* accomplish to permit their inclusion). I have been asked what to do if a parent complains that a child's depiction of his family with two same-sex parents is contrary to community values. For educators in public schools, I believe the response is simple (but often contentious): "Every taxpayer's child has the same right to be respected, accepted, and valued in this school. Every school activity must be equally open to all children. At home, one may teach whatever values one wishes, but here, we show and teach acceptance and respect for every individual." Parents who do not wish their children to be exposed to alternative lifestyles or belief systems will not like or accept this response easily, but it is my belief that no other approach is acceptable in a public school system. As discussed above, Gutmann's (2001) criteria of nonrepression and nondiscrimination are helpful guidelines.

Traditional and largely negative assumptions about children who are in some ways different from the historical norm in a given school or community represent the kinds of knowledge frameworks that must be deconstructed. To exercise ethical and transformative leadership, one must reconstruct the knowledge frameworks of the school community in ways that permit every child to be successful.

## EMANCIPATION, DEMOCRACY, EQUITY, AND JUSTICE

The foregoing discussion of changing, deconstructing, and reconstructing knowledge frameworks lays the groundwork for a leader, wanting to be equitable and transformative in a multicultural and diverse school community, to focus on what I have termed "emancipation, democracy, equity, and justice." The connotations of each word differ slightly but, taken together, provide a basis for creating learning environments that are accessible to all students.

The first of these terms, "emancipation," is likely the most unexpected and perhaps even the most contentious. To *emancipate,* according to the *Merriam-Webster* dictionary, means to "free from restraint, control, or the power of another; to free from bondage." Bondage may, of course, refer to physical constraints but more often in education implies a kind of servitude, or servility, that is imposed on one segment of the population by another. We have already noted that school systems tend to value and perpetuate the community norms and academic traditions of those who historically have held power. The impact of this with respect to test bias is fairly well known; however, the ways in which tradition may inhibit full participation and success of others in other ways is less often discussed. Sometimes examples are well publicized—stories of Muslim girls not being allowed to play soccer or another sport because, somehow, wearing a hijab might be dangerous; stories of how children learning a second (or third) language are considered rude because they have inadvertently used a word deemed to be inappropriate or have been caught speaking their home language to a classmate in an attempt to understand the nuance of an assignment. Examples are endless. The point, however, is that unless school leaders take action to create structures and cultures that are inclusive, some children do not really have full access to the benefits of schooling.

I once visited a large, diverse, urban high school with a very multicultural population that included a substantial number of indigenous students. After being shown the school's multiplicity of programs, including advanced, international baccalaureate, and gifted programs, one of our group observed that she had not seen any indigenous children in these enriched classes but that they had all seemed to be in the lower-level sections. Our guide responded, in all seriousness, "They have the same opportunities as anyone else to apply, but these programs just aren't for them." When the questioner persisted, asking if the school ever had indigenous students in these higher-level courses, we were told that there had once been one indigenous girl in the program but that she had dropped out after 2 months and that the educators did not know why. I can only speculate on how a lack of understanding of her heritage or of the challenges presented to her in being the only one of her linguistic or cultural group might have led to her feeling isolated and unwelcome. Putting the onus on a student to accommodate, rather than on the institution to help and support her success, is unethical.

Judith Green (1999) argues that we need a kind of democracy she characterizes as deep—one that expresses the "experience-based possibility of more equal, respectful, and mutually beneficial ways of community life" (p. vi); it is, at its core, a "realistic, historically grounded ideal, a desired and desirable future possibility that is yet to be" (p. ix, italics in the original). It is in this context that an ethical school leader needs to think of democracy—an approach that focuses on mutual benefit (something that indigenous girl was clearly not afforded) and that emphasizes hope and possibility for the future. As long as school is seen as primarily a means of providing a middle-class experience, the potential contributions of others will continue to be ignored and their voices silenced. When one combines recognition of the need for more equal, respectful, and mutually beneficial experience of community life within a school, one will find that equity of access and of achievement becomes a greater reality as well. Russell Bishop (personal communication, 2013) argued that it is not sufficient to

> promote solutions to educational disparities in ways that are socially just, but rather [we must] do so in ways that acknowledge the aspirations, preferences, and practices of currently marginalized peoples. Such gains must acknowledge the cultural aspirations of Indigenous and minoritized peoples because as many leaders suggest, "what is the value of 'gaining all,' if we lose who we are in the process?"

This is the crux of the need for an ethical and transformative approach to leadership that, in its quest for equity, emancipates and liberates instead of simply readjusting the inequities in ways that re-inscribe domination and marginalization.

## PUBLIC AND PRIVATE GOOD

Shields, Bishop, and Mazawi (2005) write that

> in a socially just education system, if we were to place the scores of the total population, the scores of the dominant group, and those of a minoritized group on a graph, they would be coincident. There would not be a lower range of scores for the minoritized group. Neither would there be higher drop-out rates among minoritized groups, lower school leaving grade point averages, higher rates of suspension or disciplinary incidents, or disproportionate numbers of students who fail to go on to higher levels of education.
>
> (p. 142)

In other words, the educational outcomes of all students would be equitable. This is consistent with Farrell's (1999) argument that equity involves four components: access (of which we have spoken), survival, outputs, and outcomes. Survival requires that students from diverse social groups have a roughly equal probability of completing school to the same level. Equity of *outputs* requires that students will "learn the same things to the same levels at a defined point in the schooling system" (p. 159); and equity of *outcomes* requires a focus on both the public and the private good outcomes of schooling. It suggests that

> children from various social groupings will live relatively similar lives subsequent to and as a result of schooling (have equal incomes, have jobs of roughly the same status, have equal access to sites of political power, etc).
>
> (ibid.)

Often we talk in terms of private good outcomes; those who complete a certain level of school will enjoy greater lifetime earnings, better career opportunities, and in general better heath. We neglect to identify the communal benefits that derive from greater educational equity as well: less crime, lower costs for the judicial or penal systems, more equitable incarceration rates, and more available male role models in minoritized families. Ensuring that all children achieve to high levels provides not only a greater economic benefit to a society, but greater levels of social well-being, health, and civic participation (McMahon, 1999).

## ADDRESSING POWER IMBALANCES

Oakes, Rogers, and Lipton (2006), in discussing why change does not naturally occur once inequities have been identified and acknowledged, state:

> Equity reforms are often cut short by political struggles for comparative advantage, as middle- and upper-class parents seek to ensure that their children have the same absolute and relative social and economic privileges that they enjoy. The intractability of these norms and politics cannot be understood, let alone altered, absent consideration of the larger social, economic, and political milieu

in which current inequalities between and within schools seem so sensible to so many of those who are privileged currently.

(p. 14)

Their point is that power imbalances are at the root of social inequities and that those who hold power attempt to preserve it for themselves and their children at the expense of others who strive for equal opportunities.

The need to understand and then to address power imbalances is central to Delpit's argument that power imbalances continue to marginalize those who strive for access to mainstream cultures and institutions. In a seminal article, Delpit (1993) states that although it is well known that the power operating in organizations is that of the dominant culture and reflects its rules and values, it has not been as widely recognized that

[i]f you are not already a participant in the culture of power, being told explicitly the rules of that culture makes acquiring power easier [or that] those with power are frequently least aware of—or least willing to acknowledge—its existence. Those with less power are often most aware of its existence.

(p. 86)

Leading ethically in diverse communities requires a two-pronged approach to organizational power. The first, Delpit argues, is to educate those who do not understand the rules. As an example, I have often cited an incident from my first visit to New Zealand. As I was accustomed to doing, I completed my academic presentation and then perched on the corner of a table to respond to questions. Suddenly, and to my surprise, my hostess came up behind me and whispered, "Off the table." I quickly complied, although I then had no comprehension of my misdeed; sitting on a surface that might at some time contain food, I subsequently learned, was considered offensive by my Maori hosts. Fortunately my hostess understood the need to make the rule explicit, for I have no idea how long it might have taken me, or how many people I might have offended, before I realized my error on my own. Telling a person the implicit rules of a culture is so much kinder than assuming she will be upset to be told.

Delpit (1993) goes on, however, to explain that making rules explicit and helping "outsiders" gain access to a given culture is only a first step, which must be accompanied by helping students "to learn about the arbitrariness of those codes and about the power relationships they represent" (p. 100). And, of course, if these rules are arbitrary, then that arbitrariness must also be addressed if we are to level the playing field in ways that acknowledge and value the diverse cultures represented. Delpit concludes:

This can only be done, however, by seeking out those whose perspectives may differ most, by learning to give their words complete attention, by understanding one's own power, even if that power stems merely from being in the majority, by being unafraid to raise questions about discrimination and voicelessness with people of color, and to listen, no, to hear what they say.

(p. 101)

It is easy for educational leaders to listen to those who support and are in agreement with them. However, leaders who want to ensure that their practices are ethical and transformative will take seriously these comments about seeking out and hearing those whose ideas differ from their own. Only when we listen to those who cause us to reflect on our beliefs and approaches will we begin to overcome power imbalances and learn what change may be necessary.

## INTERDEPENDENCE AND GLOBAL AWARENESS

To this point, we have focused primarily on attitudes, beliefs, and practices that lead to more equitable learning environments for all students. Ethical educational leaders must also attend to issues of pedagogy and curriculum. In other words, the learning environment and the content of what we teach and how we teach it all contribute to whether we have provided a transformative educational experience to our students.

Educators are increasingly aware of both the reality and the diversity of the global community. Students who inhabit schools and classes throughout the world increasingly come from other continents and many countries, often having experienced conflict, war, displacement, or the death of one or more family members. Sometimes, educators bemoan the time away from school when students accompany their parents on a return trip to their birth country or place of origin, perhaps failing to understand that learning occurs outside of the schoolhouse as well as within it—and that we need to learn from one another in multiple ways and in diverse places. Nevertheless, the rich diversity of humanity and the world in which we live is what nourishes and sustains us and, as we learn to live together in mutual benefit, is what offers hope for a better future.

Hence, ethical and transformative leaders will ensure not only that their educational learning environments are inclusive and respectful of all students but that they also offer opportunities for equitable access, survivability, outputs, and outcomes. We will go further. Elsewhere (Shields, 2012) I have distinguished between what I have called a socially just education (referring to ensuring a level playing field within the institution) and a social justice education. The latter, I believe, prepares students for life in a pluralistic society in which we must recognize our interdependence and global connectedness. The rate of diaspora and the intricacies of the global economy make it increasingly difficult to ignore the impact of what happens in one community on another, far distant community. Global warming, caused in part, scientists generally agree, by human activity, including the burning of fossil fuels, manufacturing, and the destruction of forests, has resulted in increasingly severe conditions worldwide. In 2012 alone, the United States experienced shrinking ice sheets, blistering heat, severe drought, and devastating storms. Volcanic ash from an erupting volcano in Iceland disrupted air traffic in Europe, affecting passengers around the world for over a week. When an Egyptian resident was arrested for killing four Americans (including the ambassador) in Libya as a result of political unrest in the Middle East, the political reverberations were worldwide.

In other words, we cannot escape the fact that what happens in one part of the world impacts many other places. Hence, I argue that it is important to teach students global awareness, critique, and understanding. Studies by Westheimer and Kahne (2004) and Vedøy and Møller (2007) demonstrate clearly that what is taught matters. The former conducted a 2-year study of three programs focused on teaching students different aspects of critical awareness—developing personally responsible citizens, participatory citizens, and justice-oriented citizens. Their findings are important in the context of this discussion about ethical leadership in that students who participated in the program that emphasized participatory citizenship showed statistically significant learning related to knowledge about how the government works and how to participate by conducting polls, interviewing, and so forth, but no gains related to understanding "broad social critiques and systemic reform" (Westheimer & Kahne, 2004, p. 261). In contrast, students who were enrolled in a program that focused on creating justice-oriented citizens showed the opposite: They emphasized social critique and posited "structural explanations for social problems" but did not emphasize "technocratic skills associated with participation" (p. 262).

Thus, as economic inequality (as measured by the income gap of a country) widens, there is an increasing responsibility on the part of educators to help students understand issues of disparity, privilege, and social justice and how to address them in their roles as future global citizens. Teaching respect and understanding may be the starting point, but it is also critically important to teach students how to be engaged in the world in which they live and in which they will take on leadership roles. This is essential because there is significant evidence that

> income inequality, measured by the Gini index, has a significant and positive effect on the incidence of crime. This result is robust to changes in the crime rate when it is used as the dependent variable (whether homicide or robbery), the sample of countries and periods, alternative measures of income inequality, the set of additional variables explaining crime rates (control variables), and the method of econometric estimation.
>
> (Fajnzylber, Lederman, & Loayza, 2002, p. 25)

Learning about the effects of income inequality on global quality of life and about possible courses of action and beginning to develop new frameworks for thinking about and living in the wider community will help to prepare students to participate appropriately in the complex world of tomorrow.

## ETHICAL, TRANSFORMATIVE LEADERSHIP: HOPE FOR THE FUTURE

I have argued here, based on numerous theories and empirical studies, that ethical, transformative leadership offers a way forward. To accomplish this, I have posited the need for moral courage, for deep and equitable change, and for both critique of our current beliefs, approaches, and systems and action that promises hope and a better, more equitable future. I have suggested that the principles of transformative leadership theory—the need to deconstruct inequitable knowledge frameworks and to reconstruct them in more equitable ways: a focus on emancipation, democracy, equity, and justice; on both public and private good; on addressing power imbalances;

and acknowledging our global interdependence—will lead to more inclusive and equitable education for all, education that includes equity of access, survival, outputs, and outcomes.

To fulfill these tenets, I have also argued that it is not simply a matter of following or upholding the rules. In fact, sometimes, in order to ensure that school is inclusive and just and that all students are welcomed and included, one must actually contravene the policy or rules in order to ensure equitable treatment for students from diverse backgrounds. Punishing students for something they have always learned was normal, or for neglecting something they have not had the opportunity to learn, is neither helpful nor equitable. Indeed, Jensen (2009) argues that punishment does not change behavior, but rather that a new knowledge framework and new understandings are prerequisites for behavior change. Disproportionate suspension, detention, or retention will not lead to the kinds of changes we want in our schools. What is required is strong and caring relationships, respect for all students, a willingness to teach them what they do not know, and holding everyone to high expectations. And, after all, isn't that what a good teacher automatically does: teach every child engaging and enriching material?

Thus, if we are satisfied with the status quo, with the widening achievement gap, with continued crime in our most diverse and disparate communities, then we might say, with my colleague of long ago, *"ethics has nothing to do with educational administration."* On the other hand, if we are concerned about the polarized and polarizing politics of many nations, with social unrest, with economic inequity, and with constant internal and external threats to our well-being, we will want to prepare today's students for a different world—one in which Greene's (1999) vision of "more equal, respectful, and mutually beneficial ways of community life" becomes a reality. A quarter of a century ago, William Foster (1986) stated that educational leadership "must be critically educative; it cannot only look at the conditions in which we live, but it must also decide how to change them" (p. 185). Ethical educational leadership for diverse and pluralistic contexts requires a critical and transformative approach to leadership, one that even goes beyond the decision of how to change the conditions in which we live but that acts ethically and courageously to ensure that change occurs.

Starting with the principles outlined here provides school leaders with some benchmarks and guidelines, but there are no easy answers. Sometimes, indeed, what we have been taught is right is not; the rules we are asked to uphold should be disregarded or torn down; the values of the community should be challenged. These are not easy or popular positions to take or uphold, but they are characteristics of ethical, transformative leadership.

## NOTES

1. During the 2012 presidential election campaign, several candidates (e.g., Todd Akin, Phil Gingrey) discussed what they called "legitimate rape," using an erroneous and spurious argument to support an unequivocal position against abortion that they believed to be a moral response. This is, in fact, antithetical to ethical leadership.
2. The term *minoritized* refers to a group of people who have been ascribed the characteristics of a minority (Shields, 2005) regardless of whether or not they are in the numerical minority. In other words, those groups that have traditionally held power may continue to exclude or marginalize others regardless of shifting numbers, resulting in people who may actually be in the numerical majority, being treated as if their position and perspective were of little worth. Minoritized populations have less influence, and their

perspectives are often silenced by the voices of the powerful. For example, schools on the Navajo reservation, with over 95% of the population being Navajo students, still use a largely Western and Caucasian-based curriculum; schools with majority Latino or African American populations may still use a Eurocentric curriculum that distorts or misrepresents history.

# REFERENCES

Culbertson, J. A. (1988). A century's quest for a knowledge base. In N. J. Boyan (Ed.), *Handbook of research on educational administration* (pp. 3–26). New York: Longman.

Culbertson, J. A. (1995). *Building bridges: UCEA's first two decades.* University Park, PA: University Council for Educational Administration.

Delpit, L. D. (1993). The silenced dialogue: Power and pedagogy in educating other people's children. In N. M. Hildago, C. L. McDowell, & E. V. Siddle (Eds.), *Facing racism in education* (pp. 84–102). Cambridge, MA: Harvard Education Review.

Fajnzylber, P., Lederman, D., & Loayza, N. (2002, April). Inequality and violent crime. *Journal of Law and Economics, 45,* 1–40.

Farrell, J. P. (1999). Changing conceptions of equality in education. In R. F. Arnove & C. A. Torres (Eds.), *Comparative education: The dialectic of the global and the local* (pp. 149–177). Lanham, MD: Rowman & Littlefield.

Foster, W. (1986). *Paradigms and promises.* Buffalo, NY: Prometheus.

Green, J. M. (1999). *Deep democracy: Diversity, community, and transformation.* Lanham, MD: Rowman & Littlefield.

Greene, M. (1998). Introduction: Teaching for social justice. In W. Ayers, J. A. Hunt, & T. Quinn (Eds.), *Teaching for social justice* (pp. xxvii–xlvi). New York: Teachers College Press.

Gutmann, A. (2001). Democratic education in difficult times. In S. J. Goodlad (Ed.), *The last best hope: A reader* (pp. 216–230). San Francisco: Jossey-Bass.

Jensen, E. (2009). *Teaching with poverty in mind: What being poor does to kids' brains and what schools can do about it.* Alexandria, VA: Association for Supervision and Curriculum Development.

McMahon, W. W. (1999). *Education and development: Measuring the social benefits.* New York: Oxford University Press.

Oakes, J., Rogers, J., & Lipton, M. (2006). *Learning power.* New York: Teachers College Press.

Palmer, P. (1998). *The courage to teach: Exploring the inner landscape of a teacher's life.* San Francisco: Jossey-Bass.

Shields, C. M. (2008). *Courageous leadership for transforming schools: Democratizing practice,* Norwood, MA: Christopher-Gordon.

Shields, C. M. (2011). Leadership: Transformative. In E. Baker, B. McGaw, & P. Peterson (Eds.), *International Encyclopedia of Education* (3rd ed., pp. 26–33). Oxford: Elsevier.

Shields, C. M. (2012). Transformative leadership: An introduction. In C. M. Shields (Ed.), *Transformative leadership: A reader* (pp. 1–20). New York: Peter Lang.

Shields, C. M. (2013a). Theorizing democratic and social justice education: Conundrum or impossibility? In B. Irby, G. Brown, R. Lara-Alecio, & S. Jackson (Eds.), *Handbook of educational theories* (pp. 1035–1046). Charlotte, NC: Information Age Publishing.

Shields, C. M. (2013b). *Transformative leadership in education: Equitable change in an uncertain and complex world.* New York: Routledge.

Shields, C. M., Bishop, R., & Mazawi, A. E. (2005). *Pathologizing practices: Deficit thinking in education.* New York: Peter Lang.

Tyack, D. B. (1974). *The one best system: A history of American urban education.* Cambridge, MA: Harvard University Press.

Vedøy, G., & Møller, J. (2007). Successful school leadership for diversity? Examining two contrasting examples of working for democracy in Norway. *International Journal of Studies in Educational Administration, 35*(3), 58–66.

Westheimer, J., & Kahne, J. (2004). What kind of citizen? The politics of educating for democracy. *American Educational Research Journal, 41*(2), 237–269.

# 4

## THE PURPOSE OF EDUCATION

### ROBERT J. STARRATT

This essay attempts to provide a framework of ethical leadership that is closely tied to the ethical integrity of educating. While this chapter would be in agreement with much of the thinking expressed in other chapters of this handbook, it attempts to focus primarily on the ethics of the educating process and the simultaneous leading of that process on any given day by a variety of members of the school community intent on cultivating the ethical integrity of educating.[1]

First, this essay omits the obvious attention all schools give to the minimum requirements that adults and students in the school observe the laws of the nation, state, and locality; many of those laws encompass clear ethical requirements. Thus schools expressly prohibit theft; violence against anyone's person; sexual harassment; bullying of any kind; racial, ethnic, and religious discrimination; destruction of property; and the like. Schools also have their particular rules against, for example, cheating, truancy, tardiness, disrespect toward teachers, misuse of library and other learning resource materials, and the like. Classrooms have particular rules that have to do with maintaining good order. Some of those rules that students and teachers are called upon to observe are not involved with ethical violations; rather they pertain to good manners, ways of dressing, procedures that ensure efficiency and good order, and the like. Often, however, they are lumped together in students' minds as rules against "bad" behavior. In some adults' thinking, they are lumped together as promoting "character education."

In what follows, I want to concentrate on more foundational perspectives that support a school's attempts to model ethical behavior, as well as introduce students to predispositions to acting ethically, and to thinking about ethical ways of living. These foundational perspectives derive from the ontology of human relationality and the psychology of enacting membership in the world. The educational mission of the school, while prohibiting those behaviors that violate the relationality of human life and frustrate the enactment of membership, should be concerned equally or more importantly with the continuous cultivation of understanding of how one is constituted by multiple relationships in the natural world, the cultural world, and the social world, and how those relationships shape and energize the fuller participation in those worlds as an authentic member. Thus we turn first to the foundational qualities or predispositions of an ethical person that the school might positively cultivate.

## FOUNDATIONAL QUALITIES OF THE MATURE PERSON

At the outset, it is important to focus on the convergence of ethical development with human development,[2] which has its foundation in the ontology of the human. Being ethical addresses the ontological relatedness of our being. We are constituted by our relationality. We live by, with, and through other human beings. We do not constitute ourselves independently of our relationships to others. We are not stand-alone, stand-apart, isolated, and independent beings who come to birth, indeed, who come to exist at all by our own power. There was a time when we did not exist, and there will be a time when, at least in our embodied state, we will not exist. We did not come into being out of our own nothingness. We came into being as children begotten by parents who belonged to an existing community within an existing society and an existing culture, with physical attributes resulting from the genes of parents and a long line of ancestors, with a body initially grown inside another body. We are constituted by our relationality to all that produced us, physically, socially, cultur-ally, inside of a history that provides possibilities for and limitations to our com-mon adventure into what we call our humanity. That adventure of an individuality constituted by relationality continues to involve struggles and dreams, beauty and terror, heroism and cowardice, triumphs and defeats, inventiveness and stubborn adherence to tradition.

Ethics is what our community and culture and society has come to recognize and name as what violates that relationality as well as honors that relationality. What choices and experiences grow us as fuller, more intentional human beings we call good and desirable; what choices and experiences frustrate or suppress us as fuller, more intentional human beings we call bad or evil, undesirable, dysfunctional, and unworthy of our humanity. Those good or bad choices and experiences either respect and honor our relationality or disrespect and dishonor our relationality.

One way humans define their relationality is through the term "membership." We are members of a family, a community, a tribe or nation, a cultural and a reli-gious tradition, an organization, and a profession. Enacting one's membership in any one of these groups is the way we enact the relationality of our essential nature, our humanity. Membership confers many "goods" for our lives—friendships, security, work, recreation, language, imagery, and rituals for self-expression and for defend-ing values tied to our relationality. Membership implies and invites participation in the life, values, struggles, and satisfactions of fellow members, by which participa-tion we learn how to overcome an exclusive preoccupation with self and discover the fulfillment of sharing our lives with others (Green, 1985). Our membership also provides us with an identity, with possibilities for contributing something unique from ourselves.

Membership brings to the fore an awareness of rights as well as responsibilities of membership. Rights and responsibilities are two of the faces of relationality for humans. One of the basic responsibilities of membership is to see that the rights of all members are protected and sustained. Furthermore, the exercise of those rights and responsibilities by each individual potentially contributes to the overall welfare of the community one belongs to.

What societies and cultures consider ethical is very close to or synonymous with what they consider a minimal or virtuous exercise of the relationality that constitutes our lives as human beings. Learning to understand the specifics of our relationality within the worlds of culture, nature, and society and learning to enact those basic responsibilities and rights of membership in those worlds is what schools promote, or are supposed to promote. Thus we begin to see the legitimacy, if not the necessity, of arguing for the interpenetration of ethics with the educating process of exploring the various meanings of our relationality to the world *so that* we might exercise that understanding as we seek to participate in those worlds.

This educating process, however, takes place largely when, developmentally, the young being educated have not yet entered those years of adulthood when society expects them to be ethical. In most of their years in pre-collegiate schools, they are considered psychologically pre-ethical—that is, lacking the maturity expected of adults in ethical matters. Most advanced cultures and nations make distinctions between juvenile and adult lawbreakers precisely based on that psychological distinction. Thus it would appear that the best that schools can hope to achieve is the development in the young, through the academic and social curriculum of the school, of those pre-ethical dispositions that provide much of the foundation for the further development of mature, adult ethical living. We therefore turn to an altogether too brief inquiry into those pre-ethical dispositions that the school can legitimately foster through its social and academic curriculum.

## PREDISPOSITIONS OR FOUNDATIONAL QUALITIES OF AN ADULT ETHICAL LIFE

We now take up what can be considered foundational human qualities (I tend to use the terms *predispositions* and *qualities* rather interchangeably) of personhood that support living an ethical life. In any culture, one might be able to identify these qualities as belonging to persons whom their fellows would consider ethical. Persons lacking in these qualities would be less likely to be called ethical, except perhaps in rather superficial ways.

As one moves away from specific actions or choices that might be considered ethical in specific situations and circumstances toward more basic, predispositional ethical qualities, one moves away from ethical disputes about what is the ethical thing to do in this specific instance, toward greater agreement that these general qualities are indeed foundational dispositions for ethical living. These qualities inform all ethical living, although, in any specific instance, the predominance of one quality over the others or the mix of all of them together will differ according to circumstances and perceptions. Those qualities will reflect the basic relationality of our humanity and provide a compass for cultivating the pre-ethical educating agenda of the school.

The truly ethical person acts as an autonomous agent, acts within the supports and constraints of relationships, and acts in ways that transcend immediate self-interest. In other words, the ethical person has developed relatively mature qualities of *autonomy, connectedness,* and *transcendence.*

In speaking about these qualities, we must first recognize that children and youngsters develop these qualities over time. At any given time in their development, youngsters will exhibit greater or lesser strength in these qualities. Likewise, adults will vary in the strength of these dispositions, depending on whether their development toward maturity has been arrested or supported by significant people and circumstances of their lives. At present, we will explore these qualities as we might find them in a more fully developed adult.

It is also important to acknowledge that the sexes will express these qualities differently. Males are socialized, for better or worse, differently toward autonomy than females.[3] Nonetheless, females will learn to express their autonomy as they develop their human personhood. That expression will not be better than or inferior to the male expression. It will be and should be different in terms of their gendered lives, but as humans, it will be recognized in both sexes as the quality of their autonomy. The same is true about the qualities of connectedness and transcendence. There are normal ways females learn and express their connectedness and transcendence that are different from males. In human beings, however, those qualities will be recognized in both males and females. Although these foundational human qualities will be critical for the ethical development of both boys and girls, the mutual interpenetration of these qualities in the different sexes will be reflected differently at different stages and with different intensities in their development. As teachers move through the various stages of constructing various learning activities for their students, the men and the women on the faculty will have to discuss these differences and their implications for the design of specific learning activities.

## AUTONOMY

Ethical persons are autonomous. That is, they are independent agents who act out of an intuition of what is right or appropriate in a given situation—in contrast to those who act out of a mindless routine or simply because others tell them to act that way, or who act out of a feeling of obligation to or fear of those in authority. Autonomy implies a sense of personal choice, of taking personal responsibility for one's actions, of claiming ownership of one's actions. Assumed in the notion of autonomy is the sense that the autonomous person is an individual who has a sense of standing out from the crowd. It does not mean necessarily an opposition to all that the crowd stands for. Rather it means a willingness to oppose the crowd in certain circumstances, to walk in a direction different from the crowd if it seems called for. It conveys a certain independence, a definition of one's self that is self-chosen, not imposed by anyone else.

Obviously one does not exist in isolation from communities of meaning and memory. To a great extent, one's identity as a person is formed as a male or female member of a specific cultural community, with its traditions, myths, and mores. Yet one becomes an individual by appropriating the community's meanings and mores in a personal and unique way. At times one breaks through the standardized, routinized habits of thinking and acting into new ways of thinking and acting. If one is to overcome the suffocation of the collective, one has to choose one's own meanings. One has, in a sense, continuously to create oneself; otherwise he or she becomes absorbed into the unreflective and undifferentiated ways of thinking and acting of the collective. For humans, it is the painful task of adolescence when one has to begin to separate from parents and from peers to forge one's own identity.

Accepting the meanings that the culture conveys can shape one's identity. There are customary ways to be feminine or masculine, to be successful, to be popular, to be good, or to be bad. By simply doing what the culture (either the peer culture or the parental culture) dictates, one chooses an identity that is hardly differentiated from the generalized identities modeled by the culture. Others will seek to reject what the culture dictates in order to validate their individuality. In adolescence, that often takes the form of distinctive hairstyles, clothing, language and countercultural music, dances, and public heroes. Although viewed by adults as unhealthy or crazy, such behavior by adolescents is often a necessary interlude when youngsters can differentiate themselves. However, the process of self-definition, begun early and with a clear focus in adolescence, goes on through young adulthood.

After the first extreme efforts at differentiation, the process settles into a less flamboyant but usually deeper journey. Assuming that one chooses not to conform to socially defined prescriptions, at least in certain defined areas of one's life, how does one justify these choices? Often such choices carry waves of anxiety with them, for they imply that one is cutting oneself off from society's definitions. Staying with what society prescribes offers security and approval. Striking out into the unknown puts one's self at risk. To assume responsibility for one's life, to assert one's autonomy, to create one's meaning where none existed before, one needs to be strong to stand up to such anxiety.

From where does the strength to assume responsibility for one's life come? One source of strength comes from knowledge and understanding gained through personal experience as well as through studying how the world works as it is presented in the humanities and arts, in history and the natural and social sciences. That knowledge and understanding helps the young begin to place themselves within the contours of the cultural, social, and natural worlds. The strength also comes from knowing that there are options and from knowing at least some of the options quite well. The study of literature and history helps to explore some of those options, in addition to contact with adult models in one's life. The strength to be free, however, comes not simply from knowledge.

The strength to be oneself can be fully gained only in relationships with other human beings. In authentic relationships, others give us the courage to be ourselves. Here we have the paradox of autonomy. One cannot be autonomous in isolation. Striving to be totally oneself by oneself reveals one's incompleteness, one's existential loneliness. One makes contact with 'reality,' with the rich world of meaning, by reaching out beyond the isolated self, to share questions, dreams, and options with others, both peers and considerate adults. Buber (1958) offers a way out of the either/ or conundrum of narrow individualism or constricting collectivism by showing that the depth of reality is essentially relational. He offers us a vision of society working toward a transcending ideal, but an ideal rooted in autonomous individuals who find their fulfillment in living relationships.

The ethical person must be autonomous. Only in one's autonomy can one bring one's unique personal gifts to an ethical exchange. Only autonomous actors can claim responsibility for their choices. Only autonomous agents add a piece of their own lives, a quality of their unique selves, to the ethical act. What constitutes the act as *ethical* is that it is the intentional act of *this person,* not the act of an unreflecting, robot-like human who is following a routine prescribed by someone else or is driven by irrational urges. Hence, we can see that one of the primary human tasks facing a young person is to become autonomous, to claim his or her own life. One can speak, then, of a deep moral obligation to become autonomous, for only then can one claim membership in a community of moral agents. It follows that the formation of autonomous young persons is an important agenda for schools educating society's young for their ethical participation in a self-governing life.

## CONNECTEDNESS

Just as the predisposition toward autonomy is inescapably embedded in our onto-logical nature of relationality, yet at the same time calls us to own ourselves, to enact our relationality as this distinct person embedded in this history and culture, so too the predisposition of connectedness likewise flows out of our ontological nature of relationality. We exist inescapably connected to the world, not as isolated individu-als forced to invent connections to an alien world, forced to subdue it or submit to its vagaries, free to exploit it for our own self-interest or recreation. We belong to the world. The world of nature, culture, and society is inside us, defining us, gifting us, challenging us, nurturing us, and offering us possibilities. We exist because the worlds of nature, culture, and society have made us possible. That does not mean that nature, culture, and society are always benign. For many persons, nature, the mainstream culture, and the class divisions of society impose limitations and in many instances are oppressive. Nonetheless the struggle against the limits and the forms of oppression involves employing the available cultural and political tools and all the gifts of one's humanity to resist the dehumanizing aspects imposed by nature and society and the mainstream culture.

Connectedness is a fact about us that requires us to be ethical. Children take the world for granted. It is *there* for the child. The child does not think to thank the world for being there when the child wakes up in the morning. When the child wakes up, it is time for the world to wake up and take care of his or her needs. Or, if the child is not ready to wake up, the child expects the world to go back to sleep until the child is ready to wake up. Later on in childhood, the child wakes up and says to various members of the family, "Get out of the bathroom, I need it." "What's for breakfast this morning?" "Where's my clean school uniform?" "Why do I always have to empty the trash?" "I don't want to go to school today." In other words, children tend to see themselves occupying the center of the universe, expecting it to respond to their needs and wants, usually right away.

Most days, the world has already anticipated the children's needs. Their hearts are still pumping blood throughout their bodies, the antibodies in their biological systems are attacking the germs that affect their health, their genes are directing the growth patterns in their bones and muscles, the sun is up, the tides are changing, birds are chirping, flowers are opening to the day, bees are processing their honey, frogs are chasing mosquitoes, worms are busy purifying the soil of toxic chemicals, cows have been producing milk for their breakfast cereals, trucks have already carried the bread that their parents bought in the store yesterday with money they worked at their jobs all week to earn. The school bus drivers have left their homes already to head for their assigned duties. Their teachers are heading out the door for their school. The newspaper fellow has already left the newspaper on the front steps. Weather satellites are sending their pictures to weather forecasters. The airports are open waiting to take them wherever they want to go. Hotel workers around the world are busy getting their rooms ready for their arrival. Doctors and nurses are getting ready to take care of them should they need them. Bank tellers are heading off to work to handle their finances. The pet dog has even gotten up to greet them. The stars and planets are doing their best. The world is ready to serve them. In the children's minds, that's as it should be.

Granted, this disposition to place oneself at the center of the universe should not be judged unethical, for that would be to place unreasonable responsibilities on infants and children. Rather, adults should recognize that this disposition flows from a necessary survival instinct. The human infant's first "responsibility" is to survive in a totally unfamiliar environment so different from the womb. Being totally dependent on the parent(s) for everything, the child can't help but be self-centered in establishing how he or she is in relationship to the unfamiliar environment. The child has to learn how to trust this environment to be consistently predictable in its response to the child's needs, and so the child continuously manipulates his or her environment to see how it responds.

"Going to school" presents a considerably different environment—one in which the child has to repeat the self-centered focus on survival, now separated from the familiar routines of give and take with parents and siblings, in an environment of many other children who themselves are focused on their own survival in a group of self-centered peers. Add to this anxiety-riddled daily experience the additional threat implied in the classroom work assigned by the teacher who evaluates and critiques their clumsy attempts to complete "the assignment," along with the accompanying threat of appearing stupid to one's classmates. Darwin's theory of the survival of the fittest written into the law of the jungle supplies an apt metaphor indeed for the childhood years of "going to school."

"Socialization," seen from the child's experience, looks considerably different from the adult's perspective. Adults have been socialized into viewing the socialization process as entirely natural—not the humiliating, even terrorizing experience it often seems to the young.

What the socialization process of schooling has to accomplish—its unspoken but necessary curriculum—is to help youngsters learn that the world beyond their self-focused survival efforts is connected in all its parts, and connected to their own lives. The point of learning how all the parts of the world work together and implicate the learners themselves in that working together is so that they, the learners, may more intelligently and responsibly live their connections to the world as they journey toward adult participation in an interconnected world.

The learning of the connectedness of the world is immediately tied, first of all, to the connectedness of humans in the agenda of sociality. The silent curriculum of negotiating interpersonal and group relationships involves cultural skills of the languages of self-expression that the young gradually learn both through their teachers' instructions and through the trial-and-error learning of the schoolyard and on the school bus. Discussion about the adventures of characters in stories assigned by the teacher leads to lessons about social behavior that can be applied to the schoolyard, the school cafeteria, the school bus, and to the life of the local neighborhood. Those lessons point to the interdependence of humans on one another in all forms of human striving—in making friends, playing games, arguing the interpretation of school rules, shopping at the local grocery store, in lifesaving surgery at the hospital, and so forth.

The study of history reveals the struggles endured and the challenges met by one's forebears, as well as the ways people have treated other people who differed from them in religion, class, gender, race, tribe, or nationality. The social fabric of the past reveals connections of oppression, power, wealth, and conquest, as well as connections of cultural and technological invention, political cooperation toward greater communal self-government, heroic resistance to injustice—the residue of which connections are evidenced in the social fabric of one's civic community and the lifeworld of one's family. In these studies the young learn how communities at various epochs have *lived* their understandings of the connectedness of social and political life in the way they treated various groups of people, some with deference, some with contempt, some with fear, some with armed resistance, and some with haughty indifference and assumed superiority. They also learn how various groups throughout history gained greater freedom from subjugation and altered the negative social relationships in ways that redefined the connectedness of their social fabric. Again, the point of studying history is to appreciate how people in the past have both *made* and *endured* their history and to come to terms with how one wants to live out the implications of the lessons history teaches, whether those lessons point to cultural, political, scientific, or other professional and career involvements.

Exposure to advances in the natural and social sciences in school lessons reveals the connectedness between elements of natural and social systems. The current international emphasis in educational policy around science, technology, engineering, and mathematics (STEM) reflects a perspective on increasing one's national competitive advancement in the global marketplace. This emphasis provides an opportunity for educators to *add* an intentional focus on understanding the connectedness of the world of nature with ecologically supportive policies on energy production and consumption. Significant portions of global communities continue to live the understanding that nature is simply there for human exploitation and financial advancement with no corresponding *lived* understanding of the ecological impact on global resources of arable land, forests, clean air, and clean water. Besides the education of scientists, mathematicians, and engineers in the basic technical performance of their disciplines, schools need to integrate a lived understanding of the connectedness these disciplines also reveal about ecological sustainability.

The emphasis on incorporating the learnings about the connectedness of the cultural, social, and natural world into commitments to live out some of the implications of that connectedness in one's own life point back to the ontological vocation of human beings to each live out the relationality that defines their very humanity. Developing that disposition during the pre-ethical years of the young as they are being socialized into what it means to be a full human being—which includes becoming an autonomous, responsible adult—is central to the mission of schools in a self-governing democracy.

## SELF-TRANSCENDENCE

Finally, the third predisposition on the way to becoming an adult, ethical person is self-transcendence. One can be an autonomous person who remains a self-centered individual. One can understand the connectedness of elements of the cultural, natural, and social worlds but still not live out that understanding beyond the connection to one's own privileged group and its agenda of dominating the cultural, social, and natural worlds so as to retain their privileged position. The ethical person brings a sense of her or his own autonomy to owning ethical choices that honor the living out of connectedness to and within the worlds of nature, culture, or society and *embody choices* that take one beyond self-interest to a larger commitment to some common good.

On a basic level, transcendence means going beyond the ordinary, beyond what is considered average. In this sense, it means striving for and achieving a level of excellence that exceeds anything one has ever done before. The standard of excellence will be relative both to the type of activity involved (playing the violin, high jumping, writing poetry) and to the person involved (a physically uncoordinated person, a mature professional athlete, a sight-challenged person). Transcendence on this level means a struggle to stretch the limits placed upon us by nature, to create a purer sound, to leap against gravity's pull, to see clear through to the essence of a feeling and capture it just so in the perfect metaphor. It is the struggle for the perfection of a human talent, and it is a struggle precisely because the possibilities of reaching that perfection, let alone of sustaining it, are limited by self-doubt and our very ordinariness as human beings (Nussbaum, 1990).

On another level, transcendence means going beyond self-absorption (which the search for excellence can sometimes promote) to engaging our lives with other people, whether to share their life journey with them or to work with them toward some goal that benefits a group or society in some way or other. Transcendence in this sense also means going beyond the ordinary. By the very ordinary nature of our social existence, we have to make room for others in our lives. People often intrude at times when we wish they wouldn't, but we respond to them with polite tact and go back to our project as soon as their intrusion is over. We learn to accommodate others, sometimes cheerfully, sometimes reluctantly. This is what minimal or ordinary social relations require. Transcending this level of social relations means taking on the burdens of others, caring for them, putting ourselves in their place—not once a month, but very often, if not habitually. It means anticipating their needs, surprising them with thoughtful gifts. It means finding our fulfillment in easing the burdens of others, making them laugh, helping them finish a project. This form of transcendence is clearly a foundation for the exercise of the ethic of care.

Transcendence also means being able to invest one's energies in a collective activity with others that serves some valued purpose beyond self-interest. That form of transcendence involves becoming a part of something larger than one's own life. Through that involvement one moves beyond an exclusive concern for one's own survival and necessities of life to an effort to serve a larger common good. That common good invests the actions of the individual with higher value, with higher moral quality.

As involvement with others becomes more total, it moves toward the third level of transcendence, which is what I call the heroic. One can invest one's energies in other people and in a cause—up to a point. At some point, people say to themselves, "OK that's enough for now. Now it's time for my life, my interests, my leisure and recreation." The more total involvement is the willingness to sacrifice some of what most people would say were one's legitimate rights to "time off" or "time for oneself." Teachers who consistently stay late and arrive early in order to help out youngsters having difficulty with their school work or just plain difficulty with life; social workers who consistently go the extra mile for their clients in getting them needed assistance; doctors who continue to spend quality time with their patients, listening to their anxieties; public officials who treat ordinary citizens with as much respect and courtesy as they do the "important people"; store managers who spend countless hours devising ways to improve staff morale and customer service—these are people who transcend the ordinary and embrace heroic ideals of making a difference in people's lives. The recognition of some of the great heroes, like Mother Teresa or Václav Havel, with public awards like the Noble Prize does not belittle the significance of the more everyday expressions of heroism.

Our interpretation of what constitutes heroic action is, of course, mediated by our culture and subcultures through the symbolic values they attach to some achievements. Olympic gold medals, a scholarship to Oxford University, an Oscar-winning performance are all culturally significant, heroic activities. On a smaller stage, the neighborhood dominoes champion walks around his turf with heroic stride, for, in that ambience, he is somebody to be reckoned with.

By claiming transcendence as a basic human quality, we recognize that it is foundational to human moral striving. If this disposition is not developed during youth and young adulthood, then a mature ethical life (barring an extraordinary conversion) is hardly possible. Green (1985) is helpful here in pointing to an educational source for nurturing this sense of transcendence: the great writers of imaginative literature. In conversations with these poets of the heroic, these prophets and utopians, youngsters are exposed to the images of possibilities for human life. By exposure to stories of great human striving, their own heroic aspirations are kindled; these exemplars provide models for possible imitation. Biographies of great leaders in history bring reality perspectives to frame the more utopian idealism of imagination. The point Green makes is important, however: Our transcendent aspirations are nurtured in and through the heroic imagination.

When transcendence is joined with the qualities of autonomy and connectedness, we begin to see how the three qualities complement and feed each other in the building of a rich and integral human life. Although we speak of these three foundational qualities of an ethical person in a somewhat abstract way, we don't want to think of them as a list of virtues that we set out to acquire. We are speaking of an ethical *person* who has a unity and integrity, whose actions reveal qualities that shine out as from a diamond. These qualities of an ethical person, however, do not fall from the sky. They are developed in action, through choices that are acted upon. These qualities are never achieved as an acquisition. They are always to be found in the action of specific persons in this moment, in these circumstances, with these people, and hence never perfectly or fully expressed. They are achieved only in the doing and in the doing-constantly-repeated (Meilaender, 1984).

What is described above is more like an ideal type of person. This person rarely if ever exists in perfect form. Most of the time human beings reflect imperfect efforts in the direction of truly autonomous, connected, and transcending actions. The ideal type, however, serves a purpose—as that toward which humans can reach. It also provides a guide for those who would educate toward ethical living. By providing opportunities for youngsters to exercise autonomy, connectedness, and transcendence, educators enable youngsters to experience the *beginning* of fulfillment and satisfaction of a way of being human.

If these qualities are foundational in a developing ethical person, then ethical educators will be concerned to nurture those qualities and discourage the development of their opposites. Teachers need to reflect on how they can use the everyday activities of youngsters in their classrooms and in other activities around the school to nurture these dispositions. Youngsters' development is not uniform. What might be appropriate for a 16-year-old may not be appropriate for a 10-year-old. How one nurtures the sense of transcendence in kindergarten would differ from an approach taken in seventh grade. The three dispositions can be nurtured in every grade, however, in ways that are suitable for the children, but it would be a mistake to expect all the children to manifest these dispositions in the same way. Gender, race, culture, and class will all nuance the child's expression of autonomy, connectedness, and transcendence. Class-bound and ethnocentric teachers will have difficulty with such varied expressions. The sensitive teacher will observe the different expressions and listen to youngsters explain their behavior. Over time such teachers will be able to promote these dispositions within an appropriate range of plurality and diversity.

## ETHICAL LEADERSHIP OF THE INSTITUTION WHERE SCHOOL LEARNING TAKES PLACE

The school is an institution that has a recognizable organizational shape and a variety of organizational structures, processes, and procedures that provide some predictability and order to the work that goes on in the school. In other words, schools, like other public and corporate institutions, have explicit ways of governing their internal life and their relationships with the external communities they serve. To be sure, schools are governed by larger governing bodies, such as state departments of education, local school boards, and school committees, as well as legal and financial statutes adopted by local municipal, state, and federal governing bodies. Within the laws, policies, and guidelines provided by those authorities, schools govern themselves through their charter, their mission statement, their statement of core values, and various internal administrative and departmental procedures.

## THE ETHIC OF JUSTICE

The ethic of justice provides guidance to many school policies and procedures, insisting on some uniform attention to equity and fairness in the way the school governs itself in all its daily activities. By modeling what justice looks and feels like in a self-governing community, the school explicitly exercises one of its educating functions. Students learn justice by living in a community that practices justice and explicitly corrects injustice when it occurs in the community's practices.

By and large the ethical demands of justice impose a balance between rights and responsibilities. Teachers have certain rights and responsibilities guaranteed by civil law and by their contract with the school, often spelled out in the teacher's handbook. Students likewise have certain rights and responsibilities, often spelled out in the school's student handbook. In supervising the work of the school on a daily basis, administrators have to attend to a practical and prudent balance of the rights and responsibilities of both students and teachers. Often specific situations will arise when there seems to be a conflict between protecting a person's rights and articulating that person's responsibilities—for example, in a disagreement during school recess over one student's right to be included in a game and his responsibility to follow the rules of the game, or in a disagreement over how carefully a teacher has to park his car in the places allotted for faculty parking. However, a general agreement by the community that they wholeheartedly endorse the ethic of justice does not guarantee that the application of that ethic automatically issues in a clear response to every, or even most, disputes that arise.

Ethicists distinguish among various applications of the ethic of justice. For example, one aspect of justice deals with distributive justice, another with retributive justice, another with restorative justice. In civil society, demands for distributive justice refer to the fair public distribution of or access to public resources such as clean air and clean water; access to housing, education, public parks and beaches, and jobs; equal protection under the law; freedom of speech; and so forth. In schools, distributive justice issues might involve relatively equal per-pupil expenditures across schools in the district, appropriate services for special needs children, equal access to advanced placement courses based on one's academic record, more responsive pedagogies for second-language learners who are unfairly penalized by insufficient opportunities to learn the material on high-stakes exams, and so forth.

In civil society, retributive justice refers to the fair imposition of sanctions for violations of laws, public policies, and organizational rules. In schools, retributive justice refers to punishments such as school suspensions for students who have knowingly violated rules against bullying, fighting, or destruction of school property. Unfortunately retributive justice can sometimes occupy the entire concern of administrators and teachers.

More recently, school systems in the United States and other countries have developed a process of restorative justice. This process requires the offending person(s)—and sometimes the person's parents—to meet with the parties that have been wronged or offended by the offender's behavior in order for the offender to understand the damage or hurt that has been inflicted, to provide the offender an opportunity to seek some kind of reconciliation with those offended, and to discuss various ways the offender might restore or make up for the harm done (Riestenberg, n.d.). Sometimes retributive justice is imposed along with restorative justice; restorative justice sometimes takes precedence over retributive justice.

Since the 1970s, restorative justice initiatives have spread to various countries, from Japan to Belgium to Canada and the United States. Beginning in 1989 New Zealand has made restorative justice the guiding force of its entire juvenile justice system (Zehr, 2002). Evaluations of some restorative justice programs in schools suggest that the most effective ones are based on a continuous, proactive, whole-school effort to build a foundation of community around relationships of caring and respect (Morrison, 2007).

One of the limitations of leading a school exclusively from an ethic of justice, however, is the frequent inability to resolve claims in conflict. What is just for one person might not be considered just by another person. Hence educators' discussions of what is just in any given situation can tend to become mired in minimalist considerations: What minimal conditions must be met in order to fulfill the claims of justice? This question can reduce issues around justice to minimalist types of formulae whose application can have dehumanizing consequences.

## THE ETHIC OF CARE

As I have argued elsewhere (Starratt, 1991, 1994, 2012), the ethic of justice does not encompass the full complexity of ethical concerns. It is complemented by an ethic of care.[4] Both ethics need one another. In a variety of cases, sometimes one is more appropriately highlighted over the other, but in many others, the human way is to keep them interpenetrating each other.

The ethic of care focuses on the demands of relationships, not from a contractual or legalistic standpoint, but from a standpoint of regard for the very "givenness" of the other. This ethic places human persons in relationships of absolute value. It enacts the belief that each person enjoys an intrinsic dignity and worth and, given the chance, will reveal genuinely admirable qualities. Thus, an ethic of caring requires fidelity to persons, a willingness to acknowledge their right to be who they are, an openness to encountering them in their authentic individuality, and a loyalty and responsibility to the relationship, even at a distance (Hollway, 2006). Such an ethic does not demand relationships of intimacy (though it may include such relationships); rather, it postulates a level of caring that honors the dignity and integrity of each person and desires to see that person enjoy a fully human life.

Caring does not deny human fallibility. Rather it acknowledges that to be human means to be vulnerable and insecure, impulsive and susceptible to immature actions, as well as capable of spontaneous generosity, courage, and enduring commitments. Nevertheless, the caring person recognizes that it is in caring relationships that the specifically human is grounded; isolated individuals functioning only for themselves are but half-persons; one becomes whole when one enters into relationships of mutuality with others, where there is some self-disclosure and sharing of ideas and feelings.

Humans are social beings who need to be validated in caring relationships. More than being fairly treated, they need someone to care for them and someone, in return, to care for (Noddings, 1992). We hear some claiming that respect is the basic virtue. However much I am respected, if I am not cared for and cherished by someone, the respect I receive from others will not be enough to feel fulfilled in life. Likewise, if I have no one to care about and for, my life is likewise truncated, diminished. Caring is an intrinsic law of life for humans. Where it is plentiful, humans flourish. Where it is thin and artificial, humans grow spiritually thin and humanly artificial. Caring is an ethic in the bones of humans. They know, intuitively if tacitly, that they are obliged to care for one another if they are to be human. We come to be a human being through being cared into existence, cared into growing, and cared into finding oneself through caring (Becker, 1971; Bellah, Madsen, Sullivan, Swidler, & Tipton, 1985; Buber, 1958).

The ethic of care is not limited to interpersonal relationships as might be found in families, friendships, and marriage partners. The ethic of care also reaches beyond to caring for other persons in need, whether sick and infirm, impoverished, or unjustly persecuted or oppressed (Hollway, 2006; Skeggs, 1997). It also extends to fellow workers on the job and to fellow citizens one encounters in everyday life. Caring is the ethic that binds communities together in sociality. Justice is the ethic that binds people together in the demands that accrue in virtue of their rights as citizens and as individual human beings. Within the ethic of care, one is not responsible for other people in view of their rights, but in view of sharing with them a common humanity, a humanity endowed with beauty, talent, and promise, but also a humanity that is fragile, continually enveloped by ambiguity, and needing care. Our common humanity that all humans share with one another is something that is given by being born a human being. The ethic of care is also a responsibility that is given by being born a human being.

A school community committed to an ethic of caring will be grounded in the belief that the school as an organization should hold the good of human beings within it as sacred. This ethic reaches beyond concerns with efficiency, which can easily lead to using human beings as merely the means to some larger purpose of productivity, such as an increase in the district's average scores on a standardized test or the lowering of per-pupil costs.

A school committed to an ethic of caring will attend to the "underside" of the diverse interactions among members of the community, that is, to those motives that sometimes intrude in an exchange with a teacher, student, or parent. Sometimes those motives involve the desire to dominate, to intimidate, or to control. Sometimes those motives involve racial, sexual, ethnic, and age stereotypes that block the possibility of honest communication. Sometimes a teacher feels insecure in the face of strong and assertive students and feels the need to put them in their place. Sometimes an administrator is not even aware of the power she or he has in the eyes of teachers and recklessly toys with the teacher's insecurity by some light-hearted ridicule of a classroom activity.

Besides developing sensitivity to the dignity and uniqueness of each person in the school, educators promote an ethic of caring by attending to the cultural tone of the school. Often the use of language in official communiqués will tell the story. Formal abstract language is the language of bureaucracy, of distance. Humor, familiar imagery and metaphor, and personalized messages are the language of caring. Through awards and ceremonies as well as school emblems, school mottos, school songs, and other symbols, the school communicates what it cares about. When the school rewards academic competition in ways that pit students against each other, when the awards are few and go only to the "top students" in the formal academic disciplines, then the school makes a clear statement of what it values. Ceremonies and awards that stress caring, cooperation, generosity, service, and teamwork send different messages. Some schools clearly promote a feeling of family and celebrate friendship, loyalty, and service. Laughter in the halls, frequent greetings of each other by name, symbols of congratulations for successful projects, frequent displays of student work, hallways containing pictures of groups of youngsters engaged in school activities, cartoons poking fun at teachers and administrators—these are all signs of a community environment that values people for who they are. When youngsters engage every day in such a school community, they learn the lessons of caring, of respect, and of service to each other. With some help from peers and teachers, they also learn how to forgive, to mend a bruised relationship, to accept criticism, and to debate different points of view (Christensen, 2009; Noddings, 1992; Schoonmaker, 2012).

Schools that model caring explicitly exercise an important educating function. Students learn the ethic of care—the virtuous way of living in a richly human community—through the daily practice of caring and being cared for, as well as correcting uncaring practices in the community. That learning provides the foundation of sociality that any democracy requires (Schoonmaker, 2012). This more general level of ethical educational leadership sets the stage for a deeper exploration of the ethical character of the teaching profession, to which we now turn.

## THE PROFESSIONAL ETHICS OF TEACHING

Every profession demands that its practitioners follow two fundamental ethical principles: (1) Do no harm in the practice of the profession and (2) promote the good intrinsic to the practice of the profession. The first principle demands that professionals—doctors, lawyers, engineers, social workers, teachers—have mastered the most current understandings about the discipline they practice, so that they will not be guilty of shoddy, misinformed, or obsolete applications of what the profession is supposed to know, thereby causing harm through their incompetence. It implies also that the practitioners of the profession will abide by the general ethical principles in society to do no harm by cheating, lying, stealing, sexual harassment, and the like in their dealings with their clients or patients.

The second ethical principle endorsed by professions enjoins them to pursue the good intrinsic to their practice. For the medical profession, this principle refers to promoting the good of health of their patients and the public in general. For the legal profession, this means promoting the good of justice for their clients and for society in general.

MacIntyre (1984) observes,

> What is distinctive of a (professional) practice is in part the way in which conceptions of the relevant goods and ends which the technical skills serve—and every practice does require the exercise of technical skills—are transformed and enriched by these extensions of human powers and by that regard for its own internal goods which are partially definitive of each particular practice or type of practice.
>
> (p. 180)

The technical skills of the professional practice of teaching serve "relevant goods and ends" and involve "the extension of human powers." In regard to the profession of teaching, I take that to mean *both* the extension of the human powers of the teachers and that of the human powers of the learners, namely the power gained through advancing the knowledge of the world.

The practice of teaching extends the human powers of teachers in a way that enables teachers to reach across the divide between themselves and their students and to bring what they know toward the grasp of their students through their dialogical co-production of knowledge. That co-production of knowledge likewise extends the human powers of the learners to perform and apply their new knowledge to situations in their lives. This seems to imply that the power gained through knowledge and understanding enables the learners to participate more fully as members of the worlds of nature, culture, and society—the ultimate "good" produced by the profession of teaching. MacIntyre (1984) goes on to refer to "that regard for its own internal goods which are partially definitive of each particular practice or type of practice." By that, I take him to refer to the goods of teachers' professional knowledge of the curriculum as well as the various pedagogical strategies that engage the students' motivation, attention, and dialogue with the lessons the teachers have designed. He seems to imply that the truly professional teacher continues to broaden and deepen her own knowledge and pedagogical strategies—those goods that increase the possibility of further enlarging the human powers of the learners.

What are the powers in the learner that good teaching extends? They are the powers of understanding that illuminates the intelligibility of the way the worlds of culture, nature, and society work, illuminates not only the structures and processes by which those worlds work, but also illuminates the aesthetics of those worlds—their harmonies and disharmonies, colors and tones, subtleties and vagaries, power and potentialities. In understanding how the world is and how it works, the learner comes to appreciate, however tacitly, his or her own intellectual agency, the very gift of intelligence that enables understanding. Beyond the appreciation of intellectual knowledge in itself, the learner begins to appreciate how to *put knowledge to use*. Knowledge enables one's participation in the human community and its cultural, social, and natural sustainability. All the learning cultivated by the professional talent and dedication of teachers extends the human powers of learners (Polanyi & Prosch, 1975). That constitutes the ethical good of the practice of teaching, and the ethical good intrinsic to the work (practice) of learning.

Initially, the learners' putting that knowledge to use involves relatively simple applications like using crayons to color a seascape, writing a five-sentence paragraph describing one's neighborhood, converting fractions into percentages, figuring out the cost of six apples, or explaining why some things float and others sink. Gradually that knowledge and understanding creates the mental sediment out of which grows other, more complex knowledge and understandings that tie together a larger network of conceptual relationships. As learners continue to probe the intelligibility of the worlds of nature, culture, and society, they begin to sense the power of knowing, how it expands their sense of themselves becoming more competent in the affairs of adult life, more competent in self-expression, more competent to talk about adult issues, more self-assured that they are taking charge of their lives because they "know what they are doing." They can enjoy the satisfactions of completing projects with others, thereby progressively developing a more mature sense of agency, rather than always having to be told what to do, how to do it, or why to do it.

## SUMMING UP

This essay has attempted to offer a perspective on leading an ethical educating process. It first proposed to ground the ethics of the educating process in the ontology of the human in its relationality. It then positioned the ethical focus of the first dozen or so years of schooling on the development of pre-ethical qualities or dispositions through the social, civic, and academic curricula the school enacts with its young learners. After the focus on students' pre-ethical development, we turned to the adults' practice of the ethics of justice and care as they shaped an ethical environment where learning takes place with the young. Finally, we explored the professional ethics of the practice of teaching—the promotion of the good of learning for young learners: their coming to know the world in which they live out their lives so that they can exercise an intelligent and responsible membership in that world.

### Concluding Remarks

Ethical education is not a simple training in the predisposition to be ethical, the lessons of which, once learned, guarantee an ethical adulthood. Ethical education is a lifelong education. It takes place simultaneously with our efforts to be human. We learn to be human in the *struggle* for integrity in our encounters with others. Virtue is not something we achieve and then continue to possess. Virtue is always out in front of us to be achieved; it involves a perpetual doing. The human person is always incomplete. In a sense, we do not create ourselves; we do ourselves. We do not make "good works"; we do good. We can't lay it out ahead of time. We can't say, now that I have developed and possess this virtue, I know how to act in this or that circumstance, in advance. The virtuous act must be continually improvised (Meilaender, 1984).

Since ethical education is a lifelong experience, it should begin in school so that the process of ethical learning can become more intentionally reflective and its lessons more clearly learned.

Paradoxically, we learn what it is to be human when we *fail* as well as when we succeed. In failure, we learn the hard lesson of our limits, the ambivalence of our motives, and the wonderful lesson of being forgiven by our fellows. We learn through failure the tacit lesson of compassion, compassion for ourselves and compassion for our brothers and sisters. In the pursuit and occasional achievement of some virtuous activity, we discover the quiet joy of enhancing someone else's life, the satisfaction of easing someone else's pain, the surprising pleasure when our honoring a relationship is acknowledged, the paradoxical fulfillment of ourselves when we give away ourselves. We gain our humanity in interaction with other humans who are struggling with all the heroic ambiguities of the human condition (Becker, 1971). A perfect ethical community would probably bore us to tears; we would not recognize it as a human community. A human community is a community that expresses the full spectrum of the vagaries of the journey toward its fulfillment, in short, a less-than-divine comedy. In school, we begin to learn that the direction of our life, collectively and individually, involves our taking responsibility for and ownership of it.

Cultivating an ethical school, then, calls for great courage; a modicum of intelligence; lots of humility, humor, and compassion; and an unyielding hope in the potential, endurance, and heroism of human beings. It is a dream worthy of educators.

## NOTES

1. This essay contains material developed earlier in my book *Cultivating an Ethical School* (Starratt 2012). While that work contains a much fuller exposition of this topic, this essay represents advances in my thinking regarding various aspects of my argument.

2. In proposing these foundational qualities as pre-ethical, I have been influenced by Ernest Becker's (1968) brilliant treatment of the ethical person in his *The Structure of Evil* (especially ch. 11). His work is a synthesis of earlier works by Martin Buber, Max Scheler, John Dewey, Josiah Royce, Max Weber, Ralph Waldo Emerson, and others. Emile Durkheim (1961), of course, has written the classic exposition on the centrality of autonomy and relationships to all moral actions in *Moral Education*. John Macmurray's (1999) *Persons in Relation* provides a scholarly source for my treatment of the ontological relationality of human being. I also found Thomas Green's (1985) treatment of moral education enormously appealing but have chosen to focus on these three basic qualities rather than on his "five voices of conscience," which I believe can easily be related to my trilogy.

3. The literature on women's development is considerable. Some significant books include Gilligan, C. (1982), *In a Different Voice: Psychological Theory and Women's Development*, Cambridge, MA: Harvard University Press; Thorne, B., Kramerse, C., & Henley, N. (Eds.) (1983), *Language, Gender and Society*, Rowley, MA: Newbury House; Belenky, M. F., Clinchy, B. M., Goldberg, N. R., & Tarule, J. M. (1986), *Women's Ways of Knowing: The Development of Self, Voice, and Mind*, New York: Basic Books; Jordan, J., et al. (1991), *Women's Growth in Connection: Writings from the Stone Center*, New York: Guilford Press; Sichtermann, B. (1986), *Femininity: The Politics of the Personal* (trans. by J. Whitlam), Minneapolis: University of Minnesota Press.

   For me, Virginia Woolf's *A Room of One's Own* (New York: Harcourt Brace, 1957) remains a pivotal book for raising awareness about women's oppression.

   For books in which the masculine and feminine are treated under the same cover, see Sanford, J. A. (1980), *The Invisible Partners: How the Male and Female in Each of Us Affects Our Relationships*, New York: Paulist Press; Pearson, C. (1986), *The Hero Within Us: Six Archetypes We Live By*, San Francisco: Harper & Row.

4. In my earlier works (Starratt, 1991, 1994, 2012), I treat a third ethic, the ethic of critique, which refers to the ethical activity of criticizing and correcting *structural* injustice in which organizations in their very policies and procedures advantage some members of their organizations or communities while disadvantaging other members. Some argue that this phenomenon should be treated under the ethic of justice. In the interests of limited space, I accept this position here and include the critique of structural injustice as an aspect of the ethic of justice.

# REFERENCES

Becker, E. (1968). *The structure of evil: An essay on the unification of the science of man.* New York, NY: George Braziller.

Becker, E. (1971). *The birth and death of meaning* (2nd ed.). New York, NY: Free Press.

Bellah, R. N., Madsen, R., Sullivan, W. M., Swidler, A., & Tipton, S. M. (1985). *Habits of the heart: Individualism and commitment in American life.* Berkeley, CA: University of California Press.

Buber, M. (1958). *I and thou* (2nd ed.). (R. G. Smith, Trans.). New York, NY: Scribners.

Christensen, L. (2009). *Teaching for joy and justice.* Milwaukee, WI: Rethinking Schools Publications.

Durkheim, E. (1961). *Moral education* (E. K. Wilson & H. Schnurer, Trans.). New York, NY: Free Press.

Fromm, E. (1956). *The art of loving.* New York, NY: Harpers.

Green, T. F. (1985). The formation of conscience in an age of technology. *American Journal of Education, 93,* 1–38.

Hollway, W. (2006). *The capacity to care: Gender and ethical subjectivity.* London, UK: Routledge.

MacIntyre, A. (1984). *After virtue* (2nd ed.). Notre Dame, IN: University of Notre Dame Press.

Macmurray, J. (1999). *Persons in relation.* Amherst, NY: Humanities Press.

Meilaender, G. C. (1984). *The theory and practice of virtue.* Notre Dame, IN: University of Notre Dame Press.

Morrison, B. (2007). Schools and restorative justice. In G. Johnstone & D. W. Van Ness (Eds.), *Handbook of restorative justice.* Devon, UK: Willan Publishers.

Noddings, N. (1992). *The challenge to care in schools: An alternative approach to education.* New York, NY: Teachers College Press.

Nussbaum, M. (1990). *Love's knowledge. Essays on philosophy and literature.* New York, NY: Oxford University Press.

Polanyi, M. & Prosch, H. (1975). *Meaning.* Chicago, IL: University of Chicago Press.

Riestenberg, N. (n.d.). *Applying the framework: Positive youth development and restorative practices.* Retrieved from http://f.p.enter.net/restorativepractices/beth06_riestenberg.pdf

Schoonmaker, F. (2012). *Living faithfully: The transformation of Washington School.* Charlotte, NC: Information Age Publishing.

Skeggs, B. (1997). *Formations of class and gender.* London, UK: Sage.

Starratt, R. J. (1991). Building an ethical school: A theory for practice in educational administration. *Educational Administration Quarterly, 27,* 185–202.

Starratt, R. J. (1994). *Building an ethical school.* London, UK: Falmer Press.

Starratt, R. J. (2012). *Cultivating an ethical school.* New York, NY: Routledge.

Zehr, H. (2002). *The little book of restorative justice.* Intercourse, PA: Good Books.

# 5

## SOCIOPOLITICAL AWARENESS

### STEVEN JAY GROSS

Currently, our international sociopolitical context can be described as turbulent, resulting in a hypercharged landscape that challenges earlier assumptions and foundational ideas on the very purposes of education. It is also a realm filled with paradoxes and potential ethical dilemmas stretching our traditional educational philosophies almost to the breaking point.

For this chapter I have included three facets that I believe help to describe our context. They are: security, the economy, and technology. Terrorism and our national responses to it raise questions possibly pitting security against freedom. But the seeds of our current situation were planted long ago and we need to understand their long-term evolution. Our economic order is shifting rapidly as we witness malaise in heretofore wealthy continents such as Europe and North America and the rise of new continents such as Asia and parts of South America. Globalism and neoliberalism raise questions about the continuation of middle-class affluence, as privatization in the form of vouchers and charter schools seems to create a world of consumers rather than citizens. Information technology offers the promise of constant access to ideas and new communities that may democratize society but also allow for new dangers such as cyberbullying.

I will consider each of these areas in turn and conclude each section by analyzing each through the lens of turbulence theory (see Chapter 17 of this text). This will include a "turbulence gauge" (Gross, 2004; Shapiro & Gross, 2008, 2013), which estimates the level of turbulence along the continuum of light, moderate, severe, and extreme (Gross, 1998) and applies the turbulence to each situation. Below each turbulence gauge will be a synopsis that briefly explains the turbulence level in terms of underlying drivers, namely positionality, stability, and cascading forces (Shapiro & Gross, 2008, 2013). The chapter will conclude with a general statement about the level of turbulence when these areas are combined with overarching ethical challenges facing educators in our era.

# THREE FACETS TO OUR CONTEXT: SECURITY, ECONOMICS, AND TECHNOLOGY

## Security

Like all other elements considered in this chapter, it is impossible to completely tease out security and consider it separately. Poverty and security are clearly linked. Technology, as well, has its own security aspects, such as prevention of cyberattacks at the state level and of cyberbullying at the personal level—hence the argument for combining all of these factors in the conclusion of this chapter. Yet, if we define the basics of security in traditional terms, meaning the state of physical safety in one's person and one's home community, there are aspects of the current state of the world that deserve special consideration by those who want to educate ethically and teach ethical leadership to the rising generation of educational leaders around our world. Perhaps it is the influence of Maslow's (1943) hierarchy that has caused me to place security first for consideration and to spend so much time on it. If there is no sense of basic security, it seems impossible, or at least improbable, for there to be much in the way of self-actualized behavior, to use Maslow's phrasing.

Because I believe that our current security rests on the fractured foundation of the past, I will take some time to reflect on the earlier decades. It is fair to assert that state-to-state security issues that have formed the foundation of our perspective on our safety were the result of agreements and institutions growing out of World Wars I and II. Victors in both cases sought to create stability by creating international organizations such as the League of Nations, an ultimate failure, and the United Nations, which still exists, albeit sporadic in impact. The impulse toward internationalizing government was understandable, given the cascading collapse of the system of interlinked treaties among the European powers that plunged that continent and North America into a devastating war (Meyer, 2006). Yet, failure to gain American support for the League, as well as its own structural limits, meant the demise of Woodrow Wilson's vision that the First World War was a war to end all wars.

Other aspects of the 1919 Versailles Treaty that pressured postwar Germany through reparations did little to secure a long-lasting peace. Also at this time, the decisions by what were called the Great Powers in dealing with colonized people in the Middle East, Africa, and Asia set the stage for security crises that haunt us to this day. It is easy to see the deficiencies of the work of politicians after nearly a century. It would do us well to remember that these people were traumatized by the experience of over 4 years of devastating trench warfare that caused the loss of millions of lives. As if that were not enough, the Russian Revolution created the first lasting state built upon Marxist-Leninist philosophies, thereby changing the course of national and international security considerations until the end of the Soviet Union in December 1991.

Reaction to all of this unrest was the giddy decade of the 1920s in Europe and America, rising support for revolution in places like China, and a growing press for independence from colonial rule in India. Withdrawal from international ties into a false security typified America's initial reflex after the war, perhaps best captured by President Warren Harding's call for a return to what he referred to as *normalcy*.

While isolationism was challenged by efforts to demilitarize the world through trea-ties, the impact of these attempts was small. Security was fractured and fragile at best.

All of these patterns represented ethical challenges to educators. What really mattered: the national interest, regional alliances, or grand international organiza-tions? Choices here would define who was meant by "we." If narrow nationalism was to trump internationalism, as it did in the post-WWI security environment, "we" would be defined in an exclusionary fashion, and "our" national well-being would be defined in contrast to our neighbors. This became the tragic unfolding reality in the 1930s across Europe and in Japan. Schools were hardly immune to the influ-ence of armed nationalism. In fact, more often than not, insecurity, heightened by the Depression, made the schools and a distorted, unethical education of the young paramount to extremist regimes' strategy of amassing ever-greater power within and beyond their national boundaries. This was clearly the case in Hitler's Germany.

Yet in some democracies, the cascade toward fascism, militarism, Nazism, and totalitarianism abroad was combated, in part, by moves to democratize educational leadership. In particular, the American democratic school administration move-ment dedicated itself to shared governance at the school level and democratic debate among educators (Koopman, Miel, & Misner, 1943). Programs sponsored by the US federal government, such as the Civilian Conservation Corps, helped millions of young men escape poverty, move into the countryside, and further their education (Uys, 1999). Similar, though more limited, programs were developed by Eleanor Roosevelt for women (Cook, 1999). These examples stood in stark contrast to youth programs in Germany that emphasized preparation for war and a blind allegiance to authority such as the Hitler Youth. Clearly the insecurity of the Depression era produced widely different outcomes for school-age youth.

The fissures of the post-WWI world seem obvious to us today and did so to thoughtful political leaders of that time. Wilson himself warned that a second world war was likely in two decades if international agreements could not be enforced. Had his political skills of persuasion within his own country been the equal of his pro-phetic remarks, America might have entered the League of Nations, thereby possibly altering the course of events. That was not to be. Again, world security collapsed and an even greater horror descended, fueled by fascist militarism in Japan and Italy and a Nazi ideology of world conquest and race hatred. Advances in industrialism only made for ever-greater destruction, on the battlefield and among civilian populations. Chief among these, though hardly an isolate, was the Holocaust.

Franklin Roosevelt, learning from the mistakes of the previous generation, led the call for an international institution to guard against the possibility of a third world war by championing the United Nations even before the allied victories over Ger-many and Japan. His widow, Eleanor Roosevelt, led in the creation of the UN's Dec-laration of Human Rights, an inspirational yet still aspirational document (Glendon, 2002). Through the United Nations' efforts and by virtue of the diminished powers of France and the UK, the colonial empires eventually saw the wisdom of independence for their dominions. Sometimes, as was the case in India, this was done with relative peace. At other times, violence and regional war broke out. The wars in Vietnam and other Southeast Asian nations are clear examples.

Perhaps the master narrative of the era was the Cold War between the US and the Soviet Union. Both nations, and their allies, had nuclear weapons at first numbering in the hundreds but soon numbering in the thousands. Weapons delivered by conventional aircraft soon were eclipsed by those attached to the tips of intercontinental ballistic missiles. The first of these, a 1957 rocket the Russians called Sputnik set off alarm bells in the US, with direct federal intervention into education, in the name of national security. Educators at the time were pressed to explain how an apparent education gap could have been ignored, thereby jeopardizing the nation and the entire West to this obvious threat from the East. In retrospect, this rhetoric seems loaded and out of touch with the facts, but in the nervous, anti-Communist 1950s, it held sway. Security threats from halfway around the world were laid at the feet of the education establishment. This pattern has persisted in the US and several other countries.

The precarious balance between the two superpowers was kept through the doctrine of mutually assured destruction, with its apt acronym MAD. Simply put, neither side dared to attack the other unless it wished to have its own nation destroyed. But the two nations lived in a complex world wherein other countries developed their own arsenals, as was the case of the UK and France. China soon joined the group, as did India and Pakistan later in the 20th century.

The ethical challenge of raising a generation whose lives could be wiped out at the push of a button far away was on the minds of many educators. Yet the moral challenge of the day could also be as brutal as wondering whether it was ethical to shoot someone who wanted to enter your own family's fallout shelter after a nuclear attack. Schools taught children to "duck and cover" in the event of war, meaning that they should crouch under their desks until all was well. The security and ethical educational leadership of half a century ago sounds surreal today but many of our generation's senior school leadership were raised in just such an environment.

Of course, the world never did fall off the nuclear cliff during the Cold War, despite the shockingly close call of the Cuban Missile Crisis of 1962 and the heated rhetoric of the Reagan years. Proxy wars became common, such as Vietnam. These also pushed the boundaries of conventional ethical reasoning for school leaders. For instance, was it appropriate for schools to sponsor antiwar demonstrations or even tolerate them? What constituted free speech for young people who wanted to make their opinions heard in the public school? Was the school an island of sane neutrality in a society split over international events or was this an amoral and unrealistic position for educators to take? If this was true for K–12 educational leaders, it was doubly the case for university presidents and their staffs. Unrest on campuses was neither rare nor only an American phenomenon. Witness the unrest in France in 1968 (Kurlansky, 2005).

The Cold War ended with the demise of the Soviet Union in 1992, and a New World Order was declared. But the legacy of previous wars was not to be ignored in the equation of post–Cold War international relationships. The US supported anti-Soviet forces in Afghanistan known as Mujahedeen. The idea was to become allies with anyone interested in opposing Soviet dominance. Looking back on this strategy, it seems almost impossible to believe that the very people who the US expected to remain comrades-in-arms would come to raise existential questions and security threats in the early 21st century. Once favored regimes, such as Saddam Hussein's Iraq, became sworn enemies as well. Just as some leaders in the West predicted a new era of peace, the world's security equation became far more complex, and risk, rather than calm, became the watchword for the future.

Educating the young in an era of fractured peace was challenging enough. Just as in the post-WWI world, considerations of who was part of "us" raised critical ethical questions. The 1990s Rwandan genocide, itself an outgrowth of Belgian colonial practice pitting Tutsi and Hutu against one another, typified the horror that people could visit upon one another. In its aftermath, guilt in the West over not acting forcefully enough to confront mass murders made many wonder, *Are we not all culpable?* What is the state of our own morality and ethical reasoning if we do not act to prevent crimes like this? Educators rightly ask, *How are we helping young people to see that insecurity at this level is everyone's business?*

If the Rwandan genocide, and the violence and "ethnic cleansing" atrocities in the former Yugoslavia, constituted security crises with clear challenges for the ethical education of school leaders and students, the events of September 11, 2001, escalated the issues to a qualitatively different plateau. In US cities such as New York and Washington, D.C., educators had to respond to the terror attacks themselves. Cases of heroic leadership by educators who faced extreme turbulence and yet acted in the best interest of their students have since emerged, showing that ethical behavior and education for school leaders can literally save lives (Shapiro, 2007).

But the terrorist attacks of that day, and the 2005 bombings in the London underground, transcend the physical; they shattered the psychological sense of security of people around the world and raised ethical questions for educational leaders that we have yet to answer. Previous national security challenges, such as those described above, represent the contest between nation-states. But today's security issues compound this challenge by adding asymmetrical combatants. Conflict between the US and Iran, for instance, has one definition, but what does that mean in the midst of a war on terror itself? All of this comes amidst political conflicts at home. As we strive to create a secure world for our children in and out of school, what boundaries are we willing or not willing to cross? For instance, the US Patriot Act has been criticized by some for giving governmental authorities too much power over citizens, thereby diminishing individual freedom in the pursuit of security. Drone aircraft are now used where piloted planes and ground forces once pursued foreign terrorists. But this raises the question of making violence too antiseptic, and thus too readily employed. This problem is heightened in the case of drones being used to kill US citizens suspected of working with terrorist groups outside of the US. These questions raise clear ethical dilemmas that should cause reflection for educators and those in our public and independent school systems as well as at the tertiary levels.

It seems impossible to divide current challenges to security from the rise of religious fundamentalism. On the one hand, a broadened acceptance of various faiths and traditions seems obligatory in a democratic society. On the other hand, when do the dictates of a given tradition stretch openness beyond its limits? Who is to mediate these dilemmas? Threats to journalists in Europe, such as those leveled at a Danish cartoonist for derogatory depictions of the Prophet Mohammad, raise this issue again, as do cases of threats to Muslim women in countries such as Sweden (Norberg & Tornsen, in press). Just as in earlier eras described above, a central question seems to be, how do we define exactly who "we" are? How bounded is that definition and what processes can educators at all levels put into place to facilitate a reasoned dialogue leading to improved understanding?

There is also the continuing question of state-to-state security threats in the form of nuclear proliferation. Iran and North Korea are key examples, and yet these too reflect a more complex picture that raises ethical dilemmas, since both are players in regional arenas where challenges to stability have dire consequences. Iran's case raises the whole Middle East security question that has been front page news for decades. North Korea's nuclear ambitions bring with them potential conflict with South Korea, Japan, the US, and possibly even China, since experts predict that any large-scale conflict between the two Koreas will result in massive emigration from North Korea into China. It is understandable for any nation to guard against any further nuclear weapons in the hands of any regime, and especially in the keeping of regimes with unsavory reputations. However, it is hard to lay claim to a monopoly of the moral high ground when so many advanced nations themselves have nuclear arsenals as bedrocks of their national defense plans.

Finally, we need to consider security at the school building itself. The 2012 murder of 20 schoolchildren and 6 adults at the Sandy Hook Elementary School in Connecticut is only a recent example of the tragedy of gun assaults on our most vulnerable citizens. While most mass shootings have occurred in the US, other nations have experienced the same shattering of security. That same year, children were shot to death in France. In 2011, 68 children were killed in Norway and 12 children lost their lives in Brazil at the hands of a gunman. Germany, Finland, Canada, and Argentina also suffered losses of life in schools over the past decade. Statistically, schools are safe places and children are protected. However, the fact that it is predictable that children and teachers will likely be the targets of deranged killers is not only alarming, it represents a challenge to educational ethicists. In countries such as the US, citizens have a right to gun ownership. However, that right is not boundless. Citizens may not possess machine guns, for instance. How can we help guide discussions that protect citizen rights while simultaneously protecting the children and adults in our schools?

Since a central mission of schools is to raise the next generation of responsible citizens, it is critical for educators to consider how they will help students in their charge to reason through this issue carefully and flexibly. Moreover, it is just as important for educators, and those they work with, to consider how they will act as citizens in helping their societies to deal with such consequential problems. Simply leaving security concerns, such as those illustrated above, to national or international leaders seems to be the equivalent of quitting the field. Sadly, once relevant secondary courses, such as Problems of Democracy, previously common in countries such as the United States, are no longer widely taught due to high-stakes testing in other subject areas. Our field must develop new avenues in which to engage students.

**Table 5.1** Security turbulence gauge and synopsis

| Level of Turbulence | General Definition | Applied to This Situation |
|---|---|---|
| Extreme | Structural damage to the current order | General outbreak of global war. |
| Severe | Sense of crisis | **Threats of war. Regional outbreaks of war. Violence at all levels. Serious impact on personal lives throughout the world.** |
| Moderate | Widespread awareness of serious issues | **Tensions exist but are largely controlled at local, regional, and international levels.** |
| Light | Little or no disruption | Few tensions exist. Violence is low, as is crime in general. Safety seems assured throughout the world. |

**Synopsis:  We are cycling back and forth between moderate and severe turbulence in the area of security.**

There is a fractured perspective of what we mean by "we" and "us" when we consider security issues. International relations are destabilized with the fading of the post-WWII world order and without its replacement in place. Series of cascading problems keep tensions high but still manageable for now. This is threatened by nuclear proliferation, cyber and physical terrorism, and general insecurity due to poverty in the developing world.

**Ethical questions facing educators in the security facet** (Table 5.1):

- How much power should we give to governments in order to achieve security?
- How can we reach a balance between personal rights and the shared values that impact our security?
- How can educators best promote ethical discussions of national security issues?

Below is my estimate of how turbulent our current state of security is when measured in the turbulence gauge.

## *Economics*

Just as our physical security is complex and rests on historical evolution and trends, all with important consequences to the way we learn about and teach ethical leadership, so too is our global economic condition. At the time of this writing, the world is still not out of the severe turbulence caused by the Great Recession of 2008. Unlike cyclical recessions, that economic nosedive created the most dangerous and widespread financial losses since the Great Depression of the 1930s. But the effects of the Great Recession have not been evenly distributed around the world.

At the time of this writing the European Union has gone back into recession, and in several of its member nations unemployment has hit record levels. In April 2013, the European average unemployment reached 12%. Here too, the impact of hard times is not felt evenly. Germans have been asked to help out other member nations, most notably Greece, causing the German government to require austerity measures in Greece in return for infusions of financial aid. Spain and Italy are facing similar problems, with Spanish unemployment reaching 26.3% in February 2013 (European Commission Eurostat, 2013).

European financial insecurity has caused many to wonder what price is too great for staying in the European Union, even as that body has been awarded the Nobel

Peace Prize for its work in bringing stability to a continent so devastated by conflict. Just as strategic security issues in the first part of this chapter brought us back to the question of how we define "we," economic security issues have the same effect. Germany, under Chancellor Angela Merkel, proposes austerity for member states it helps to bail out of debt. To some, these changes are referred to as "reforms," but to others these restrictions in social welfare benefits represent a dismantling of the social compact in Europe that helped to create decades of post-World War II stability and security. Breaking that covenant, in their view, represents an erosion of the foundation undergirding educational achievement. Therefore, the debate has profound implications for schools and those who care about ethical conduct in educational policy.

"We" may all be Europeans in a European Union, but that does not mean that those asked to give financial support always feel that their aid is well deserved, and those who receive this aid do not always feel that the strings attached are reasonable. The relationship between potential disunion and a reversion to traditional nationalistic conflicts in Europe is something leaders in many capitals, and their citizens, are reflecting upon. Clearly, these questions bring with them ethical problems that educational leaders need to take up.

In the United States, an agonizingly slow recovery has been under way, bringing with it a return to tepid economic growth, an uptick in the housing market, and some movement toward regaining millions of lost jobs. Yet, with this modest progress has come a protracted battle between the executive and legislative branches of government, shocking levels of income inequality not seen since the 1920s, and a downward trend of jobs from those that once could support a family to those that are poorly paid, non-unionized, and often lacking in benefits.

Just as the wealthy European nations are divided from those in greatest need, the wealthy in the US are divided from those with less economic clout. The Occupy Wall Street movement of 2011 used the rallying cry "We are the 99%!" for good reason. Over the past 30 years, income inequality and, with it, political inequality have soared in the US, so that now CEOs in America's largest companies make over 380 times what the average workers in the same companies make (Mishel & Sabadish, 2012). In 1980, the ratio was 42:1. Put another way, CEO salaries grew a startling 726% in annual compensation from 1978 to 2011, while the annual compensation rise for workers was 5.7% for the same period. Moreover, the existence of a shocking childhood poverty rate of 23% in the US is of particular concern to educators whose focus is on ethics and moral reasoning (Gould & Wething, 2012).

But there are also winners in the current global economy. Australia's economy has done remarkably well, as has that of Canada. Likewise, Brazil has become an economic power transcending its regional position. Perhaps the biggest story of all is that of China. In 2013, the new Chinese leadership called for a 7.5% increase in economic growth. This is normal, or even modest, by recent Chinese standards but would be shockingly high in Europe or in North America. As the world's second largest economy and soon to be its largest, China is perhaps on its way to being the world's second superpower.

But ethical challenges exist for China in the form of vast income inequality and corruption. Lack of food safety (*The Economist*, 2011) and the safety of school buildings (Yardley, 2008) have resulted in tragic loss of life. The blame, in both cases, seems to be on well-connected business people selling their customers shoddy products to make greater profits. There is no doubt that China is a powerful nation, but if it is to live up to the greatness of its culture and its astoundingly important history, change leading to openness is in order. One promising sign is the recent proposal for a food and drug administration to ensure purity and safety.

China has risen from poverty to uneven but dynamic prosperity. India is moving along the same lines. Both cases offer important opportunities for those who seek to educate ethical leaders, since both cultures have their own profound ethical traditions. For instance, how will those in the West learn about, and then learn to integrate, perspectives such as Confucianism and Taoism into their own ways of looking at the world? Ethical leadership may be a universal goal but it is not likely expressed best uniformly. The economic development of these two nations does more than represent internal ethical dilemmas. East truly does meet West, and that gives us a chance to reconsider just what is meant by "we" once more.

What do the historical shifts in the distribution of wealth mean for us as educators? This is not simply a problem for the United States. In countries such as Israel, the widening gap between haves and have-nots raises questions about basic fairness. Social democracies, such as those in the Nordic nations, have created solidly middle-class societies where poverty is rare. In the US, calls for such a society echo as ancient memories from distant leaders, such as Franklin Roosevelt and his ideal of a Second Bill of Rights, while the present budget fights seem aimed at diminished support for old age pensions and medical care funded by the government.

Once, states in the US offered high-quality tertiary education at almost no cost to students, many of whom were the first in their families to attend universities. In return, these people became doctors, lawyers, accountants, teachers, and business professionals. Generations of wealth were built upon their endeavors. But the current climate discourages such investments, and states have pulled away from their earlier levels of support.

The result is crushing levels of student debt that cannot be alleviated, even through bankruptcy. Even state universities are scenes of students bearing crushing levels of debt payable soon after graduation. For instance, at Temple University, where I teach, bachelor degree students graduate with an average of $30,000 of debt. Contrast this to the early 1970s, when I attended the same university as an undergraduate, when tuition was nearly free.

Students who borrow heavily in the US also take on a burden that even our own bankruptcy laws do not cover. Simply put, the debt incurred by college students cannot be put aside by the protection of any law at this time. Combined with high levels of unemployment, this burden itself represents a serious ethical challenge for educational leaders to explore. Since education is an international field, it is possible for nations suffering under these conditions to be aided by the work of colleagues from nations with more humane priorities. It is helpful to know of other societies that educate at the university level with quality and without massive debt burdens. Sweden and Australia represent two such cases. It is also useful to see nations such as these that have not turned education from a community responsibility into a mere consumer privilege.

Yet even the Nordic nations, with their emphasis on cooperation and social cohesion, are not immune from the pressures of global competition that typifies today's economy. A clear case is that of what I will call the Finnish effect. This refers to Finland's recent series of successes in international tests such as the Programme for International Student Assessment (PISA). While this drew attention worldwide, it was particularly striking to Finland's neighbors, such as Sweden. Questions such as, How did the Finns do so well? were soon followed by, What are we doing wrong?

Unlike the US, where either distance or willful distortions caused the wrong lessons to be learned (such as ignoring the fact that Finland has a strong social welfare system and a traditional respect for teachers, both lacking in the US), Finland's neighbors understand local conditions and are left to ponder the problem of competition versus cooperation in the region. This raises the question of how to help educational leaders frame such overarching ethical issues for themselves and for the students in their schools. The course of globalism may be set, but at least we can ask for perspective from our field.

A critical aspect of globalism is the agenda of neoliberalism found in North America, Australia, New Zealand, and western Europe. Starting in the 1960s and 1970s, economists like Nobel Prize winner Milton Friedman proposed that markets not only created wealth, they also created freedom. Following this analysis, governments and their tax-and-spend policies became the enemies of wealth creation and personal freedom. Political conservatives from Margaret Thatcher to Ronald Reagan embraced this philosophy, thus becoming sort of antichrists to traditional Keynesian models, such as the New Deal in the US and the welfare state in the UK (Harvey, 2005). In his first inaugural address, Reagan famously quipped, "In this present crisis, government is not the solution to our problem; government is the problem."

Education writ large felt the impact of neoliberalism almost at once with a drive to privatize public schools in the form of vouchers. The 1983 *A Nation at Risk* report (National Commission on Excellence in Education, 1983) framed the problem with the haunting image of a "rising tide of mediocrity" coming from our schools if immediate steps were not taken. Parental choice in school selection became a rallying cry, along with calls for greater accountability for school performance. This has only increased in recent years, to the point where, in the past decade, most advanced economies have increased high-stakes testing among their publicly funded schools.

At the same time, increased privatization, in the forms of vouchers and, especially, charter schools in poor urban areas, has taken off. It is notable that private academies, and many charter schools, have dispensed with teacher unions, thereby lowering operating costs and further concentrating managerial power. While rhetorical arguments prophecy a renaissance of educational achievement if schools are turned over to market forces in the form of charters and private academies, the systematic study of their impact has been much less certain. In the US, studies have shown that charter schools are sometimes more effective than comparable public schools, and sometimes less effective, but most are hardly distinguishable from their public counterparts. One thing that they do almost predictably is to further segregate populations of students (Miron, Urschel, Mathis, & Tornquist, 2010). This should give us cause to wonder why these models proliferate and whose interests are served by their growth? The community of educational ethicists is well positioned to pursue such foundational questions.

In Sweden, privatization has taken the form of public funding of private schools held by for-profit corporations that often take their earnings overseas. This places privately controlled schools in much the same position as any corporation, thereby raising the ethical question: If the corporately managed school has primary fiduciary responsibilities to its shareholders, how can it simultaneously hold the interests of students above other concerns? What happens when these two interests are in conflict?

The prospects for this kind of ethical education dilemma seem greater, given the push to privatize by large foundations such as those run by Bill and Melinda Gates, the Walton family (founders of Walmart), and Eli Broad. Each of these offers millions of scarce dollars to schools, districts, and governing bodies that are willing to embrace neoliberalism and its market-forces strategies. Unlike earlier support for education from the foundation world, this group emphasizes what the literature calls venture philanthropy. It is a form of investment that sees district leaders as managers with a portfolio of schools, each managed in turn by staff responsible for predetermined results. Just like their counterparts in the corporate world, these holdings need to show gains (in this case, increased test scores) or they can be dispensed with. This means that staff and the principal can be dismissed or that whole schools can be terminated and reopened in some other form. Just like stock portfolios, district holdings can, in this way, be churned for maximum return on investment (Saltman, 2010).

Clearly, this kind of thinking represents the experience of the business tycoons in question. The Gates, Walton, and Broad fortunes were the result of business acumen and an intense drive for profit and market share. However, to what extent can schools, and the children they serve, be treated as objects in a business enterprise? Sandel (2012) warns us of the marketplace's inability to make moral judgments. Once again, those educators concerned with ethical decision making need to consider this quandary and suggest reasoned responses, even if these responses challenge neoliberal privatization and the power structure that supports it.

Next, our economic order has a monstrous side that we must recognize and deal with as teachers of ethical leadership. Human trafficking, in all of its forms, is simply a hideous form of slavery. Whether as prostitution, forced child labor, or the kidnapping of workers held as serfs, it is real, yet we sometimes act as though it does not exist. Those of us living in wealthy countries have an added responsibility to face this ugly reality, since our comfortable lives are in such stark contrast to those victimized by this facet of our global economy. The collapse of a clothing factory in Bangladesh in 2013, killing over 1,000 workers who made clothing for export, is just one current example. We rightly decry the growing gap between the rich and poor internally, yet the gap between the richest and poorest nations is far more appalling and deserves more than passing attention.

Before closing this section, I suggest that we reconsider how we define wealth itself and that we reflect upon the implications of that definition. Currently, it seems that we remain stuck with a definition that excludes nearly everyone, since only the top small percentage of our population considers itself to be wealthy. The other 95% or more remain outside of the privileged circle, or rather, are further down the pyramid. This has its own consequences in terms of our spirit of community.

But more than that, our consumer society encourages excess to the point where wealth seems really to be the condition wherein one can spend to the point of spectacular waste and seem to get away with it. Owning multiple mansions, private jets, numerous yachts, and so on is not a crime, of course. But in a world where children starve, one wonders when is enough, enough? More than that, the waste involved in energy consumption and pollution caused by this kind of spending is considerable. Ironically, the small percentage of people in the position to spend this freely seem to be rich in things, yet poor in time—odd, when considering the fact that time is the one resource that cannot be replenished. Since our field of ethical decision making requires us to think in large, societal terms, it seems appropriate for us to reflect on newer, more constructive ways to redefine wealth. Perhaps this means having both the material and time resources to pursue one's goals with like-minded associates. No matter the form our suggestions might take, a serious reflection on alternative ways to think about wealth that are less destructive to our planet and our souls is in order.

**Ethical questions facing educators in the economic facet** (Table 5.2):

- How shall we advocate for our most needy schoolchildren and their families in a time of budget cutting?
- What kind of economic security do we envision for our youth and how might we advocate for that vision?
- How broadly can we define "we"?

**Table 5.2** Economic turbulence gauge and synopsis

| Level of Turbulence | General Definition | Applied to This Situation |
| --- | --- | --- |
| Extreme | Structural damage to the current order | Depression, including massive unemployment and suffering. Economic and social collapse. |
| Severe | Sense of crisis | **Regional breakdowns. Record unemployment, national animosity, exploitation of people in affected nations.** |
| Moderate | Widespread awareness of serious issues | **Newly thriving national economies. Uneven recovery from downturns. Continued high unemployment. Growing income distribution gap. Mistrust of markets along with growing reliance on them rather than governments.** |
| Light | Little or no disruption | General prosperity. Wealth/poverty gap diminishing. National and international economies at healthy levels of competition, including reasonable pressures to innovate. Power balance between public and private interests. New definitions of wealth considered. |

**Synopsis: Our economic situation is cycling between moderate and severe levels.**

The concept of "we" and "us" is defined in polarizing ways so that we envision rich versus poor nationally and internationally in a kind of seesaw metaphor. For one to be up, the other must be down. This is destabilizing, since we seem to disagree on a balance between equity of opportunity and equity of results. Stabilizing international agreements that formed the basis of the post-WWII economic order such as the World Bank and the International Monetary Fund (coming from the 1944 Bretton Woods Conference) seem to be breaking down. Debts of sovereign nations are an issue, but austerity measures seem to lead to new recessions. Regional agreements such as the Euro Zone have internal cascading potential, thereby threatening more widespread cascading of tensions.

*Technology*

Little more typifies our era, or serves as a better emblem of our fixations, than information technology. Unlike earlier sections of this chapter, nearly every observation I can make applies nearly evenly in advanced economies and, increasingly, to nearly everyone with access to electricity around the world. To illustrate the point, a 2013 UN study found that 6 billion of the Earth's 7 billion people have access to mobile phones, while only 4.5 billion have access to working toilets (Wang, 2013). Currently, about one third of the world has Internet access. In the US, about 95% of teens (ages 12–17) use the Internet, and 80% of those use social media (Madden et al., 2013).

Constant change in technology is the rule. In the past 30 years, we have seen the development and proliferation of personal computers, the Internet, smart phones, and social media. Memory was once measured in the byte, then the megabyte and kilobyte. When multigigabyte hard drives came out, people were astounded at the immensity of memory, but those days seem long ago in a world where computer memory held in one device is rapidly replaced by access to cloud computing. Most know the meaning of a nanosecond, and many feel that their lives are divisible by such brief flashes of time. And it may be best to describe the cascading revolution of technologies in terms of nanoseconds, since that captures the speed with which change seems to have enveloped global life. Email, once considered the height of efficiency, is now looked upon despairingly by the young as a relic fit only for the aged among us. Facebook, itself once a darling of youth culture, may become too overwhelmed by extended families and commercials to be hip, so it can be replaced by faster vehicles such as Twitter. Even here, text can be replaced by images that friends can edit and enhance, such as Instagram. Devices such as smart phones now connect to Global Positioning Systems linked to databases that steer customers to shopping centers of possible interest while steering them away from traffic jams. Companies like Google experiment with wearable technology—in their case, modified high-tech eyeglasses. But all such novelty in the technology world is transient. By the time this chapter gets into the hands of readers, these references are likely to seem passé.

Whole industries reel with the impact of such rapid change. Consider the extreme turbulence facing the publishing world. E-readers are cheap and of high quality. Many who used to support traditional bookstores have abandoned them for e-books or for traditional texts purchased at a discount by e-commerce firms such as Amazon, itself maker of the Kindle e-reader. Newspapers barely hang on in many of their traditional strongholds and are wiped out elsewhere. The few at the top, such as the *New York Times* and the *Wall Street Journal* in the US, seem to have found a way to transition into the new e-universe, but they are the exceptions. Journalism is challenged by these new circumstances, and cuts in budgets have yielded reductions in critical areas such as investigative reporting. On the one hand, free applications such as Zite can organize the daily news contoured to a person's priorities. On the other hand, even these services can easily lose out to one's preferred blogs.

Self-published books, self-recorded music, and self-produced websites are cheaper and of better quality than ever, resulting in almost unlimited potential exposure. But the key word in that sentence is *potential*. Who actually goes to these homegrown sites or downloads these recordings? In a world where nearly everyone can produce near professional-grade material, even the good gets lost in the deluge of media stimuli. Recording contracts were once the gold standard for a musical artist. Now that world is turned upside down, and it is concerts that sell music recordings, not the other way around. Looked at one way, technology has democratized the world of mass communication and publication, delivering it into the hands of billions around the globe. Looked at another way, it is only a mirage, since real exposure, and its accompanying rewards, belongs to a small elite at the top of the cultural pyramid.

Given the place that information technology has in the society in general, it is no wonder that schools have been a place where IT possibilities have been trumpeted and where its impact may be seen. A brief reflection on our history shows that this is nothing new. Schools in the early 20th century were sold technology as well, and with great vigor. Typewriters turned the product of young writers into something resembling texts prepared by publishers. Photographic images were projected onto screens as early as the 1840s, through the use of "magic lanterns," and by the dawn of the last century, these too could be found in schools. Adding to the original multimedia of its day was the use of phonographs, which brought not only orchestral music to schools for the first time, but also the speeches of leading politicians of the era. In the US presidential election of 1912, for instance, candidates Theodore Roosevelt, William Howard Taft, and Woodrow Wilson made waxed cylinder recordings of speeches that were distributed widely around the country.

All of these were promoted as the latest marvels, destined to revolutionize the learning experience for the world's young people. Subsequent decades brought similar claims for using motion pictures, radio, and television in the classroom. While these "marvels" may not have had the world-changing impact by which they were promoted, more humble technologies such as the mimeograph and its replacement, the more malleable photocopier, certainly did become rooted into the classrooms, albeit to both positive and negative results. Prosaic technologies such as these augmented the drill-centered instructional world of the 1950s and 1960s and became part of the fabric of early school memories for those now in the latter years of their career. But they are also important precursors to the tools and the rhetoric facing today's educators.

Fast forward to our era. The school day may seem to start around 8 and end at 3, but that is only a superficial shell that hides the morphed reality. We are told that we need to switch to a frame where learning can take place anytime and anywhere. The teacher is no longer held as the central source of information but the person who makes connections and facilitates learning in a flexible way, matching student investigations with sources of information and ways to share new ideas. Groups of students might work in teams, both in their own classes and with others around the world, in a global enterprise of rich discovery connected to authentic problem solving.

These are possible visions of the future, and this type of learning may exist in spots today. The trouble is, it is all too rare. In these glorified images of the possible, one can hear echoes of the same kind of promise from years past. *The photograph will liberate students from their parochial circumstance and elevate them to the world of international culture. The radio will melt away the miles separating people and will lead to universal peace and understanding. Through television, people will experience great theater and learning will be there for all.* Slender shards of reality exist in each of these visions.

However, educators need to ask, what is the likely outcome of the current technology, given what we know about the promises of the past?

Without becoming defensive, and risking the label of Luddite, educators need to reason as a community and ponder the deep ethical challenges ahead. Please note that the image of creative teams of students engaged in hands-on exploration and problem solving with the aid of the latest technology may be possible, but what chance does this highly evolved pedagogy have when it meets up with a high-stakes testing system that micro-manages instruction by punishing any activity that is not on the test? There are, of course, exceptions to this pattern, such as the school district in Danville, Kentucky, where project-based learning is central. Its story, featured on national television in the US (PBS News Hour, 2013), demonstrated two things: that creativity is possible and that leaders with the wisdom and courage to pursue this avenue are rare. Short of this kind of use for technology in the classroom, critics will continue to assert that schools are being used as unprotected markets for enterprising technology companies that can mesmerize educators with the latest media light show.

But the dual-edged sword of technology extends much further. Consider the seemingly ubiquitous access to social media and Internet-based learning familiar to most of us living in advanced economies. Are these the tools of an educational renaissance where authentic learning really does exist for anyone, anywhere, anytime, like the rhetoric would have us believe? Or is this merely a slick sales pitch for us to accept a second-class student citizenship wherein no one ever sees a teacher, much less gets to be mentored in any meaningful fashion? My own students thank me for offering a course online so that they will not have to travel to class every week, or even monthly, as students in hybrid courses do. I don't blame them because the pressure of their lives dictates harsh choices, wherein there is no time to commute to campus and join a real community. Their appreciation seems less related to the quality of the course than it is to the frenetic quality of their lives.

The attraction of our new technology world also stems from economic pressures. For instance, current budgetary conditions lead to encouraging faculty to teach online because it is more profitable for the institution, thereby accelerating the growth of this kind of education. While these realities make technology attractive to some, critics consider virtual education a poor substitute for authentic schools.

At the university level, we are witnessing the advent of Massive Open Online Courses (MOOCs), where thousands of students participate in credit-bearing classes organized by companies such as Coursera, and edX. Higher education partners in this emerging enterprise include Harvard, Princeton, Stanford, and the University of Pennsylvania. MOOCs have gained favor with state legislators as well. In May 30, 2013, the California Senate unanimously passed legislation requiring state colleges to accept MOOC courses for students in that system who need them to fulfill graduation requirements (Meyer, 2013). This too is related to the economics of education, since California has experienced serious financial challenges in recent years, preventing full funding of its state institutions of higher education. So those colleges and universities could not offer required courses in sufficient numbers to satisfy demand, thereby leaving students waiting for needed courses. Instead of raising revenue to support their own institutions, this quasi-private alternative was found, fitting into the growing trend of market forces and neoliberal responses to education funding problems. Questions were also raised about professorial intellectual property rights, which are being threatened by MOOCs, because universities can claim ownership of these courses and alter them after they are taught (Schmidt, 2013). Finally, the MOOCs have the potential to follow the pattern established by technology's impact on the recording and publishing industries described above: A few at the top of the pyramid could become rich, while those at its base labor along as mere assistants. The damage this could do to our traditional academic community has yet to be imagined.

Current and future technology presents clear school-based ethical dilemmas that need consideration. For instance, e-readers will soon be able to track what pages a student reads in a given assignment and what ideas that student highlights. Faculty at all levels will be able to track these and respond, possibly with sanctions for skipping over sections of reading. On the one hand, conscientious teachers may be concerned about the quality of student study habits. On the other hand, this raises privacy questions heretofore beyond our experience.

Another area of direct concern to educators is cyberbullying. While everyone is concerned with the traumatic impact of cyberbullying, it does not seem to be diminishing, and its victims suffer almost relentless attacks from anonymous foes hiding behind their computer screens and mobile devices. Some have been caught and punished, but the danger still exists, raising another challenge for educators: How can we heighten awareness among students to prevent this kind of attack on their fellows? In physical bullying situations, we encourage students not to stand by and watch the event but to intervene. How can this be accomplished successfully in the online world? Echoing the question posed throughout this chapter, we must ask for an expanded definition of who "we" are. If the cyberbullying victim is seen as part of "us," then we, perhaps, have a greater prospect of seeing supportive responses that may save a young victim's life. How might those teaching ethical reasoning enhance that child's chances?

Regardless of how any of us feel about technology in our lives, there is no doubt that it has been, and will continue to play, a critical role. Opening up new avenues of information more broadly than earlier generations could even imagine is one of its qualities, while opening up the risk of financial exploitation and the destruction of privacy is clearly another. There seems to be little more important than educating those leading schools and universities in sound ethical reasoning if we are to benefit from the former while hoping to diminish the impact of the latter.

**Ethical questions facing educators in the technology facet** (Table 5.3):

- How can we move our systems toward valuing students more than corporate profits?
- How do we encourage technologies that do not exploit fellow educators (the MOOC and online challenge)?
- What can we do to help our young *use* technology rather than being *used by* technology (including cyberbullying, hyperconsumerism, hurried lives)?

**Table 5.3** Technology turbulence gauge and synopsis

| Level of Turbulence | General Definition | Applied to This Situation |
|---|---|---|
| Extreme | Structural damage to the current order | **Industries undone by tectonic changes. Rates of change seem to accelerate. Leadership and power positions transitory at best. Constant claims of novelty, but are they real?** |
| Severe | Sense of crisis | **"Borders" redefined in many dimensions. Space and place redefined. Massive wealth transfers. New imperative for change in traditional institutions.** |
| Moderate | Widespread awareness of serious issues | New ways of working through technology emerging. Early adopters foreshadow potential of coming changes. Rising but arithmetic demand for change in processes. |
| Light | Little or no disruption | Small, incremental changes leading to sequential adjustments in the current way of doing things. Intergenerational continuity is common. |

**Synopsis:** **We seem to be cycling between severe and extreme turbulence in technology, with the edge given to extreme levels.**

There is nearly ubiquitous access to transformative technology in the form of smart phones, but not in other areas of technology. As in other areas reviewed in this chapter, definitions of "we" and "us" vary widely, leading to differing positions in technology use and availability. National governments able and willing to use technology against citizens, always the case but this opportunity is enhanced with ever-greater levels of technology available. Privacy issues abound as well as questions of who gets to benefit from technology. Substance of technological changes is at issue. Destruction of the old order, in publishing, for example, are numerous. Stability is a thing of the past. Cascading, accelerating change is the norm.

## CONCLUSION: THE LARGER CONTEXT

In this chapter I have reviewed turbulent sociopolitical conditions in three pivotal areas: security, economy, and technology. Levels of turbulence applied to each of these were estimated and all three showed elevated turbulence ranging from moderate/severe, in the cases of security and economy, to severe/extreme for technology.

While analyzing these separately is helpful in identifying specific drivers that create increases in turbulence, we know that all three interact in the real world. For instance, the connection between security and technology can be seen in revelations of US governmental reviews of mobile telephone calls and Internet traffic for millions of citizens, raising the question of where we draw the line between security and privacy rights. Likewise, the connection between technology and the economy can be seen in the drive to use distance learning and online courses to lower administrative costs in higher education. This raises the possibility of a two-tiered system wherein the privileged receive concentrated help from faculty while most students may become relegated to the virtual campus. Finally, the connection among all three is evident in the electric grid that keeps our economy, our security apparatus, and our technology going. On the one hand, this dynamic system defines our world, but its very centrality creates a new and potentially catastrophic vulnerability—witness the current outcry over future cyberattacks.

Combining all three areas into one turbulence gauge would look like Table 5.4.

**Table 5.4** Turbulence gauge for the combined elements of security, economy, and technology with synopsis

| Level of Turbulence | General Definition | Applied to This Situation |
|---|---|---|
| Extreme | Structural damage to the current order | Technology is ubiquitous, thus accelerating seismic changes in security and the economy that, in turn, propel dynamic shifts in technology, thus setting off the cycle of radical change again. |
| Severe | Sense of crisis | **Technology expands to include more people around the world, thus shifting the balance of power in security and economy, resulting in the destruction of older institutions. Yet sufficient stability exists for elements of the current order to sustain themselves.** |
| Moderate | Widespread awareness of serious issues | Technology evolves dynamically but in an orderly way. Adjustments to the economy and security are made ongoing with occasional disruptions that cause temporary crises followed by reversion to previous norms. |
| Light | Little or no disruption | Security, technology, and economy blend harmoniously and predictably. They develop slowly, their dynamics are understood, and changes are measured and appear to be controlled. |

**Synopsis:**

If, as suggested above, we expand our definition of "we" to be more inclusive, then the position to consider is not simply our personal one, nor that of those in our immediate context, but a more universal perspective. This broader view changes how we estimate the combined forces away from the small minority of privileged groups. Security dislocations are evident around the world, at times eroding stability and cascading into greater conflict. As of this writing, the civil war in Syria has the world pondering this very possibility. Similarly, the economic crisis of 2008 has cast a shadow of varying intensity around the world and is still threatening many. The stability of governmental intervention seems to have prevented the kind of wild cascading seen in the 1930s. Finally, the sweeping turbulence in technology change impacts nearly everyone with a mobile device while it erodes whole institutions, thereby destabilizing them and causing a cascade of unpredictable change.

The impact of technology, and its likely influence on security and the economy, is driving the combined turbulence toward severe and even extreme levels, in my opinion. Whether this represents a dismal forecast or opens up a creative opportunity depends upon our ability to respond to the inherent ethical challenges of this dynamic sociopolitical context with creative, flexible, and deeply considered democratic ethical wisdom. While we do stand on a precarious stage, we ought not to forget this critical opportunity.

# REFERENCES

Cook, B. W. (1999). *Eleanor Roosevelt*. New York: Viking.

European Commission Eurostat. (2013). "Unemployment statistics"—statistics explained (2013/6/5). Retrieved from http://epp.eurostat.ec.europa.eu/statistics_explained/index.php/Unemployment_statistics

Glendon, M. A. (2002). *The world made new*. New York: Random House.

Gould, E., & Wething, H. (2012). *U.S. poverty rates higher, safety net weaker than in peer countries*. Retrieved from www.epi.org/publication/ib339-us-poverty-higher-safety-net-weaker/

Gross, S. J. (1998). *Staying centered: Curriculum leadership in a turbulent era*. Alexandria, VA: Association of Supervision and Curriculum Development.

Gross, S. J. (2004). *Promises kept: Sustaining school and district innovation in a turbulent era*. Alexandria, VA: Association of Supervision and Curriculum Development.

Harvey, D. (2005). *A brief history of neoliberalism*. Oxford: Oxford University Press.

Koopman, O., Miel, A., & Misner, P. (1943). *Democracy in school administration*. New York: Appleton-Century.

Kurlansky, M. (2005). *1968: The year that rocked the world*. New York: Random House Trade Paperback.

Madden, M., Lenhart, A., Cortesi, S., Gasser, U., Duggan, M., Smith, A., & Beaton, M. (2013). Teens, social media, and privacy [Pew Internet and American Life Project]. Retrieved from www.pewinternet.org/Reports/2013/Teens-Social-Media-And-Privacy.aspx

Maslow, A. H. (1943). A theory of human motivation. *Psychological Review, 50*(4), 370–396.

Meyer, G. J. (2006). *A world undone: The story of the great war, 1914 to 1918*. New York: Delta.

Meyer, L. (2013). California bill allowing credit for MOOCs passes senate. *Campus Technology*. Retrieved from http://campustechnology.com/articles/2013/06/06/california-bill-allowing-credit-for-moocs-passes-senate.aspx

Miron, G., Urschel, J., Mathis, W. J., & Tornquist, E. (2010). *Schools without diversity: Education management organizations, charter schools, and demographic stratification* (National Education Policy Center Research Brief). Retrieved from http://nepc.colorado.edu/publication/schools-without-diversity

Mishel, L., & Sabadish, N. (2012). *CEO pay and the top 1%: How executive compensation and financial sector pay have fueled income inequality*. Retrieved from www.epi.org/publication/ib331-ceo-pay-top-1-percent/

National Commission on Excellence in Education. (1983). *A nation at risk: The imperative for educational reform*. Washington, DC: US Government Printing Office.

Norberg, K., & Tornsen, M. (in press). In the name of honor: Swedish school leaders' experiences of honor-related problems. *Journal of Educational Administration*.

PBS News Hour. (2013, April 3). *Kentucky school district wants project based learning to outshine testing*. Retrieved from www.pbs.org/newshour/bb/education/jan-june13/learning_04-03.html

Saltman, K. J. (2010). *Urban school decentralization and the growth of "portfolio districts."* Boulder, CO and Tempe, AZ: Education and the Public Interest Center & Education Policy Research Unit. Retrieved from http://epicpolicy.org/publication/portfolio-districts

Sandel, M. J. (2012). What isn't for sale? *The Atlantic*. Retrieved from http://m.theatlantic.com/magazine/archive/2012/04/what-isnt-for-sale/308902/

Schmidt, P. (2013, June 12). AAUP sees MOOCs as spawning new threats to professors' intellectual property. (The Chronicle of Higher Education). Retrieved from http://chronicle.com/article/AAUP-Sees-MOOCs-as-Spawning/139743/

Shapiro, S. H. (2007). *In the Playdough trenches: Early childhood directors' experiences on 9/11/01*. Thesis (Ed.D.) New York: New York University, Steinhardt School of Culture, Education and Human Development.

Shapiro, J. P., & Gross, S. J. (2008). *Ethical educational leadership in turbulent times: (Re)Solving moral dilemmas*. New York: Lawrence Erlbaum Associates.

Shapiro, J. P., & Gross, S. J. (2013). *Ethical educational leadership in turbulent times: (Re)Solving moral dilemmas* (2nd ed.). New York: Routledge.

*The Economist*. (2011). Food safety in China: In the gutter. Retrieved from www.economist.com/node/21534812

Uys, E. L. (1999). *Riding the rails: Teenagers on the move during the Great Depression*. New York: TV Books.

Wang, Y. (2013, March 25). More people have cell phones than toilets, U.N. study shows. *Time Newsfeed*. Retrieved from http://newsfeed.time.com/2013/03/25/more-people-have-cell-phones-than-toilets-u-n-study-shows/#ixzz2VvzkjRH5

Yardley, J. (2008, May 28). Chinese are left to ask why schools crumbled. *New York Times*. Retrieved from www.nytimes.com/2008/05/25/world/asia/25schools.html?pagewanted=all

# 6

# LEADERSHIP, SUSTAINABILITY, AND ETHICS

## MIKE BOTTERY

This chapter is concerned with what educational leaders can learn about the ethics of their practice from a study of environmental systems. It examines three sources for such learning. One source is from an understanding of the epistemology of these two systems, particularly from a greater understanding of the complexity of actions, as well as a necessarily greater provisionality of judgments than is normally recognized. A second source of ethical learning stems from examining when these two systems get into trouble, for both education and the environment suffer from a number of similar kinds of stressors, and similar kinds of crisis points. A final source of ethical learning derives from the fact that both systems appear to benefit from similar prescriptions for remediation and greater sustainability.

## DERIVING ETHICAL PRINCIPLES FROM UNDERSTANDING THE NATURE AND CONSEQUENCES OF LIVING IN COMPLEX SYSTEMS

The argument that education and the environment are both highly complex systems is central to an understanding of their functioning and raises some surprising ethical obligations for educational leaders. Writers like Johnson (2009) and Mitchell (2009) point to a number of similarities of complex systems, arguing that they contain many agents that interact with each other and possess the ability to remember previous events. Because of this, they are able to adjust their thinking and behavior in the light of previous experience. One agent's actions will then change the context for others in the same system and thus condition how they each respond.

Both educational and environmental systems fit this broad definition of complex systems very well. Such systems can be relatively small, such as the interactions in a classroom or school or life within a pond or wood, but the notion of a system is also able to encompass larger complexities, such as national educational systems, and larger environments, such as that of the Amazon basin, or of the arctic tundra. Both are influenced by human activity, clearly so with educational systems, but also with the environment, as while humanity may not be physically present in some environments, our huge global population (currently 7 billion and rising) and its extensive influence upon the environment across the globe means that we still heavily affect most environmental systems. Such far-reaching human presence also means that both systems are influenced by, as Wallace and Fertig (2007) point out, the human ability to "meaning make"—to imagine situations, to act as if they were real, and thereby in many cases to make those situations realities. A number of consequences follow from such understandings of complexity.

A first is that such systems will, necessarily, exhibit large elements of unpredictability. In environmental terms, one example is species extinction. As Wilson (2003) points out, extinctions are caused by a combination of factors—habitat destruction, pollution, invasive species, overpopulation, and human overharvesting—and yet the combination of causes is different in each case, depending upon the nature of a particular species and the ecosystem within which it exists. In education, unpredictability is also exhibited in a variety of ways. With respect to leadership practice, for instance, Hoyle and Wallace (2005) point out that leadership involves dealing not with one particular stakeholder, but with a whole variety of stakeholders, who all may have very different views of educational purposes and what should be done to attain these. Part of the art of leadership—and its sustainability—then lies in managing the balance between these diverse claims. If there is one group (for instance, government) that fails to recognize this, they can place great pressure upon such leadership.

If such systems exhibit such unpredictability, a second consequence is that these systems will probably change and evolve in unexpected—and sometimes undesirable—ways. Many actions, which are proposed as 'solutions' to perceived problems, may then generate other problems more serious than those originally confronted. In the environment, for instance, chemicals used to eradicate insect pests in order to boost crop yields may produce highly damaging effects, through killing off the natural predators of these pests, as well as filtering down into ecosystems and causing long-term damage (Carson, 1962). In education, Bangs, MacBeath, and Galton (2011) have shown how attempts to engineer more effective educational systems through control mechanisms of high-stakes testing and punitive accountability may lead to pupil disaffection through soulless and sterile lessons, increasingly lowered teacher morale, and threats to educational leadership sustainability through increasing numbers wishing to leave the profession, or others not wishing to take up the role.

A final consequence is that such uncertainty and unpredictability increases the further into the future one travels. This uncertainty and unpredictability occur because of a combination of both external and internal causes. As just noted, the way in which actors interact is so complex as to be increasingly difficult to predict. Yet this ability to understand and predict future interactions is made even more difficult by the necessary limitations of an actor's sensory and reasoning abilities, as is any attempt to stand outside behaviors and interactions to understand them. What both actors and observers perceive is then very likely to be a small amount of what is actually occurring. Indeed, an observer's presence is likely to complicate the issue further, as any behavior is liable to be altered by such presence. The result, once again, is a problem of understanding, which escalates exponentially as one moves forward in time. As someone once said, if you want to make God laugh, tell him your plans.

## COMPLEXITY AND THE NEED FOR AN ETHICAL RESPONSE

Such a description enables a better appreciation of the complex reality actors face, as well as the stressors within systems that lead to their unsustainability. This is not only because the stressors are, in part, caused by a lack of appreciation of such complexity, but also because any remediation needs to be couched in such understandings, which involve an ethical commitment to an appreciation of such a complex reality, and actions within them. What is being proposed here is not dissimilar to the position taken by Popper (1966) on the need for an ethical commitment to decision making, based upon rationality and logic, rather than the acceptance of decision making based upon others' political authority, because of the kinds of totalitarian horrors he saw under Hitler and Stalin. For Popper, then, the decision to adopt a quest for truth through rationality, or an acceptance of a totalitarian version of truth, is an ethical commitment and "deeply affect[s] our whole attitude towards other men, and towards the problems of social life" (p. 232).

In a similar manner, the acceptance and adoption of an understanding of a complex reality is an ethical commitment, perhaps extending even further than Popper's claim, for it reaches beyond our relations with other human beings and includes our relations with other living things on this planet.

When such complexity is recognized, the result is almost inevitably the adoption of what Bore and Wright (2009) describe as "wicked" rather than "tame" understandings of problems and resolutions, in both environmental and educational systems. "Tame" problems tend to be those that are simple and linear, easy to describe and understand. However, in accepting them as representing the nature of reality, they probably underdescribe the nature of difficulties faced. The result is liable to be the adoption of solutions that mirror the problems described: neat, simple, linear, and short term in nature, but because they do not adequately address the problem, they are unlikely to produce a suitable complexity of solution. They may well then threaten the system's sustainability and damage those within it. So, for example, if school success is defined as the performance by pupils and teachers of measurable demonstrations of behavioral competence, or the achievement of raw attainment scores, such a definition will probably fail to describe the complex sets of interests, personalities, events, interactions, and contexts that generate such demonstrations and such scores. It can then radically under- and misdescribe the kinds of work that need to be performed to achieve these. Even worse, it will highly likely ignore the huge effort put in by individuals, which may, because of events beyond their influence, fail to reach stipulated criteria. This amounts to a huge injustice and to punitive regimes that lead to undeserved punishments. Such simplistic perspectives may then lead to the long-term unsustainability of both the actors involved and the system itself. In this way, then, an epistemological understanding requires an ethical position.

## THE ETHICAL NEED FOR PROVISIONALITY

This discussion also has major implications for the certainty with which judgments are made. Complex situations and problems will not always be fully understood: There will be many times when what is known by actors within a system is no more than a fragment of the problem. If this is the case, then it needs to become the epistemological basis for educational leaders' views of what they and others can know. Once again, this was well put by Popper (1982) when describing the empirical base of science. He argued, contrary to many "commonsense" views, that science has nothing final or absolute about it. It doesn't rest upon some "solid bedrock," but instead must be likened to a building built on a swamp, where piles are driven down into the swamp. However, it must never be assumed that these will provide some final foundation for the structure. His conclusion is still startling to some today: "We simply stop when we are satisfied that the piles are firm enough to carry the structure, *at least for the time being*" (p. 111, italics in original).

This is not only a statement about the kind of reasoning processes needed in scientific endeavors, but also an ethical requirement with respect to both environmental and educational practice. If one accepts the complexity of systems and of the limitations of actors and observers within these systems, then the limitations of particular judgments about them need to be recognized as well. This then raises concerns about humanity's historic certainty in the boundlessness of environmental resources, still displayed today in what Boulding (1968/1989) described as "cowboy economics," in which an inexhaustible supply of resources and of sufficient new land to dump pollution are assumed. Such certainty needs replacing by a greater humility and provisionalism of understanding and actions. This is encapsulated in Boulding's notion of a spaceship world, on which what is used may be irreplaceable, and what pollutes the living space may never be fully removed. In acknowledging that the full picture may never be known, humanity becomes much more careful in its actions with respect to its environmental resources.

A similar provisionality and humility also needs to be seen within educational systems, particularly with respect to educational leadership. Not only must leaders recognize their limitations, but this recognition should form a cornerstone of policymaking. The effects of educational policies in many parts of the world over the last three decades on those working in education are well documented (Bottery, 2007; Hargreaves, 2003; Hargreaves & Fink, 2003; Levin, 2003). These policies share a number of characteristics: a lack of trust and consultation in professionals, more systematic and high-stakes testing, and more punitive accountability, leading to a greater culture of compliance. In such a culture, many individuals may fail to reflect upon policy purposes and cease to intelligently adapt to concerns, both current and future. As Lauder, Jamieson, and Wikeley (1998) argued, the long-term effect might be to create "a trained incapacity to think openly and critically about problems that will confront us in ten or twenty years time" (p. 51).

Such policies have also been embedded within a "fast" policy climate (Ball, 2008) in which educational results are produced as much for electoral success as for long-term learning benefits. Such time frames, created by short-term political demands rather than educational requirements, hinder proper conceptualization of problems, as well as their local contextualization. In so doing, they also fail to address the personal survival strategies created by "street level bureaucrats" (Lipsky, 1980), which help them manage workloads that do not always permit full attention to all clients.

Because such policies fit electoral rather than educational timetables, they are likely to be hurried and poorly framed and lead to practitioner stress and lowered morale, as those within the system cannot, or do not, want to adapt their values and practices to such aims and time frames. Threats to such actors and the greater likelihood of policy failure both contribute to system unsustainability.

A greater awareness of the provisionality of understanding and of the judgments and policies stemming from this would probably lead to policies that are less adventurous, less risky, and ultimately less damaging to those in the system. Again, this constitutes an ethical injunction, for the adoption of approaches that threaten system sustainability and thereby increase harm to those within the system cannot be ethically acceptable. Once more, epistemology and ethics link arms and suggest new ways of envisaging the work of educational leaders.

## DERIVING ETHICAL POSITIONS FROM UNSUSTAINABLE SITUATIONS

Besides deriving ethical positions from an understanding of a shared complex reality and from a greater acceptance of a provisionality of judgments in both systems, the environment and education suffer similar kinds of problems. This occurs particularly when there is both an excessive exploitation of "resources" within these systems and when substances, practices, or ideas are introduced that "pollute" them. In such cases, crises are likely to arise, as actors within them find it difficult to adapt. Once again, these effects cause harm to actors within the systems and therefore call for ethical stances on how such actors should be treated.

## OVEREXTRACTION AND DAMAGE TO RESOURCES

There is a copious literature on unsustainable environmental resource extraction. Deforestation (Diamond, 2005), marine life (Wilson, 2003), fresh water (Klare, 2008; Smith, 2011), and fossil fuels (Holmgren, 2009; Strahan, 2007) are but a few examples now widely understood. What is perhaps less widely appreciated is the effect that this overextraction has on species survival. Wilson (2003, p. 102) argues that the five previous great species extinctions in geological history are now being added to by a sixth, man-made episode, in which up to half of current species may be extinct by the end of this century. One strong link between species extinction and human activity is argued by Greider (2004), who describes how current neoliberal models of economic activity drive the excessive extraction of environmental resources forward, through its pursuit of consumption and growth as primary values. Moreover, ecological damage is not regarded in such thinking as a cost but as an addition to a country's gross domestic product (GDP) through the action required to clean up the damage. The theory also argues that if firms manage to push such costs onto someone else, they should not be penalized but rewarded, thus encouraging firms to produce products without taking account of potential environmental damage.

Just as in the environment, many kinds of *educational* resources can be overextracted or damaged, particularly those of the human kind. Human actors in educational systems across the globe are being placed under increasing pressure through forms of management based upon low trust, high accountability, and high-stakes testing regimes. These changes are underpinned by the same kinds of neoliberal thinking, for just as the extraction of environmental resources is driven by a desire to extract as much as possible to increase growth and consumption, with little thought for the sustainability of such resources, the same kind of thinking applies in education. In the same drive to raise growth and consumption, neoliberal strategies aim to develop competitive workforces, extracting more work from these "human resources" (Bottery, Ngai, Wong, & Wong, 2008; Gronn, 2003; Levin, 2003; Wright, 2011). Worker flexibility, the casualization of labor, the increasing use of fixed term contracts, and the "democratisation of insecurity" (Brown & Lauder, 2001) are all utilized to achieve these ends, in both the private and public sectors, within "greedy organisations" (Gronn, 2003). Through policies of surveillance and punishment, more time and personal commitment are extracted. The initiatives, the rush of policies, and the kinds of management favored in delivering these combine in education to produce what Galton and MacBeath (2008) describe as "initiative overload," with the inevitable issues of increased stress, earlier retirement, and fewer individuals wishing to take up leadership positions (e.g., Levin, 2003; Rhodes & Brundrett, 2009). As with the environment, the requirement to address the effects on human "resources" is fundamentally an ethical one.

## THE POLLUTION OF NORMAL FUNCTIONING

System sustainability is threatened not only by the excessive extraction of resources, but also by the introduction of substances, ideas, or practices that undermine or pollute normal functioning. In environmental terms, this occurs through the introduction of invasive nonnative species and through pollution being left behind after extraction. While some of this occurs through natural processes, human activity has had the largest effect. The deliberate or accidental human introduction of invasive species can devastate a native species population, as it may have no natural protection (Wilson, 2003), while the effects of pollution are probably even more stressful, as demonstrated by oil, nuclear, and synthetic chemical leaks.

In education, the most toxic form of damage has probably been through the importation of noneducational ideas based upon an inappropriate ethic, and the consequent reduction of first-order educational values to a second-order role. While the consideration of ideas and practices from other sectors can be a valuable stimulus to new thinking, the introduction of ideas or practices that run against healthy systemic functioning should be treated with caution. The importation of business ideas into education, such as the primacy of efficiency, consumption, and private advantage, with the downplaying of values, like those of the public good, the championing of equity, and the nurturing of care and trust, are particularly noteworthy. Barber (1984), for example, argues that values central to the development of a citizenship education, like the pursuit of community and public good, have increasingly been replaced by those of individual consumerism. In the process, the notion of education as a collective action for the public good is replaced by the driving force of individual and organizational competition for private gain (Grace, 1994). When this happens, information is seen not as an open process enabling public and community action, but as a commodity to be used for individual and competitive advantage. In like manner, the concept of trust has been used by Fukuyama (1996) to argue its value as a predictor of economic success, rather than as a foundational social and educational relationship attribute. Finally, as the priority of the equity of need has been supplanted by the priority of individual choice, evidence continues to amass of the increasing wealth disparities over the last 20 years (Facer, 2011). The subversion of systemic first-order system values by second-order ones is particularly problematic because these second-order values depend upon first-order ones for a healthy society within which to function. Such subversion then poses genuine problems for systemic sustainability.

## REACHING CRISIS POINT

When changes are large and/or occur rapidly, system actors may be incapable of adapting, and crisis situations may develop, ultimately leading to system collapse. Rising global temperatures, for example, have led to the concern that many species may be unable to adapt swiftly enough to survive (e.g., Intergovernmental Panel on Climate Change, 2007; Lynas, 2008; Stern, 2006; Wilson, 2003). Such concerns are strengthened by fossil and geological evidence that such rapid climate change has been a contributory factor to previous species extinctions (Benton, 2003; Ward, 2008), as well as archaeological evidence of the rapid and unpredictable collapses of early civilizations (Diamond, 2005). The same kinds of crisis points and system collapse in education are suggested by the examples of evidence detailed above about stress, early retirement, and concerns about leadership sustainability. The behavior of actors in different national systems—not just the teachers and their leaders, but pupils as well—suggest severe compromise.

## ETHICS AND CHANGES IN PRACTICE
## WITHIN SUCH SYSTEMS

Educational and environmental systems then share a number of similar threats to their sustainability; they also exhibit similar symptoms when crisis points arise. This section will suggest that they could also employ similar changes to practice to help in remediation, changes that are underpinned by particular ethical principles. These remediative changes are:

(a) from adopting efficiency as the major criteria for resource usage to sufficiency as the major criterion
(b) from a conception of well-being based on resource consumption to conceptions based more on how well resources are nurtured and maintain themselves

(c) from the adoption of short-term visions for short-term gains to longer-term visions for the benefit of future generations
(d) from environmental concerns being at the periphery of educational leadership and policymaking to being a central player.

### From Efficiency as the Major Criteria for Educational Resource Usage to Sufficiency as the Major Criterion

Boulding's (1968/1989) description of the need to move from cowboy to spaceship economics in how humanity treats the planet it depends upon has been further developed by Princen (2005). He argues for a move from a "frontier world" (a cowboy world where environmental needs are not considered) to an "environmental protection world" (where the environment is one factor in decision making) to a "sustainability world" (where environmental considerations are the priority). Championing this last position, Princen calls for an embrace of "imperative sufficiency" over all other considerations, including over values like efficiency, growth, and consumerism. He argues that where there is a realistic possibility of environmental systemic collapse, then actions to ensure the maintenance of the environment to at least present levels should take precedence over all other considerations. If transferred to education (see Bottery, 2012), this position would argue that major systemic problems caused by the demands on "human resources" would lead to the same need to adopt an imperative educational version—where the protection of those humans who resourced the system is paramount.

Environmentally, the position of imperative sufficiency can be based on the ethical argument that other species need to be viewed as more than a means to the end of human economic growth and consumption; as Singer (2006) and others have argued, species have rights to existence irrespective of their usefulness to human beings. This ethical argument can be extended to education, for it can be argued that the activity of education should not be primarily a matter of enhancing economic supply and demand. In this model, governments, private organizations, and consumers decide on what is needed from the education system and trained human resources supply those needs. An ethical—and inherently educational—position would, instead, argue that a primary function of education is the nurturing of learning relationships among human beings, where the primary concern is in the growth of potentials beyond any purely economic concerns. Educators should, by this argument, be viewed as resourceful humans engaged in a meeting and development of minds. Furthermore, on this basis, as much concern for the welfare of the educators should be displayed as is for their students. Having worth and value in their own right, an imperative version of sufficiency would better recognize their existences, their needs, and their rights.

### From a Conception of Well Being Based on Resource Consumption, to One Based on How Well Resources Are Nurtured and Maintained

Such a notion of sufficiency then argues that both the environment and those within educational systems need to be regarded not as means to ends but as ends in themselves. For those within education systems, it places center stage the perennial question of what is good for them and what constitutes their well-being. In the light of the discussion so far, it argues that human well-being should not be measured by how fast resources (human or nonhuman) can be consumed, but by how well they are nurtured and maintained. As Princen (2005, p. 24) puts it, current policy attitudes tend to support the idea that "goods are good, so more goods are better." Yet, while a degree of consumption will always be essential for physical well-being, a strong literature now argues that consumption satisfies only up to a certain point. Thus, while the GDP of countries like the US and the UK has risen consistently since the 1950s, other measures like the general progress indicator (GPI), which have much broader conceptions of well-being beyond the purely economic, have remained static or actually declined (Bok, 2010; Haidt, 2006; Hamilton, 2004; Layard, 2006). Beyond a certain point, then, consumption hasn't produced better overall well-being. Instead, as writers like Seligman (2011), Diener and Biswas-Diener (2008), and Layard (2008) argue, a sense of genuine long-term well-being comes from very different factors—like the satisfaction derived from striving for personally fulfilling accomplishments, engagement in meaningful relationships, and the nurturing of physical and mental health. The message seems clear: Individuals (and their societies) would be healthier and more fulfilled if they spent more time nourishing things like their social connectedness.

### From a Reduced Focus on Short-Term Visions for Short-Term Gains, to the Greater Adoption of Longer-Term Visions for the Benefit of Future Generations

The implications for educational leaders are clear: The discussion of the good life, of what constitutes well-being, is not to be left to others—they are integral to the role of the educator. As importantly, this argument, when framed within a longer-term perspective, also asks educational leaders to move beyond consideration of the well-being of those within any personal circle, society, or generation. It calls for a reassessment of the kinds of resources needed to nurture such relationships now and in the future.

Such changes in perception then lead necessarily to changes in perceptions of time scale. When the dominant societal motif is consumption, and usually immediate consumption, societal attention will almost inevitably be on the short term. A focus on both resource maintenance and the rights of other living things requires, however, a review not only of current conditions, but perhaps more importantly of projections of their likely condition into the future. This is, perhaps, the seminal point of the most quoted definition of sustainable development: that from the Brundtland Report (World Commission on Environment and Development, 1987), which argued that sustainability is achieved when "the needs of the present are met . . . without compromising the ability of future generations to meet their needs" (p. 8).

Brundtland was talking about the needs of future human generations, but the argument can and should be extended to other species: Sustainability is achieved not only when the present needs of species are met, but when thought is given to how the needs of future generations of different species are not compromised. Such future focus is also picked up in the discourse on educational sustainability (most notably in the form of leadership sustainability). Derived from the earlier environmental discourse, writers like Hargreaves and Fink (2003) argue that "educational reform in recent years has sacrificed depth of learning to the achievement of standardized testing" and that this has prevented the ability "to plan for a more sustainable future" (p. 694).

The argument for longer-term visions—both environmentally and educationally— are then very powerful. They demand from educational leaders a focus on the needs of those not yet born, and therefore on the need for a concern for intergenerational equity. While there are arguments questioning the rights of the unborn (Partridge, 2003), an approach that fails to take account of the needs of those not yet born, because of a focus on the needs of those currently in existence, seems a highly questionable self-serving position—particularly if it focuses on only one species. In an age when global resources currently need to supply the needs of 7 billion people (probably 10 billion by midcentury), educational leaders need to move beyond thinking of both intragenerational human equality and intergenerational human equality to include the needs of other species as well. This requires them to facilitate views of society, population, resources, and the environment that recognize, as perhaps never before, that those in the present need to consider the needs of those yet to be born.

### Conclusion—Moving Environmental Concerns from the Periphery of Educational Leadership and Policy-Making Concerns to Being a Central Player

The fourth major change then becomes the conclusion to this piece. This chapter has argued that an understanding of environmental and educational systems requires both more complex and provisional views and that ethical injunctions, deriving from these, argue for a deliberate avoidance of "tamer" understandings that harm those within the systems involved. From such a position, it was then argued that environmental and educational systems suffer a number of similar problems, particularly the damaging effects that occur when "resources" are excessively exploited and when system functioning is damaged by the introduction of external substances, practices, or ideas. Similar kinds of problems, however, also allow for similar kinds of remediative actions. These include the adoption of sufficiency, rather than efficiency, as a dominant principle for societal functioning, a broader consideration of the meaning and achievement of well-being, not just for human beings but for other species as well, and the need for longer time lines. In doing so, it has demonstrated the importance of a number of ethical concerns—of seeing people and other species as ends rather than as means to ends, of the need to debate the meaning and achievement of environmental and human well-being, and of both intra- and intergenerational equity.

Perhaps the final sobering conclusion, though, is this: While educational leaders have much to learn from a study of the environment for the values, policies, and practice they bring to their work, this addresses only the tip of the iceberg. If thought on the environment is used only as an aid to leadership thinking and development, then a much bigger, and more important, picture is missed. If there are real possibilities that the world's icecaps are on the point of irreversible meltdown, if the world's climate is at a tipping point, which could lead to the collapse of present environmental systems, then taking note of these for the sake of improving leadership practice may well be looking down the wrong end of the telescope. Shouldn't these challenges mean the forefronting of environmental and species values for educational leaders? If the environment is not made a central concern of educational leadership, there may be, in the not too distant future, few educational systems within which to make it such. The question to ask, then, is: If we have not inherited the world from our ancestors but, rather, have borrowed it from all life to come, in what condition will we return it? Perhaps, then, this is the critical ethical issue with which educational leaders should be concerned and from which their ethical leadership should be developed.

## REFERENCES

Ball, S. J. (2008). *The education debate*. Bristol, UK: The Policy Press.

Bangs, J., MacBeath, J., & Galton, M. (2011). *Reinventing schools, reforming teaching*. London: Routledge.

Barber, B. (1984). *Strong democracy*. Berkeley: University of California Press.

Benton, M. (2003). *When life nearly died*. London: Thames and Hudson.

Bok, D. (2010). *The politics of happiness*. Princeton, NJ: Princeton University Press.

Bore, A., & Wright, N. (2009). The wicked and the complex in education: Developing a trans-disciplinary perspective for policy formulation, implementation and professional practice. *Journal of Education for Teaching, 35*(3), 241–256.

Bottery, M. (2007). Educational leaders in a globalising world: A new set of priorities? *School Leadership and Management, 26*(1), 5–23.

Bottery, M. (2012). Leadership, the logic of sufficiency, and the sustainability of education. *Educational Management Administration and Leadership, 40*(4), 449–464.

Bottery, M., Ngai, G., Wong, P. M., & Wong, P. H. (2008). Leaders and contexts: Comparing English and Hong Kong perceptions of educational challenges. *International Studies in Educational Administration, 36*(1), 56–71.

Boulding, J. (1989). The economics of the coming spaceship earth. In M. Allenby (Ed.), *Thinking green: An anthology of essential ecological writing* (pp. 133–138). London: Barrie and Jenkins. (Original work published 1968)

Brown, P., & Lauder, H. (2001). *Capitalism and social progress*. Basingstoke, UK: Palgrave.

Carson, R. (1962). *Silent spring*. New York: Houghton Mifflin.

Diamond, J. (2005). *Collapse*. London: Penguin.

Diener, E., & Biswas-Diener, R. (2008). *Happiness: Unlocking the mysteries of psychological wealth*. Oxford: Blackwell.

Facer, K. (2011). *Learning futures: education, technology, and social change*. London: Routledge.

Fukuyama, F. (1996). *Trust: The social virtues and the creation of prosperity*. London: Penguin.

Galton, M., & MacBeath, J. (2008). *Teachers under pressure*. London: Sage.

Grace, G. (1994). Education is a public good: On the need to resist the domination of economic science. In D. Bridges & T. McLaughlin (Eds.), *Education and the marketplace* (pp. 126–138). London: Falmer.

Greider, W. (2004). *The soul of capitalism*. New York: Simon and Schuster.

Gronn, P. (2003). *The new work of educational leaders*. London: Paul Chapman.

Haidt, J. (2006). *The happiness hypothesis*. London: Arrow Books.

Hamilton, C. (2004). *Growth fetish*. London: Pluto Press.

Hargreaves, A. (2003). *Teaching in the knowledge society*. Milton Keynes, UK: Open University Press.

Hargreaves, A., & Fink, D. (2003). *Sustainable leadership*. San Francisco: Jossey-Bass.

Holmgren, D. (2009). *Future scenarios*. Dartington, UK: Green Books.

Hoyle, E., & Wallace, M. (2005). *Educational leadership: Ambiguity, professionals, and managerialism*. London: Sage.

Intergovernmental Panel on Climate Change. (2007). *Contribution of working panel II to the fourth assessment report of the Intergovernmental Panel on Climate Change: Summary for policymakers*. Retrieved from www.ipcc.ch/pdf/assessment-report/ar4/wg2/ar4-wg2-spm.pdf on 7/08/08

Johnson, N. (2009). *Simply complexity.* London: Oneworld Press.

Klare, M. (2008). *Rising powers, shrinking planet.* London: Oneworld Press.

Lauder, H., Jamieson, I., & Wikeley, F. (1998). Models of effective schools: Limits and capabilities. In R. Slee, G. Weiner, & S. Tomlinson (Eds.), *School effectiveness for whom?* (pp. 51–69). London: Falmer.

Layard, R. (2006). *Happiness: Lessons from a new science.* London: Penguin.

Levin, B. (2003). Educational policy: Commonalities and differences. In B. Davies & J. West-Burnham (Eds.), *Handbook of educational leadership and management* (pp. 165–176). Thousand Oaks, CA: Sage.

Lipsky, M. (1980). *Street-level bureaucracy.* New York: Russell Sage Foundation.

Lynas, M. (2008). *Six degrees.* London: Harper Perennial.

Mitchell, M. (2009). *Complexity: A guided tour.* Oxford: Oxford University Press.

Partridge, E. (2003). Future generations. In D. Jamieson (Ed.), *A companion to environmental philosophy* (pp. 377–390). Oxford: Blackwell.

Popper, K. (1966). *The open society and its enemies* (2 vols). London: Routledge and Kegan Paul.

Popper, K. (1982). *The logic of scientific discovery.* London: Hutchinson.

Princen, T. (2005). *The logic of sufficiency.* Cambridge, MA: MIT Press.

Rhodes, C., & Brundrett, M. (2009). Growing the leadership talent pool: Perceptions of heads, middle leaders and classroom teachers about professional development and leadership succession planning within their own schools. *Professional Development in Education, 35*(3), 381–398.

Seligman, M. (2011). *Flourish: A new understanding of happiness and well-being.* London: Nicholas Brearley Publishing.

Singer, P. (Ed.). (2006). *In defence of animals: The second wave.* Oxford: Blackwell.

Smith, L. (2011). *The new north: The world in 2050.* London: Profile Books.

Stern, N. (2006) The Stern review. Executive summary. Retrieved from www.hmtreasury.gov.uk/media/9/9/CLOSED_SHORT_executive_summary.pdf

Strahan, D. (2007). *The last oil shock.* London: John Murray.

Wallace, M., & Fertig M. (2007). Applying complexity theory to public service change: Creating chaos out of order? In M. Wallace, M. Fertig, & E. Schneller (Eds.), *Managing change in the public services* (pp. 36–56). Oxford: Blackwell.

Ward, P. (2008). *Under a green sky.* New York: HarperCollins.

Wilson, E. O. (2003). *The future of life.* London: Abacus.

World Commission on Environment and Development. (1987). *Our common future.* (The Brundtland Report). Oxford: Oxford University Press.

Wright, N. (2011). Between 'bastard' and 'wicked' leadership? School leadership and the emerging policies of the UK coalition government. *Journal of Educational Administration and History, 43*(4), 345–362.

# 7

## SEEKING SOCIAL JUSTICE

### RACHEL MCNAE

He aha te mea nui o te ao? He tangata! He tangata! He tangata![1]

[When asked, "What is the most important thing in the world?
The reply is: It is people, it is people, it is people!"]

(Maori proverb)

The passion of people, and the reality of our limitations when meeting the needs of many, or just a few, as the case may be—is immense.

Social justice is about people, their interaction and actions with and for one another.

Socially just educational leadership comes about through asking what direction are we going in and does this indeed have the importance of 'people, people, people' at the forefront?

(Reneti, 2012)

The Maori *whakatauki* (Kōrero Māori, Whakatauki proverbs) shared above frames the focus of this chapter. It encourages those who read it to focus their attention on nurturing the people around them and the relationships that connect and embrace these people. It is my belief that such a whakatauki is pertinent for educational leaders as they bring forward past stories and experiences to navigate the increasingly complex challenges within their centers for learning, schools, and wider communities while at the same time holding relationships central to their work. Reneti (2012), an educational leader working in the area of early childhood education, has contextualized this whakatauki in her work to illuminate its relevance to the relational focus of socially just educational leadership.

To this end, the purpose of this chapter is twofold. First, it examines the concept of social justice within an educational context. Complexities associated with defining social justice leadership are identified and core principles of social justice are illustrated in educational contexts as an attempt to make sense of the key facets of leading with socially just intent. Second, the building of respectful relationships, through the engagement of student voice, is presented as an example of socially just leadership practice within educational settings. Through presenting a detailed case study, actions toward raising socially just consciousness and upholding core principles of social justice are described. Overall, this chapter provides an insight into ethical educational leadership, which is epitomized through a commitment to social justice. The intention is to engage the reader in broader social action to transform oppressive and exploitative circumstances in educational settings that not only marginalize and exclude student voice from school decision-making processes but also impact on student learning.

## DEFINING LEADERSHIP FOR SOCIAL JUSTICE

*Leadership and social justice are not natural bedfellows; nor are leadership and inclusion. The extent to which leadership meshes with social justice or inclusion depends on the way in which leadership is conceived, that is, in the way that relationships are envisioned among members of institutions, in the roles that are prescribed for individuals and groups, and in the ends to which leadership activities are directed.*

(Ryan, 2006, p. 7)

Radical shifts in educational leadership arising from increasing globalization continue to challenge traditional notions of what it means to be an educational leader. With an increasing emphasis on the growing complexity and diversity of educational contexts, paramount have become the protection and promotion of equal rights and justice and care required to ensure that differing perspectives are valued and included when ensuring the effectiveness of educational leaders (Rapp, 2002). While there is an expectation for educators to lead this continuous change in order to keep up with accelerated globalization across broader social, political, and economic contexts, there is an implicit expectation for educational leaders to also protect and uphold principles of social justice (Blackmore, 2002). It is therefore not surprising that school leaders in their increasingly diverse communities play a key role in supporting social justice practices in schools.

Thus, recent scholarship scoping the role of leadership preparation programs in developing "socially just" leaders is becoming increasingly prominent as educationalists seek support to manage the increasing diverse communities that walk through their school gates. However, as outlined above by Ryan (2006), the relationship between leadership and social justice is neither clear-cut nor well defined, and defining social justice leadership becomes a complex task. With a multitude of definitions in the literature illustrating varying understandings of what social justice leadership can be (for example, Blackmore, 2002; Bogotch, 2002; Furman & Gruenewald, 2004; Rapp, 2002; Strachan, 2005), the topic itself is rife with complexities and uncertainties. Not surprisingly, then, Furman (2012) laments the paucity of social justice research particularly in relation to its essential role in the practice of educational leadership.

So, the question needs to be asked: What is meant by the phrase "social justice"? Research *on* and *for* social justice holds increasing prominence in scholarship. As this concept has received more attention, a number of definitions have been promoted as reflecting the contextualized nature of social justice leadership. In this burgeoning body of literature, some common themes prevail. Lee's (2007) definition below encapsulates many of the discourses considered essential by scholars when describing social justice:

> Social justice involves promoting access and equity to ensure full participation in the life of a society, particularly for those who have been systematically excluded on the basis of race/ethnicity, gender, age, physical or mental disability, education, sexual orientation, socio-economic status, or other characteristics of background or group membership. Social justice is based on a belief that all people have a right to equitable treatment, support for their human rights, and fair allocation of societal resources.
>
> (p. 1)

Within the limitations of this chapter, providing a definition that encapsulates all of these areas of social justice is unrealistic, therefore it is useful to examine this definition with the purpose of highlighting themes that permeate the literature specific to socially just, ethical educational leadership.

Firstly, leading in socially just ways involves addressing and eliminating marginalization in schools. Giving attention to issues of social justice encourages educational leaders to focus "on the experiences of marginalized groups and inequities in educational opportunities and outcomes" (Furman, 2012, p. 194).

Secondly, themes of inclusion underscore most social justice work as educational leaders seek to break down barriers to opportunity. Ryan (2006) believes that "if people are meaningfully included in institutional practices and process" (p. 5), social justice can be achieved. However, meaningful inclusion requires thoughtful and embedded change. For example, integrating marginalized groups into an already existing system can actually become an unjust practice. These new members may become situated in a system that further perpetuates their marginalization, as they may not have the skills or resources to participate within the system. Ryan argues, "Inclusion involves more than engineering minor problems; it can only be achieved when the structure and inherent features of an already unequal system are changed" (p. 7).

Thirdly, there is an implicit understanding that educational leaders will not only come to *know* instances of injustice and systems that perpetuate marginalization, but they will also *act* with socially just intent to eliminate the discourses and systems that create these situations in the first place. Leaders who are cognizant of social justice are concerned with the common good and, as Howell and Avolio (1992) note, will sacrifice self-interest for the sake of the collective good. The essential actions of educational leaders in bringing stakeholders together to understand their role in an unjust system, to transform the people who are part of the problem so they become part of the solution, and to access capabilities to reverse injustice cannot be over-looked. It is these actions of socially just educational leaders that shift institutional arrangements and systems toward participation and inclusion as they strive to create equity through transforming traditional discourses and conditions. Consequently, a key role of the socially just educational leader is to reveal instances of injustice and to disrupt and subvert arrangements that promote marginalization and exclusionary processes (Lyman, Strachan, & Lazaridou, 2012). Thus, educational leaders are called to action simply by the nature of their profession, and Stevenson (2007) argues, "The school principal, with the authority and influence that their position confers, is clearly a pivotal individual in shaping the organisational culture" (p. 774).

Whether it is through the implementation of programs that address the needs of marginalized groups or actions that seek to interrogate and change systems that exclude individuals, educators play a key role in modeling socially just action and supporting others to do the same. Theoharis (2007) calls for educational leaders to "make issues of race, class, gender, disability, sexual orientation, and other histori-cally and currently marginalizing conditions . . . central to their advocacy, leadership practice, and vision" (p. 223). However, such action must be informed, and Lyman and colleagues (2012) highlight the importance of having knowledge or experience of "local manifestations of global issues" so that leaders and school communities are moved individually and collectively to leadership commitments that emphasize social justice.

## OVERCOMING BARRIERS TO SOCIALLY JUST LEADERSHIP

Leading for social justice is frequently touted as the magic bullet to solve societal woes and address academic underachievement in schools. However, Scanlan (2012) purports that although "socially just educational leadership focuses on reducing inequalities within schools" (p. 348), such practice can be difficult, and eliminating educational inequalities is "an ambitious and elusive goal" (p. 349). Significant barri-ers exist to addressing social justice. Most commonly experienced is what Theoharis (2004) terms "internalized oppression" (p. 6), whereby existing structures and sys-tems may provide benefits for particular communities or individuals, and there may be resistance to changing the status quo, as these actions may disrupt current enti-tlements or advantages. Strachan (1997) calls for leaders to develop ongoing resis-tance to these oppressive contexts. By committing to actions of social justice, such as democratic decision making, establishing meaningful relationships, and integrating stakeholders in decision-making processes, educational leaders can seek to disrupt oppressive practices.

Furthermore, a lack of understanding, knowledge, and commitment to issues of social justice can prevent social justice issues being addressed. Darling-Hammond (2002) indicates that social justice issues may not be well understood and educators may not want to engage in such issues, either because they may not know they exist or tackling them is perceived as too difficult. Rusch and Horsford (2008) believe that "social justice is much easier to study and intellectualize than to actualize in practice"

(p. 354). Shields (2004) warns that a "commitment and good intentions are not enough" (p. 8) and suggests that educational leaders can be supported in their work through embracing core principles of social justice in their leadership practice. It is therefore useful to illustrate this literature in such a way as to be able to emphasize the core principles that support the work of socially just leaders in educational contexts.

## SOME CORE PRINCIPLES OF SOCIAL JUSTICE

Shah (2010) reminds us that in order to encapsulate the "concepts, practices and perceptions in diverse contexts" (p. 27), it is useful to define and theorize about educational leadership in multiple ways. This chapter has highlighted the importance of including social justice as integral in any definition or theorization of educational leadership. Thus, the following core principles of socially just leadership are described so as to aid this outcome.

Socially just leaders are reflective. Hence, educational leaders lead in socially just ways when they critically reflect upon, and understand, how their "underlying beliefs, values, and attitudes may be counterproductive in our quest for education that is both just and excellent" (Shields, 2004, p. 8). Reflection is an important part of developing a conscience of and for social justice. Through the processes of reflection, McKenzie and colleagues (2008) believe that educational leaders can develop a critical consciousness that not only allows them to become attuned to injustices along with the educational practices in their schools and wider communities that generate and perpetuate these. Reflection of this kind is key to creating action within socially unjust situations.

Socially just leaders are action orientated and transformative (Shields, 2010). Making the case for transformative leadership as a core part of socially just leadership practice, Shields (2009) states that such leadership raises questions in relation to "justice and democracy; it critiques inequitable practices and offers the promise not only of greater individual achievement but of a better life lived in common with others. It inextricably links education and educational leadership with the wider diverse social context within which it is imbedded" (p. 55).

Socially just leaders are purposeful. Within this transformational approach to leadership, actions that reflect inclusive and democratic behaviors are displayed, which are linked to a clear agenda of achieving social justice. As McCashen (2005) suggests, "Lobbying, campaigning, advocating, taking direct action, and protesting are important forms of action for social justice" (p. 35). Central to this work is the importance of relationships and recognizing this; a key focus for educational leaders must be that they ensure that their schools are culturally responsive to the needs of students. To this end, the needs of young people should be central, whereas frequently students' voices (the very means by which these needs can be expressed), are ignored, which therefore is an issue of social justice.

Finally, socially just leaders are orientated to socially just pedagogy. A social justice orientation is embedded within leadership practice and cannot be separated from the business of leadership itself. In acknowledging this fact, Theoharis (2008) lays down a challenge for conceptualizing social justice leadership:

To better understand social justice leadership, it is necessary to come to grips with the notion that social justice leadership is not a job someone does from a distance and is not a position for which a principal punches in and punches out. This work with all the bold possibilities and all the turmoil requires grounding in social justice and a complex, highly intelligent, passionate, personal, and humble leader.

(p. 19)

With such a challenge in mind, it is therefore not surprising that leading with socially just intent requires courage and resilience, as well as conviction, for socially just leaders are compelled to be fully involved participants in their own initiatives. Socially just leadership requires the full embodiment and immersion of the leader in any action that seeks to address social injustice.

## SOCIALLY JUST EDUCATIONAL LEADERSHIP IN ACTION

Within educational contexts, it is frequently the teachers who are the designers of curriculum and instruction (Scratchley, 2003). Beane (1990) has suggested that many students, although the key stakeholders in this context, have little control over their learning experiences because the conditions under which they learn have been determined almost entirely by adults. Within the school environment, this culture positions the students as passive recipients of adult protection and knowledge (Smith, Taylor, & Gollop, 2000) and places the students in powerless situations with no meaningful role other than what Kress (2006) describes as passive consumers of information that lacks relevance to their lives. Increasing contributions of scholarship to the area of youth participation research call for the students to be involved in the creation of their learning experiences so that their needs can be more adequately met. Examining the needs of the students and contextualizing this issue within a socially just ontology underpin these relational approaches.

### Engaging Student Voice to Shape Teaching and Learning Approaches

Research investigating student voice is rapidly expanding and many researchers espouse the benefits of involving students in school decision-making processes and curriculum design (Lodge, 2005; MacGregor, 2007; Rudduck & Flutter, 2004; Thomson & Gunter, 2005). This body of research challenges assumptions made about the way young people want to learn with the aim of further meeting their needs. Young people's perceptions about their learning provide researchers and educators with a much-needed source of knowledge, and this can play a key role in creating better conditions for learning in the future.

The literature surrounding students' involvement in decision making within school communities is generally based on one of two United Nations initiatives: the 1989 Convention on the Rights of the Child and the 1998 Lisbon Declaration on Youth Policies and Programs (the Lisbon Declaration). However, in New Zealand, the Treaty of Waitangi[2] is also relevant as Maori draw on cultural knowledge to establish appropriate ways in which *rangatahi* (youth) can best participate in decision making. Despite these conventions, declarations, and treaties, the processes of involving youth in decision making in schools is still in its infancy, as evidenced by those calling for further action in this area (for example, Bolstad, 2011; Campbell, 2000; McNae, 2010; Saunders, 2005; Zeldin, Petrokubi, & MacNeil, 2007).

According to Scratchley (2003), adults make assumptions about what is important for young people to know and do and fail to ask young people what they think, resulting in the creation of "one-size-fits-all" and "top-down" approaches to learning. These are frequently based on their own experiences, and Stanton-Rogers, Stanton-Rogers, Vyrost, and Lovas (2004) warn that there is a need for adults to step away from using their own personal experiences to shape learning experiences:

> If we [school staff] have a concern for what current life is like for today's generation of young people, or what may help them in their futures, we cannot use our own experiences of being young or the aspirations we then held as much of a guide. If we want to promote the life opportunities of young people, if we want to help them to prepare for their futures and make well-informed choices about them, then we need to find out about this 'new world' in which they are growing up.
>
> (p. 117)

Bishop and Glynn's (1999) research emphasizes the importance of changing power relations and creating a learning environment where the learners' sense-making processes are used and developed so they can successfully participate in gaining and constructing knowledge. It is refreshing that they stress the importance of the role of the teacher when interacting with the students so that knowledge is co-created. Including and valuing student voice therefore becomes central to this process, as it is believed by many researching in the area (e.g., Archard, 2013; Mansfield, 2013; McNae, 2010; Mitra, 2003; Saunders, 2005) that if students were engaged in school decision-making approaches and were viewed as active agents of change, which would extend their roles beyond a consultative function, they would be more likely to engage in conversations about learning and how schools can better meet their learning needs.

It is timely to introduce an example of socially just leadership in action. This example is situated within the New Zealand educational context and illustrates the importance of building, establishing, and sustaining relationships in order to address inequities in educational participation. "Revolution" is a leadership development program generated with young women through the formation of youth–adult partnerships and the engagement of student voice. This case study illuminates the power of voice and makes a case for educational leaders to consider the importance of including the voices of students in school decision-making processes.

## "REVOLUTION": ENGAGING STUDENT VOICE TO CO-CONSTRUCT A LEADERSHIP PROGRAM WITH YOUNG WOMEN IN A NEW ZEALAND HIGH SCHOOL

### Situating the Case Study

This qualitative action research study was located in an urban girls' Catholic secondary school and examined the leadership perceptions and experiences of 12 young female students. The focus of this research was to develop an alternative model of leadership curriculum development and engage students in co-constructive pedagogies as a means for them to share their voices. Prior to embarking on this research, I was a teacher at a girls' secondary school in New Zealand. It was during my time there as the Year 13 Dean,[3] that I observed young women being required by staff to take on leadership roles within the school. Moreover, there was minimal preparation for the few opportunities that were available to these students, and in most years, leadership preparation was generally nonexistent except for a loosely termed "leadership camp."

As a feminist, I was concerned on a number of levels. Firstly, the way that leadership was promoted within the school, solely through formal leadership roles that provided opportunities for only a handful of students, gave students the message that leadership was reserved for "the finest." Secondly, I was concerned by the lack of inclusive and contemporary leadership development opportunities provided to the young women. Thirdly, I was disheartened by the message that the young women received from seeing student leadership existing only in the final years of school. As a result, many of the young women were not engaging in leadership practice within or outside of the school prior to this year level or once they had left school after their final year. This led to my first encounter with leadership development with young secondary school women and, from this, to my ongoing research activities in this area.

### Background to the Research

> Sarah shuffles into the hostel meeting room, her slippers scuffing the already worn carpet as she slowly and deliberately moves across the floor. With a MILO carefully balanced on top of a Cosmo magazine, she looks at me and exhales a sigh of what could only be read as frustration. Placing her mug on the coffee table, she looks over to one of her peers, rolls her eyes, and plunges herself into a space on the awaiting couch. "How long will this take, I've got study," her eyes piercing mine, "AND I've got better things to do."

As a teacher of young women in a secondary school I recall the occasion described above as stemming from the invitation by a school principal to provide leadership guidance for a group of young women in their final year of schooling. I responded to this request by designing and implementing what I thought to be an effective leadership development program for a group of 16- and 17-year-old young women. Supported by postgraduate study in the area of leadership, I scoured my lecture notes, theories, and course readings to design a program that focused on defining, explaining, and practicing leadership. The program took place the following term, and upon reflection I am now not surprised about the "not-so-positive" response I received from the students. As Sarah illustrated in the above example from my research journal, the desire to learn, be involved, and be engaged in what should be a positive learning experience was nonexistent. Upon reflection, I can now see that the content of the program was far removed from the actual contexts in which the young women exercised their leadership, and the definitions and theory were irrelevant to their day-to-day experiences. I cringe as I reflect and feel apologetic, and even embarrassed, that I subjected anyone to such a learning (or not) opportunity.

After completing the delivery of this leadership program, I thought to myself that there had to be a better way to teach young women about leadership. I was a feminist who was supported by my core value of social justice. What should have been important was the leadership experiences of the young women, not the theories and definitions of leadership. These experiences, and the context in which they exercised their leadership, should have been central. I therefore set about redesigning how I might go through this process differently.

### The Purpose of the Research

The underpinning philosophy for the design and implementation of the second leadership program described in this case study was that it had to be a collaborative process between the young women and myself (Saunders, 2005). Also, it was critical that the program be relevant for this group. An imported leadership program created by adults, for adults, was not likely to meet the needs of the young women in a secondary school. This research used a collaborative action research approach to examine the leadership perceptions and experiences of young women in order to co-construct and evaluate a leadership development curriculum to meet their needs. I believed that by understanding their leadership beliefs, and their leadership contexts, learning experiences could be designed to develop their leadership practice in a meaningful and relevant way. From my study of the literature, and previous work in this area, I believed that the use of adult–student partnerships (presented in the form of learning communities) and the inclusion of student voice in the negotiation and evaluation of a leadership development curriculum would assist in the creation of a leadership program that met the needs of this particular group of students.

### Description of the Research

Having the voices of the young women as a central part of this research required detailed planning, using a variety of research methods and ensuring that the methods selected allowed for this to happen in a safe and valid way. Methods that also contributed to the formation of the strong youth–adult partnerships were essential. Semi-structured interviews allowed the young women to individually share their voices. Focus group discussions allowed for engaging and interactive discussions among the young women, as well as between the young women and myself. Field notes and artifacts of students' work from workshop activities provided further means by which to gather important information and observations throughout the research.

Over 12 months, a number of key phases were located within an action research framework. The first phase of the research involved making initial contact with the school involved, fulfilling school access requirements, and selecting students for the leadership program and associated research. The second phase involved gaining informed consent for the research from the students and their parents. The third phase involved creating a community of learning so that students got to know each other. Team-building activities and icebreaker games were used as a means for group members to get to know each other. Initial focus group interviews were held to ascertain the young women's views of leadership and their perceptions and beliefs about what it meant to be a leader. The fourth phase involved developing the content and creating the structure for the leadership program. This was done through a second series of focus groups. During these conversations, students shared what they wanted to learn, how they would like to learn it (different learning strategies, both practical and theoretical), and what order the content should follow. Working together, we negotiated a framework that illustrated what the students felt was important to learn, what order to learn it in, and what activities they would use to allow the learning to happen. I also drew on my leadership knowledge and teaching experience to contribute to this and expand the students' ideas about what leadership could be and offer a variety of teaching and learning approaches.

The fifth phase involved facilitating and participating in the leadership program. At the end of each session, the students evaluated what worked in the leadership session and what did not and made suggestions for future improvements and changes. In the sixth phase, a final evaluation of the content and structure of the Revolution program was made by the participants, and changes to the leadership program were suggested. Using evaluation field notes from each of the previous leadership sessions, students participated in focus group conversations and evaluated the whole of the program, making suggestions as to what might work better and what might have more impact or have been more relevant. During this phase, the students also made a presentation to the board of trustees outlining what the program looked like, why and how they created it, the benefits and challenges of the program, and the changes and ideas they would make for the following year.

### Summary of the Research Findings

The findings demonstrated that the process of co-construction provided a valuable opportunity to work with the young women in a youth–adult partnership and create a contextually relevant leadership program. As Kate stated:

> Well I don't really know that much about leadership, so how helpful am I going to be? Like shouldn't we just get told what to do?' . . . But then it got me thinking that maybe the whole thing of being a leader is being able to create stuff and then . . . with your help, of course, which thank God we have your help because I wouldn't know where to start. But then, you didn't know the school, or us so

we helped you there. So, it was good that we sort of realized what a leader needs and then with your input of how we can achieve getting these things with the activities and stuff. That was quite good.

Although the young women initially found the co-construction process difficult, as it challenged the traditional pedagogical approaches they were familiar with, it was also personally rewarding and a source of enjoyment, with the majority of the reasons for this relating to the youth–adult partnerships that were created. The students appreciated the opportunity to work alongside an adult, be consulted about their prior knowledge and learning needs, and see their opinions acted upon. Anna commented:

So, why don't all teachers do this [ask us what and how we want to learn]? I mean, if they did, I reckon we would learn more, and enjoy it. I mean, teachers could have made Revolution, but it would've been lame. Had like heaps of those peer support games and theory 'cause that's what teachers like. But, I reckon, it's cool because our ideas are there and they suit us. Like heaps of drama stuff, discussions, and different activities . . . we have all included how we like to learn.

Other benefits of this youth–adult partnership included enhancing the young women's sense of agency in school decision making about learning as they actively sought solutions to instances of marginalization in their school context. Some students felt the need to challenge the lack of leadership development opportunities that existed within the school and made plans to bring the school on board with what was happening. Kate took it upon herself to write to the principal and ask for funding to support the program. She received over $400 to buy resources for the following year to ensure that the leadership learning was sustained for another group of students. In her discussions afterward, she reported:

I know, cool, eh? But I just wished she had read my letter, she kinda went . . . skim . . . as she flicked through to the numbers . . . she didn't even read it and I had spent heaps of time on it . . . we even had a letterhead from Revolution . . . she just gave me a slip and sent me to the office [for the money].

The findings reported that it was important to the students that adults showed they valued what the students contributed to the school community. These findings support key themes in the literature, such as the work of Meier (1993), who highlighted the need for connection, inclusivity, participation, and collaboration. Furthermore, the sense of *agency* (Watkins, 2005) assisted the group to work as a collective, generating a belief from all members of the learning community that they could make informed choices and take action on issues that mattered to them. By being a part of the learning community, there was also a sense of *belonging* through membership. Respect, inclusion, acceptance, and support were key ingredients for this to occur, reflecting what Watkins deems as important elements of an inclusive, socially just learning community. Through developing a sense of belonging, there was a growth of commitment within the community, which illustrated the *cohesion* among the community members. This cohesion assisted in the creation of joint action when required. Lastly, recognizing and embracing the differences of others illustrated that *diversity* was a key facet in the creation of the learning community. This may have assisted in creating an inclusive community of difference as described by Shields and Seltzer (1997), in which culturally diverse viewpoints and practices are accepted and celebrated.

## SOCIALLY JUST LEADERSHIP—CREATING SPACES FOR VOICES, ACTING UPON CHOICES

> *The tide is turning from the antiquated notion of students as passive recipients of teaching, to a new recognition on the interdependence that is necessary between students and adults.*
>
> (Fletcher, 2004, p. 4)

This case study is an example of engaging students' voices to challenge the traditional notion of the teacher–student relationship and, as emphasized by Fletcher above, set out to reshape the relationship between the teacher and the student. Founded on the notion that young people and adults could work together in partnership within a learning community to share their voices and make decisions about teaching and learning, this work illustrates leaders purposefully engaging in socially just leadership practices as they seek to include and act upon the voices of students.

Boomer, Lester, Onore, and Cook (1992), among others, call for both students and teachers to work in partnership to create curricula in schools that are truly meaningful and beneficial to all involved. This is often termed "negotiating the curriculum," and to this end, Libby, Sedonaen, and Bliss (2006) assert:

> Youth have the right to participate in the decision-making that affects their lives not only because it provides a key developmental process, but also because the systems in place to address their needs will be better positioned to achieve positive youth outcomes when they have integrated young people into their planning and decision-making processes.
>
> (p. 14)

Acquiring knowledge that is selected by people outside their contexts may cause students to become passive recipients and not motivated or encouraged to become lifelong learners (Bishop & Glynn, 1999). It is vital, therefore, for teachers to listen to the voices of students, allowing them to help shape the content, process, style, and language of their learning experiences. Hart's (1992) ladder of participation is a model frequently used by many in the area of youth development and student engagement. In this model he uses the illustration of a ladder and its rungs to show how the level of student engagement, and the influence of adults, can impact on the learning experience and engagement for young people. At the bottom of the ladder he shows a tokenistic approach to involving students in decision making that results in minimal student engagement. As they move up the rungs of the ladder, they pass through increasing levels of engagement. At the top rung, students have meaningful and student-driven ownership of learning processes and a high level of engagement. This model illustrates the important aspect of not just listening to the voices of students (which he describes as tokenism, decoration, and often manipulation), but also creating action from this, which can result in a high degree of participation (which he describes as child-initiated processes with shared decision making). Similarly, Fielding (2004) emphasizes key aspects of student engagement, calling for a move from dissemination, through discussion and teacher-led dialogue, to student-led dialogue. Hargreaves (2006) similarly focuses on the aspect of student voice and states: "Co-construction focuses heavily on the talk that takes place between teacher and learner—their learning conversations" (p. 18).

Drawing on research within the New Zealand context, the process of co-construction with students is a journey that uses group members' voices as an essential tool to move us from power-imposing models to power-sharing models of interrelationships (Bishop & Glynn, 1999). Bruner (1996) also believes in restructuring power relations and states that we need to:

> characterize the new ideas as creating communities of learners. Indeed, on the basis of what we have learned in recent years about human learning—that it is best when it is participatory, proactive, communal, collaborative and given over to constructing meanings rather than receiving them.
>
> (p. 84)

Bishop and Glynn (1999) purport that this kind of learning environment can be created through providing contexts where learning can take place actively and reflectively. The work of Beane and Apple (1995) is central to creating such an environment. They draw attention to the principles of democratic education, advocating for a learning environment that encourages the open flow of ideas, a concern for the common good, trust in the group's ability, and the active use of critical thinking to evaluate experiences and ideas—all facets of socially just leadership. A variety of learning styles needs to be included and students must be given the power to determine which learning styles they need to use in order to learn best. Denner, Meyer, and Bean (2005) support this collaborative approach to learning when working with young women. They believe that settings in which young women have the opportunity to work together and practice a range of leadership styles in a supportive environment provide them with a forum where they do not have to choose between maintaining relationships or hiding their opinions (which is often the case in female youth peer groups). On a slightly broader agenda, Cook-Sather (2002) argues that "authorizing students' perspectives is essential because of the various ways it can improve education practice, re-inform existing conversations about educational reform and point to the discussions and reform effects yet to be undertaken" (p. 3). It is unfortunate, however, that the voices of young people are not utilized and are rarely heard in educational leadership research, even though they are paramount to educational processes (Brooker & Macdonald, 1999). Highlighting the importance of drawing attention to this as an issue of social justice.

## CONCLUDING THOUGHTS—IMPLICATIONS FOR ETHICAL EDUCATIONAL LEADERS

*Until we can understand the assumptions in which we are drenched, we will not know ourselves.*

(Adrienne Rich, cited in Rapp, 2002)

To lead with socially just intent highlights a number of implications for educational leaders. Leaders for social justice in educational contexts work with strong moral purpose and seek to educate the public on human rights and obligations toward others (Blackmore, 2002). However, as Rapp (2002) points out, the increasingly telescopic focus on performativity can lead to reduced attention paid to issues of social justice, or what Blackmore calls "the 3 R's of socially just learning systems, networks, alliances and partnerships" (p. 214)—responsibility, recognition, and reciprocity. Rather than being inspired by a shared vision for a just society, Rapp (2009) argues that "the activities of students and educators are increasingly governed by irrational criteria of efficiency, profit, and quick returns" (p. 81). Accountability and performance can easily become the key foci of educational leaders and dominate systems of education. The responsibility commonly lies with the educational leader to make sense of these complex times and place importance on the relationships within their educational contexts.

Educational leaders have a responsibility to ensure that spaces are created for the voices of all stakeholders in their communities. It is within these spaces that information can be shared to enhance the teaching and learning actions that take place.

Through coming to know the teaching and learning relationship as one of reciprocity, the Maori principles of *ako* can be emphasized to break down traditional discourses associated with models of power and ownership of knowledge. In Maori culture, the term *ako* is used to describe a teaching and learning relationship where the educator is also learning from the student and "effective teaching and learning is based on reciprocal relationships and incorporating the people and contexts of children's wider lives" (Ministry of Education, 2009, p. 10). A key part of achieving this will be coming to understand the complexities associated with student voice initiatives and supporting staff to develop respectful youth–adult partnerships that allow students and teachers to learn together.

With these ideas in mind, Theoharis (2004) suggests three vital steps for leaders of and for social justice. These steps include learning, infusing, and sustaining. An essential part of learning about social justice is to examine personal perspectives in deep-set assumptions associated with their current leadership contexts. Personal views of the world are formulated, determined, and shaped by experiences, culture, gender, and upbringing (Bishop, 1997). A key action of a socially just educational leader will be the ability to reflect upon the needs of the community and the direction the school must take to ensure appropriate provision for all (Furman, 2012; Thrupp & Lupton, 2006). To lead in socially just ways, educational leaders are required to critically reflect and understand how their "underlying beliefs, values, and attitudes may be counterproductive in our quest for education that is both just and excellent" (Shields, 2004, p. 8).

It will be through dialogue and collaboration that educational leaders will be able to meet the needs of significantly diverse groups. Time and resources must be made available to consider other perspectives (Kana & Aitken, 2007). Through doing so, there can be an increased opportunity for school leaders and teachers to "honor the diverse cultural, linguistic, physical, mental, and cognitive capacities of their students" (Landorf & Nevin, 2007, p. 712). Campbell-Stephens (2009) argues that educational leaders must be aware of these views and the different lenses through which increasingly diverse communities view their rights and responsibilities. Providing opportunities through leadership development programs, for leaders to interrogate and reflect upon these values and beliefs, is a significant part of developing socially just leadership capabilities. However, Brown (2004) states that substantive changes must occur in the ways that educational leaders are prepared and in later work makes suggestions as to what is required for successful leadership training programs to enable leaders to lead effectively with a social justice understanding and the ability to critically reflect and question unjust practices. She believes:

> Courses . . . should require critical thought and systematic reflection . . . [where] students should be introduced to a variety of ideas, values and beliefs surrounding social life, cultural identity, educational reform, and historical practices. They could then be challenged to explore these constructs from numerous, diverse, changing perspectives. Personal biases and preconceived notions they hold about people who are different from themselves by race, ethnicity, culture, gender, socioeconomic class, sexual orientation, and physical and mental abilities could be identified and discussed. As such, these courses would require an active, sustained engagement in the subject matter and an openness of mind and heart.
>
> (Brown, 2004, p. 15)

Infusing and sustaining practices that reflect equity and social justice throughout schools and the communities in which leaders work is an essential aspect of shifting social justice agendas forward, especially as they also have the responsibility of facilitating learning about social justice for others. Knowing the important role of educational leaders in teaching *and* leading for social justice within schools, most importantly, is the understanding of how they came to be, know, and act in socially just ways. As indicated by Rusch and Horsford (2008), these actions are not without their own challenges:

> Learning about social justice is far different from engaging in the emotion-laden work of learning social justice. Frequently, instructors of aspiring educational leaders find that when social justice content is introduced, the adult classroom

becomes a messy community, filled with the untidy and unexamined viewpoints, multiple stereotypes, and carefully crafted biases. Transforming perspectives about critical social justice issues seems an insurmountable task.

(p. 353)

With little research in this area about the development of socially just leadership practice (Furman, 2012), and even less focus on the New Zealand context, further research will be critical in addressing the injustices and inequalities in schools, both in New Zealand and internationally. The recent work of Lyman, Strachan, and Lazaridou (2014) makes a significant contribution to this body of work and pushes boundaries with regard to researching socially just leadership. Termed *critical evocative portraiture,* this new methodology explores the embodied nature of socially just leadership through the examination of narratives that describe lived experiences in leadership. There are a number of distinguishing features that set this methodology apart from other types of narrative inquiry, and it is not in the scope of this chapter to address these. However, one interesting feature of this work is the focus on voice, resonating with the underpinning messages provided by the case study described in this chapter.

Coming to understand social justice leadership as a way of being, a practice that embodies the personal and seeks to disrupt the political, is not easy work. Responding to the call to action requires a diverse range of skills that allows educational leaders to lead in socially just ways. It takes courage, thoughtful and informed action, and reflective processes. Leading in this way and modeling socially just ethical educational leadership can open the door to others, as the attention is drawn back to the central notion of why schools exist—for the students, the students, the students!

## NOTES

1. This is a *whakatauki,* which is a quote or phrase in the Maori language that draws together the thoughts, values, and advice of past generations. Frequently used in Maori culture to share key messages between families and generations, they reflect metaphoric representations of past knowledge related to Maori culture and actions.
2. A significant and historical New Zealand document signed in 1840, outlining an agreement in which Maori gave the Crown rights to govern and to develop British settlement, while the Crown guaranteed Maori full protection of their interests and status and full citizenship rights (Waitangi Tribunal, 2013).
3. A position of pastoral care where a teacher on staff oversees a year group of students alongside her teaching position.

## REFERENCES

Archard, N. (2013). Adolescent leadership: The female voice. *Educational Management Administration Leadership, 41*(3), 336–351.

Beane, J. (1990). *Affect in the curriculum: Towards democracy, dignity and diversity.* New York: Teachers College Press.

Beane, J., & Apple, M. (1995). (Eds.). *Democratic schools.* Alexandria, VA: Association for Supervision and Curriculum Development.

Bishop, R. (1997). Interviewing as collaborative storytelling. *Education Research and Perspectives, 24*(1), 28–47.

Bishop, R., & Glynn, T. (1999). *Culture counts: Changing power relations in education.* Palmerston North, New Zealand: Dunmore Press.

Blackmore, J. (2002). Leadership for socially just schooling: More substance and less style in high-risk, low-trust times? *Journal of School Leadership, 12*(2), 198–222.

Bogotch, I. (2002). Educational leadership and social justice: Theory into practice. *Journal of School Leadership, 12*(2), 138–156.

Bolstad, R. (2011). From "student voice" to "youth–adult partnership." *Research Information for Teachers, 1,* 31–33.

Boomer, G., Lester, N., Onore, C., & Cook, J. (1992). *Negotiating the curriculum: Educating for the 21st century.* London: Falmer Press.

Brooker, R., & Macdonald, D. (1999). Did we hear you? Issues of student voice in curriculum innovation. *Journal of Curriculum Studies, 31*(1), 83–87.

Brown, K. (2004). Leadership for social justice and equity: Weaving a transformative framework and pedagogy. *Educational Administration Quarterly, 40*(1), 79–110.

Bruner, J. (1996). *The culture of education.* Boston: Harvard University Press.

Campbell, J. (2000, October). Time for action. *Young People Now, 138,* 19–24.

Campbell-Stephens, R. (2009). Investing in diversity: changing the face (and the heart) of educational leadership. *School Leadership and Management, 29*(3), 321–331.

Cook-Sather, A. (2002). Authorizing students' perspectives: Towards trust, dialogue and change in education. *Education Researcher, 31*(4), 3–14.

Darling-Hammond, L. (2002). Learning to teach for social justice. In L. Darling-Hammond, J. French, & S. P. Garcia-Lopez (Eds.), *Learning to teach for social justice* (pp. 1–7). New York: Teachers College Press.

Denner, J., Meyer, B., & Bean, S. (2005). Young women's leadership alliance: Youth–adult partnerships in an all female after-school program. *Journal of Community Psychology, 33*(1), 87–100.

Fielding, M. (2004). 'New wave' student voice and the renewal of civic society. *London Review of Education, 2*(3), 197–217.

Fletcher, A. (2004). *Broadening the bounds of involvement: Transforming schools with student voice.* Retrieved from www.studentinvolvement.net

Furman, G. (2012). Social justice leadership as praxis: Developing capacities through preparation programs. *Education Administration Quarterly, 48*(2) 191–229.

Furman, G. C., & Gruenewald, D. A. (2004). Expanding the landscape of social justice: A critical ecological analysis. *Educational Administration Quarterly, 40*(1), 47–76.

Hargreaves, D. (2006). *A new shape for schooling.* London: Specialist Schools and Academies Trust. Retrieved from http://curriculumdesign.ssatrust.org.uk

Hart, R. A. (1992). *Children's participation: From tokenism to citizenship. Innocenti essays no. 4.* Florence, Italy: UNICEF International Child Development Centre.

Howell, J., & Avolio, B. (1992). The ethics of charismatic leadership: Submission or liberation? *The Executive, 6*(2), 43–54.

Kana, P., & Aitken, V. (2007). "She didn't ask me about my grandma"—using process drama to explore issues of cultural exclusion and educational leadership. *Journal of Educational Administration, 45*(6), 697–710.

Kōrero Māori, Whakatauki proverbs. (n.d.). Retrieved from www.korero.maori.nz/forlearners/proverbs.html

Kress, C. A. (2006). Youth leadership and youth development: Connections and questions. *New Directions for Youth Development, 109,* 45–56.

Landorf, H., & Nevin, A. (2007). Inclusive global education: Implications for social justice. *Journal of Educational Administration, 45*(6), 711–723.

Lee, C. C. (2007). *Social justice: A moral imperative for counselors.* Alexandria, VA: American Counseling Association.

Libby, M., Sedonaen, M., & Bliss, S. (2006). The mystery of youth leadership development: The path to just communities. *New Directions for Youth Development, 109,* 13–25.

Lodge, C. (2005). From hearing voices to engaging in dialogue: Problematizing student participation in school improvement. *Journal of Educational Change, 6*(2), 125–146.

Lyman, L., J. Strachan, J., & Lazaridou, A. (2012). *Shaping social justice leadership: Insights of women educators worldwide.* Lanham, MD: Rowman & Littlefield Education.

Lyman, L., Strachan, J., & Lazaridou, A. (2014). Critical evocative portraiture: Feminist pathways to social justice. In I. Bogotch & C. Shields (Eds.), *International handbook of educational leadership and social (in) justice* (pp. 253–274). Netherlands: Springer International Handbooks of Education.

MacGregor, M. G. (2007). *Building everyday leadership in all teens.* Minneapolis, MN: Free Spirit Publishing.

Mansfield, K. (2013). How listening to student voices informs and strengthens social justice research and practice. *Educational Administration Quarterly.* First published online October 17, 2013. doi: 10. 1177/0013161X13505288.

McCashen, W. (2005). *The strengths approach.* St. Lukes Innovative Resources. Maryborough, Australia: Centre Stage Printing.

McKenzie, K., Christman, D., Hernandez, F., Fierro, E., Capper, C., Dantley, M., & Scheurich, J. (2008). From the field: A proposal for educating leadership for social justice. *Educational Administration Quarterly, 44*(1), 111–138.

McNae, R. (2010). Young women and leadership: Sharing conversations to create meaningful leadership learning opportunities. *Journal of Educational Administration, 48*(6), 677–688.

Meier, D. (1993). Transforming schools into powerful communities. *Teachers College Record, 94*(3), 654–658.

Ministry of Education. (2009). *Kia hikitia.* Wellington, New Zealand: Author.

Mitra, D. L. (2003). Student voice in school reform: Reframing student–teacher relationships. *McGill Journal of Education, 38*(2), 289–304.

Rapp, D. (2002). Social justice and the importance of rebellious, oppositional imaginations. *Journal of School Leadership, 12*(3), 226–245.

Reneti, K. (2012). *Educational leadership for social justice.* (Unpublished master's paper). University of Waikato, Hamilton, New Zealand.

Rudduck, J., & Flutter, J. (2004). *How to improve your school: Giving pupils a voice.* London: Continuum.

Rusch, E. A., & Horsford, S. D. (2008). Unifying and integrating messy communities: Learning social justice in educational leadership classrooms. *Teacher Development, 12*(4), 353–367.

Ryan, J. (2006). Inclusive leadership and social justice. *Leadership and Policy in Schools, 5*(1), 3–17.

Saunders, R. (2005). Youth leadership: Creating meaningful leadership programmes for young women through a process of co-construction. *New Zealand Journal of Educational Leadership, 20*(2), 15–30.

Scanlan, M. (2012). A learning architecture: How school leaders can design for learning social justice. *Educational Administration Quarterly, 49*(2), 348–391.

Scratchley, M. (2003). *Hearing their voices: The perceptions of children and adults about learning in health education* (Unpublished doctoral thesis). University of Waikato, Hamilton, New Zealand.

Shah, S. (2010). Re-thinking educational leadership: Exploring the impact of cultural and belief systems. *International Journal of Leadership in Education: Theory and Practice, 13*(1), 27–44.

Shields, C. (2004). Dialogic leadership for social justice: Overcoming pathologies of silence. *Educational Administration Quarterly, 40*(1), 109–132.

Shields, C. (2009). Transformative leadership: A call for difficult dialogue in courageous action in radicalized contexts. *International Studies in Educational Administration, 37*(3), 53–68.

Shields, C. (2010). Transformative leadership: Working for equity in diverse contexts. *Educational Administration Quarterly, 46*(4), 558–589.

Shields, C. M., & Seltzer, P. A. (1997). Complexities and paradoxes of community: Towards a more useful conceptualization of community. *Educational Administration Quarterly, 33*(4), 413–439.

Smith, A. B., Taylor, N. J., & Gollop, M. (2000). *Children's voices: Research, policy and practice.* Auckland, New Zealand: Pearson Education.

Stanton-Rogers, W., Stanton-Rogers, R., Vyrost, J., & Lovas, L. (2004). Worlds apart: Young people's aspirations in a changing Europe. In J. Roche, S. Tucker, & R. Flynn (Eds.), *Youth in society* (pp. 76–90). London: Sage.

Strachan, J. M.B. (1997). Feminist educational leadership in a 'new right' context in Aotearoa/New Zealand. Unpublished Doctoral thesis, University of Waikato, Hamilton, New Zealand.

Strachan, J. M. B. (2005). Working out of my comfort zone: Experiences of developing national women's policy in Vanuatu? *Delta, 7*(1), 47–65.

Stevenson, H. (2007). A case study in leading schools for social justice: When morals and markets collide. *Journal of Educational Administration, 45*(6), 769–781.

Theoharis, G. (2004). *The rough road to justice? A meta-analysis of the barriers to teaching and leading for social justice.* Paper Presented at the University Council of Educational Administration, November 12–15, 2004, Kansas City, MO.

Theoharis, G. (2007). Social justice educational leaders and resistance: Toward a theory of social justice leadership. *Educational Administration Quarterly, 43*(2), 221–258.

Theoharis, G. (2008). Woven in deeply: Identity and leadership of urban social justice principals. *Education and Urban Society, 41*(1), 3–25.

Thomson, P., & Gunter, H. (2005). *Researching students: Voices and processes in a school evaluation.* Paper given at the annual meeting of the American Educational Research Association, Montreal, Canada.

Thrupp, M., & Lupton, R. (2006). Taking school contexts more seriously: The social justice challenge. *British Journal of Educational Studies, 54*(3), 308–328.

Waitangi Tribunal. (2013). The Treaty of Waitangi. Retrieved from www.waitangi-tribunal.govt.nz/treaty/

Watkins, C. (2005). Classrooms as learning communities: A review of research. *London Review of Education, 3*(1), 47–64.

Zeldin, S., Petrokubi, J., & MacNeil, C. (2007). *Youth–adult partnerships in community decision making: What does it take to engage adults in the practice?* National 4H Council. Retrieved from www.fourhcouncil.edu/pv_obj_cache/pv_obj_id_7288E7A

# 8

# LEADING WITH EMPATHY

## QIAN HAIYAN AND ALLAN WALKER

Empathy is acknowledged as an important leadership quality. There is general agreement that empathetic leaders "enhance mutual communication and generate mutual trust . . . between the leader and the follower" (Mackay, Hughes, & Carver, 1990, p. 57). Empathetic leaders do more than just sympathize with the people around them; they use their emotional intelligence to improve their organizations in subtle but important ways (Goleman, 2005).

Whether defined as an affective capacity, i.e., to share others' feelings, or as a cognitive ability, i.e., to understand others' feelings and perspectives, empathy is an "other-focused" rather than an "ego-focused" emotional characteristic (Aaker & Williams, 1998; Ketelle & Mesa, 2006). Other-focused emotion is more consistent with the need for unity, harmony, and the alignment of one's actions with those of another. Such values have been found to be more characteristic of collectivist than individualist societies (Aaker & Williams, 1998; Hofstede, 1980).

Research has consistently found Confucian and neo-Confucian societies[1] to be highly collective and Anglo-American English-speaking countries[2] to be individualistic[3] (Hofstede, 1980, 1997, 2001; House, Hanges, Javidan, Dorfman, & Gupta, 2004). While there is an expanding knowledge base about empathetic leadership in individualist societies (e.g., Bennis, 2003; Ketelle & Mesa, 2006; Sugrue, 2005), little has been written about leaders or leading with empathy in non-Western societies, including East Asia. This is despite the fact that empathy is deeply rooted in traditional belief systems across the region, where empathy has long been recognized as an important personal attribute for both leaders and nonleaders. For example, a student once asked the ancient Chinese philosopher Confucius whether there was one word that could be practiced for one's whole life. The Great Master answered with the word empathy (*shu*), that is, do not impose on others what you yourself do not desire (*Analects*).

This chapter attempts to add to our knowledge base of how contemporary Chinese school leaders understand empathy and what it might look like in their work environments. We do this through a single-principal case study of a leader deemed to lead with empathy. The study is guided by two questions:

- How does a leader with empathy lead in a collectivist society?
- How do empathetic understandings underpin and influence the leadership practices in such societies?

Given that it is a single-person case study, we do not claim any generalizability. Our aim is to provide a very initial snapshot of an empathetic school leader in China and hope that this can promote more research in the area. The principal was therefore selected not as a typical Chinese school leader, but rather as one recognized as upholding values such as mutual understanding, respect, and trust in a context largely dominated by an emphasis on accountability and quality assurance. Thus, the paper makes no attempt to provide a generalizable portrait of Chinese empathetic leadership. Rather, it portrays a "real flesh and blood" individual with "motives and emotions" (Ball & Goodson, 1985, p. 13) and attempts to connect the leader's narrative with his political and cultural context. As such, the single case study aims to supply important insights into the relationships among culture, empathy, and leadership.

The chapter has six sections. The first section outlines the values found to describe collectivist societies. To do this requires a concomitant discussion of individualism. The second section reviews relevant literature about empathy and leadership. The third section describes Confucian understandings of empathy and leadership. The fourth section introduces the background of the school, the principal, and the research. The fifth section presents the major research findings with illustrations of critical incidents the principal narrated. The final section discusses the relationships among culture, empathy, and leadership.

## COLLECTIVISM–INDIVIDUALISM

It is accepted that societal culture has a marked influence on how leaders lead and organizations work (Hofstede, 1997). Over the years scholars in international comparative management and cross-cultural business psychology have studied in considerable depth this influence and how it impacts organizational performance (e.g., Bigoness & Blakely, 1996; Hofstede, 2001; Hoppe, 1993; House et al., 2004; Ralston, Holt, Terpstra, & Yu, 2008). Similar interest in the field of education leadership has increased over the last decade but has only occasionally attempted serious empirical investigation (Dimmock & Walker, 2005; Hallinger & Leithwood, 1996; Hallinger, Walker, & Bajunid, 2005; Walker, Bridges, & Chan, 1996; Walker & Dimmock, 2002a). This is important given that perhaps even more so than in private-sector organizations, school leadership is centrally concerned with the interpretation and enactment of the values embedded in the society (Hallinger et al., 2005).

Perhaps the most informative work in the area remains that of Geert Hofstede (2001) and, more recently, the Global Leadership and Organizational Behavior Effectiveness (GLOBE) study (House et al., 2004). Both sets of work focus on a number of key dimensions of national culture that capture multiple features of the social relationships that describe organizational life. One of the most researched of Hofstede's cultural dimensions is the collectivism–individualism dimension.

This collectivism–individualism dimension aims to capture the degree to which individuals are integrated into groups and to which there is closeness between persons in a relationship. Vecchio (1995) describes it as the extent to which a person is "inner directed" or "other directed." In individualist societies, individuals place their personal goals above those of their in-group; the ties among individuals are loose. People are expected to look after themselves and their immediate families. In collectivist societies, people place group goals above their personal goals; they are brought up to be loyal to and integrated in strong cohesive groups, which often include extended families. In individualist societies, people are driven by an "I" consciousness and obligations to the self, including self-interest, self-actualization, and guilt; at school, emphasis is placed on permanent education and learning how to learn; and in the workplace, values tend to be applied universally to all, other people are seen as potential resources, tasks prevail over relationships, and the employer–employee relationship is described as "calculative." In collectivist societies, by contrast, family members are brought up with a "we" consciousness, opinions are predetermined by the group, and strong obligations to the family emphasize harmony, respect, and shame; at school, learning is viewed as an activity primarily for the young and focuses on how to do things and on factual knowledge; and in the workplace, value standards differ for the in-group and out-groups, relationships prevail over task, and employer–employee relationships have a moral basis (Walker & Dimmock, 2002b).

## CONNECTING EMPATHY, LEADERSHIP, AND CULTURE

Leading is a profoundly emotional form of work (Hargreaves, 1998; Walters, 2012). Empathy is part of the makeup of this work, and when enacted by a leader, it can positively affect the organization (Fullan, 2001, 2003). Much has been written about the strengths of leading with empathy. This section first reviews what we know about empathy and empathetic leadership. This is followed by a discussion of the relationship between empathy and culture and of how empathy is understood in relation to leadership in China. This review shows that little is known about empathetic leadership in contemporary school settings in China.

### Empathy and Empathetic Leadership

Over the past three decades or so, the concepts of multiple intelligence (Gardner, 1983) and emotional intelligence (Goleman, 1995, 1998; Salovey & Mayer, 1990) have become increasingly popular in the leadership discourse, particularly business success stories. The literature holds that "emotional intelligence can be an inoculation that preserves and encourages growth" (Goleman, 1998, p. 312).

One of the fundamental characteristics of emotional intelligence is empathy (Fullan, 2001). Empathy, by definition, refers to the awareness of another person's feelings. In relation to leadership, Goleman (2005) defines empathy as thoughtfully considering employees' feelings in the process of making intelligent decisions. A leader who works with empathy believes and respects his or her employees, acknowledges their power, and accepts their weaknesses (Poymilis, 2010).

Leading with empathy is a common denominator that can be observed across a range of different leadership types. Polymilis (2010) argues that terms such as transformational leadership, servant leadership, spiritual leadership, and values-based leadership, at least in part, can all be collected under the "umbrella of empathy" (p. 11). For example, individualized consideration, one of the inherent elements of transformational leadership, describes the characteristic of empathy (Pillai, Williams, Lowe, & Jung, 2003). Servant leaders consciously put themselves in the place of their followers when they make decisions—this is a key component of their desire to serve others (Greenleaf, 1970). Empathy can also enhance the spiritual dimension of the relationship between leaders and followers and evoke the feeling that followers follow their leaders because they want to, not because they have to (Polymilis, 2010). Empathetic leading is also integral to values-based leadership, where the leader focuses on the strengths of the led (Begley, 2001).

Evidence suggests that empathetic leaders are usually more effective (Gronn, 2011; Robinson, 2010). Empathy plays a particularly important role in motivation and trust building. In motivating followers, empathetic leaders understand that everyone wants to "be valued" (Donadio, 2012, p. 13) and that no one wants to be "treated as unimportant" (Manning & Curtis, 2003, p. 150). As such, they take a personal interest in their followers and provide individualized support (Hargreaves, 1998). Teachers working with empathetic leaders are thus prepared to "work above and beyond the official call of duty, entirely of their own volition" (Hargreaves, 1998, p. 315).

When working to build trust, empathetic leaders understand that the social costs of an overdependence on managerial control can be detrimental to human relationships and to organizational performance (Moos, 2005). Thus, they do not rely on their formal power to win trust; rather they recognize that informal power, based on their own legitimacy, is a precursor to genuine trust (Moos, 2005). Empathetic leaders win the respect of followers by establishing their own trustworthiness.

In summary, empathy is an overarching term that is implicitly embedded across a range of contemporary leadership concepts and models. Empathetic leaders are generally effective because they promote trusting relationships within organizations and so are more likely to win the trust of others.

### Empathy and Culture

Emotional experiences have been found to be quite common across cultures (Aaker & Williams, 1998; Matsumoto, 1989). However, different cultures attach different levels of importance to the same type of emotions. In other words, in some cultures people are more likely to have stronger feelings about certain emotions than in other societies (Aaker & Williams, 1998).

Cultural psychology suggests that emotions can be categorized into *ego-focused* and *other-focused*. These labels refer to "the degree to which specific emotions systematically vary in the extent to which they follow from, and also foster or reinforce, an independent versus interdependent self" (Markus & Kitayama, 1991,

p. 235). Some examples of *ego-focused* emotions include pride, happiness, frustration, and anger. These tend to be associated with an individual's internal state or attributes. Examples of *other-focused* emotions include empathy, indebtedness, and shame. These are often associated with others in a social context and are consistent with the need for unity, harmony, and alignment of one's actions with those of another.

As discussed earlier, in individualist cultures, people tend to have more independent self-construal; rather, in collectivist cultures, people see themselves as inseparable from others and the social context (Aaker & Williams, 1998; Hofstede, 1980). Research shows that there is a closer relationship between collectivist societies and other-focused emotions, while individualist values are more closely connected with ego-focused emotions. For example, Morris and Peng (1994, cited in Aaker & Williams, 1998) compared how a murder was reported in an English-language US newspaper (the *New York Times*) and a Chinese-language US newspaper (*World Journal*). The case involved a Chinese postgraduate student who shot his US advisor, several fellow students, and then himself after he had lost an award competition and unsuccessfully appealed the decision. The English-language report tended to highlight the personality traits, or internal attributes, of the student (e.g., "very bad temper," "darkly disturbed man"), while the Chinese report highlighted others in the social context and the situation in which the student found himself (e.g., "did not get along with his advisor," "isolation from Chinese community"). The example hints that collectivist cultures tend to house more intense feelings of empathy.

Thus, although recognition and experiences of empathy appear to be robust cross-culturally, empathy is more widely expected and observed in collectivist societies. China is generally categorized as a collectivist society (Child, 1994; House et al., 2004). Perhaps the greatest influence on Chinese culture is Confucianism (Gu, 1981; Louie, 1984). The next section outlines traditional beliefs around empathy and leadership in China.

## EMPATHY AND LEADERSHIP IN CONFUCIAN CULTURES

Empathy is frequently mentioned in Confucian writings. A number of examples taken from the Analects are recounted below:

> The gentleman is judged wise by a single word he utters; equally, he is judged foolish by a single word he utters. That is why one really must be careful (hence be empathetic) of what one says.
>
> If you love others, they will love you; if you despise others, they will despise you. Since you know how to treat yourself, you should know how to treat others.
>
> Never impose upon others what you don't desire yourself.

Confucius himself was seen a model of empathy. The Analects recorded that "Confucius did not sing for the rest of the day as he usually would do after he had wept at a funeral" (VII, verse 10), and "Confucius never ate enough food at a meal when he found himself seated next to someone who had been bereaved" (VII, verse 9).

Thus, empathy is a quality traditionally expected of a Chinese leader. In traditional Confucian thinking, leaders are expected to exemplify three concepts: humaneness (*ren*), which involves sympathy and empathy; ritualism (*li*), where the leader is expected "to comply with established social norms and to set himself as a model for the populace"; and moralism (*de*), where the leader is expected to provide a role model for establishing moral order (Guo, 2002, p. x). Empathy is a highly valued quality of leaders from a Chinese cultural perspective.

Confucianism holds that a leader with empathy is a warm (*wen*) person (Low, 2012). Such a person is soft and gentle and can always be depended upon. Only when leading with empathy can leaders win genuine obedience and loyalty. For example, according to Mencius, Confucius's later disciple, when people are subdued by force, their hearts are not truly won over; they submit just because they do not have enough strength to fight or resist. However, when people are won by virtue (such as being empathetic and caring), they submit or accept sincerely and are glad in their hearts (Cai, 1991, p. 27, cited in Low, 2012, p. 825).

Despite the messages embedded in traditional philosophy, an examination of Chinese school leadership in contemporary literature (e.g., Lee & Yin, 2010; Qian & Walker, 2011a, 2011b; Walker & Qian, 2011; Yin, Lee, & Wang, in press) portrays a very different image of leaders. This is an image of leaders who are more authoritarian than caring and place more emphasis on upward rather than inward accountability. Leaders extend care to teachers, but this is underpinned by instrumental exchange and respect for status (e.g., Qian & Walker, 2011a; Yin, Lee, & Wang, in press). Leaders advocate mutual trust, but they also tend to control conflicts and opposition to maintain harmony (Qian & Walker, 2011a; Walker, Qian, & Zhang, 2011). Under the increasing pressure of quality assurance and accountability, managerial strategies such as rewards and sanctions are often adopted by school leaders in China to maximize teacher productivity (Qian & Walker, 2011b).

Given the contradictions between widely touted traditional values and apparent organizational reality, it is useful to look more deeply at empathetic leadership as it is played out in Chinese schools today. We will do this through an in-depth case of one principal in Shanghai. The case sets out to see how traditional values around empathy influence the leadership philosophy and practices of the leader. Given that most recent studies focus on the managerial roles of principals, using empathy as a lens for understanding aims to expose another, often neglected, side of school leadership in China.

## THE STUDY

We first met Principal Ning in a master program organized by our institute. All the attendees in the program were school principals or midlevel leaders from Shanghai. In the 40-person cohort, Ning was by no means a star. He was quiet, almost hidden within the group. However, since most of the students came from the same district, they knew each other's schools well. His classmates often made reference to Mr. Ning's school as having a particularly effective teacher development program.

Even though others often mentioned him, Principal Ning remained silent and humble. The only time he spoke out was toward the end of the course when he volunteered to share some of the teacher development practices at his school. Many of his practices did not aim explicitly to enhance teacher competence; instead the thrust was to improve teachers' sense of belonging and ownership. His words aroused our interest to know more about him. We therefore set up a short interview with him to talk about his teacher development policies, and the word "empathy" kept reappearing in our notes from this interview. His school policies and his leadership "wisdom" seemed to flow from the concept of 'empathy.'

We therefore decided to visit his school and talk with him further. Our discussion was still mainly about his approach to teachers and the rationale behind the strategies he adopted. We encouraged him to share stories/examples of working relationships in the school. A definite picture of a principal leading with empathy emerged from the data.

### The Principal

Principal Ning is in his late forties. He was born and grew up in North China. After studying philosophy at university, he was assigned to work at a local teachers' college in his province. The main responsibility of the college was to provide in-service training to local educators. Ning taught a wide range of courses, such as politics, educational psychology, and educational management.

Due to a shortage of high-quality teachers in the late 1990s, Shanghai organized open recruitment and invited teachers across China to apply for teaching positions. In 1997 both Ning and his wife were successfully recruited by a middle school in Shanghai. Ning admitted that it was his wife that the school really wanted. His wife was a mathematics teacher, while he could only teach politics. Mathematics is a major course (together with Chinese and English) in middle schools, while politics (as a subject) is considered less important. The school wanted his wife, so they had to take Ning as well.

Although he did not impress the school with his academic and professional background at the interview, it did not take long for him to win the reputation of being trustworthy and competent. He was subsequently promoted to director of teaching and instruction in only his second year at the school. In his fifth year he was promoted to vice principal, and a few months later he became the party secretary of the school. One year later he became the principal. Even as a newcomer to the school, and to the City of Shanghai, it took him less than 7 years to be promoted from a subject teacher to school principal. What made Ning particularly proud was that before the principal election, the district bureau sent a team to the school to collect teachers' opinions. Ning got support from 100% of the teachers; all of his colleagues expected and nominated him to be the principal.

Ning believes he is known as a democratic, scholastic, and kind leader; he never attempts to "put on an authoritarian face giving orders from above." He holds that his leadership approach accentuates care for, and understanding of, teachers. To use his words:

> Managing people is to manage their hearts [guanxin]. You can never manage others' hearts if you do not care for them [guanxin]. Caring for others requires that you use your own heart [yongxin], and using your heart means you show empathy to others and understand their needs, interests, and motivations [dongxin].

## *The School*

Ning came to School A in 2007. The school is located in downtown Shanghai and has 800 students (Years 1 to 9) and 90 teachers, and it was facing unprecedented difficulties when Ning arrived. The school's reputation was originally built on extracurricular courses in painting and calligraphy, but this had almost disappeared because it could no longer attract talented students. Worrying that the school would be less and less competitive, some teachers (particularly art teachers) sought to transfer to other schools. The then-principal also suddenly resigned and left the job.

Ning was assigned to School A as a "firefighter." He met the challenge of "saving" the school through helping teachers see *their* place in the school through his care, understanding, and empathy. He believed that the school had progressed significantly since his arrival. One indicator of this was that teachers now want to stay and have stopped applying for jobs elsewhere—this demonstrates a strong sense of belonging to the school.

## *The Data*

The data were mainly collected from two interviews with Principal Ning in August and December 2012. The focus was how he constructed and maintained trusting relationships with teachers, how he approached teacher development, and how he generally understood the needs of teachers. He narrated his approach to teacher development and his relationship with teachers and shared stories to illustrate his approaches and relationships. In the interviews, a set of "why" questions were asked to check the consistency between the narratives and to probe Ning's beliefs and values about leadership.

The picture, which emerged from the data, was of a principal who seemed to have deeply internalized Confucius' advocacy for empathy: *Do not do to others what you do not desire yourself.*

## PRINCIPAL NING AS A LEADER WITH EMPATHY

This section presents the data collected from Ning about his interpretation and practice as an empathetic leader under three themes: caring and showing concern, recognizing others' strengths and appointing people on their merit (*yongren suochang*), and putting himself in the place of another (*tuiji jiren*).

### *Caring and Showing Concern*

As Ning held a strong belief that "managing people is managing their hearts," one of the most important tasks he set for himself was to win teachers' hearts. In his opinion, to win teachers' hearts, a leader needs to extend care and concern to every member of the school. He was fully aware that every person was watching him closely, as he was new to the school. Then, how could he let teachers know what kind of person he was? He believed that teachers could form their judgment about who he was by observing how he treated the most disadvantaged people in the school. He therefore chose to improve the status and promote the importance of these least advantaged people:

I asked myself: Who are most disadvantaged? The answer is: those school cleaners and toilet cleaning ladies. Then for the first time in the history of the school, I invited these people to attend the School Teachers' Conference and placed them on the presidency table. I asked them to introduce themselves. When they spoke of their names and jobs, laughter burst out among the teachers. I told the teachers: It is the first time I have heard this laughter and I hope it is the last time. We should respect them and their jobs. From that time on, every time we have the annual Teacher's Conference, I invite them to sit on the stage and no one would laugh any longer.

His care for disadvantaged staff extended beyond inviting them to the school conference. He invigorated a new school policy where the principal would host a New Year's dinner for the cleaners. Since the cleaners came from outside Shanghai, they would go back to their hometowns for the Chinese New Year. Each year, before they left Shanghai, Ning invited them to have a get-together dinner. The cleaners deemed this a great honor. They would take a shower and put on their finest clothes for the occasion. They felt respected and a strong sense of belonging to the school. By this relatively simple act, Ning also established his populist appeal, and the teachers saw him as being concerned for every member of the school:

The money I paid for the dinner came from the school budget, but no one at the school would criticize me for misusing the money. In contrast, I suppose there would be gossip if I spent the school budget on a dinner with other school leaders.

Ning was also concerned about teacher well-being. He believed that when teachers were happy, they had a more positive attitude and stronger motivation toward their jobs. Ning implemented a number of specific strategies to boost teachers' sense of happiness. First, he redesigned the physical environment. Every corner of the school was decorated with student artwork according to a particular theme, such as calligraphy, painting, science, or celebrity. He invested in a sound system to pipe music throughout the school and built a self-service coffee corner so that teachers had a space to interact with colleagues. Although these initiatives were expensive, the payback was high in terms of teacher morale and closer professional relationships.

Second, Ning designed activities to enrich teachers' spiritual lives. There was a yoga class for female teachers on Monday night, calligraphy and Ping Pong classes on Tuesday, and chalk microcarving, dancing, and chorus lessons from Wednesday to Friday, respectively. The teachers enjoyed these activities and felt they had something to look forward to when they came to school every morning. As the teachers' chorus group and the Ping Pong team became increasingly famous and won several awards in the district, the teachers developed a stronger sense of achievement and appreciated that the school gave them room for personal development.

Although many of these strategies were not intentionally designed to enhance teachers' professional engagement or improve their classroom teaching competence, an apparent difference could be observed among teachers. For example, since Ning's arrival, the district education bureau has promoted four teachers to the prestigious senior-class teacher status.[4] By contrast, no single teacher had gained this promotion in the decade before Ning came to this school.

## Recognizing Others' Strengths and Appointing People on Merit

In addition to showing care and concern, another quality that distinguished Ning from many of his counterparts was that he never complained about teachers. He recognized that most of his teachers were middle-aged women devoted to families and thus lacked a strong incentive to work hard or pursue career success. However, Ning also believed that it was the leader's responsibility to improve and develop teachers instead of criticizing or threatening them with the loss of their jobs. In his words:

> I trust teachers and I also have faith in myself. I believe I have the ability to improve and transform teachers. If he or she is not doing the job well, I need to analyze why. It is probably my problem; I did not put him or her in the right position. The real touchstone for a leader is whether you can improve the teacher instead of laying him/her off.

Thus, Ning never turned to sanctions and punishment to motivate teachers; he believed that such a motivational strategy would incur more trouble:

> Instrumentally you can also calculate which approach will pay you more. One is to always criticize teachers and threaten to dismiss the least performing one. Another is to always recognize their strength and encourage them. My experiences have taught me that the latter is far more effective. We need to have faith that no teacher has the intention not to do the job well or not to improve their students' academic outcomes. [Then if you lay off the least performing teacher], how will other teachers judge you? They would think you are too cold [*hen*]. Moreover, if a teacher is often criticized or punished, there will be a passive impact on him or her mentally or psychologically.

With faith that all teachers wanted to improve, Ning seemed able to see strength in each teacher. His belief was that "every teacher can be one with his or her own uniqueness" (*techang xing jiaoshi*). This belief impacted his evaluation strategies:

> It is probably a stronger motivation if we can evaluate teachers' strengths and focus on what they are good at. Every teacher is unique and their value and contribution can also be distinctive [from those of others]. We cannot compare them with others. Instead we need to compare them with their past and to examine whether they have reached their potential. Every person has some weaknesses, but we need to emphasize strengths more. If we evaluate all the teachers with a single criterion, the criterion was often students' academic performance. However, this criterion is not objective, just, or reasonable. Those who are evaluated as unqualified will be less and less confident.

Therefore, in Ning's opinion, boosting and maintaining each teacher's self-confidence was extremely important. His policy was to "pick up teachers' strengths, magnify these, and publicly recognize them." Using this policy, Ning successfully shifted the work attitudes of several colleagues who used to be labeled as "disobedient" or "a headache" by previous principals. Ning was proud of this and regularly recounted supporting stories throughout our discussions.

For example, he talked about one teacher who had worked at the school for a long time and kept challenging the school authority. The teacher was widely liked and respected by other teachers. Because of his impact on teachers, the previous principals did not dare to sanction him if his job did not meet expected standards. Gradually, the teacher became sloppier in his work and developed a very negative attitude toward his job. After studying the teacher, Ning found that he was a big Ping Pong lover. Thus, Ning assigned him a new part-time job as the coach of the staff Ping Pong team. Every Tuesday afternoon, he would remind his team members one by one to attend the training; Ning was also a member of the team. The teacher was strict with his team members during the training; his teammates respected his expertise. Under his leadership the team won the district-level championship. The staff member developed a huge sense of belonging to the school and became a supportive "spokesperson" for the school policies. Ning said that the teacher's new nickname was "Vice Principal," even though he did not occupy the position.

## Putting Himself in the Place of Another

Like all principals, Ning encountered unexpected problems in his work life, many of which revolved around teachers' personal problems. To Ning, the most important, if not single, principle he applied to such situations was putting himself in the place of others (*tuiji jiren*).

Ning shared an incident that took place not long before our second interview. One afternoon, two teachers came to his office. They were emotional, trembling, and crying. When Ning saw this, his first reaction was to ask the three vice principals who shared the office with him to stop what they were doing and sit down together to listen to the teachers. The two teachers complained that their photos had been viciously defaced (there were pictures of all faculty on the staff canteen wall). They considered the defacement an unbearable personal insult. One teacher even mentioned giving up her life.

After listening to the two teachers, Ning's second decision was to accompany them to the "crime scene" to investigate the issue with the vice principals. They also called the police. The police carefully examined the photos to see if they could identify the culprits. Ning did everything he could to support the police and to make the two teachers feel better. For example, he asked the school janitors to retrieve the videos that showed who and when people came to the school that day. The school allowed parents to use the staff canteen if they arrived before the students were dismissed. Ning immediately asked the head of the school logistics department to put a poster on the school gate to announce the end of the policy.

At the end of the day, the two teachers felt much better, even though the suspect was not identified. Ning justified his actions in this way:

When these two colleagues came to my office, I immediately got the impression that it was such a blow to them. Therefore, I needed to deal with it extremely seriously. That is why I asked the other members of the leadership team to stop what they were doing and attend to the needs of the two teachers. By doing so, I could make the two colleagues feel that we understood their suffering and we put their incident as the first priority; the whole high-level leadership team devoted their whole afternoon to accompanying them and investigating the incidents.

By contrast, Ning believed that if he had not shown enough empathy and had merely asked a vice principal to deal with the crisis, this incident could have become unmanageable.

As Ning consciously put himself in the place of others, it was not surprising to find that this was mirrored in school policies and the work environment. For example, on the walls next to the staircases there were signs such as "Younger sisters and brothers are small. Please walk slowly on the stairs." This was a sign to remind higher-grade students to be more considerate of lower-grade students. Understanding that some Primary 1 students did not have a proper understanding of how to unlock the toilet doors and how to use flushing water, the school also videotaped how to use the toilet and showed it to the Primary 1 students.

## A CHINESE PERSPECTIVE ON EMPATHETIC LEADERSHIP?

The case study of Principal Ning portrays an image of a Shanghai principal leading with empathy. As argued elsewhere, Ning was by no means a typical principal in China. However, he did display some features that have a strong connection with Confucian cultural values.

First, it was not difficult to delineate the impact of Confucian understanding of empathy (*shu*): Do not impose upon others what you do not want yourself. Ning internalized the concept and transfused it into school policies and norms. For example, he gave less advantaged staff more visibility because he understood that every person, regardless of social or professional background, needed to be respected. He recognized teachers' strengths instead of weaknesses because he understood that no one would enjoy working with a pedantic leader.

Second, Ning saw the school as an organic entity. Every part of the school was connected with the others; one policy could have a chain effect and cause unexpected teacher behaviors and practices. This is the Chinese way of viewing an organization (Walker, 2011). Thus, he had to ensure the alignment among his actions, speeches, and policies. For him, he often reminded himself of these questions: What kind of school do we have? How can we cultivate our students and for whom are we cultivating them? Ning also understood that a principal's decisions and actions were always in the spotlight. He maintained a strong sense of self-awareness that "all the teachers are watching me." When he invited school cleaners to go to the stage to introduce themselves, Ning was proud of his decision, as were all the teachers watching. When Ning explained why he would not dismiss poorly performing teachers, the reason he gave was also that "all the teachers were watching what you do."

The third feature was the importance attached to school harmony. In East Asia a traditional expectation of leaders is that they maintain harmony (Blunt & Jones, 1997). Ning automatically assumed responsibility for this. When he was asked to describe his successes, he explained that it was how he had changed the public image of the school. No teacher sought to move to another school; everyone seemed to be content with and devoted to the school. His responsibility to maintain harmony was also related to his strong awareness that all the teachers were watching him. He was careful not to arouse any potential conflict with and among teachers, as these could threaten the school harmony.

Fourth, Ning did not seek any personal benefits. This is also in line with the high levels of power distance (Hofstede, 1980, 2001). Leaders in Confucian contexts were expected to possess "non-utilitarian" qualities (Pye, 1991). Ning recognized that his personal merit was that he never tried to seize an honorary title or award for himself. If there was any opportunity to win such a title, he passed it on to his colleagues. Although these could be seen as personal losses, Ning was actually rewarded by holding the teachers' trust. In Ning's words, "Teachers will remember everything. If you only crave personal fame and gain, you are losing the greater for the less."

In this chapter we have attempted to glean some understanding of the formation and practice of empathetic leadership through the eyes of one Chinese school principal in Shanghai. Although the scope of the study prevents generalization in traditional terms, it does prompt a number of insights or issues that may provoke further investigation into the place and exercise of empathetic leadership from a cross-cultural perspective. For example, from the case presented, it appears that many of the leadership practices associated with empathy are common across cultures. These include practices such as fostering mutual trust, making others feel cared for, and avoiding exercising overt managerial control over employees. However, some differences began to emerge. For example, Ning's empathy was at least partly driven by a concern for his own image within the collective, as well as concern for how the school was seen by outsiders. Ning always had a strong awareness of how he and his school would be evaluated *by others*. Such considerations may show a close relationship with collectivist values.

Data flowing from this initial investigation of leadership empathy across cultures prompt a number of further questions that may inform future study:

- How does the conceptualization and exercise of empathetic school leadership play out in schools between and within different cultures?
- How does the conceptualization and exercise of empathetic school leadership play out in schools internationally as they face constant performativity demands and are held increasingly accountable for measurable outcomes, usually in the form of standardized test scores?
- How can leaders in different cultures gear empathetic beliefs and practices toward improving school performance and equity? For example, how can empathy influence the cultural foundations and structure of professional development, pastoral care, curriculum development, collaborative practices, and pedagogical innovation?

- Where is the line between genuine empathy and instrumentally construed or "faked" empathy? Is contrived empathy possible, and if so, is it acceptable?
- Can empathy be "taught" through leader development programs? And, if so, what form might these development approaches take?

## NOTES

1. Confucian and neo-Confucian societies include, for example, Mainland China, Hong Kong, Taiwan, Japan, and Korea.
2. Anglo-American English-speaking countries include, for example, the US, UK, and Australia.
3. We acknowledge the pitfalls of the generic labeling of societies and that this risks overplaying the influence of culture and of downplaying value differences between and within societies. For a discussion of the problems associated with researching cross-cultural values, see the study by Walker (2003).
4. Teachers in China have a professional ranking. Teachers are classified into these ranks: third-class teacher (the lowest), second-class teacher, first-class teacher, senior-class teacher, and special-class teacher (the highest).

## REFERENCES

Aaker, J. L., & Williams, P. (1998). Empathy versus pride: The influence of emotional appeals across cultures. *Journal of Consumer Research, 25*(3), 241–261.

Ball, S. J., & Goodson, I. (1985). *Teacher's lives and careers.* London: Falmer Press.

Begley, P. T. (2001). In pursuit of authentic school leadership practices. *International Journal of Leadership in Education: Theory and Practice, 4*(4), 353–365.

Bennis, W. (2003). *On becoming a leader.* Cambridge, MA: Perseus Publishing.

Bigoness, W. J., & Blakely, G. L. (1996). A cross-national study of managerial values. *Journal of International Business Studies, 27*(4), 739–752.

Blunt, P., & Jones, M. L. (1997). Exploring the limits of Western leadership theory in East Asia and Africa. *Personnel Review, 26*(1/2), 6–23.

Cai, Z. Z. (Ed.). (1991). *The sayings of Mencius: Wisdom in a chaotic era.* Singapore: Asiapac.

Child, J. (1994). *Management in China during the age of reform.* Cambridge, UK: Cambridge University Press.

Dimmock, C., & Walker, A. (2005). *Educational leadership: Culture and diversity.* London: Sage.

Donadio, G. (2012). *Changing behavior: Immediately transform your relationships with easy-to-learn, proven communication skills.* Boston: SoulWork Press.

Fullan, M. (2001). *Leading in a culture of change.* San Francisco: Jossey-Bass.

Fullan, M. (2003). *Change forces with a vengeance.* London: Routledge Falmer.

Gardner, H. (1983). *Frames of mind: The theory of multiple intelligence.* New York: Basic Books.

Goleman, D. (1995). *Emotional intelligence.* New York: Bantam.

Goleman, D. (1998). *Working with emotional intelligence.* New York: Bantam.

Goleman, D. (2005). What makes a leader. In D. L. Taylor & W. E. Rosenbach (Eds.), *Military leadership: In pursuit of excellence.* Boulder, CO: Westview Press.

Greenleaf, R. K. (1970). *The servant as leader.* New York: Paulist Press.

Gronn, P. (2011). Risk, trust and leadership. In C. Sugrue & T. Solbrekke (Eds.), *Professional responsibility: New horizons of praxis* (pp. 89–101). London: Routledge.

Gu, S. S. (1981). *A historical account of educational systems in China* [in Chinese]. Nanjing, China: Jiangsu People's Publishing House.

Guo, X. (2002). *The ideal Chinese political leader: A historical and cultural perspective.* Westport, CT: Praeger.

Hallinger, P., & Leithwood, K. (1996). Culture and educational administration: A case of finding out what you don't know. *Journal of Educational Administration, 34*(1), 98–116.

Hallinger, P., Walker, A., & Bajunid, I. A. (2005). Educational leadership in East Asia: Implications for education in a global society. *UCEA Review, 45*(1), 1–4.

Hargreaves, A. (1998). The emotional politics of teaching and teacher development: With implications for educational leadership. *International Journal of Leadership in Education: Theory and Practice, 1*(4), 315–336.

Hofstede, G. H. (1980). *Culture's consequences: International differences in work-related values.* Beverly Hills, CA: Sage.

Hofstede, G. H. (1997). *Cultures and organizations: Software of the mind.* London: McGraw Hill.

Hofstede, G. H. (2001). *Culture's consequences: Comparing values, behaviors, institutions, and organizations across nations* (2nd ed.). Thousand Oaks, CA: Sage.

Hoppe, M. (1993). The effects of national culture on the theory and practice of managing R&D professionals abroad. *R&D Management, 23*(4), 313–325.

House, R. J., Hanges, P. J., Javidan, M., Dorfman, P. W., & Gupta, V. (Eds.). (2004). *Culture, leadership, and organizations: The GLOBE study of 62 societies.* Thousand Oaks, CA: Sage.

Ketelle, D., & Mesa, R. P. (2006). Empathetic understanding and school leadership preparation. *Leadership Review, 6,* 144–154.

Lee, J. C. K., & Yin, H. B. (2010). Curriculum policy implementation in China: Interactions between policy designs, place and people. *Curriculum and Teaching, 25*(2), 31–53.

Louie, K. (1984). Salvaging Confucian education (1949–1983). *Comparative Education, 20*(1), 27–38.

Low, K. C. P. (2012). Being empathetic: The way of Confucius. *Educational Research, 3*(11), 818–826.

Mackay, R. C., Hughes, J. R., & Carver, E. J. (1990). *Empathy in the helping relationship.* New York: Springer.

Manning, G., & Curtis, K. (2003). *The art of leadership.* New York: McGraw Hill.

Markus, H., & Kitayama, S. (1991). Culture and the self: Implications for cognition, emotion and motivation. *Psychological Review, 98*(2), 224–253.

Matsumoto, D. (1989). Cultural influences on the perception of emotion. *Journal of Cross Cultural Psychology, 20*(1), 92–105.

Moos, L. (2005). Regulation and trust: Negotiating relationship. In C. Sugrue (Ed.), *Passionate principalship: Learning from the life histories of school leaders* (pp. 105–122). London: Routledge Falmer.

Morris, M., & Peng, K. P. (1994). Culture and cause: American and Chinese attributions for social and physical events. *Journal of Personality and Social Psychology, 67*(6), 949–971.

Pillai, R., Williams, E. A., Lowe, K. B., & Jung, D. I. (2003). Personality, transformational leadership, trust, and the 2000 presidential vote. *Leadership Quarterly, 14*(2), 161–192.

Polymilis, C. (2010). *Empathetic leadership in critical situations: How can leaders lead with empathy in times of trauma?* (Unpublished master's thesis). Naval Postgraduate School, Monterey, CA. Retrieved from www.hsdl.org/?view&did=10517

Pye, L. W. (1991). The new Asian capitalism: a political portrait. In P. L. Berger & H. H. Hsiao (Eds.), *In search of an east Asian development model.* New Brunswick, NJ: Transaction Publishers.

Qian, H. Y., & Walker, A. (2011a). Leadership for learning in China: The political and policy context. In T. Townsend & J. MacBeath (Eds.), *International handbook of leadership for learning* (pp. 209–224). Dordrecht, Netherlands: Springer.

Qian, H. Y., & Walker, A. (2011b). The "gap" between policy intent and policy effect: An exploration of the interpretations of school principals in China. In T. Huang & A. W. Wiseman (Eds.), *The impact and transformation of education policy in China* (pp. 187–208). Bingley, UK: Emerald.

Ralston, D. A., Holt, D. H., Terpstra, R. H., & Yu, K. C. (2008). The impact of national culture and economic ideology on managerial work values: A study of the United States, Russia, Japan, and China. *Journal of International Business Studies, 39*(1), 8–26.

Robinson, V. M. J. (2010). From instructional leadership to leadership capacities: Empirical findings and methodological challenges. *Leadership and Policy in Schools, 9*(1), 1–26.

Salovey, P., & Mayer, D. (1990). Emotional intelligence. *Imagination, Cognition and Personality, 9,* 185–211.

Sugrue, C. (Ed.). (2005). *Passionate principalship: Learning from the life histories of school leaders.* London: Routledge Falmer.

Vecchio, R. (1995). The impact of referral sources on employee attitudes: Evidence from a national sample. *Journal of Management, 21*(5), 953–965.

Walker, A. (2003). Developing cross-cultural perspectives on education and community. In P. Begley & O. Johansson (Eds.), *The ethical dimensions of school leadership* (pp. 145–160). Dordrecht, Netherlands: Kluwer Academic.

Walker, A. (2011, May 18–20). *Reaffirming resonance.* Keynote address at the Reform of School Evaluation and Teacher Professional Development Conference, Taipei Municipal University of Education, Taipei, Taiwan.

Walker, A., Bridges, E., & Chan, B. (1996). Wisdom gained, wisdom given: Instituting PBL in a Chinese culture. *Journal of Educational Administration, 34*(5), 12–31.

Walker, A., & Dimmock, C. (2002a). *School leadership and administration: Adopting a cross-cultural perspective.* New York: Routledge-Falmer.

Walker, A., & Dimmock, C. (2002b). Moving school leadership beyond its narrow boundaries: Developing a cross-cultural approach. In K. Leithwood & P. Hallinger (Eds.), *Second international handbook of educational leadership and administration* (pp. 167–204). Dordrecht, Netherlands: Kluwer.

Walker, A., & Qian, H. Y. (2011). Successful school leadership in China. In C. Day (Ed.), *The Routledge international handbook of teacher and school development* (pp. 446–457). London and New York: Routledge.

Walker, A., Qian, H. Y., & Zhang, S. (2011). Secondary school principals in curriculum reform: Victims or accomplices? *Frontiers of Education in China, 6*(3), 388–403.

Walters, D. (2012). One vision, many eyes: Reflections on leadership and change. *International Journal of Leadership in Education: Theory and Practice, 15*(1), 119–127.

Yin, H. B., Lee, J. C. K., & Wang, W. (in press). Dilemmas of leading national curriculum reform in a global era: A Chinese perspective. *Educational Management Administration and Leadership.* doi: 10.1177/1741143213499261.

# 9

## A CONCERN FOR CARING

### LEA KUUSILEHTO-AWALE

For the Nordic peoples, the establishment of the welfare society model following World War II is a distinguishing feature that engenders great pride. At the societal level, I would argue that since World War II, the Nordic peoples have been able to establish a commitment to ethically responsible civil leadership with a particular emphasis on an ethic of care and caring leadership for all. This civil leadership commitment was founded upon a strong "no citizen left behind" societal consensus and thereby created an investment in social stability, which has accumulated and guaranteed economic success in this part of the world, as indicated, for example, by the Human Development Index Country reports of 1980–2013 published by the United Nations Development Programme (UNDP). This form of societal model emerged as a result of broad political consensus in decision making and visionary thinking among our leaders in the post–World War II decades. This was a time when many of the Nordic people were poor and did not even dare to dream about the levels of wealth we are now enjoying.

During that particular time, humane outcomes came to be considered as important as material outcomes. The prewar poverty and the traumatic effects of the war had caused the Nordic peoples to aim at building an inclusive society with communal and civil benefits for all. Thus, we Nordic people consider our welfare society model to be a cornerstone of this commitment to caring for others and, thereby, a strong influence upon the promotion of ethical leadership.

But is this proud feature now under threat? During the past few decades it has become necessary to distinguish our current Nordic circumstances from those that helped to nurture and sustain a welfare state. It is essential for us to realize that we are now citizens of the globe such that our societies are increasingly becoming interconnected with many others in the most diverse ways, including economically, socially, ecologically, environmentally, culturally, educationally, and psychologically. The impact of globalization on our Nordic societies and their basic principles and values cannot be ignored. Here, globalization is understood to be the borderless interconnection and interdependence among nations made manifest through financial, trade, knowledge, and societal ties, which have been enhanced and strengthened by rapid advancements in transport and communication technologies (Castells, 1996, 1997, 1998).

Moreover, due to our extensive access to communication technology in this globalized context, the wider world now enters our everyday Nordic lives and becomes part of our learning environment. Consequently, the question must be faced as to what moral and ethical messages and learning we are conveying to our students as a result of the frequent reports of serious unethical and immoral actions of individuals, enterprises, financial institutions, religious personnel, and governments that regularly flood our media. For educational leaders concerned with the learning experienced by our students from such sources, and the impact that this might have on what is deemed to constitute a welfare society, the implications of this question assume even greater importance.

As a response to this concern, this chapter first seeks to provide a summary of some of the human-made situations of deepest concern in today's world that convey potentially detrimental messages to our students about how they should learn to live and work with others. While these situations in themselves are of deep concern, there is an additional important concern for teachers and educators. What are our students learning from what they see happening around them, not only in their own country but also in other countries, in regard to how they should act toward themselves and others? Secondly, this chapter endeavors to provide a means for overcoming this concern by describing a reflective outline of how an ethically sound learning environment can be created and maintained. The model to be presented is based on the writer's extensive practical experience as a school leader and an educator of school leaders in Finland.

Given the structural limitations of this chapter, it is possible to mention only four examples of serious media reports that have the potential to influence the ethical understandings of students and, thereby, to erode the fundamental values and principles underpinning the Nordic welfare state. These four examples include the Global Financial Crisis (GFC) of 2008, Muslim unrest, African famines, and the impact on education and schooling of the Global Education Reform Movement (GERM).

In many ways, the impact of the GFC in Europe has been the forgotten part of this devastating era. From a global perspective, most of the attention has been upon the USA and how its economy is recovering from its self-imposed economic crisis. Yet, the economies of so many European countries similarly collapsed as a result of the unethical leadership actions of some financial institutions in the USA (Harvey, 2005; Stiglitz, 2002, 2012) and in Europe. Furthermore, while the USA economy seems to be well on the way to recovery, the economies of other countries, like Greece, Spain, Italy, Ireland, and Iceland, remain weak and underperforming. For a number of such countries, national bankruptcy remains a distinct possibility, and so they are reliant upon financial assistance from the European Union to remain viable. However, this assistance has come with stringent externally imposed conditions from the EU, including the implementation of agreed economic sanctions if there are violations to these conditions. For many citizens of these countries, it seems that it is the victims of the GFC who are the ones having to also pay the price for restoring the country's economic stability. This has led to very public displays of social disobedience in the form of violent street marches and the destruction of property.

For the common people, it seems that the unethical perpetrators of the financial crisis—some wealthy financiers—have benefited the most from their misdeeds. They were not held accountable for the devastation they caused in the lives of so many people while, at the same time, they do not appear to be as adversely affected by the financial strategies being imposed upon the everyday worker as a means for reestablishing the economic viability and stability of the country. It is not hard to imagine how the message conveyed by the GFC is not about caring for others but, rather, about the economics of greed—a message unconsciously accepting the view that the income of a few can rise exponentially while for many there is little or no benefit; worse still, a message that promotes economics before people, that any economic activity is acceptable even if it brings about the traumatic and devastating disenfranchisement of millions of individuals and families and seriously disrupts many societies and environments (Stiglitz, 2012).

Further, in the course of the Muslim unrest in North Africa and the Middle East, we have witnessed citizens trying to speak their minds against oppression by peacefully demanding democracy but being attacked and crushed by the violence of their own leaders. What once seemed to be more influenced by differences between Muslim and non-Muslim ideologies now no longer seems to be the case. The present situation appears far less differentiated on clearly identifiable religious grounds and, thus, is much more complex and confusing from an outside perspective. But what cannot be ignored or mistaken is the clear indifference to the loss of civilian life for the sake of political gain. Local and national leaders seem far more intent on military rather than moral victory. Moreover, the involvement of the leaders of the economically powerful nations is more about maintaining military sales and economic advantage than saving innocent lives. Again, what are our students learning from such images and messages, which are regularly appearing in the Nordic media? What priority is being given to caring for people in such circumstances?

Similarly, we are regularly witnessing repeated devastating droughts in the Horn of Africa caused by poor civil infrastructure associated with the outcomes of climate change. These cyclic famines continually threaten the lives of over 10 million people, especially the most vulnerable, the children. In the case of the former Somalia, the situation is aggravated by the prolonged war among several tribes that places cultural dominance over social peace and harmony. Yet despite the repetitiveness of this inhumane situation, our Western world appears largely indifferent. The facts and the knowledge about the southern African drought and famine situations were well known among international nongovernmental organizations (NGOs) in the autumn of 2010. Also, the International Coffee Organization predicts that by 2020 the coffee production in East Africa will decrease by 50% due to the climate change causing increased and sustained aridity. Yet, the international media did not inform the public about this serious concern until the middle of 2011. The role of the media in this situation is in stark contrast to the previous example describing the Muslim unrest.

Why are civilian deaths caused by war thought to be more important to report upon than civilian deaths caused by droughts and famine? What does a lack of media attention to an issue of caring for the needs of drought-stricken people in the Horn of Africa convey about a commitment to caring for others in general? Can we be selective in whom we care for? If I am not expected to care for other, non-Nordic peoples, then why should I care for all Nordic people? Why not just care for those I personally want to care for?

Finally, in education, neoliberal reform strategies have been advocated through GERM, which has imposed the doctrine of school improvement through a commitment to nationalized curricula, heavy standardized testing, and mandatory evaluation. The desired accountability strategy has been essentially performance based and has been realized through policies that evaluate, reward, and sanction schools on the basis of measured student performance. To a great extent, the result of these policies has seen an increase in teaching for testing and simplified ranking lists of "the best performing schools." All too frequently, the public and the politicians use these student performance outcome ranking lists to victimize both the schools and the teachers. Yet, the results illustrated by these ranking lists are highly debatable. For example, there is no solid evidence that increasing student assessment and evaluation regimes would effect an increase in student learning outcomes (Elmore, 2005; Sahlberg, 2006, 2007). Despite these known concerns, politicians have a tendency to use these outcomes to justify the draining off of essential educational resources instead of finding ways for helping the schools and teachers to tackle the root causes of poor student performance often imbedded in other social ills. Rather than condemning teachers and schools, government leaders should be increasing resources to community building, teacher education, and student support.

From a global perspective, this nationalized and standardized student testing policy implementation, often made mandatory as a condition for investments and loans to a country from the World Bank and the International Monetary Fund (IMF), has proven to achieve only meager improvements to student academic results while widening the academic achievement divide between students from wealthy and poor families (Harvey, 2005). In the current educational discourse, the ancient objective of education, which was to foster the holistic growth of the learner as a moral, emotional, intellectual, spiritual, and skilled person, is outdated. Education today appears to be all about competitiveness and individualism. Moreover, what appears as being of greatest value and, therefore, of most importance to the country is the quality of education for those who are already advantaged by it. Education is no longer a public means for showing care for each and every student but rather a social mechanism that cares for some students and some schools more than others. What might the hidden message for our students be from this situation?

## TOWARD A SOLUTION

Given the potential influence of media coverage on the ethical understandings of school students as a result of such social catastrophes like those presented above, it is essential to situate any solution within the global context. If the genesis of the problem is a global matter, it is unlikely that a solution formulated on purely local criteria would suffice. For instance, endeavoring to prevent the ethical understandings of Nordic students being adversely influenced by international media reports through censorship or restricted viewing or by introducing rules to mandate ethical behavioral outcomes in young people may be a well-intentioned but erroneous response.

Thus, I wish to draw upon the scientific concept of entropy to guide this discussion toward the finding of a suitable solution to this problem. In the field of science, the concept of entropy acknowledges the level of energy contained within a system occupying a clearly defined region. Moreover, the greater the entropy contained by a system, the more energy it has, and the more "active" are its components. Similarly, the components in a system can be made to become more "active" by increasing the system's entropy through the addition of more energy into the system. However, it is also true that a system can become unstable if its entropy is increased too much such that its components become far too active, to the point of bursting out of the system.

When applied to our discussion, the "system" is the global world, and the important entropy is more social than physical. Here, social entropy is the tangible level of social interaction across and throughout the world. Moreover, it is being argued that global communication technologies, largely in the form of media coverage, increase this social entropy in two ways. First, it enables social interaction on a global scale. What happens in one country can be readily observed in most other countries. Secondly, the involvement of the media has the potential to increase the level or intensity of the activity. It is becoming clear that many initiators of social unrest not only welcome media interest in their issues and activities but also can escalate the intensity of their actions so as to maximize the media's interest and attention. Under such circumstances, the promotion of ideological perspectives onto a world "stage" through the media is considered to be a more worthwhile outcome than restrained protest regardless of any unfortunate consequences. It is in this way that it can be said that the social entropy of the world is increasing and, if left unrestrained, at some future point in time it could destabilize the world. In the short term, at least, I argue that this increased global social entropy is destabilizing the Nordic social welfare state by undermining its acceptance of, and commitment to, caring for others among school students.

However, as we witness an increase in this social entropy, it is important that we learn from the scientific world about how the unwanted destabilizing outcomes of such social entropy can be contained. According to the laws of thermodynamics and chemical engineering, there is no amount of resources that can repair all of the damage caused by excessive entropy. Moreover, trying to do too much to control the situation only adds more energy into the system and thereby increases the entropy. Hence, science argues that the converse is what is needed. Entropy is prevented from emerging by anticipation and education, or if it is in process, by taking small steps to slightly reduce the entropy and thereby regain some control of the system (K. Annala, personal communication, 2011).

What does this mean in practical, real-life terms? It means the nurturing of ethical behavior as well as cognizance of and, as Paolo Freire put it, conscienticization to the forces shaping our worldview today. This is about growing a deep conscious awareness of the inherent issues within the situation. In other words, ensuring that each and every Nordic student has a sincere commitment to caring for others must become an integral provision of his or her education. This is a challenge to the objective of schooling, to the teachers and the principals, as well as to their professional education. Education for competitiveness and individualism is not a sufficient objective for this end. Rather than the commitment to caring for others being a social norm, a Nordic value, it should become a personal virtue, an innate personal principle. Moreover, this virtue should be inculcated into the very being of each student through their schooling. Just as literacy and numeracy are deemed to be fundamental capacities of an educated person, so too should there be an ethical capacity in the form of a sincere and authentic concern for caring for others. Since the end of World War II, we Nordic peoples have depended on our legislative leaders to maintain and sustain our proud commitment to an inclusive welfare state, but in a global world this responsibility must be assumed by the individual and developed in his or her formative years at school. This is not to negate the importance of leadership, as it is now even more essential that our leaders at all levels willingly and readily act as ethical role models. If we wish to counter the diluting effect of leadership and societal acts of misconduct conveyed by the global media upon the ethical development of our students, then it behooves us to make ethical behavior, cognizance of it, and conscienticization to it a far more explicit and universal outcome of education.

To this end, this chapter explores the uniquely important role of the educational leader toward achieving this desired outcome. More specifically, the remainder of this chapter describes how it is possible for the educational leader to create a socially responsible learning environment in which ethical behavior and a commitment to caring for others will be natural outcomes. This is about the establishment of morally responsible school leadership.

## MORALLY RESPONSIBLE, CARING SCHOOL LEADERSHIP

The word "responsible" was documented back in 1599 to mean that one is "answerable to another for something." Moreover, the Latin root, *responsus*, is the past participle of *respondere*, to "respond" (Online Etymological Dictionary, n.d.). Thus, to be responsible and thereby answerable to another embraces more than compliance or obedience because it is an action initiated in response to another person. It is not a passive reaction to another person's expectations or demands but rather a dynamic interaction in which the responsible person considers the diverse needs of all resulting in a particular preferred response. It is in this sense that being responsible takes on a moral dimension, since a responsible person takes care to consider the outcomes of their own actions on the lives of others. A responsible person is invariably *morally accountable* for their actions.

Consequently, responsible school leadership is not only "answerable to another for something" but also responds in a morally accountable way. Hence, in the Nordic countries in particular, the call is for today's school leaders to be morally responsible. According to Starratt (2005), as the world changes from a national to a global community, where there is a need to be managing the Earth's fragile resources and to achieve international peace and security, a different kind of school leader is required: *a multidimensional leader,* who understands the various dimensions of the learning tasks the schools must cultivate. Adjusting to the new and unique demands of today's world begins in our schools and requires a particular type of school leader. Such a leader, according to Starratt, must have a moral vision of what is required from the whole community, and that leader must carry a proactive responsibility for making this kind of learning take place. Today, the world needs morally responsible school leaders.

Furthermore, Starratt (1994, 2005) provides a framework for clarifying the breadth and depth of what constitutes a morally responsible school leader. There must be a breadth to their leadership. In Starratt's five domains of moral responsibility, a school leader should be (1) a human being, (2) a citizen and a public servant, (3) an educator, (4) an educational administrator, and (5) an educational leader. Within and across each of these five domains, he posits that a morally responsible school leader attends to the three ethics of justice, critique, and care. These three ethics provide the depth to the actions of a morally responsible school leader. The ethic of justice requires the morally responsible school leader to always be concerned with fully knowing the rights, law, and policies specific to a situation in question. The ethic of critique requires the morally responsible school leader to be alert to when it might be necessary to redefine or reframe existing categories of privilege, power, culture, and language in order to advocate on behalf of the disadvantaged. The ethic of care requires the morally responsible school leader to ensure that all decisions have no unwanted, unexpected, or unnecessary detrimental consequences for others. This chapter posits that the fundamental question for educators to ask every day is, "Do I make the conscious choice to care?" If the answer is yes, educators remember every day why they open the school door. The ethic of justice and critique follow from this decision.

Although Starratt's framework is intended for universal application, its particular significance for the Nordic context is acknowledged. This chapter has argued that while we Nordic people are proud of our welfare society with its emphasis on a commitment to caring for others, this is being threatened as the values and understandings of our students come under the influence of the detrimental behaviors and decisions conveyed through the international media. Hargreaves (2005) describes caring school leadership as the work of attentive love, which Greenleaf (1977) depicts as the encountering and acknowledging of the individual fellow human with respect, attentiveness, and gentleness and building a learning environment where these attributes are consistently and sustainably exercised. For Noddings (1992, 2005), the practice of care is incorporated into a *relationship* based on mutual agreement or alignment. Furthermore, she argues that within this relationship there is a guarantee of true accountability. Here, Noddings' interpretation of accountability for caring is that it must be *a relationship between the carer and the cared for.* The relationship must be based on the carer perceiving, listening to, and hearing the expressed and inferred needs of the cared for, and in responding to these, the carer's actions must be based on consent and acceptance of the cared for.

Hence, for Noddings, a caring school leader asks, "What should schools be accountable for?" She replies that, in the first instance, schools should be accountable for being *responsive to and caring* about the learning needs of the students. She claims that schools should be responsive to the students' learning needs while simultaneously providing a pastorally caring learning environment. She is bringing the learner into the primary focus of schooling just as Caldwell and Spinks (2008) challenge us to rethink teaching, learning, and school administration so that the students and their needs are its key focus.

What is the philosophy of education in such a school? Again according to Noddings, the legitimate philosophy of education of a caring school leader fosters a school where reasonable people are readily able to express differing conceptions of experience and truth. This philosophy turned into practice offers the students many choices to study, many ways of learning, and many different ways of being assessed. It does not abandon differing learners and potentials and is based on relational caring for all. As regards accountability, the natural outcome from this philosophy is that instead of focusing on holding the school responsible for its stated purposes, it is held *responsible for the opportunities and choices* it offers its students.

For Noddings (2005, 2006), it is vitally important for schools to offer their students a diversity of opportunities and choices in order to better prepare them to cope with deep social change. She claims that, by and large, many teachers are alienated from the practical realities of their students' lives and so they tend to teach compartmentalized disciplines infused with "methodolatry." Many teachers respond with the equipment of the industrial era to the demands of postindustrial social change. As proposed by Hargreaves (2006), basic skills of earlier times to be learned at school were literacy, numeracy, and obedience and punctuality, whereas the current demand is for an education that provides learners with skills to learn multiliteracies, creativity, information and communication technologies, teamwork, lifelong learning, adaptation, change, and environmental responsibility.

More specifically, caring school leaders need to exhibit five essential qualities. First, a caring school leader must be committed to growing themselves toward educational leadership. Caring school leaders are committed to continually seeking to learn more about how best to lead themselves as well as others. This is about caring school leaders understanding themselves as fully human beings with strengths and weaknesses, preferences and biases, and likes and dislikes, and yet always striving to act for the common good. Hence the fundamental outlook of caring school leaders is that of equality and the nature of learning and knowledge as being essentially humanistic, socioconstructivist, and experiential. Learners acquire knowledge within a sociorelational context; it is not given to them from a more knowledgeable other. Hence, leaders empower the teachers and the students as fellow human beings of equal importance and worth, and so engage with them in developing the pedagogy and the school's administration. In a caring school, learning, teaching, and leading are relational, shared efforts.

Second, caring school leaders must strive to ensure that the teachers engage in sharing their expertise and thus develop their professional capacity together. An example of this from the Finnish context is the mandatory teacher self-evaluation process introduced in 1994, which has evolved into a shared method to compare and distribute professional and pedagogical experiences and inventions. This process has shown that the development of transparency in one's own teaching methods, practices, and know-how by working interdependently with other teachers greatly improves the performance of the entire teaching faculty. Despite its initial personal challenges, in the long run both pride and joy in each other's professional and pedagogical learning is perceived and shared. In such a rich professionally learning environment, trust among the teachers increases and enhances the overall school culture to support improved student learning (Müller & Hernandez, 2010).

The third essential quality of caring school leaders is that they create the understanding that every student counts and matters. Such leaders seek to establish a school culture in which all students can confidently seek the guidance and help from at least one staff member so that at all times students know that they matter to someone. In support of this pastorally caring culture, the administrative structures and follow-up systems are thoroughly discussed and agreed upon with teachers, students, and parents so as to ensure full community involvement to prevent student dropout. Caring for the well-being of each student becomes a whole-school responsibility.

Fourth, caring school leaders ensure that the school curriculum supports the learning of each student to live a life committed to caring. Learning to care becomes an essential of not only the school curriculum but also the culture of the school, the teaching methodology, and how life is lived in the school. Each student should be taught *in* and *through* caring. The curriculum teaches the student how to care, while the nature of the culture and the quality of the interpersonal relationships inside and outside of the classroom teach the student how to care through being cared for by others. With respect to the curriculum, Noddings (1992, 2005) proposes that each student be immersed in the following six themes of care: caring for self; caring in the inner circle; caring for strangers and distant others; caring for animals, plants, and the earth; caring for the human-made world; and caring for ideas. According to Hargreaves (2005), caring is bringing passion into the classroom and changing the structures in such a manner that every teacher can engage in caring. Thus, it is the caring school leader's responsibility to ensure that all teachers engage in caring in the way they teach and in the way they relate to others.

Finally, caring school leaders need to recognize the phenomenological or emotional dimension of schooling as an essential part of not only student learning but also teaching and coping with change. Emotions are important natural human qualities and, therefore, are an integral part of all human endeavors. Hence, the emotional side of life should be embraced and not avoided. Emotional learning is necessary for intellectual learning. The emotional side of relationships provides the necessary feelings of safety and security, as well as the gaining of meaningfulness through finding mutual interests, which create a sense of worth, optimism, and happiness. As Hargreaves (2005) states, emotions and caring are ambers of hope and thus can empower both teachers and students in all that they do.

## SUMMARY

Parallel to the Nordic peoples witnessing repeated gross miscarriages of justice and violations against sustainable codes of conduct in economic, environmental, religious, cultural, social, and educational issues in their our own countries is the growing awareness that these very same issues are being experienced on a global scale. Modern media technologies ensure that such issues are brought to the attention of the Nordic peoples regardless of their origin or context. Importantly, these media reports are readily available to Nordic students. As a result, the highly valued Nordic welfare society, with its emphasis on a commitment to caring for others, is being threatened as the values and understandings of our students come under the influence of the international media in a global world. In response to this threat, it is argued that it becomes essential to include the learning of ethical behavior as an innate educational outcome. Moreover, the achievement of this outcome necessitates the development of morally responsible school leadership, which requires a commitment to an ethic of care from school leaders in all domains of their leadership. Simply stated, if the proud Nordic welfare society is to be maintained, a commitment to caring for others must become the quintessential feature of school leadership.

Hence, this chapter has reflected on the concept of morally responsible school leadership from a Nordic perspective. To this end, it utilized Starratt's (2005) five domains of moral responsibility essential to school leadership and his (1994) three ethical dimensions of justice, critique, and care as its points of departure for creating a morally responsible leadership theoretical framework. More specifically, this chapter has argued that within a Nordic society, the ethic of care assumes a primal position for the genesis of morally responsible leadership. In such a society, caring leadership is the primary means for carrying out this form of school leadership. Thus, the concept of care, or caring, was discussed as a crucial relationship between school leaders and those they lead, and this was followed by a description of the actual leadership practices required in a school with a tangible commitment to teaching all students to care despite the troubled global world in which they live.

## REFERENCES

Caldwell, B. J., & Spinks, J. M. (2008). *Raising the stakes*. New York: Routledge.

Castells, M. (1996). *The rise of the network society, the information age: Economy, society and culture* (Vol. I). Cambridge, MA: Blackwell.

Castells, M. (1997). *The power of identity, the information age: Economy, society and culture* (Vol. 2). Cambridge, MA: Blackwell.

Castells, M. (1998). *End of millennium, the information age: Economy, society and culture* (Vol. 3). Cambridge, MA: Blackwell.

Elmore, R. (2005). Accountable leadership. *Educational Forum, 69*(2), 134–142.

Greenleaf, R. K. (1977). *Servant leadership: A journey into the nature of legitimate power and greatness*. New York: Paulist Press.

Hargreaves, A. (2005). Introduction. In A. Hargreaves (Ed.), *Extending educational change* (pp. 1–14). Dordrecht, Netherlands: Springer.

Hargreaves, A. (2006). *Sustainable leadership*. Retrieved from www.edu.gov.on.ca/eng/policyfunding/leadership/pdfs/hargreaves.pdf

Harvey, D. (2005). *A brief history of neoliberalism*. Oxford: Oxford University Press.

Müller, J., & Hernandez, F. (2010). On the geography of accountability: Comparative analysis of teachers' experiences across seven European countries. *Journal of Educational Change, 11*(4), 307–322.

Noddings, N. (1992). *The challenge to care. An alternative approach to education*. New York: Teachers College Press.

Noddings, N. (2005). *The challenge to care. An alternative approach to education* (2nd ed.). New York: Teachers College Press.

Noddings, N. (2006). Educational leaders as caring teachers. *School Leadership and Management, 26*(4), 339–345.

Online Etymological Dictionary. www.etymonline.com Retrieved on September 10, 2007.

Sahlberg, P. (2006). Education reform for raising economic competitiveness. *Journal of Educational Change, 7*(4), 259–287.

Sahlberg, P. (2007). Education policies for raising student learning: The Finnish approach. *Journal of Education Policy, 22*(2), 147–171.

Starratt, R. (1994). *Building an ethical school. A practical response to the moral crisis in schools.* London: Falmer.

Starratt, R. (2005). Responsible leadership. *Educational Forum, 65*(2), 124–133.

Stiglitz, J. (2002). *Globalization and its discontents.* New York: Norton.

Stiglitz, J. (2012). *Price of inequality: How today's divided society endangers our future.* New York: W. W. Norton.

UNDP Human Development Index Country reports. Retrieved from http://hdr.undp.org/en/countries/

# 10

## THE PREVALENCE OF SILENCE

### KJERSTI LIEN HOLTE

Professional reflection on unethical or negative organizational issues is absolutely essential in a strategy for the development of ethical leadership. For several reasons, it is difficult for leaders to have important critical conversations with employees in regard to the perceived quality of their performance. It can, therefore, be difficult to build a solid base for ethical decision making so that important meetings supporting moral learning do not take place. Some people blame these communication difficulties on organizational structure or the personality of the leader. Another perspective on the problem is that there are hidden mechanisms within the organization that prevent transparency about difficult issues. The fact that these mechanisms are hidden makes it difficult for leaders to expose them.

My aim in this chapter is to expose the presence of hidden mechanisms of silence that may surround unethical practices already happening in schools by answering the following questions: Why does silence about ethical and negative issues exist in schools? How can a school leader facilitate open and honest communication so as to encourage ethical reflection and action with school staff? This is a theoretical study where existing theories are used to answer these questions. I present three main reasons why an aura of ethical silence may exist in schools and four different motives that influence teachers and others to maintain their silence when they are confronted with unethical issues. The reasons for the existence of ethical silence are: exclusion and inclusion rituals, forms of employment, and cultural characteristics. Embedded within these reasons are the different motivational behaviors of prosocial behavior, indulgence behavior, defensive behavior, and passive aggressive behavior. Hence, this chapter argues that educational leaders seeking to instill and maintain high ethical standards need to engage with the potential presence of hidden silencing mechanisms in their schools in order to facilitate honest communication, ethical reflection, and, ultimately, moral behavior.

## THE PREVALENCE OF SILENCE

Silence is a pivotal problem for the practice of ethical educational leadership because the complexity of the school community can camouflage its perceived requirement or hide its essential objective. According to Argyris and Schön (1978), for organizational learning and development to occur, the organization needs to follow a cycle of discovery, invention, production, and evaluation. Thus, if school leaders not only wish to personally practice but also to promote ethical behavior, they need to be able to discover where unethical behaviors are occurring, invent a means for redressing this behavior, ensure that the new ethical behavior is produced by the intervention, and then, later, evaluate the whole process to ensure that what is desired is actually occurring.

Assumed within this understanding is that an openness to acknowledging the presence of such unethical behavior in the school community will occur automatically. Indeed, openness based upon honesty and forthrightness is crucial in all of these phases of organizational learning if the school is to truly come to know, learn, and thereby improve itself (Kraman & Hamm, 1999). If a school community is to really discover some of its unethical problems, then school leaders need to ensure that they can come to know what and where unethical practices are happening currently. Inventing solutions necessitates communication about what is the actual core dysfunctionality and naming the unethical behavior if it exists.

In order to achieve this, school leaders are dependent on honest communication with other school personnel if the leaders are to invent or find solutions to produce alternative ethical behaviors. Also, to then be able to authentically and comprehensively evaluate this solution to ensure that it is producing ethical behaviors, school leaders need each and every person associated with the situation to be willing and open when communicating their impressions and experiences following the intervention.

However, for several reasons, it is difficult for school leaders to have important critical conversations with other school personnel in regard to the perceived existence of unethical practices. It can, therefore, be difficult to build a solid base for ethical decision making, which means that important meetings supporting moral learning and the development of alternative ethical practices do not take place. In reality, there are hidden mechanisms within many school communities that prevent honesty and transparency about unethical behaviors. The fact that, by and large, these mechanisms are hidden makes it difficult for school leaders to expose and redress such practices.

Moreover, the fidelity of the assumption that the presence of unethical practices will be automatically and openly acknowledged is further eroded if the school leader is perceived to be personally culpable. School leaders are subjected to a variety of situations that involve value choices and ethical considerations. They have to deal with the distribution of benefits, the prioritizing of principles, and subjective interpretations of situations (Strand, 2001). Often school leaders face dilemmas where there is no clearly right or wrong choice. Sometimes they have to compromise and temporarily disregard particular problems despite their personal reluctance to do so. Such choices and compromises are founded upon personal beliefs and values, rather than facts and predictable outcomes, which means that errors of judgment and mistakes are possible. Furthermore, given that personal beliefs and values are influential in the school leaders' decision-making processes, self-interest is ever-present (Popper, 1986). Personal preferences and biases are never far from the school leader's interpretation of a given situation. In this way, the school leader's approach to resolving dilemmas is inherently an ethical decision. Moreover, this circumstance makes the school leader prone to acting unethically on occasions. As is the case for leaders in many other contexts, school leaders can be tempted to hide or rationalize their unethical decisions and/or practices through either denial or justification based upon false moral grounds (Habermas, 1999).

Swedish researchers (Hedin, Månsson, & Tikkanen, 2008) have identified the following six areas where unethical behavior can arise within a school community (pp. 46–47):

1. Downsizing and reorganizations that have consequences for members of the school community
2. Impractical or unjust work methods
3. Suppressing or silencing reports or information
4. Financial disorder
5. Harassment and discrimination
6. Inappropriate leadership and an unhealthy working environment

In many ways, these areas for potential unethical behavior seem so publicly observable that one could falsely assume that they would be readily and promptly addressed. However, many employees report that they do not dare speak up or complain about such unethical practices (Aronsson & Gustafsson, 1999; Jensen, 2004; Skivenes & Trygstad, 2005). More specifically, Aronsson and Gustafsson (p. 202) emphasize that the results within the school system are particularly alarming, with some 40% of the teachers in their research reporting that they met resistance from the school leader if they raised questions about ethical issues. It would seem that silence, rather than speaking out, about unethical practices is far too common. The question is, therefore: Why does silence about unethical issues exist in school communities?

## DEVELOPING A WAY TO OVERCOME THE PREVALENCE OF SILENCE

The empirical evidence that is available on employee silence in ethical matters shows that employees fail to speak out for a number of different reasons. Some studies explain it by focusing on the organization and its leadership (Hennestad, 1990; Roethlisberger & Dickson, 1939/1964; Tourish & Robson, 2006; Vakola & Bouradas, 2005), while other studies have focused on group relationships and employee differences (Bowen & Blackmon, 2003; Premeaux & Bedeian, 2003; Van Dyne, Soon, & Botero, 2003), on learning perspectives (Berlinger, 2003; Bryant, 2003; Milliken, Morrison, & Hewlin, 2003), or on normative relationships (Hirschman, 1970). These explanations touch upon some central factors but are often somewhat deficient because they emphasize some elements more than others or because investigations tend to focus on one particular perspective only. Several of these earlier explanations mention hidden, informal, and unofficial learning processes. A common aspect of these studies is that these learning processes are only partially described and analyzed. However, Holte (2009) presents a theory of the hidden curriculum of silence based on qualitative interviews with teachers. The data from the participating teachers were compared with answers from nurses at a nursing home and workers in a factory in the process industry. Hence, this silence theory is based on both empirical and theoretical data and provides an answer to the question: Why does silence about unethical issues exist in school communities?

Within her research, Holte (2009) identified a hidden curriculum of silence in schools with respect to acknowledging and addressing unethical practices. She refers to this phenomenon as the "curriculum silentium," and claims that it influences the ethical judgments made by school employees to the point of encouraging them to remain silent when observing unethical situations because speaking out is considered far too risky. Furthermore, Holte posits that this influential curriculum silentium process that leads to such employee silence comprises five phases. First, the awareness phase occurs when the employee, through observation or personal experience, develops an opinion that certain practices by an individual or a group are unethical. The second phase is that of the employee's reaction in which he or she considers what alternative forms of action to take based on the perceived seriousness of the situation. Should the employee speak out, remain silent, or leave the organization? The third phase is referred to as the "voice-loop" phase, where the employee decides to try to speak out or protest but gains no apparent beneficial result and so becomes inclined to suppress his or her judgment and remain silent. During this phase, the school employee may experience negative sanctions or may simply be ignored. For some school employees, this phase may last a long time, while others may never enter it because they choose not to ever make their negative point of view known to others. Instead, they go directly to the fourth phase: deliberate silence. In this phase, all criticism is stifled. In reality, some determined school employees might choose to return to the voice-loop phase after periods of silence because they are not yet willing to give up. Others, in contrast, will move on toward the fifth phase, the phase of redirected attention. They redirect their attention from the concern that is troubling them by, for example, avoiding exposure to the unethical practice or by rationalizing why silence is the best option for them.

The curriculum silentium is a hidden or subconscious force, yet it has its genesis in very explicit elements such as organizational goals, content, learning situations, information dissemination strategies, organizational culture, leadership style, and employee motivation. It is a hidden or subconscious force because people are seldom aware of their own involvement in the learning and practice of the elements that constitute the curriculum silentium. Furthermore, both leaders and employees can adopt and promote these elements. However, given the structural limitations of this chapter, I will be able to describe only the influence of employee motivation, organizational culture, and leadership style in contributing to the presence of ethical silence within an organization.

## Employee Motivation

There are four different employee motives for choosing to remain silent about unethical issues in an organization. These motives are: prosociality, indulgence, defensiveness, and passive aggression. The strength of each of these motives may fluctuate depending on the situational circumstances, and they are seldom found alone.

In the case of *prosociality* as a motive for maintaining silence, the priority is to strengthen their relationships with colleagues rather than to speak out about a perceived unethical situation. Moreover, it has been found (Van Dyne et al., 2003) that such ethical inaction is self-justified based on the awareness that we can all make mistakes in our professional practice, and so we require mutual dependency with our colleagues, who not only understand our human limitations but also will not judge and condemn us, just as we will not judge and condemn them. Underlying this mutual dependency is the belief that a good colleague is a workplace friend who will overlook another's imperfections and weaknesses no matter the consequences. What is considered "the right thing to do" is, therefore, to safeguard the social bond and to ignore the ethical implications. Furthermore, this prosocial motive may be grounded in misplaced courtesy, gratitude, and fellowship among employees. If someone has helped you in a difficult situation, you then feel obliged to return the favor. Silence about an unethical practice can be one way of fulfilling this obligation.

Moreover, this acceptance of the need for mutual dependency within an organization can further undermine the establishment of ethical practices because it also makes honest conversations difficult to initiate. To initiate a conversation that challenges another's ethics is seen as an act of disloyalty. In Scandinavian communities, in particular, there exists an informal law called the Jante law, which describes a pattern of group behavior toward any individual who seeks to portray the actions of another as unworthy and inappropriate (Sandemose, 1933). In light of the Jante law, it can be considered rude, or even unacceptable, to protest something one finds unethical about another person.

Hence the purpose of prosocial silence is to achieve and maintain good relationships in the workplace (Holte, 2009). Good social relationships among colleagues are considered to be far more important than countering unethical practices.

The second type of employee motivation for maintaining silence in the face of perceived unethical behavior in an organization is *indulgence*. Silence motivated by indulgence comes from the person's experience of being powerless or submissive when confronted with widely accepted and supported traditional practices, cultural codes, and/or organizational structures (Van Dyne et al., 2003). If an unethical practice is seen as being the inevitable result of widely accepted organizational structure, culture, or traditions, then most people believe it is far too difficult to change. Why participate in a conversation about ethical issues when the chances for change are small? Rather than question such a seemingly entrenched and immutable practice, most choose to tolerate or overlook the situation.

The third type of employee motivation for maintaining silence in the face of perceived unethical behavior in an organization can be described as *defensiveness*. In this case, silence is motivated by the need to protect oneself against the negative consequences of exposing unethical practices (Van Dyne et al., 2003). For many within an organization, the more negative the anticipated consequences from an open and honest conversation about perceived unethical practices, the stronger the defensive motive is likely to be. If a person has previously observed the social and/or organizational exclusion of another employee, who had spoken up about a perceived unethical or negative condition in the organization, then he or she is far less likely to personally risk the same outcome. In the extreme case of exclusion, a violation of the expected social code to maintain silence might mean losing one's job. Naturally, most people want to protect both themselves and others against such a possibility. Even in far less extreme circumstances, the perception can be that simply talking to someone in authority about a possible unethical situation involves too much work and effort, particularly if there is no explicit evidence, with no guarantee of success. Raising questions about the possibility of unethical practices is considered to be a high-risk action. In this situation, it seems more beneficial to say nothing and maintain current workplace relationships than to speak out, only to be engulfed in organizational tension, disunity, and isolation.

The final type of employee motivation for maintaining silence in the face of perceived unethical behavior in an organization is that of *passive aggressive* inaction. A person is said to be motivated by such passive aggressive inaction if he or she is fully aware of unethical practices in the organization but deliberately chooses to not participate in discussions or conversations about the topic because the person is hoping for more serious consequences for the perpetrator of the unethical behavior (Nelson, Pasteernack, & Van Nuys, 2005). In the mind of such people, a conversation about certain unethical behaviors might stop these from happening and thereby protect the "bad" leader or "underperforming" colleagues and prevent them from losing their jobs, which is the nonpreferred outcome from the perspective of the passive aggressive person. Hence, instead of telling the leader about unethical practices in the organization, these people allow it to happen in the hope that it will eventually reveal itself in the form of a scandal, to the career detriment of the perpetrator.

### Organizational Culture

The second influence contributing to the presence of ethical silence within an organization is organizational culture. The tendency for school employees to remain silent when they either observe or experience unethical behavior can be reinforced by the culture of the organization. Although it is seldom possible to identify a particular organizational culture as being homogeneous, as there are not only numerous different types of organizational cultures but also the likelihood of subcultures (Schein, 2004), there are particular cultural characteristics that tend to induce curriculum silentium (Holte, 2009). These characteristics include those of a threatening, an ignoring, or a feel-good culture.

In a threatening culture, the employee is intimidated to remain silent through direct or indirect threats. Indirect threats are often presented as narratives that are not necessarily specific to the particular organization (Bryant, 2003). Regardless of the particular details described in the narrative, its intention is to provide a message, or an impression, about why it is important to ignore the unethical deeds of others and what might happen if this advice is not adhered to. Direct threats can be an instruction or directive to remain silent, with sanctions or unpleasant consequences for anyone who chooses to not adhere to this instruction or direction.

Regardless of its nature, a threatening culture builds up fear and anxiety within employees as they struggle to overcome their tense feelings caused not only by their reaction to the unethical situation but also by their inner conflict over whether to speak out or keep silent and having to confront their own level of ethical conviction if influenced by self-interest when their decision to remain silent is based on avoiding negative personal consequences (Athern & McDonald, 2002; Hedin et al., 2008; Skivenes & Trygstad, 2005). Thus, it can be seen how a threatening organizational culture primarily enhances defensive silence among employees because it enhances prosocial motives as it places an emphasis on the primary importance of protecting social relations and securing personal safety and security. Also, the irrationality of a threatening organizational culture can reinforce a passive aggressive motive for silence among employees as it encourages individuals to concentrate on their own safety and security at the expense of others.

On the other hand, the *ignoring* organizational culture establishes a commitment to silence about unethical behavior because it signals to each employee that such behavior can be overlooked or ignored, that openness about such matters is not realistic or intolerable, and that the opinions of employees are unwelcome or do not count. This culture enhances silence because the employees believe they have no influence on the situation. This can happen if the employees have previously tried to take up a sensitive issue but experienced discouragement or failure. In ignoring cultures, ethical opinions and contributions from employees will be cast aside or treated in a superficial way. Deliberately slowing down an ethical review process can also have a silencing effect. In such a situation, it appears to the employee who has spoken out about a perceived unethical situation that the leader is responding so slowly to his or her complaint that the issue will never be suitably redressed and so it is better to ignore the issue. This can lead to experiences of powerlessness and indulgence and enhance forbearing silence. An ignoring culture can also cause frustration and anger and therefore enhance passive aggressive silence as well.

Finally, a feel-good organizational culture is one in which the protection of positive and harmonious feelings is given a higher priority than a commitment to ethical behavior. Being enthusiastic, thinking positively, acting supportively, and being nice, happy, and engaged are all deemed to be important social outcomes. Moreover, it is accepted that an effective way to protect and maintain this feel-good culture is to not talk about potential problems or mistakes or unethical practice. Any attempt to initiate a discussion about something thought to be unethical practice is understood as being disrespectful, acting unnecessarily, and bad for the organization as a whole. This culture enhances prosocial and defensive silence, since it encourages strategies that not only values employee relationships as the pivotal cultural characteristic but also protects, strengthens, and normalizes the existing relationships.

*Leadership Style*

The third and final influence contributing to the presence of ethical silence within an organization is leadership style. One essential insight that should be gained from all of the previous discussion is that the presence of curriculum silentium is widespread and can readily occur in any school community. With or without the direct involvement of the school leader, curriculum silentium can easily become an unwanted facet of a school's culture and thereby undermine the achievement of ethical behavior within the school. Thus, the attainment of ethical educational leadership relies upon the school leader being vigilant in eradicating any hint of curriculum silentium from the school's culture.

To this end, the most important action school leaders can initiate is to establish processes that will enable the school community to suitably gain and share knowledge about perceived unethical behavior and/or erroneous beliefs about the need for ethical silence. This will open up more options for actions that can lead the school community toward the desired ethical outcome. The knowledge should be shared with the employees so it can build a foundation for honest, open, and supportive communication. This will show to each and every person that they can trust the school, and especially the school leader, to listen to their concerns and to sincerely investigate the situation.

When it comes to reviewing the school's culture as a potential unintended source of promoting curriculum silentium, it is important for the school leader to stridently ask questions about the present state of the organization: What can be done to facilitate an open discussion about ethical issues? What is ethical behavior? How do we recognize unethical behavior? How should a person react when observing unethical behavior? Why is ethical behavior important in our school community? Is it important that each and every person in our school community acts ethically? Do we feel anxious when raising concerns about the ethical behavior of others in the school community and, if so, why? What do we ignore that might be an ethical issue and why? Are we aware of what we ignore, or is it out of ignorance?

When conducting such a cultural review as this, it is important not to overlook critiquing the traditional, taken-for-granted rituals that are often considered to be fundamental to defining the school's uniqueness and distinctiveness. Rituals are "fostered activities [that] provide opportunities for people to identify with others" in the school community so as to "provide [the] people in a school with a sense of belonging and hope" (O'Mahoney, Barnett, & Matthews, 2006, p. 12). It is possible that these benefits can also hide unwanted explicit practices and unhelpful implicit messages. Thus, it is important for the school leader to seek knowledge about these rituals, which may well be excluding or hurting certain individuals in the school community. If the rituals send a different ethical message than that desired by the school community, then it could be extremely difficult to achieve ethical leadership.

To assist in this process, Holte (2009) introduces a process called *critical didactic relations analysis,* which can be used in school communities to reveal "sacred cows" and "blind spots" when it comes to ethical issues. Sacred cows are those widely accepted practices that have widespread superficial appeal but have hidden unwanted consequences, whereas blind spots are those parts of the culture deliberately, or unintentionally, avoided or ignored during formal review or critique processes. A substantial contribution of this analytical method is that it can be used to improve the ethical decision-making process. It is a process that can lead to more sincere openness about hidden unwanted phenomena in the school community. Such an analysis can also engender a more critical awareness of how the school community's understanding of itself actually contributes to unfortunate behavioral tendencies. It is in the nature of hidden processes that often people are not consciously aware of their own contribution to unwanted outcomes. Using the critical didactic relations analysis process can provide people with a chance to relate in a different, more responsible, and agentive fashion to situations that initially seemed to lie outside of their input or control.

The critical didactic relations analysis process comprises three steps:

1. The identification of a gap between a formal and an experienced policy
2. The analytic construction of the hidden policy, as if it were a planned policy, using didactic categories applicable to organizations
3. The analysis of the relationships among the didactic categories

The first step forms the point of departure for the ethical investigation of the particular situation. Differences among the ideological, formal, perceived, operationalized, and experienced policies/processes/actions show that there is a gap between the intention and the reality, which indicates that there are ongoing unofficial, partially hidden learning processes inherent in the school culture in general and/or the common practices associated with the situation in particular. The second step involves the analytical construction of a policy or a detailed outline of a process that would achieve the unwanted reality as it is currently experienced. In other words, treat the current practice as though it were the outcome of a planned policy or desired process but create the policy or process based on what is happening using the didactic categories applicable to organizations. These didactic categories are: goals, content, dissemination strategies, and the motivation of all participants. The third and final step in the critical didactic relations analysis process involves the analysis of each of the didactic categories within this newly created policy or process in order to explain the inherent motives, beliefs, assumptions, and values within this commonly accepted practice that, in fact, legitimate unethical practice.

The relationships among the different categories is central to the completion of a coherent and comprehensive understanding of the implied ethical imperatives associated with this situation. It is essential to realize this because, ultimately, this analysis provides the school leader with insight into what aspects of each category needs to change so as to remove the unethical features of the situation. However, changes in one of the categories are likely to affect the others and vice versa. None of the categories is dominant, and this, in many ways, explains their functionality in the analysis of the hidden learning. Empirical insights connected to changing one category can help the school leader to interpret and predict adjustments required to other categories, as these can be seen to be logical consequences because they can be both outcomes from or catalysts for the implemented change.

Theoretically, this critical didactic relations analysis process is a new contribution to the mix of ways in which a school leader can redress unofficial or hidden unethical practices in the school community. Arguably, such actions have been previously directed by more diffuse, unsystematic guidelines or have been avoided completely. A critical didactic relations analysis process makes it easier to employ a truly multidisciplinary perspective on how to redress complex ethical issues.

The most important contribution of the critical didactic relations analysis is that it enables the school leader to create analytic constructions of relationships that are difficult to grasp otherwise. In this way, one can identify hypotheses and thematic areas that have perhaps previously not been queried. Let us say, for example, that a hidden policy exists that leads to discrimination of dyslexic pupils in a school. In this instance, a critical didactic relations analysis would immediately lead us to ask the following questions: What is the goal of such a policy? What content is disseminated through the policy? How is it disseminated? Which dissemination strategies and learning situations are prominent? How are teachers and pupils motivated by the goals of such a policy, and to what ends? This could help structure the collection and analysis of data in the work with ethical issues. Such questions would also apply, for example, to studies of school resistance and different types of racism and discrimination. The reciprocal nature of the didactic categories simplifies the work involved in discovering what is often hidden.

## SUMMARY

In this chapter I have exposed the presence of hidden mechanisms of silence that may surround unethical practices already happening in schools. Often, hidden mechanisms of silence within the school community prevent transparency about unethical issues and make it difficult to carry out ethical leadership. I have described these mechanisms as the curriculum of silence because they teach employees to remain silent about difficult issues. Specifically, I have presented three main reasons for the existence of this "curriculum silentium" and four different motives that influence teachers and others to maintain their silence when they are confronted with unethical issues. The three reasons for the existence of a curriculum of silence were presented as: employee motivation, organizational culture, and leadership style. Embedded within these reasons were the four different motivational behaviors of: prosocial behavior, indulgence behavior, defensive behavior, and passive aggressive behavior. Prosocial behavior illustrates how people remain silent to show gratitude or secure good relations with colleagues or their leader. Indulgence behavior describes how often people do not see themselves as qualified to judge the ethicalness of a situation or in a position to make any difference to unethical practices. Defensive behavior occurs when people protect themselves, colleagues, or their leader from potential negative consequences by not revealing the presence of unethical issues. Losing one's job seems to be a main concern. Passive aggressive behavior exists when people remain silent, hoping for more serious consequences to eventually result for those causing the unethical action. Also, I have argued that threatening, ignoring, and feel-good organizational cultures are conducive to the establishment and continuance of a curriculum of silence.

Hence, this chapter argues that educational leaders seeking to instill and maintain high ethical standards need to engage with the potential presence of these hidden silencing mechanisms in their school in order to facilitate honest communication, ethical reflection, and, ultimately, moral behavior. To assist the facilitation of open and honest communication, it has been suggested that a process called critical didactic relation analysis can be employed. This process can readily reveal the existence of sacred cows and/or blind spots of unethical practice in schools. Critical didactical relation analysis comprises three steps. First, a gap between the expected outcomes from a formal policy with the real outcomes experienced has to be identified. Second, using the real outcomes as a guide, the staff and the school leader construct a policy that would actually produce these unwanted outcomes. Some didactic categories have been provided so as to assist in this analytical construction of this fictitious policy. Finally, an in-depth analysis of this fictitious policy with respect to its inherent values, beliefs, and assumptions precipitates an awareness of the previously hidden unethical principles at play in the everyday activities and practices of the school staff. Now the school leader and staff are in a position to change these activities and practices so that the desired ethical outcomes are achieved. These three steps make it possible to find better ways to change unwanted into desirable ethical practices.

However, the most significant message provided by this chapter is that silence rather than conviction can be the greatest obstacle to the achievement of ethical educational leadership. It is all very well to want to be an ethical educational leader, but if unethical behavior is being ignored, overlooked, or condoned because no one is willing to publicly acknowledge its existence, then any conviction toward the establishment of ethical educational leadership is idealistic at best, if not exacerbating and demoralizing at worst. Thus, it can be seen that the development of authentic ethical educational leadership is both an individualistic and a cultural phenomenon. The establishment of ethical educational leadership demands that school leaders strive to ensure that not only their own behavior is ethical but also that their schools' culture supports and promotes a commitment to ethical practices by all. Employee silence in regard to the possible existence of unethical behavior is not necessarily a source of comfort and confidence to an intuitive and diligent ethical educational leader.

## REFERENCES

Argyris, C., & Schön, D. (1978). *Organizational learning*. Reading, MA: Addison-Wesley.

Aronsson, G., & Gustafsson, K. (1999). *Kritik eller tystnad.—En studie av arbetsmarknads- och anställnings-förhållandens betydelse för arbetsmiljökritik* [Criticism or silence: A study of the labor and employment relationship, the importance of occupational criticism]. *Labour & Working, 5*(3), 189–206.

Athern, K., & McDonald, M. C. (2002). The beliefs of nurses who were involved in a whistleblower event. *Journal of Advanced Nursing, 38*(3), 303–309.

Berlinger, N. (2003). *What is meant by telling the truth: Bonhoeffer on the ethics of disclosure*. London: Continuum.

Bowen, F., & Blackmon, K. (2003). Spirals of silence: The dynamic effects of diversity on organizational voice. *Journal of Management Studies, 40*(6), 1393.

Bryant, M. (2003). Persistence and silence: A narrative analysis of employee responses to organisational change. *Sociological Research Online, 8*(4). Retrieved from www.socresonline.org.uk/8/4/bryant.html

Habermas, J. (1999). Between facts and norms: An author's reflections. *Denver University Law Review, 76*(4), 937–942.

Hedin, U. C., Månsson, S. A., & Tikkanen, R. (2008). *När man måste säga ifrån. Om kritikk och whistelblowing i offentliga organisationer.* [When one has to tell. About criticism and whistleblowing in public organizations.] Stockholm: Natur og kultur.

Hennestad, B. (1990). The symbolic impact of double bind leadership: Double bind and the dynamics of organization culture. *Journal of Management Studies, 27*(3), 265–280.

Hirschman, A. O. (1970). *Exit, voice, and loyalty: Responses to decline in firms, organizations, and states.* Cambridge, MA: Harvard University Press.

Holte, K. L. (2009). *Hysj. En kritisk didaktisk relasjonsanalyse av Curriculum Silentium; den skjulte policyen for taushet om arbeidsrelatert kritikk hos ansatte.* [Shhh! A Critical Didactic Relations Analysis of the Curriculum Silentium. The Hidden Policy of Silence Regarding Work Related Criticism from Employees.] Karlstad, Sweden: Karlstad University Press.

Jensen, A. (2004). *Frimodige ytringer ere enhver tilladte.* [Free Speach is everyone allowed.] Oslo: Rapport fra norsk redaktørforening.

Kraman, S. S., & Hamm, G. (1999). Risk management: Extreme honesty may be the best policy. *Annals of Internal Medicine, 131,* 963–967.

Milliken, F. J., Morrison, E. W., & Hewlin, P. F. (2003). An exploratory study of employee silence: Issues that employees don't communicate upward and why. *Journal of Management Studies, 40*(6), 1453–1476.

Nelson, G. L., Pasteernack, B. A., & Van Nuys, K. E. (2005, October). The passive aggressive organization. *Harvard Business Review.*

O'Mahoney, G., Barnett, B., & Matthews, R. (2006). *Building culture: A framework for school improvement.* Heatherton, Victoria, Australia: Hawker Brownlow Education.

Popper, K. (1986). *Unended quest. An intellectual autobiography.* Glasgow: Flamingo.

Premeaux, S. F., & Bedeian, A. G. (2003). Breaking the silence: The moderating effects of self monitoring in predicting speaking up in the work place. *Journal of Management Studies, 40*(6), 1359–1392.

Roethlisberger F. J., & Dickson W. J. (1939/1964). *Management and the worker: An account of a research program conducted by the Western Electric company, Hawthorn Works, Chicago.* Cambridge, MA: Harvard University Press.

Sandemose, A. (1933). *En flyktning krysser sitt spor.* [A refugee crosses his tracks.] Oslo: Aschehoug.

Schein, E. H. (2004). *Organizational culture and leadership* (3rd ed.). San Francisco: Jossey-Bass.

Skivenes, M., & Trygstad, S. (2005). *Varslere: en bok om arbeidstakere som sier ifra!* [Whistelblowers: A book about employees who use their voice.] Oslo: Gyldendal Akademisk.

Strand, T. (2001). *Ledelse organisasjon og kultur.* [Leadership, Organization and Culture.] Bergen, Norway: Fagbokforlaget.

Tourish, D., & Robson, P. (2006). Sense making and the distortion of critical upward communication in organizations. *Journal of Management Studies, 4*(6), 711–730.

Vakola, M., & Bouradas, D. (2005). Antecedents and consequences of organisational silence: An empirical investigation. *Employee Relations, 27*(5), 441–458.

Van Dyne, L., Soon A., & Botero, I. C. (2003). Conceptualizing employee silence and employee voice as multidimensional constructs. *Journal of Management Studies, 40*(6), 1359–1392.

# II

## Developing Ethical Educational Leadership

# II

Developing Ethical Educational Leadership

# 11

## AN ETHICAL LEADERSHIP DEVELOPMENTAL FRAMEWORK

### NANCY TUANA

Effective and responsible educational leaders must also be ethical leaders. By this I mean not only that their leadership decisions and practices must be based on ethical values and principles, but also that they "lead with ethics" in the sense of being committed to, and taking a leadership role in, ensuring the development of moral literacy throughout their communities. Effective ethical educational leadership, the focus of this handbook, is grounded in the recognition that ethical leadership, in the sense of *putting ethics in the foreground of all activities,* is essential for the entire educational community. It is not possible for one person, no matter how ethical or how effective a leader, to make a community ethical. An ethical community exists because the commitment to ethical leadership permeates the entire community. Too often, the focus on ethical leadership is limited to the education of the leaders of a school unit but neglects the second, and I would argue, more essential component of educating the entire community to *lead with ethics.* Such a limited focus can result in the mistaken impression that the field of ethical leadership should focus on the education of principals and administrators, rather than being a key element of education for all teachers at all levels.

For the same reason, when educators consider the ethical dimensions of teaching, it is not sufficient to be attentive only to creating a fair and equitable classroom environment. Educators must also have the skills needed to enhance the abilities their students require to learn how to lead with ethics as well. In other words, it is not sufficient to focus on the moral agency of the educator. *Ethical educational leadership also requires that teachers be effective ethics educators.* In holding this position, I agree with and build on Starratt's (2007) argument that authentic learning is intrinsically ethical. "By authentic learning I mean a learning that enables learners to encounter the meanings embedded in the curriculum about the natural, social and cultural worlds they inhabit, and, at the same time, find themselves in and through those very encounters. That kind of authentic learning, I argue, is intrinsically ethical" (p. 165).

However, ensuring that teachers are able to promote moral literacy means that training for ethical leadership in education should include the skills teachers need to support the development of the knowledge and skills students, at all grade levels, need to be moral agents. *Good education must therefore include the development of moral literacy.* Unfortunately, teacher preparation is often sorely lacking in providing educators the skills and knowledge needed for this aspect of leading with ethics.

This section of the handbook focuses on a framework for educators to ensure that they have the essential foundation they need not only to be ethical leaders, but also to ensure that their classrooms and institutional settings contribute to the enhancement of the moral literacy of their students. This framework was originally developed in my 2007 essay "Conceptualizing Moral Literacy," which was included in a special issue of the *Journal of Educational Administration* on the topic of moral literacy. Subsequent scholarly work on the topic of moral literacy by members of the University Council for Educational Administration's Center for the Study of Leadership and Ethics (UCEA CSLE, 1999) has provided important resources for developing and extending the original model. The chapters in this section continue to build on this framework and are designed to provide resources for a more ethically responsible approach to educational leadership in both senses of the phrase introduced above.

I use the phrase "moral literacy" for various reasons. The term "literacy" is intended to stress a twofold connotation. The first is that it involves a complex set of skills and abilities that must be developed over time. Moral literacy is a lifelong achievement, for we find ourselves confronted with new, and sometimes unique, ethical issues throughout our lifetimes. The second is to underscore the importance of education for developing this essential form of literacy. Just as math, science, or reading literacy evolves over time and with effective educational support, so too moral literacy must be developed in stages and with repeated and age-appropriate instruction. Just as we do not learn everything we need to know about science in kindergarten or informally from our parents or our communities, so too moral literacy is best supported by making it a formal subject of study throughout the educational process. Moral literacy should become as essential to a good education as literacy in math, science, history, or literature. I intentionally use the term "moral" rather than "ethical" for the type of literacy I espouse in order to distance it from the typical focus on ethical reasoning training common in philosophical approaches to ethics or the rule-based approach common to codes of ethics. While ethical reasoning is certainly an important component of moral literacy, it is, as I will illustrate below, only one part of the knowledge and abilities needed to be a morally literate individual.[1]

The framework I and others in this handbook advocate for moral literacy consists of three elements (Figure 11.1):

1. Ethical sensitivity
2. Ethical decision-making skills
3. Ethical motivation

While my essay serves to provide a broad introduction to each of these elements, the essays in this section of the handbook further explicate and build upon this framework.

**Figure 11.1** The ethical leadership development framework

## ETHICS EDUCATION FOR/IN LIFE

Ethics education is for life. Effective ethics pedagogy leads with ethics. This conception of leading is woven into the very heart of education, as the term "pedagogy" comes from the Greek παιδαγωγέω (paidagōgeō): παῖς (país, genitive παιδός, paidos) means "child" and ἄγω (ágō) means "lead." Hence, we design our curriculum to lead. But good education *leads to,* in the sense of cultivating skills. Education is not a rote memorization of facts but an education of the person into agency in which she or he becomes an inquirer and a creator. If pedagogy does not lead to the development of such lifelong skills, it is a failure.

Effective ethics pedagogy leads with ethics in the sense of enabling students to appreciate and understand the ethical dimensions of the subjects they are studying and the experiences they are having in all the domains of their life. All educational institutions are committed to both formal and informal education, and both domains should lead with ethics.

The formal educational domain is rife with issues of ethical significance. Social science classes present students with ways of living different from their own. They present opportunities for moral literacy through understanding how different value systems shape ways of living, thereby providing a basis for better understanding not only other cultures, but also people within the students' communities who hold values different than their own. History classes are filled with opportunities to understand justice and injustice: from a careful examination of the values and ethical principles that led to a war or how unethical motives and/or problematic assumptions about human nature led to slavery or servitude for some groups of people. Our science and technology classes are wonderful opportunities for thoughtful attention to the impact of these fields on society and reflection on the types of knowledge deemed valuable to know, as well as who is impacted by what we elect not to know. Literature and the arts are the perfect setting for engaging the moral imagination of students and providing them the opportunity to better understand ways of living.

The informal educational context also serves as an opportunity for leading with ethics by illuminating the importance of moral literacy for life. Schools provide various informal educational programs such as school anti-bullying programs, academic integrity programs, and anti-drug/alcohol efforts. While these programs may include a "compliance" component, i.e., the penalties for cheating or for bullying, they are most effective when they provide students with the ethical values and principles underlying the desired actions, i.e., respect, truthfulness, responsibility. In this way, students are not simply acting so as to avoid being punished, or simply following rules, but are coming to understand the principles and actions that constitute a value-led life.

But effective ethics education must also be *in the midst of living*, which is what I mean by ethics education *in* life. One mistake made by some ethics educators is to deploy artificial examples to illustrate ethical issues. The classic case of this is the "trolley problem" that has been used extensively in philosophy classes and publications to tease out moral intuitions. The philosopher Judith Jarvis Thomson (1976), offered the original description of the trolley problem:

> A trolley is running out of control down a track. In its path are five people who have been tied to the track by a mad philosopher. Fortunately, you could flip a switch which will lead the trolley down a different track to safety. Unfortunately, there is a single person tied to that track. Should you flip the switch?
>
> (pp. 8–9)

The issue with the trolley problem is not only that it is a fiction, but also that it is a caricature of the complexity of the types of ethical problems we face. Creating an artificial "landscape," so to speak, for isolating one or another aspect of a moral problem—Is it acceptable to kill one innocent to save five? Is there a morally significant difference between killing and letting die?—obscures not only the complexity of the nature and context of the types of ethical issues our students are likely to face in their lives, but also their everydayness. The fiction of a trolley-like example does not impart the myriad ways in which ethical values and decisions are woven into the fabric of everyday life. Every time students interact with other students, they are making judgments and choices about what constitutes respectful behavior. Every time students work on an assignment, they are making judgments and choices about academic integrity.

If we do not educate *for life*, our students will be ill equipped to deal with ethics *in life*. It is not only naïve but ethically irresponsible to think that our students will not face challenging and complex ethical issues throughout their lives. Ethically responsible education must prepare them for these challenges. For this reason, ethical educational leadership must ensure that moral literacy is as key a subject matter in the schools as is math, science, or reading literacy.

Should one have any doubt about the difficulty, complexity, and indeed the "everydayness" of the ethical challenges our students will face not only in life, but in their educational settings, one need only stand where I am situated—at the

Pennsylvania State University in 2012. Since November of 2011, the entire Penn State community has been shaken to its very core by the Jerry Sandusky scandal. The extent of the child sex abuse was horrendous. Sandusky is a former Penn State University football assistant coach and founder of The Second Mile, a non-profit charity whose mission was to serve Pennsylvania underprivileged and at-risk youth and where Sandusky allegedly met the children he sexually assaulted. In 2012, he was tried for 52 charges of sexual crimes against children and found guilty on 45 counts of sexual abuse. While serial child molestation may be difficult to comprehend, the ethical wrongness of the action is not at all obscure. However, the ethical complexity of the situation at Penn State was fueled by allegations that some university officials covered up the incidents or did not do enough to protect children from Sandusky. The president of the university, Graham Spanier, was forced to resign, and the head football coach, Joe Paterno, and athletic director, Tim Curley, were fired. Sandusky maintains his innocence; his appeal for a retrial has been denied.

Over time, the investigation revealed that others might also have known that Sandusky was assaulting children but did not report it. We read reports of janitors who either witnessed the assaults directly or were told of the assaults by other janitors who claimed to have directly witnessed them. None of them reported the incidents. In one interview, it was suggested that the janitors did not report the incidents for fear of losing their jobs. Others, such as assistant coach Mike McQueary and the mother of one young boy, who found reasons to be concerned about the nature of Sandusky's interactions with her son, did report the incident. The molestations continued long after their reports.

While it is not appropriate for Penn State students or faculty or even our community members to pass judgment on the university or local officials who dealt with the various reports over time, we have, nonetheless, been called to examine what ethics would demand of us should we be in a similar position to those who witnessed or received a report or even had a suspicion about the abuse. Given the prevalence of child sexual assault (Table 11.1), it is unfortunately not likely that those of us who work with children will find ourselves in a similar situation. What counts as evidence and how strong must it be? What actions are ethically required of us? Is it sufficient to simply report the suspected abuse or are we morally obligated to press for action if our report does not have the desired effect? What are the virtues most salient to being the kind of person who would act, even if you thought your actions might not be effective or could result in someone's loss of a job or credibility? What principles and values should govern an institution like a university or a nonprofit organization, and how would it be best to instill and enact those principles and values to better ensure that a scandal like this could not occur?

Effective ethics education is, thus, essential for each of us to be able to act responsibly as we find ourselves in the midst of complex ethical issues. The framework below provides an outline of the abilities and skills needed to live a value-led life and provides a blueprint of the various components of effective ethics education.

**Table 11.1** The global prevalence of child sexual abuse

The study "Prevalence of Child Sexual Abuse in Community and Student Samples: A Meta-Analysis," by Pereda et al. (2009) provides a snapshot of this offense. Based on an analysis of 65 research studies across 22 countries, the authors concluded:

- The mean prevalence of child sexual abuse globally was 7.9% for males and 19.7% for females.

- The highest prevalence rate of child sexual abuse geographically was found in Africa (34.4%). Europe showed the lowest prevalence rate (9.2%). America and Asia had prevalence rates between 10.1% and 23.9%.

- "South Africa has the highest prevalence rates for both men (60.9%) and women (43.7%)."

- "Jordan presents the second-highest prevalence rate for men (27.0%), followed by Tanzania (25.0%). Rates between 10% and 20% are reported for males in Israel (15.7%), Spain (13.4%), Australia (13.0%) and Costa Rica (12.8%), while the remaining countries all have prevalence rates below 10%."

- Except for South Africa, the highest reports of child sexual abuse for females were in the following countries: Australia (37.8%), Costa Rica (32.2%), Tanzania (31.0%), Israel (30.7%), Sweden (28.1%), the United States (25.3%), and Switzerland (24.2%). All report prevalence rates above 20%. The figures for New Zealand (18.7%), Spain (18.5%), Great Britain (18.2%), El Salvador and Norway (each 16.9%), Singapore (15.9%), Canada (15.2%), and China (10.8%) fall between 10% and 20%.

- The authors concluded that the lower rate for males may be inaccurate due to underreporting resulting from the "possibility of greater shame and the fear that they will be labeled as homosexual (if the aggressor was another man) or weak (if the aggressor was a woman), which may combine with the fact that they are more often accused of having provoked the abuse."

- A general conclusion was that "the results obtained in the present study confirm that the experience of child sexual abuse is a problem of considerable magnitude in all the societies analysed" (pp. 333–334).

## ETHICAL SENSITIVITY

The conception of ethical sensitivity (Figure 11.2) I introduced in 2007 deviated from standard accounts in a number of ways. Bebeau, Rest, and Yamoor (1985) defined moral sensitivity as an awareness of how our actions affect other people. Narvaez (2001) defined ethical sensitivity as the interpretation of a situation in determining who is involved, what actions to take, and what possible reactions and outcomes might ensue and listed seven components: (1) reading and expressing emotion, (2) taking the perspectives of others, (3) caring by connecting to others, (4) working with interpersonal and group differences, (5) preventing social bias, (6) generating interpretations and options, and (7) identifying the consequences of actions and options. While these accounts identified important features of moral literacy, the first is too narrow to adequately encompass the nature of ethical sensitivity, and the latter mixes categories and types of moral literacy that involve different types of abilities and will be clearer if they are demarcated. Generating interpretations and options and identifying the consequences of actions and options, for example, are better understood as components of ethical decision making rather than of ethical sensitivity.

**Figure 11.2** Ethical sensitivity

I define ethical sensitivity as consisting of three major components:

1. the ability to determine whether or not a situation involves ethical issues;
2. the ability to identify the moral virtues or values underlying an ethical issue; and
3. awareness of the moral intensity of the ethical issue (Figure 11.3).

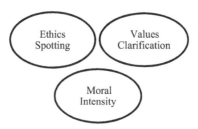

**Figure 11.3** The three components of ethical sensitivity

### The Ability to Determine Whether a Situation Involves Ethical Issues

The first component of ethical sensitivity, or what I call the ability to "ethics spot," is often overlooked. As with the trolley example, we assume that what constitutes an ethical issue will be obvious. Unfortunately, this is not the case for a variety of reasons. First, the ability to ethics spot requires training in basic ethical principles and ethical values. Small children often do not understand that lying is ethically unacceptable because they do not yet appreciate the importance of honesty and integrity. Ethics education must, thus, include the ability to understand and appreciate ethical values and principles, for this is an essential foundation for ethics spotting.

Second, even with such training, some issues are so complex that it is difficult to determine whether or not they involve ethical issues. Take the case of individual contributions to greenhouse gas emissions. We know that the aggregated overall increases in greenhouse gases are resulting in anthropocentric climate change, which is already having harmful impacts on a number of regions and is expected to have exponentially larger negative impacts in the future if emissions continue at the present rates. However, the impact of the amount of greenhouse gases one individual emits, even if aggregated, has an imperceptibly small impact on climate change. Given this, does the fact that some of my actions result in greenhouse gas emissions constitute an ethical issue given how small an impact each of my actions will have on global warming? For example, is it an ethical issue to buy nonlocal foods or foods out of season? Is it an ethical issue to drive rather than to take public transportation to work? Is it an ethical issue to keep my home temperature at 70°F rather than 60°F?

But there is a third reason: What counts as an ethical issue will not always be transparent—in this case due not to the complexity of the issue but to *ethical insensitivity.* Ethical insensitivity occurs when an individual's or community's ability to recognize that an action or situation involves an ethical issue has been hampered by other factors. Christopher Branson (2009), in his account of "wisdom-led leaders," calls attention to self-deception as a key element of what I'm labeling ethical insensitivity. These are instances in which self-deception obscures the true nature of one's action. As he explains:

> The consciousness of wisdom-led leaders is influenced by authenticity and moral integrity. Authenticity is about being true to the values, motives, and beliefs that the leader really wants to live by. As such, authenticity is about achieving an inner victory over self-deception. It is about accessing one's second level of consciousness through, again, self-reflection and self-inquiry. Achieving authenticity is through one's consciousness scrutinising one's consciousness— one's thinking reflecting on the appropriateness and accuracy of one's thinking.
> (Chapter 4, p. 3)

There are a variety of additional factors that result in what I am calling ethical insensitivity. In the following sections I will discuss three of them, namely, community shared prejudices, moral blind spots, and habituating wrongdoing.

*Community Shared Prejudices*

Community shared prejudices can make it difficult to see that our actions have ethical significance. The classic case of community shared prejudices is the history of slavery, where many people believed that it was morally acceptable to enslave a group of people because they believed that these individuals were not "fully human." At certain historical moments, there was little opposition to certain forms of slavery due to the prevalence of the view that there was nothing morally problematic about the practice. Being able to ethics spot in such a context is very difficult and requires the ability to question the very values and worldview in which one has been raised.

In a similar way, community shared prejudices occur in many contexts and can be difficult to identify, particularly for those who are raised in or trained to be a member of that community. Examples of current prejudices might be the following: counting monetary gains or losses in an economic cost/benefit analysis as a way to make decisions about vehicle safety in car manufacturing; the moral standing of nonhuman animals and the practice of farming animals; the assumption and insistence that there are two and only two sexes.

### Moral Blind Spots

Bezzina and Tuana (forthcoming) discuss the concept of "moral blind spots" to elaborate on the category of ethics spotting. In the context of business organizations, Dennis Moberg (2006) explained the high incidence of corporate scandals in the early 21st century as resulting, in part, from blind spots that undermined the moral capabilities of corporate executives. His argument is that the problem resulted not simply because of the actions of the wrongdoers, but from a system in which neither they nor the business community in which they worked grasped the ethical wrongness of the actions. Moberg argues that communities internalize "frames," which are "well-learned sets of associations that focus people's attention on and label some aspects of a situation to the exclusion of others" (p. 414). These frames, in turn, "create blind spots, those defects in one's perceptual field that can cloud one's judgment, lead one to erroneous conclusions, or provide insufficient triggers to appropriate action. For example, if people frame an interpersonal conflict situation as a fundamentally competitive one in which benefits can only be distributed in inflexible parcels, they are blinded to the possibilities of collaborative action" (ibid).

Moral blind spots, while in some sense similar to community shared prejudices, are significantly different. Community shared prejudices result in people *seeing an action as either not within the domain of ethics or as ethically justifiable:* Slavery is acceptable because some races are not fully human; women are naturally subservient to men because they are incapable of self-governance and thus must be controlled; farming and eating animals is not an ethical issue because animals have no moral standing. Moral blindness is, rather, a way of seeing the world that obscures one to the fact that an action *that one would agree is unethical* is occurring. There is reason to believe, for example, that the startlingly high rates of incest coupled with the low reportage rates is, in at least some cases, due to blind spots caused by false interpretive frames, i.e., that incest is a rare occurrence that happens in only severely dysfunctional families and that, were it happening, it would be easy for a nonmolesting relative to know that it was. Moral blind spots can also result from something being too painful to acknowledge, and thus we unconsciously suppress or turn away from it; again not an uncommon reaction with incest or other forms of child sexual abuse, where there can be denial even in the face of evidence of the abuse (cf. Gladwell, 2012).

### Habituating Wrongdoing

In addition to the complexity of issues, self-deception, community shared prejudices, and moral blindness, habitual wrongdoing can blunt an individual's ethical sensitivities. Repeated small thefts from one's business setting, "little white lies" on one's tax statements, "pirating" music by illegally downloading it from the Internet, can become so "normalized" that individuals stop seeing those actions as unethical.

Here, unlike the other two domains, habituating a behavior can make the ethical significance of the behavior fade into the background. Downloading becomes so "normalized" that the same people who would not hesitate to illegally download a song or an album from the Internet would refuse to walk into a music store and take a CD by slipping it into their pocket or bag because they would see that as stealing. Similarly, a worker who would not even think about taking $100 out of the till might nonetheless take office supplies home from work for personal use without even seeing that doing so is unethical.

The cultivation of ethical sensitivity, the ability to determine whether a situation involves ethical issues, is augmented in a variety of ways. The *cultivation of empathy or compassion* is a frequent element of the development of the ability to ethics spot. Being sensitive to the impact of injustice—feeling compassion for the victim of a bully or for the suffering of those living in poverty—is often a way to understand that there is an ethical issue. Compassion does not address the question of responsibility or enable us to formulate ethical obligations, but it can both help us see that we are in the moral domain and help to move us to action. Given this, the cultivation of empathy and compassion is a frequent component of moral literacy. In addition, the removal, or minimizing, of ethical insensitivity requires the cultivation of the ability to critically analyze our own and our society's practices.

Another key element of ethics spotting is the *ability to identify the values underlying the situation* and what virtues are relevant to the situation. This leads us to the second domain of ethical sensitivity.

### The Ability to Identify the Moral Values or Virtues Underlying an Ethical Issue

One important technique to strengthen the ability of students to ethics spot is to provide them training about ethical values. In his analysis of authentic school leadership practices, Paul Begley (2003) argued that "the skills of authentic and expert leaders will extend beyond management. All leaders consciously or unconsciously employ values as guides to interpreting situations and suggesting appropriate administrative action" (p. 11). I agree with Begley and extend his position to argue that leading with ethics, in the sense of foregrounding ethics in all activities, is essential for the entire educational community. This means that the ability to identify underlying ethical values is a key element of moral literacy but is often a skill that one must cultivate over time. It is also an ability that education can help students develop.[2]

There are two components of this aspect of ethical sensitivity. These are an appreciation and ability to identify what is or is viewed as:

(a) the intrinsic value of things or states and
(b) ethical values and the co-related virtues.

Intrinsic value is perhaps the most foundational, yet most controversial, of all aspects of ethical values. What things or states possess intrinsic ethical value has been a site of contention not only between cultures and even within one culture, but also throughout the history of ethical theory. Some posit that there is only one thing with intrinsic ethical value; others hold that there are multiple things or states that possess intrinsic ethical value. Human life, human flourishing, human freedom, human happiness, and human pleasure are common referents of intrinsic ethical value. Some have also argued that knowledge, wisdom, love, and spiritual enlightenment have intrinsic ethical value. While less common, there are cultures and theorists who hold that nonhuman animals or even ecosystems possess intrinsic ethical value.

What we view as holding intrinsic ethical value shapes many of our ethical beliefs. Indeed, there is a clear correlation between what we hold as having intrinsic ethical value and those traits we see as being ethical values. Common ethical values include: freedom, trustworthiness, respect, loyalty, responsibility, fairness, caring, and sanctity. Many of these are correlated with the view of human life and/or human flourishing as having intrinsic value.

Ethics education that includes this aspect of ethical sensitivity will incorporate various elements into the curriculum at age-appropriate levels. One important component is to help students develop the ability to identify what different cultures, or even groups of people within a culture, understand as constituting intrinsic value and to be able to trace the impact of those beliefs on actions, institutions, laws, and the like. This might include a discussion of times when beliefs about intrinsic value were in tension with practices. For example, how prejudice resulted in violations of beliefs regarding the intrinsic value of human life. This component of the curriculum might also include a discussion of the meaning of the various ethical values and their relevance to particular policies or practices. A discussion of academic integrity would provide an opportunity for students to identify the ethical values underlying school policies, as well as provide the basis for a discussion about the virtues a person with integrity would want to cultivate, such as honesty, trust, respect, fairness, and responsibility.

A valuable classroom exercise is to identify a community—the classroom, the township, a profession—and ask students to identify the values and correlated virtues that they believe are important to ensuring that it is an ethical community. In addition to identifying the various values and virtues, students can be encouraged to begin to see linkages among values and between values and virtues. For example, a virtue like trustworthiness is typically linked to traits such as honesty, reliability, keeping confidences, and honoring commitments. Students will sometimes not agree about the list of relevant values. This in turn presents a pedagogical opportunity to discuss why there might be differences in values and to think about how value differences among individuals or groups can lead to different judgments about right and wrong actions.

Discussions of values and related virtues can, in turn, help students ethics spot even in difficult cases. They can begin to understand why someone who views animals as having intrinsic ethical value might oppose farming animals or might advocate vegetarianism. A discussion of honesty and fairness can help them begin to appreciate why an action where their ethical sensitivities have become dulled—downloading music or texting test answers—is ethically problematic. The ability to ethics spot is, of course, only the first step. But it is a crucial ability nonetheless.

### Awareness of the Moral Intensity of the Ethical Issue

The third component of ethical sensitivity is particularly important for those difficult ethical situations where there are competing ethical demands or competing ethical values. It can also help students appreciate differences in ethical sensibilities among people or cultures.

The moral intensity of an action is often linked to the seriousness of the harm that could result from the action and/or the urgency of a response. An appreciation of the moral intensity of an ethical issue can be enhanced by efforts to cultivate students' moral imagination and their empathy, so that they can better appreciate the impact of actions.

The ability to weigh the moral intensity of a situation is an important ability to assist students when they are faced with competing ethical demands. They may face a situation where they have promised to help tutor a friend before an upcoming test but then get a call from another friend who is experiencing an emotionally difficult situation and needs their support. Moral intensity can be one factor in the process of deciding among competing ethical demands. How urgent is the problem the second friend is facing? How quickly does he need help? How does his need compare with that of the friend who wants tutoring help? Another illustration can be found in the types of conflicts professional engineers sometimes face between the principles of their professional code of ethics. A not uncommon example is a tension between the maxims of "Hold paramount the safety, health, and welfare of the public" and "Act for each employer or client as faithful agents or trustees." If a client is asking that the engineer keep the budget of the job within the parameters of the contract but the engineer identifies an issue that could impact public health but would be expensive to fix, the engineer faces competing ethical demands. Again, while not the complete answer, the moral intensity of the situation is a relevant factor. If risks and impacts from not fixing the issue are high, that argues against ignoring the issue. But if the impacts would be small and/or the risks not high, then that makes the tension less salient.

The moral intensity of an issue is, however, also linked to values. Those with different value systems can have very different views of the moral intensity of an issue. Those, for example, who see animals as having intrinsic value may view loss of species diversity due to climate change as an issue with high moral intensity, while others might see it as not being an ethical issue unless the loss of diversity impacts human flourishing.

Training in identifying the moral intensity of a situation and how various people or groups view this moral intensity can therefore help students understand the basis of ethical disagreements. Being able to determine whether the conflict is due to differences in the values groups hold to be relevant to the issue or the moral intensity of the ethical issue can help students appreciate positions different than their own and understand the nature of ethical disagreements. This is an invaluable ability in understanding other cultures or engaging in cross-cultural dialogue. It can enable them to identify the particular nature of the disagreement and help disputing groups better appreciate the source of their disagreement.

These three components of ethics sensitivity provide students with the skills they need to both identify when a situation involves an ethical issue and better understand the reasons why people disagree about ethical issues. While not sufficient for full moral literacy, ethics sensitivity is a key ability for those who lead with ethics.

## ETHICAL DECISION MAKING

Ethical decision-making skills involve a set of abilities (Figure 11.4):

1. An understanding of the various ethical frameworks and how they might apply to the issue:
   a. What are the consequences of actions or inactions and what is the ethical relevance of those consequences?
   b. Are there rights that must be taken into consideration? What are the relevant moral obligations?
   c. What virtues are relevant to the situation and what actions would best support those virtues?
   d. What relationships are relevant to the situation and what would an ethics of care require?
2. Identifying and assessing the facts relevant to the ethical issue
3. Identifying the relevant stakeholders
4. Identifying and assessing the values individuals or groups hold to be relevant to the ethical issue
5. Generating and evaluating options for action.

### Ethical Frameworks

Rather than advocating for a particular ethical framework, I encourage an integrated approach to ethical frameworks for moral literacy. The different ethical frameworks

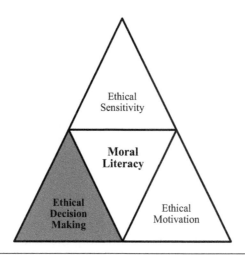

Figure 11.4 Ethical decision making

are not inherently incompatible if seen as guidelines for ethical analysis. Further-more, an integrated approach to ethics education provides students with the abilities to identify the consequences of actions, determine the rights that are relevant and discuss corresponding obligations, and consider the ethical import of different types of relationships. It also continues the attention to values and the corresponding vir-tues initiated in the curriculum on ethical sensitivity.

As I argued in my original 2007 essay, a robust approach to this component of ethical decision making is to consider questions like the following:

- What would be the likely consequences of acting in this way? How do I fac-tor in uncertainty about the impacts of actions? Who is responsible for unin-tended consequences of such an action? Have I anticipated the effects of this decision on all who are involved? What are the impacts of this action on future generations?
- Is the intention of the action relevant to its ethical worth? That is, if good conse-quences result from an action taken due to an unethical intention, is the action ethical or unethical? What if the action was ethically motivated but resulted in harm, does that make the action unethical?
- What duties are relevant to this situation and which rights should I be attentive to? Are there any competing rights or duties, and if so, how are they to be balanced?
- What would a virtuous person do? What kind of person would I be if I acted in this way? Does this decision uphold my basic moral values and have I been attentive to and respectful of the values of others involved?
- Does my decision nurture good relationships and address the particular needs and interests of those relationships? Do certain individuals or groups have a greater stake in the outcome either because we have special obligations to them or because they have greater needs?[3]

Another approach is that of Shapiro and Stefkovich's (2011) multiple ethical para-digms (see also Chapter 14 of this handbook). They offer four paradigms: the ethics of justice, the ethics of critique, the ethics of care, and the ethics of the profession. While not identical to the frameworks noted above, there are various overlaps between them. And similar to my advocating an integrated approach to ethical frameworks in ethics education, Shapiro and Stefkovich note that using the different paradigms allows educators and students to be attentive to different approaches to ethics, but they also stress that the approaches are not to be seen as mutually exclusive and urge attention to instances where use of more than one of the paradigms leads to a better approach to an ethical issue.

### Identifying and Assessing the Facts Relevant to the Ethical Issue

An often overlooked aspect of ethical decision making is ensuring that one has an accurate understanding of all the facts relevant to the issue. While it seems obvi-ous that any type of empirical reasoning should be grounded on a solid evidentiary basis, too often we forget that ethical analyses also involve an empirical component. We cannot, for example, analyze the ethical acceptability of genetic manipulation without understanding what types of genes are being modified, for what purposes, and with what consequences. Thus, a key component of any ethical analysis is developing a robust understanding of the issue, including all the relevant facts, as well as making sound inferences from those facts. In addition, moral literacy in this domain requires understanding which facts are uncertain and the nature of that uncertainty. Ethical decision making thus involves critical reasoning skills. What we sometimes discover is that what appear to be ethical disagreements are actually empirical disagreements about the relevant facts or appropriate inferences from those facts.

### Identifying the Relevant Stakeholders

The notion of a *stakeholder* was initially introduced in a business context to contrast with stockholders and to signal that there are other parties that have a stake in the decisions made by corporations in addition to those who hold equity in them. In his book *Strategic Management: A Stakeholder Approach,* R. Edward Freeman (1984) introduced the term as follows: "A stakeholder in an organization is (by definition) any group or individual who can affect or is affected by the achievement of the organization's objectives" (p. 46). Similarly, in the analysis of an ethical issue, it is important to identify all the relevant stakeholders who are affected by the issue at stake, whether positively or negatively, or who should have a say in how the situation is addressed.

The question of who to count as a stakeholder often leads to questions concerning moral standing. For example, many believe that when we are making decisions that will have long-term impacts on health or well-being, stakeholders should include not only those people currently alive, but also future generations. The notion of inter-generational justice, for example, entails the view that all present generations may be obligated by considerations of justice not to pursue policies that create benefits for themselves but impose costs on those who will live in the future. A more controversial question is whether anything other than humans has moral standing. Some, for example, argue that some nonhuman animals should be accorded at least partial moral standing, while others would argue that species and ecosystems also have moral standing.

Reflection on the relevant stakeholders is an important component of ethical reasoning in that it helps to identify the range of impacts of an action or policy and consider which are ethically relevant, the types of rights and duties that are relevant and to whom, and the nature and significance of the relationships that result in someone or something being a stakeholder, as well as to reflect upon who should have a say in the decision and why.

### Identifying and Assessing the Values Individuals or Groups Hold to Be Relevant to the Ethical Issue

Ethical reasoning skills include the value clarification skills of ethical sensitivity but builds on them by developing the ability to assess them. Assessing values includes the following skills:

    (a) Determining the ethical import of the values I, or others, hold to be relevant to an issue: The ability to identify relevant values does not provide us with all that is required to make responsible ethical choices. Take the case of a teacher whose student is requesting that she be allowed to redo a failed assignment because a personal problem prevented her from properly focusing on the assignment by the time it was due. While compassion is very likely to be a value relevant to this situation, exactly how we should see it as factoring into an ethically responsible decision regarding the request requires careful analysis. The degree to which compassion is relevant to our decision has to do with other factors—for example, the impact of the problem on the student and how we see that impact affecting them. If it was a relatively minor personal problem, we will likely weigh the relevance of compassion differently than if it was a difficult or high-intensity problem. In particular, we often have to weigh competing ethical values and their import, which leads us to the next skill.

(b) Being able to weigh competing values: While I may see compassion as relevant to the above instance, I will also have to balance it against other values, such as fairness. Decisions about how to compare and calculate the import of competing values is a crucial element of moral literacy, for some of the most difficult ethical issues are those involving having to decide how to ethically balance different values, such as compassion and fairness.

(c) Identifying mistakes in value assessments: Another important ethical reasoning skill related to values is the ability to analyze whether all and only the values relevant to the situation were taken into consideration. Mistakes in value assessments can happen in a variety of ways. An analysis of the ethical acceptability of an action may have overlooked a value that was relevant to the analysis or mistakenly included values that were not actually relevant. It might also have misinterpreted the salience of the values so identified, underestimating the significance of some values relative to others.

### Generating and Evaluating Options for Action

Ethical decision-making skills are also needed to generate and assess options for action when we find ourselves confronted with an ethical issue. When I teach ethics or train other faculty to integrate ethics into their classes, I advocate that when students are examining an ethical issue, they should not only go through the steps identified above (what is the ethical issue, who are the relevant stakeholders, what are the relevant facts, etc.), but should identify and then assess five different courses of action. My point in this advocacy is to help students see two things. First, while for complex ethical issues there may not be a uniquely correct ethical choice, the students will typically identify some choices that are clearly wrong when asked to identify multiple courses of action. Second, being asked to compare the different action choices provides them with additional training in ethical reasoning skills. Assessing what it is about a proposed action that makes it an unacceptable choice (violation of rights, overlooking crucial values, etc.) helps to strengthen all of the skills listed above. In addition, being asked how they would rank the different options that seem to them to be ethically acceptable, and to justify that ranking, not only helps students develop their ethical decision-making skills, it also helps them understand the complexity of ethical choices and reinforces the importance of their becoming morally literate in order to be ethically responsible in all aspects of their lives, whether in their professions, in the personal domain, or as citizens.

## ETHICAL MOTIVATION

The third domain of moral literacy is ethical motivation. As I have endeavored to explain in this essay, moral literacy involves a progression of skills that begin with the ability to ethics spot, or to appreciate that a situation involves an ethical dimension, and evolve to include the ability to assess different ethical positions or understand and appreciate the complexity of ethical issues. But full moral literacy is not simply a cognitive endeavor; a central and essential element is ethical motivation, which involves a number of components (Bezzina & Tuana, forthcoming), including (Figure 11.5):

1. Moral purpose
2. Moral courage
3. Moral hope

The link between literacy and action is as crucial to moral literacy as it is to reading literacy. If education leads to the *ability* to read but not to the *will* to read, then education has failed. The goal of education is not simply to impart a series of skills, but to provide the type of environment in which students engage in those skills in practice and experience how they are of benefit to their and others leading better lives. Similarly, moral literacy includes not just knowledge and skills, but also the types of moral habits and sentiments that are essential to *acting morally*, to facing ethical problems in our everyday experiences. Moral literacy is about *engagement* with everyday moral issues in which we take a stand, learn from our mistakes as well

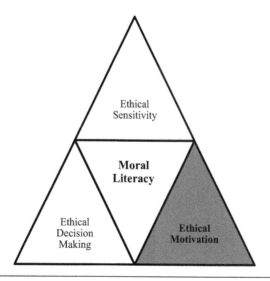

**Figure 11.5** Ethical motivation

from our good choices, and appreciate how ethical issues are intertwined with a host of issues. The simple act of buying a new car, for example, raises aesthetic issues (Do I like this shape or color?), as well as economic issues (Can I afford this?) and ethical issues (How much will driving a car like this contribute to rising greenhouse gases and global warming?). Moral literacy, thus, cannot be separated from the real-life contexts in which it arises (the argument against "trolleyology" noted above). Nor can it be separated from moral motivation and, ultimately, ethical action.

### Moral Purpose

Moral purpose is a key element of ethical motivation. It is a state of commitment to a set of ethical values and goals. Moral purpose can be individual or community shared. Many scholars have identified individual moral purpose and clear personal values as central elements of authentic leadership (e.g., Begley 2003; Hodgkinson 1991). But while one goal that education may aspire to is that students develop moral literacy and lead value-led lives, to do this, education itself must be shaped by shared moral purpose. As John Dewey (1909) explained, "We need to translate the moral into the conditions and forces of our community life, and into the impulses and habits of the individual" (p. 58). Similarly, Michael Fullan (1993) insists: "Teaching at its core is a moral profession. Scratch a good teacher and you will find a moral purpose" (p. 12).

Moral purpose signals the importance of acknowledging that the image of ethical action, or indeed ethical education, as focused on the viewpoint of individuals who are isolated moral agents making decisions solely through conscious cognitive processes (Kohlberg, 1984) is lacking. Moral action happens in the midst of living and in and through our interactions with others—our family, our friends, our coworkers. And it is in the midst of these relationships that we enact moral literacy. As Dewey (1897) phrases it:

> I believe that moral education centers about this conception of the school as a mode of social life, that the best and deepest moral training is precisely that which one gets through having to enter into proper relations with others in a unity of work and thought. The present educational systems render it difficult or impossible to get any genuine, regular moral training.
>
> (p. 78)

Similarly the moral purpose of a profession, such as the moral purpose of education, arises from a community that embraces a shared sense of moral purpose via a shared commitment to explicit values.

Building shared moral purpose is a sophisticated enterprise that requires leaders to navigate the complexities of modern schools in times that are ethically ambiguous. The challenge for leaders is often to choose between two "goods" rather than a good and a "bad" (Duignan, 2003). Educational leaders in complex times find themselves constantly engaged in discerning the moral purpose of a community and how best to bring it alive and nurture it in a way that will allow it to shape the educational experience (Bezzina, 2012, p. 249).

Shared moral purpose must be explicitly cultivated and emerge out of the particulars of the circumstances in which the schools are part, including the national curricular standards and expectations and the economic situation of the school and the community of which it is a part. Shared moral purpose is a key to ethical motivation, but to be effective, it must be continually reinforced, reflected upon, and engaged in the context of the complexities of shaping curriculum and cultivating educationally responsible relationships. According to Michael Bezzina (2008), clear and explicit dialogue about the moral purpose of education, in turn, reinforces shared ethical leadership across the school community, which is the more expansive sense of leading with ethics, with which I opened this essay.

## Moral Courage

Rushworth Kidder (2005) explains the importance of moral courage in his book by the same title in the following way:

> [W]hile many have fine values and develop great skill at moral reasoning and ethical decision making, such mental activity counts for little if their decisions sit unimplemented on the shelf. What's so often needed is a third step: the moral courage to put those decisions into action. More broadly, what's needed is the courage to live a moral and ethical life.
>
> (p. viii)

While not all ethical actions require moral courage, living by our values can take tremendous courage. As we know from the battlefield, as well as from the instances of the good Samaritans who have gone into burning buildings to rescue others trapped within, living our values may mean risking physical well-being to save another. But the risk can also be to reputation or financial well-being. The janitor who did not report Sandusky feared that he would lose his job. Arthur Anderson and the many other accountants and executives who failed to report the financial misdeeds at Enron likely feared economic and criminal damages would result from doing so. The student who fails to report bullying may fear personal physical or reputational damage.

Like moral purpose, moral courage can be individual, but it can also be collective, cultivated within a community. Indeed, this is what student honor codes often aim to do—to encourage the entire educational community to strengthen and enact moral courage. Whether in the commitment to take responsibility for one's own educational development, even when that may mean not getting the high grades one hoped for, or the courage it takes to report wrongdoing by another, honor codes are designed to strengthen both individual and community moral courage (McCabe & Trevino, 1993, 1997; McCabe, Trevino, & Butterfield, 1999). Moral courage gives us the strength needed to remain people of integrity, that is, to reinforce and live our commitment to ethical values and principles in the face of danger and hardships resulting from doing so and to accept and endure that risk to well-being.

A component of moral courage is also the willingness to acknowledge our ethical lapses and take responsibility for them, even when we know that doing so will come at a cost to ourselves. Too often, the domain of moral courage is limited to future actions, that is, choosing to stand by our values even when we know that doing so will put us at risk. But such an account overlooks the fact that moral courage is also required to acknowledge ethical failures to ourselves and others. These admissions may result in the loss of respect from those whose opinions we care about, as well as other impacts, such as losing one's job.

### Moral Hope

If we do not believe that ethical change is possible or our ethical goals are attainable, we will not commit to a moral purpose. Indeed, moral courage goes hand-in-hand with moral hope and motivates us to risk hardships to do what is right and attain what is just. Without hope, we experience despair or cynicism, and perhaps even indifference. But not all forms of hope are in the moral domain. We often hope for a bright future for ourselves or our loved ones. We might hope to win the lottery or to get a promotion. These are not instances of moral hope. Moral hope is aimed at the achievement of moral purpose, at the belief not only that it is the moral purpose of education (to take one instance) desirable but that it is *possible* and that the choices I and others make are relevant to its success. Bezzina and Tuana (forthcoming) have argued that moral hope is a vital element for moral agency: "Hopelessness or despair leads not only to suffering, but also to an impaired ability to act, not only in one's own interests, but also in the interests of others" (p. 12).

Moral hope, however, is not parochial. It cannot be limited to achieving moral purpose in my classroom or for my school, but rather encompasses the hope that all education achieves moral purpose. It is an important element of ethical motivation because hope is not an abstract concept or merely a belief, but a state of being in which we are called to action. Moral hope is not a belief, but a disposition to act. Moral purpose combined with moral courage and moral hope leads to moral agency.

## CONCLUSION: MORAL AGENCY

Moral literacy (Figure 11.6) aims, always, at moral agency and ethical action—not just that we know what is right, or that we can identify appropriate values, or can provide a justification of why one action choice is better than an alternative, but that we *do what is right*. Any account of moral literacy that does not include a focus on what motivates right action would be lacking. Ethical sensitivity and ethical reasoning skills must be translated into ethical action through ethical motivation.

The three elements of moral literacy are mutually sustaining and reinforcing. For example, dialogue about shared moral purpose helps to minimize ethical insensitivity caused by blind spots. Moral courage also enables individuals and groups to question community shared prejudices and, thereby, reassess unethical behavior, such as racism or sexism, that has been normalized by being habituated. Moral hope and moral courage combine to catalyze us from knowing what is right to doing what is right.

Moral hope and moral courage are also the wellspring from which actions toward justice emerge, for acting consistently with moral purpose requires the belief that

**Figure 11.6** Moral agency

one can affect change, and this means believing both that change is indeed possible (moral hope) and that I am capable of having an impact (moral courage). This combination of moral hope and moral courage has been labeled moral potency. Hannah and Avolio (2010) define moral potency as

> a psychological state marked by an experienced sense of ownership over the moral aspects of one's environment, reinforced by efficacy beliefs in the capabilities to act to achieve moral purpose in that domain, and the courage to perform ethically in the face of adversity and persevere through challenges.
>
> (p. 261)

They argue that moral potency provides the psychological resources that "bridge moral thought to moral action" (p. 292). For example, "before [teachers] will act in a way that aligns consistently with moral purpose (moral agency), they need a sense of their own role as an influential player in this domain (moral potency) reflected in their sense of a capacity to act in ways that make a difference; their ownership of, and commitment to, moral purpose; a sense of hope; and the requisite courage to act" (Bezzina & Tuana, forthcoming, p. 6).

The school culture, indeed the broader culture in which schools are located, has a huge impact on moral agency. As the essays in this volume repeatedly stress, our schools need to create a "virtuous cycle" (Weaver, 2006, p. 351) in which resources and opportunities for exercising moral agency are offered to all members of the school—not just principals or teachers, but to all the students as well as the staff—and in this way, each person, in turn, contributes to strengthening the moral culture of the school.

Ultimately action will be taken by individuals who are morally literate and who have moved through their sense of moral potency to a position of moral agency. Thus leaders will need to work with their communities in ways that will promote this transition. The likelihood of this happening is enhanced within a community in which moral purpose is explicit, in which norms and structures enhance commitment and the sense of efficacy, and in which an underlying sense of hope shapes courageous ethical action (Bezzina & Tuana, forthcoming, p. 19).

Moral literacy is, thus, not an end in itself, but a path to moral agency and ethical action.

## NOTES

1. There is no agreed-upon distinction between the moral and the ethical. Individual theorists will sometimes mark a distinction between the terms, but there is little agreement on the uses of these terms among theorists. For this reason, my distinction between 'moral' and 'ethical' is simply pragmatic.
2. Begley's (2003) concept of spheres of values is one tool designed to promote this ability.
3. For a more detailed discussion of these different frameworks, see the study by Tuana (2007).

## REFERENCES

Bebeau, M., Rest, J., & Yamoor, C. (1985). Measuring dental students' ethical sensitivity. *Journal of Dental Education, 49*(4), 225–235.

Begley, P. T. (2003). In pursuit of authentic school leadership practices. In P. T. Begley & O. Johansson (Eds.), *The ethical dimensions of school leadership* (pp. 1–12). Dordrecht, Netherlands: Kluwer Academic Publishers.

Bezzina, M. (2008). We do make a difference: Shared moral purpose and shared leadership in the pursuit of learning. *Leading and Managing, 14*(1), 38–59.

Bezzina, M. (2012). Transforming learning and learners project paying attention to moral purpose in leading learning: Lessons from the leaders. *Educational Management Administration and Leadership, 40*(2), 248–271.

Bezzina, M., & Tuana, N. (forthcoming). *From awareness to action: Some thoughts on engaging moral purpose in educational leadership.*

Branson, C. (2009). *Leadership in an age of wisdom.* Dordrecht, Netherlands: Springer.

Dewey, J. (1897). My pedagogic creed. *School Journal, 54*(3), 77–80.

Dewey, J. (1909). *Moral principles in education.* Boston: Houghton Mifflin.

Duignan, P.A., (2003). Leading in an age of paradox and dilemma. In J. Hurley (Ed.), *Leaders lead* (pp. 12–16). Adelaide: Australian Principals Associations Professional Development Council (APAPDC) in association with Commonwealth Department of Education, Science & Training (DEST).

Freeman, R. E. (1984). *Strategic management: A stakeholder approach.* Boston: Pittman Publishing.

Fullan, M. G. (1993). Why teachers must become change agents. *Educational Leadership, 50*(6), 12–17.

Gladwell, M. (2012, September 24). How child molesters get away with it. *The New Yorker.* Retrieved from www.newyorker.com/arts/critics/atlarge/2012/09/24/120924crat_atlarge_gladwell?currentPage=all

Hannah, S. T., & Avolio, B. J. (2010). Moral potency: Building the capacity for character based leadership. *Consulting Psychology Journal: Practice and Research, 62*(4), 291–310.

Hodgkinson, C. (1991). *Educational leadership: The moral art.* Albany: SUNY Press.

Kidder, R. M. (2005). *Moral courage.* New York: Harper.

Kohlberg, L. (1984). *The psychology of moral development.* New York: Harper and Row.

McCabe, D. L., & Trevino, L. K. (1993). Academic dishonesty: Honor codes and other contextual influences. *Journal of Higher Education, 64*(5), 522–538.

McCabe, D. L., & Trevino, L. K. (1997). Individual and contextual influences on academic dishonesty: A multi-campus investigation. *Research in Higher Education, 38*(3), 379–396.

McCabe, D. L., Trevino, L. K., & Butterfield, K. D. (1999). Academic integrity in honor code and non-honor code environments: A qualitative investigation. *Journal of Higher Education, 70*(2), 211–234.

Moberg, D. J. (2006). Ethics blind spots in organizations: How systematic errors in person perception undermine moral agency. *Organization Studies, 27*(3), 413–427.

Narvaez, D. (2001). Ethical sensitivity. Activity booklet 1. Retrieved from http://cee.nd.edu/curriculum/documents/actbklt1.pdf

Pereda, N., Guilera, G., Forns, M., & Gómez-Benito, J. (1999). The prevalence of child sexual abuse in community and student samples: A meta-analysis. *Clinical Psychology Review, 29*(4), 328–338.

Shapiro, J. P., & Stefkovich, J. A. (2011). *Ethical leadership and decision making in education: Applying theoretical perspectives to complex dilemmas.* New York and London: Routledge.

Starratt, R. J. (2007). Leading a community of learners. *Educational Management Administration and Leadership, 35*(2), 165–183.

Thomson, J. (1976). Killing, letting die and the trolley problem. *Monist, 59*(2), 204–217.

Tuana, N. (2007). Conceptualizing moral literacy. *Journal of Educational Administration, 45*(4), 364–378.

UCEA CSLE (University Council for Educational Administration's Center for the Study of Leadership and Ethics). (1999). Retrieved from http://ucea.org/leadership-ethics

Weaver, G. R. (2006). Virtue in organizations: Moral identity as a foundation for moral agency. *Organization Studies, 27*(3), 341–386.

# 12

## THE INTERPLAY OF VALUES

### ROSS NOTMAN

To believe that the art of educational leadership is simply a matter of technical capabilities and skills is to underestimate the complex web of personal and interpersonal influences at work beneath the leadership surface. Within the personal dimensions of educational leadership, ethical leadership and its associated sensitivities frequently lie at the heart of such complexity (Branson, 2010; Duignan, 2006; Shapiro & Stefkovich, 2005; Starratt, 2010).

This chapter sets out to background two leadership components that relate strongly to ethical sensitivities in schools. First, the concept of values-based leadership is examined through its formative theoretical phases, from scientific interpretations of educational administration to more humanistic approaches to educational administration theory, including values and ethical dimensions. Second, the concept of contextually responsive leadership is reviewed in relation to selected leadership theories and the internal and external contexts in which schools function.

The discussion then moves to describe the impact of leaders' values and school contexts through the findings of two Australasian research studies about school principals' engagement in ethical decision making. Ethical questions arising from the research are posed at appropriate stages for the reader's consideration. This is followed by an exploration of ethical implications for leadership theory and practice that involve features of leaders' self-reflection; dilemma management; and an ecological interpretation of context and the leadership self. The discussion closes by arguing for a stronger presence of ethical elements in leaders' professional learning programs. Finally, the chapter concludes with questions for further research into the processes of principals' ethical sensitivities and decision making.

## VALUES-BASED LEADERSHIP

In a report on UK findings of a 3-year national research project on the impact of leadership on student learning outcomes, Day and colleagues (2010) make 10 strong claims about successful school leadership, of which Claim 3 identifies head teachers' values as key components in their success. This finding reflects a cumulative body of research that supports values-based leadership as an emerging factor in the success of school leaders' practice (Beatty, 2005; Begley, 2006; Milstein & Henry, 2008; Notman, 2008). This section of discussion will set the scene for ethical understanding by summarizing earlier developments in values theory and their links to a philosophy of values-based leadership.

### Early Developments in Values Theory

In relation to the field of values-based educational leadership, a major conceptual framework is located in the early work of Hodgkinson (1978) and Greenfield (1986) on values theory. There had been a consensus, among a growing group of supporters of values theory, that values were a springboard for human action (Greenfield, 1986) and that values were central to the successful practice of leadership and administration (Greenfield, 1986; Hodgkinson, 1991; Willower, 1987). The definition of a value had been drawn together by Leithwood, Begley, and Cousins (1994), building on the attributes of values in the work of Rokeach (1973) and Hodgkinson (1978). A *value*:

- is an enduring belief about the desirability of some means; and
- once internalised, a value also becomes a standard or criterion for guiding one's own actions and thought, for influencing the actions and thought of others, and for morally judging oneself and others. (Leithwood et al., 1994, p. 99)

Earlier theories of educational administration as a science had been promulgated in the 1950s and 1960s by theorists such as Simon (1957), Griffiths (1959), and Halpin (1966). Research activity became theoretically oriented, and training programs for educational administrators were based more on the scientific concepts of Taylorism than on educational principles. Also, role expectations, defined in the form of job descriptions, made their entrance into the field of school leadership.

During the 1970s, in recognizing the limitations of such scientific theoretical approaches, educational theorists began to promote a values perspective as an alternative theory of educational administration. Evers and Lakomski (1996) wrote:

The first of these [theories] was developed by the Canadian scholar Christopher Hodgkinson (1978, 1983, 1991), and declares administration not to be a science at all, but rather, a humanism. This is because, for Hodgkinson, science deals with factual matters whereas administration is values-laden. Hodgkinson also maintains that decision-making is central to administration. Because knowledge of logic and value constitute the essentials of decisions, administrators' training will involve some training in philosophy where these matters can be dealt with systematically.

(p. 5)

Hodgkinson (1978) initially conceived of a values framework that comprised three categories of values. He contended that type 1 values were largely metaphysical in nature and were grounded in ethical principles. He referred to these as "transrational" values, which were often found in ideological or religious systems and which he regarded as more authentic than the other two types. Type 2 values were differentiated into two separate classifications based on a sense of "rightness" because they account for the will of the majority (Cunningham & Cordeiro, 2003). Hodgkinson referred to them as "rational" values. Type 2a values were grounded in consequences so that "rightness" was defined in relation to "a desirable future state of affairs or analysis of the consequences entailed by a value judgment" (Leithwood et al., 1994, p. 100). Type 2b values were grounded in consensus or the will of the majority. Finally, the "subrational" values of type 3 were based on a personal preference of what an individual perceived to be "good." These values were located in the affective or emotional domain.

Hodgkinson (1983) later expanded on this initial values classification to look more broadly at implications of values theory for leadership behaviors that were informed by an underlying philosophy of leadership:

> Affect, motives, attitudes, beliefs, values, ethics, morals, will, commitment, preferences, norms, expectations, responsibilities—such are the concerns of leadership proper. Their study is paramount because the very nature of leadership is that of practical philosophy, philosophy-in-action. Leadership is intrinsically valuational. Logic may set limits for and parameters within the field of value action but value phenomena determine what occurs within the field. They are indeed the essential constituents of the field of constituents of the field of executive action, all of which is to say that the leader's task is essentially affective.
>
> (Hodgkinson, 1983, p. 202)

A second major contributor to the link between values theory and educational leadership and administration was Thomas Greenfield. Greenfield (1983) contended that the focus for social science inquiry was not based on observation and fact but rather on people's subjective understandings. His interpretive approach rejected prevailing positivist theories that separated organizations from the people in them: "Organisations are inside people and are defined completely by them as they work out ideas in their heads through their actions in the practical world" (Greenfield, 1983, p. 1). Greenfield believed that the assumptions of the positivist paradigm were incorrect; they presumed that schools constituted an orderly environment, where people behaved predictably, instead of the reality where the school environment was often chaotic and, some believe, inherently anarchistic.

However, Greenfield's subjective assertions were not beyond criticism from those who held positivist views of educational administration. Griffiths (1978) took exception to such "Great Man" theories and maintained a deductive conception of administrative theory as "a set of assumptions from which propositions can be deduced by mathematical or logical reasoning" (Griffiths, 1978, p. 82). Willower (1979) also refuted Greenfield's propositions by maintaining a pragmatic outlook on educational administration, described by Gronn (1983) as a "kind of conveyor belt or delivery system" (p. 26). Nevertheless, there was considerable tension between the two competing perspectives of scientific and humanist approaches to the development of educational administration theory. This is represented by Foster (1986):

> Greenfield's thesis has profound implications for the study of educational administration and for the preparation of administrators. Two extreme preparatory models suggest themselves. The administrator-as-scientist, schooled in the scientific method and concerned with quantifiable results, applies the findings of social science research as best he or she can, and brings progress to the school by performing all other required scientific or pseudoscientific activities. The administrator-as-humanist, trained in the arts and sciences and experienced in the ways of the world, brings feeling and intuition to the profession. Orthodox theory endorses the scientist model, but the humanist model may offer a more accurate description of the effective administrator.
>
> (p. 62)

In 1986, Greenfield added another dimension to this debate with the publication of his paper *The Decline and Fall of Science in Educational Administration*. In setting out an agenda for future inquiry in the administration field, Greenfield (1986) advocated "a humane science which would use interpretive and qualitative methods of inquiry; which would focus upon power, conflicts, values and moral dilemmas in educational leadership" (cited in Grace, 1995, p. 52). Not only did this broaden the parameters of the scientific/humanist debate but it also rekindled an awareness of theoretical views, such as Hodgkinson's (1978), about ethical and values dimensions of educational administration.

Subsequent studies supported the theoretical claims made by Hodgkinson (1978, 1983) and Greenfield (1986); in particular, research carried out by Leithwood and Steinbach (1991) and Begley (1999). Leithwood and Steinbach's (1991) study of chief education officers' problem-solving strategies identified four categories of values at work. "Basic human values," such as freedom, happiness, knowledge, respect for others and survival, equate to Hodgkinson's (1978) type 1 values based on principles. They also link to Rokeach's (1973) terminal values or "end states of existence." Categories entitled "general moral values" (carefulness, fairness/justice, courage) and "professional values" (responsibility, consequences) represent values that guide decision making and can be linked to Hodgkinson's (1978) type 2a values of consequence. "Social and political values," which incorporate Hodgkinson's (1978) type 2b values of consensus, "recognize the essentially social nature of human action and the need for individuals to define themselves in relation to others to make their lives meaningful" (Leithwood et al., 1994, p. 103).

In order to reinforce the complexity of values derivation and implementation, Begley's (1999) study of academic and practitioner perspectives on values illustrated a syntax of values terminology through an adaptation of a graphic found in several of Hodgkinson's books (1978, 1991). This graphic is shown in Figure 12.1.

The outer ring of the "onion" represents the observable actions and speech of the individual, the *only* way available for making empirical attributions of the values

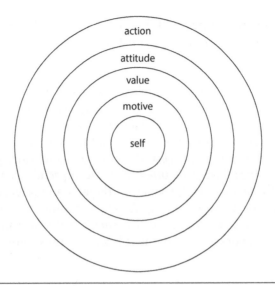

**Figure 12.1** Syntax of value terms (Source: Begley, 1999)

orientations of the individual. The next layer represents attitudes. This is the thin, permeable membrane situated between values and actions or speech. The following layer portrays the idea that attitudes often foreshadow actions that are influenced by the specific values a person holds for whatever reasons.

The key to understanding the nature and function of values, Begley claimed, is found in the next layer of the onion: motivational base. It represents the motivating force behind the adoption of a particular value. Finally, at the core of the onion, there is the self, the essence of the individual: "the biological self, as well as the existential or transcendent self" (Begley, 1999, pp. 55–56).

### The Role of a Values-Based Leadership Philosophy

An integral part of ethical leadership is the nature of the values employed by school leaders in the operation of their educational environment. Hodgkinson (1978, 1991) advocated for the role of values in effective educational administration from philosophical and analytical positions. In contrast, a political perspective on the values underpinning moral leadership focuses on the "nature of the relationships among those within the organisation and the distribution of power between stakeholders both inside and outside the organisation" (Leithwood, Jantzi, & Steinbach, 1999, p. 11). A cultural perspective, on the other hand, focuses on those shared values and beliefs that lie at the heart of the school organization (Nias, Southworth, & Yeomans, 1989).

The central orientation of a values-based leadership philosophy, building on the foundational work of Hodgkinson and Greenfield, is toward what leaders think about and value. As Fairholm (1998) claimed, "Leadership partakes of the values and principles of life as well as operational action. Therefore, it is a question of philosophy, of the principles of reality and of human nature and conduct" (p. 57). It is also a question of reflection on self: a critical examination of one's knowledge and values systems in comparison with the experience of others and the mores of the broader school context. Examining one's "personal compass" (Brock & Grady, 2012) is a first step in knowing how values inform a leader's behavior and where values might provide congruence between a leader's personal belief system and the school's philosophical directions. In addition, such a critical examination may inform how the leader might act ethically and with integrity.

This development and interrogation of the self is an ongoing process, one that does not assume closure but rather encourages an openness to critical analysis and justification of what the educational leader believes and why. The result of this critical self-examination may confirm or question a leader's fundamental beliefs and levels of self-awareness. This may, in turn, "lead to a willingness of participants to enter a place of vulnerability in order to challenge and then change assumptions and ways of being and thinking in education" (Robertson, 2011, p. 223).

The discussion now shifts focus from a values perspective on leadership to the milieu in which values are enacted. Here, the focus is on how leaders respond to the contingencies of their educational context in what can be termed contextually responsive leadership.

## CONTEXTUALLY RESPONSIVE LEADERSHIP

One of the capabilities that successful educational leaders display is a capacity to understand, and respond to, challenges presented to them by the contexts in which they work. The mediation of different contextual influences is an important leadership skill that underpins school improvement processes. As Gu and Johannson (2012) claim, such processes are likely to be "a product of the interaction between the moderating effects of schools' external contexts and the mediating effects of their internal contexts" (p. 6). In this examination of contextual elements that may impact on educational leaders, the role of context will be explored in relation to selected leadership theory, external environment considerations, and internal factors relating to the school itself.

### Selected Leadership Theory

Day and colleagues (2011) use a sample of four general leadership theories to illustrate the importance of context to educational leaders. Yukl's (1994) multiple linkage model points to the impact of "situational variables" such as the size of an organization, its procedures and policies, and the professional development and experience of its staff. Leader–member exchange theory such as that proposed by Graen and Uhl-Bien (1995) offers a second perspective that centers on leader–follower relationships and leaders' perceptions of their staff's attributes and work experience.

A third perspective focuses on an information processing approach (e.g., Lord & Maher, 1993), whereby leaders' actions are shaped by the internal contexts of their own knowledge base and personal dispositions and characteristics and by external contexts, where others respond to the actions of the leader, a response "which in part depends on the nature of the leadership 'prototypes' (internalised models of ideal leaders) possessed by colleagues and/or followers and judgments by those colleagues about how well the leader matches those prototypes" (Day et al., 2011, p. 5). Finally, cross-cultural leadership theory (e.g., House, Hanges, Javidan, Dorfman, & Gupta, 2004) makes links between cultural norms and values and preferred types of leadership practice that align and are accountable to an associated culture(s). Such theoretical links provide a useful background to appreciating a number of contextual variables confronted by schools and their leaders.

### External and Internal School Contexts

Across a range of contextual literature, there are commonly recognized features that constitute a school's external environment. These pragmatic considerations encompass the *micro* world of students and their family/community, with features such as personal well-being (Mongon & Leadbeater, 2012), financial hardship linked to a lower socioeconomic status of the school's intake zone (Notman, 2011), varying degrees of social responsibility, and cultural diversity (Merchant et al., 2012). The external context also contains features that represent the *macro* political world of educational policy and regulatory requirements of various government administrative and school review agencies, and the broader social world of community values and expectations of education. In this way, the educational leader is subject to overarching social, economic, cultural, and political spheres of influence and need, all of which are found outside of the school.

The internal context of the school environment has been commonly described as including the following influence factors: school culture, teacher experience and competence, staff morale, financial resources, school size, and bureaucratic and labor organization (Hallinger, 2003). In addition, universal trends toward greater public participation in education (Woods, 2005) and the advent of self-managing schools, particularly in New Zealand, have brought about increasing demands for the democratization of leadership in the form of distributed leadership and shared decision making among staff, along with a greater appreciation of the need for student voice to be heard in the running of the school.

What types of challenging situations or contingencies do school leaders typically confront? School type, staff capacities and morale, and community support are among factors that may impact on the contextual setting for leadership responsibilities. In addition, leaders need to be ethically sensitive to the educational situation in which they work and operate, particularly in relation to the human dynamic. As Southworth (1998) commented earlier, "Leaders need to be aware of the power relations in their school, their organisational contexts, individual colleagues' professional maturity levels and groups' expectations" (p. 39). The important point of interest then focuses on the manner in which educational leaders respond to the unique set of contextual circumstances presented to them. This view has been reinforced by a key proposition underpinning the values of school leaders, that they must embrace the distinctive and inclusive context of the school (National College for School Leadership, 2001), especially in regard to raising and sustaining levels of school performance (Gu & Johannson, 2012). Such contextual interactions can be linked back to situational or contingent leadership approaches to school leadership of the 1970s and 1980s. These theoretical positions came to prominence with a contingency theory proposed by Fiedler (1967) and Hersey and Blanchard's (1977) notion of situational leadership, which Day, Harris, Hadfield, Tolley, and Beresford (2000) summarized as the "conjunction of the person and the situation" (p. 10).

Given this theoretical overview of development within the respective fields of values-based leadership and contextually responsive leadership, how might the ethical application of such concepts be viewed through a research lens?

## ETHICAL APPLICATION OF CONCEPTS THROUGH RESEARCH

The theme of ethical sensitivity is a major focus for this chapter, particularly in its links to educational leaders' behaviors that are informed by an intersection of understanding one's own values system, and how those values are aligned, contested, or compromised by different contexts in which schools work. Such educational leaders "are deeply aware of how they think and behave, and are perceived by others as being aware of their own and others' values, knowledge, and strengths; aware of the context in which they operate; and who are confident, hopeful, optimistic, resilient, and high on moral character" (Avolio, Gardner, Walumbwa, Luthans, & May, 2004, p. 4).

For the purpose of research illustration, two Australasian research studies will be examined to show how school principals engage in ethical decision making within the domains of values-based leadership and contextually responsive leadership. First, Dempster (2001) reported selected results from the Principals' Ethical Decisionmaking Study (PEDMS) carried out in partnership with Education Queensland in Australia. The study was designed around intensive principal interviews ($n = 25$) from a range of urban and rural schools, along with a survey of Queensland government school principals ($n = 552$). Its aim was to "identify and describe situations in which school principals face ethical dilemmas, to record the decisions they make, to explain their reasoning and why they take the action they do" (Dempster, p. 6).

The second research study was a New Zealand qualitative case study that examined the personal and professional lives of an urban and a rural secondary school principal in the South Island of New Zealand over a period of 35 months (Notman, 2005, 2008). Data collection methods included participant observation and intensive interviewing of each principal and of others significant to their work. The primary purpose of this study was to determine the personal dimensions of a secondary principal's job and, subsequently, how each school leader's personal and professional values acted as a motivating force behind their leadership behaviors. Using Dempster's reporting framework, I present relevant research results from both studies using three focus headings. These outline some of the frequent and troublesome circumstances involving ethical decision making reported by principal respondents.

## Ethical Sensitivities

### Circumstances Involving Students

In the Australian study, the issue of dealing with conflict between the internal context of the school's values and the external context of values taught to students at home was identified as the most frequent and troublesome. Dempster (2001) reported: "One third (32%) of principals indicated that they encountered this kind of ethical problem often or very often, and 38% of principals reported having much or a great deal of trouble with it" (p. 12). This finding was replicated in the contested values results of the two New Zealand principals. Here, it was evident from both principals that values contestation with adolescents constituted an ipso facto situation. They accepted an inevitability of a conflict in values between those of a middle-aged school principal and those of a developing adolescent. As Begley (1999) noted: "Students live in a world that reflects postmodern values and they regularly confront teachers and principals that represent, within educational organisations, a proceeding modernist generation" (p. 53). In a similar manner, the principals also regarded parents as holding values with which they did not necessarily agree, and as wishing to take different directions for their children than that espoused by the school's ethos, policies, or procedures.

### Circumstances Involving Staff

Dempster's (2001) study revealed that for this category, the challenge of monitoring staff performance was identified in the survey results as the most frequent and troublesome for principals. As an example, the researcher cites a case where a secondary school principal placed a teacher on diminished work performance. The teacher had returned to work after a mild heart attack but continued to be affected by poor health, and his teaching performance continued to be unsatisfactory. In assessing the situation, the principal was cognizant of two competing interests: On the one hand, he was concerned about the well-being of the teacher; on the other, he was mindful of his responsibility for student learning. Similarly, "Helen Aiken," the female principal in the New Zealand study, was faced with a critical incident involving a teacher who left a class unattended during an important inspection visit by the Education Review Office. Helen's dilemma was whether to confront the teacher directly over the unprofessional behavior or to ignore the situation in the interests of staff stability, at a time of considerable tension in the school.

In this case, Helen's decision to chastise the teacher might be understood in terms of contested values between those held by the principal and the values represented by the teacher's behavior. A total of seven of Helen's core values seemed confronted by this act, and this was subsequently confirmed by her: her student-centered focus where student interests and well-being were paramount; high standards of behavior expected of staff as professional role models; a work ethic and demand for excellence and academic achievement that demonstrated real engagement in the learning process between teacher and students; an ethic of care that showed concern for the safety of one's students; an inherent honesty about one's intentions in leaving the class so frequently; and a betrayal of Helen's and the staff's efforts to present a united front of effective teaching to a team of external reviewers. Such was the extent of the affront to Helen's core values that any consideration of a persuasive or compromise approach was simply out of the question. Fortified by the "rightness" of her values stance, Helen felt a moral justification in her direct action of taking the teacher to task about the incident.

### Circumstances Involving External Relations

The most frequent and troublesome circumstance in the Australian study was the issue of dealing with overly demanding parents, where "30% of principals reported that this type of circumstance occurred often or very often, and 40% of them reported having much or a great deal of trouble in dealing with it" (Dempster, 2001, p. 13). One example of this kind of circumstance cited a principal dealing with an insistent father who felt his daughter should have received an achievement award and challenged the school's selection procedures. Staff, on the other hand, believed the father to be overbearing and unreasonable and that his claims should be ignored. The principal responded as follows:

> However, I explained that we couldn't do that [ignore the father], because we had a responsibility to respond in the way that the father had approached the issue: lucidly and logically. And at the end of the day we did. We explained to the father how we went about the award task and we apologised for not better informing parents about the rules until after the event. As it turned out that was his core concern, and so he accepted with more or less good grace what the situation was. In this case, I had to hose down those staff members who were responding emotionally and ensure that the parent was not belittled or treated like a fool.
>
> (Dempster, 2001, p. 16)

In this situation, the task for the principal's ethical decision making was to consider the "rightness" of each perspective, so that a negotiated settlement of the issue could result in a win-win situation for both parties.

There was also another area that posed interesting ethical situations for school principals. This centered on the interactions between a school and related government agencies. The issue of dealing with policy or directives from the central office created frequent ethical problems for 62% of Australian principal respondents. Their two New Zealand counterparts had different perceptions of values conflict between themselves and government agencies such as the Education Review Office and the Ministry of Education. Helen stated firmly that she had no difficulty in accepting the bureaucratic values of efficiency and accountability where they helped her to make improvements in student learning.

However, "Max James," the rural school principal, was just as determined that there was a definite conflict between bureaucratic values and his own personal and professional values that focused on specific learning and social needs of students living in a rural community. He had an aversion to what he termed a "bean counting" mentality of government agencies that compelled him to react to *their* demands in assessment and curriculum objectives, rather than to students' unique learning needs. This values tension for Max is replicated by Bailey's (2000) belief that "teachers may be placed in the position of violating their own deeply-felt beliefs about what children in their care need when they are told how and what to teach" (p. 118). Max also believed that the market forces model of education, which aimed to achieve higher performance standards through interschool competition for students, was in direct opposition to his values of cooperation and consensus.

In Max's case, despite concerted disapproval of government agencies' values stance, he had adopted the approach of "pragmatism with principles" (Moore, George, & Halpin, 2002, p. 185) by mediating government policy and procedures through his own values lens. On a superficial level, Max conducted a localized form of political resistance. At a deeper level, his defense was built around values resistance. Here, he worked within national demands but at the same time held strongly to fundamental personal and professional values of his current philosophy as it pertained to the needs of his small rural school. It appeared that from a values perspective, Max's accountability to his rural community comprehensively exceeded his obligations to the demands of central government.

### Managing Ethical Dilemmas

From this sample of research case studies, we gain some insight into the complex field of managing ethical dilemmas. Local dilemmas in the Australasian schools reflected a range of ethical, professional, and political dilemmas, whereby individual interests were often in conflict with and assessed against the common good of the wider group. For example, in the New Zealand research schools, Helen dealt with students wanting a second-chance education, staff employment issues, and intergroup conflict resolution. For Max, the observed dilemmas included the potential outcomes of student expulsion from a rural school, teacher professional conduct, and weighing staff personal employment issues against long-term school public relationships with the community.

From a personal perspective, the ramifications of their dilemma management were ever-present in their thinking. Helen and Max both felt the weight of decision making on their shoulders, whether it involved a compromise to elicit a win-win situation for the individual and for the group, or whether it involved the power of persuasion of logical argument to change people's minds or to take a contrary stand on the basis of policy or regulation. Their judgment calls were often centered on competing human needs that had them asking themselves: Who benefits? Who loses the most? What is the worst-case scenario that the school can withstand if this particular decision is taken? This was evidenced, in particular, by Helen's direct treatment of the teacher absent from class.

The dilemma management positions of these school principals can be seen as predominantly ethical ones. Research results from both countries also underlined the concept of principals as moral agents by the manner in which they lead and manage their schools, particularly in respect of an ethical consideration of competing individual and group needs. Further examples from earlier leadership literature had included school appraisal activity, where individual needs and development were often at odds with organizational goals (Cardno, 1994), and loyalty dilemmas, where the principal was asked to assess the case of a student(s) against that of a teacher (Moller, 1998).

## ETHICAL IMPLICATIONS FOR THEORY AND PRACTICE

What, then, are some of the ethical implications for the theory and practice of educational leadership, as they arise from a sample of Australasian research studies outlined above and from the extant literature? This section will explore implications as they relate to the themes of: critical self-reflection; dilemma management reconceptualized as the management of contested values; an ecological interpretation of the juncture between school context and the leadership self; and professional learning for principals.

### Critical Self-reflection

There are evident links among the notions of critical self-reflection, leaders' values, and the different contexts within which an educational leader carries out his or her daily work. A self-examination of core values and belief systems enables leaders to become more aware of the motivating principles behind their leadership behaviors (Fink, 2005; Smyth, 2001). Such an examination should also assist principals to understand how their personal and professional values may align with, and differ from, those values held by others in the broader contexts of the school. These concepts mirror Smyth's phases of critical self-reflection, whereby "interrogation and questioning of one's values may confirm their legitimacy or suggest their renegotiation in a contested situation, and where reconstruction of one's values stance may enable the principal to reflect on alternative courses of action" (Notman, 2008, p. 9).

This self-critical process is especially applicable when one considers current contexts in which principals operate. Increased public demand for educational services and reduced financial support for schools place further pressure on ethical dilemmas of educational leadership that make administering schools "different from such work in other contexts" (Goldring & Greenfield, 2002, pp. 2–3). This will require principals, in turn, to reflect on their values priorities in terms of where to spend a shrinking financial resource. For instance, does a principal's value of academic excellence support the development of a gifted and talented program for high-achieving students, or is it outweighed by the value of social justice that supports the employment of an English as a Second Language teacher to assist new immigrants in English language acquisition? Such ethical dilemmas continue to confront principals' philosophical and values-based positions.

### Reconceptualizing Dilemma Management

The concept of values contestation and its management by the two New Zealand secondary school principals constituted a major finding of that research study. The study revealed principals' rationales behind their decision making in dilemma situations.

A sample of critical incidents demonstrated the principals' recourse to their core personal and professional values when searching for a resolution to the dilemma. In this way, using Begley's (1999) framework of values terminology, critical incidents surrounding principals' management of dilemmas can be conceptualized and interpreted as a values-based decision-making process. In Max James's case, one critical incident displayed the most profound form of values contestation in which values of principle of both staff and educational leader were in conflict. As Hodgkinson (1991) pointed out in his values typology, the contestation of values of principle or transrational values, and the contestation of values of preference or subrational values, are frequently the most difficult to resolve.

In addition, there are two other considerations within values contestation that may enhance an understanding of ethical dilemma management. First, it may be assumed that the notion of values conflict occurs *between* people on an interpersonal basis. Hodgkinson (1983) offered a less publicized but subtle view that true value conflict is always *intra*personal, deep within the self: "The essential subjectivity of value dictates that any conflict *between values* must occur within the individual consciousness; it must be part of the affective life of the individual and private to that phenomenology" (p. 106). Helen Aiken and Max James both underwent intrapersonal values conflict to varying degrees, exemplified best in Helen's self-review of her values position on school alcohol issues in the face of a lack of community support for her moral stance. This must constitute a watershed moment for any principal, who contemplates the prospect that the resolution of values contestation may well result in the principal's own values being superseded by the greater legitimacy of others' values or not perceived to be of any values currency at all. It is important for principals to be aware of the impact of this intrapersonal values conflict and the possibility of its occurrence at any stage of dilemma management decision making.

A second consideration within values contestation is a reemphasis of an underlying moral purpose behind educational leadership and values-based contingency leadership in particular (Day et al., 2000; Harris & Chapman, 2002). Max and Helen's decision-making processes, employed during their management of contested values, were influenced by the strength of their convictions, by doing what was right in the best interests of their school. Their decision making was also influenced by key personal values of honesty and integrity. These affected the ways in which they gave feedback to others, the levels of honesty within their own self-assessment of leadership performance, and the manner with which they resolved intrapersonal values conflict.

This moral purpose in educational leadership, and its origins in principals' unique sets of core values, has been underlined in the literature, for example, by Sergiovanni's (2001) frequent assertions that leadership is a far more cognitive process than simply being personality or rules based: "Cognitive leadership has more to do with purposes, values, and frameworks that oblige us morally than it does with needs that touch us psychologically or with bureaucratic things that push us organizationally" (Sergiovanni, p. ix). Equally, the proposed dangers of ethical relativism for administrators (Strike, Haller, & Soltis, 1998), and interest in the concept of "ethical intelligence" as a moral imperative (Day, 2004), have supported a need for educational leaders to have a personal platform of clear values, beliefs, and a sense of moral purpose if their dilemma management is to be well informed.

It should be noted that there are no easy solutions to moral decision making, nor is it prudent to develop a definitive listing of values necessary to engage in effective values-based leadership. As Begley (2002) stated: "The processes of valuation in school leadership situations are much too context-bound to permit this quick fix" (p. 51). Of greater importance is to develop awareness within principals of how to make problematic leadership choices in dilemma situations, particularly those in which there are no clear right or wrong answers, where the choice is often between "right" versus "right." This latter perspective is cogently summarized by Hodgkinson (1996) in his writing on values theory:

> It comes down to this: an administrator, any administrator, is constantly faced with value choices. To govern is to choose. One can accept or not accept the value dictates imposed by the particular organizational culture in which one works. One can aspire to or disdain any of a number of systems of 'ethics' from workaholism to neo-Confucianism. One can allow, or not allow, one's leadership to be swayed by values deriving from hedonism, ambition, careerism, or by the prejudices and affinities one has for colleagues and peers. And one can do all of this in the open or in secret or somewhere in between. But each day and each hour provides the occasion for values judgements with each choice having a determining effect upon the value options for the future.
>
> (p. 109)

### An Ecological Interpretation of Contextually Responsive Leadership

Under the concept of self-management in New Zealand schools, educational leaders have been asked to take up a responsive role in regard to internal contingencies, to be contextually aware of external influences, and to build trusting relationships with their school communities. This responsive role has been accentuated in New Zealand education by an expectation that leaders will meet multiple needs and be answerable to multiple accountability points within their educational constituencies:

> For example, the learning needs of students; the social, economic and cultural needs of families and ethnic groups, as they relate to well-being, financial hardship and diversity respectively; the professional needs of teachers and boards of trustees; and the policy and regulatory requirements of educational agencies such as the Ministry of Education and the Education Review Office.
>
> (Notman, 2011, p. 147)

This ecological approach to understanding the realities of the leadership role illustrates that educational leadership does not exist in a vacuum but rather within a broader sociocultural-economic-political context (Bottery, 2004). This blended context can impact on school directions and has the potential to both enhance and constrain one's capability to lead and to manage. In this way, an ecological view of educational leadership supports a contextually responsive role, as educational leaders react to and engage with different contextual layers of influence and need. The educational leader, whether a principal, deputy principal, middle manager, or teacher leader, is in a challenging position, caught between the "micro" world of students and their family/community and the "macro" world of educational agencies and society's educational expectations and values.

Thus, we can gain an appreciation of the ethical demands facing educational leaders, where their values-based and contextually responsive leadership functions are subject to other forces within and outside the school. Hargreaves (2011) describes this as "fusion leadership," which moves beyond traditional notions of technical competencies and skills:

> Instead, it is the psychological integration of a personality and a community combined with the knowledge, empathy and strategic capability to know what parts of one's own and one's colleagues' leadership are the right ones, for the right time and for the challenges at that moment. Leadership beyond expectations is not a fission of competencies but a fusion of qualities and characteristics within oneself, one's community and over time.
>
> (p. 239)

### Leadership Professional Learning

Increasingly, in the literature and research of educational leadership, there are calls to emphasize professional learning over professional development (Parsons & Beauchamp, 2012; Timperley, 2011). Timperley recommends that a clear distinction be made between higher-order professional learning and lower-order professional development. She argues that an increased depth of professional knowledge "may challenge existing beliefs, attitudes and understandings" (p. 4). One can point to the role of ethical leadership as an example of higher-order learning, and a worthy area for inclusion in a leadership preparation or in-service professional learning program.

From his research, Dempster (2001) suggests three areas of development that could help principals meet the ethical challenges of school decision making:

(i) *The policy context of ethical decision making,* where "principals should be engaged, formally and informally, in the reflective analysis of broad political and economic policy affecting education" (p. 17).
(ii) *Ethical values,* where such values might be built into in-service programs, particularly in relation to "contestable values dualities experienced in education" (ibid).
(iii) *Case studies of ethical issues,* where principals can juxtapose their own ethical dilemmas against others' in-school scenarios.

There still appears to be reluctance on the part of organizations to develop an ethical sensitivity among their staff and leaders (Cranston, Ehrich, Kimber, & Starr,

2012; Langlois & Lapointe, 2010; Shapiro & Hassinger, 2007). This is evident in the professional learning area of self-knowledge, where earlier research literature had advocated a paradigm shift in school leadership and administrator training that differs from previously dominant technical models. For example, Daresh and Male (2000) argued for an emphasis on personal values and ethical stances, while Day (2000) proposed a "formation" approach to principal learning that encouraged self-reflection and personal understanding of one's values to reveal the inner motives and ethical positions of the person behind the principal.

This chapter's discussion has drawn attention to the interwoven links between values-based leadership, with a focus on the personal and professional self, and contextually responsive leadership, with its focus on the situation or environment in which schools operate. This represents a duality of concept and practice, within which challenging ethical decisions must be made. In order to help school leaders meet these future challenges, professional learning strategies will have to adapt to a changing educational, social, and political world, as they encounter interactions of increasingly diverse values held by students, teachers, parents, community members, and those who work in educational bureaucracies. The changing knowledge bases held by each principal will be important features to be addressed in future principal learning programs. These will include the knowledge of the craft of educational leadership and administration; knowledge of students, teachers, and parents in their learning and social contexts; and, most importantly, knowledge of self and the belief systems that inform one's ethical behavior.

## QUESTIONS FOR FURTHER RESEARCH

Within the general domain of ethical sensitivities, it is recommended that further exploration be directed to the pathways chosen by principals in their ethical decision making, their management of contested values, and subsequent conflict resolution processes. How *do* principals arrive at complex ethical decisions in the context of competing personal, social, and professional interests? It is suggested that future research examine, in detail, the nature of critical incidents that principals have to confront and the manner in which contested values are resolved. Additional research questions are proposed in this regard: To what extent can principals appreciate how others determine right and wrong? Is there a sequence of steps that principals take before arriving at a solution to ethical dilemmas, not unlike Kohlberg's (1984) six stages of moral judgment? Is there a series of prioritizations as principals weigh up implications of critical decisions for themselves personally, as educational leaders, for the school as an organization, or for the greater good of the wider community?

## SUMMARY

There are multiple layers of meaning that contribute to our understanding of how school principals engage with ethical sensitivities during the course of their daily work. An eclectic approach has been used in this chapter to show how ethical sensitivities in general, and school ethical decision making in particular, might be worked out against a backdrop of the interdependent influence of values-based leadership and contextually responsive leadership: The former reveals the workings of the intra-personal leadership of self, where one's values and attitudes affect subsequent ethical actions; the latter demonstrates the relational connectedness of the principal to the range of constituents within each educational community. This can be viewed as a symbiotic relationship of person, place, and people, where the ethical sensitivities of the principal can be seen at work in a demand environment that is both bounded and situational.

## REFERENCES

Avolio, B. J., Gardner, W. L., Walumbwa, F. O., Luthans, F., & May, B. R. (2004). Unlocking the mask: A look at the process by which authentic leaders impact follower attitudes and behaviours. *Leadership Quarterly, 15*(6), 801–823.

Bailey, B. (2000). The impact of mandated change on teachers. In N. Bascia & A. Hargreaves (Eds.), *The sharp edge of educational change* (pp. 112–128). London: Routledge Falmer.

Beatty, B. (2005). Emotional leadership. In B. Davies (Ed.), *The essentials of school leadership* (pp. 122–144). London: Paul Chapman Publishing & Corwin Press.

Begley, P. T. (1999). Academic and practitioner perspectives on values. In P. T. Begley & P. E. Leonard (Eds.), *The values of educational administration* (pp. 51–69). London: Falmer Press.

Begley, P. T. (2002). Western-centric perspectives on values and leadership. In A. Walker & C. Dimmock (Eds.), *School leadership and administration* (pp. 45–59). London: Routledge Falmer.

Begley, P. T. (2006, October 4–8). *Self-knowledge, capacity and sensitivity: Prerequisites to authentic leadership by school principals.* Paper presented at Values-based Leadership Conference, Victoria, Canada.

Bottery, M. (2004). *The challenges of educational leadership.* London: Paul Chapman Publishing.

Branson, C. (2010). Ethical decision making: Is personal moral integrity the missing link? *Journal of Authentic Leadership in Education, 1*(1), 1–8.

Brock, B. L., & Grady, M. L. (2012). *The daily practices of successful principals.* Thousand Oaks, CA: Corwin Press.

Cardno, C. (1994). *Dealing with dilemmas: A critical and collaborative approach to staff appraisal in two schools.* (Unpublished PhD thesis). University of Auckland.

Cranston, N., Ehrich, L., Kimber, M., & Starr, K. (2012). An exploratory study of ethical dilemmas faced by academic leaders in three Australian universities. *Journal of Educational Leadership, Policy and Practice, 27*(1), 3–15.

Cunningham, W. G., & Cordeiro, P. A. (2003). *Educational leadership: A problem-based approach.* Boston: Allyn & Bacon.

Daresh, J., & Male, T. (2000). Crossing the border into leadership: Experiences of newly appointed British headteachers and American principals. *Educational Management and Administration, 28*(1), 89–101.

Day, C. (2000). Beyond transformational leadership. *Educational Leadership, 57*(7), 56–59.

Day, C. (2004). *A passion for teaching.* London: Routledge Falmer.

Day, C., Harris, A., Hadfield, M., Tolley, H., & Beresford, J. (2000). *Leading schools in times of change.* Buckingham, UK: Open University Press.

Day, C., Sammons, P., Hopkins, D., Harris, A., Leithwood, K., Gu, Q., & Brown, E. (2010). *10 strong claims about successful school leadership.* Nottingham, UK: National College for Leadership of Schools and Children's Services.

Day, C., Sammons, P., Leithwood, K., Hopkins, D., Qu, Q., Brown, E., & Ahtaridou, E. (2011). *Successful school leadership: Linking with learning and achievement.* Maidenhead, UK: Open University Press.

Dempster, N. (2001, August 2). *The ethical development of school principals.* Paper presented at the International Leadership Institute, Adelaide, New Zealand.

Duignan, P. (2006). *Educational leadership: Key challenges and ethical tensions.* New York: Cambridge University Press.

Evers, C., & Lakomski, G. (1996). *Exploring educational administration: Coherentist applications and critical debates.* New York: Pergamon Press.

Fairholm, G. W. (1998). *Perspectives on leadership: From the science of management to its spiritual heart.* Westport, CT: Quorum.

Fiedler, F. (1967). *A theory of leadership effectiveness.* New York: McGraw-Hill.

Fink, D. (2005). Developing leaders for their future not our past. In M. J. Coles & G. Southworth (Eds.), *Developing leadership: Creating the schools of tomorrow* (pp. 1–20). Maidenhead, UK: Open University Press.

Foster, W. (1986). *Paradigms and promises: New approaches to educational administration.* Buffalo, NY: Prometheus Books.

Goldring, E., & Greenfield, W. (2002). Understanding the evolving concept of leadership in education: Roles, expectations and dilemmas. In J. Murphy (Ed.), *The educational leadership challenge: Redefining leadership for the 21st century. One hundred-first yearbook of the National Society for the Study of Education* (pp. 1–19). Chicago: National Society for the Study of Education.

Grace, G. (1995). *School leadership. Beyond education management: An essay in policy scholarship.* London: Falmer Press.

Graen, G. B., & Uhl-Bien, M. (1995). Relationship-based approach to leadership: Development of leader-member exchange (LMX) theory of leadership over 25 years: Applying a multi-level multi-domain perspective. *Leadership Quarterly, 6*(2), 219–247.

Greenfield, T. B. (1983, May). *Environment as subjective reality.* Revised version of a paper presented to the Symposium on School Organisations and Their Environments at the annual conference of the American Educational Research Association, Montreal.

Greenfield, T. B. (1986). The decline and fall of science in educational administration. *Interchange, 17*(2), 57–80.

Griffiths, D. E. (1959). *Administrative theory.* New York: Appleton-Century-Crofts.

Griffiths, D. E. (1978). Contemporary theory development and educational administration. *Educational Administration, 6*(4), 80–93.

Gronn, P. (1983). *Rethinking educational administration: TB Greenfield and his critics.* Victoria, Australia: Deakin University.

Gu, G., & Johannson, O. (2012). Sustaining school performance: School contexts matter. *International Journal of Leadership in Education: Theory and Practice.* doi: 10.1080/13603124.2012.732242.

Hallinger, P. (2003). Leading educational change: Reflections on the practice of instructional and transformational leadership. *Cambridge Journal of Education, 33*(3), 329–351.

Halpin, A. W. (1966). *Theory and research in administration.* New York: Macmillan.

Hargreaves, A. (2011). Fusion and the future of leadership. In J. Robertson & H. Timperley (Eds.), *Leadership and learning* (pp. 227–242). London: Sage Publications.

Harris, A., & Chapman, C. (2002). Democratic leadership for school improvement in challenging contexts. *International Electronic Journal for Leadership in Learning, 6*(9). Retrieved from www.ucalgary.ca/~iejll/volume6/harris.html

Hersey, P., & Blanchard, K. (1977). *Managing organizational behaviour: Utilizing human resources.* Englewood Cliffs, NJ: Prentice-Hall.

Hodgkinson, C. (1978). *Towards a philosophy of administration.* Oxford: Blackwell.

Hodgkinson, C. (1983). *The philosophy of leadership.* Oxford: Blackwell.

Hodgkinson, C. (1991). *Educational leadership: The moral art.* Albany: State University of New York Press.

Hodgkinson, C. (1996). *Administrative philosophy: Values and motivations in administrative life.* New York: Pergamon Press.

House, R. J., Hanges, P. J., Javidan, M., Dorfman, P. W., & Gupta, V. (2004). *Culture, leadership and organizations: The GLOBE study of 62 societies.* Thousand Oaks, CA: Sage.

Kohlberg, L. (1984). *Essays on moral development. Vol. 2. The psychology of moral development.* San Francisco: Harper & Row.

Langlois, L., & Lapointe, C. (2010). Can ethics be learned? Results from a three-year action-research project. *Journal of Educational Administration, 48*(2), 147–163.

Leithwood, K., Begley, P., & Cousins, L. (1994). *Developing expert leadership for future schools.* London: Falmer Press.

Leithwood, K., Jantzi, D., & Steinbach, R. (1999). *Changing leadership for changing times.* Buckingham, UK: Open University Press.

Leithwood, K., & Steinbach, R. (1991). Components of chief education officers' problem solving strategies. In K. A. Leithwood & D. Musella (Eds.), *Understanding school system administration: Studies of the contemporary chief education officer* (pp. 127–153). New York: Falmer Press.

Lord, R., & Maher, K. (1993). *Leadership and information processing: Linking perceptions to performance.* New York: Routledge.

Merchant, B., Arlestig, H., Garza, E., Johansson, O., Murakami-Ramalho, E., & Tornsen, M. (2012). Successful school leadership in Sweden and the US: Contexts of social responsibility and individualism. *International Journal of Educational Management, 26*(5), 428–441.

Milstein, M. M., & Henry, D. A. (2008). *Leadership for resilient schools and communities.* Thousand Oaks, CA: Corwin Press.

Moller, J. (1998). Action research with principals: Gain, strain and dilemmas. *Educational Action Research, 6*(1), 69–91.

Mongon, D., & Leadbeater, C. (2012). *School leadership for public value.* London: Institute of Education, University of London.

Moore, A., George, R., & Halpin, D. (2002). The developing role of the headteacher in English schools. *Educational Management and Administration, 30*(2), 175–188.

National College for School Leadership. (2001). *Leadership development framework.* Nottingham, UK: NCSL.

Nias, J., Southworth, G., & Yeomans, R. (1989). *Staff relationships in the primary school: A study of school culture.* London: Cassell.

Notman, R. (2005). *The person of the principal: A study of values in secondary school leadership.* (Unpublished PhD thesis). Massey University, New Zealand.

Notman, R. (2008). Leading from within: A values-based model of principal self-development. *Leading and Managing,14*(1), 1–15.

Notman, R. (2011). Building leadership success in a New Zealand education context. In R. Notman (Ed.), *Successful educational leadership in New Zealand: Case studies of schools and an early childhood centre* (pp. 135–154). Wellington: New Zealand Council for Educational Research Press.

Parsons, J., & Beauchamp, L. (2012). Practical ethical leadership: Alberta-based research studies on instructional leadership. *Journal of Educational Leadership, Policy and Practice, 27*(2), 26–36.

Robertson, J. (2011). Partnership in leadership and learning. In J. Robertson & H. Timperley (Eds.), *Leadership and learning* (pp. 213–226). London: Sage.

Rokeach, M. (1973). *The nature of human values.* New York: Free Press.

Sergiovanni, T. J. (2001). *Leadership: What's in it for schools?* New York: Routledge Falmer.

Shapiro, J. P., & Hassinger, R. E. (2007). Using case studies of ethical dilemmas for the development of moral literacy: Towards educating for social justice. *Journal of Educational Administration, 45*(4), 451–470.

Shapiro, J. P., & Stefkovich, J. A. (2005). *Ethical leadership and decision making in education: Applying theoretical perspectives to complex dilemmas* (2nd ed.). Mahwah, NJ: Lawrence Erlbaum Associates.

Simon, H. A. (1957). *Administrative behaviour.* New York: Macmillan.

Smyth, J. (2001). *Critical politics of teachers' work: An Australian perspective.* New York: Peter Lang Publishing.

Southworth, G. (1998). *Leading improving primary schools: The work of headteachers and deputy heads.* London: Falmer Press.

Starratt, R. J. (2010). Developing ethical leadership. In B. Davies & M. Brundrett (Eds.), *Developing successful leadership* (pp. 27–37). Dordrecht, Netherlands: Springer Educational.

Strike, K. A., Haller, E. J., & Soltis, J. F. (1998). *The ethics of school administration* (2nd ed.). New York: Teachers College Press.

Timperley, H. (2011). *A background paper to inform the development of a national professional development framework for teachers and school leaders.* Melbourne: Australian Institute for Teaching and School Leadership.

Willower, D. J. (1979). *Ideology and science in organization theory.* Paper presented at the annual meeting of the American Educational Research Association, San Francisco, 8–12 April.

Willower, D. J. (1987). Inquiry into educational administration: The last twenty five years and the next. *Journal of Educational Administration, 25*(1), 12–28.

Woods, P. (2005). *Democratic leadership in education.* London: Paul Chapman.

Yukl, G. (1994). *Leadership in organizations.* Englewood Cliffs, NJ: Prentice-Hall.

# 13

## THE POWER OF PERSONAL VALUES

### CHRISTOPHER M. BRANSON

The purpose of this chapter is not only to describe one of the most fundamental components of ethical educational leadership—personal values—but also to illustrate their power. Personal values have power because they are a primary influence in each and every person's decision-making processes. Each and every choice, judgment, or evaluation that a person makes is influenced, consciously or unconsciously, by his or her personal values. Hence, if the life of today's educational leader is now rife with having to solve extremely difficult, complex, or ambiguous problems and/or having to choose between outcomes that are neither right nor wrong but, rather, varying degrees of better, then it follows that his or her personal values are directly active in guiding that person's leadership. From this chapter, leaders will be able to understand how their personal values are able to influence their leadership practice. Moreover, they will know how to ensure that their personal values are positively influencing such practice.

Fundamental to the importance of this handbook generally and this chapter in particular is the awareness that ethical leadership is not a natural outcome. Ethical leadership is only achievable through deliberate and conscious intention (Taylor, 2003). It is far less likely to be achieved instinctively or unwittingly. Regrettably, many leaders have had little or no formal exposure in regard to the nature of ethical decision making such that they are likely to lack a vocabulary to name ethical issues or to be able to articulate a moral landscape from which to generate an appropriate ethical response (Starratt, 2004). Hence, enhanced ethical leadership depends on leaders knowing how to interpret their personal realities more faithfully, and this is not attained naturally (Wilber, 2000a). Indeed, according to Langlois (2004, p. 89), "It seems necessary to train [leaders] in moral judgement and in ethics to render them capable of managing according to a renewed and responsible form of leadership." The educational leader must learn how to become an ethical leader.

To learn how to become an ethical leader begins with understanding the essence of what it means to be an ethical leader. Simply stated, ethical leaders are able to deliberately attend to the needs of others at the expense of their own personal needs and desires. Most often, such attention to the needs of others is founded upon leaders' personal observations, intuitions, subjective impressions, and transcendent beliefs rather than explicit facts. Hence, ethical leadership development is about nurturing leaders' moral sensitivity through awakening their subjective consciousness and their transpersonal instincts in relation to the choices that confront them. It is about enabling leaders to accept their intuitions and instincts, their feelings and emotions, as valid sources of wisdom toward determining what is the best outcome that can be achieved for the good of others. The formation of any intuitions, instincts, feelings, and emotions in response to a given situation are formed within educational leaders from their own personalized values, beliefs, and motives rather than from externally prescribed and explicit analytical processes. In other words, the genesis of ethical leadership comes from within the leader and not from without. In this way it can be seen how the development of ethical leadership begins through the nurturing of a heightened moral sensitivity (Tuana, see Chapter 11), which compels leaders to examine the motives, values, and beliefs steering their decisions so as to ensure that it is the needs of others and not their own self-interests that are being attended to. As proposed by Burns (1978), ethical leadership "is a process of morality to the degree that leaders engage with followers on the basis of shared motives and values and goals—on the basis, that is, of the followers' true needs as well as those of leaders" (Burns, 2010, p. 36). The awareness that motives, values, and beliefs are at the heart of ethical leadership is not new; it is more that to date we have not striven to learn how to make this ideal a reality. This chapter provides a means for achieving it.

To this end, professional self-reflection is widely regarded as a valid approach to enhancing the moral sensitivity of leaders beyond technical expertise (Richmon, 2003). In particular, it is argued that "a process oriented focus on values contemplation seems to be gaining momentum, and in some ways, provides a far more promising direction for the future, than calls for the objectification of values through rational arbitrary criteria" (p. 43). Since values are normally unconscious dimensions of a person's inner self (Branson, 2005, 2009), such a self-reflective values contemplation process is about developing the leader's moral sensitivity by providing a means for making these unconscious values conscious. It is about nurturing a moral consciousness, as explained by Frattaroli (2001, p. 323):

> When we talk about the goal of making the unconscious conscious we are really talking about the concept of free will—the idea that as we become more conscious we are less controlled by our desires and have more possibility of autonomous conscious choice that is not biologically determined. Where once [leaders were] controlled by the unconscious neurobiological forces of the drives, [they] will become free to direct [their lives] from the centre of [their] self-reflective moral consciousness.

Using self-reflection in this way to develop moral sensitivity involves gaining self-knowledge of one's inner world, to the finely differentiated layers and qualities of private experiencing, and being faithfully aware of one's responses to any moral dilemmas

(Branson, 2009; Mackay, 2004). It is the self having knowledge of both the mind and the body as experiences. Through the gaining of self-knowledge, people are better able to transcend both their minds and their bodies and thus can be aware of themselves as objects in awareness, as experiences. Hence, developing a moral sensitivity requires taking "the less travelled path whereby we look honestly at ourselves and take responsibility for our own faults" (Frattaroli, 2001, p. 225). This is not about being self-judgmental or self-condemning but rather self-accepting as the first step toward self-actualization. Truly coming to know one's self is the necessary first step toward developing a better self. In this sense, moral sensitivity is about using self-knowledge to create a new personal meaning from all that one does and thinks about (Taylor, 2003). It is about creating an "inner voice" (p. 26) that tells you what is the right thing, the ethical thing, to do.

From a more precise perspective, the nurturing of moral sensitivity through self-reflection is about finding a practical way to gain self-knowledge of personal motives, values, and beliefs (Hodgkinson, 1996). Given that all ethical decisions involve the making of choices, which are directly influenced by personal motives, values, and beliefs, this means that the ethical decision-making process is inextricably influenced by personal motives, values, and beliefs. Through the gaining of self-knowledge about one's personal motives, values, and beliefs, it is possible to ensure that these are commensurate with achieving desired ethical outcomes. Educational leaders are better able to judge their own behavior in order to ensure that it achieves their personally desired ethical standards through knowing their own personal motives, values, and beliefs. The knowing of personal motives, values, and beliefs nurtures moral sensitivity, which then enhances the educational leader's ethical decision-making capacity.

Previous research (Branson, 2005, 2007) suggests that in order to gain self-knowledge of the role played by personal motives, values, and beliefs in influencing personal behavior, it is first necessary to know how these are formed. Unless the formational elements of personal motives, values, and beliefs are clarified, they remain subliminal and notional components of the inner self, and the relationship between these and behavior remain concealed or misunderstood. Hence, it is essential to come to know the inner antecedents of personal motives, values, and beliefs.

Drawing on literature from the fields of cognitive and behavioral psychology and values theory, it can be seen that the self is constituted from the integration of one's self-concept, self-esteem, motives, values, beliefs, emotions, and behaviors (de Bono, 2009; Griseri, 1998; Hultman & Gellermann, 2002; Leary & Tangney, 2003; Osborne, 1996; Weisinger, 2009). All of these components of the self are formed during one's life experiences and become powerful influences on how one experiences, perceives, and reacts to reality. This means that one's own self-concept is at the heart of how one behaves and this self-concept indirectly influences behavior through the sequential components of the self of self-esteem, motives, values, emotions, and beliefs. The integration of all of these components of the self influences the manner in which the individual thinks about, perceives, and responds to his or her world. These components come together to form the core of the self, and the complexity of the self evolves from these through the addition of other cognitive, psychological, social, and kinesthetic processes.

In addition, the literature proposes that this indirect connectedness between the self-concept and behaviors is made more complex by the decreasing degree of consciousness that one has of one's beliefs, emotions, values, motives, self-esteem, and self-concept (Westwood & Posner, 1997). These components of the self appear to be ever-increasingly subliminal components and are little influenced by sensory feedback from one's reality. They are inner, tacit, and increasingly intangible behavior-governing components of one's being. Hence, the seeking of self-knowledge about one's inner self is not a natural process and requires a deliberate undertaking. In order to be able to effectively gain self-knowledge, people require guidance in knowing what to look for in their selves, and they need to learn self-reflective ways (Cashman, 1998; McGraw, 2001; Wilber, 2000b). Mostly, people have limited self-knowledge.

The diagrammatical representation in Figure 13.1 has been designed to illustrate the understandings provided by the literature of how a person's behavior is influenced by the various components of the Self.

This diagrammatical representation not only highlights that one's self-concept is at the heart of one's self, by placing it at the core of the representation, but it also illustrates the sequential order of the components as one moves from self-concept to behaviors. Also highlighted is the understanding that one's level of conscious awareness of the role played by each component in influencing the achievement of a desired purpose typically increases as one moves out from the center of the representation. People have little or no conscious awareness of how their self-concept is influencing the achievement of a particular desired purpose, whereas they are usually fully conscious of how the achievement of this desired purpose is being influenced by their

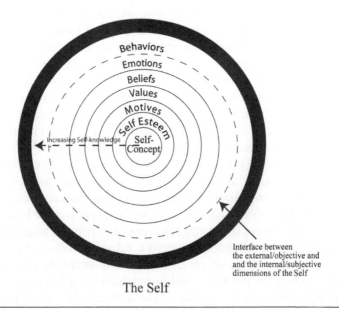

The Self

Figure 13.1 A diagrammatical representation of the various components of the Self as presented by the literature, which shows how these components are able to interact in order to influence a person's behavior (Branson, 2010, p. 51).

behavior. The final understanding conveyed by this diagrammatical representation is that each component is not a discrete entity but rather is interrelated and interactive. The inner components are each antecedents of their adjacent outer component, but they in turn depend on feedback from their outer neighboring component to maintain relevance. In this way, each component helps to create the united self.

Although it is possible to view these common general components as forming a united self, it must be realized that each self is unique to the individual person (Elliott, 2001). The manner by which these components interact is very idiosyncratic because each person's subliminal interactive processes are unique and distinctive. A similar act evinced by two different people, even in apparently identical circumstances, is likely to reflect quite unique ways of blending these components of their self. Furthermore, these components of their self influence how they understand and interact with all of their reality and are not limited to just one aspect of their life. One's emotions, beliefs, values, motives, self-esteem, and self-concept are not only unique to the individual but they are also relatively consistent and impact in a similar way on all aspects of one's life.

This means that in order to develop ethical leadership by nurturing leaders' moral sensitivity, it is necessary to devise a means by which they are able to gain self-knowledge of their inner self. Leaders must be able to come to know how their self-concept and self-esteem influences their motives, values, beliefs, and emotions, thereby impacting on their ethical leadership behavior. In this way, leaders are able to consciously monitor their inner influences as they attend to ethical issues in order to ensure that they are able to act freely in achieving the best ethical outcome. It is through the bringing of naturally existing unconscious inner phenomena into their consciousness that initiates educational leaders' progress toward becoming ethical leaders.

Once it is understood what knowledge of the self educational leaders need to bring into their consciousness so as to develop their ethical leadership capacity, the next step is to appreciate how this can happen in a natural and easily achievable way. Wilber (2000a, p. 243) posits that consciousness "is not part of the brain. The mind, or consciousness, is the interior dimension, the exterior correlate of which is the objective brain. The mind is an 'I', the brain is an 'it'. You can look at a brain, but you must talk to a mind, and that requires not just observation but interpretation." Moreover, this essential task of interpretation can be accomplished only through introspection and self-reflection (Frattaroli, 2001). People must learn to interpret the depths of their inner self more adequately and more faithfully so that their inner influences on their lives become more transparent (Wilber, 2000b). However, most people do not have such self-knowledge, as this commitment to introspection through reflective self-inquiry and reflective self-evaluation is not something people do naturally or accurately or that automatically influences their behavior (Bandura, 1986; Branson, 2007, 2009; Hall, Lindzey, & Campbell, 1998; Hodgkinson, 1996, 2003). Genuine self-knowledge depends upon an avoidance of being false to one's real self, and this requires deep personal honesty and arduous effort (Trilling, 1972). Self-knowledge can be formed only within people who have a strong motivation to know more about their own inner self and to value gaining an accurate image of their authentic self. People need to learn how to be appropriately introspective as a means of increasing their consciousness.

Hence, the research approach (Branson, 2005, 2007) used to explore self-reflection and its influence on the development of ethical leadership followed the lead presented in the literature of a deeply structured approach to introspection and self-reflection (Lord & Hall, 2005). Deeply structured self-reflection incorporates learning how to "personally articulate one's self-concept and core values" so as to "construct sophisticated understandings of situations that can be used to guide thoughts and behaviors" (Lord & Hall, 2005, p. 592). At the heart of such a deeply structured process of self-reflection is the need to assist people to come to know their self-concept. Increasing people's knowledge of their self-concept is essential for the nurturing of personal authenticity (van Knippenberg, van Knippenberg, De Cremer, & Hogg, 2005). It is through coming to know and understand their self-concept that people are able to develop an appropriate meaning system from which to feel, think, and act with authenticity (Shamir & Eilam, 2005). This meaning system arises from having a deeper awareness of their emotions, beliefs, values, motives, and behaviors (Leary & Tangney, 2003). As a result, the person is then able to act in accordance with appropriate emotions, beliefs, motives, and values. In this way, according to Taylor (2003), introspection and self-reflection provide "moral salvation" (p. 27) because they help to recover the person's own "authentic moral contact" (p. 27) by pointing "towards a more self-responsible form of life" (p. 74). Furthermore, the literature proposes that it is through reflecting upon their "personal narratives" (Sparrowe, 2005, p. 11) or "life-stories" (Shamir & Eilam, 2005, p. 6) that people are able to come to know their self-concept.

Based on these understandings, Branson's (2007) research used an *inside-out approach* in implementing a deeply structured self-reflective process. By this it is meant that the participants were provided with a comprehensive set of guiding self-inquiry questions that commenced with the innermost core component of their self, their self-concept, and then progressed sequentially outward through their self-esteem, motives, values, beliefs, and, finally, behaviors. The aim of this process was to, first, isolate and examine a key influential personal image held in the participants' self-concept and then to sequentially trace the impact of this image through their self-esteem, motives, values, beliefs, emotions, and behaviors. According to the literature, these key influential personal images are formed during a unique life experience, called a "trigger event" (Gardner, Avolio, Luthans, May, & Walumbwa, 2005, p. 344) or "defining moment" (McGraw, 2001, p. 98), which can occur at any time throughout the life of a person.

The initial self-reflection research (Branson, 2005, 2007) followed the lead presented in the literature whereby the educational leader participants used general trigger events or defining moments from within their personal lives. These were life experiences that were deemed to be highly significant, the detail of which could be readily recalled. However, once the process of deconstructing each of these experiences into insights aligned with the participants' understandings of their own self-concept, self-esteem, motives, values, beliefs, emotions, and behaviors proved achievable and beneficial, subsequent successful application of this process in leadership development courses and workshops has allowed participants to reflect upon, and similarly deconstruct, key experiences in their professional careers. It would seem that any moment that appears to a person to be a vitally important experience, such that it can be easily and richly remembered, provides an opportunity for critical and constructive reflection and thereby offers a vehicle for coming to know one's inner self.

However, a vital understanding about such an image of the self is that it is created from an interpretation of the particular life experience. It is not formed on factual evidence but rather on subjective perceptions and interpretations. Despite this lack of objectivity associated with the created image, the person's physical and emotional response to this very important life experience then becomes a guiding influence for how the person reacts to subsequent situations through a process known as "repetition compulsion" (Frattaroli, 2001, p. 196). Whenever the mind interprets another life experience as having very similar demands and characteristics, people will automatically react as they did when responding to the initial important experience. Hence, the self-concept image, formed during this important life experience, continues to be at the center of the response to new life experiences. Reflecting on the original life experience, and its inherent personal images, emotions, and behaviors helps to clarify current behavioral responses to situations perceived as having similar defining characteristics. In other words, people have gained essential self-knowledge, which enables them to more closely critique their behavior.

Specific to the development of ethical educational leadership, such a deeply structured self-reflective process enables leaders to not only more accurately determine their actual values but also to ensure that they are being influenced by those values that they would wish to influence their behavior. When unacknowledged values are influencing our behavior, these values control our behavior. Under such conditions, while we might desire to be influenced by values that would ensure that we act ethically, if our actual values are not commensurate with our acting ethically, then in the most crucially important times, when circumstances and demands are most challenging and when it is absolutely essential that we act ethically, we will be influenced under such pressure by our actual values and not our desired values such that it is unlikely that we would act ethically.

However, while unacknowledged values control behavior, acknowledged values can lead behavior. Once we are able to come to know our actual values, we can control them. On the one hand, those of our values that we truly wish to influence our behavior can be more strongly supported toward doing so. On the other hand, those of our values that we recognize as not always enabling us to act in the way we would wish to can be closely monitored in order to minimize their effects or be deliberately suppressed if necessary when facing a complex ethical dilemma. It is in this way that we are able to work toward ensuring that the right values are leading our behavior.

## A DEEPLY STRUCTURED SELF-REFLECTION PROCESS

With these general principles in mind, the following deeply structured self-reflection process is offered for guidance toward the gaining of relevant self-knowledge about one's own personal values. The process begins with the person recalling to memory, and in as much detail as is achievable, a personal or professional life experience that has left a lasting impression. While, in most instances, such life experiences are likely to have occurred over a finite time span, on some occasions individuals have reflected on a significant life experience that occurred over a more prolonged period of time. The most critical feature for guiding the choice of a life experience to reflect upon is its perceived high level of significance and not the relative length of transpiration. Furthermore, the level of significance is often directly related to the depth and clarity of recalled details. The more details that can be recalled, the more profound will be the knowledge gained about the self from the reflection process (Table 13.1).

**Table 13.1** Questions to guide a person's deeply structured self-reflection process focusing on a previous personal or professional experience perceived as being character defining

| COMPONENT | GUIDING QUESTIONS |
|---|---|
| Self-concept | • Describe this defining experience. What happened that made this experience so significant?<br>• What impressions/feelings about yourself did you sense at this time? Was this what you expected to happen? Were you proud? Relieved? Excited? What impressions/feelings do you gain about yourself now when you recall this time? Why?<br>• What benefits (physical and/or social and/or affective) did you gain from this time?<br>• Who was there with you? What part did they play in how you felt about this time?<br>• What was your mental/physical experience? Were you able to fully comprehend and enjoy the moment? Were you in control or a little shocked?<br>• What were you saying to yourself?<br>• How would you have felt about yourself if you had not achieved the outcome that you did?<br>• How would you change the way you responded to the situation if you could?<br>• What image or understanding about your self did this achievement instill in your memory? |
| Self-esteem | • What was your previous understanding about your capacity to deal with the demands of this experience prior to this time?<br>• In what ways did this experience change your understanding of yourself?<br>• How did this moment influence your sense of self-worth? What level of self-esteem does it create in you as you now reflect back on it?<br>• Have you ever previously experienced a similar situation but did not achieve the same outcome? If yes, how did this previous occasion make you feel about yourself? How does this previous experience still influence your thinking about yourself? |
| Motives | • From this experience, what are your motives when having to respond to similar situations? What do you try to do to ensure you are able to achieve the best outcome?<br>• How is your thinking about yourself in such similar situations influenced by other motives (e.g., personal/professional reputation, loyalty to family, gaining a better career, responsibility to your community, cultural expectations)?<br>• What were the reasons behind how you chose to respond to this experience? Why were these reasons important to you? |
| Values | • What qualities/characteristics do you value most in your self in the way you responded to this situation? Why is each of these important to you? Do these values always provide you with a sense of success? Do these values sometimes cause you to become annoyed with yourself?<br>• What qualities/characteristics do you value least in your self in the way you responded to this situation? Why do you dislike these values? Do these values put pressure on you? Why? In what ways, if any, are these values ever of any help to you?<br>• What qualities/characteristics would you like to have had in your self that you feel would have helped you to respond even more capably to this situation? Why would these have helped you? |

*(Continued)*

**Table 13.1** (Continued)

| COMPONENT | GUIDING QUESTIONS |
|---|---|
| Beliefs | • What are your personal beliefs about yourself now when you face similar situations?<br>• How would you describe yourself to someone you have just met based upon how you responded to this experience?<br>• What personal/professional strengths enabled you to deal with this experience? In what other ways do these strengths help you?<br>• What, if any, personal/professional weaknesses became apparent to you during this experience? In what other ways do these weaknesses influence your life? |
| Emotions | • What was your emotional reaction to this life experience? What do you think caused you to feel this emotion(s)?<br>• Where else in your life do you experience very similar emotions?<br>• In what ways have any of your desires, hopes, or dreams about yourself been affected by this experience?<br>• In what ways, if any, has this experience left some uncertainty or fear in you about having to cope with other similar situations in future? |
| Behaviors | • When responding to this or similar life experiences, which of your particular behaviors: (a) make you feel very pleased about yourself? (b) make you wish that you could do this differently?<br>• As a result of this important experience in your life, what behaviors/routines/habits: (a) Do you really like to do? (b) Do you avoid doing?<br>• What other, if any, behaviors/routines/habits would you like to develop in order to respond to life experiences like this with even more confidence and capacity? |

Such a deeply structured self-reflection process not only helps the leader to itemize and explicate the many and diverse outcomes that resulted from the particular chosen life experience but also it helps to create an awareness and an appreciation of the holistic nature of how his or her behavior is affected by the interconnectedness of all of the inner components of the self. This is because this deeply structured self-reflection instrument directly reflects the previously presented conceptual framework in Figure 13.1, which was designed to illustrate the understandings provided by the literature of how a person's behavior is influenced by the various components of the self. The extreme left-hand column displays these components in the order of importance established in the literature, commencing with the self-concept and progressing through to the actual behavior. Hence, this instrument provides an essential insight into the coherence and comprehensiveness of unconscious cognitive processes associated with not only the particular life experience under reflection but also of human behaviors in general.

Through the application of this comprehensive, deeply structured self-reflection process to an important personal or professional life experience, a leader is able to comprehend how a particular self-concept image influences the adoption of certain personal motives, values, and beliefs. In so doing, it is far more likely that leaders will come to know their actual values. It must be remembered that people are normally not aware, or only partially aware, of their values (Branson, 2005; Hultman & Gellermann, 2002) because these are often tacit, subliminal, intangible, inner influences on their behavior (Sarros, Densten, & Santora, 1999). Thus, having to name your values is not a simple and straightforward task. This means that not only are people often unaware of many of their values but also when they endeavor to openly clarify their values, there is a strong possibility that they may unintentionally or intentionally state false values (Cashman, 1998; McGraw, 2001). People can lay claim to values that in reality are not the values that are truly impacting their behavior. This tendency for people to make false judgments about their personal values has resulted in the formation of three categories of personal values. Espoused personal values are those that people falsely say they value; desired personal values are those that people would like to have guiding their behavior; and actual personal values are those that are consistently guiding the person's behavior. When given lots of time to think and plan, particularly when what constitutes an appropriate response is more obvious, people can choose to act so as to suggest that their behavior is being influenced by espoused or desired values. However, when a response is called for within a more ambiguous, intense, complex, high-stakes, and immediate context, it is the person's actual values that will come to the fore and influence the person's behavior unless the person is able to intentionally control them. As has been said before, people can control their actual values only if they know their actual values. It is when the conditions are more ambiguous, intense, complex, high stakes, and immediate that it becomes essential for leaders to know their actual values. In order to be ethical, leaders must come to know their actual values.

In addition to coming to know their actual values, this deeply structured self-reflection process enables leaders to reflect more critically on their actual values in order to determine whether or not these are always positive and helpful influences on their leadership behavior. The data generated by the deeply structured self-reflective process provide leaders with the opportunity to nurture their moral consciousness by enabling them to take control of any actual personal values that have previously been tacitly influencing their leadership behavior in ways that were contrary to what they would have wanted. For instance, people might value the quality of assertiveness as one of their innate personal attributes. However, by consciously recognizing this as a personal actual value, they have the capacity to apply it when it helps to achieve an ethical outcome or they can suppress its influence on them when it is likely to achieve a self-interested and/or unethical outcome. In this way, the self-reflective process provides a means for leaders to ensure that they act in a more ethically desirable and acceptable way.

## HARNESSING THE POWER OF PERSONAL VALUES

Where once what it meant to live an ethical life was dictated by external sources such as religious institutions and reinforced through social roles and responsibilities, now being ethical is linked to our understanding of what it means to be truly human. As Starratt (2003, p. 137) attests, "One's morality flows from one's humanity." Furthermore, Starratt argues that there are "three qualities of a fully human person; autonomy, connectedness, and transcendence. These are the foundational human qualities for a moral life; it would be impossible to be moral without developing these qualities." Thus, by nurturing leaders' moral consciousness, the deeply structured process of self-reflection enhances leaders' ethical leadership capacity because it enables leaders to consolidate their achievement of autonomy, connectedness, and transcendence.

First, striving for autonomy as a means of enhancing one's ethical leadership is about developing "self-truth" (Starratt, 2003, p. 137), "self-determining freedom" (Taylor, 2003, p. 27), or "free will" (Frattaroli, 2001, p. 323). As leaders become more conscious of all the factors that are impacting on their ethical judgments, they are less controlled by their self-centered desires and have more possibility of making an autonomous conscious ethical choice. Leaders become free to direct their lives from their self-reflective ethical consciousness. Moreover, the greatest source of influence over the behavior of leaders comes from their own inner self where unconscious values "influence at least 70% of their daily behaviour" (O'Murchu, 1997, p. 138). A leader's will is not free when it is being largely controlled by unconscious influences. This is manipulated will rather than free will. Hence, the development of a leader's autonomy is dependent upon bringing these normally powerful but unconscious instinctual influences into consciousness and, thereby, under direct control.

By means of this structured approach to self-reflection, leaders are more readily able to clearly distinguish the inner influences on their leadership behavior, including their self-concept, self-esteem, motives, values, beliefs, and emotions. They are able to become very definite and specific about the previously unconscious influences upon their chosen response to the particular life experience. Knowledge of the likely antecedent determinants of their leadership behavior enables leaders to have enhanced clarity and greater certainty about their behavior because they have gained self-knowledge about its antecedents. The structured self-reflection process allows leaders to become explicitly conscious of what had previously been unconscious influences on their leadership behavior and, thereby, are more readily able to initiate freely chosen and explicitly desired behavior. On the one hand, if they are sincerely satisfied with the behavioral response to the particular life experience, because it was influenced by appropriate and desirable values, then leaders can initiate a similar response in the future with confidence and certitude. On the other hand, if leaders on reflection become dissatisfied with the behavioral reaction to the particular life experience, because it was influenced by inappropriate or undesirable values, then they can consider alternative better ways to respond to similar experiences in the future. It is in this way that such leaders are acting autonomously, and thus more ethically, because they are becoming the authors of their own self-truths, the creator of their own true selves, because they are freely and deliberately choosing how they wish to respond to particular life experiences rather than being unconsciously reactive based upon preexisting unacknowledged inner influences.

Secondly, the pivotal role of connectedness in ethical consciousness, claims Harris (2002, p. 215), can be clearly seen by examining the roots of the word "consciousness." Here, it is found that "consciousness" comes from the Latin *con*, which means "with," and *scio*, which means "to know." Consciousness is "knowing with," and this makes it a relational activity. Consciousness requires an "I" and a "we"—two distinct entities capable of forming a relationship. Developing an ethical consciousness is not only about coming to know ourselves, but it is also about knowing how to relate to others in a more mutually beneficial and rewarding way. A person's ethicalness crucially depends on dialogical relations with others (Taylor, 2003). In particular, developing an ethical consciousness is about realizing that we all create self-fulfilling prophecies in our interactions with others. "We expect people to behave according to our projective expectations and without intending it we elicit in them reactions that confirm those expectations" (Frattaroli, 2001, p. 231). Hence, an important aspect of nurturing an ethical consciousness is about recognizing personal, unconscious, self-imposed relationship inhibitors. Once these are made conscious, they can be removed in order to expand the range of people with whom we can empathize and whom we can recognize as part of our ethical responsibility.

This structured self-reflection process generates this outcome because it asks leaders to go on a journey of self-discovery to uncover their inner self but also to become more aware of how some of their inner values might be enhancing or restricting aspects of their interpersonal relationships. By knowing and understanding their inner self, leaders can become more discerning about their leadership behaviors, particularly in regard to how the inappropriate application of some of their values could be hampering their leadership behaviors by diminishing the quality of their interpersonal relationships with some members of their school community.

Finally, the concept of transcendence within the context of ethical leadership encapsulates the essential commitment to be continually striving to be a better person. To this end, Wilber (2000b, p. 264) proposes that "increasing interiorization = increasing autonomy = decreasing narcissism." In other words, the more self-knowledge leaders have of their inner self, the more detached from that self they become. The more detached from the self they become, the more they can rise above that self's limited perspective. And the more they can rise above the self's limited perspective, the less self-centered leaders become. The more clearly and faithfully leaders can subjectively reflect on their selves, the more they can transcend their innate personal desires in order to consider what is in the best interests of others. This is supported by Taylor's concept of "horizons of importance" (2003, p. 39), where he suggests:

> The ideal of self-choice supposes that there are other issues of significance beyond self-choice. The ideal couldn't stand alone, because it requires a horizon of importance, which helps define the respects in which self-making is significant. Unless some options are more significant than others, the very idea of self-choice falls into triviality and hence incoherence. Self-choice as an ideal makes sense only because some issues are more significant than others.

As long as most of the inner influences on our behavior remain within our unconscious, there is little choice in how we respond to ethical dilemmas. However, by making these inner influences part of our consciousness, then we do have self-choice in regard to whether or not they are appropriate. As unconscious influences, our inner influences automatically seek largely self-interests. On the other hand, as conscious influences, our inner influences can be controlled and directed toward seeking horizons of greater importance where consideration is given to what is ultimately in the best interest of all. In this way, such transcended behavior achieves ethical outcomes. When applied to leadership, this understanding necessitates that ethical leaders become conscious of how their personal values can be harnessed and, thereby, redirected toward achieving better, more transcendental and ethical consequences.

## CONCLUSION

It is in these ways that the structured self-reflection process illustrates both the power and potential of personal values. Moreover, it highlights how important it is for a leader to become conscious of their personal values if they wish to nurture their ethical consciousness. This process of structured self-reflection enables the leader to clarify their thinking about their leadership practices, to raise their self-awareness of the power of their personal values, to get in touch with their inner world, and to develop more mutually beneficial professional relationships in their school community. In this way, this self-reflective process is able to enhance each leader's autonomy, connectedness, and transcendence thereby increasing their ethical leadership capacity.

Moreover, this suggests that if the attainment of ethical leadership practice is desirable, then there is a need for the professional development of leaders to move beyond a dominant focus on professional behavior and to challenge leaders to overcome their natural shortcomings in the development of their ethical consciousness by engaging in deeply structured self-reflection. As claimed by Lord and Hall (2005, p. 592):

> An adequate model of leadership skill development needs to go beyond traditional discussions of training or self-directed learning, which tends to focus on the acquisition of . . . surface structure skills. Such surface approaches minimize consideration of the deeper, principled aspects of leadership that may be especially important for understanding the long-term development of effective leaders.

This chapter supports the view that leaders need help and guidance in the essential area of making explicit their inner self so that they can more fully critique the antecedents of their behavior in order to build their ethical leadership capacity. This view promotes the importance in the professional development of leaders for focusing on reviewing the formation of their inner self as established during character forming personal and professional experiences. Such professional development should challenge leaders to achieve a greater congruence amongst their inner self, the ethical standards that they would aspire to, and their leadership behavior. A commitment to deeply structured self-reflection, as illustrated in this chapter, can offer a very important contribution to the professional development of ethical leaders.

It must be noted, however, that research (Branson, 2005, 2007) in the beneficial use of structured self-reflection found that the full engagement with the process requires a "tranquility of mind" in order to benefit from this process. Not only do leaders need to be at peace in their minds with respect to the impact of their self-reflection on their understanding of their selves from their chosen life experiences, but also they need to have some high degree of confidence in themselves in their current performance as educational leaders. They not only need to be able to mentally and emotionally escape from any immediate school-related demands but also they need to be able to accept that while they might be doing a good job as educational leaders, they can still improve.

A final insight gained by the research into the effects of structured self-reflection is that this approach takes a considerable amount of time and a great deal of commitment and courage. To ensure the proper continuity is maintained as the procedure moves through the sequential inner components of the self, sufficient time must be assigned for appropriate discernment at each component. The quality of the discerned data at each subsequent component is dependent upon the quality of the previously discerned data. Also, only one key life experience can be reviewed through this process at a time. While all of the data gathered from this single experience will provide powerful insights, a more holistic and balanced perspective can only be gained from completing the procedure with a number of different experiences. To do this not only takes commitment but also courage. To do so, leaders require commitment, as they need to repeat the whole procedure a number of times and carefully consider each element of the procedure throughout this demanding time. In addition, leaders need to have courage because the procedure requires that they look at defining moments in their personal and professional experiences not only accurately but also with complete openness and honesty.

If leaders are able to find the time, commitment, and courage to learn from the insights and knowledge that can be gained only through structured self-reflection, then, and only then, will they be able to fully comprehend and appreciate the power of their personal values. Only then will they be provided with a specific means for personally achieving not only more fully human lives but also an ethically accountable form of leadership. Structured self-reflection is the pathway to authentic ethical leadership.

## REFERENCES

Bandura, A. (1986). *Social foundations of thought and action: A social cognitive theory.* Englewood Cliffs, NJ: Prentice-Hall.

Branson, C. M. (2005). Exploring the concept of values-led principalship. *Leading and Managing, 11*(1), 14–31.

Branson, C. M. (2007). The effects of structured self-reflection on the development of authentic leadership practices among Queensland primary school principals. *Educational Management Administration and Leadership Journal, 35*(2), 227–248.

Branson, C. M. (2009). *Leadership for an age of wisdom.* Dordrecht, Netherlands: Springer Educational.

Branson, C.M. (2010). *Leading educational change wisely.* Rotterdam, Netherlands: Sense Publishers.

Burns, J. M. (1978). *Leadership.* New York: HarperCollins.

Burns, J. M. (2010). *Leadership.* New York: HarperCollins.

Cashman, K. (1998). *Leadership from the inside out: Becoming a leader for life.* Provo, UT: Executive Excellence.

de Bono, E. (2009). *Think: Before it's too late.* London: Vermilion.

Elliott, A. (2001). *Concepts of the self.* Malden, MA: Blackwell.

Frattaroli, E. (2001). *Healing the soul in the age of the brain: Becoming conscious in an unconscious world.* New York: Penguin Books.

Gardner, W. L., Avolio, B. J., Luthans, F., May, D. R., & Walumbwa, F. (2005). "Can you see the real me?" A self-based model of authentic leader and follower development. *Leadership Quarterly, 16*(3), 343–372.

Griseri, P. (1998). *Managing values: Ethical change in organisations.* Hampshire, UK: Macmillan Press.

Hall, C. S., Lindzey, G., & Campbell, J. B. (1998). *Theories of personality.* New York: John Wiley.

Harris, B. (2002). *Sacred selfishness: A guide to living a life of substance.* Makawao, HI: Inner Ocean Publishing.

Hodgkinson, C. (1996). *Administrative philosophy: Values and motivations in administrative life.* Trowbridge, UK: Redwood Books.

Hodgkinson, C. (2003). Conclusion: Tomorrow, and tomorrow, and tomorrow: A postmodern purview. In P. T. Begley & O. Johansson (Eds.), *The ethical dimensions of school leadership* (pp. 221–231). Dordrecht, Netherlands: Kluwer Academic Publishers.

Hultman, K., & Gellermann, B. (2002). *Balancing individual and organizational values: Walking the tightrope to success.* San Francisco: Jossey-Bass.

Langlois, L. (2004). Responding ethically: Complex decision-making by school superintendents. *International Studies in Educational Administration Journal, 32*(2), 78–93.

Leary, M. R., & Tangney, J. P. (2003). *Handbook of self and identity.* New York: Guilford Press.

Lord, R. G., & Hall, R. J. (2005). Identity, deep structure and the development of leadership skill. *Leadership Quarterly, 16*(4), 591–615.

Mackay, H. (2004). *Right and wrong: How to decide for yourself.* Sydney: Hodder Headline.

McGraw, P. (2001). *Self matters: Creating your life from the inside out.* New York: Simon and Schuster.

O'Murchu, D. (1997). *Quantum theology: Spiritual implications of the new physics.* New York: Crossroad Publishing.

Osborne, R. E. (1996). *Self: An eclectic approach.* Needham Heights, MA: Simon and Schuster.

Richmon, M. J. (2003). Persistent difficulties with values in educational administration: Mapping the terrain. In P. T. Begley & O. Johansson (Eds.), *The ethical dimensions of school leadership* (pp. 33–47). Dordrecht, Netherlands: Kluwer Academic Publishers.

Sarros, J. C., Densten, I. L., & Santora, J. C. (1999). *Leadership and values: Australian executives and the balance of power, profits, and people.* Sydney, NSW: Harper Collins.

Shamir, B., & Eilam, G. (2005). "What's your story?" A life-stories approach to authentic leadership development. *Leadership Quarterly, 16*(3), 395–417.

Sparrowe, R. T. (2005). Authentic leadership and the narrative self. *Leadership Quarterly, 16*(3), 419–439.

Starratt, R. J. (2003). *Centering educational administration: Cultivating meaning, community, responsibility.* Mahwah, NJ: Lawrence Erlbaum.

Starratt, R. J. (2004). *Ethical leadership.* San Francisco: Jossey-Bass.

Taylor, C. (2003). *The ethics of authenticity.* Cambridge, MA: Harvard University Press.

Trilling, L. (1972). *Sincerity and authenticity.* Cambridge, MA: Jossey-Bass Publishers.

van Knippenberg, B., van Knippenberg, D., De Cremer, D., & Hogg, M. A. (2005). Research in leadership, self, and identity: A sample of the present and a glimpse of the future. *Leadership Quarterly, 16*(4), 495–499.

Weisinger, H. (2009). *The genius of instinct: Reclaim mother nature's tools for enhancing your health, happiness, family, and work.* Upper Saddle River, NJ: Pearson Education.

Westwood, R. I., & Posner, B. Z. (1997). Managerial values across cultures: Australia, Hong Kong and the United States. *Asia Pacific Journal of Management, 14*(1), 31–66.

Wilber, K. (2000a). *A brief history of everything.* Boston: Shambhala.

Wilber, K. (2000b). *Sex, ecology, spirituality* (2nd ed.). Boston: Shambhala.

# 14

## ETHICAL DECISION MAKING

JOAN POLINER SHAPIRO, JACQUELINE A. STEFKOVICH, AND
KATHRINE J. GUTIERREZ

## DEVELOPING THE MODEL[1]

In the early 1990s, after reviewing a number of books that focused on ethical decision making for educational leaders, Shapiro and Stefkovich noted both omissions
and limitations. They felt the books, at that time, were focused on nonconsequential
ethics having to do primarily with the ethic of justice. Laws, rules, and rights were
placed at the center of the decision-making process. Instead, Shapiro and Stefkovich wanted something more nuanced and more comprehensive to assist educational
leaders in making ethical decisions.

They turned to the work of R. J. (Jerry) Starratt for guidance. Starratt's (1994a)
book *Building an Ethical School* looked beyond the ethic of justice. He wrote about
the need for the ethic of critique and care as well. This book served as a springboard
for the development of the multiple ethical paradigms (MEPs). While Starratt spoke
of the ethics of critique and care, there was a need to delve in more detail into these
paradigms. Stefkovich and Shapiro also felt that there seemed to be a grave omission.
As they presented and reflected, over a few years, the concepts underpinning the
ethic of the profession took shape.

In this chapter, MEPs will be introduced. This model for ethical decision making
includes the ethics of justice, critique, care, and the profession. Additionally, an ethical dilemma, taking place in the island of Guam, will be presented. Following the
dilemma, questions will be raised to help resolve or solve the ethical dilemma.

To understand MEPs, it is important to define ethics itself. This concept has had
numerous meanings over time. Initially, it came from the Greek word *ethos*, which
meant customs or usages, especially belonging to one group as distinguished from
another. Later, ethics came to mean disposition or character, customs, and approved
ways of acting. Dewey (1902), for example, defined ethics as the science that dealt
with conduct insofar as this is considered as right or wrong, good or bad. Although

Dewey's characterization of ethics as a science might be disputed, his focus on behavior cannot be in doubt. Reflecting upon these definitions, using a critical lens, one might ask: Good or bad by whose standards? Right or wrong according to whom? Or even, approved ways of acting by whom?

In an attempt to answer these and other important questions, the ethics of justice, critique, care, and the profession will be described. As will be shown, these ethics emanate from diverse traditions, emerge from different starting points, and may even clash with each other. In this depiction, we have been careful to keep in mind how MEPs have an impact on school administrators, teacher leaders, and higher educational administrators' decision-making processes in the contemporary world.

## THE ETHIC OF JUSTICE

The ethic of justice deals with laws, rights, and policies and is part of a liberal democratic tradition that, according to Delgado (1995), "is characterized by incrementalism, faith in the legal system, and hope for progress" (p. 1). The liberal part of this tradition is defined as a "commitment to human freedom," and the democratic aspect implies "procedures for making decisions that respect the equal sovereignty of the people" (Strike, 1991, p. 415). Present-day philosophers and writers, coming from a justice perspective, frequently have dealt with issues such as rights and impartiality that are very much a part of distributive justice. In fact, Rawls (1971) defined justice as fairness.

Educators and ethicists from the ethic of justice have profoundly affected approaches associated with education and educational leadership. Modern-day ethical writings in education using the foundational principle of the ethic of justice include, among others, works by Beauchamp and Childress (1984); Goodlad, Soder, and Sirotnik (1990); Kohlberg (1981); Sergiovanni (2009); Strike (2006); and Strike, Haller, and Soltis (2005).

The ethic of justice, from a contemporary perspective, takes into account a wide variety of issues. Viewing ethical dilemmas from this vantage point, one may raise queries regarding the interpretation of the rule of law as well as deal with the more abstract concepts of fairness, liberty, and responsibility. These may include, but are certainly not limited to, questions related to equality versus equity, moral absolutism versus situational ethics, and the rights of individuals versus the greater good of the community.

Moreover, the ethic of justice frequently has served as the framework for legal principles and ideals, particularly as they affect education. In many instances, courts in the United States have been reluctant to impose restrictions on school officials, thus allowing them considerable discretion in making important administrative decisions (*Board of Education v. Pico*, 1981). At the same time, these court opinions have frequently reflected the values of the education community and society at large (Stefkovich & Guba, 1998). Accordingly, what is legal in some places might be considered illegal in others. For example, as of this writing, corporal punishment is still legal in 19 US states (Center for Effective Discipline, 2012). Strip-searching is illegal in only 7 US states (Stefkovich, 2012). In those states where such practices have not been deemed illegal, it is left up to school officials and the community whether they are to be supported or not. Here, ethical issues such as due process and privacy rights are often balanced against the need for civility and the good of the majority.

Examples of law and its relationship to the justice paradigm are even more dramatic when viewed from an international perspective. Frequently, the United States stands alone (or nearly alone) in its approach to a variety of human rights issues related to school-age youth. For example, the United States, Somalia, and South Sudan are the only countries in the world that have yet to sign the United Nations Convention on the Rights of the Child (OHCHR, 1989). Somalia is planning to sign and South Sudan only became its own country in 2011. The US is alone in expressing concerns that ratifying this document would interfere with the country's states' rights to discipline children, mostly because the Convention document was viewed as abolishing corporal punishment in schools (Stefkovich, 2012).

Broadly framed, then, the ethic of justice takes into account questions such as: Is there a law, right, or policy that relates to a particular case? If there is a law, right, or policy, should it be enforced? Is the law enforced in some places and not in others? Why or why not? And if there is not a law, right, or policy, should there be one?

## THE ETHIC OF CRITIQUE

Often the ethic of critique opposes, or highlights, problems inherent in the ethic of justice. Many writers and activists (e.g., Apple, 2003; Bakhtin, 1981; Bowles & Gintis, 1988; Foucault, 1983; Freire, 1970; Giroux, 2006; Greene, 1988; Gross & Shapiro, 2002; Larson & Murtadha, 2002; Purpel, 2004; Purpel & Shapiro, 1995; Rapp, 2002; Reitzug & O'Hair, 2002; H. Shapiro, 2006, 2009; Shapiro & Purpel, 2005; J. Shapiro, 2006) are not convinced by the analytic and rational approach of the justice paradigm. Some of these scholars find a tension between the ethic of justice, rights, and laws and concepts such as democracy and social justice. In response, they raise difficult questions by critiquing both the laws, rights, and policies themselves and the process used to determine whether the laws, rights, and policies are just. They also ask questions related to circumstances when a ruling can be wrong, such as in the case of earlier Jim Crow laws supporting racial segregation (Starratt, 1994b).

Instead of accepting the decisions and values of those in authority, these scholars and activists challenge the status quo by applying an ethic that deals with inconsistencies, formulates the hard questions, and debates and challenges the issues. Their intent is to awaken us to our own unstated values and make us realize how frequently our own morals may have been modified and possibly even corrupted over time. Not only do they force us to rethink important concepts such as democracy and social justice, they also ask us to redefine and reframe other concepts such as privilege, power, culture, language, and even justice itself. While deconstructing the accepted concepts, they also provide us with a language of empowerment, transformation, and possibilities.

The ethic of critique is based on critical theory, which has at its center an analysis of social class and its inequities. According to Foster (1986), critical theorists are scholars who have approached social analysis in an investigative and critical manner and who have conducted investigations of social structure from perspectives originating in a modified Marxian analysis (p. 71). More recently, critical theorists have turned to the intersection of race and gender, as well as social class, in their analyses. A modern example of the work of critical theorists can be found in their argument that schools reproduce inequities similar to those in society (e.g., Bourdieu, 1977, 2001; Lareau, 2003).

Along with critical theory, the ethic of critique is also frequently linked to critical pedagogy (Freire, 1970). Giroux (2006) asked educators to understand that their classrooms are political sites as well as educational locations, and as such, ethics is not a matter of individual choice or relativism, but it should also provide forums to discuss issues of poverty and human suffering. In this vein, critical theorists are often concerned with hearing the voices of those who are silenced, particularly students (Giroux, 2003; Weis & Fine, 1993).

To Giroux (2003, 2006), Welch (1991), and other educators who work within this tradition, the language of critique is central. Many of these scholars, however, feel that discourse alone will not suffice; they are frequently activists who believe discourse should be a beginning leading to some type of action, preferably political. For example, Shapiro and Purpel (2005) emphasized empowering people through the discussion of options. Such a dialogue, hopefully, would provide what Giroux and Aronowitz (1985) called a "language of possibility" that when applied to educational institutions, might enable them to avoid reproducing the "isms" in society (i.e., classism, racism, sexism, and heterosexism).

Turning to educational leadership in particular, Parker and Shapiro (1993) argued that one way to rectify some wrongs in school and in society would be to place more attention upon the analysis of social class in the preparation of principals and superintendents. They believed that social class analysis "is crucial given the growing divisions of wealth and power in the United States, and their impact on inequitable distribution of resources both within and among school districts" (pp. 39–40). Through the critical analysis of social class, there is the possibility that more knowledgeable, moral, and sensitive educational leaders might be prepared.

Beyond the US, Apple (2010) deals well with inequality in education in an edited book, *Global Crisis, Social Justice, and Education*. This book discusses inequities at an international level with chapters exploring social, educational, and economic movements in Japan, Israel/Palestine, and Mexico/Latin America, all of which are globally interconnected. Apple's emphasis is on opposing movements in Japan that inhibit egalitarian approaches to education, supporting efforts that foster democratic education in Israel and Palestine, and advocating for community-based education projects in Latin America. As with his earlier works, but even more explicitly (Apple, 2003), Apple equates the critical scholar's role with that of an activist in education. He challenges all of us to self-reflection as we ask difficult questions and make hard decisions.

The ethic of critique, then, asks educators to examine and grapple with those possibilities that could enable all children, whatever their backgrounds, to have opportunities to grow, learn, and achieve. Such a process should lead to the development of options related to important concepts such as oppression, power, privilege, authority, language, voice, and empowerment. This ethic, inherent in critical theory and critical pedagogy, is aimed at awakening all of us to inequities in society and, in particular, to injustices within education at all levels. It asks us to deal with the difficult questions regarding social class, race, gender, and other areas of difference, such as: Who makes the laws, rules, and policies? Who benefits from them? Who has the power? Who are silenced? Once such difficult questions are answered, this ethic then considers: What could make a difference to enable those who have been silenced, ignored, and oppressed to become empowered? What new possibilities could be presented to lead toward social justice and the making of a better society?

## THE ETHIC OF CARE

The ethic of care is often juxtaposed with the ethic of justice in the Western contemporary world. For example, Strike (1999) created a distinction between the two ethics by saying:

> Justice aims at a society and at personal relationships in which people are treated fairly, where they get what they are due, in which they are respected as equals, and where mutually agreeable conditions of cooperation are respected. Caring aims at a society and at personal relationships in which nurturance and relationships are highly valued.
>
> (p. 21)

Roland Martin (1993) continued with the dissimilarity between the ethic of justice and that of care. She created a sharp difference between the male productive and the female reproductive processes and how they are valued in society.

Some feminist scholars (e.g., Beck, 1994; Belenky, Clinchy, Goldberger, & Tarule, 1986; Gilligan, 1982; Gilligan, Ward, & Taylor, 1988; Ginsberg, Shapiro, & Brown, 2004; Grogan, 1996; Marshall & Gerstl-Pepin, 2005; Marshall & Oliva, 2006; Marshall, Patterson, Rogers, & Steele, 1996; Noddings, 1992, 1999, 2003; Sernak, 1998; Shapiro, Ginsberg, & Brown, 2003; Shapiro & Smith-Rosenberg, 1989) have challenged the dominant—and what they consider to be often patriarchal—ethic of justice and have made the ethic of care more central to moral decision making and to society in general. They have paid special attention to concepts such as loyalty, trust, and empowerment. Similar to critical theorists, these feminist scholars have emphasized social justice as a pivotal concept associated with the ethic of care.

Gilligan (1982), in her classic book *In a Different Voice*, introduced the ethic of care in the resolutions of moral dilemmas. In her research as a former graduate student of Kohlberg's, she used initially the same types of moral dilemmas as he did in his work. However, Gilligan discovered that unlike Kohlberg's male interviewees, who adopted rights and laws for the solution of moral issues, women and girls frequently turned to another voice of care, concern, and connection in finding answers to ethical cases.

Not content to simply hear the other voice at a private level, Noddings (1992) moved the ethic of care into the public forum, as it relates to education, by creating an educational hierarchy placing "care" at the top. She wrote, "The first job of the schools is to care for our children" (p. xiv).

Although the ethic of care, most recently, has been associated with feminists, men and women alike attest to its importance and relevancy. Beck (1994) made this point when she wrote, "Caring—as a foundational ethic—addresses concerns and needs as expressed by many persons; that it, in a sense, transcends ideological boundaries" (p. 3). Male ethicists and educators, including Buber (1965) and Sergiovanni (1992), have helped to develop this paradigm. These scholars have sought to make education a "human enterprise" (Starratt, 1991, p. 195).

In fact, within the philosophy of utilitarianism, Bentham, Mills, and Hume spoke of an ethic of care that was part of the public sphere (Blackburn, personal communication, 2006). The concept of the greatest happiness of the greatest number, according to Blackburn (2001, p. 93), moved care into the civic realm.

The ethic of care is important not only to scholars in the past and in the present, but also to educational leaders, who are often asked to make moral decisions. Beck (1994) stressed that it is essential for educational leaders to move away from a top-down, hierarchical model for making moral and other decisions and instead turn to a leadership style that emphasizes relationships and connections.

When an ethic of care is valued, educational leaders can become what Barth (1990) has called "head learner(s)" (p. 513). What Barth meant by this term is the development of outstanding leaders who listen to others when preparing to make important moral decisions. For example, Shapiro, Sewell, DuCette, and Myrick (1997), in their study of inner-city youth, listened and identified three different types of caring: attention and support, discipline, and "staying on them," or prodding them over time.

Another aspect of this paradigm is that it tends to sometimes deal with emotions. Highlighting this complexity, Begley (2010) has queried whether the ethic of care is a completely rational model or if emotion is part of this ethic (p. 42). Hence, portions of this model coincide well with the emerging brain research regarding decision making, in general, in which emotions and reason are blended in intricate ways (Lehrer, 2009).

Thus, the ethic of care directs individuals to consider the consequences of their decisions and actions. It asks them to raise questions, such as: Who will benefit from what I decide? Who will be hurt by my actions? What are the long-term effects of a decision I make today? And if someone helps me now, what should I do in the future about giving back to this individual or to society in general?

## THE ETHIC OF THE PROFESSION

Shapiro and Stefkovich (2011) gave considerable attention to the ethic of the profession in their work on MEPs. They felt that there was a need to bring this ethic to the attention of educational leaders. They were aware that other fields had ethical requirements for their professions (e.g., law, medicine, dentistry, business) and believed that educational leadership needed ethics to play a central role both for the legitimacy of the profession and, in particular, for the students in this field.

Stefkovich and Shapiro were not alone in their interest in the ethic of the profession for educational leaders. A number of writers (e.g., Beck, 1994; Beck, Murphy, & Associates, 1997; Beckner, 2004; Begley & Johansson, 2003; Bon & Bigbee, 2011;

Branson, 2009, 2010; Burford, 2004; Dantley, 2005; Frick, 2009; Goldring & Green-field, 2002; Greenfield, 2004; Murphy, 2005; Normore, 2004; Starratt, 1994a, 1994b, 2004; Strike, Haller, & Soltis, 2005; Zaretsky, 2005) advocated for prospective school leaders to have some preparation in ethics, and especially in ethical decision making. This call also applies to teacher leadership (Campbell, 2004; Hansen, 2001; Strike & Ternasky, 1993).

Turning to the preparation of educational leaders in the US, in the mid-1990s, the Interstate School Leaders Licensure Consortium (ISLLC), along with the National Policy Board for Educational Administration (NPBEA, 1996), identified ethics as one of the competencies necessary for school leaders. This consortium, working under the auspices of the Council of Chief State School Officers and in collabora-tion with the NPBEA, consisted of representatives from 24 states and 9 associations related to the educational administration profession.

In *Educational Leadership Policy Standards: ISLLC 2008* (NPBEA, 2008), school leaders again set forth six standards for the profession. Of these, Standard 5 remained: "An education leader promotes the success of every student by acting with integrity, fairness, and in an ethical manner" (pp. 4–5). Standard 5, with its functions, officially continues to recognize the importance of ethics in the knowledge base for school administrators. Along with the six standards, many states now require principals to pass an exam measuring related competencies, including ethics, and the standards are now incorporated into the National Council for the Accreditation of Teacher Education (NCATE) (Murphy, 2005).

In the past, professional ethics has generally been viewed as a subset of the justice paradigm. This is likely the case because professional ethics is often equated with codes, rules, and policies, all of which fit neatly into traditional concepts of justice (Beauchamp & Childress, 1984). A number of states and most education-related pro-fessional organizations have developed their own professional ethical codes. Defined by Beauchamp and Childress as "an articulated statement of role morality as seen by members of the profession" (p. 41), some of these ethical codes are longstanding, while some are considerably more current. One of the more recent and unique codes is the *UCEA Code of Ethics for the Preparation of Educational Leaders,* developed by the University Council of Educational Administration (2011). This organization's hope was to create a code that was meaningful by combining the voices, perspectives, and values of many of those within the field of educational leadership over a 6-year period. The intention is that this will be a living code and that it will be discussed and modified very often.

Despite the attempts to make the codes and standards more significant, generally there is a paradox regarding ethical codes set forth by the states and professional associations. On the one hand, they have tended to be limited in their responsiveness in that they are somewhat removed from the day-to-day personal and professional dilemmas educational leaders face. Nash (1996), in his book on professional eth-ics for educators and human service personnel, recognized these limitations as he observed his students' lack of interest in such codes.

On the other hand, it should not be forgotten that professional codes of ethics serve as guideposts and aspirations for a field, offering statements about its appearance and character (Lebacqz, 1985). They personify "the highest moral ideals of the profession," thus "presenting an ideal image of the moral character of both the profession and the professional" (Nash, 1996, p. 96). Seen in this light, standardized codes can provide a most valuable function. Thus, it is possible that the problem may not lie as much in the codes themselves, but in the fact that sometimes too much is expected from them with regard to moral decision making (Lebacqz, 1985; Nash, 1996).

Despite a positive approach to standardized codes, Nash (1996) and Shapiro and Stefkovich (2001, 2005, 2011) did observe a lack of connection between their students' own personal and professional codes and those set forth by states or professional groups. The majority of their students found it more valuable to create their own codes. Over time, Stefkovich and Shapiro discovered that aspiring educational leaders should be given the opportunity to create their own personal codes of ethics based on life stories and critical incidences as well as their own professional codes based on their work experiences and expectations.

Actions by school administrators are likely to be strongly influenced by personal values (Aiken & Gerstl-Pepin, 2005; Begley, 2010; Begley & Zaretsky, 2004; Friedman, 2003; Willower & Licata, 1997). Personal codes of ethics build on these values and experiences (Shapiro & Stefkovich, 1997, 1998; Stefkovich & Shapiro, 1994). It is not always easy, however, to separate professional from personal ethical codes. Other factors that should play roles in the development of individual professional codes include considerations not only of personal codes but also of formal codes of ethics established by professional associations and written standards of the profession (e.g., ISLLC). In addition, an awareness and understanding of community standards, including both the professional community and the community in which the leader works, require attention and recognition.

The development of professional ethics is far from a clear process and often presents pitfalls. In fact, Shapiro and Stefkovich (1998, 2011) identified four clashes that could affect the creation of one's own professional ethical codes. First, there may be clashes between an individual's personal and professional codes of ethics. Second, there may be clashes within the professional code itself. This may occur when an individual's personal ethical code conflicts with an ethical code set forth by the profession or when the individual has been prepared in two or more professions. Third, there may be clashes of professional codes among educational leaders; what one administrator sees as ethical, another may not. Fourth, there may be clashes between a leader's personal and professional code of ethics and customs and practices set forth by the community (i.e., either the professional community, the school community, or the community in which the educational leader works). For example, behavior that may be considered unethical in one community might, in even a neighboring community, merely be seen as a matter of personal preference.

Furman (2003, 2004; Furman-Brown, 2002), expanding on what she characterized as a separate ethic of the community, challenged educational leaders to move away from heroic (solo) managerial decisions and turn toward community involvement in the decision-making process. Her definition of community appeared to be a comprehensive and participatory process and seemed to dovetail well with a distributive model in which the work and the decisions expected of the educational leader are shared with appropriate others (Gronn, 2001; Katzenmyer & Moller, 2001; Kochan & Reed, 2005; Spillane & Orina, 2005).

To deal with the four clashes previously discussed, and professional ethics in general, it is important to ground the decision-making process in something meaningful. Greenfield (1993) contended that schools, particularly public schools, should be the central sites for "preparing children to assume the roles and responsibilities of citizenship in a democratic society" (p. 268). Gross and Shapiro (2008) also spoke of the importance of fostering the development of young people, moving them forward to become critical and moral citizens.

Not all those who write about the importance of the study of ethics in educational leadership discuss the needs of children; nonetheless, this focus on students is clearly consistent with the backbone of the profession. Other professions often have one basic principle driving it. In medicine, it is "First, do no harm." In law, it is the assertion that all clients deserve "zealous representation." In education, Shapiro and Stefkovich (2011) believe that if there is a moral imperative for the profession, it is to serve the best interests of the student. Consequently, they believe that this ideal must lie at the heart of any professional paradigm for educational leaders from pre-K–16 and beyond.

This focus on the best interests of the student is reflected in most educational professional association codes. For example, the American Association of School Administrators' (2007) *Statement of Ethics for School Administrators* begins with an assertion focusing on the well-being of students. Serving the best interests of the student is also consistent with the ISLLC's standards for the profession (NPBEA, 2008.). This emphasis on a student's best interests is also in concert with Noddings' (2003) ethic of care that places students at the top of the educational hierarchy, as reflective of the concerns of many critical theorists who believe that students' voices and concerns are too often silenced (Giroux, 2003; Mitra, 2004, 2008; Mitra & Gross, 2009; Weis & Fine, 1993).

But the concept of addressing student voice is not simple. In this era, moral dilemmas become very complex as cases increasingly involve a variety of student populations as well as parents and communities comprising diversity in broad terms that extend well beyond categories of race and ethnicity. In this respect, differences—encompassing cultural categories of race and ethnicity, religion, social class, gender, disability, and sexual orientation, as well as individual differences that may take into account learning styles, exceptionalities, and age—often cannot be ignored (Banks & Banks, 2006; Davis, 2000, 2001; Shapiro, Sewell, & DuCette, 2002; Shapiro, 1999; Sleeter & Grant, 2003; Tooms & Alston, 2005).

The literature does not define "best interests of the student" (Stefkovich, O'Brien, & Moore, 2002). In the absence of such clarification, school leaders have often referred to a student's best interests to justify adults' interests (Walker, 1998). Attempts have been made, however, to fill this gap (Stefkovich, 2014; Stefkovich & O'Brien, 2004; Walker, 1995, 1998). Stefkovich (2014) conceptualizes decisions related to a student's best interests as those incorporating individual rights, teaching students to accept responsibility for their actions, and respecting students. These three Rs—rights, responsibility, and respect—are key, according to Stefkovich, to making ethical decisions that are in a student's best interests and, in turn, to fulfilling one's professional obligations as an educational leader.

In this chapter, a paradigm for the profession has been described that expects educational leaders to formulate and examine their own professional codes of ethics in light of individual personal codes of ethics, as well as standards set forth by the profession, and then calls on them to place students at the center of the ethical decision-making process. It also asks them to take into account the wishes of the community. The ethic of the profession, then, goes beyond the ethics of justice, critique, and care to inquire: What would the profession ask me to do?

## AN ETHICAL DILEMMA

What follows is an ethical dilemma, written by Kathrine Gutierrez, which posits a hypothetical case scenario that takes place on the island of Guam, considering the realities of the makeup of multiple ethnicities that are reflective of the island residents. The case focuses on the dominant religion on Guam, Catholicism, as the context for the case scenario. The scenario is an adapted version of the work cited by Shapiro and Stefkovich (2011, pp. 105–108). The dilemma highlights diverse issues surrounding both conflict and consideration of an administrator's decision to grant time off for faculty to attend religious services and the effect on students being placed into a "break period," as opposed to students engaging in instructional activities during a regular class period. Following the dilemma, there are questions to assist the reader in working through the decision-making process using multiple ethical paradigms.

### Time off for Religious Services[2]

Guam, a US territory, is a small island community with a population of about 165,000 (Guam Economic Development Authority, 2014b). The population comprises a melting pot of ethnicities: Chamorros (the indigenous people of the island), Japanese, Koreans, Filipinos, Vietnamese, Chinese, Palauans, Micronesians (people from the Federated States of Micronesia: Chuuk, Yap, Pohnpei, Kosrae), white Americans (non-Hispanic), African Americans, Indians, and others. Specifically, the ethnic percentages represented on the island, according to a census, were: "Chamorro 37.1%, Filipino 26.3%, other Pacific islander 11.3%, white 6.9%, other Asian 6.3%, other ethnic origin or race 2.3%, mixed 9.8% (2000 census)" (Central Intelligence Agency, 2014a). The cultural diversity on the island of Guam is typified by the existence of the various ethnic groups who compose the residents of the island. The nationality of individuals born on Guam is classified as Guamanian (Central Intelligence Agency, 2014b). "Guam's culture has also been influenced and enriched over the last 50 years by the American, Filipino, Japanese, Korean, Chinese, and Micronesian immigrants who have each added their unique cultural contributions" (Guam Economic Development Authority, 2014a). The island is also home to both a US Air Force base and naval base, which work in a partnership known as Joint Region Marianas.[3]

Public education on Guam is overseen by the Guam Department of Education, which is a single unified school district for grades K–12 with 26 elementary schools, 8 middle schools, 5 high schools, and an alternative school with over 30,000 students

(Guam Department of Education, n.d.). Public schools on Guam are patterned after school systems in the continental United States, and "the Chinese and Japanese communities each support schools to preserve their respective language and cultures" (Guam Economic Development Authority, 2014c). The teachers in each of the schools are as diverse as the community residents. Like the community, many of the public school teachers are Chamorro or of Chamorro ancestry and devout Catholics. According to the Central Intelligence Agency (2014c), 85% of the community residents are Roman Catholics. In any given week of the year, Catholic rosary services are held in cathedrals, residents' homes, or both. What follows is a hypothetical case scenario that considers the realities of a diverse island community in which a large number of the population follow the same faith.

*Scenario*

On May 30, the day after the Memorial Day weekend and just 2 weeks shy of the end of the school year, teachers and administrators were busily preparing for year-end testing and budget review. At Central Elementary School, teachers had just been notified that one of their recent retiree colleagues, Mrs. Maria Cruz, had passed away over the weekend. A well-liked teacher, Mrs. Cruz had worked at Central Elementary for 30 years. On this Tuesday, Catholic rosary services for Mrs. Cruz were to take place at noon and 6 p.m. at the town cathedral.

Principal Robert Perez circulated a written notice to all teachers regarding the rosary services for Mrs. Cruz. The notice read:

> One of our former teachers, Mrs. Maria Cruz, sadly passed away over the weekend. Noon rosary services for Mrs. Cruz will be held at the cathedral. Any teachers wishing to attend the noon rosary service for Maria may do so as long as their classes are covered by other teachers for the time they are away. No official leave form is required to attend the rosary services. Kindly inform my secretary, Ms. Anita Baza, of your intentions and who will be covering your class.

Later that morning, Principal Perez saw first-grade teacher Ms. Rose Torres in the hallway. "Hi Rose! Are you planning to attend the rosary for Maria anytime this week?"

Ms. Torres replied, "Yes, I am. Tina Mafnas [another first-grade teacher] and I are combining our classes and will take turns covering for the hour."

Principal Perez responded, "Great. As always, you do not have to sign a leave form if you stagger the coverage of your classes. Just be sure the kids are working on the set curriculum for that time period and let my secretary, Ms. Baza, know your schedule."

On receipt of the notice, fourth-grade teachers Mrs. Sashi Takagumi (a Japanese resident in the community) and Ms. Meifeng Wei (a Chinese resident, originally from Hong Kong) fumed over the notice in the teachers' lounge. "The fact is that Principal Perez has practiced a no leave deduction policy during our entire 5 years of employment here," Mrs. Takagumi complained. "Just last week, I wanted to visit the Shinto shrine, and I signed annual leave to do so—in which I returned back to work within one hour." She continued, "Meifeng, this is really unfair! Maybe I should say that I am going to attend a rosary service next time so that I do not have to sign annual leave."

"Yeah, but what can we do? We are in the minority when it comes to religious beliefs in this community. And the fact that Principal Perez is a devout Catholic only perpetuates this 'school culture' of taking care of your own kind," retorted Ms. Wei.

"We need to stand up for what is right," replied Mrs. Takagumi. "We are foolish to let it escalate further. We are no longer new teachers trying to pass our probationary period. We do not need to keep a low tone about this any longer. Either we are allowed the same no leave policy to attend our religious services or else everyone has to sign for annual leave for any kind of absence related to attending a religious event."

"I see your point, Sashi," said Ms. Wei. "But the real focus should be on what is the appropriate action to take as professionals. I mean, shouldn't church and state issues stay out of our public schools? I don't think that central office, in particular Superintendent Salas, will be happy to know that classes are being combined even if it is only for one hour. And what about the parents of these children in combined classes—what will they think? You know that regardless of what religion these children practice, their parents will be upset over lumping two classes into one huge classroom. It really has become more of a break period than a focus on teaching the curriculum for that hour. It is too difficult to oversee so many students and keep their concentration. By the time the classes combine, which usually means going to the library or study hall room, 30 minutes have gone by," explains Ms. Wei.

"Yes, I agree with you, Meifeng," Mrs. Takagumi firmly stated. "We need to petition Superintendent Salas to investigate this 'time off without leave' practice. The children are the ones at a disadvantage with this practice, not us. We really should focus on doing our best job to educate our students."

Mrs. Takagumi and Ms. Wei decided to write a formal letter to Superintendent Salas concerning this dilemma. In addition, they planned to attach a petition containing signatures of other teachers from Central Elementary School who were opposed to Principal Perez's "time off without leave" practice.

Four teachers in favor of the "time off without leave" practice heard about the petition and stormed into Principal Perez's office. One of these teachers, Mrs. Baza, began: "Principal Perez, you have to talk with Mrs. Takagumi and Ms. Wei. If their petition ends up in Superintendent Salas' office, we all lose out on the practice of taking time off to show respect and attend ceremonies and events for our specific religious beliefs."

"Yes," agreed Joe Cruz, another teacher and cousin of the deceased teacher, Maria. "You need to communicate our culture of caring and concern for others."

"Joe is right. However, Mrs. Takagumi and Ms. Wei are still relatively new to our island and our school. We need to embrace their concerns too and let them know that the school respects their religious beliefs and practices," replied teacher Cecilia Mafnas.

"They have nothing to complain about," a fourth teacher observed. "You let them take time off when they need to pick up their children. It is not your fault, Principal Perez, if they submit a leave form to the payroll officer for taking time to attend a funeral service. They never asked not to sign one for their services. They do not

222 • Shapiro, Stefkovich, and Gutierrez

understand the culture and tradition of the school. We care about our colleagues. That is the kind of teachers we are. Regardless of the type of religious funeral services, we care enough to pay our last respects to the families of our deceased teacher."

On hearing the comments of these four teachers, Principal Perez called Mrs. Takagumi and Ms. Wei into his office for a chat. "Sashi and Meifeng, thank you for coming to my office. I know you are upset about the 'time off without leave' practice to attend religious services. You have been part of our school for 5 years. You should understand and be aware of the cultural tradition of paying last respects to a deceased teacher of our school. I understand your strong resolve to obey the rules and regulations of the profession and that any absence away from work should require signing a leave form. On the other hand, I am committed to the concern and caring nature of this community and the traditions of our school. I ask that you give me 2 days to think over how to best handle this situation before you submit your petition to Superintendent Salas."

Mrs. Sashi Takagumi and Ms. Meifeng Wei were quite cordial with Principal Perez and respected him as the school leader. They agreed to wait 2 days to submit the letter and petition to Superintendent Salas. Now, Principal Perez needs to decide how to address this dilemma as he sees the merits of both those in favor of and those against the "time off without leave" practice.

## QUESTIONS FOR DISCUSSION AND REFLECTION

Each of the following questions asks the reader to consider responses to the dilemma from each of MEPs. The case can be best understood by framing the circumstances as a definite dilemma for both the principal and superintendent. It is not a clear-cut or "routine problem" (Cuban, 2001). This dilemma is laden with multiple value conflicts:

1. *Questions for the ethic of justice:* The ethic of justice takes into account questions such as: Is there a law, right, or policy that relates to a particular case? If so, should it be enforced? If not, should there be one?
2. *Questions for the ethic of critique:* The ethic of critique asks us to deal with the difficult questions regarding social class, race, gender, and other areas of difference, such as: Who makes the laws, rules, and policies? Who benefits from them? Who has the power? Who are silenced? What could make a difference to enable those who have been silenced and/or ignored to become empowered? Finally, and particularly relevant to this case, what new possibilities could be presented to lead toward social justice, making school a better place for all stakeholders?
3. *Questions for the ethic of care:* This ethic directs individuals to consider the consequences of their decisions and actions. It asks them to consider questions such as: Who will benefit from what I decide? Who will be hurt by my actions? What are the long-term effects of a decision I make today? And if someone helps me now, what should I do in the future about giving back to this individual or to society in general?

4. *Questions for the ethic of the profession:* The professional paradigm expects educational leaders to formulate and examine their own professional codes of ethics in light of individual personal codes of ethics, standards set forth by the profession, and community expectations and then calls on them to place students at the center of their ethical decision-making process. This paradigm asks: What would the profession ask me to do, taking into account the best interests of the student?

## CONCLUSION

In this chapter, we introduced multiple ethical paradigms (MEPs), consisting of the ethics of justice, critique, care, and the profession, and discussed each of these in some detail, focusing particularly on the professional paradigm, as it encompasses the other three ethics and considers community needs as well as the educational leader's individual personal and professional ethics. We then introduced an ethical dilemma with an international focus and applied the frames to the analysis of this scenario. The questions we present leave it up to the reader to respond to the dilemma. It is our hope that the MEP will serve as both a model and a tool to help educational leaders in our global society to make wise, thoughtful, and truly ethical decisions under often challenging circumstances.

## NOTES

1. This chapter comes, in part, from Chapter 2 by Shapiro and Stefkovich (2011) and from Chapter 2 by Shapiro and Gross (2013).
2. This case is an adaptive version of the original case in the text by Shapiro and Stefkovich (2011, pp. 105–108).
3. For more information about Joint Region Marianas, see: http://cnic.navy.mil/Marianas/AbouttheRegion/History/index.htm

## REFERENCES

Aiken, J., & Gerstl-Pepin, C. (2005, November). *The New DEEL: Democratic responsive practice for school leaders.* Paper presented at the annual convention of the University Council of Educational Administration, Nashville, TN.

American Association of School Administrators. (2007) *Statement of ethics for school administrators.* Arlington, VA: American Association of School Administrators.

Apple, M. W. (2003). *The state and the politics of knowledge.* New York: Routledge Falmer.

Apple, M. W. (Ed.). (2010). *Global crises, social justice, and education.* New York: Routledge.

Bakhtin, M. (1981). *The dialogic imagination.* Austin: University of Texas Press.

Banks, J. A., & Banks, C. A. M. (2006). *Multicultural education: Issues and perspectives* (6th ed.). San Francisco: Jossey-Bass.

Barth, R. J. (1990). *Improving schools from within: Teachers, parents, and principals can make the difference.* San Francisco: Jossey-Bass.

Beauchamp, T. L., & Childress, J. F. (1984). Morality, ethics and ethical theories. In P. Sola (Ed.), *Ethics, education, and administrative decisions: A book of readings* (pp. 39–67). New York: Peter Lang.

Beck, L. G. (1994). *Reclaiming educational administration as a caring profession.* New York: Teachers' College Press.

Beck, L. G., Murphy, J., & Associates. (1997). *Ethics in educational leadership programs: Emerging models.* Columbia, MO: University Council for Educational Administration.

Beckner, W. (2004). *Ethics for educational leaders*. Boston: Pearson Education.

Begley, P. T. (2010). Leading with moral purpose: The place of ethics. In T. Bush, L. Bell, & D. Middlewood (Eds.), *The principles of educational leadership and management* (pp. 31–54). London: Paul Chapman–Sage.

Begley, P. T., & Johansson, O. (Eds.). (2003). *The ethical dimensions of school leadership*. Boston: Kluwer Academic Publishers.

Begley, P. T., & Zaretsky, L. (2004). Democratic school leadership in Canada's public school systems: Professional value and social ethic. *Journal of Educational Administration, 42*(6), 640–655.

Belenky, M. F., Clinchy, B. M., Goldberger, N. R., & Tarule, J. M. (1986). *Women's ways of knowing*. New York: Basic Books.

Blackburn, S. (2001). *Being good: A short introduction to ethics*. Oxford: Oxford University Press.

*Board of Education v. Pico*. (1981). *Island Trees Union Free School District No. 26 v. Pico,* 457 U.S. 853 (1981).

Bon, S. C., & Bigbee, A. J. (2011). Special education leadership: Integrating professional and personal codes of ethics to serve the best interests of the child. *Journal of School Leadership, 21*(3), 324–359.

Bourdieu, P. (1977). Cultural reproduction and social reproduction. In J. Karabel & A. H. Halsey (Eds.), *Power and ideology in education* (pp. 487–511). New York: Oxford University Press.

Bourdieu, P. (2001). *Masculine domination*. Stanford, CA: Stanford University Press.

Bowles, S., & Gintis, H. (1988). *Democracy and capitalism*. New York: Basic Books.

Branson, C. M. (2009). *Leadership for an age of wisdom*. Rotterdam, Netherlands: Springer.

Branson, C. M. (2010). *Leading educational change wisely*. Rotterdam, Netherlands: Sense Publishers.

Buber, M. (1965). Education. In M. Buber (Ed.), *Between man and man* (pp. 83–103). New York: Macmillan.

Burford, C. (2004, October). *Ethical dilemmas and the lives of leaders: An Australian perspective on the search for the moral*. Paper presented at the 9th annual Values and Leadership Conference, Christ Church, Barbados.

Campbell, E. (2004). *The ethical teacher*. Maidenhead, UK: Open University Press.

Center for Effective Discipline. (2012). *U.S.: Corporal punishment and paddling statistics by state and race*. Retrieved from www.stophitting.com/index.php?page=statesbanning

Central Intelligence Agency. (2014a). *The World Factbook. People and society: Guam, ethnic groups*. Retrieved from www.cia.gov/library/publications/the-world-factbook/geos/gq.html

Central Intelligence Agency. (2014b). *The World Factbook. People and society: Guam, nationality*. Retrieved from www.cia.gov/library/publications/the-world-factbook/geos/gq.html

Central Intelligence Agency. (2014c). *The World Factbook. People and society: Guam, religions*. Retrieved from www.cia.gov/library/publications/the-world-factbook/geos/gq.html

Cuban, L. (2001). *How can I fix it? Finding solutions and managing dilemmas: An educator's road map*. New York: Teachers College Press.

Dantley, M. E. (2005). Moral leadership: Shifting the management paradigm. In F. W. English (Ed.), *The Sage handbook of educational leadership: Advances in theory, research, and practice* (pp. 34–46). Thousand Oaks, CA: Sage Publications.

Davis, J. E. (2000). Mothering for manhood: The (re)production of a black son's gendered self. In M. C. Brown II & J. E. Davis (Eds.), *Black sons to mothers: Compliments, critiques, and challenges for cultural workers in education* (pp. 51–67). New York: Peter Lang.

Davis, J. E. (2001). Transgressing the masculine: African American boys and the failure of schools. In W. Martino & B. Meyenn (Eds.), *What about the boys?* (pp. 140–153). Philadelphia: Open University Press.

Delgado, R. (1995). *Critical race theory: The cutting edge*. Philadelphia: Temple University Press.

Dewey, J. (1902). *The school and society*. Chicago: University of Chicago Press.

Foster, W. (1986). *Paradigms and promises: New approaches to educational administration*. Buffalo, NY: Prometheus Books.

Foucault, M. (1983). On the genealogy of ethics: An overview of work in progress. In H. L. Dreyfus & P. Rabinow (Eds.), *Michel Foucault: Beyond structuralism and hermeneutics* (2nd ed., pp. 229–252). Chicago: University of Chicago Press.

Freire, P. (1970). *Pedagogy of the oppressed*. (M. B. Ramos, Trans.). New York: Continuum.

Frick, W. C. (2009). Principals' value-informed decision making, intrapersonal moral discord, and pathways to resolution: The complexities of moral leadership praxis. *Journal of Educational Administration, 47*(1), 50–74.

Friedman, I. A. (2003). School organizational values: The driving force for effectiveness and change. In P. T. Begley & O. Johansson (Eds.), *The ethical dimensions of school leadership* (pp. 161–179). Boston: Kluwer Academic Press.

Furman, G. (2003). Moral leadership and the ethic of the community. *Values and Ethics in Educational Administration, 2*(1), 1–8.

Furman, G. C. (2004). The ethic of community. *Journal of Educational Administration, 42*(2), 215–235.

Furman-Brown, G. (Ed.). (2002). *School as community: From promise to practice.* Albany: SUNY Press.

Gilligan, C. (1982). *In a different voice.* Cambridge, MA: Harvard University Press.

Gilligan, C., Ward, J., & Taylor, J. (1988). *Mapping the moral domain: A contribution of women's thinking to psychology and education.* Cambridge, MA: Harvard University Graduate School of Education.

Ginsberg, A. E., Shapiro, J. P., & Brown, S. P. (2004). *Gender in urban education: Strategies for student achievement.* Portsmouth, NH: Heinemann.

Giroux, H. A. (2003). *The abandoned generation: Democracy beyond the culture of fear.* New York: Palgrave Macmillan.

Giroux, H. A. (2006). *America on the edge: Henry Giroux on politics, education and culture.* New York: Palgrave Macmillan.

Giroux, H. A., & Aronowitz, S. (1985). *Education under siege.* South Hadley, MA: Bergin & Garvey.

Goldring, E., & Greenfield, W. (2002). Understanding the evolving concept of leadership in education: Roles, expectations, and dilemmas. In J. Murphy (Ed.), *The educational leadership challenge: Redefining leadership for the 21st century. 101st yearbook of the National Society for the Study of Education* (pp. 1–20). Chicago: University of Chicago Press.

Goodlad, J. I., Soder, R., & Sirotnik, K. A. (Eds.). (1990). *The moral dimension of teaching.* San Francisco: Jossey-Bass.

Greene, M. (1988). *The dialectic of freedom.* New York: Teachers College Press.

Greenfield, W. D. (1993). Articulating values and ethics in administrator preparation. In C. Capper (Ed.), *Educational administration in a pluralistic society* (pp. 267–287). Albany: State University of New York Press.

Greenfield, W. D. (2004). Moral leadership in schools. *Journal of Educational Administration, 42*(2), 174–196.

Grogan, M. (1996). *Voices of women aspiring to the superintendency.* Albany: State University of New York Press.

Gronn, P. (2001). Distributed leadership as a unit of analysis. *Leadership Quarterly, 13*(4), 423–451.

Gross, S. J., & Shapiro, J. P. (2002). Towards ethically responsible leadership in a new era of high stakes accountability. In G. Perrault & F. Lunenberg (Eds.), *The changing world of school administration* (pp. 256–266). Lanham, MD: Scarecrow Press.

Gross, S. J., & Shapiro, J. P. (2008, November). *New DEEL townhall: Leadership for learning/democratic ethical educational leadership: Are these two educational movements compatible or incompatible?* Paper presented at annual convention of University Council of Educational Administration, Orlando, FL.

Guam Department of Education. (n.d.). *Home[page].* Retrieved from https://sites.google.com/a/gdoe.net/gdoe/

Guam Economic Development Authority. (2014a). *Guam: American in Asia.* Retrieved from www.investguam.com/guam/

Guam Economic Development Authority. (2014b). *Guam: Guam quick facts.* Retrieved from www.investguam.com/guam/

Guam Economic Development Authority. (2014c). *Guam: Quality of life: Education.* Retrieved from www.investguam.com/guam/quality-of-life/

Hansen, D. T. (2001). Teaching as a moral activity. In V. Richardson (Ed.), *Handbook of research on teaching* (4th ed., pp. 826–857). Washington, DC: American Educational Research Association.

Katzenmeyer, M., & Moller, G. (2001). *Awakening the sleeping giant: Helping teachers develop as leaders* (2nd ed). Thousand Oaks, CA: Corwin.

Kochan, F. K., & Reed, C. J. (2005). Collaborative leadership, community building, and democracy in public education. In F. W. English (Ed.), *The Sage handbook of educational leadership: Advances in theory, research, and practice* (pp. 68–84). Thousand Oaks, CA: Sage Publications.

Kohlberg, L. (1981). *The philosophy of moral development: Moral stages and the idea of justice* (Vol. 1). San Francisco: Harper & Row.

Lareau, A. (2003). *Unequal childhoods: Class, race and family life.* Berkeley: University of California Press.

Larson, C., & Murtadha, K. (2002). Leadership for social justice. In J. Murphy (Ed.), *The Educational Leadership Challenge: Redefining Leadership for the 21st Century* (pp. 134–161). Chicago: University of Chicago Press.

Lebacqz, K. (1985). *Professional ethics: Power and paradox.* Nashville, TN: Abingdon.

Lehrer, J. (2009). *How we decide.* Boston: Houghton Mifflin Harcourt.

Marshall, C., & Gerstl-Pepin, C. (2005). *Re-framing educational politics for social justice.* Boston: Allyn & Bacon.

Marshall, C., & Oliva, M. (2006). *Leadership for social justice: Making revolutions in education.* Boston: Allyn & Bacon.

Marshall, C., Patterson, J. A., Rogers, D. L., & Steele, J. R. (1996). Caring as career: An alternative perspective for educational administration. *Educational Administration Quarterly, 32*(2), 271–294.

Mitra, D. L. (2004). The significance of students: Can increasing 'student voice' in schools lead to gains in youth development? *Teachers College Record, 106*(4), 651–688.

Mitra, D. L. (2008). *Student voice in school reform: Building youth–adult partnerships that strengthen schools and empower youth.* Albany: State University of New York Press.

Mitra, D. L., & Gross, S. J. (2009). Increasing student voice in high school reform: Building partnerships, improving outcomes. *Educational Management Administration and Leadership, 37*(4), 462–473.

Murphy, J. (2005). Unpacking the foundations of ISLLC standards and addressing concerns in the academic community. *Educational Administration Quarterly, 41*(1), 154–191.

Nash, R. J. (1996). *"Real world" ethics: Frameworks for educators and human service professionals.* New York: Teachers College Press.

National Policy Board for Educational Administration. (1996). *Interstate School Leaders Licensure Consortium: Standards for school leaders.* Washington, DC: Council of Chief School Officers.

National Policy Board for Educational Administration. (2008). *Educational leadership policy standards: ISLLC 2008* (pp. 1–5). Washington, DC: Council of Chief State School Officers. Retrieved from www.ccsso.org/content/pdfs/elps_isllc2008 pdf

Noddings, N. (1992). *The challenge to care in schools: An alternative approach to education.* New York: Teachers College Press.

Noddings, N. (1999). Care, justice and equity. In M. S. Katz, N. Noddings, & K. A. Strike (Eds.), *Justice and caring: The search for common ground in education* (pp. 7–20). New York: Teachers College Press.

Noddings, N. (2003). *Caring: A feminine approach to ethics and moral education* (2nd ed). Berkeley: University of California Press.

Normore, A. H. (2004). Ethics and values in leadership preparation programs: Finding the North Star in the dust storm. *Values and Ethics in Educational Administration, 2*(2), 1–8.

OHCHR [Office of the United Nations High Commissioner for Human Rights]. (1989). *Convention on the rights of the child.* Retrieved from www.ohchr.org/Documents/ProfessionalInterest/crc.pdf

Parker, L., & Shapiro, J. P. (1993). The context of educational administration and social class. In C. A. Capper (Ed.), *Educational administration in a pluralistic society* (pp. 36–65). Albany: State University of New York Press.

Purpel, D. E. (2004). *Reflections on the moral and spiritual crisis of education.* New York: Peter Lang.

Purpel, D. E., & Shapiro, S. (1995). *Beyond liberation and excellence: Reconstructing the public discourse on education.* Westport, CT: Bergin & Garvey.

Rapp, D. (2002). Social justice and the importance of rebellious oppositional imaginations. *Journal of School Leadership, 12*(3), 226–245.

Rawls, J. (1971). *A theory of justice.* Cambridge, MA: Harvard University Press.

Reitzug, U. C., & O'Hair, M. J. (2002). From conventional school to democratic school community: The dilemmas of teaching and leading. In G. Furman-Brown (Ed.), *School as community: From promise to practice* (pp. 119–141). Albany: State University of New York Press.

Roland Martin, J. (1993). Becoming educated: A journey of alienation or integration? In S. H. Shapiro and D. E. Purpel (Eds.), *Critical social issues in American education: Toward the 21st century.* White Plains, NY: Longman.

Sergiovanni, T. J. (1992). *Moral leadership: Getting to the heart of school improvement.* San Francisco: Jossey-Bass.

Sergiovanni, T. J. (2009). *The principalship: A reflective practice perspective* (6th ed.). Boston: Allyn & Bacon.

Sernak, K. (1998). *School leadership—balancing power with caring.* New York: Teachers College Press.

Shapiro, H. S. (2006). *Losing heart: The moral and spiritual miseducation of America's children.* Mahwah, NJ: Lawrence Erlbaum.

Shapiro, H. S. (Ed.). (2009). *Education and hope in troubled times: Visions of change for our children's world.* New York: Routledge.

Shapiro, H. S., & Purpel, D. E. (Eds.). (2005). *Social issues in American education: Democracy and meaning in a globalized world* (3rd ed.). Mahwah, NJ: Lawrence Erlbaum Associates.

Shapiro, J. P. (2006). Ethical decision making in turbulent time: Bridging theory with practice to prepare authentic educational leaders. *Values and Ethics in Educational Administration, 4*(2), 1–8.

Shapiro, J. P., Ginsberg, A. E., & Brown, S. P. (2003). The ethic of care in urban schools: Family and community involvement. *Leading & Managing, 9*(2), 45–50.

Shapiro, J. P., & Gross, S. J. (2013). *Ethical educational leadership in turbulent times: (Re)Solving moral dilemmas* (2nd ed.). New York: Routledge.

Shapiro, J. P., Sewell, T. E., & DuCette, J. P. (2002). *Reframing diversity in education.* Lanham, MD: Rowman & Littlefield.

Shapiro, J. P., Sewell, T. E., DuCette, J., & Myrick, H. (1997, March). *Socio-cultural and school factors in achievement: Lessons from tuition guarantee programs.* Paper presented at the annual meeting of the American Educational Research Association, Chicago.

Shapiro, J. P., & Smith-Rosenberg, C. (1989). The 'other voices' in contemporary ethical dilemmas: The value of the new scholarship on women in the teaching of ethics. *Women's Studies International Forum, 12*(2), 199–211.

Shapiro, J. P., & Stefkovich, J. A. (1997). The ethics of justice, critique and care: Preparing educational administrators to lead democratic and diverse schools. In J. Murphy, L. G. Beck, & Associates (Eds.), *Ethics in educational administration: Emerging models* (pp. 109–140). Columbia, MO: University Council for Educational Administration.

Shapiro, J. P., & Stefkovich, J. A. (1998). Dealing with dilemmas in a morally polarized era: The conflicting ethical codes of educational leaders. *Journal for a Just and Caring Education, 4*(2), 117–141.

Shapiro, J. P., & Stefkovich, J. A. (2011). *Ethical leadership and decision making in education: Applying theoretical perspectives to complex dilemmas* (3rd ed.). New York: Routledge.

Shapiro, S. (1999) *Pedagogy and the politics of the body.* New York: Garland.

Sleeter, C. E., & Grant, C. A. (2003). *Making choices for multicultural education: Five approaches to race, class, and gender* (4th ed.). New York: J. Wiley & Sons.

Spillane, J. P., & Orina, E. C. (2005). Investigating leadership practice: Exploring the entailments of taking a distributed perspective. *Leadership and Policy in Schools, 4*(3), 57–176.

Starratt, R. J. (1991). Building an ethical school: A theory for practice in educational leadership. *Educational Administration Quarterly, 27*(2), 185–202.

Starratt, R. J. (1994a). *Building an ethical school.* London: Falmer Press.

Starratt, R. J. (1994b, April). *Preparing administrators for ethical practice: State of the art.* Paper presented at the annual meeting of the American Educational Research Association, New Orleans.

Starratt, R. J. (2004). *Ethical leadership.* San Francisco: Jossey-Bass.

Stefkovich, J. A. (2014). *Best interests of the student: Applying ethical constructs to legal cases in education.* New York: Routledge.

Stefkovich, J. A. (2012, October 4). *School searches from an international perspective.* Paper presented at the annual conference of the Australia New Zealand Education Law Association, Rotorua, New Zealand.

Stefkovich, J. A., & Guba, G. J. (1998). School violence, school reform, and the Fourth Amendment in public schools. *International Journal of Educational Reform, 7*(3), 217–225.

Stefkovich, J. A., & O'Brien, G. M. (2004). Best interests of the student: An ethical model. *Journal of Educational Administration, 42*(2), 197–214.

Stefkovich, J. A., O'Brien, G. M., & Moore, J. (2002, October). *School leaders ethical decision making and the 'best interests of students.'* Paper presented at the 7th annual Values and Leadership Conference, Toronto, Canada.

Stefkovich, J. A., & Shapiro, J. P. (1994). Personal and professional ethics for educational administrators. *Review Journal of Philosophy and Social Science, 20*(1–2), 157–186.

Strike, K. A. (1991). The moral role of schooling in liberal democratic society. In G. Grant (Ed.), *Review of research in education* (pp. 413–483). Washington, DC: American Educational Research Association.

Strike, K. A. (1999). Justice, caring, and universality: In defense of moral pluralism. In M. S. Katz, N. Noddings, & K. A. Strike (Eds.), *Justice and caring: The search for common ground in education* (pp. 21–36). New York: Teachers College Press.

Strike, K. A. (2006). *Ethical leadership in schools: Creating community in an environment of accountability.* Thousand Oaks, CA: Corwin Press.

Strike, K. A., Haller, E. J., & Soltis, J. F. (2005). *The ethics of school administration* (3rd ed.). New York: Teachers College Press.

Strike, K. A., & Ternasky, P. L. (Eds.). (1993). *Ethics for professionals in education: Perspectives for preparation and practice.* New York: Teachers College Press.

Tooms, A., & Alston, J. (2005, November). *What's democracy and ethics got to do with them? Administrative aspirants' attitudes towards the gay community.* Paper presented at the UCEA annual convention, Nashville, TN.

University Council of Educational Administration. (2011). *UCEA code of ethics for the preparation of educational leaders.* Charlottesville: University of Virginia.

Walker, K. (1995). The kids' best interests. *Canadian School Executive, 15*(5), 2–8.

Walker, K. (1998). Jurisprudential and ethical perspectives on 'the best interests of children.' *Interchange, 29*(3), 283–304.

Weis, L., & Fine, M. (1993). *Beyond silenced voices: Class, race, and gender in U.S. schools.* Albany: State University of New York Press.

Welch, S. (1991). An ethic of solidarity and difference. In H. Giroux (Ed.), *Postmodernism, feminism, and cultural politics: Redrawing educational boundaries* (pp. 83–99). Albany: State University of New York Press.

Willower, D. J., & Licata, J. W. (1997). *Values and valuation in the practice of education administration.* Thousand Oaks, CA: Corwin Press.

Zaretsky, L. (2005). *Moving beyond the 'talk' toward the 'enactment' of democratic ethical educational leadership: A conversation between two principals.* Paper presented at the annual convention of the University Council of Educational Administration, Nashville, TN, November.

# 15

## MANAGING ETHICAL DILEMMAS

### NEIL CRANSTON, LISA C. EHRICH, AND MEGAN KIMBER

Over the past decade there has been considerable growth in the literature pertaining to ethics, ethical decision making, and ethical dilemmas. While this attention has, to some extent, been a consequence of scandals within both the public sector and the private sector, it also needs to be recognized that with organizational changes based on globalization and neoliberalism, more leaders at more levels in a variety of contexts are experiencing ethical dilemmas. As one of our interview respondents asserted, ethical dilemmas are the "bread and butter" of leaders' work. In this chapter, we review a decade of research and writing we have undertaken to investigate the ethical dilemmas experienced by organizational leaders. We draw out the differences and similarities in the ethical dilemmas faced by leaders in schools, universities, and the public service, highlighting the complexities and challenges inherent in them. This discussion leads us to a conceptual model for identifying and resolving ethical dilemmas. We then introduce a scenario similar to those we have work-shopped with principals across Australia. Use of this scenario by practitioners and researchers enables them to experience the complex web of ethical dilemmas that leaders confront. A set of recommendations is posited. These recommendations are drawn from the ideas of leaders who have worked with us on this and similar dilemmas. Such recommendations provide a practical, albeit still challenging, means to better understand and resolve the ethical dilemmas that are prevalent in schools today. To provide a context for this review, we begin by discussing several theoretical approaches to ethics, ethical decision making, and ethical dilemmas.

## THEORETICAL APPROACHES TO ETHICS AND ETHICAL DILEMMAS

### Ethics

The term "ethics" comes from the Greek *ethos*, which means "character"; therefore, an ethical person is someone who has character. Defining the nature of character is likely to be difficult and highly contextually based. Not surprisingly, the meaning of ethics has been, and continues to be, a subject of debate. Plato is attributed as saying that ethics is what we ought to do or how we ought to live our lives. Similarly, Hosmer (1987, p. 91) maintains that ethics is "the study of proper thought and conduct." Yet what constitutes "ought" and "proper conduct" is a value-laden question. Because of the considerable differences in cultures and societies across the world, it is understandable that there is a "plurality of ethical views" (Robinson, 2010, p. 178), and what is considered proper in one context may not be in another.

Ethics can be understood in terms of what it is not. For instance, corruption, fraud, illegal behavior, and abuse of power are deemed unethical practices (Hunter, 2012), in contrast to practices such as honesty, integrity, and professionalism (Kuther, 2003). Francis and Armstrong (2003) put forward a set of ethical principles for organizations to help minimize the risk of litigation. These include dignity, equitability, prudence, honesty, openness, goodwill, and avoidance of suffering. While principles such as the aforementioned have been codified by professional bodies to provide guidance on acceptable practice for members of those respective professions (Ehrich, Kimber, Cranston, & Starr, 2011), principles are limiting, as they do not make any allowance for competing priorities or contextual constraints (Sumsion, 2000).

### Ethics and Leadership

In recent decades, ethics has emerged as an important field of inquiry for leaders in a variety of contexts such as schools, the public sector, universities, and other organizations (Ciulla, 2006; Cranston, Ehrich, & Kimber, 2006; Cranston, Ehrich, Kimber, & Starr, 2012; Kane & Patapan, 2006; Preston, Samford, & Connors, 2002; Robinson, 2010). The reason for its emergence can be explained in two key ways. First, there has been heightened media and public awareness of unethical behaviors such as corruption and fraud among organizational leaders (Trevino, 1986). This awareness has led to stronger calls for accountability and transparency, leading to the establishment of university programs in applied ethics, widespread use of professional codes of conduct in private and public sectors, and the establishment of anti-corruption committees or bodies (Kimber, Carrington, Mercer, & Bland, 2011).

Second, writers and researchers in the field of leadership have begun to acknowledge that leadership is not a technical or rational endeavor. Rather it consists of moral and ethical dimensions (Campbell, 1997; Duignan, 2006; Starratt, 1996), since leaders are actively engaged in decision making based on values (Robinson, 2010; Walker & Shakotko, 1999). Hodgkinson (1991, p. 11) supports this when he says, "values, morals and ethics are the very stuff of leadership and administrative life."

The realization that ethics lies at the heart of leadership (Ciulla, 2006) has enabled a more humanistic understanding of leadership and a wider appreciation of the complexity facing leaders as they make values-based decisions.

Leaders often make decisions with little or no knowledge of theoretical approaches to ethics. Yet Ciulla (2006) maintains that an understanding of theory is important in understanding what ethics is all about. Freakley and Burgh (2000) concur when they state that an understanding of ethical theories is useful for helping leaders to organize their perspectives and beliefs in a more coherent manner. The next section considers a number of well-known theoretical approaches to ethics.

### Ethical Theories

The first ethical theory considered here is "*consequentialism,* where ethical decisions are based primarily on calculating the *good* in terms of consequences" (Preston, 2007, p. 36, emphasis in original). A person who follows this type of perspective would make a decision after weighing up the likely consequences and then would choose an alternative that produced the best result (Freakley & Burgh, 2000). Utilitarianism is an example of a consequentialist approach (Preston, 2007; Preston, Samford, & Connors, 2002). Its advocates maintain that the best result would be one that maximized the good, or happiness, for the most people (Robinson, 2010). Identifying what constitutes this "good" is highly subjective and problematic.

In contrast to consequentialism is *non-consequentialism* or *deontology.* Those who adopt a non-consequentialist perspective refer to absolute or general principles that are said to be applicable in all situations (Robinson, 2010). For these theorists, it is rules rather than consequences that count (Stewart, 2000). Subscribers to this perspective would make ethical judgments based on duty, rights, laws, motive, intuition, or reason. The Golden Rule of "do unto others as you would have them do unto you" illustrates this understanding of ethics (Preston, 2007). There are two versions of non-consequentialism—divine command theory and Kantian moral theory (Preston, 2007; Stewart, 2000). In divine command theory, "the duty or right to obey is revealed by a divine authority," such as in the Bible or the Qur'an (Preston, 2007, p. 40). The Ten Commandments from Christianity is an example here (Preston, 2007; Robinson, 2010). In Kantian moral theory, the categorical imperative is important. Here right and wrong actions are determined through "*universalizing* the action's *maxim* and seeing if this can be done *consistently*" (Stewart, 2000, p. 36, emphasis in the original).

Another understanding of ethics is that of *justice.* From this perspective, social cohesiveness depends on a "shared understanding of, and commitment to" both the rights of members and the "just distribution of the society's resources" (Preston, 2007, p. 42). Social contract theory is one example here. However, Rawls's (1999) work might be seen as having Kantian overtones.

A fairly contemporary theory of ethics emanating from feminist writers such as Noddings (1992) and Gilligan (1982) is an *ethic of care,* where care is the foundation of an ethical approach (Robinson, 2010). This theoretical approach "emphasises the quality of relationships and contextual factors in an ethical life" (Preston et al.,

2002, p. 24). Relationships with others are central and these are given predominance over other principles (Freakley & Burgh, 2000).

One of the oldest ethical theories is *virtue ethics*. This theory originates from Aristotle and is related to a person's good character, since its advocates hold that good character will lead to good ethical behavior and decision making (Robinson, 2010). Proponents of virtue ethics "argue in favour of a connection between character and reasoning[,] for without good character I may reason about what is right but still choose not to do so" (Freakley & Burgh, 2000, p. 125). Thus the key question is not necessarily "what ought we *do*, but who ought we *become*" (Preston, 2007, p. 49, emphasis in original). The proponents of this view of ethics see a relationship among people, society, and institutions in the pursuit of a common good (Preston et al., 2002). Virtues are "dispositions of the soul" that are "activated in actions towards the best or the most appropriate ends according to wise judgements of contingent necessities" (Kane & Patapan, 2006, p. 713). A key contemporary virtue ethicist, Alisdair MacIntyre, distinguishes between the internal goods of practices, as it is through the pursuit of these that we develop virtues, and the external goods of institutions. External goods such as the pursuit of power, money, or fame are considered unethical (Higgins, 2010a; MacIntyre, 1984; Overeem & Tholen, 2011; Preston, 2007).

A central element of virtue ethics is phronesis, which means practical wisdom. Practical wisdom is the highest virtue, as it involves intellectual capacity and virtue. It encompasses:

> *all* the virtues: courage, temperance, generosity, magnamity, mildness, humour, and truthfulness. [For Aristotle, p]ractical wisdom was, in other words, a matter of personal character—specifically a character that had been habituated to virtue tempered by long and experience.
> (Kane & Patapan, 2006, p. 713, emphasis in original)

The final ethical theory, sometimes referred to as an "applied theory," is *institutional ethics*. Institutional ethicists focus on individuals within institutions and ask that they be accountable to their institutions and to the wider community (Preston et al., 2002). As discussed by Preston and colleagues (2002), it builds ethics "into the operations and decision-making of the institution" (p. 50) so that ethics becomes part of the "ethos, policies and practices" (ibid). Thus all individuals have a role to play in upholding institutional ethics, not least, the leaders.

### Ethical Dilemmas

Given the complex sociocultural milieu in which leaders operate, it is not surprising that they would find themselves, from time to time, faced with ethical dilemmas. Ethical dilemmas are decisions "that require a choice among competing sets of principles, often in complex and value laden contexts" (Ehrich, Cranston, & Kimber, 2005, p. 137). These competing choices have been described as pulling leaders in different directions (Badaracco, 1992) and have been found to cause leaders great stress and anxiety (Cranston et al., 2006). Difficulties are said to arise when leaders are faced with choices that are considered "right." For example, Kidder (1995) states that many ethical dilemmas facing professionals do not concern right versus wrong options but right versus right. In other words, the choices could all be seen as right. Alternatively, when all of the options are deemed "wrong," it would also potentially cause angst for leaders. How leaders interpret, respond to, and resolve ethical dilemmas is likely to depend on a variety of factors and forces both internal and external to the leader. Some of these factors and forces are discussed later in the chapter.

## RESULTS FROM THREE CONTEXTS

Our research with school leaders, university middle-level leaders, and public sector leaders indicates that leaders at various organizational levels are experiencing ethical dilemmas (Kane & Patapan, 2006). Indeed, a number of the ethical dilemmas discussed by middle-level leaders in universities in 2011 had similar dimensions to, and were as equally complex as, the dilemmas discussed by senior public service leaders in 2004 and school principals in 2006. Our research points to the pervasiveness of ethical dilemmas experienced by leaders in their work lives. School leaders and senior public sector leaders, whom we interviewed, saw addressing ethical dilemmas as "core business" of their practice. As much as one of the school principals argued that ethical dilemmas were "the bread and butter of school leaders' lives" (Cranston et al., 2006), a university middle-level leader argued that much of the work of their position has required them "to act ethically, in dealing with matters related to students, staff and in teaching and research." This leader considered it essential that they were "informed about being ethical and to be alert for occasions when this might be challenged" (Ehrich et al., 2012, p. 99).

Interestingly, university middle level-leaders indicated that generally, the workplace culture of their organization was ethical. Yet, only a third of them had viewed colleagues acting ethically in the workplace. One explanation for this incongruence is the centrality of personal values and of relationships to the ethical decision-making practices of these leaders (Cranston et al., 2012; Ehrich, Cranston, & Kimber, 2004). In another study we conducted, a middle-level public sector leader noted that ethical dilemmas kept him awake at night (Cranston, Ehrich, & Kimber, 2005). This leader also stated that he was the person who had "to make that ethical decision, do I do anything about it or do I just let it go and let somebody else worry about it when it all blows up?" (Cranston et al., 2005, p. 4). It could be argued, therefore, that ethical dilemmas are common, complex, and challenging for leaders across different organizational settings.

While, not surprisingly, some of the critical incidents that sparked the ethical dilemmas experienced by these leaders varied according to their particular context and organizational position (e.g., student issues were important for school leaders and university middle-level leaders but not for public servants, while the misuse of money concerned senior public servants and school leaders), many of the dilemmas were similar across all three contexts. Essentially, these dilemmas were about:

- student/staff welfare or behavior;
- responsibility and accountability (including blurred accountability);
- supervisor directive and supervisor issues (such as inaction over serious issues);

- staff (under)performance;
- the misuse of funds; and
- conflicts of interest.

These dilemmas concerned conflict or choice between:

- personal values and professional ethics;
- personal values and professional ethics and organizational culture;
- the "best interest" of an individual or a subgroup and the "best interest" of the community (whether that be the polity, the school, or the university);
- the immediate community and the wider community;
- the public interest and supervisor directive;
- professional ethics and the law; and
- ethical principles (justice and mercy, justice and care, or efficiency and equity).

Thus, as noted earlier, ethical dilemmas are not simply between right and wrong. They can be challenging and complex because they can involve choice between right and right or wrong and wrong (Kidder, 1995).

In resolving ethical dilemmas, leaders often encounter multiple (and at times competing) factors or forces. These factors include political and public interest imperatives, financial issues, impact of globalization, community concerns, and workplace culture. Survey respondents from the public sector and from universities identified personal ethics and values, professional ethics, and organizational culture as the most significant (greater than 80%) factors in the ethical dilemmas that they faced. The next most important factors identified by respondents were supervisor directive and the public interest or public good. Following from these, community and societal, legal, and political issues were stressed. Respondents also referred to economic and financial factors and global factors (Cranston et al., 2005, 2012; Ehrich et al., 2012). It might be argued that such findings are unsurprising because it is in these arenas "that contestation of values across individuals and institutions come into play" (Cranston et al., 2012, p. 9). Recent research by Hanhimäki and Tirri (2009), in respect to teachers in Finland, confirms both the types and classification of critical incidents and ethical dilemmas that we have identified in our research in Australia.

Quotations from interviewees and survey respondents across the three contexts we have examined also draw attention to the ways in which leaders are mindful of the implications their decisions have, not only for themselves but also for their organizations and their communities. For instance, one school principal had anxiety over being able to "sleep at night" if responsible for a particular decision. This principal continued:

Do I feel good in myself? It's deeply very personal. I have difficulty making an unethical decision and living with it unless someone can point out that my values that underpin that decision were a bit skewed.

(Cranston et al., 2006, p. 114)

This response again highlights the centrality of personal values in resolving ethical dilemmas.

Some respondents referred to asking themselves the question of how their proposed decision would look to a member of the community or to their family members. This was, in essence, one of their "value tests." This attention to community perception was used by senior public servants and by university middle-level leaders in particular, which might be due to the view that public administration or education is a public good that was articulated by some of these leaders (Cranston et al., 2012). For instance, in a survey response, one university leader stated:

> At the end of the day, I always ask the question: What would I want someone to do if the action they took or did not take would have an effect on my family members. . . . the most important elements to me are personal ethics and values and serving the public good.
>
> (Cranston et al., 2012, p. 12)

It can be suggested that many of the university middle-level leaders who responded to the survey, like many of the senior public servants and school leaders who were interviewed, viewed personal values and professional ethics as being "at the core of these dilemmas and complex decision-making processes. . . . Ethical dilemmas are conflicts that involve values or moral principles" (Cranston et al., 2012, p. 12).

As suggested from the quotations above, one of our research findings has been that ethical leaders appear to engage in reflection around ethics and ethical dilemmas in their workplaces. While such reflection might be attributed to the interview and survey questions, it is also possible that reflection is an important way in which these leaders evaluate their ethical decision making and adjust their decision-making processes or responses, if necessary. Additionally, the ability to justify one's decisions and to reflect on those decisions might be seen as aspects of professional ethics.

In respect to justification, one school principal commented, "The leadership team worked through the dilemma to ensure that they fully justified [it] to the school community" (Cranston et al., 2006, p. 114). Thus, leaders considered the impact or outcome of their decision not only on themselves but also on other individuals, their institution, and their community. School leaders, for example, were most cognizant of the implications of their decisions on others, with several "continually reflecting on their actions . . . [such that] one participant knew that further decisions would be necessary. Another indicated that he would act differently in future" (ibid). Indeed, one principal was clear "that leadership was about 'coming back' to a core set of beliefs you have about education and about what the school is about. . . . [Another principal stated that] school leaders must 'walk the talk.' They needed to 'practice what they preached'" (ibid). Respondents in the other contexts that we have examined made comments that implied a similar moral understanding of leadership and the expected behavior of those in leadership positions.

Such comments remind us of Samier's (2008) discussion of "moral mute managers," who adhere to rules, codes, and formalized goals rather than exercise what might be viewed as "higher order moral principles" (Kimber & Ehrich, 2011). It could be argued, therefore, that good character rather than institutional codes is critical to good leadership. Such a position resonates with the work of Preston and colleagues (2002), MacIntyre (1984), and Uhr (2005). Indeed, MacIntyre (also see Higgins, 2010a, 2010b) distinguishes between "internal goods" and "external goods." Those who focus primarily on external goods are viewed as unethical. For MacIntyre, "the moral problem of management . . . is that it is mainly occupied with the attainment of external goods at the cost of internal goods and with the development of institutions at the cost of practices" (Overeem & Tholen, 2011, p. 731). For institutions to support practices, therefore, ethics should be "built into the ethos, policies and practices of an institution" (Preston et al., p. 50). If leaders reflect in this manner, then it might be suggested that development of the virtue of practical wisdom is a necessary attribute for ethical leadership.

## A MODEL FOR IDENTIFYING AND RESOLVING AN ETHICAL DILEMMA

We now turn our attention to a conceptual model of ethical dilemmas we have been using for some time derived initially from the literature but refined through various iterations from empirical research with leaders across three organizational contexts: schools, universities, and the public sector (Cranston et al., 2003; Ehrich et al., 2004, 2012).

As can be seen from Figure 15.1, the model consists of five core components. The first component is the critical incident that generates the ethical dilemma for the decision maker. Critical incidents are "issues or situations in [leaders'] work that produce ethical reflection and moral emotions" (Hanhimäki & Tirri, 2009, p. 107). The leaders who have participated in our research have identified a variety of critical incidents, including:

- dealing with staff underperformance or behavior such as different interpretations of institutional policies;
- observing student actions such as breaking school rules or plagiarizing sources;
- being given a directive from a supervisor that conflicts with their personal values and professional ethics or with their notions of wider accountability;
- confronting institutional changes that conflict with the ethos of the organization, such as the managerial imperative to make money versus maintaining standards of academic excellence; and
- uncovering the misuse of public money.

A variety of factors (or forces) can highlight the critical incident and influence the choices a decision maker sees open to him or her (second component of the model). These factors are:

- The public interest or public good—what a community decides is in the best interest of its members as a whole as "expressed through the ballot box, interest groups and ongoing debate and discussion" (Ehrich et al., 2004, p. 31). It entails ensuring that public officials are accountable to the community for making and

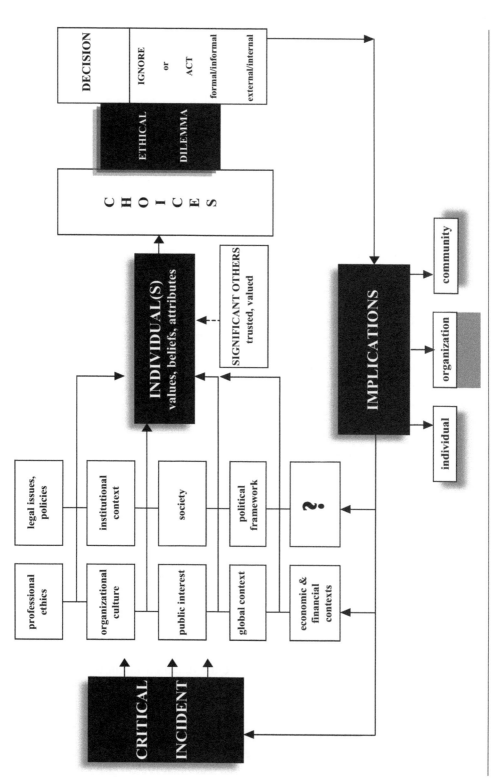

**Figure 15.1** A model for examining and understanding ethical dilemmas (Cranston et al., 2003; Ehrich et al., 2004, 2012).

administering policies. Any organization that receives public money (money collected through the taxation system) is accountable to the community for the use of that money. Thus public officials must act in the public interest or for the public good.

- The political framework—the political ideology, system, and structure of a jurisdiction socializes people and enhances or constrains the decisions and actions they take.
- The community or society—the multiple and competing stakeholders (individuals and groups) that impact on and react to leaders' decisions.
- Professional ethics—the ethical standards and values held by members of a particular profession that guide their actions and that the community expects of a member of that profession (Ehrich et al., 2004, 2012; Kimber et al., 2011; Uhr, 2005).
- Legal institutions are required to comply with legislation and judicial rulings.
- Economic and financial contexts could develop from the impact of the dominant economic paradigm on the policies and actions of an organization such the impact of a preference for neoliberal economic thinking leads to policies that result in the privatization of public sector goods and services.
- International or global social, political, cultural, and economic trends impact on institutions.
- The institutional context and factors beyond the immediate workplace—the operational milieu within which leaders work, which includes policies, procedures, and accountabilities.
- The organizational or workplace culture—the ethos of an organization can be ethical or unethical, and can be strong or weak.
- The unknown—represented as "?" and might be identified as duty of care in educational contexts.

As discussed in the previous section, leaders' personal values can be critical to how they identify, determine, and consider the choices available to them (third component of the model). These personal values stem from the ideology and beliefs that they have been socialized into and connect with the theoretical perspectives on ethics discussed in the first section of this chapter—e.g., consequentialist, Kantian, religious, care, character. The ethical dilemma that leaders find themselves in can arise as they contemplate the choices that they believe are open to them. Here, leaders might consult with a "significant other" in their lives, such as a partner or a trusted deputy in the institution. These choices are dilemmas because they might entail choosing between right and right or wrong and wrong (Kidder, 1995).

The action (or non-action) taken to resolve the dilemma might be formal or it might be informal. A formal action could entail following institutional procedures in re-marking a student's work or issuing a staff member with a warning notice. An informal action might involve meetings with staff members to resolve a dispute. These actions are internal to institutions. However, actions can be external to institutions, such as leaking information to the media to raise awareness of an issue of public concern. From the discussion in the previous section, it is clear that this action or non-action is likely to have implications for the individual—the decision maker and the person the decision is made about; the institution, such as through either setting a precedent or maintaining the status quo; and the community, such as affecting the reputation of the institution.

## ETHICAL DILEMMA SCENARIO

This section provides some practical ideas to stimulate thinking and responses to the more theoretical ideas raised earlier in the chapter. In particular, it presents an ethical dilemma scenario located in a school setting with related stimulus questions. These can be used in workshop situations with school leaders to exemplify some of the key learnings of the chapter. The workshop scenario is followed by some practical suggestions for school leaders to think carefully about, both in preparation for meeting ethical dilemmas in their schools and in practical matters to consider as they work their way through such dilemmas as they unfold.

### Ethical Dilemma: "To Expel or Not!"

*"Only the Best College" is a large well-established preparatory to year 12 college in inner Bloomtown, a thriving city of almost a million people. The college is located near two other schools—one a government school and the other a nongovernment school. All three schools are competing for local students, as well as for those students who are serviced by good public transportation to and from the area. The principal (Peter Perfect) has been at the school for 5 years and has worked hard to turn the school around from one with an undesirable reputation to one that is strong on discipline; indeed, the school has the highest student exclusion numbers in the area. Many parents are attracted to this tough discipline approach, and student numbers are increasing. The two deputy principals (Mary Soft and Barry Firm) work hard to support the principal in this regard, although Mary often reflects on the negative impact such a tough line has on some students, some of whom eventually completely drop out of school as a result.*

*One of the very able academic senior students in Mary's year 12 pastoral care group, Cathy Future, has just been to Mary's office to tell her she has been "kicked out of" home and is now living with her boyfriend. Cathy knows that the school will not look kindly on this situation because of its potential negative impact with some members of the school community and she expects that the principal, if he knew, would remove her from the school. This is a critical time for Cathy, as the final exams for her schooling are less than a month away and she is striving to achieve sufficiently high scores to enter law at the local university. Mary knows that Cathy is at the breaking point given her family situation and that she needs support and stability if she is to make the best of the remaining days at school and achieve her goal of university entry.*

*When Mary arrives at school the next day, she is met by Peter in a highly agitated state. He has just been confronted by a group of parents who claim that one of the senior girls is living with her boyfriend. They demand she be removed from the school, as she is clearly a bad influence on others and her actions will damage the reputation of the school. Mary begins to brief Peter about the full background to the situation, arguing that the school needs to support the student. Peter knows that the parents are likely to make a real issue of the matter and that one of them who met him earlier is linked to the local newspaper. Potentially, the school's reputation stands to be seriously damaged. The subsequent impact on enrollments could be significant. Peter knows that he must make the decision about the future of Cathy at "Only the Best College" as quickly as possible because some students and teachers are talking about the situation.*

What follows is a series of steps that could be taken in thinking about this scenario and the ethical dilemma that emerges from it.

First, it is essential to put yourself in the middle of the scenario (try to be Peter, then Mary, then Cathy, then a parent, etc.) and to think about what the school might be like, its culture, its parent body, the views about the school the wider community might hold, and so on.

Second, spend about 10 minutes thinking about the questions below and any others that come to mind.

1. What are the key issues that need to be considered in trying to understand the dilemma?

   a. Think about: the key forces at play; the actual ethical dilemma; what might be Peter's values, beliefs . . . what might be Mary's?; and what about the choices and decisions available to Peter?

   b. What are the implications of the various choices and decisions—for Cathy, for Peter, for the school, for the school community?

2. How do you think the scenario plays out?
3. What would *you* have done if you were in Peter's shoes? In Mary's shoes?

Finally, thinking about these questions and any others that come to mind, share your ideas with others in your group (again for about 10 minutes). You might want to consider:

4. Were there differences and similarities in group members' responses?
5. Why might there be these similarities and differences?
6. Who are the "winners" and "losers" as a result of the various decisions taken?
7. Is there a "right" answer?
8. What are some key learnings from this ethical dilemma for the future?

## WAYS FORWARD FOR LEADERS TO "MANAGE" ETHICAL DILEMMAS: RECOMMENDATIONS FOR ACTION

Extending the scenario presented in the previous section, in this section we offer some practical suggestions for leaders to consider as they manage the "bread and butter" (Cranston et al., 2006) ethical dilemmas so prevalent in organizations today. In large part, the suggestions have been drawn from informal feedback from school leaders during workshops using scenarios such as the one presented in the previous section. While discussed here in the context of ethical dilemmas, not surprisingly they are matters for school leaders to consider and respond to in more general ways as they undertake their complex roles and responsibilities (Australian Institute for Teaching and School Leadership, 2011; Cranston & Ehrich, 2009; Department of Education and Early Childhood Development, 2012; Gurr & Drysdale, 2012).

The recommendations are categorized under the following subheadings:

- *Precursors*—these are matters that need to be clear for school leaders *before* they are confronted by an ethical dilemma. While they are likely to be dynamic due to personal and professional growth of individuals, as well the operational contexts within which leadership is being enacted, they are the "fundamentals" on which, and against which, determinations in ethical dilemmas are founded. In a sense, these are the strategic issues that will drive how an individual school leader responds to the dilemma.
- *Practical*—these are matters that need careful consideration when the ethical dilemma arises. In the model presented earlier in this chapter, they are relevant once the *critical incident* occurs. Such matters play out during the (successful or otherwise) resolution of the ethical dilemma.

In thinking through the issues raised below, it is helpful to revisit the model discussed earlier in this chapter.

### Precursors

Because ethical dilemmas are so value laden, it is essential that school leaders understand their *own* values and value positions. They need to be able to articulate, and defend if necessary, what they, as school leaders, really stand for. Consequently, school leaders should make clear what their non-negotiables are in circumstances where rules and precedents may be vigorously tested. Noteworthy is that these values are located as central in the model.

Connected to these personal values is an understanding of the values of the school. Most importantly here is that the espoused *and* the enacted values may not be fully aligned. That is, the rhetoric of "this is what we believe in and practice in this school" might be different from what parents, students, and teachers see in their everyday experiences and interactions in the school.

Thus a related concern is a need for school leaders to understand the values of the parent community. While it might be expected that these values should be consistent with that of the school—and they may be in some cases—it is more likely that the parents will not hold homogenous views. Nor should it be expected that teachers, and other school community members, would hold similar values. Rather, there is likely to be a diversity of value positions across different community members. Thus there is a need for school leaders to try to understand and manage the values of *all* in the school community, not just those of the powerful and vocal few.

## Practical

It is essential that the school leader gather the relevant and full "facts" specific to the ethical dilemma. Such fact gathering is necessary because, in the first instance, the issue that arises may not, on the surface, seem to be of an ethical nature. By gathering and understanding the full "facts," a school leader can avoid what might be termed a knee-jerk reaction where the first response or reaction to an issue might not be the most appropriate one in the longer term once the situation is better understood.

The model provides some useful reminders in understanding the issues at play in the dilemma, as well as some of the outcomes likely to result. Importantly, it is essential to think through the implications, consequences, and precedents various alternative decisions flowing from the dilemma will create—for individuals, for the school, and for the community. Critically, it is rare that there will be one "right" answer or response; often more than one equally attractive alternative may emerge. It is also important to remember that decisions often create precedents; if the decision maker(s) make this decision this time, they will need to make the same decision next time, otherwise they are potentially demonstrating inconsistency and bias.

If a student or students are involved, a key question is: What are the duty-of-care issues that need to be considered? This question might also be relevant if a teacher is involved. We raise the duty-of-care question because ethical dilemmas involve people, and it is necessary to ensure that individuals are safe, both in the short term and in the long term. Moreover, a duty of care closely resonates with the idea of the moral accountability of leadership, which maintains that leaders act and work in the best interests of staff and students.

Given the central nature of values in ethical dilemmas, as discussed earlier in this chapter, it will be essential to revisit (and possibly clarify) the value positions of the school leader, the school, and the community. A key question here is, how does the intended decision align with these? And further, how will they be seen to align by students, teachers, parents, and the wider community? One stark way to quickly revisit the value issues is for school leaders to put *themselves* in the position of the individual(s) at the center of the ethical dilemma. That is, *all* the individuals involved: the final decision maker (the school leader), the person(s) at the center of the dilemma, and others who might be impacted by the decision that is made. A focusing questions here is: "How would I like my child (myself, my friend, . . .) to be treated in this situation?"

Once a decision has been made, it is then important to "manage" the outcomes, although typically it is likely that these will have been considered, at least in some part, already. The notion here is that the decision will, inevitably, not be the endpoint to the matter, as often there will be significant implications, consequences, and precedents flowing from the initial decision. It may be that a communication strategy, whether that be small (e.g., within the student body) or large (e.g., dealing with the media), is required because the ability to justify one's decision—in terms of values and in terms of the good—is a necessary skill in ethical leadership. If this is not carefully and thoughtfully done, a range of impressions as to what has transpired may arise among the student, teacher, parent, and wider community groups. The "truth" may be lost in the rush by some to make judgments as to the voracity, or otherwise, of the decision—and hence the decision maker, the school leader, needs to ensure that clarity (and often confidentiality) is respected in any wider communication.

Most importantly is the need to *learn* from the experience. The learnings from critical reflection as to what happened, how it happened, and how it was managed and resolved will be vital in seeking to avoid such dilemmas arising again. As a final exercise, it might be instructive to think back over the earlier scenario (and reactions to this) and see if there are other matters that could be added to the ideas above, at both the precursor and practical stages.

## CONCLUSION

In this chapter we have presented some ethical theories that leaders might use to help them frame their understanding of ethical dilemmas. Our discussion was operationalized through summarizing results of our research into ethical dilemmas experienced by leaders in schools, universities, and the public sector. Following from this discussion, we presented a model to assist leaders to identify and resolve ethical dilemmas. The model contained five parts—the critical incident, individual decision makers, and their personal values; the factors or forces that illuminate the ethical dilemma; the choices available in resolving the dilemma; the action that is taken; and the implications of the decision or action for the individual, the organization, and the community. This model was further explicated through an ethical dilemma scenario and recommendations to assist school leaders in using the model in their decision making. Key themes in this chapter have been the pervasive, complex, and challenging nature of ethical dilemmas; the importance of personal values and of relationships; professional ethics; and practical wisdom as expressed through wise judgments, critical reflection, and justification of decisions.

## REFERENCES

Australian Institute for Teaching and School Leadership. (2011). *National professional standard for principals.* Melbourne: AITSL.

Badaracco, J. (1992). Business ethics: Four spheres of executive responsibility. *California Management Review, 34*(3), 237–253.

Campbell, E. (1997). Administrators' decisions and teachers' ethical dilemmas: Implications for moral agency. *Leading & Managing, 3*(4), 245–257.

Ciulla, J. (2006). Ethics: The heart of leadership. In T. Maak & N. M. Press (Eds.), *Responsible leadership* (pp. 17–32). London: Routledge.

Cranston, N., & Ehrich, L. C. (2009). *Australian school leadership today.* Brisbane: Australian Academic Press.

Cranston, N., Ehrich, L., & Kimber, M. (2003). The 'right' decision? Towards an understanding of ethical dilemmas for school leaders. *Westminster Studies in Education, 26*(2), 135–148.

Cranston, N., Ehrich, L. C., & Kimber, M. (2005, June). Ethical dilemmas and middle and senior-level managers in the public service: Managing the tensions. *The Public Interest,* 5–9.

Cranston, N., Ehrich, L. C., & Kimber, M. (2006). Ethical dilemmas: The "bread and butter" of educational leaders' lives. *Journal of Educational Administration, 44*(2), 106–121.

Cranston, N., Ehrich, L. C., Kimber, M., & Starr, K. (2012). An exploratory study of ethical dilemmas faced by academics in three Australian universities. *Journal of Educational Leadership, Policy and Practice, 27*(1), 3–15.

Department of Education and Early Childhood Development. (2012). *New directions for school leadership and the teaching profession (discussion paper)*. Melbourne: State of Victoria. Retrieved from www.education.vic.gov.au

Duignan, P. (2006). *Ethical leadership: Key challenges and ethical tensions*. New York: Cambridge University Press.

Ehrich, L. C., Cranston, N., & Kimber, M. (2004). Public sector managers and ethical dilemmas. *Journal of the Australian and New Zealand Academy of Management, 10*(1), 25–37.

Ehrich, L. C., Cranston, N., & Kimber, M. (2005, July 3–7). *Academic managers and ethics: A question of making the right decision*. Paper presented at the 28th HERDSA annual conference "Higher Education in a Changing World: Research and Development in Higher Education," New South Wales, Sydney, Australia.

Ehrich, L. C., Kimber, M., Cranston, N., & Starr, K. (2011). Ethical tensions and academic leaders. *Higher Education Review, 43*(3), 50–69.

Ehrich, L. C., Cranston, N., Kimber, M., & Starr, K. (2012). (Un)ethical practices and ethical dilemmas in universities: Academic leaders' perceptions. *International Studies in Educational Administration, 40*(2), 99–114.

Francis, R., & Armstrong, A. (2003). Ethics as a risk management strategy: The Australian experience. *Journal of Business Ethics, 45*(4), 375–385.

Freakley, M., & Burgh, G. (2000). *Engaging with ethics: Ethical inquiry for teachers*. Katoomba, NSW, Australia: Social Science Press.

Gilligan, C. (1982). *In a different voice: Psychological theory and women's development*. Cambridge, MA: Harvard University Press.

Gurr, D., & Drysdale, L. (2012). Tensions and dilemmas in leading Australia's schools. *School Leadership & Management, 32*(5), 403–420.

Hanhimäki, E., & Tirri, K. (2009). Education for ethically sensitive teaching in critical incidents at school. *Journal of Education for Teaching, 35*(2), 107–121. doi: 10.1080/02607470902770880

Higgins, C. (2010a). Worlds of practice: MacIntyre's challenge to applied ethics. *Journal of Philosophy of Education, 44*(2–3), 237–273. doi: 10.1111/j.1467-9752.2010.00755.x

Higgins, C. (2010b). A question of experience: Dewey and Gadamer on practical wisdom. *Journal of Philosophy of Education, 44*(2–3), 301–333. doi: 10.1111/j.1467-9752.2010.00757.x

Hodgkinson, C. (1991). *Educational leadership: The moral art*. Albany: SUNY Press.

Hosmer, L. T. (1987). *The ethics of management*. Homewood, IL: Irwin.

Hunter, S. T. (2012). (Un)ethical leadership and identity: What did we learn and where do we go from here? *Journal of Business Ethics, 107*(1), 79–87. doi: 10.1007/s10551-012-1301-y

Kane, J., & Patapan, H. (2006). In search of prudence: The hidden problem of managerial reform. *Public Administration Review, 66*(5), 711–724.

Kidder, R. M. (1995). *How good people make tough choices: Resolving the dilemmas of ethical living*. New York: William Morrow.

Kimber, M., Carrington, S., Mercer, K. L., & Bland, D. (2011). Enhancing professional ethics: Service-learning in teacher education. In J. Millwater, L. C. Ehrich, & D. Beutel (Eds.), *Practical experiences in professional education: A transdisciplinary approach*. Brisbane: Post Pressed.

Kimber, M., & Ehrich, L. C. (2011). The democratic deficit and school-based management in Australia. *Journal of Educational Administration, 49*(2), 179–199.

Kuther, T. L. (2003). A profile of the ethical professor: Student views. *College Teaching, 51*(4), 153–160.

MacIntyre, A. (1984). *After virtue* (2nd ed.). Notre Dame, IN: University of Notre Dame Press.

Noddings, N. (1992). *The challenge to care in schools: An alternative approach to education*. New York: Teachers College Press.

Overeem, P., & Tholen, B. (2011). After managerialism: MacIntyre's lessons for the study of public administration. *Administration & Society, 43*(7), 722–748. doi: 10.1177/0095399711413728

Preston, N. (2007). *Understanding ethics* (3rd ed.). Sydney: Federation Press.

Preston, N., Samford, C., & Connors, C. (2002). *Encouraging ethics and challenging corruption*. Sydney: Federation Press.

Rawls, J. (1999). *A theory of justice*. Cambridge, MA: Harvard University Press.

Robinson, S. (2010). Leadership ethics. In J. Gold, R. Thorpe, & A. Mumford (Eds.), *Gower handbook of leadership and management development* (5th ed., pp. 175–196). Farnham, UK: Gower.

Samier, E. (2008). The problem of passive evil in educational administration: Moral implications of doing nothing. *International Studies in Educational Administration, 36*(1), 2–21.

Starratt, R. (1996). *Transforming educational administration: Meaning, community and excellence.* New York: McGraw Hill.

Stewart, N. (2000). *Ethics: An introduction to moral philosophy.* Cambridge, UK: Polity Press.

Sumsion, J. (2000). Caring and empowerment: A teacher educator's reflection on an ethical dilemma. *Teaching in Higher Education, 5*(2), 167–179.

Trevino, L. K. (1986). Ethical decision making in organizations: A person–situation interactionist model. *Academy of Management Review, 11*(3), 601–617.

Uhr, J. (2005). *Terms of trust: Arguments over ethics in Australian government.* Sydney: UNSW Press.

Walker, K., & Shakotko, D. (1999). The Canadian superintendency: Value-based challenges and pressure. In P. T. Begley (Ed.), *Values and educational leadership* (pp. 289–313), Albany: State University of New York Press.

# 16

## USING TURBULENCE THEORY TO GUIDE ACTIONS

### STEVEN JAY GROSS

Ethical dilemmas and their possible resolution are a consistent issue facing educational leaders at all levels in today's pre-K through graduate schools. While these dilemmas are serious, they are not all of the same magnitude, and the question often relates to the intensity of any given issue. It is in this vein that turbulence theory[1] has been successfully applied as an aid in understanding and responding to challenges of ethical decision making in educational settings around the world. This chapter will examine the origins of turbulence theory, the four levels of turbulence, and the use of the turbulence gauge, the underlying dynamics that escalate and reduce levels of turbulence, and turbulence theory's relevance to ethical decision making for educators.

## IT STARTED ON A NEW YEAR'S EVE FLIGHT

As a child, I *was* a good flyer. From the time of my first flight in 1956 from Idlewild Airport in New York (later renamed in honor of President Kennedy) to Nassau in the Bahamas, and throughout his teenage years, getting on an airplane was nothing short of a dream trip in a modified spaceship. Even as a small child, he always held fast to the idea that no matter how cloudy, rainy, or snowy the surface conditions, a few minutes after takeoff, and a few thousand feet of altitude, the sun was shining and he would be able to look down on a vista of earth unimaginable only a hundred years earlier.

This enthusiasm came naturally enough. My grandfather had the same perspective and was one of the first builders of biplanes when he worked for the Glenn Curtiss Company, an early competitor to the Wright brothers. Later, during World War I, he joined the navy and was sent to southern France to assemble early naval aircraft, where his unit entertained then Assistant Secretary of the Navy Franklin Delano Roosevelt during FDR's tour of the front.[2] A generation later, during World War II, my father left the infantry to join the precursor to today's Air Force, the Army

Air Corps. Showing an inherent ability with multi-engine airplanes and leading a crew, he became a pilot in the 8th Air Force flying 30 missions over occupied Europe, including the D-Day invasion in a B-17 named *Wolf Pack.* Among his many medals at the end of the war was the Distinguished Flying Cross. To add to this list of airborne enthusiasts closely connected to me is the case of my father-in-law, a graduate of the Chinese Air Academy, a national hero for his daring fighter-pilot exploits against the Japanese in World War II, a general in the Republic of China's Air Force, and later commandant of that nation's air academy.

With this background, and with scores of beautiful flights behind me, I anticipated a lifelong love of flying. That was an illusion and it was with that illusion fully intact that I cheerfully boarded a jet bound from Miami to Philadelphia on New Year's Eve, 1970. Sitting next to me was a retired couple, who seemed nervous. "Oh, please don't pay much attention to us," said the wife, "it's just that this is our first airplane ride and we're a little on edge." It was not hubris but a sense of community that inspired me to reply: "Look, I have been on airplanes since I was 6 years old, here and around the world. You're never going to be safer than you are right now. The ride to the airport was by far the most dangerous part of the trip." Reflecting on my little speech now, I sounded like a brainwashed lobbyist for the airlines, but this was a genuine enthusiasm and proved correct until dinner was served (please remember, it was a different era and hot meals were still the norm, even on 2-hour flights). There were the passengers with hot turkey, mashed potatoes, and brilliant green peas steaming in front of them. My new friends and I were enjoying the meal and I even got the husband to wink at his wife as he was teased about his recent angst. Then, with the suddenness of a runaway rollercoaster careening down a vertical drop, the plane fell. Turkey, mashed potatoes, and peas became airborne, quickly decorating the passengers' clothing. Screams and panicked cries foreshadowing gruesome deaths spread throughout the cabin and the elderly man sitting next to me, his dentures rocking wildly in a half-spilled glass of water in front of him, started to cry.

A quality that later helped me to become a caring teacher took over. As the plane steadied itself, I tried to keep a calming dialogue going (which ended up being nothing more than a monologue). "Oh, that was terrible, but it was only an air pocket. It happens now and again but is nothing serious. We'll be there soon and all we've had was a scare and a little dinner spread over our clothing." It was useless. The man's crying did slow but I could see by the couple's nervous frowns that their brittle confidence in flying, and in my advice, was shattered. My counsel to them was really my own way of dealing with the fissures now evident in my idealistic image of flight. By the time I reached my parent's home and started to mix into their New Year's Eve party, I knew the damage was done. I felt traumatized and now would look at flying as a risky business. In truth, I had my first experience with severe turbulence.

For years, I was a white-knuckled flyer, not ceasing flight altogether, but dreading it. As in other cases of trauma, even a small stimulus, like the report of thunderstorms en route, let alone a small amount of bumpiness on board, was enough to reawaken my fears and unleash squadrons of menacing butterflies in my stomach. I became so focused on the fear of turbulence that I once asked my father if he shared my concern when he was flying missions over Nazi Germany. With an amused, kindly, but ironic expression, my father replied, "Actually, Steve, compared to flak and enemy aircraft, turbulence was not exactly high on my list of worries."

I had fear but no context for the next 25 years. All of that changed at a place called The World's Biggest Bookstore in Toronto, Canada. I was in town doing research on a book about initiating serious innovation in public schools and, frankly, I was in a bit of a funk. The high school I was studying seemed to match an emerging and disturbing pattern. No matter how thoughtful the change in curriculum, instruction, and assessment, and no matter how carefully and sensitively the plans were constructed with the surrounding community, there always seemed to be a strong level of disturbance associated with significant change. Why? I felt that it was somehow unfair for these considerate, talented educators to have to face angry groups of parents as they unveiled their designs for school reform.

Certainly, I understood that change always brought with it opposition. I had enough theory and philosophy to see that Hegel's (1892) dialectic applied and that these new concepts could easily be labeled as today's antithesis resulting from the current thesis leading to some new synthesis that, in turn, would attract a new antithesis. That, however, was little comfort as I tried to frame the world of educational innovation. What I needed was a way of understanding four looming questions:

- How might the levels of disturbance facing innovating schools be described so that different degrees of challenge could be compared?
- How might the emotional strength of that disturbance be more thoroughly understood?
- How might the school look at its own disturbance in a measured way so that reasoned action could be more likely?
- Might there be a positive aspect to the disturbances facing schools that decide to innovate? Or was turbulence always a detrimental force always to be avoided or at least diminished?

I had come to this mother of all bookstores simply to wander in a comfortable space. Aimlessly browsing among countless aisles filled with books was like a balm and freed me to let my mind float. It was nearly closing time when I happened on the how-to section of the store and spotted a manual for beginning pilots. Given my attitude about flight, I had no idea why my hands reached for it so automatically. I rapidly turned the pages to the section on turbulence and there it was, a pilot's set of definitions for turbulence. Of course, there were times when there seemed to be no movement at all during flight, the book stated—this was known as smooth-as-glass flying. But, normally, there were four levels of turbulence: light, moderate, severe, and extreme. The text went on to describe each of the four levels:

- *Light:* little or no movement of the craft
- *Moderate:* very noticeable waves
- *Severe:* strong gusts that threaten control of the craft
- *Extreme:* forces so great that control is lost and structural damage to the craft occurs

Even in texts dedicated to the study of turbulence under many conditions, these four basic levels were fundamental (Lester, 1994).

The more I thought about it, the more these categories started to have meaning for the problems facing innovating schools. Continuing my research trips to schools in North America, I began to apply the four levels of turbulence to conditions that I witnessed.

During that year of investigations, I found clear examples of three turbulence levels. For example, one elementary school found it difficult to engage all families, since they came from two disjointed communities, one upper-middle-class living near the campus and the other a working-class community residing miles away. This was a concern to the school leaders, and the local PTA, because it meant that one group of parents would have access to the school and be able to influence it, while the second might feel disenfranchised. While no immediate crisis existed, the issue of a disjointed community led to a series of responses and regular monitoring. In this way, it was much like the light turbulence level, since there was little disturbance but attention needed to be paid.

A high school in the study seemed to face a more concentrated challenge. While this school was doing well and was following through on its innovative ideas, it suddenly had to absorb students from a sister school in the same district that was forced to close. This issue was hardly a case of light turbulence, since the consequences of not accommodating the new students and their families would be serious for the school and its reform agenda. Responding to this challenge, the school leaders made welcoming new students their highest priority and took the position that the new students had the right to influence their new school as much as they had the obligation to be influenced by it. A pre-semester in-service for the school's professional staff led to specific responses, including an orientation for new students, inclusion of the school's student advisory program, and a buddy system linking new to current students. This school faced and responded to moderate turbulence. The influx of many new students represented a noticeable wave to the school. This was not a case of business as usual but a specific issue requiring focused attention. It is useful to note that cases of moderate turbulence compel action, sensitivity, and creativity. Often, existing committee structures, called to action in time and given clear focus, can respond to this level of turbulence.

A Midwest district faced a qualitatively different challenge. This district was known for its high performance, including its solid results in state-sponsored tests. School and district leaders worked for several years to infuse new curriculum and instructional practices into their programs. While many community members supported the new set of learning objectives, another group found these too close to the principles of outcomes-based education (OBE) (Spady, 1988). Since OBE had become a politically charged issue, it was not long before the two camps saw each other as diametrically opposed. Soon, names were hurled across the growing divide, tempers flared, and long-time friendships withered in the heat of acrimonious debate. Neither light nor moderate turbulence could describe this condition, since the shockwaves of this crisis threatened the entire reform program of the district and its schools.

It was clear that short of an intense effort to regain control, the district was headed for disaster. Fortunately, district and community leaders did rally. A highly respected community member, not identified with either side, became board chairperson. Another community member, with professional group facilitation skills, organized and conducted a series of forums including all sides in the debate. These meetings were taped and broadcast over the local cable access channel. After weeks of intensive listening and sharing, the community saw that their common interests outweighed their differences. Compromises and a modified direction were found. The community and its school district experienced an episode of severe turbulence. The entire enterprise was at risk in much the same way as severe turbulence threatens the aircraft with total loss of control. In the air, extraordinary maneuvers may be required to recover from this level of turbulence. This applies to reforming schools as well. No existing organizational structure was used to get this district back on its reform flight path—new leaders inventing new responses were needed.

The original study making up "Staying Centered: Curriculum Leadership in a Turbulent Era" (Gross, 1998) did not uncover an example of extreme turbulence. This was not surprising, since extreme turbulence would mean the destruction of the reform program and I was only studying ongoing innovations. My speculation on the existence of extreme turbulence kept the place open for such a possibility and I was certain that eventually I would find such a case, since regrettably, educational reform often missed its mark (Sarason, 1990).

It was not long before an example did reveal itself (Gross, 2000). On my initial visit to this school, I found a smoothly working reform that had a well-organized curriculum, strong parental support, solid teacher participation, well-coordinated after-school programs, and positive relations with the area superintendent. Given the challenges of high levels of poverty in the families the school served, their success was even more remarkable. What a contrast my next visit turned out to be only 2 years later. Gone was the relationship with the district after the departure of the supportive area superintendent. On top of that, the school was compelled to grow too rapidly in size and in grade level. Instead of a small K–5 elementary school, the building now accommodated grades K–8 in much larger numbers. This growth led to hiring many new teachers, some of whom did not seem to support the original reform agenda. Adding to the stress was the problem that one of the grades had not performed adequately on a state test, thereby placing the entire school on a need-to-improve list. Finally, the foundation that financed the original reform was ending its support, since the funding cycle was at its end. When I arrived, I found that the gifted principal, who initiated the reform, was preparing to retire. With a degree of regret, I concluded that I had found an example of extreme turbulence leading to the destruction of the reform itself. Like extreme turbulence in an airplane, this condition does more than grab attention—it creates a crisis that even the inventiveness of talented school and community leaders may not be equal to.

With the example of extreme turbulence, the metaphor seemed complete. Each level of turbulence had an equivalent from the data on innovating schools. Just as important, there were responses to each of the first three levels (light, moderate, and severe) that seemed instructive to academics and practitioners. Answers to three of my four questions were starting to emerge. With turbulence, I could now describe different degrees of challenge facing innovating school. Likewise, I could speak to the relative emotional strength of disturbances. By using the four levels of turbulence, schools could reflect upon their issues in measured ways and pursue responses that reflected their current condition. While all metaphors are limited (Morgan, 1997), the metaphor of turbulence seemed to fit three of my questions well and I gained a new vocabulary to share with fellow educators.

## THE POSITIVE ASPECTS OF TURBULENCE

Giving a paper on turbulence theory and its relationship to ethical decision making at a University Council of Educational Administration (UCEA) conference with my co-author, Joan Shapiro (Shapiro & Gross, 2002), led to a question that pushed my thinking further. A colleague in the audience challenged the idea of turbulence being simply a negative force that leaders needed to defend against. "Steve, isn't turbulence also the force that opens up new possibilities for the organization?" Two aspects of this question immediately struck me. First, it seemed quite credible. Why would turbulence merely be a problem? Weren't the very innovations that attracted my initial research a kind of turbulence compared with the traditions that they sought to replace? In fact, the concept of turbulence being a positive force had recently been described in the literature on business management (Gryskiewicz, 1999). I also recalled that Lewin's (1947) pioneering work in action research involved unfreezing, change, and refreezing in organizations. This can also be seen as the purposeful escalation of turbulence in an organization aimed at positive change.[3]

Almost at once, I saw that at the micro level, turbulence was needed for flight to occur in the first place. Lift simply could not occur in a vacuum. Molecules of air, moving faster over the top of the wing than the bottom, are required (Braybrook, 1985). It also became obvious that even modern aircraft take off and land facing the wind. The turbulence of that air movement is needed to send airplanes aloft and help them to land safely. Out of control, turbulence could lead to disaster, but well understood and monitored, it was an essential element of life in the air.

Further thought caused me to see where I had limited my perspective. My own traumatic experience caused me to color my attitude toward disturbances. Until challenged by this question, I had created categories that made turbulence a problem for innovators to avoid or handle, just as I hoped that radar and good piloting skills would help aircraft avoid or handle turbulence. Now, I realized that this was important but not the complete story.

I needed to deepen my understanding of the nature of turbulence and so I opened myself up to considering its different manifestations that might add new dimensions to the existing metaphor beyond air movement and airplanes. I expanded my explorations as soon as the 2002–2003 academic year ended and I had the opportunity to literally go into the field back home in Vermont. At first, I tried to simply look at air movement closer to the ground and spent time watching the impact of even small bursts of wind on plants and trees. Although I did learn a great deal from these observations, such as the uneven impact of barely perceptible breezes, I was not satisfied with this tack. Hiking in the Green Mountains National Forest one morning, I heard the sound of a brook and stopped to simply enjoy it. While I had walked past this small body of water scores of times, on that day it had an unanticipated attraction. What I saw was a complex swirling of water, first moving rapidly, and then slowing, taking twigs and leaves along, only to treat these differently as its motion shifted. Throughout that summer, I spent weeks observing creeks, rivers, waterfalls, and small streams. I recorded everything that I could possibly see each day, waiting until much later to attempt to analyze my observations. I allowed the flowing bodies of water to show new aspects of this kind of turbulence. In the spirit of grounded theory (Glaser & Strauss, 1967), I allowed insights gained from one day's fieldwork to inform my perspective on the following day's work.

## POSITIONALITY

One new element of turbulence theory, emerging from expanding the metaphor to include the behavior of flowing water, was *positionality*. I noticed that a moving river did not have the same impact on twigs and leaves at its center as it did on those similar objects at its edges. In fact, careful examinations caused me to see that the impact of the water's flow had many varying levels of impact, all depending upon the position of the object relative to the center of the stream or its banks. Leaves at the center of the flow moved rapidly, while leaves the same size on the sides might move much slower, get caught on the banks, or become trapped in small whirlpools.

Position mattered in bodies of moving water and I soon found parallels in organizational turbulence. Turbulence might seem uniform viewed from far away, but at the level of the specific case where one was, in relation to the organization, it seemed very meaningful. Reflecting on my earlier work on turbulence in the air, it was clear to me that my own sense of concern when the seat belt sign illuminated was likely far greater than that of the pilot. In schools, the case of severe turbulence described above meant different things to the superintendent, the high school principal, the parents, and area business leaders.

### Defining Positionality in Turbulence Theory

This variety of movement in the same stream with objects the same size seemed very much like the concept of positionality theory (Alcoff, 1991–1992; Hauser, 1997; Kezar, 2000; Maher & Tetreault, 1993) and standpoint theory (Collins, 1997) used in social science.

Recent scholarship has revealed a debate between these two perspectives. Defending standpoint theory, Collins (1997) states:

> First, the notion of Standpoint Theory refers to historically shared, group experiences. Groups have a degree of permanence over time such that group realities transcend individual experiences. For instance, African Americans, as a stigmatized racial group existed long before I was born and will probably continue long after I die. While my individual experiences with

institutionalized racism will be unique, the types of opportunities and constraints that I encounter on a daily basis will resemble those confronting African Americans as a group.

(p. 375)

Countering this claim for the utility of standpoint theory, Kezar (2000) describes the utility of positionality theory:

Positionality Theory acknowledges that people have multiple, overlapping identities, and thus make meaning from various aspects of their identity, including social class, professional standing, and so forth. Therefore, it is more complex and dynamic than Standpoint Theory while retaining its epistemological concerns. Positionality Theory assumes that power relationships can change and that social categories are fluid, dynamic, affected by history and social changes.

(p. 725)

The type of positionality I suggest for turbulence theory combines elements of both of these perspectives. When thinking of positionality as developed in turbulence theory, it is important to understand the relative situation of individuals in the organization in *a multidimensional fashion*. In the case of educational institutions, this means not only attempting to be empathetic to the turbulence as students might experience it, for example, but also acknowledging that groups of students (as organized by gender, race, age, socioeconomic status, or years in the community, for instance) may experience it differently. Equally, it means seeing individuals in each of their group affiliations and simultaneously as separate beings. This is not a linear, easily nested process.

While this sounds perplexing at first, the result can become a systematic process in which those facing a dilemma can ask a series of questions leading to a richer understanding of the authentic positions and perspectives of others without condescending or, as Alcoff (1991–1992) describes it, *speaking for others*. A reasonable sequence of questions to illuminate positionality during turbulence might be:

1. What different groups exist in our organization (younger students, older students, staff, faculty, administration, parents)? How might the current turbulence affect each of them?
2. What different demographics exist in our organization (e.g., gender, race, social class, neighborhood, English as a second language, special education)? In each group? What might their perspectives be?
3. What do we know about individual situations? How might this alter the way this turbulence is perceived?

While light or moderate levels of turbulence might allow for detailed speculation, data gathering, and analysis, as a means of working through the problem, severe or the threat of extreme turbulence is likely to offer no such opportunity, since the need for a rapid, well-considered response is too acute. Therefore, a deep, ongoing understanding of this type of positionality within our organizations is highly recommended.

## CASCADING

The second addition to turbulence theory, coming from my examination of flowing water, was *cascading*. Anyone who has seen even a small river or creek is familiar with the nature of water as it tumbles over a series of small rocks. While I had experienced this all of my life, it was not until I took the time to think about this phenomenon as a metaphor that I saw its meaning for the study of organizations and the people in them. Water picks up speed as it cascades. The turbulence of the water is easily increased as it moves from one downturn to the next.

The effect of cascading had its parallel in organizations facing turbulence. In the case of extreme turbulence described earlier in this chapter, none of the destabilizing blows facing the innovating school—rapid growth, disappointing test results, withdrawal of superintendent support, loss of foundation funds, and departure of the founding principal—were isolated. Each, in turn, escalated the level of turbulence facing the school just as a series of vertical drops amplifies the speed of water as it cascades. The same phenomena could be seen in the horrifying firestorms created by massive bombing in World War II in cities like Dresden, Germany (McKee, 1984). Each explosion intensified city fires, thereby raising the air temperature. Hot air rising sucked cool air from the ground into the fire, thereby fueling fires and causing them to grow, thereby magnifying the intensity of the fire. The combined forces led to ground winds with such power that people were literally hurled into an inferno. A third example of multiple forces assembled to heighten turbulence through cascading is the case of massive student protests in France during 1968. Kurlansky (2004) notes:

> In chemistry it is found that some very stable elements placed in proximity to other seemingly moribund elements can spontaneously produce explosions. Hidden within this bored, overstuffed, complacent society were barely noticeable elements—a radicalized youth with a hopelessly old-fashioned geriatric leader, overpopulated universities, angry workers, a sudden consumerism enthralling some and sickening others, sharp differences between generations, and perhaps even boredom itself—that when put together could be explosive.
>
> (p. 218)

With these examples in mind,[4] the concept of cascading, like positionality, became a new addition to turbulence theory that helped me to understand dynamic forces within organizations in a richer context. For those experiencing turbulence even at the light level, it is important to consider forces in the environment that may propel that turbulence to higher levels. Community concern over a new social studies curriculum in isolation may represent a moderate level of turbulence. However, that same issue in the wake of a badly handled labor dispute, a rise in property taxes, and a report of failure in standardized tests is quite another matter. Therefore, understanding cascading is a matter of understanding context and the force of a series of turbulent conditions. By using turbulence theory and carefully measuring the degree of turbulence represented by each issue, it is possible for educational leaders to prioritize their response.

## STABILITY

Cascading and positionality are clearly related to turbulence, but something was nagging me because something seemed missing. A third force that also might escalate or diminish turbulence levels became clear as I compared pairs of schools going through roughly the same kinds of challenges yet experiencing different levels of turbulence. What could account for the difference?

I reflected on one earlier study (Gross, 1998) that included the case of Verona, Wisconsin, a community just outside of Madison. Verona schools went through a serious clash of opinions about what direction they should take—so serious, in fact, that it threatened to turn the district upside down. In an early interview, one district leader said that if the schools had not developed a reputation for being successful, things might have gotten out of hand. In other words, the schools had a solid reputation coming into the turbulent period. A different district, facing the same issues but without the advantage of a solid reputation, would likely suffer greater fallout from the same kind of turbulence. The third force became much clearer. Besides cascading and positionality, schools seemed to differ in the degree of their perceived *stability*.

Just as I used physical examples to study the rudiments of cascading, new examples seemed relevant to examine stability. Recalling the famous case of the Tacoma Narrows Bridge illustrates the point. This suspension bridge, over Washington State's Puget Sound, first opened in July 1940 and collapsed only 4 months later in the face of high winds. Even before construction was completed, the span earned the infamous nickname of Galloping Gertie. Although the reasons for the collapse are complex, the general problem can be described as a lack of rigidity of the bridge's deck, thereby making the whole structure inherently unstable. Fortunately, its replacement does not have the same structural weaknesses and has withstood conditions at the site since opening in 1950.

Stability, therefore, appears to be a relationship between the object we are examining (e.g., an organization, a bridge, a country, a person) and the dynamic force(s) confronting it. More stable organizations appear to withstand the dynamic forces confronting them, and their reputation for stability seems to insulate them from some of the harshest turbulence. That explains the case of the Verona school district. Organizations operating as learning systems seem to take this a step further by turning the turbulent experience into an opportunity to reflect and actually profit, thereby further enhancing their resilience and stability.

But there is a serious difference between stability and simply being stuck in behaviors that seem to repeat themselves. Stability in turbulence theory is a dynamic concept. It is achieved and sustained through movement, not by being rigid. In fact, a rigid response may appear to be solid, and an artifact of stability, but it rarely is. Think of a deer "frozen in headlights" and you'll get the idea. Confidence in the inherent worthiness of the organization, when it is authentically felt, provides the needed energy to respond in measured, flexible ways.

In March 1933, Franklin Roosevelt assumed the office of President of the United States. The nation was experiencing the severe turbulence of the Great Depression. The whole banking system seemed ready to collapse. FDR's famous words "The only thing we have to fear is fear itself" embodied the spirit of his inaugural address, aimed at creating a sense of needed stability. Yet, while we remember that phrase nearly 80 years afterward, the greatest response from the crowd at the time was the president's insistence on action and flexibility needed to respond to the crisis. In his words, "This Nation asks for action, and action now" (Grafton, 1999). FDR's real recipe to infuse stability was his reliance on vigorous experimentation to create needed change, and the first hundred days of his administration, leading to the creation of many New Deal programs, is still held up as a yardstick for all incoming administrations.

In one high school (Gross, 2001), I found that a culture emphasizing dialogue, democratic practices, and innovation helped to create stability, even when the school faced the turbulence of conflict with city and state education officials wanting to interfere with its operation.

But there are limits to stability. I considered the case of a downed branch I saw one day while walking in Vermont. Clearly, this was a result from the previous day's thunderstorm. From the look of it, there was some degree of rot where the branch once connected to the rest of the tree, perhaps making that point the weak link. So, what happened? A forceful thunderstorm came through that neighborhood. It came in contact with the branch and broke it off. We could say that relative to the force of the wind, the branch was unstable, meaning that it could not stay connected to the tree, and so it fell.

In the physical world, stability is found in structures able to withstand the forces to which they are exposed. In normal circumstances (late spring thunderstorms with high winds are to be expected in this part of the world), that branch (or that part of the tree's organization) broke off. Relative to normal forces, it was inherently unstable. Now, if a tornado touched down (tornados, though rare in Vermont, were predicted), an abnormal condition would exist. Relative to that force, nearly everything in its path would be unequal to the tornado's force, meaning that nearly everything would be unstable. So, we are back to the idea of stability being a concept best described in relation to the dynamic forces that impact upon it. Nothing is stable in an unqualified sense. The universe itself came into being through the very unstable moment we refer to as the Big Bang. Given sufficient dynamic force, all organizations will become unstable, as is the case of business collapses and social revolutions.

**Moving from the universe to schools and universities, stability may be seen as:**[5]

- Reputation in general, status, awards received
- Academic achievement of students (real or perceived)
- Size, numbers of students, numbers of campuses (applying more likely to higher education)
- Exclusivity, selectivity of admission (applying to selective independent schools, magnet public schools, selective charter schools, and selective higher education institutions)
- Reputation of the faculty
- Reputation for efficient and transparent management (especially in K–12 public schools)[6]

To summarize, stability includes three key ingredients:

First, things are stable in relation to the forces acting upon them. Stability is only a relative, not an absolute, condition.

Second, achieving and maintaining stability requires flexibility and change. This may sound ironic but it is clearly the case.

Third, at some point, stability will always give way to sufficient dynamic force acting upon it. This is the problem facing designers. What is the likely threshold that a given structure is ever going to face? Normally, one would build for something reasonably beyond that level. But that is not as simple as it sounds *because conditions change.*

## THE THREE FORCES COMBINED

Positionality, cascading, and stability therefore impact systems, both physical and human, in ways that can increase or decrease turbulence. It is important to view these forces in combination with one another, and not in isolation, to grasp their effect on turbulence levels. Asking simple questions such as, How are different people in this situation experiencing events? What has happened in this organization's recent past? In general, how stable are things around here? can go a long way in starting the process of seeing these forces as powerful drivers of turbulence. It can also start an analysis of how to act in ways that might modify the current levels of turbulence as you respond to ethical dilemmas at hand.

## TURBULENCE THEORY'S RELATIONSHIP TO CHAOS THEORY

While it is beyond the scope of this chapter to enter into a detailed comparison and contrast between turbulence theory and related concepts, some brief mention at the chapter's close seems useful. Below, Gross describes his perspective on turbulence theory's connection to, and distinction from, chaos theory as well as reflecting on turbulence theory's strengths and limits as a metaphor.

I am often asked to describe the differences between turbulence theory and chaos theory and usually begin my answer by sharing some of the similarities that I see. Both focus upon the combined importance of seemingly small changes, thereby asking us to remember that detail and pattern matter, especially in complex systems. Both make us think about the ebb and flow of life from seeming instability to renewed and transformed models of stability. Both seem to be elements in the natural world with strong parallels in our organizational lives.

Yet, key differences also exist between turbulence theory and chaos theory. Though inspired by natural phenomena,[7] turbulence theory is designed to help us better understand life in micro and macro human organizations. Further, turbulence theory's use of a turbulence gauge (Gross, 2004), and its combination with rich concepts such as multiple ethical paradigms, make it operational for people in organizations to employ it when they wish to observe, plan, and act. Turbulence theory recognizes complexity but is constructed to provide useful tools to help those employing it to flow with rapidly evolving change, thereby taking advantage of its benefits and minimizing its potential for harm.

Besides pointing to the similarities and differences between turbulence theory and chaos theory, it is useful to explain that the two theories can be combined with potentially beneficial results. For example, we might consider an escalating pattern of turbulence as an episode of an organization being stuck on one side of a Lorenz attractor (a kind of swirling figure 8 wherein each side behaves like a powerful whirlpool). Further consideration of the benefits of combining these theoretical lenses seems worthwhile, since, in their application to organizations, they are each metaphors with strengths and limits.

## TURBULENCE THEORY AS A METAPHOR

Morgan (1997) describes the use of metaphors in understanding organizational life in rich, flexible ways:

> Metaphor is often regarded just as a device for embellishing discourse, but its significance is much greater than this. The use of metaphor implies *a way of thinking* and *a way of seeing* that pervade how we understand our world generally.
>
> (p. 4, emphasis in the original)

Noting the limits of any given theory, Morgan cautions:

> In recognizing theory as metaphor, we quickly appreciate that no single theory will ever give us a perfect or all-purpose point of view. We realize that the challenge is to become skilled in the art of using metaphor: to find fresh ways of seeing, understanding, and shaping situations that we want to organize and manage.
>
> (pp. 5–6)

In this context, turbulence theory is a metaphor for both the episodic and continuing forces that we live with each day in our organizations. As Morgan observes, each successful metaphor, each well-considered theory, illuminates an aspect of reality. Coinciding with this illumination, however, each metaphor simultaneously obscures something of reality. Turbulence theory illuminates levels of change in our organizations and helps us to frame them. This chapter describes some of the ways in which it can be used to gain a deeper understanding of these forces. However, turbulence theory is not intended to be, in Morgan's words, an all-purpose point of view. The careful application of turbulence theory is intended to add a new dimension to our understanding of organizational life and, in the context of this book, to our understanding of the forces surrounding ethical dilemmas.

## GUIDANCE FOR THE APPLICATION OF
## TURBULENCE THEORY

While not intending to impose a formulaic approach to using turbulence theory, some guidance is in order. As the earlier parts of this chapter indicate, there are key variables to consider when using turbulence theory. These include contextual forces, such as positionality, stability, and the possibility of the cascading of events, the degree of turbulence in any given situation, and the possible consequences of a changed level of turbulence. Each of these variables, in turn, is made up of several elements that are described below. At the conclusion of each, summary questions are suggested.

*Contextual forces.* Early on, it is important to explore contextual variables surrounding any given situation. In turbulence theory, the relevant issues of context include cascading, relationships among key individuals, and the current stability or volatility of the organization. When examining cascading, it is useful to collect data on the forces that are at play in the current situation. If a school is facing an ethical dilemma over a controversial new curriculum, for instance, other seemingly unrelated events might contribute to turbulence such as a teacher strike, budget defeat, poor test scores, or a combination of all three. What is the relationship among them? How have they emerged in the recent past? What does this particular organization's history tell us about the potential for cascading to have a serious impact on turbulence? Seeing relationships between key individuals in context causes us to ask similar questions. What past history exists, both constructive and combative, between these individuals that bears on this situation? Remembering the architectural example of Galloping Gertie, we come to the issue of the current stability or volatility of the organization itself. This requires considering its recent history from an internal and external perspective. One way of viewing this contextual variable is to ask the question, Is the current turbulence an exception or part of a larger pattern of disruption?

*Positionality.* Once the contextual forces have been explored in some detail, a series of questions about positionality will further illuminate turbulence as different individuals and groups within the organization may be experiencing it. The purpose of the discussion on positionality earlier in this chapter was designed to define that term as it applies to turbulence theory. Clearly, one's position in an organization during turbulence is also a key variable, and one that deserves examination from multiple perspectives suggested in the questions raised earlier. As those questions imply, there are three places to begin to explore positionality as it relates to turbulence. First, there is the job of defining the functional groups involved in the issue. In schools, functional groups typically include younger and older students, faculty, staff, administration, parents, board members, and the wider community. What does the dilemma look like from each of these perspectives? While this is crucial information, stopping at this point risks overgeneralizing about individuals within these functional groups and assuming that every teacher, for instance, will feel similarly about a given turbulent issue. Therefore, the next lens of positionality is one of demographics. This includes categories that are obvious, such as gender, age, ethnicity, race, religion, sexual orientation, level of formal education, and social economic status. It also includes perspectives not so commonly considered, such as years living in a given community. Judgment needs to be exercised in this phase of analysis, since an individual's multiple demographic affiliations are complex. Larger patterns that relate to the specific turbulent condition are what matter most. Finally, there is the position of the individual. Does this turbulence mean something of particular significance to one or more of the key actors in the current situation?

***Establishing the current level of turbulence.*** After the forces of context and positionality are considered, it is more likely that a reasonable estimate of the level of turbulence may be made. The turbulence gauge can be seen in Table 16.1. Having thought through contextual and positionality variables, it is now time to look at the four levels of turbulence (light, moderate, severe, and extreme) found in the left-hand column as well as the corresponding general definitions found in the second column and select the closest fit. Those working through the problem may then describe their situation in the appropriate cell of the right-hand column entitled "Turbulence as Applied to This Situation." The turbulence gauge is completed when all of the cells in the right-hand column are filled in. This is normally done by estimating the conditions one would find if turbulence was either higher or lower than the current level. Since establishing a level of turbulence is the result of complex conceptual analysis, it is highly useful for individuals to compare their findings at this point and explore their insights through dialogue. This will allow divergent views to be aired and may lead to greater confidence in the current level of turbulence.

***Possible consequences of changing levels of turbulence.*** Context, positionality, and current level of turbulence are obviously key variables whose qualities and interactions merit early analysis. However, since turbulence theory is not a static construction, change in turbulence level is an additional variable requiring attention. Individuals or groups working through turbulence would be wise to explore questions such as these: What is likely to happen to the current level of turbulence if no attention is paid to the situation in the short and medium term (raising the issue of cascading)? Would more turbulence help or harm the organization's pursuit of its goals (reflecting the potential for positive results from turbulence)? How might contemplated actions reduce the level of turbulence (when that level is considered too high and, consequently, harmful)? This exercise will help formulate relevant predictions of turbulence.

**Table 16.1** The generic turbulence theory gauge

| Degree of Turbulence | General Definition | Turbulence as Applied to This Situation |
|---|---|---|
| Light | Associated with ongoing issues, little or no disruption in normal work environment, subtle signs of stress | |
| Moderate | Widespread awareness of the issue, specific origins | |
| Severe | Fear for the entire enterprise, possibility of large-scale community demonstrations, a feeling of crisis | |
| Extreme | Structural damage to the institution's normal operation is occurring | |

By carefully examining the key variables—contextual forces, positionality, current level of turbulence, and consequences of changing levels of turbulence—in this order, relationships between pairs and among groups typically emerge, leading to a richer understanding of the flow of turbulence in a given situation. Using turbulence theory in this way fulfills four of the relevant requirements that Glaser and Strauss (1967) make for theories described in Chapter 1 of this text. Contextual forces and positionality help to explain and interpret turbulence in multidimensional ways that capture the dynamic flow of volatile conditions in our schools. Determining the current level of turbulence and possible changes in turbulence helps scholars and practitioners make relevant predictions that can guide decision making. In so doing, turbulence theory has become a useful tool applied to dynamic, challenging conditions that abound in the schools of our era.

## CONCLUSION

That evening, long ago, when I experienced a few moments of severe turbulence in flight thrust me into a new way of looking at the world. Today, it seems that nearly everyone accepts that we live under turbulent conditions of some kind. Events like September 11, 2001, and its aftermath are easy to spot. So are natural crises like Hurricane Katrina and the tsunamis that killed over two hundred thousand people in December 2004. The fast pace of change, represented by the post-industrial information economy and its dislocations, seems to fit this metaphor as well. The purpose of turbulence theory transcends the need to describe these sudden, and sometimes wrenching, changes. It is meant to help us gain perspective on this movement, see potential benefits, and retain needed flexibility. The hope of turbulence theory is that it may help us work with the conditions of our era.

## NOTES

1. This chapter is adapted from a chapter in Shapiro and Gross (2013), *Ethical Educational Leadership in Turbulent Times* (New York: Routledge). The author is grateful to Routledge for granting permission to use this version of the work in the present handbook.
2. Those interested in Roosevelt's personal story will remember that it was on the return to the US from this European tour that Eleanor Roosevelt, opening his trunk, came across romantic letters sent to her husband from her personal secretary Lucy Mercer.
3. Yet, the concept of positive change resulting from turbulence is relative. Traditionalists in that same organization may see the action research process as an unwelcome interference with the normal life of the group.
4. Cases of cascading during turbulence are connected to the process of positive feedback loops in organizational theory (Senge, 1990) wherein trends seem to reinforce and increase one another's impact. This is the case of the firestorm, since it only grows more deadly due to its own cycle described above. In an earlier study (Gross, 2004), I found that avoiding just such a positive feedback loop was a crucial adjustment for reforming schools to make if they hoped to sustain innovations over time.
5. Note that in most of these examples, perceptions may be subject to a lag time before moving on one way or another—so that a school once considered unstable but which has improved markedly may remain unstable in the minds of people for some time after things have actually gotten better. The reverse is also the case.
6. Note that each of the ways stability may be seen in schools and universities is relative to some dynamic, opposing force and that achieving and sustaining stability requires flexibility and action, due to the need to respond to or utilize the energy of that force in a planned manner.

7. While illustrations supporting turbulence theory may derive from the movement of small particles such as the turbulent flow of water droplets in a stream or the dynamics of molecules on an airplane wing, we may learn just as much about turbulence from examples in architecture. One illustrative case is of the Tacoma Narrows suspension bridge nicknamed Galloping Gertie, which fell apart in a graphic demonstration of extreme turbulence (Levy & Salvadori, 2002).

## REFERENCES

Alcoff, L. (1991–1992, Winter). The problem of speaking for others. *Cultural Critique, 20*, 5–32.

Braybrook, R. (1985). *The aircraft encyclopedia*. New York, NY: Simon and Schuster.

Collins, P. H. (1997). Comment on Hedeman's "The truth and method: Feminist standpoint theory revisited": Where's the power? *Signs, 22*(2), 375–381.

Glaser, B. G., & Strauss, A. L. (1967). *The discovery of grounded theory: Strategies for qualitative research*. Chicago, IL: Aldine.

Grafton, J. (Ed.). (1999). *Franklin Delano Roosevelt: Great speeches*. Mineola, NY: Dover.

Gross, S. J. (1998). *Staying centered: Curriculum leadership in a turbulent era*. Alexandria, VA: Association for Supervision and Curriculum Development.

Gross, S. J. (2000, October). *From turbulence to tidal wave: Understanding the unraveling of reform at one innovative and diverse urban elementary school for children at risk*. Paper presented at the Northeast Educational Research Association annual conference, Ellenville, New York.

Gross, S. J. (2001). Navigating a gale: Sustaining curriculum-instruction-assessment innovation in an urban high school for immigrants. *Journal of Research in Education, 11*(1), 74–87.

Gross, S. J. (2004). *Promises kept: Sustaining school and district innovation in a turbulent era*. Alexandria, VA: Association of Supervision and Curriculum Development.

Gryskiewicz, S. S. (1999). *Positive turbulence: Developing climates for creativity, innovation, and renewal*. San Francisco, CA: Jossey-Bass.

Hauser, M. E. (1997). How do we really work? A response to "Locked in uneasy sisterhood: Reflections on feminist methodology and research relationships." *Anthropology & Education Quarterly, 28*(1), 123–126.

Hegel, G. W. F. (1892). *The logic of Hegel*. Oxford: Clarendon.

Kezar, A. (2000). Pluralistic leadership: Incorporating diverse voices. *Journal of Higher Education, 71*(6), 722–743.

Kurlansky, M. (2004). *1968: The year that rocked the world*. New York, NY: Ballantine Books.

Lester, P. F. (1994). *Turbulence: A new perspective for pilots*. Englewood, CO: Jeppesen.

Levy, M., & Salvadori, M. (2002). *Why buildings fall down*. New York, NY: W. W. Norton & Co.

Lewin, K. (1947). Frontiers in group dynamics II. *Human Relations, 1*(3), 143–153.

Maher, F. A., & Tetreault, M. K. (1993). Frames of positionality: Meaningful dialogues about gender and race. *Anthropological Quarterly, 62*(3), 118–126.

McKee, A. (1984). *Dresden 1945: The devil's tinderbox*. New York, NY: E. P. Dutton.

Morgan, G. (1997). *Images of organization* (2nd ed.). Thousand Oaks, CA: Sage Publications.

Sarason, S. B. (1990). *The predictable failure of educational reform: Can we change course before it's too late?* San Francisco, CA: Jossey-Bass.

Senge, P. (1990). *The fifth discipline*. New York, NY: Doubleday.

Shapiro, J., & Gross, S. J. (2002, October). *Understanding educational leadership in a time of turbulence*. Paper presented at the University Council of Educational Administration annual conference, Pittsburgh, PA.

Spady, W. G. (1988). Organizing for results: The basis of authentic restructuring and reform. *Educational Leadership, 46*(2), 4–8.

# 17

## MAINTAINING MORAL INTEGRITY

### CHRISTOPHER M. BRANSON

Ever since Foster (1986, p. 284) so insightfully declared: "Leadership must be ethical [because] it carries a responsibility not just to be personally moral, but to be a cause of 'civic moral education' which leads to both self-knowledge and community awareness" tertiary institutions throughout the world have striven to inculcate ethical decision-making units into their educational leadership courses. Yet our current educational leadership literature is still brimming with calls to recognize the place of ethics in the professional development of leaders (Begley, 2006; Duignan, 2006; Fullan, 2003; Greenfield, 2004; Hollimon, Basinger, Smith, & Leonard, 2009; Richmon, 2003; Starratt, 2003; Tuana, 2007). Why, after more than 20 years of knowing that ethical decision making is integral to appropriate leadership behavior, does it still remain a major concern within our educational leadership literature? Surely, this is a clear indication that we have yet to find the most effective way to help prepare our current and future educational leaders for being able to confidently and effectively deal with their complex, problematic, and unavoidable ethical decision-making responsibilities.

To this end, this chapter proposes that our failure to date to adequately prepare our current and future educational leaders for being able to effectively deal with ethical decision-making responsibilities is caused by an inherent oversight in our existing ethical decision-making frameworks. Essentially, these frameworks do not cater to the pivotal role played by personal moral integrity in every ethical decision. Moral integrity is about instinctively and consistently doing what is right for the good of others in the absence of incentives or sanctions. People often try to explain moral behavior by referring to a personal benefit, such as the good feeling we experience when we act ethically. But to characterize moral behavior as conferring some form of personal benefit is a perverse way of seeing it. A more informed understanding of what constitutes moral acts are that they are carried out for their own sake and not because the actor expects any benefit, psychic or otherwise. In this way, possessing moral integrity is about achieving a personal victory where the interests of others, rather than self-interests, are the spontaneous motivation.

Hence, this chapter seeks to redress this oversight, first, by describing the role of moral integrity within every ethical decision, and second, by explaining the nature of personal moral integrity. While self-reflection and self-inquiry can play a large part in ensuring that one's leadership actions reflect moral integrity, more needs to be known about what to reflect on, or what to inquire into, about one's self before such processes can be beneficial. Thus, this chapter will conclude by describing how our educational leadership development programs associated with ethical decision making can be easily adjusted so as to cater to the concurrent development of the leader's crucially important component of personal character that is moral integrity.

## THEORETICAL DEVELOPMENTS IN OUR UNDERSTANDING OF MORAL INTEGRITY

As described more fully by Branson (2009), our general understanding of moral integrity has been so altered during the past 400 years that we are now very unsure, if not dismissive, of its nature, its importance, and its relevance in today's society (Hamilton, 2008; Lennick and Kiel, 2005; Taylor, 2003). This being the case, how can moral integrity be an essential part of leadership? How can we expect our leaders to reflect upon the ethicalness of their actions if they do not understand what is really meant or expected of them?

Our confusion or ambivalence about the concept of morality is very much an outcome of its history. Ferrè (2001) reminds us that the "arbitrariness" of ethics has been a recurrent theme since the breakdown of the medieval society in late pre-modern and early modern thinking. Here, arbitrariness does not mean erratic but rather it means that ethics does not always obey rational or objective rules. From when the world first entered what has become known as the Enlightenment or modern era, ethics and moral decision making were recognized as being a distinctively different form of judgment from that of reasoned, rational, or objective judgment.

The Scottish philosopher David Hume (1711–1776) held the view that the subjective realm of impressions, sentiments, feelings, and moral thoughts were far superior to that of reason. "Reason," wrote Hume (1955, p. 415), "is and ought to be only the slave of the passions and can never pretend to any other office than to serve and obey them." Moreover, Hume emphasizes his view of the clear distinction between ethical and reasoned thinking when he draws his often cited conclusion that "ought" can never be derived from "is." According to Hume, matters of fact and reason are questions of "is" and "is not," containing no trace of an "ought." In other words, what we ought to do so as to act with moral integrity can never, in Hume's opinion, be directed by rules based on supposed facts. No matter how closely we commit to facts or rules, there will only ever be a need for more facts and rules to guide our actions, and not values or beliefs, which are "entirely different." From Hume's perspective, rules and regulations can never develop a sincere commitment to moral integrity in a person. For Hume, it is the person's passions, feelings, desires, and subjectivity that form the foundation for moral decision making.

Although accepting Hume's clear distinction between ethical and reasoned thinking, the German philosopher Immanuel Kant passionately opposed the view presented by Hume. For Kant, according to Cottingham (2006), rationality was the only source of true knowledge. Kant's (1949) assertion was that any actions influenced by subjectivity did not merit moral esteem because only when someone acts "without inclination, from the sake of duty alone, does his action for the first time have genuine moral worth" (p. 11). Kantian philosophy perceives a moral person as someone who acts according to a universally accepted principle or rule.

Moreover, Kant provided the cornerstone for morality in the modern era by locating the source of moral value in the autonomous free will of the individual person. From a Kantian perspective, it is assumed that people will each exercise their free will in a rational way so as to maximize their respect for others and, thereby, enhance their own sense of self-respect. However, when describing the nature of free will, Kant (1956) added: "For the law of pure will, which is free, puts the will in a sphere entirely different from the empirical, and the necessity which it expresses, not being a natural necessity can consist only in the formal conditions of the possibility of a law in general" (p. 34). This means that, in Kant's view, the person's free will, the core component in moral decision making, is not considered to be empirical, or knowable through reason. Thus, the concept of free will cannot be used to judge the worthiness of the moral decision. Rather, the moral decision can be judged only from the degree of alignment of the resultant action with a universally accepted moral rule. In other words, questions about how people were to make appropriate moral decisions were irrelevant, and the only concern in morality was being able to rationally explain how your behavior met some predetermined social expectation.

However, a third important perspective on the nature of moral integrity is that of utilitarianism as proffered by John Stuart Mill in 1861. Mill argues that the level of moral integrity of an act depends not on any intrinsic worth, as had been promoted by Kant, but on the amount of goodness or happiness it produces or tends to produce (Ferrè, 2001; Hamilton, 2008). The standard of happiness inherent within a moral act is referred to as its utility. Moreover, an action's relative level of utility is directly proportional to the amount of happiness that it generated. This has been referred to as the *greatest happiness principle:* Actions are right in proportion as they tend to promote happiness, but wrong if they tend to produce the reverse of happiness. Mill also took pains to point out that a utilitarian does not try to make each individual decision by direct reference to this greatest happiness principle but instead will stick to rules or guidelines based on past experience of the kind of conduct that tended to maximize his or her happiness. This understanding later became known as indirect, or rule, utilitarianism and enabled Mill's philosophy to have a strong influence over what was perceived as appropriate moral behavior for market economics and accepted organizational behavior. In sum, utilitarianism asserts that an action is morally right or wrong according to its consequences, rather than because of any intrinsic features such as being based on honesty, truthfulness, or compassion.

In essence, these two moral philosophies that have dominated our moral understandings—Kantianism and utilitarianism—share the common trait of being consequentialist philosophies. That is to say, each of these philosophies, in its own way, proposes that the consequence of an action determines its relative adherence to moral acceptability. It is the perceived consequences of the action that motivates the person to act with moral integrity. For Kantianism, if the consequence, or the outcome, of an action can be seen to abide by a universally accepted principle or rule, then it is deemed to be a suitably moral action. Similarly, utilitarianism also asserts that an action is morally acceptable according to its consequences, but in this instance its degree of moral acceptability is not determined by how closely it abides by a universal rule but by how able it is in bringing about goodness and happiness for the most people.

Ultimately, though, as Ferré (2001) so rightly points out, a moral philosophy is only as good as the level of motivation it provides to the person to act morally. Batson (2008) discusses some recent moral motivation research that sheds interesting light on this issue. Data from this research support the view that, by and large, people are not really motivated to act morally. Rather, most people are moral hypocrites because "they try to appear moral yet, if possible, avoid the cost of being moral" (p. 51). Batson (p. 52) makes clear the link between this apparent lack of moral integrity and moral motivation:

> In moral motivation, generality and abstractness can be an Achilles' heel. The more general and abstract a principle is, the more vulnerable it is to rationalization. Most people are adept at moral rationalization, at justifying to themselves—if not to others—why a situation that benefits them or those they care about does not violate their principles. . . . The abstractness of most moral principles makes such rationalization especially easy. Principles may be used more reactively than proactively, more to justify or condemn action than to motivate it.

This observation of moral hypocrisy is similar to that formulated by economist Robert Frank in 1988, which included insights into reciprocal altruism previously presented by Trivers in 1971. Frank posited that people are motivated to present themselves as passionately committed to moral principles in order to gain the self-benefits that the ensuing trust provides. However, the key to success in this endeavor is in having the ability to appear as being committed to a genuine moral purpose. To this end, Batson (2008) adds that if people can convince themselves that serving their own interests does not violate their moral principles, then they can honestly appear moral and so avoid detection without paying the price of actually upholding the principles. In this form of moral masquerade, self-deception may be an asset, making it easier to look genuine while actually deceiving others.

But if moral masquerading is a natural and prevalent human trait, then the development of moral integrity and, thereby, ethical leadership is an unrealistic expectation. If moral integrity cannot be realistically nurtured and developed, then the achievement of ethical leadership is merely a tantalizing dream. Conversely, if we hope to be able to enhance moral integrity and develop ethical leadership, then we need to know how to reduce the prevalence of moral masquerading.

Hence, the difficulty is in finding an alternative source for moral motivation. There is no point in aligning ethical leadership with moral integrity if we cannot point to what it means to be moral and why people should aspire to it. Today, it is still held to be true that people need some form of strong persuasion or incentive in order to personally commit to adopting a particular moral point of view. Generally, a commitment to moral integrity won't happen automatically. It is true that under particularly dangerous, life-threatening circumstances certain individuals will act with extraordinary selflessness for the benefit of another. While this clearly shows that humans are not adverse toward embracing moral behavior, it does not prove that every person is committed to acting with moral integrity. Our task is to determine how it is possible to bring out this commitment to moral integrity in not just the exceptional person, the hero, but in each of our leaders. If our natural processes of reasoning and rationality tend to automatically undermine our moral integrity, how can it remain as a viable and credible part of ethical leadership?

## UNDERSTANDING THE NATURE OF MORAL INTEGRITY

Arguably, these difficulties associated with moral integrity theorizing have arisen from seeing it as a primary rather than as a secondary phenomenon. We have concentrated on the phenomenon of moral integrity as a stand-alone entity and not as one that is constituted from other more primary or fundamental phenomena. This section seeks to extend our theoretical understanding of the nature of personal moral integrity by exploring how it is constituted. Once we are more aware of how moral integrity is constituted, then it becomes possible to describe a means for developing it. Again, a more comprehensive explanation is provided in my 2009 text, *Leadership for an Age of Wisdom.*

In further considering the concept of moral masquerades, it is interesting to note the German philosopher Friedrich Nietzsche's famous claim in his 1886 moral treatise in *Beyond Good and Evil*, that "there are no facts, only interpretations" (see Solomon, 1999, p. 196). Nietzsche was an early critic of modernity's overreliance on reason and rationality and pressed for the acknowledgment of the integral role of perspective in human affairs. Here, Nietzsche was not suggesting that all moral decisions are merely individualized viewpoints. Rather, he is arguing that the decision-making process, by necessity, involves the interpretation of reality as formed by the person making the decision.

This does not mean that Nietzsche advocated complete autonomy and therefore adhocracy in the moral decision-making process. On the contrary, he held a dual understanding of the concept of perspective. First, he acknowledged that a moral decision is made from the perspective of the person making the decision. However, secondly, he also acknowledged that the person making the decision is also aware that the outcome from the decision will be morally judged from the perspective of those observing the outcome. Each of these perspectives is subject to individual interpretation by the person making the decision, and reasoning helps the person to balance his or her own desires with the perceived moral expectations of others. Achieving this balance between his or her own desires and the perceived expectations of others does not mean that the person's moral commitment was directly aligned with the moral expectations of those observing the behavior; it just means that they appeared so. In this way, Nietzsche pointed to the unreliability of reasoning within moral integrity and pressed for the need to use whatever means possible to better understand the way humans make interpretations so as to reduce the prevalence of moral masquerades and, thereby, enhance moral integrity.

I argue that this call by Nietzsche for each of us to better understand the way we make interpretations begins with exploring the nature of our free will. As mentioned earlier in this chapter, people want others to act morally even though their own moral integrity might be questionable. This clearly indicates that acting morally is a choice. People want others to choose to act morally while they, themselves, might choose not to act as morally. Freedom of choice is integral to moral integrity. So, a way to deepen our understanding of moral integrity is to examine our freedom to choose what is truly best when making an ethical decision. Von Hayek (1960) refers to this as the person's inner freedom or metaphysical liberty, which he described as

> the extent to which a person is guided in his actions by his own considered will, by his reasoning or lasting conviction, rather than by momentary impulse or circumstance. But the opposite of inner freedom is not coercion by others but the influence of temporary emotions, or moral or intellectual weakness. If a person does not succeed in doing what, after sober reflection, he decides to do, if his intentions or strength desert him at the decisive moment and he fails to do what he somehow wishes to do, we may say that he is 'unfree', the slave of his passions.
>
> (p. 15)

However, it must be acknowledged that von Hayek was not the first to raise the possibility of the existence of inner freedom in people. Indeed, Kant had previously suggested that "free will" could play a pivotal part in moral behavior. Unfortunately, he never really expanded upon his views of the nature of free will. Consequently, as later philosophers extended and refined his philosophies, the existence of free will was challenged. For example, in 1819 the French mathematician and philosopher Pierre Simon de Laplace published an essay arguing that all events are connected with previous ones by the tie of universal causation. His argument gained much support because of the apparent success of Newtonian physics in not only being able to find some of these predetermined natural universal causations but also in being able to describe them in mathematical equations. Laplace concluded that human actions, too, were part of this same natural deterministic system. He insisted that it was an absurd belief that people had free will. Rather, he proposed that when people believe they are able to apply their free will, this is due to their ignorance of the hidden universal causes, which are in fact moving them to select one rather than the other outcome.

This view of free will being absent from human nature became known as determinism. The rise in support for determinism throughout the nineteenth and twentieth centuries is a key factor in the undermining of beliefs about the importance of moral behavior in society. It seems most fitting that to be moral, a person must choose to act in the best interests of others, and choosing to act implies a degree of freedom or the application of free will. Conversely, if people have no free will, then their behavior is not chosen but determined by some other cause beyond their selves. If their behavior is determined for them, then they cannot be held responsible or accountable for it, which means that moral behavior is an illusion.

Thus, attempting to understand the concept of inner freedom, or free will, has been a lingering philosophical conundrum. For example, in 1986 Thomas Nagel, in his publication *The View From Nowhere*, finds himself in two minds on the issue of free will and writes: "I change my mind about the problem of free will every time I think about it" (p. 110). On the one hand, Nagel can find no way to give a coherent explanation for the nature of freedom but, on the other hand, he cannot help presupposing freedom in practice. Similarly, in 1984 John Searle wrote that he acknowledges people's conception of themselves as free agents such that it is "impossible for us to abandon the belief in the freedom of the will" but asserts that "science allows no place for the freedom of the will" (p. 92). Thus, on the issue of free will, our current dominant philosophies seem incapable of providing a credible explanation for its existence—something I address in the text *Leadership for an Age of Wisdom* (Branson, 2009). So, despite our everyday experiences that promote the conviction that we possess free will, its existence remains questionable and, thus, confusing because it cannot be explained.

While I truly believe that there is a great deal of similarity between von Hayek's concept of inner freedom and Kant's concept of free will, I prefer to use the term *inner freedom*. To me, free will sounds too definitive, too concrete, and too inflexible. It conjures up an image of having the freedom to decide right from wrong, true from false, good from bad, with some determined sense of certainty and confidence. Self-willed people act in a headstrong way; they can be perversely obstinate or intractable. Hence, I prefer *inner freedom* because it is able to remain faithful to my conviction that freedom is a variable. The particular level of freedom a person has lies somewhere along a continuum and this means it can be increased or decreased.

Hamilton (2008) describes the ideal of inner freedom as "the freedom to act according to one's own considered consciousness, by the full consideration of one's objective and subjective reasoning" (p. 25). Inner freedom is one's ability to use consciousness and a sense of what is right to stave off influences that would prevent one from behaving or living in keeping with one's considered judgment. It is an integral part of our everyday thinking and decision making. Our inner freedom does not depend on external authority; instead, it ultimately depends on how we defend ourselves. It is the freedom we gain by repelling interference, manipulation, temptation, and social pressure. It is the freedom that, though often hard won, is nevertheless there to be won. Furthermore, in the absence of inner freedom we might act in a manner contrary to our own interests. Despite the benefits that inner freedom provides, few among us would doubt that we can, and often do, act in a manner contrary to our own interests.

The obvious question then becomes—how is our inner freedom related to our moral integrity? The first thing to see is that our moral integrity is directly influenced by how we see ourselves as individuals and as active members of society. Moreover, this "seeing" is at the second level of our consciousness. Seeing ourselves with respect to our physical characteristics and actions and how we relate to others are examples of the first level of our consciousness. At the second level of consciousness we are making critical observations, interpretations, and judgments about ourselves in relation to what we have noticed at the first level of consciousness. Our second level of consciousness utilizes subjective and objective reasoning in order to inform ourselves about ourselves so as to create a self-image. It is our capacity to create self-images that distinguishes us from other, nonhuman living things. Furthermore, it is this possibility of understanding ourselves as both an image and as an object of our own consciousness that engenders our moral sensibilities. The degree to which we are willing to act morally depends on the extent to which we live according to our self-image and our understanding that we have an existence beyond merely our appearance. In other words, when we adopt a moral attitude to other people, we relate to them through our second level of consciousness rather than our first level. However, we are most likely unaware of our moral decision making because it is occurring within our second level of consciousness, which happens automatically and often beyond our awareness unless we make a special effort to attend to it. Nevertheless, it still determines our moral behavior.

If our moral attitude arises out of our second level of consciousness, then this means that we are attending to not just objective features but also subjective features as well. If we are making critical observations, interpretations, and judgments about ourselves, then we are activating our subjectivity. Subjectivity involves potentialities, possibilities, relativities, comparisons, and the like. But if we are subjectively thinking about ourselves, from where do we find another to compare with? It can only be from what we see in others. We can see ourselves in others. We can see that in our opinion, we are better than others or worse than others. Or, we can want to be more like the good we see in another. Thus, if we can see ourselves in others, this means we assume we share a common unitary nature. Through a form of intuition, we are able to understand that the inner nature of each of us is identical. We automatically accept that human nature is universal—the universal self. So, in opposition to our everyday consciousness, in which we identify with our own bodies and egos, convinced that we are real and distinct, we are also capable of ontological identification with the being of all or the universal self.

When we identify with the universal self, the illusion of our independent existence falls away and the personal self merges with the universal shelf, which is shared by all. We recognize in another our own inner nature. Abolition of the distinction between subject and object and the participation of self in others give rise to what can be called "metaphysical empathy" (Hamilton, 2008, p. 146), and it is this that forms the grounds of morality and the basis for our moral integrity.

Metaphysical empathy is the awareness of participation in the being of others that arises from identification of the self with the universal self. If the universal self is the subtle essence of each of us, the moral self is the most personal expression of that universal self as experienced in the everyday, physical world. Metaphysical empathy is the innermost voice within our second level of consciousness, where all personal interests, social conventions, duties, and obligations are left behind. Furthermore, responding to the demands of this innermost voice provides the reason for taking the moral path. The moral self is the arbiter, the inner judge, who speaks to us with an immediacy and authority no external legislation or contract can possess. Our moral integrity is the tangible outer sign of the degree to which we have embraced our moral self.

The basis of morality cannot be found embedded in a categorical imperative, enshrined in principles of justice worked out behind a veil of religious dogma, or inscribed in a social contract that is beyond our comprehension. Nor can it be found in the library of rules that have evolved as a means of creating a rational social order. The basis of morality lies in identification of the self with the universal self, and the moral self that emanates from there. The grounds for morality lie in being able to intuitively identify one's self with a universal self. It is this intuition that offers the possibility of moral integrity. Our moral integrity finds expression in our moral self, the locus of ethical impulses that prefigures all social conditions and rational deliberations.

The moral self connects our everyday life experiences with our very essence through our consciousness. Our moral self is at the heart of our existence, it is uniquely our own, yet it links us to everybody. Using our inner freedom, then, involves allowing our self to be guided by our moral self. Thus freedom is always first in our being rather than in our doing. Our inner freedom is acting according to our own considered will only if our will is understood as our inner guide that is provided by our moral self. In this way, virtue and freedom form an inseparable pair.

In more recent times, being able to apply our free will has meant being able to do whatever one wants, following one's own wishes unconstrained by rules or external authority. Yet this cannot be true freedom, inner freedom. Even if we are free to do as we will, we are not free to choose what it is that we will. If we have to exercise free will, we must be responding to no inducements, preferences, pressures, or predispositions. Our actions must be independent of influences. We are autonomous, and thus free, only when we act entirely volitionally, according to our own will. We are free only when we act according to goals and principles that we have given ourselves. In other words, we must initiate our own actions, free of attachments, yearnings, social pressures, and impulses and without regard to the influence of peers, parents, churches, or fashions. At the deepest level, our very subjectivity arises in relation to other things, through the resistance to or effects from outside influences, and true personal authenticity must lie beyond all these courses of actions.

Having real freedom is having the ability to begin an event by one's self. But what is the self we are referring to? In people who are truly free, the will that guides their actions must belong to the self that owes its origin to its own consciousness—its moral self. Thus, it is only by acting according to the lessons of our moral selves that we can achieve authenticity. So the basis of inner freedom is our life lived in accordance with our discerned consciousness. And it is only when our personal selves act in accordance with the will of our moral selves that we rid ourselves of all influences and coercions, all determinations, and all other external laws, secular or divine. Moreover, the degree to which our personal selves act in accordance with the will of our moral selves defines the level of our moral integrity. In this way, our moral integrity is what liberates us from behaving unethically and endangering the well-being of others.

The idea that individuals find liberation through their own moral integrity represents a profound break from modern ethical systems. It repudiates all external forms of ethical authority and invests moral authority in the individual. As Hamilton (2008) explains, if we ask why we should not lie, Aristotle would say we should not lie because lying is not part of a good character; Kant would say we should not lie because we have a duty to be truthful; Mill would say we should not lie because it reduces the social good. In truth, we should not lie because it is contrary to our moral selves. Each of us must decide what is right. We must accept that we are lawgivers and only then decide to be law followers. There is no need for God to give us laws or injunctions that must always be mediated by those who claim to represent God on Earth. Being free individuals, we do not need any rulebooks as ethical guides. Nor do we need to appeal to duties derived from the principle of non-contradiction or intellectual constructions that prove the mutual benefit of social justice or contracts that are often beyond our comprehension. These rob us of our true authenticity as moral agents. They coerce us to act according to an external understanding of what it means for us to be moral. In fact, all we have ever needed to become moral agents was a greater awareness of our own moral integrity. All we need to be able to do is to exercise our inner freedom in a deliberate and considered way.

Exercising inner freedom in order to maintain our moral integrity means acting according to our considered consciousness and lasting conviction. To do this, we must reflect on what is in our interests and then have the conviction to act on that judgment. However, in keeping with our understanding of freedom as a variable rather than as a constant, this means that our level of commitment to maximizing our inner freedom has the potential to not always be as we would wish it to be. Hence, our level of moral integrity can be diminished accordingly. There are three factors that have the potential to adversely affect our level of commitment to maximizing our inner freedom: self-deception, impulsiveness, and a lack of self-control.

There is a considerable amount of philosophical literature on the idea of self-deception (see for instance Ferrè, 2001; Hamilton, 2008; Lennick & Kiel, 2005; Sergiovanni, 1992; Taylor, 2003; Terry, 1993; Trilling, 1972). Some have argued that self-deception is impossible because it involves forming the intention to deceive oneself. Others have posited various ways of partitioning the mind and operating as if there were two people inhabiting it. In this case, knowledge of the plans, intentions, and motives of one is, one way or another, denied the other; we can imagine a deceiver and a deceived. On the other hand, psychology offers a less radical construction by supposing that instead of two contradictory beliefs being held, our true beliefs can be held unconsciously while we act on a consciously held but false belief.

Extending this latter view of self-deception further, psychology also proposes that these unconscious processes also involve techniques we use to manage our attention in ways that exclude from our decision making uncomfortable or subversive facts and feelings. We unconsciously, but deliberately, edit what our senses detect in order to maintain our preconceptions. As Mele (see Edward, 1998, p. 630) noted, "The fundamental strategy in self-deception is to distort the standards of rationality for belief by exaggerating favourable evidence for what we want to believe, disregarding contrary evidence, and resting content with minimal evidence for pleasing beliefs." As long as we are deceiving ourselves, we are not being true to ourselves and so are not authentic; we have closed ourselves off from the knowledge of what is in our long-term best interests. Ultimately, self-deception damages our own interests. Although ubiquitous in everyday life, self-deception is inconsistent with the exercise of inner freedom and the enhancement of our moral integrity.

Impulsiveness is also inconsistent with the exercise of inner freedom. However, we must distinguish between impulsiveness and spontaneity, for there is no doubt that there are pleasures in spontaneity, and a life ruled by planning would be dull and would probably reflect a degree of neuroticism. The nature of spontaneity is aligned with other essential human qualities, such as intuition, creativity, and instinct, while the nature of impulsiveness is aligned with a lack of awareness, consideration, and self-control. It is difficult to imagine people living a life of inner freedom unless they repeatedly exercise a deep and genuine capacity for being fully aware of what is happening around them and being able to rationally consider all aspects of the situation. In this way, they are able to resist the daily inducements to impulsiveness.

Finally, a lack of self-control is similar to impulsiveness because it also allows people to act without restraint. This occurs when people act in a way that is contrary to their considered judgment. This should not be taken to imply a sharp distinction between reason and emotions, since our desires are naturally included when we make considered judgments. A lack of self-control occurs when we hold particular convictions but, instead of weighing them against our private best interests, we allow our personal desires to overwhelm the decision because we are too weak to prevent this. There are times in our lives when we are more prone to this sort of behavior—when we feel alone, vulnerable, upset, or ill-treated. We might feel a need to comfort ourselves as a result of grief over a loss or a rebuff from friends or our boss. We might feel resentful and want to punish others for transgressing ethical rules, or we might persuade ourselves that moral rules are all well and good when we can afford them emotionally or financially.

Our moral integrity is directly linked to the relative level of our self-control toward living up to our sincerely expressed beliefs about what it would be morally best to do. It depends on the degree to which we decide to act against our better judgment due to self-deception or impulsiveness. Every time our consciousness is influenced by a lack of self-control, or by self-deception, or by impulsiveness, our moral integrity is compromised and our selfish desires outweigh our moral arguments. When we succumb to these, we sacrifice our inner freedom because outside forces have led us to do something we feel is wrong. These outside forces are not only other people or the state; they are also forces that we create ourselves through our beliefs, opinions, attitudes, and values. Forces we are not always conscious of yet are powerful enough to cause us to disregard our true selves and to compromise, to some degree, our moral integrity. We relinquish part of our inner freedom to such forces and, in so doing, we adversely affect our moral integrity. It is in this way that we can say our moral integrity resides in the realm of our inner freedom and its role is to adjudicate on the best course of action, taking account of our own interests and those of others represented by our moral values or commitments. These moral interests can include the personal standards of integrity we set for ourselves.

If our level of moral integrity is directly related to the degree to which we exercise our inner freedom, this means that any improvement in how we exercise our inner freedom will, simultaneously, enhance our moral integrity. If it is possible to reduce a leader's tendency to be influenced by self-deception, impulsiveness, and a lack of self-control, then not only is the leader's inner freedom reinforced but also his moral integrity is consolidated. The leader's capacity to act morally is improved. The critical importance of being able to achieve this outcome is echoed in the words of Storr (2004, p. 415), who writes

> Leadership is not a person or a position . . . it is a complex, paradoxical and moral relationship between people, which can cause harm between some groups, accompanied by benefits to others . . . and is based on trust, obligation, commitment, emotion and a shared vision of the good—no one can be a leader without willing followers.

In a diverse and chaotic world, moral integrity has to be at the very heart of leadership. In times of chaos, people expect leaders to bring certainty and order to their world. While leaders cannot offer control over the seemingly chaotic external world that is affecting their organization, they can fill the need of their followers for stability by having moral integrity. A leader's moral integrity allows people to feel that there is order in their relationship with others. It provides a kind of internal order even when there is no external order. This is why there is so much concern over the moral integrity of leaders in all walks of life. We want to know and trust our leaders, rather than be dazzled by their charisma. We want our leaders to have moral integrity. Thus, it is imperative that we are able to enhance a leader's moral integrity.

To this end, Hamilton's (2008) claim that the foremost capacity that allows us to exercise inner freedom is conscious deliberation is noted. What is implied is a particular type of introspection in which all self-interests, all pressures, and all rational considerations are cast aside and moral judgment occurs spontaneously. Similarly, von Hayek (1960, p. 15) refers to one's considered will or lasting conviction and says that "to assert this will, as opposed to the caprice of passion or desire, requires no more than sober reflection and the courage to see one's actions governed by the conviction formed by it." Of course, it is not reason alone that provides the basis of our moral integrity. Instead, it is a full awareness of our ethical standards and an understanding of what contributes to our welfare in the longer term. What is required is an unambiguous process of honest, deliberative self-reflection and self-inquiry that requires us to be under no misconceptions as to what we really want, so that when we achieve our aims we do not decide we were mistaken and want something else. In other words, this process of honest, deliberative self-reflection and self-inquiry is able to ensure that we are fully informed and have clear, unambiguous preferences. Leaders' moral integrity can be enhanced by means of a coherent and comprehensive self-reflective process, which allows them to avoid falling victim to short-term urges and inappropriate manipulation of their desires.

Some may refer to this process of conscious deliberation as introspection. I personally prefer to use *self-reflection*, but I acknowledge that in the minds of some, the two terms could be interchangeable. For me, introspection is too close to the concept of inspection. Inspection conjures up an image of objective judgment—right/wrong, good/bad, true/false type of thinking. This is not what is being proposed. As leaders reflect on their thinking, they are endeavoring to see where and why their thinking has led to misunderstanding and unhelpful actions. They are not judging themselves; they are analyzing and interpreting their thinking. This is neither a natural or easy task because it takes effort, commitment, and practice. To access our consciousness, we must deliberately exercise our consciousness.

The opportunity for us to engage in conscious deliberation through self-reflection and self-inquiry is always present, but the voice of the moral self is usually drowned out by the thoughts and inclinations that continually occupy our minds. Rawls (1972) acknowledges that in practice we are rarely fully informed about the likely consequences of our actions but we do the best with the information that is readily available, so that the plan we then follow can be said to be subjectively rational. Gathering information and consciously deliberating involves effort, and the amount of effort to be expended on each decision is itself the subject of a decision. In this rational mode, at some point we decide that the possible benefit of more information and more deliberation is less than the cost of the additional effort required. If we make the wrong decision and regret it under these conditions, it is not because we acted impulsively or with a cavalier attitude toward the facts: It is because we made the decision not to make the effort to gather more information. This is why we are harder on ourselves when things go wrong because we failed to think the situation through rather than for reasons that could not be foreseen.

The good news is that we can easily redress any preexisting limitations on our ability to fully engage in conscious deliberation. We can readily learn self-reflective techniques that enable us to become more aware of any sources of self-deception, impulsiveness, and a lack of self-control. Also, such self-reflective processes help to illuminate situations in which our inner freedom is being suppressed by some form of coercion or deception. Coercion occurs when our actions are made to serve another's will, not for our own best interests but for the other person's purpose. Deception, like coercion, is a form of manipulating the data on which a person counts, in order to make that person do what the deceiver wants. As previously discussed, we can be the cause of our own deception in order to gain self-centered outcomes. Both coercion and deception take the form of unreasonable attempts to influence people to act in ways that are contrary to their considered interests. The reality of coercion and deception is to deprive us of our inner freedom, to induce us to act on impulse or from our weaknesses, even though we might willingly comply. Importantly, von Hayek (1960, p. 139) says that "since coercion is the control of the essential data of an individual's action by another, it can be prevented only by enabling the individual to secure for himself some private sphere where he is protected against such interference. This private sphere is one in which an individual can weigh up the consequences of their actions, being confident that the facts on which they make an assessment are not shaped by another." Self-reflection and self-inquiry provide this private sphere.

As Christian de Quincey (2002) reminds us, we can train people's brains in order to change their behavior, but we need to dialogue with their consciousness, their minds, if we want them to change their beliefs, attitudes, assumptions, and perceptions. Until leaders are capable of deeply and honestly exploring their own physical and cognitive reactions to their experiences, they will still be prone to self-deception, impulsiveness, and a lack of self-control. That is, they will be prone to external or internal coercion or deception. It is essential that leaders can become aware of any personal or external modes of deception or coercion limiting their inner freedom. They need to learn how to challenge their usual and natural ways of thinking and to get in touch with their habitual ways of reacting. Rather than noting their thoughts, they need to understand and critique their own thinking. They need to understand how and why they are constructing their reality as they are doing. This is not a natural or simple task. For leaders to be able to gain such deep and genuine self-knowledge depends solely on their avoiding being false to their real selves, and this requires deep personal honesty and arduous effort and may not be possible, in the first instance, without the critical input from another person, a mentor (see Branson, 2009).

In summary, then, this chapter has argued that not only does moral behavior remain a deeply desired character trait in today's society; it is an essential component of ethical leadership. Moral integrity is a fundamental prerequisite of ethical leadership. However, moral integrity is not, necessarily, a natural human trait—but it can be nurtured and enhanced. Hence ethical leadership founded upon personal moral integrity can be developed. Thus, the key to developing ethical leadership is to improve the moral integrity of leaders by strengthening their inner freedom. An ethical leader's inner freedom needs to be exercised in order for it to become truly effective. Moreover, leaders learn how to better exercise their inner freedom and, thereby, enhance their moral integrity through self-reflection. Self-reflection illuminates their habitual ways of thinking that naturally restrict their inner freedom. Self-reflection is the way leaders can examine and change their second level of consciousness; their way of thinking about how they are thinking. Thus it can be seen that the leader's second level of consciousness is both the arbiter and the creator of ethical leadership.

However, this description of how moral integrity plays an integral role in ethical leadership means absolutely nothing unless it can be explained how this process could actually happen inside the human person. In other words, the credibility and viability of ethical leadership depends on being able to present a coherent and achievable explanation of how leaders can exercise their inner freedom and, thereby, enhance their moral integrity. The next section of this chapter provides a simple way in which this can be accomplished.

## DEVELOPING PERSONAL MORAL INTEGRITY

What is being proposed here is not a single, stand-alone process but rather the final or additional stage of a comprehensive ethical decision-making process. This assumption is reflected by means of this particular chapter's placement within this handbook's order of chapters. In other words, before commencing the following proposed self-reflection process for guiding personal moral integrity thinking and deciding, it is assumed that you will have completed an explicit ethical decision-making process similar to those offered in the previous three chapters. Having completed such a process, whichever is preferred, it can then be assumed that you are consciously "exposed to differing paradigms and diverse voices—of justice, rights, and law; care, concern, and connectedness; critique and possibility; and [where applicable] professionalism" (Shapiro & Stefkovich, 2005, p. 29). Moreover, participation in such a process has "not only [led] to stimulating conversations, but they will also encourage reflection and guidance for wise [and ethical] decision-making in the future" (p. 30). Essentially, such descriptive ethical decision-making processes enable you to not only reach a decision but also, and perhaps just as importantly, know the reasons as to why the preferred decision has been chosen.

The introduction of the self-reflection process for guiding personal moral integrity thinking and deciding acknowledges the awareness that the application of any of the ethical decision-making processes is more likely to provide a multiplicity of alternative actions rather than precipitate a singular best solution to the ethical dilemma. In other words, the leader still has to make a choice from all of the alternative insights, options, and possibilities provided by each of the different ethical perspectives. Arguably, the leader is more informed but not necessarily more able to make the appropriate ethical decision. To fully complete the ethical decision-making process, the leader is still required to make an ethically appropriate choice based on all of the information he or she now possesses. Moreover, for this to be an ethically appropriate choice, it necessitates that the leader act with moral integrity.

As has been previously described, moral integrity is about instinctively and consistently doing what is right for the good of others in the absence of incentives or sanctions. Thus, ethical leadership is made manifest in acts carried out for their own sake and not because the leader expects any personal or professional benefit. Hence, possessing moral integrity for a leader is about achieving a commitment where the interests of others, rather self-interests, are the spontaneous motivation. To this end, Branson (2006) published a model for guiding structured self-reflection, which utilizes the understanding that a deeper awareness of one's self can be gleaned from a self-directed inquiry into one's self-concept, self-esteem, motives, values, beliefs, emotions, and behaviors associated with a particular situation. Adapting this framework to the exploration of a particular ethical dilemma would produce the framework in Table 17.1.

## CONCLUSION

While the benefits to be gained in ethical decision making from such self-reflection can only really be assessed in their actual application to a real situation, Starratt's (2004) insights are noteworthy and encouraging. Here, in his analysis of what constitutes ethical leadership, he claims that there are three qualities of a truly ethical leader—autonomy, connectedness, and transcendence. First, he explains that striving for autonomy as a means of enhancing one's moral integrity is about developing "self-truth" or, in Taylor's (2003, p. 27) words, "self-determining freedom" or inner freedom (Branson, 2009). As people become more conscious of all the factors impacting on their moral judgments, they are less controlled by their self-centered

**Table 17.1** Questions to guide a self-reflection process toward the achievement of personal moral integrity

| COMPONENT OF SELF | QUESTIONS FOR SELF-REFLECTION |
|---|---|
| Self-concept | • How will I be affected by the likely outcome generated by all of the other ethical perspectives?<br>• What are my desires, hopes, or preferences about this issue? Are these realistic or idealistic? Why? How might these influence my decision?<br>• Am I avoiding anything in what I have considered to be relevant information? If so, why? |
| Self-esteem | • What strengths or previous knowledge do I bring to this issue? Has this influenced my thinking and analyzing? Is this strength or knowledge truly relevant?<br>• What weaknesses or lack of knowledge do I bring to this issue? Has this influenced my thinking and analyzing? Is this perceived weakness or lack of knowledge truly relevant? |
| Motives | • What is my primary motive in resolving this issue?<br>• Is my thinking unquestionably aligned with this motive?<br>• What outcome do I personally prefer? Why?<br>• What outcome do I personally dislike? Why?<br>• Are my actions reflecting a commitment to self-control?<br>• Are the decisions about what I have considered to be irrelevant information justified? |
| Values | • Do I personally benefit in any way from a particular outcome?<br>• Which values or principles do I want guiding my decision? Are they?<br>• Is my thinking free from self-interest, self-deception, and impulsiveness? |
| Beliefs | • What personal biases do I bring to this issue?<br>• What is my regular outlook toward those who will benefit most from each possible outcome? Has this influenced my thinking?<br>• What is my regular outlook toward those who will be adversely affected by each possible outcome? Has this influenced my thinking? How could these adverse effects be minimized or negated?<br>• Is my thinking more influenced by personal beliefs rather than an unbiased assessment of the knowledge gained from each of the other ethical perspectives? |
| Emotions | • What are my fears about resolving this issue? Are these realistic or idealistic? Why?<br>• Am I aware of my emotions in relation to this issue? What does this say about my involvement in this issue?<br>• What are my true feelings about the preferred outcome?<br>• What is the source of these feelings?<br>• Are these feelings based on the immediate issue, from past experiences, or from perceived consequences of the anticipated decision? |
| Behaviors | • How has my analysis of each ethical perspective been influenced by my previous actions and decisions?<br>• How can the outcome be implemented in the most ethical, respectful, and empathic way?<br>• Will the implementation of the intended outcome reflect all of the values and principles that I want guiding my decision-making process?<br>• What do I need to do to best prepare myself to implement the chosen decision in the best possible way? |

desires and have more possibility of making an autonomous conscious moral choice. People become free to direct their lives from their self-reflective moral consciousness because they are freed from self-deception, impulsiveness, and a lack of self-control. O'Murchu (1997) claims that the greatest source of influence over the behavior of people comes from their inner selves where unconscious motives, values, and beliefs influence at least 70% of their daily behavior. A person's will is not free when it is being largely controlled by unconscious influences. This is manipulated will rather than free will. Hence, the development of a leader's autonomy is dependent upon bringing these normally powerful unconscious instinctual influences into consciousness and under direct control. This is about nurturing inner freedom through self-reflection.

Secondly, the pivotal role of connectedness in personal moral integrity, claims Harris (2002, p. 215), can be clearly seen by examining the roots of the word "consciousness," the source of our ethical decision-making processes. Here it is found that "consciousness" comes from the Latin *con,* which means "with," and *scio,* which means "to know." Consciousness is "knowing with" and this makes it a relational activity. Consciousness requires an "I" and a "we"—two distinct entities capable of forming a relationship. Developing personal moral integrity is not only about coming to know ourselves, but it is also about knowing how to relate to others in a more mutually beneficial and rewarding way. A person's morality, urges Taylor (2003), crucially depends on dialogical relations with others. In particular, developing moral integrity is about realizing that we all create self-fulfilling prophecies in our interactions with others. "We expect people to behave according to our projective expectations, and without intending it, we elicit in them reactions that confirm those expectations," writes Frattaroli (2001, p. 231). Hence, an important aspect of nurturing an ethic of personal moral integrity is about recognizing personal, unconscious, self-imposed relationship inhibitors. Once these are made conscious, they can be removed in order to expand the range of people with whom we can empathize and whom we can recognize as part of our moral responsibility. The process of self-reflection, as presented above, enables the leader to become aware of, and strive to overcome, any personal, unconscious, self-imposed relationship inhibitors.

Finally, the concept of transcendence within the context of personal moral integrity encapsulates the essential commitment to continually strive to be a better person. To this end, Wilber (2000, p. 264) proposes that "increasing interiorization = increasing autonomy = decreasing narcissism." In other words, the more self-knowledge people have of their inner selves, then the more detached from those selves they become, the more they can rise above the limited perspectives of those selves, and so the less self-centered they become. The more clearly and faithfully people can subjectively reflect on their selves, the more they can transcend their innate personal desires in order to consider what is in the best interests of others. This is supported by Taylor's (2003, p. 39) concept of "horizons of importance," where he suggests that

[t]he ideal of self-choice supposes that there are other issues of significance beyond self-choice. The ideal couldn't stand alone, because it requires a horizon of importance, which help[s] define the respects in which self-making is

significant. Unless some options are more significant than others, the very idea of self-choice falls into triviality and hence incoherence. Self-choice as an ideal makes sense only because some issues are more significant than others.

As long as most of the inner influences on our behavior remain within our unconscious, there is little choice in how we respond to ethical dilemmas. However, by making these inner influences part of our consciousness, then we do have self-choice in regard to whether or not they are appropriate. As unconscious influences, our inner influences automatically seek largely self-interests. On the other hand, as conscious influences, our inner influences can be controlled and directed toward seeking horizons of greater importance where consideration is given to what is ultimately in the best interest of all. In this way, such transcended behavior achieves moral outcomes. When applied to educational leadership, this understanding necessitates that ethical leaders need to become conscious of how their inner dimensions of their selves can be controlled and redirected toward achieving better, more transcendental, consequences. Moreover, it is only through a commitment to self-reflection that such conscious awareness can be nurtured and enhanced.

## REFERENCES

Batson, C. D. (2008). Moral masquerades: Experimental exploration of the nature of moral motivation. *Phenomenology and the Cognitive Sciences, 7*(1), 51–66.

Begley, P. T. (2006). Self-knowledge, capacity and sensitivity: Prerequisites to authentic leadership by school principles. *Journal of Educational Administration, 44*(6), 570–589.

Branson, C. M. (2006). Beyond authenticity: Contemporary leadership from a worldview perspective. *Values and Ethics in Educational Administration Journal, 4*(4), 1–8.

Branson, C. M. (2009). *Leadership for an age of wisdom.* Dordrecht, Netherlands: Springer Educational.

Cottingham, J. (Ed.) (2006). *Western philosophy: An anthology.* Malden, MA : Blackwell.

de Quincey, C. (2002). *Radical nature: Rediscovering the soul of matter.* Montpelier, VT: Invisible Cities Press.

Duignan, P. (2006). *Educational leadership: Key challenges and ethical tensions.* New York, NY: Cambridge University Press.

Edward, C. (1998). *Routledge encyclopedia of philosophy.* New York, NY: Routledge.

Ferré, F. (2001). *Living and value: Toward a constructive postmodern ethics.* Albany, NY: State University Press of New York Press.

Foster, L. A. (1986). *Paradigms and promises: New approaches to educational administration.* Amherst, NY: Prometheus Books.

Frank, R. H. (1988). *Passions within reason: The strategic role of the emotions.* New York, NY: W. W. Norton.

Frattaroli, E. (2001). *Healing the soul in the age of the brain: Becoming conscious in an unconscious world.* New York, NY: Penguin Books.

Fullan, M. (2003). *The moral imperative of school leadership.* Thousand Oaks, CA: Corwin.

Greenfield, W. D. (2004). Moral leadership in schools. *Journal of Educational Administration, 42*(2), 174–196.

Hamilton, C. (2008). *The freedom paradox: Towards a post-secular ethics.* Crows Nest, New South Wales, Australia: Allen & Unwin.

Harris, B. (2002). *Sacred selfishness: A guide to living a life of substance.* Makawao, HI: Inner Ocean Publishing.

Hollimon, D., Basinger, D., Smith, R. G., & Leonard, P. (2009). Promoting moral literacy teaching competency. *Values and Ethics in Educational Administration Journal, 7*(2), 1–8.

Hume, D. (1955). *Treatise.* L. A. Selby-Bigge (Ed.). Oxford, UK: Clarendon Press.

Kant, I. (1949). *Fundamental principles of the metaphysics of morals.* (T. K. Abbott, Trans.). New York, NY: Liberal Arts Press.

Kant, I. (1956). *Critique of practical reason.* (L. W. Beck, Trans.). Indianapolis, IN: Bobbs-Merrill.

Lennick, D. & Kiel, F. (2005). *Moral intelligence: Enhancing business performance and leadership success.* Upper Saddle River, NJ: Wharton School Publishing.

Nagel, T. (1986). *The view from nowhere.* New York, NY: Oxford University Press.

O'Murchu, D. (1997). *Quantum theology: Spiritual implications of the new physics.* New York, NY: Crossroad Publishing.

Rawls, J. (1972). *Theory of justice.* Cambridge, MA: Harvard University Press.

Richmon, M. J. (2003). Persistent difficulties with values in educational administration: Mapping the terrain. In P. T. Begley & O. Johansson (Eds.), *The ethical dimensions of school leadership* (pp. 33–47). Dordrecht, Netherlands: Kluwer Academic Publications.

Searle, J. R. (1984). *Minds, brains and science: The 1984 Reith Lectures.* London, UK: British Broadcasting Corporation.

Sergiovanni, T. (1992). *Moral leadership: Getting to the heart of school improvement.* San Francisco, CA: Jossey-Bass.

Shapiro, J. P., & Stefkovich, J. A. (2005). *Ethical leadership and decision making in education: Applying theoretical perspectives to complex dilemmas* (2nd ed.). Mahwah, NJ: Lawrence Erlbaum.

Solomon, R. (1999). *A better way to think about business: How personal integrity leads to corporate success.* New York, NY: Oxford University Press.

Starratt, R. J. (2003). *Centering educational administration: Cultivating meaning, community, responsibility.* Mahwah, NJ: Lawrence Erlbaum Associates.

Starratt, R. J. (2004). *Ethical leadership.* San Francisco, CA: Jossey-Bass.

Storr, L. (2004). Leading with integrity: a qualitative research study. *Journal of Health Organisation and Management, 18*(6), 415–434.

Taylor, C. (2003). *The ethics of authenticity* (11th ed.). Cambridge, MA: Harvard University Press.

Terry, R. W. (1993). *Authentic leadership: Courage in action.* San Francisco, CA: Jossey-Bass.

Trilling, L. (1972). *Sincerity and authenticity.* Cambridge, MA: Harvard University Press.

Trivers, R. L. (1971). The evolution of reciprocal altruism. *Quarterly Review of Biology, 46,* 35–57.

Tuana, N. (2007). Conceptualizing moral literacy. *Journal of Educational Administration, 45*(4), 364–378.

von Hayek, F. (1960). *The constitution of liberty.* London, UK: Routledge & Kegan Paul.

Wilber, K. (2000). *Sex, ecology, spirituality* (2nd ed.). Boston, MA: Shambhala Publications.

# 18

## AN INSIGHT INTO THE NATURE OF
## ETHICAL MOTIVATION

### MICHAEL BEZZINA AND NANCY TUANA

Almost universally, when asked why they chose their profession, teachers will say that they wanted to make a difference in the lives of their students. Dewey (1909) put it this way in his *Moral Principles in Education*: "The business of the educator is to see to it that the greatest possible number of ideas acquired by children and youth are acquired in such a vital way that they become *moving* ideas, motive forces in the guidance of conduct" (p. vii). In a few short lines, Dewey has captured ideas that go to the very core of the work of teachers as a moral enterprise and, in turn, place an obligation on educational leaders to make this enterprise possible. Together they are challenged by Greenfield's question: "Leading and teaching to what ends and by what means?" (2004, p. 174). This question lies at the heart of the moral purpose of education.

This chapter seeks to engage with the particular challenges faced by leaders who seek to engage their colleagues with a compelling moral purpose and then to galvanize them into action around this purpose, so that it goes beyond mere rhetoric, to become a genuine motivating force. Doing this will draw on what has been learned from an ongoing Australian research project known as Leaders Transforming Learning and Learners (LTLL)—a study of the ways by which moral purpose can be given a higher profile in the work of teachers and leaders, and the consequences of doing this. Burford and Bezzina describe this study in Chapter 25 in this collection.

This present chapter will seek, particularly, to focus on those aspects of the LTLL research, and related literature, that have contributed to an emerging conceptual framework that describes the movement from moral literacy through to moral agency—action in a culture of hope. This has the potential to inform leadership practice as leaders seek to build and then capitalize on the moral and ethical capacity within their schools. In this way, this chapter provides an insight into the nature of ethical motivation—the personal inner force that compels a leader to act ethically.

## WHAT DO WE MEAN BY MORAL PURPOSE?

In the context of this chapter, it is taken that an ethically motivated leader consistently acts with moral purpose. "Moral purpose" is a term that is widely used in the literature but seldom defined, and still less often operationalized. Thus, this chapter attempts to respond to this shortcoming.

For the purposes of this discussion, moral purpose can be understood as the commitment to ends that express underlying values and ethics. In the particular context of schools, the commitment is ultimately to the transformation of the learner into a fuller, richer, deeper human being. Teachers engage with this moral purpose when they seek to infuse academic learning with a dimension of personal meaning, thereby enriching the educative process (Starratt, 2004) by giving students a better sense of their lives and of how they can contribute to their community and to society (Hodgkinson, 1991). The task of school leaders, then, is to engage teachers more fully in the pursuit of this type of authentic learning, both as individuals and as an educating community. According to West-Burnham and Farrar (2010), there are four major categories of moral purpose at work in schools: social justice, performance and standards, the development of the individual, and cultural transmission.

The LTLL project was designed so as to explore the way in which an emphasis on moral purpose might impact on learning and leading in schools. Its methodology and broad outcomes are more fully described in Chapter 25.

## THE LEADERS TRANSFORMING LEARNING AND LEARNERS PROJECT

The LTLL project had its origins in both the world of practice and the world of academe and has always maintained a focus in both of these domains. The conceptual framework, discussed in Chapter 25, is included here for ease of reference (Figure 18.1).

The conceptual framework at the heart of the LTLL initiative is an attempt to capitalize on the growing consensus in the literature around leadership and learning behaviors that have been shown to enhance student learning. This consensus extends to such issues as the importance of the quality of the teacher, primacy of assessment for learning, whole-school approaches to planning and implementation of curriculum, shared moral purpose, and the need to link leadership and learning (Bezzina, 2008). Thus, in the model on page 284, moral purpose (as reflected in values and ethics that drive a vision of the transformed learner) shapes and interacts with educative leadership and authentic learning. A detailed discussion of the elements of this model can be found in Bezzina (2012).

The conceptual framework was validated in the various phases of the LTLL project. As well as asking school teams to complete a reflective tool at the commencement of and completion of each school's engagement with its chosen initiative, the researchers engaged school teams in focus group interviews. These interviews were transcribed and are the principal source of illustrative data for this chapter.

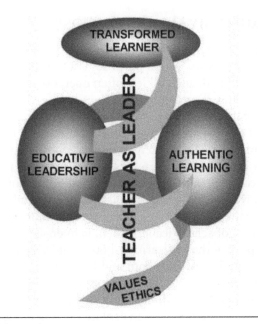

**Figure 18.1** The revised LTLL framework.

## WHAT THE RESEARCH TELLS US

The results of the various forms of data gathering have been reported in a variety of publications (Bezzina, 2007, 2011, 2012; Bezzina & Burford, 2010a, 2010b). This chapter uses some of the data from this research as a means of illustrating an emerging understanding of the ways moral literacy, moral potency, and moral agency can enhance understanding of, first of all, how teachers give expression to moral purpose, and then secondly, how leaders can create the circumstances in which this might be best enabled. It is argued that working with both the individual and the community is essential to this form of leadership, in a move from stipulating behavior to stimulating purpose.

In brief, the process of moving from a sense of moral purpose to action embodies three elements: being aware of and appreciating the ethical dimension of the work of education; owning the ethical elements of the situation, having a sense of efficacy and the courage to act, and, finally, taking action in this regard. These dimensions of the process are referred to as moral literacy, moral potency, and moral agency. The goal that leaders pursue is that of developing moral agents who are committed to the deep purposes of the school and act on them. The sections that follow will provide an outline of the three concepts and then move on to an exploration of the ways in which leaders might best utilize this understanding in their work.

## MORAL LITERACY

Moral literacy has been defined by Herman (2007) as "a basic, learned capacity to acquire and use moral knowledge in judgment and action" (p. 207). This definition has two important elements from the perspective of informing leadership behaviors.

First of all, moral literacy is seen as being a part of the foundation for moral action. This makes it—the development of moral literacy—an important focus for leaders. Secondly, it can be learned, which means that it is susceptible to intentional influence by leaders. The skills and knowledge specific to making ethical choices in life are learned capabilities requiring skills in which individuals can be more or less competent (Tuana, 2007, p. 365).

A key dimension of moral literacy is the capacity to be sensitive to the moral and ethical dimensions of situations. Research has demonstrated that we cannot take such sensitivity for granted. Moberg's (2006) work drew attention to what he called "ethical blind spots"—aspects of work in which participants were desensitized, or "blind" to the ethical import of their actions. This has been explored in some detail elsewhere (Bezzina, 2011). This phenomenon is not depicted as malicious, or even deliberate. Weaver (2006, p. 350) describes the ways in which unethical behavior often emerges from the overall organizational process, without awareness or unethical intent on the part of many organization members. These blind spots have also been described as "unexamined ethics" (Begley & Stefkovich, 2007, p. 404). Moral sensitivity, the state of being "tuned in" to the ethical content of one's work, embodies a capacity to determine whether or not a situation involves ethical issues; to determine the moral intensity of the ethical concerns; and to identify the moral virtues or values underlying the situation (Tuana, 2007, p. 366).

A second aspect of moral literacy is a capacity for ethical reasoning—for example, in applying ethical frameworks, assessing facts, and identifying relevant values (Tuana, 2007). This is a long way from what Begley and Stefkovich (2007, p. 403) called "the sheer austerity and abstractness" of some ethical frameworks. One LTLL participant described her experience with this aspect of moral literacy in these terms:

> For me also it gave literally a structure, if you like, for me mentally to hang a new principalship on because when I arrived we did a survey of what was needed and it was like this massive tower but it gave a real sense of making a manageable thing in terms of looking at the moral purpose. We used a lot of the terminology in the [Reflection Guide] document, in particular to help us.

The third element of moral literacy is referred to by Tuana (2007), drawing on the work of Johnson (1993), as moral imagination. This has to do with the capacity to think ahead to likely consequences of particular actions and to place a value on these consequences (Ajzen, 2005). Moral imagination draws on the first two elements of moral literacy by bringing to bear both rational and emotional faculties. Without this imagination, the combination of ethical sensitivity and ethical reasoning skills would likely never be translated into moral behavior. In the words of an LTLL teacher, imagining a possible future scenario:

> Learning about this transformational learning, I can't go back. I can't go back and teach any other way. If I go to another school I have no idea what I'm going to do because I now have to teach this way, I've had to change me personally.

This person felt compelled to act in particular ways (actually foreshadowing moral potency), but the key issue here is her imagining a future without the ability to respond to the compulsion. Being sensitive to the ethical dimension of their work, having ways of describing it in ethical terms, and being able to imagine the consequences of possible actions are important but not in themselves sufficient to move educators to action. The key element linking moral literacy with action is moral potency.

## MORAL POTENCY

Hannah and Avolio (2010, p. 261) developed the concept of moral potency and define it as:

> a psychological state marked by an experienced sense of ownership over the moral aspects of one's environment, reinforced by efficacy beliefs in the capabilities to act to achieve moral purpose in that domain, and the courage to perform ethically in the face of adversity and persevere through challenges.

Thus, using this insight, moral potency requires not just ownership, but courage and a sense of efficacy. Efficacy is an expression of the extent to which people have an internal locus of control—a view that they can shape their own lives (Brown & Treviño, 2006, p. 604). In addition to both ownership and efficacy, moral potency calls on the courage to see an action through—even in the face of adversity. In writing about leaders' own motivations for action, Hannah and Avolio (2010) propose that moral potency provides the psychological resources that "bridge moral thought to moral action" (p. 292).

One high school teacher in LTLL captured both the sense of responsibility and the need for courage in this observation:

> It's nobody's one responsibility, and I think that has been the . . . biggest change around evidence—more a willingness to look and not be afraid, as Karen identified, that we're not scared anymore. It might be good, it might be bad, but you know what, we're all going to own it, we're all going to work together towards it.

Significant in this observation, too, is the strong emphasis on the communal experience. The courage that was evoked was not that of individuals but of a community.

## MORAL AGENCY

The concept of agency comes from the work of social psychologists like Albert Bandura (2006, p. 164), who describes it in these terms:

> To be an agent is to influence intentionally one's functioning and life circumstances. In this view, personal influence is part of the causal structure. People are self-organizing, proactive, self-regulating, and self-reflecting. They are not simply onlookers of their behavior. They are contributors to their life circumstances, not just products of them.

This subsumes and extends the notion of potency. It takes the *disposition* to act morally and translates it into moral *action*. In other words, this is a commitment to being a moral actor.

The importance of being a moral actor is well documented in research on moral development by the developmental psychologist Darcia Narvaez. She identifies the importance of ethical action that, in her account, embraces the commitment to being a moral actor. "Ethical action skills include resolving conflicts, taking initiative as a leader, asserting respectfully, planning and implementing decisions" (Narvaez, 2010).

Turning again to our LTLL experience, how did this come to be expressed? One of the reports of the study (Bezzina, 2011) identified significant changes in practice as a consequence of engagement with LTLL. These included a greater focus on authentic learning, changed classroom practice, particularly with an emphasis on student-centered approaches and meaningful learning, a shift to greater levels of teacher leadership, and greater collaboration among teachers—built on increased levels of trust (see also Bezzina, 2008). Each of these changed behaviors is a form of moral action. One teacher described the dynamic as follows:

> I think that one of the biggest impacts has been on moral purpose for the school. We've gone down a process with the staff over the last two years of first of all giving them the language of what moral purpose is all about. . . . So that whole sense of why are we doing it? . . . That's impacted on not only the teaching but also the learning that's going on, because as a consequence of that, some of the pedagogy has really shifted.
>
> (Bezzina, 2011, p. 12)

This quotation captures, succinctly, the dynamic that seems to be at work as teachers move from awareness of moral issues to changed practice—and ultimately to the improved outcomes for students that are reported in more detail elsewhere (Bezzina, 2011).

The movement described in the previous quotation illustrates some of the aspects of the way in which moral aspiration might be understood to bridge to behavior. Ultimately, individuals who are morally literate and have moved from this through their sense of moral potency to a position of moral agency take ethically motivated action. Thus, leaders will need to work with their communities in ways that will promote this transition. The likelihood of this happening is enhanced within a community in which moral purpose is explicit (Bezzina, 2008, 2012) and in which norms and structures enhance commitment and the sense of efficacy. This builds a culture of hope and a shared sense of courageous ethical action (Bezzina & Tuana, 2013).

## THE IMPORTANCE OF CULTURE

A powerful tool for building toward moral agency and ultimately shaping moral purpose is the culture of the school itself. Despite this, it has been noted (Furman, 2004) that in the educational literature, at least, there has been little attention given to the consensual processes necessary to "achieve the moral purposes of the school in the twenty first century" (p. 220). While this highlights a gap in the literature of educational leadership, social psychologists have developed a sense of the strong and reciprocal relationship between the perceptions of the community and those of the individuals within it. For example, Hannah and Avolio (2010, p. 10) put it this way:

> Group and individual character are thus likely reciprocally related, with each influencing the other across levels through mechanisms such as organizational climate and culture as individuals interact and promote higher levels of moral potency in one another.

Weaver (2006, p. 351) describes this reciprocal process as a "virtuous cycle." The experience of the LTLL participants serves to illustrate this cycle. One teacher commented on the way in which learning together has helped to shift the culture of learning among teachers:

> I think the other thing is that the learning culture of the teachers is different. We learn much more collaboratively now than we did. I think by my observation, there's more forward thinking . . . I think the learning culture of the staff is different. I think that's really important.

This teacher had become aware of the role played by culture in shaping behavior, as well as (and perhaps more importantly) underlying beliefs.

Recognizing the power of culture is one thing. Acting in ways that might shape this culture is another. Hannah and Avolio (2010) argue for transformational approaches in which, over time, individuals come to take on the sense of moral ownership previously described. The emerging literature on authentic leadership further reinforces this type of understanding. In a recent literature review (Gardner, Cogliser, Davis, & Dickens, 2011), a tabulation of definitions of authentic leadership is provided. A significant number of these name an ethical or moral quality of that leadership and identify the capacity of such leadership to shape the context and behaviors of others.

The question that prompted this chapter was how leaders might facilitate this journey. Hannah and Avolio (2010) would argue that collectives develop norms that influence the moral thinking of their members. Leaders play a key role in the development of these norms, and their capacity to engender hope is significant.

## HOPE AND THE VIRTUOUS CYCLE

A comparison of some of the scholarly understandings of leadership, and those of hope, reveals some significant parallels. This section compares the work of authors like Kouzes and Posner (1995) and Kotter and Cohen (2002) and the four qualities of hope identified by Ludema, Wilmot, and Srivastva (1997).

Hope emerges from *relationships*. It shapes, and is shaped by, people who are connected to one another. This echoes Fullan's (2002) emphasis on relationship and provides the channels within which the virtuous cycle can operate.

Hope is inspired by the conviction that *the future can be influenced*. It is this hope that gives rise to the capacity that Kouzes and Posner describe as a "challenging the process" (1995) and underpins the direction-oriented strategies of Kotter and Cohen (2002). Only those with a sense that the future can be influenced will be likely to spend time in planning for the future.

Hope is sustained by *dialogue about high ideals*. This echoes the dimensions of leadership variously described as shared vision and organizational direction (Kotter & Cohen, 2002; Kouzes & Posner, 1995). In their communication with others, effective leaders focus on the deep moral purpose that is the wellspring of their motivation and, ultimately, of their community.

Lastly, hope *gives rise to action,* and the actions that leaders take awaken hopeful thinking and hope-filled action in others (Snyder & Shorey, 2002). Given a climate of hope, leaders are still challenged to attend to developing moral literacy and facilitating moral potency on the road to moral action. The literature gives some insights into how this might be done.

This discussion has profiled hope in a significant way. Moving from the theoretical to the practical, the LTLL teacher quoted below exemplifies the role of hope in teacher thinking:

> I think the title "Transforming Learning and Learners" . . . really does capture it. I believe that we have transformed the learning. And I hope we have—or we will in the future—transform the learners.

Note the use of "we"—a relational term. Note also the ideal of transformation, a sense that the future can be influenced, and an action focus.

A second teacher's observation makes the point of the capacity of a shift to a hope-filled perspective quite graphically. This teacher describes the reaction of an experienced teacher returning to the school after a long break:

> He said one of the significant things he has seen is a change in educational culture, and pedagogical culture and he said, that's the hardest thing to do. He said, I can really see that shift there. . . . I was as guilty as anyone around here of thinking, these kids can't achieve very much academically, so why bother? And I would have thought he was a fairly conscientious guy, but he said that, you know, there was a culture of saying, well, look, these kids are never going to be fantastic, so therefore we just set the mark there. . . . I think we've moved beyond that, and I get a real sense that, you know, that there's a shift there.

The situation that existed prior to engagement with LTLL might be characterized as "hope-less"—a fatalistic sense that little difference would, or could, be made. The change was in teachers' attitudes. In the post-LTLL world, expectations and possibilities had changed.

## BRINGING THE DISCUSSION TOGETHER

Leaders have a dual responsibility for action. Like everyone else, they are responsible for their own actions, but beyond this they are charged with the exercise of influence on others. Thus, the imperative to build the bridges between moral thought and moral action expresses itself both in the leaders' own behaviors (as a necessary but not sufficient way of promoting ethical action) (Hannah & Avolio, 2010) and in the ways in which they exercise influence in order to provide a foundation of hope and help to develop moral potency and moral agency among colleagues. These behaviors embody the insights of social learning theory with respect to the roles of both modeling and situational influences (Brown & Treviño, 2006).

In one school-based study it was found that there was a reciprocal relationship between shared moral purpose and shared leadership, which was facilitated by an explicit treatment of ethical issues and a common language (Bezzina, 2008). The argument put forward by Bezzina (2008) was that by bringing the moral dimension of teaching and learning to the fore, creating the opportunities for all teachers to engage with the issues, and releasing their potential as educational leaders, moral purpose was both stimulated and enriched by the experience of shared leadership. Moral purpose was clarified and reinforced through explicitly developing moral literacy amongst the school community. That moral purpose, fueled by hope, led to an increased experience of individual and collective moral potency, that is, of courage and a sense of efficacy. This, in turn, triggered moral agency. Once again, there is a virtuous cycle in operation, and its operation has been illustrated by some of the quotations from the LTLL participants used in this chapter.

The discussion so far in this chapter provides some insight that can shape the work of leaders seeking to make moral purpose a real driver for action. It is suggested that, based on these insights, such leaders will seek to create opportunities in which the diverse individual community members will be engaged with the moral import of their work, sensitive to external factors and individual differences among staff. Over time, the appreciation of the ethical dimension of the work of the school will be enhanced by the use of shared understandings and the exercise of a shared moral imagination. This calls for leaders to take an educative stance in providing opportunities for individuals to deepen and extend their moral literacy. Beyond this, it calls for a focus on the shared understandings that will grow from this educative work and from the work of culture building. Teachers, individually and collectively, will need to be challenged by the "so what" question: If we say we understand the ethical dimension of our work and together see it as important, how should we respond as individuals—and as a school community?

As the process continues—as individuals, as groups, and as a whole staff—people will take action. Opportunities will be created for reflection on experience. This will deepen understandings and appreciations (moral literacy). This, in turn, will foster commitment to act and enrich and spread the commitment to shared moral purpose and the sense of capacity to respond to this (moral potency). In other words, increasing agency can become self-reinforcing—a virtuous cycle. Figure 18.2 is an attempt to capture this dynamic.

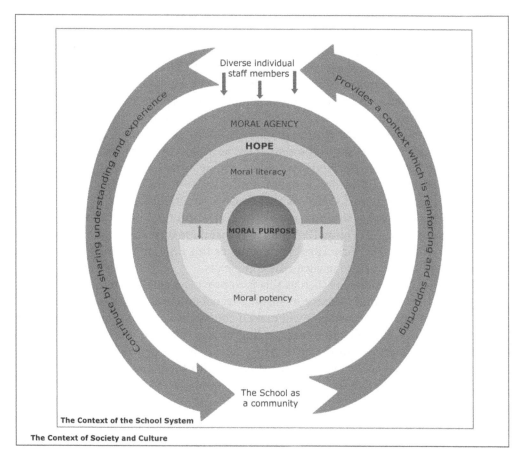

**Figure 18.2** From moral literacy to moral agency—leadership perspective.

## CONCLUSION

This chapter began by identifying the gap between the oft-espoused rhetoric about the importance of moral purpose and ethical perspectives in education, and the dearth of research that explores how this comes to be lived out in practice.

The Leaders Transforming Learning and Learners project is an initiative that has attempted to respond to the gap in the research by exploring the ethical dimensions of school improvement activities while simultaneously supporting schools in their implementation. Its diverse findings provide us with significant insights into the ways in which practitioners actually engage with moral purpose in action, and the consequence of this engagement for both leadership and learning practice and student outcomes. Some of the results of various aspects of LTLL have been brought to bear in this chapter as a means of illustrating an emerging way of understanding the way in which individuals and communities can move from a rhetoric of espousal to a very practical expression of practice motivated by moral purpose.

The overview provided in this chapter points to a conceptual framework that proposes a series of relationships among the key concepts of moral literacy, moral potency, and moral agency, and of a culture of hope, situating them in the context of the work of educational leaders with both individuals and the community as a whole.

Conceptual frameworks such as this come with attendant risk. In closing this chapter, it is fitting that this be named. The real world does not exist in neat compartments like those in Figure 18.2. It is likely that there is no single path through the elements of the framework. However, as long as this limitation is recognized, such frameworks can help us to navigate the complexity.

The point of frameworks such as this is to provide a synthesis of what we know about the role of moral purpose in shaping leadership and learning. In the sphere of academic inquiry, hopefully it will make a contribution to addressing yet another blind spot—this time in the understanding of an important dimension of ethical educational leadership. In the sphere of practice, it can provide a language with which educational leaders can begin to engage with their own practice, with their colleagues, and with their communities. It may not be perfect, but it is a start.

## REFERENCES

Ajzen, I. (2005). *Attitudes, personality, and behavior* (2nd ed.). Milton-Keynes, UK: Open University Press/McGraw-Hill.

Bandura, A. (2006). Toward a psychology of human agency. *Perspectives on Psychological Science (Wiley-Blackwell), 1*(2), 164–180.

Begley, P., & Stefkovich, J. (2007). Integrating values and ethics into post secondary teaching for leadership development: Principles, concepts, and strategies. *Journal of Educational Administration, 45*(4), 398–412.

Bezzina, M. (2007, August 12–14). *Moral purpose and shared leadership: The Leaders Transforming Learning and Learners pilot study.* Paper presented at the conference "The Leadership Challenge—Improving Learning in Schools," Melbourne.

Bezzina, M. (2008). We do make a difference: Shared moral purpose and shared leadership in the pursuit of learning. *Leading and Managing, 14*(1), 38–59.

Bezzina, M. (2011, September 25–27). *Moral purpose: A blind spot in ethical leadership?* Paper presented at the 16th annual Values and Leadership Conference, Victoria, BC, Canada.

Bezzina, M. (2012). Paying attention to moral purpose in leading learning: Lessons from the Leaders Transforming Learning and Learners Project. *Educational Management Administration & Leadership, 40*(1), 1–24.

Bezzina, M., & Burford, C. (2010a). Leaders Transforming Learning and Learners: An Australian innovation in leadership, learning and moral purpose. In A. H. Normore (Ed.), *Global perspectives on educational leadership reform: The development and preparation of leaders of learning and learners of leadership* (Vol. 11, pp. 201–211). Bingley, UK: Emerald.

Bezzina, M., & Burford, C. (2010b, September 20–24), *Moral purpose in leading for learning.* Paper presented at the 15th annual International Values and Leadership Conference, Umea, Sweden.

Bezzina, M., & Tuana, N. (2013). *From awareness to action: Some thoughts on engaging moral purpose in educational leadership.* Sydney: Australian Catholic University.

Brown, M. E., & Treviño, L. K. (2006). Ethical leadership: A review and future directions. *Leadership Quarterly, 17*(6), 595–616.

Dewey, J. (1909). *Moral principles in education.* Boston: Houghton Mifflin.

Fullan, M. (2002). Moral purpose writ large. *School Administrator, 59*(8), 14–17.

Furman, G. C. (2004). The ethic of community. *Journal of Educational Administration, 42*(2), 215–235.

Gardner, W. L., Cogliser, C. C., Davis, K. M., & Dickens, M. P. (2011). Authentic leadership: A review of the literature and research agenda. *Leadership Quarterly, 22*(6), 1120–1145. doi: 10.1016/j.leaqua.2011.09.007

Greenfield, W. D. (2004). Moral leadership in schools. *Journal of Educational Administration, 42*(2), 174–196.

Hannah, S. T., & Avolio, B. J. (2010). Moral potency: Building the capacity for character based leadership. *Consulting Psychology Journal: Practice and Research, 62*(4), 291–310.

Herman, B. (2007). *Moral literacy.* Boston: Harvard University Press.

Hodgkinson, C. (1991). *Educational leadership: The moral art.* Albany: SUNY Press.

Johnson, M. (1993). *Moral imagination.* Chicago: University of Chicago Press.

Kotter, J. P., & Cohen, D. S. (2002). *The heart of change: Real-life stories of how people change their organizations.* Boston: Harvard Business School Press.

Kouzes, J. M., & Posner, B. Z. (1995). *The leadership challenge: How to get extraordinary things done in organisations* (2nd ed.). San Francisco: Jossey-Bass.

Ludema, J. D., Wilmot, T. B., & Srivastva, S. (1997). Organizational hope: Reaffirming the constructive task of social and organizational inquiry. *Human Relations, 50*(8), 1015–1052.

Moberg, D. J. (2006). Ethics blind spots in organizations: How systematic errors in person perception undermine moral agency. *Organization Studies, 27*(3), 413–428. doi: 10.1177/0170840606062429.

Narvaez, D. (2010). Moral complexity: The fatal attraction of truthiness and the importance of mature moral functioning. *Perspectives on Psychological Science (Wiley-Blackwell), 5*(2), 163–179.

Snyder, C. R., & Shorey, H. S. (2002). Hope in the classroom: The role of positive psychology in academic achievement and psychology curriculum. *Psychology Teacher Network, 12*(1), 1–9.

Starratt, R. J. (2004). *Ethical leadership.* San Francisco: Jossey-Bass.

Tuana, N. (2007). Conceptualising moral literacy. *Journal of Educational Administration, 45*(4), 364–378.

Weaver, G. R. (2006). Virtue in organisations: Moral identity as a foundation for moral agency. *Organisation Studies, 27*(3), 341–386.

West-Burnham, J., & Farrar, M. (2010). *Every child matters: The moral purpose of education.* Nottingham, UK: National College for Leadership of Schools and Children's Services.

# 19

## DECONSTRUCTING ETHICAL MOTIVATION

### CHRISTOPHER M. BRANSON

Despite the 2008 global shock caused by the unscrupulous and opportunistic practices of a few individuals and institutions within the banking and investment world, the reality is that this incident was only one of a growing number of very serious unethical activities in the political, media, and corporate spheres (Foote & Ruona, 2008; Ncube & Wasburn, 2006). During the past two decades, political, media, and corporate scandals have shaken public trust and spawned the implementation of many new regulatory policies and laws to help ensure that organizational leaders comply with the ethical standards expected by society (Clark, 2004; Kist, 2002; Wooten, 2001). There is now an emphasis being identified on the essential role of ethical judgment in leadership (Campbell, 1997; Cooper, 1998; Richmon, 2003; Starratt, 2003). Today, perhaps more so than ever before, people want their leaders to act ethically whereby they will not produce harm but, rather, will show the virtues of doing good, of honoring others, of taking positive stands, and of behaving in ways that clearly show that their own self-interests are not the driving motivation behind their leadership (Branson, 2009). People want leaders with ethical codes that are deep, innate, and instinctive so that they will not lose direction in the face of uncertainty or external pressure (Badaracco, 2006). There is now a clear expectation that leaders will always act justly and rightly and will promote good rather than harm (Evers, 1992). Today's leaders are expected to demonstrate ethical judgment by being accountable to those they serve (Eraut, 1993). Restoring trust and maintaining ethical standards are now considered to be the required hallmarks of proper organizational leadership.

However, the desire for ethical leadership does not translate, necessarily, to actually having ethical leadership. Ethical leadership is an achievement and not a given. A leader has to strive to become an ethical leader, as it is unlikely to happen automatically. Ethical behavior is not a natural outcome, particularly for leaders, even under the threat of punitive accountabilities (Gonzalez, 2003; Goodpaster, 2004; Kermond,

2009). As Langlois (2004, p. 89) laments, "It seems necessary to train [leaders] in moral judgement and in ethics to render them capable of managing according to a renewed and responsible form of leadership." Moreover, Tuana (2007) claims:

> Simply because one can identify that a situation involves an ethical issue and be able to employ ethical reasoning skills to provide an analysis of what would be a good or bad action in the context, does not mean that they experience the action as ethical or feel any personal investment in the situation or in trying to respond ethically. Moral agency requires a rich and affective commitment to being ethical.
>
> (p. 12)

Following Tuana's lead (see Chapter 11 of this text), it can be seen that the development of ethical leadership can be described as incorporating three distinctive but interwoven components: ethical sensitivity, ethical reasoning, and ethical motivation. Research indicates that to be ethical, people need to not only know what constitutes ethical behavior, but also how to act ethically and, more importantly, they need to really want to act ethically. While much has already been done to help leaders understand what constitutes ethical leadership and how to implement ethical decision-making practices, little has been done to explore the nature and practice of ethical motivation (Branson, 2009).

Notably, however, the research of Batson (2008) found that the desire to be ethical when combined with a strong predisposition for individual gain tends to produce "moral masquerading" (p. 51). Such moral masquerading involves people acting not with ethical commitment but, rather, with ethical hypocrisy whereby they try to appear ethical yet, if possible, avoid the cost of being ethical. There is a strong tendency for people to want others to act according to some preconceived ethical standard while maintaining their own individual right to act according to their own wishes and, furthermore, are readily able to devise some form of ethical justification for their personal actions. Frank (1988) posited that people are motivated to present themselves as passionately committed to ethical principles in order to gain the self-benefits that the ensuing trust provides. This research suggests that people are motivated more toward appearing ethical rather than actually being ethical. Moreover, it highlights the importance of exploring the concept of ethical motivation as a precursor to the successful development of ethical leadership practice.

## EXPLORING THE CONCEPT OF HUMAN MOTIVATION

Human behavior is "agential" (Bandura, 1997), as it is directed toward achieving a particular motive (Hodgkinson, 1996). A person is not just a reactive entity but, rather, he or she directs action as well as seeks information (Osborne, 1996). People make choices about what they do and they initiate behavior that they believe will result in their gaining feedback supporting the image of their selves that they are striving to build. Hence, human behavior is motivated action, as it seeks to fulfill a particular personal motive. The literature describes a motive as a mental function that is cause and director of behavior and, at the same time, a seeker of information to direct and confirm behavior to ensure it has achieved the desired outcome (Cavalier, 2000; Wagner, 1999).

Arguably, Maslow's (1954) proposed hierarchical needs theory has significantly influenced our views about the nature of human motivation, but not without some criticism (see, for instance, Cianci & Gambrel, 2003; Hofstede, 1984; Wahba & Bridgewell, 1976). Although acknowledging these criticisms, there appears to be a timeless dimension to Maslow's theory that warrants further attention. Maslow, like Aristotle, posits that there is a deepening significance or meaningfulness amongst the array of human motivations. Not everything people choose to do is equally valuable, or equally good, or equally just, or provides the same depth of meaning and purpose in their lives. For Aristotle and Maslow, there are several "goods" in life, but some of them are "more good" than others (Wilber, 2000).

When applied to moral motivation, the least significant are the physiological or sensual needs that result in hedonistic behavior, but these are viewed as still a potential "good" and not to be condemned per se, yet there are also other, more significant and meaningful, pursuits. More significant and meaningful behaviors than those motivated by the physiological or sensual needs are those aligned with the person's materialistic, objective reality that generates safety, production, and consumption behaviors. Even more significant and meaningful are those that Aristotle associated with the life of a citizen (Wilber, 2000). That is, a life as a fully contributing member of a community based on intersubjective relationships, interpersonal friendships, mutual appreciation, and a feeling of belonging. However, the most significant and meaningful behavior is said to arise from being motivated by what is the very essence of our own being, our fullest potential, and our fundamental self. This has been variously referred to as our innate desire to fulfill potentialities (May, 1967), to achieve self-actualization (Maslow, 1968), to reach for self-completion (Hultman & Gellermann, 2002), or to attain self-enhancement (Osborne, 1996). People gain the greatest sense of personal significance and meaningfulness through their capacity to determine what is of ultimate worth to them beyond their objective, observable reality. Through this motive to seek the greatest sense of personal significance and meaningfulness, people strive to act in ways that appear to enable them to achieve their full potential in life. Ultimately, each person harbors a desire to become more and more the person he or she really is and to become everything that he or she is capable of becoming.

Importantly, though, the idiosyncratic conclusion as to which source of motivation has priority is determined in one's consciousness rather than being based upon rational thinking alone. In other words, the capacity to fulfill one's potentiality, to achieve self-actualization, to reach self-completion, or to attain self-enhancement involves a transformation in consciousness. As Annas (2008) suggests, "Virtuous people are people whose deliberations, leading to their acting virtuously, are, at least in part, in terms of virtue, rather than in terms of meeting obligations, or of producing good consequences" (p. 22). First and foremost, it is not so much about deciding what must be done, and in what order, but why it should be done, and this takes into consideration the perspective from the reality being experienced by the other, and not just the self, which is formed from subjective, relational, interpersonal reasoning.

Moreover, such virtuous actions are founded upon an awareness of the sort of person that the person wants to be; to not act with virtue in this instance would make the person feel less of a person. Virtuous people are not trying to emulate an image of someone else; rather, they are trying to live to their own highest standards.

Annas' (2008) real-life example in support of this point is that when we find people who have acted with incredible bravery, invariably we find that they have not included the thought of being brave in their deliberations prior to acting. Indeed, in many situations of incredible bravery, the virtuous person is motivated by a complex combination of rational, subjective, and proprioceptive thinking. Such people are being influenced by a transformed consciousness—a consciousness that is able to utilize the benefit gained from their objective thinking, which they can add to the benefits gained from their subjective thinking and the benefits they can gain from being proprioceptive. Bohm (2006) describes proprioception as the ability of people to think about the accuracy, the comprehensiveness, the limitations, the aspirations, the motivations, the consequences, and the pertinence of their thinking. Proprioception is the simple act of paying attention to one's own inner thinking world, to the finely differentiated layers and qualities of one's own private experiencing, to actively and deliberately create a deepening awareness of each aspect of this thinking, and thereby contribute in an important way in the creation of their own being (Branson, 2009).

This is the highest form of thinking (Frattaroli, 2001), in which people not only think about what they are doing, how they are feeling, and how they are relating to others as they make their decision, but they also reflect upon this thinking in search of errors, omissions, misinterpretations, and misunderstandings. This is about people wanting to learn from their experience, to enhance their practical wisdom, to be continually striving to do better, and to be authentic to their own perception of their highest potential. Through the gaining of proprioceptive self-knowledge, people are able to act more purposefully and with greater awareness of the cognitive thoughts that underpin their actions. It enables people to acknowledge their physical and cognitive limitations, to be aware of the propensity for their thoughts to be influenced by personal desires and inaccurate information, and to account for the interdependency of their actions with the lives of others. People with such self-knowledge are able to analyze and review their own motivations and underlying values in order to confirm or amend them as valid guides for action.

However, as Bohm (2006) warns, proprioception is not something people do naturally or automatically, it is not a given, but rather it takes effort and intention. Its personally perceived importance grows out of a willingness to become reflective, to contemplate reflectively and analytically upon one's experiences not so much from the practical reality point of view but more from one's sense of efficacy, self-worth, and ideal purpose that has been achieved through this experience. To do this not only takes a specific commitment but it also necessitates a heightened level of emotional, social, and psychological maturity. Essentially, proprioception calls upon people to deliberately strive to change the focus of their perceptions and to transform their consciousness, in order for them to find a deeper significance and meaningfulness in their lives.

Moreover, this transformation of one's consciousness requires the person to act with freedom and autonomy. Self-enhancement is achieved through the transformation of one's consciousness and not through the translation of one's present state (Wilber, 2000). We translate our present state when we use less significant and meaningful levels of motivation to achieve higher human aspirations. A prime example of this mismatch is our current dependence upon systems of rewards and punishments, incentives and accountabilities, as our primary means of encouraging the best from employees at all levels within our institutions and organizations. While employees are looking for a sense of purpose, significance, and meaning within their work-place to stimulate and motivate themselves to give of their best (Wheatley, 2006), the organizational culture remains locked into "a merely empirical-sensory motiva-tion" (Wilber, 2000, p. 440) regime that suppresses the very quality that it is trying to nurture. Rather than stimulating, motivating, energizing, and enthusing employees, systems based on incentives and accountabilities are more likely to cause frustra-tion, apathy, disillusionment, and mediocrity. Thus, people wanting to rise above such endemic restrictive levels of motivation must grasp their individual freedom to achieve their potential; they need to deliberately act with personal autonomy in order to gain self-enhancement and to reach their full human potential. Otherwise, our organizational and social propensity to apply systems of motivation that essen-tially rely upon deficiency needs—physical, security, belonging, and esteem needs—will prevent the person from being influenced by the personal betterment needs (Maslow, 1954).

## IMPLICATIONS FOR THE DEVELOPMENT OF ETHICAL LEADERSHIP

In the context of ethical leadership, such motivation is about instinctively and con-sistently doing what is right for the good of others in the absence of incentives or sanctions. People often try to explain ethical behavior by referring to a personal ben-efit, such as being respected more by others when we act ethically. But to characterize ethical leadership as conferring some form of generally recognizable personal ben-efit is a perverse way of seeing it. According to Kriegel (2008), if people are adapting their behavior in order to be seen to be achieving a predetermined desired outcome, like compliance obligations or presumably a better life, then they are responding to a mental representation of what their behavior should be like. This means that their action is based on a cognitive, rationalized thought process rather than an inner ethical imperative. Rather than emanating from their ethical being, it is coming from their brain influencing their behavior in order for them to be considered ethical. However, in instances of authentic ethical motivation, the inherent mental function has a transcendent quality where its focus is of the self but not on the self. Its focus is of a personal potentiality that goes beyond the physical self.

However, although this personal potentiality, this level of living based on an innate desire to achieve self-enhancement, is a natural human quality, it has to be striven for, rather than simply waited for, as it is not developed automatically. This means that given the growing demand for ethical leadership, it is imperative that practically achievable means are found that can encourage, support, and hasten the leader's natural progress toward being motivated by personal betterment or self-enhancement needs.

To this end, it is noted that people pursue this motive for personal betterment or self-enhancement through two secondary motives (Rokeach, 1973). Firstly, people seek self-enhancement through the motive to achieve success, which focuses on competence. Secondly, people seek self-enhancement through the motive to do things properly, which focuses on integrity. To have worth, people must believe that they are both competent and have integrity in what they are doing and in what others see them doing (Hultman & Gellermann, 2002). People are motivated to do things that not only show to their selves that they are competent and have integrity but also so that they can believe that others share this same positive understandings of them. This suggests that competence and integrity have both a personal and a social dimension. In other words, the fundamental human motive for self-enhancement causes people to strive toward personal and social competence as well as striving to have personal and social integrity.

However, this perspective requires some further development to make it more specific to the role of a leader. It is argued that leaders are not only motivated to do things that show to their selves and others that they are competent and have integrity but also that they show expected leadership qualities within their organization. Leadership does not happen in a vacuum; leadership occurs within a particular designated social group or organization. Also, the credibility within the leader's own eyes, and the eyes of others, is very dependent upon the leader's performance in enabling the organization to achieve a meaningful and successful outcome. This means that not only is the organizational context a source of motivation for the leader but also the leader strives to display expected leadership behavior. Within our current leadership literature, such outcomes are described as the leader's pursuit of authenticity. Authenticity implies a genuine, personal kind of leadership that is hopeful, open-ended, visionary, and creative (Johansson, 2003, p. 211). In addition, leadership based on authenticity has a social dimension, as it is described as being sophisticated, knowledge based, and skillful in its response to the social demands of people having to work together. Being authentic means that the leader is able to acknowledge and accommodate in an integrative way the legitimate needs of individuals, groups, organizations, communities, and cultures rather than being only concerned by the organizational perspectives that have been the "usual preoccupation of much of the leadership literature" (Begley, 2003, p. 2).

In summary, then, this chapter argues that the fundamental human motive for personal betterment or self-enhancement causes an ethical leader to strive toward displaying:

- Personal, social, and organizational competence
- Personal, social, and organizational integrity
- Personal, social, and organizational authenticity

Based upon this understanding of the importance of the fundamental human motive for personal betterment or self-enhancement, the following personal characteristics matrix is used to further clarify and describe the values that can be nurtured as a means of intentionally developing ethical leadership practices. Once our

**Table 19.1** A matrix of values for sustaining the self-enhancement motivation, fundamental to development of ethical leadership

| | | Context | | |
| --- | --- | --- | --- | --- |
| | | Personal | Social | Organizational |
| Desired Outcome | **Competence** | Self-Knowledge | Connectedness | Transcendence |
| | **Integrity** | Ethicalness | Trustworthiness | Responsibility |
| | **Authenticity** | Autonomy | Presence | Wise Judgment |

motives assign preference to certain choices, those choices have embedded values, and these become important influences upon our beliefs and behaviors (Branson, 2007; Gellermann, Frankel, & Ladenson, 1990). Moreover, if it is our values that align our behavior to our motives, then it becomes possible to deconstruct the fundamental human motive to attain personal betterment or self-enhancement into its constituent values and, thereby, make this motive far more accessible for ethical leadership development processes. For, as Cairnes (1998), argues, if we want ethical leaders with heart and soul, leaders with courage based on inner strength, wisdom, and grace, if we want leaders with breadth of vision and depth of character, then we will need to support them in developing themselves to their real depths, not by following some formula devised by studying leaders of old, but by supporting them in finding out who they are, what they are made of, who it is that they really want to become, and what values will help them to become this person. If it is possible to help individuals to develop the skills and knowledge necessary to cater to their physical, safety, belonging, and esteem needs, then it must be similarly possible to help them develop their skills, knowledge, and character so that they are able to reach their full human potentiality. Table 19.1 presents those values that are able to sustain the self-enhancement motive, which is fundamental to the development of ethical leadership.

This matrix of values suggests that the development of ethical leadership can be more readily accomplished by encouraging and supporting leaders' growth in applying the values of self-knowledge, connectedness, transcendence, ethicalness, trustworthiness, responsibility, autonomy, presence, and wise judgment in guiding all of their leadership activities. A brief outline of each of these values follows.

## PERSONAL COMPETENCE (SELF-KNOWLEDGE)

Self-knowledge in leaders is about leaders having the capacity and commitment to use self-reflection to form an accurate, veridical model of their selves and to be able to use this unique source of knowledge to operate more effectively in their role as leader (Gardner, 1993). Through this self-reflective knowledge, the leader's mind observes and investigates personal experience itself, including the emotions associated with it (Goleman, 1995). In this way, self-knowledgeable leaders are not only striving to improve their own map of reality, but also acknowledging that they have the mental habit of constructing particular kinds of maps, which can be unreliable or unhelpful

(Mant, 1997). Through acknowledging and accepting their personal reality, leaders are able to make sense of and act appropriately in their changing environment.

Such self-knowledge enables leaders to clarify their thinking, raise their self-awareness, develop their relationships on an intimate level, and get in touch with their emotions, thus unleashing their intuition and putting their selves in immediate contact with the world as it changes. Such leaders have the courage and commitment to work with the reality of their thoughts, feelings, and environment, going at their own pace on a journey of self-discovery, developing their inner selves, growing in their courage to take risks, and building supportive and sustainable relationships.

## SOCIAL COMPETENCE (CONNECTEDNESS)

Connectedness in leadership promotes the belief that it is imperative for today's leader to know that given the bounded rationality of individuals, and even of whole organizations, discussion, dialogue, and soliciting divergent points of view is the only way to develop better solutions to problems (Starratt, 1993). Moreover, to do this well, leaders not only have to have self-knowledge but also a deep knowledge about those they are leading. Unlike earlier notions of individual leadership based on particular traits or behaviors, connectedness in leadership acknowledges that no single person alone is likely to have the combined knowledge and capacities necessary to engage in effective leadership. Hence, connected leadership is concerned with exploring conventional relationships and organizational understandings such that there is involvement between persons in which leaders and followers raise one another to higher levels of motivation and morality (Burns, 1978, 2010). Connectedness means that leadership is interactive and multidirectional. It is leadership that does not revert to rewards, orders, requirements, seduction, or threats but, rather, followers are influenced through influence, persuasion, and mutuality (Sergiovanni, 1994, p. 199).

Furthermore, connectedness in leadership acknowledges that contemporary leaders need to be more sensitive and caring in their attitudes and relationships and more adaptable and flexible in their practices if they are to release the potential and tap the diversity of talents of those who work with them (Starratt, 1994). Connected leaders transcend the ordinary level of social relations by listening to the burdens of others, caring for them, and putting their selves in the place of others. It means that the leader has to find his or her own fulfillment in easing the burdens of others, making them laugh, and helping them to finish a project with confidence and pride.

Such connected leadership is more than simply a union, as it is based upon a commitment to mutuality, since the giving and the receiving go both ways (Whitehead & Whitehead, 1991). In this mutual relationship, each party brings something of value; each receives something of worth. In this way, a combined richness of thought and activity, superior to that of any single leader, is achieved (Telford, 1996). By building connectedness, leaders engage their followers such that there is mutual commitment to the shared purpose of building the best organization possible, as the followers are motivated to give more of their selves.

## ORGANIZATIONAL COMPETENCE (TRANSCENDENCE)

*The greatest people are the ones who have not sought greatness, but served greatly the causes, values, and missions that were much bigger than [they].*

(Cloud, 2009, p. 242)

Transcendence in leadership means that leaders have moved beyond, or transcended, their personal ordinary self-interested or self-centered ways and, thereby, live in a very different reality from only thinking that life revolves around them. Transcended leaders realize that there are far more important considerations than those that focus on their selves and that their leadership role is really not just about their own interests, but ultimately about the things that are important to the people and the organization that they are leading.

Moreover, the transcended leader's life is about knowing the right things to do and doing them well. They can see the bigger picture and are willing to become a part of the team that is striving to make this a reality. Those being led can see and follow the leader's dedication, commitment, and convictions, can discern and appreciate the leader's values and motives, and can be inspired by the leader's sense of purpose and sincerity.

Leaders, who take a transcended approach automatically create the appropriate culture, services, policies, products, tools, and equipment that people in the organization need in order to be successful (DePree, 1989). But there is more to what they do than just this functional competence. Transcended leadership also involves being able to challenge, inspire, enable, model, and encourage others so that they can attain their very best toward achieving the organizations goals (Kouzes & Posner, 1995). An important part of such leaders is their ability to model the organization's values, beliefs, and behaviors. Through their transcended approach, leaders becomes capable of inspiring others by their truthfulness and virtuousness in what they say and do, and in the honesty and transparency in the way they make clear why they are doing it (Sofield & Kuhn, 1995).

## PERSONAL INTEGRITY (ETHICALNESS)

It is not enough for leaders just to make the right moves for any purpose that suits them or for any vision that they might have of what organizations should be like—leaders must consider carefully the impact of all they do on the livelihood of others (Sergiovanni, 1992). Leaders are called upon to act ethically such that their purposes and visions are socially useful, serve the common good, meet the needs of their followers, and elevate their followers to a higher moral level (Burns, 1978). Ethical behavior in regard to leadership requires the leader be a person of courage and integrity who is passionately committed to doing the right thing regardless of the consequences (Terry, 1993).

This commitment to an ethical approach acknowledges that an essential characteristic of leadership is centered upon the interpersonal influence of leaders over their followers. Hence, leadership behavior is infused with moral choices. This requires the leader to confidently deal with and explore the realms of meaning, mission, and power (Duignan & Bhindi, 1997). Furthermore, this means going into the complex heart of human life and dealing with moral and ethical questions, building upon the foundations of people's basic principles and values. It involves leaders collaborating and consulting with people, listening to them, and motivating and challenging them.

All of this can arouse fear and anxiety in people, because dealing with these complex issues means putting into action basic principles that uphold significant values, including those that are right and worthwhile but also those associated with sensitivity, empathy, and reconciliation. In other words, leaders need to be value led; they need to be ethical, whereby they are continually monitoring their own behavior to ensure that it is being influenced by the right values. Ethicalness in leadership implies that leaders know what personal values they wish to have influencing their behavior, they are open and honest about informing others as to these being the values that will influence their behavior, and they will strive to ensure that it is these values that are influencing their behavior.

## SOCIAL INTEGRITY (TRUSTWORTHINESS)

People need to be able to trust others, but particularly their leaders (Hultman & Gellermann, 2002). They want to know that they can trust their leaders to be doing what is in their best interests and not out of self-interests (Goleman, 1998). Being trustworthy is about the leader willingly acting openly, honestly, and consistently. It is more than simply telling the truth. Trustworthiness in leaders means that they consistently display total congruence between who they say they are and what they do (Cashman, 1998). Such congruence builds not only trustworthiness but also acceptance. This congruence translates into letting others know one's values, principles, intentions, and feelings, and acting in ways that are reliably consistent with them. Furthermore, trustworthy leaders are forthright about their own mistakes and confront others about their lapses. They are frank, even willing to acknowledge their feelings, which contribute to their aura of having social integrity.

Trustworthy leaders do not seek to be treated more advantageously than those they lead (Haslam, Reicher, & Platow, 2011). They do not seek more from others than they are willing to give of themselves. A truly trustworthy leader is seen and accepted by followers as being one of them, someone who is truly a part of their group, their organization. This is a leader who willingly and readily lives the organization's norms and principles and, more, advocates and champions the benefits to be gained for all who follow suit. Trustworthy leaders are consistent and fair in the way they treat each of their followers. All are treated equitably, with no one gaining benefit or advantage from the leader through preferential treatment, unacknowledged actions, or exclusive opportunities.

## ORGANIZATIONAL INTEGRITY (RESPONSIBILITY)

Responsibility comes from self-reference and self-organization, which automatically flow from a clear understanding of meaning. Compliance comes from regulations and policies; responsibility comes from a conscious commitment to what is meaningful. Responsibility results from leaders willingly committing to something meaningful to them and being free to adjust their own behavior according to what this meaning mandates.

Leaders who willingly embrace their need to show responsibility take ownership of the results achieved by the organization and do not try to make excuses for poor performances or blame someone else for them. They accept that they are accountable for the choices they make and take responsibility for what is happening in the organization as well as for their own performance (Cloud, 2009). "When you are too quick to lay blame on others . . . you create risks for yourself. Obviously, you risk misdiagnosing the situation. But you also risk making yourself the target by denying that you are part of the problem and that you, too, need to change" (Heifetz & Linsky, 2002, p. 90). Responsible leaders learn from errors or omissions in judgment regardless of who makes them, and rather than seeing faults, they see opportunities to learn and grow both in themselves and others.

Moreover, leaders take responsibility not when they recognize a task and its requirements but when they feel it is theirs (Badaracco, 2006). Responsible leaders have a deep conviction that they must make something happen and they devote themselves to making it happen despite obstacles, frustrations, resistances, mistakes, and competing demands. But they do this in a way that shows that they accept their moral responsibility for the welfare of others. The responsible leader strives to infuse a morally appropriate organizational culture in which everyone respects the dignity, integrity, and worth of each of their coworkers.

## PERSONAL AUTHENTICITY (AUTONOMY)

Hamilton (2008) describes autonomy as "the freedom to act according to one's own considered consciousness, by the full consideration of one's objective and subjective reasoning" (p. 25). It is leaders' ability to use their consciousness and sense of what is right to stave off influences that would prevent them behaving or living in keeping with their considered judgment. As such, it must be an integral part of the leader's everyday thinking and decision making. Leaders' autonomy does not depend on external authority; instead, it ultimately depends on how they understand and remain true to their selves. It is the freedom the leader gains by repelling interference, manipulation, temptation, and social pressure. It is the freedom that, though often hard won, is nevertheless there to be won. Furthermore, in the absence of autonomy, the leader might act in a manner contrary to his or her personal self-interests. Despite the benefits that autonomy provides, few among us would doubt that we can, and often do, act, in our organizations and elsewhere, in a manner contrary to our own interests.

Autonomous leaders are consistently authentic to their selves. They are not expected to copy someone else's way of being a leader. As authentic leaders, they are expected to find the style of leadership that brings out the best in them and offers the best help to those they lead. It is not a form of leadership that endorses total freedom. Rather, it is a form of leadership that expects the optimum from leaders and presumes that leaders will continually strive to be the best they can be by always working to maintain their authenticity regardless of the presence of external constraints and contrary expectations.

## SOCIAL AUTHENTICITY (PRESENCE)

The seminal writing of Rost (1993) unequivocally articulated the centrality of influence within the role of a leader when he posited, "If there are few other unifying elements to our collective thought about leadership, the notion of leadership as influence is one that clearly stands out" (p. 79). Subsequent theorists (Bush & Glover, 2003; Duignan, 2006; Maxwell, 2005; Neck & Manz, 2007) have consolidated this understanding to the point where there is now widespread acceptance that effective leadership inherently necessitates an influence relationship "among leaders and followers who intend real changes that reflect their mutual purposes" (Rost, 1993, p. 13).

More recently, greater emphasis has been placed on describing the specific requirements of the leader in being able to nurture this influence relationship. Here, the concept of "presence" has gained prominence. Briefly, presence involves "being fully conscious and aware in the present moment [through] deep listening, [and] of being open beyond one's preconceptions and historical ways of making sense" (Senge, Scharmer, Jaworski, & Flowers, 2007, p. 13). Being able to consciously feel, understand, analyze, and employ one's immediate experience is an essential aspect of being present. Hence, it is about "paying close attention to whatever is unfolding here and now" (de Quincey, 2005, p. 238), which involves being present to one's self and being present to the others. Being present to one's self is about thinking differently whereby both objective and subjective data from the immediate experience are brought into awareness and, together, these inform the person's deliberations rather than simply repeating past habitual ways of thinking.

On the other hand, being present to the others does not only mean being there physically and hearing what others have to say but rather it necessitates the need to be there fully for the others. As Starratt (2004) argues, presence in leadership implies that leaders willingly and consistently direct alert attention and empathic sensitivity to each of the others they are leading so that their presence activates not only their own authenticity but also the authenticity of these others. Similarly, Tolle (2005) writes that a genuine relationship can only be established when "there is alert attention toward the other person" (p. 84) and involves a transformation of consciousness because "only presence can free you of the ego" (p. 78) and its selfish desires. For Duignan (2009, p. 5), "Presence means being there for the other in the sacred stillness of the precious space created between people within relationships."

## ORGANIZATIONAL AUTHENTICITY (WISE JUDGMENT)

Bolman and Deal (2008) yearn for "wise leaders" who can turn around the plight of "organizations everywhere [that] are struggling to cope with a shrinking planet and a global economy" (p. 438). Such wise leaders are those described as requiring "high levels of personal artistry if they are to respond to today's challenges, ambiguities, and paradoxes. They need a sense of choice and personal freedom to find new patterns and possibilities in everyday life at work. They need versatility in thinking that fosters flexibility in action. They need capacity to act inconsistently when uniformity fails, diplomatically when emotions are raw, non-rationally when reason flags, politically in the face of vocal parochial self-interest, and playfully when fixating on task and purpose backfires" (p. 435). Duignan (2004) echoes this sentiment by arguing that capable leaders in today's context "need to have the capability to make sensible and wise judgements when faced with new and changing situations, often involving dilemmas and conflict" (p. 18). He goes on to add that "many leaders may have the skills but do not perform well, seeming to lack the confidence, commitment, character and wise judgement to apply these skills in unfamiliar and changing circumstances." Having access to wisdom, being able to make wise judgments, is at the heart of Duignan's vision of what it takes to be a successful leader.

But what is wisdom? More particularly, what is wise judgment? Strom (2007) suggests: "Wisdom is like this. It lives in people. We see it when we think of those who have deeply influenced our lives for good. We may not be able to define wisdom exhaustively but our recollections enable us to recognise and comprehend wisdom well enough to talk about it meaningfully" (p. 16). Furthermore, de Bono (1996) suggests: "Wisdom is not instead of logic. Wisdom is the operating system of 'perception'. Logic only begins when perception ends" (p. 278). In other words, de Bono is arguing that logic (objectivity) and perception (subjectivity) are the two integral parts of wisdom. Together, objectivity and subjectivity, equally considered, create wisdom. In the context of authenticity in leadership, wise judgment is the synergetic insight leaders gain when they honestly, equitably, and explicitly consider both objective and subjective information within their decision-making process. As a synergetic process, a leadership judgment based on wisdom is able to arrive at a far more creative and beneficial outcome than that which could come from the sole consideration of the objective or the subjective information alone.

## IMPLEMENTING ETHICAL LEADERSHIP DEVELOPMENT

So far, this chapter has discussed the why and the what of ethical leadership—now it is important to describe the how. First, it was argued that the universally devastating effect of unethical leadership has strengthened the call for ethical leadership. Secondly, in the light of the acknowledged failure of compliance laws and accountabilities to generate ethical leadership, theorists and practitioners have turned their attention toward understanding how leaders make decisions rather than prescribing what decisions should be made by an ethical leader. Simply, the leader needs to learn how to commit to making ethical decisions. This involves the leader in three phases of professional development: ethics sensitivity, ethical reasoning skills, and ethical motivation. Of these three phases, to date, the least understood is that of ethical motivation. Hence, it has been argued that the foundation values for the creation of ethical motivation are self-knowledge, connectedness, transcendence, ethicalness, trustworthiness, responsibility, autonomy, presence, and wise judgment.

But, how can a leader be helped to develop each of these values in order to become an ethical leader? As has been mentioned previously, people have a tendency to practice moral masquerading, whereby they tend to act not with ethical commitment but, rather, with ethical hypocrisy as they try to appear ethical yet, if possible, avoid the cost of being ethical (Batson, 2008). This awareness highlights the importance of ensuring that the means by which ethical motivation is developed is considered very carefully. How each of the foundation values for the creation of ethical motivation is to be nurtured is a serious question. Each of these values must become a natural part of leaders' being and not just a concept within their minds that can be ignored, suppressed, manipulated, amended, or selectively applied to suit a self-interest.

It is here that complexity theory may well provide guidance. Arguably, complexity theory supports the view of "the survival of those that fit," whereby it posits that in nature it is the species that are able to learn how to share and cooperate with other species within their immediate environment that ultimately are able to survive and multiply (see Morrison, 2002). Hence, when isolated from its environment, a particular natural object might appear as possessing very random, radical, uncontrollable, and individualistic properties, but when viewed as an integral member of its natural ecosystem, it is part of an intricate pattern formed from cooperation, sharing, unity, collusion, and mutuality. It would appear that in nature, seemingly "ethical" behavior is not only the norm but is the only way that each species can survive.

Importantly, this seemingly ethical behavior found at the fundamental level of nature is formed from the four basic principles of avoidance, alignment, attraction, and feedback (Fisher, 2009; Johnson, 2010; Mitchell, 2009). In complexity theory terms, avoidance is about an object or agent avoiding doing anything that will separate it from the system it wants to be a part of. Alignment implies that the object or agent does what each other object or agent is doing in order to survive and prosper in the system. Attraction is about each object or agent striving to ensure that it is completely in sync with each and every other object or agent that it has specific contact with. Finally, feedback refers to the essential need for each object or agent to be constantly gaining accurate and current information about the state of the system's total environment in general and the impact of its own activities upon the sustainability of this system in particular.

While it is easily possible to see how the complexity theory principles of avoidance, alignment, and attraction are deeply embedded within each of the foundational values of ethical motivation of self-knowledge, connectedness, transcendence, ethicalness, trustworthiness, responsibility, autonomy, presence, and wise judgment, this cannot be claimed for the principle of feedback. This is a critically important observation because, in complexity theory, feedback is the "magic ingredient . . . [that] operates at the level of the individual. . . . This magic ingredient is the feedback of information to the individual" (Johnson, 2010, pp. 25–26). It is through being able to regularly receive relevant and accurate information about its achievement of the required levels of avoidance, alignment, and attraction that a natural body is able to survive and thrive in a highly competitive, seemingly chaotic, but sustainable natural environment.

When applied to the development of sincere ethical motivation, the application of this "magic ingredient" suggests that it is essential that an explicit feedback process be established as an integral part of any ethical leadership development program. In simple terms, such a feedback process is designed to ensure that leaders are regularly gaining relevant and accurate information about their level of attendance to the nine foundational values of ethical motivation. Hence, the importance of establishing the role of ethical mentors comes to the fore.

## ESTABLISHING ETHICAL MENTORS

In the light of our human tendency to deceive ourselves, and others, about our commitment to being ethical, this essential feedback process cannot be self-directed feedback. Thus, other people must become the catalysts for ensuring that the most relevant and accurate information is provided to leaders in regard to their level of commitment to each of the nine foundational values of ethical motivation. It is proposed that such other people would be ethical mentors. Just as the role of qualified personal trainers has become widespread in the Western world to help individuals to better coordinate and manage their personal fitness and health regimes, so it is argued that qualified ethical mentors become available to work individually with leaders to support their generation of ethical motivation and thereby to become sincere and committed ethical leaders.

Such mentoring is about having the professional knowledge and skills to help unlock leaders' potential to maximize their performance (Renton, 2009). It is about helping them to learn rather than teaching them. The role of this ethical mentor contains four key elements (Fenwick, 2000). First, as communicators, they assist leaders to name what is unfolding around them and inside them, to continually rename any changing nuances, to unlock any limiting influences from past habits, understandings, and procedures, and to acknowledge the presence of any restrictive or destructive language that inhibits emerging possibilities. Second, as storymakers, ethical mentors help leaders to trace, and meaningfully record, the interactions they have with the people and objects in their daily experiences. Third, as interpreters, ethical mentors help leaders to make sense of the patterns emerging among the complex expectations, responsibilities, and interrelationships within their everyday experiences as well as helping leaders to more fully understand and appreciate their own involvement in these patterns. Finally, as credible role models, ethical mentors show leaders how to be deeply honest and arduously committed ethical people. Together, each of these key elements in the role of the ethical mentor provides leaders with the most appropriate knowledge, wisdom, sensitivity, and insight for ensuring that they can willingly and successfully utilize their ethical leadership knowledge in their workplaces with dignity, integrity, and confidence.

What is fundamental about this essential feedback from ethical mentors is that it forces leaders to objectively and subjectively confront each and every real ethical issue that is immediately impressing upon their leadership role. Hence, their ethical leadership is not solely cognitive; it automatically engages their whole being as well. The consequences of their ethical actions are inescapably experienced practically, consequentially, and emotionally. They have to take responsibility for what level of ethical behavior they have decided to invoke, they have to acknowledge the unavoidable ethical outcomes that result from this decision, and they have to recognize their authentic feelings and sense of self-worth that are aroused by these outcomes. Through feedback, leaders are challenged to continuously, courageously, and purposefully face the myriad of ethical contestations invariably embedded in their interrelationships with everyone influenced by their leadership. The development of ethical leadership can only be fully successful when a key part of it is focused squarely upon leaders' actual ethical reality as it unfolds in every moment of their work-related lives.

These four key elements of communicator, storymaker, interpreter, and role model in the position of the ethical mentor are then directed upon the leader's relative engagement with, and adoption of, the nine foundational values of ethical motivation. These nine values become the touchstones for discussing and discerning the experienced nature of the leader's behavior, especially during times of having to deal with tangible ethical dilemmas. In this way, the outcomes generated by leaders as they strive to grow in each of the nine foundational values is not only acknowledged and understood, but also felt. Not only are the tangible and explicit benefits recognized, but also the often overlooked internal and implicit benefits that feed one's sense of personal betterment and self-enhancement is made tangible and recognizable too. In this way, not only are leaders able to affirm their improvement as leaders but also to feel their own enriched physiological, psychological, spiritual, and social characteristics too. In this way, their becoming ethical leaders is more about their sense of being, their sense of self, than simply knowing the degree of correctness in what they have done. When this level of awareness is reached, the practice of ethical leadership becomes deeply meaningful rather than being essentially desirable. Furthermore, when leaders find meaning, they do not need motivation. When leaders find meaningfulness in being sincerely committed ethical leaders, they do not need external motivation to act accordingly; the meaningfulness becomes the motivation. Then, ethical leadership is not something they practice, but rather, it is an integral part of who they are as people.

## REFERENCES

Annas, J. (2008). The phenomenology of virtue. *Phenomenology and the Cognitive Sciences, 7*(1), 21–34.

Badaracco, J. L. (2006). *Questions of character: Illuminating the heart of leadership through literature.* Boston: Harvard Business School Press.

Bandura, A. (1997). *Self-efficacy: The exercise of control.* New York: W. H. Freeman.

Batson, C. D. (2008). Ethical masquerades: Experimental exploration of the nature of ethical motivation. *Phenomenology and the Cognitive Sciences, 7*(1), 51–66.

Begley, P. T. (2003). In pursuit of authentic school leadership practices. In P. T. Begley & O. Johansson (Eds.), *The ethical dimensions of school leadership* (pp. 1–12). Dordrecht, Netherlands: Kluwer Academic Publishers.

Bohm, D. (2006). *On dialogue.* (L. Nichol, Ed.). London: Routledge.

Bolman, L. G., & Deal, T. E. (2008). *Reframing leadership: Artistry, choice, and leadership* (4th ed.). San Francisco: Jossey-Bass.

Branson, C. M. (2007). The effects of structured self-reflection on the development of authentic leadership practices among Queensland primary school principals. *Educational Management Administration and Leadership Journal, 35*(2), 227–248.

Branson, C. M. (2009). *Leadership for an age of wisdom.* Dordrecht, Netherlands: Springer Educational.

Burns, J. (1978). *Leadership.* New York: Harper & Row.

Burns, J. (2010). *Leadership* (2nd ed.). New York: Harper & Row.

Bush, T., & Glover, D. (2003). *School leadership: Concepts and evidence.* Nottingham, UK: National College of School Leadership.

Cairnes, M. (1998). *Approaching the corporate heart: Breaking through to new horizons of personal and professional success.* Sydney: Simon & Schuster.

Campbell, E. (1997). Administrators' decisions and teachers' ethical dilemmas: Implications for moral agency. *Leading & Managing, 3*(4), 247–257.

Cashman, K. (1998). *Leadership from the inside out: Becoming a leader for life.* Provo, UT: Executive Excellence.

Cavalier, R. P. (2000). *Personal motivation: A model for decision making.* Westport, CT: Praeger.

Cianci, R., & Gambrel, P. A. (2003). Maslow's hierarchy of needs: Does it apply in a collectivist culture? *Journal of Applied Management and Entrepreneurship, 8*(2), 143–161.

Clark, M. E. (2004). Hamstrung or properly calibrated? Federalism and the appropriate role of government in the post–Sarbanes-Oxley world. *International Journal of Disclosure and Governance, 1*(4), 385–412.

Cloud, H. (2009). *Integrity: The courage to meet the demands of reality: How six essential qualities determine your success in business.* New York: HarperCollins.

Cooper, T. L. (1998). *The responsible administrator: An approach to ethics for the administrative role.* San Francisco: Jossey Bass.

de Bono, E. (1996). *Textbook of wisdom.* London: Penguin Press.

de Quincey, C. (2005). *Radical knowing: Understanding consciousness through relationship.* Rochester, VT: Park Street Press.

DePree, M. (1989). *Leadership is an art.* Melbourne: Australian Business Library.

Duignan, P. (2004). Forming capable leaders: From competencies to capabilities. *New Zealand Journal of Educational Leadership, 19*(2), 5–12.

Duignan, P. (2006). *Educational leadership: Key challenges and ethical tensions.* Melbourne: Cambridge University Press.

Duignan, P. (2009). Leadership: Authentic presence, influencing relationships and influence fields. Retrieved from www.cie.org.za/images/uploads/Lead_Influence_Presence_Rels_CAT_2008_(2)-1.pdf

Duignan, P., & Bhindi, N. (1997). Authenticity in leadership: An emerging perspective. *Journal of Educational Administration, 35*(3), 195–209.

Eraut, M. (1993). Teacher accountability: Why is it central in teacher professional development? In L. Kremer-Hayon, H. C. Vonk, & R. Fessler (Eds.), *Teacher professional development: A multiple perspective approach.* Amsterdam: Swets & Zeitlinger.

Evers, C. (1992). Ethics and ethical theory in educational leadership: A pragmatic and holistic approach. In P. Duignan & R. Macpherson (Eds.), *Educational: A practical theory for new administrators and managers.* London: Falmer.

Fenwick, T. J. (2000). Expanding conceptions of experiential learning: A review of the five contemporary perspectives of cognition. *Adult Education Quarterly, 50*(4), 243–272.

Fisher, L. (2009). *The perfect storm: The science of complexity in everyday life.* New York: Basic Books.

Foote, M. F., & Ruona, W. E. A. (2008). Institutionalizing ethics: A synthesis of frameworks and the implications for HRD. *Human Resource Development Review, 7*(3), 292–308.

Frank, R. H. (1988). *Passions within reason: The strategic role of the emotions.* New York: W. W. Norton.

Frattaroli, E. (2001). *Healing the soul in the age of the brain: Becoming conscious in an unconscious world.* New York: Penguin Books.

Gardner, H. (1993). *Frames of mind: The theory of multiple intelligences* (2nd ed.). New York: Basic Books.

Gellermann, W., Frankel, M. S., & Ladenson, R. F. (1990). *Values and ethics in organization and human systems development: Responding to dilemmas in professional life.* San Francisco: Jossey-Bass.

Goleman, D. (1995). *Emotional intelligence.* New York: Bantam Books.

Goleman, D. (1998). *Working with emotional intelligence.* London: Bloomsbury Publishing.

Gonzalez, C. (2003, January 14). Declining public trust foremost a leadership problem. *Embargo* [World Economic Forum press release].

Goodpaster, K. E. (2004, March–April). Ethics or excellence? conscience as a check on the unbalanced pursuit of organizational goals. *Ivey Business Journal.* Retrieved from http://iveybusinessjournal.com/topics/the-workplace/ethics-or-excellence-conscience-as-a-check-on-the-unbalanced-pursuit-of-organizational-goals#.UwfJTvldXeI

Hamilton, C. (2008). *The freedom paradox: Towards a post-secular ethics.* Crows Nest, New South Wales, Australia: Allen & Unwin.

Haslam, S. A., Reicher, S. D., & Platow, M. J. (2011). *The new psychology of leadership: Identity, influence and power.* Hove, Sussex: Psychology Press.

Heifetz, R. A., & Linsky, M. (2002). *Leadership on the line: Staying alive through the dangers of leading.* Boston: Harvard Business School Press.

Hodgkinson, C. (1996). *Administrative philosophy: Values and motivations in administrative life.* New York: Pergamon.

Hofstede, G. (1984). The cultural relativity of the quality of life concept. *Academy of Management Review, 9*(3), 389–398.

Hultman, K., & Gellermann, B. (2002). *Balancing individual and organizational values: Walking the tightrope to success.* San Francisco: Jossey-Bass.

Johansson, O. (2003). School leadership as a democratic arena. In P. T. Begley & O. Johansson (Eds.), *The ethical dimensions of school leadership* (pp. 201–219). Dordrecht, Netherlands: Kluwer Academic Publishers.

Johnson, N. (2010). *Simply complexity: A clear guide to complexity theory.* Oxford: Oneworld Publications.

Kermond, C. (2009, November 9). Banks and telcos biggest losers of the public's trust. *Sydney Morning Herald.*

Kist, A. W. (2002). Decentralisation of enforcement of EC Competition law. *Intereconomics, 37*(1), 36–41.

Kouzes, J. M., & Posner, B. Z. (1995). *The leadership challenge: How to keep getting extraordinary things done in organizations.* San Francisco: Jossey-Bass.

Kriegel, U. (2008). Moral phenomenology: Foundational issues. *Phenomenology and the Cognitive Sciences, 7*(1), 1–19.

Langlois, L. (2004). Responding ethically: Complex decision-making by school superintendents. *International Studies in Educational Administration Journal, 32*(2), 78–93.

Mant, A. (1997). *Intelligent leadership.* Sydney: Allen & Unwin.

Maslow, A. (1954). *Motivation and personality.* New York: Harper & Row.

Maslow, A. (1968). *Towards a psychology of being* (2nd ed.). Princeton, NJ: Van Nostrand.

Maxwell, J. C. (2005). *The 360 degree leader: Developing your influence from anywhere in the organization.* Nashville, TN: Thomas Nelson.

May, R. (1967). *Psychology and the human dilemma.* Princeton, NJ: Van Nostrand.

Mitchell, M. (2009). *Complexity: A guided tour.* New York: Oxford University Press.

Morrison, K. (2002). *School leadership and complexity theory.* London: Routledge Falmer.

Ncube, L. B., & Wasburn, M. H. (2006). Strategic collaboration for ethical leadership: A mentoring framework for business and organizational decision making. *Journal of Leadership and Organizational Studies, 13*(1), 77–92.

Neck, C. P., & Manz, C. C. (2007). *Self-leadership: Leading yourself to personal excellence.* Retrieved from www.emergingleader.com/article4.shrml

Osborne, R. E. (1996). *Self: An eclectic approach.* Needham Heights, MA: Simon & Schuster.

Renton, J. (2009). *Coaching and mentoring: What they are and how to make the most of them.* London: Profile books.

Richmon, M. J. (2003). Persistent difficulties with values in educational administration: Mapping the terrain. In P. T. Begley & O. Johansson (Eds.), *The ethical dimensions of school leadership* (pp. 33–47). Dordrecht, Netherlands: Kluwer Academic Publications.

Rokeach, M. (1973). *The nature of human values.* New York: Free Press.

Rost, J. C. (1993). *Leadership for the twenty-first century.* London: Praeger.

Senge, P., Scharmer, C. O., Jaworski, J., & Flowers, B. S. (2007). *Presence: Exploring profound change in people, organizations and society.* London: Nicholas Brealey.

Sergiovanni, T. (1992). *Moral leadership: Getting to the heart of school improvement.* San Francisco: Jossey-Bass.

Sergiovanni, T. J. (1994). The roots of school leadership. *Principal, 75*(2), 6–9.

Sofield, L. K., & Kuhn, D. H. (1995). *The collaborative leader: Listening to the wisdom of God's people.* Notre Dame, IN: Ave Maria Press.

Starratt, R. J. (1993). *The drama of leadership.* London: Falmer Press.

Starratt, R. J. (1994). *Building an ethical school.* London: Falmer Press.

Starratt, R. J. (2003). *Centering educational administration: Cultivating meaning, community, responsibility.* Mahwah, NJ: Lawrence Erlbaum.

Starratt, R. J. (2004). *Ethical leadership.* San Francisco: Jossey-Bass.

Strom, M. (2007). *Arts of the wise leader.* Auckland, NZ: Sophos.

Telford, H. (1996). *Transforming schools through collaborative leadership.* London: Falmer.

Terry, R. W. (1993). *Authentic leadership: Courage in action.* San Francisco: Jossey-Bass.

Tolle, E. (2005). *A new earth: Awakening to your life's purpose.* New York: Penguin.

Tuana, N. (2007). Conceptualizing ethical literacy. *Journal of Educational Administration*, 45(4), 364–378.

Wagner, H. (1999). *The psychobiology of human motivation.* London: Routledge.

Wahba, A., & Bridgewell, L. (1976). Maslow reconsidered: A review of research on the need hierarchy theory. *Organizational Behavior and Human Performance, 15*(2), 212–240.

Wheatley, M. J. (2006). *Leadership and the new science: Discovering order in a chaotic world* (3rd ed.). San Francisco: Berrett-Koehler Publishers.

Whitehead, J. D., & Whitehead, E. E. (1991). *The promise of partnership: Leadership ministry in an adult church.* San Francisco: Harper Press.

Wilber, K. (2000). *Sex, ecology, spirituality* (2nd ed.). Boston: Shambhala.

Wooten, K. C. (2001). Ethical dilemmas in human resource management: An application of a multidimensional framework, a unifying taxonomy, and applicable codes. *Human Resource Management Review, 11*(1), 159–175.

# III

# Examples From the Field

# 20

## HOLISTIC AND MORAL DEVELOPMENT OF EDUCATIONAL LEADERS

### PAULINE E. LEONARD, TAMMY SCHILLING, AND ANTHONY H. NORMORE

In keeping with the premise that "if we understand the world narratively . . . then it makes sense to study the world narratively" (Clandinin & Connelly, 2000, p. 17), this chapter takes the form of narrative inquiry. The focus of our inquiry is holistic leadership, particularly in terms of examining holistic approaches to the moral development of educational leaders. Through narrative inquiry, we engage in reflexivity—the process of reflecting critically on our experiences as both inquirers of and respondents to those experiences (Lincoln, Lynham, & Guba, 2011). To that end, we first provide a brief review of the scholarly literature pertaining to holistic leadership. Second, through storytelling, we each share our "lived experience" (Chase, 2011, p. 422) with a variety of educational leadership projects to provide a backdrop for examining and understanding holistic leadership. We also explain why narrative inquiry is an appropriate approach for examining this topic. Third, we identify and present five themes that emerged through the comparative analysis of our stories.

## HOLISTIC LEADERSHIP

Current educational leadership discourse is typically characterized by discussions that serve to broaden our conceptualization of what constitutes effective leadership. Moreover, this turn in the leadership discussion has served to promote "dialogue across local, national, and international boundaries" (Normore, 2010, p. xiii) with the goal of "cross-fertilization of ideas and experiences" (p. xiv). One important outcome of this cross-fertilization is the increasing interest in exploring the multidimensionality of leadership and leadership development. From the perspective of the business world, it has been suggested that the recent high-profile corporate failures have raised many questions about the narrow focus of traditional leadership programs (Quatro, Waldman, & Galvin, 2007). Similarly, in education, Branson (2007) suggests that the uncertainties inherent in today's world have caused people to "want their leaders to act morally" (p. 469). As a result, the role of moral judgment and, more recently, moral literacy (Tuana, 2007) are now widely identified in the educational leadership literature.

While there may be increasing emphasis on the moral dimension of leadership in education, less sustained attention has been given to other, nontraditional dimensions that characterize holistic leadership. Nevertheless, a review of the literature revealed that holistic leadership, as a concept worthy of study, is gaining momentum. References to leadership development programs are beginning to include examining ways to "integrate mind, body, and spirit to become more effective leaders" (Shinn, 2010, p. 58). For example, Quatro and colleagues (2007) propose that corporate leadership development programs and initiatives, which traditionally have focused on the analytical aspects of leadership, should be "more holistic in scope" (p. 248). Alternatively, spiritually enlightened leaders would be skillful in enabling followers to connect their work to moral and ethical values. Accordingly, cultivating the spiritual domain would include a focus on self-reflection and meditative thinking, similar to Branson's (2007) structured self-reflection for educational leaders.

Discussions of holistic leadership vary in terms of which aspects of humanity appear to warrant our focus and sustained attention. For example, based on her academic background in organizational learning and social work, as well as her experiences with leadership training in a variety of organizations, Julie Orlov (2003) states that holistic leadership is "being able to lead from the mind, the heart, and the soul" (p. 1). Clearly, there is no reference to the physical (i.e., the body) aspect of holistic leadership development. In stark contrast, Sinclair (2007), in her treatise on how to become an enlightened leader, emphasizes the importance of paying attention to the body for gaining new insights for leadership. Alternatively, Taggart (2010), a self-described student of leadership for over 20 years and creator of a leadership consulting organization, omitted any references to mind, body, and spirit in presenting his model of holistic leadership. Therefore, we may infer that the apparent lack of consensus regarding holistic leadership may be the result of authors' use of different terminology, at least to some extent.

Inherent in discussions of holistic—mind, body, spirit—leadership development is the challenge of countering criticisms from those who may conceptualize effective leadership solely as an activity of the disembodied mind—one where rationality, reason, cognitive mastery, and objectivity prevail (Sinclair, 2007). Riaz and Normore (2008) acknowledge that challenge in their examination of the spiritual dimension of educational leadership: "Spirituality is a significant dimension of human existence that is often silenced in the public school system" (p. 1).

On the "body" front of the holistic leadership development discussion is the challenge of resisting or subverting the dominant paradigm that leadership is just a cognitive activity; it is also a physical one. According to Shinn (2010), effective leaders understand the connections among their physical, mental, and emotional capabilities. Consequently, some innovative leadership training programs are incorporating physical exercise and personal reflection into the curricula. Similarly, Sinclair (2007) claims that traditionally, leadership has been seen as a bodiless activity of the mind. She also advocates that focusing on breathing in a conscious way can help foster composure and attentiveness, and may even change the practice of leadership.

Despite the differing definitions and terminology embedded in discussions of holistic leadership, there is growing consensus that leadership is more than an activity of the mind. Moreover, there is increasing recognition that leadership development programs need to be broader in scope to incorporate the multidimensionality of humanity.

## NARRATIVE INQUIRY

Narrative has been described as a "fundamental means of imposing order on otherwise random and disconnected events and experiences" (Tedlock, 2011, p. 335). There are many conceptualizations of what constitutes narrative inquiry; however, we align our approach with those researchers who "treat *their* stories about life experience . . . as a significant and necessary focus of narrative inquiry" (p. 423). In doing so, we explore holistic leadership by telling *our* stories as a trilogy. As such, we narrate three separate, but connected, stories—each author's respective experience with projects intended to cultivate the development of morally literate, responsive, authentic leaders. The connectedness unfolds as we examine our shared experiences and emergent themes through the multifocal lens of narrative inquiry. The first story is told from the perspective of a college of education department chair, particularly in terms of her roles as facilitator of course and program development initiatives and as an administrative leader of faculty and staff in that department. The second story is told from the perspective of a faculty member with a background in physical education teacher education and community youth sport development, particularly in terms of her role in facilitating leadership development among middle and high school youth. The third narrative is told from the perspective of a university faculty member with a background in educational leadership. Among his various experiences in facilitating leadership development is his crusade aimed at helping incarcerated populations to self-rehabilitate as a result of the Education-Based Incarceration program at the Los Angeles County Sheriff's Department.

## PAULINE'S STORY

Since 1996, the annual Values and Leadership Conference has provided an ongoing forum for educational theorists, researchers, and practitioners to present and discuss ethical paradigms, perspectives, and frameworks for understanding moral leadership in education. This forum has been invaluable in my professional role as a university faculty member and, subsequently, as chair in a department responsible for initial, advanced, and alternative teacher and leader certification programs. As a result of my immersion in the values and leadership discourse, I have been able to apply relevant ethical principles and values theory to reflect on my own professional practices. Elsewhere, I have written about this reflective process (see, for example, Leonard, 2005, 2007). My engagement in the processes of structured self-reflection for the purpose of examining, understanding, and practicing moral leadership continues. What follows is an account of some of my experiences with attempting to connect theory and practice. In relating my reflections on these processes, a major goal is to underscore the lack of attention to, as well as the importance of, addressing the *holistic* development of moral leaders.

## Moral Responsibility

In 2003, the educational leadership faculty in our department designed and implemented a new educational leadership master's program. As our educational leadership team collaborated to develop the program, many of us shared our struggle of authenticity—reconciling beliefs with practice. We faced a tremendous challenge in developing the program within redesign guidelines, national and state standards, as well as our own conflicting views of what a leadership preparation program should look like for real-world applications. What was quite interesting, upon reflection, is that, as a committee, we took our responsibility very seriously, but the nature of that responsibility often differed. In applying Starratt's (2004) work on ethical leadership and the ethics of responsibility, I was able to more fully understand that process.

Starratt (2004) has stated that educational leaders must be morally responsible, not only in a preventative sense but in a proactive one as well. Responsibility, in the latter sense, is three-dimensional in that the leader is responsible as, responsible to, and responsible for. I believe that the educational leadership team members felt responsible in all three of these ways, with each member being responsible in different ways on different issues. One example is that of meeting the redesign guidelines, particularly the request for identifying the empirical basis for educational practices and teaching methods covered in the newly developed courses for the program. There was considerable deliberation about which research studies to include, with some of the program development team members placing substantial importance on integrating studies from journals and organizations that were reportedly considered to be embraced by the state board of regents and board of education. This position suggested they felt a primary responsibility *as* state employees, *to* state governing agencies, *for* developing an educational program based on strict adherence to state guidelines. Alternatively, other team members expressed dismay at such an approach and advocated that there was enough expertise on the committee to locate, examine, and utilize empirical studies that were deemed most appropriate for meeting course and program goals and objectives. This stance indicated that they felt a primary responsibility *as* program developers, *to* prospective program candidates, *for* developing an educational leadership program informed, but not constrained, by state guidelines.

In my work as a member of the educational leadership team, I was able to experience firsthand the challenges of working collaboratively to develop a new program. And while there were differences in how we conceptualized our responsibilities as, to, and for when developing the program, reflecting upon the process allowed me to ask important questions about how we worked through our differences while remaining true to our beliefs. The experience, and reflection upon the experience, has helped me realize the importance of knowing who we are, of attempting to clarify our identity, and of understanding whom we are responsible as, to, and for. The quest for authenticity demands that we participate in this process.

## Structured Self-reflection

While my work in the area of administrator preparation program development has tended to focus on emphasizing the moral aspects of leadership, my involvement in teacher preparation program development evolved to include an emphasis on the *holistic* development of teachers. This emphasis on holism emerged from the realization that there existed a lack of cultural and ethnic diversity among graduates of teacher education programs, which necessitated our focusing on culturally responsive teaching. In an effort to address that challenge, we explored the notion of the reflective practitioner as being very powerful in the process of cultivating whole teachers. Branson's (2007) deeply structured reflective process provided an avenue for facilitating the process of preservice and inservice teachers in connecting their respective life experiences to their stated teaching behaviors.

As an example, in 2008, a colleague and I conducted a qualitative case study (Leonard & Basinger, 2008) to field test an instructional technique—structured self-reflection—based on Begley's (2003) values framework and Branson's (2007) components of self. The instructional technique was a modified version of Branson's deeply structured reflective process, which we implemented in a required teacher education course. The instructional technique assisted teacher candidates in the process of critically reflecting on their life experiences and the impact of those experiences on the development and interaction of their respective Self components: self-concept, self-esteem, motives, values, beliefs, and teaching behaviors. The findings supported the premise that facilitating teacher candidates' understanding of Self through structured self-reflection enhances moral literacy and helps to create *whole* teachers who are culturally responsive in their teaching.

## Holistic Development

The essential message in sharing the preceding examples is that I have always tried to connect and align my work and responsibilities as a professor-teacher, a professor-scholar, and a professor-administrator, and while my efforts have been rewarding in many ways, I realize that I have fallen short in terms of conceptualizing and exploring a fully *holistic approach to moral leadership.* Moreover, my contention is that this is the norm, and providers of administrator preparation programs typically have focused on the intellectual aspects of leadership development to the detriment of other important aspects of our humanity, all of which are integral for the holistic development of moral leaders. In other words, I propose that sustainable effective leadership performance is best achieved when leaders recognize the critical interdependence of mind, body, and spirit (Quatro, Waldman, & Galvin, 2007) and the importance of purposefully aligning, developing, and integrating these domains as essential components of organizational culture.

As I reflect on my journey as a faculty member and current administrator, I realize that typically, I have tried to separate or compartmentalize the emotional, physical, spiritual, and intellectual experiences or aspects of my being. For example, invariably my "to do" lists are categorized under personal and professional, even though some clearly impact both private and public life. This begs some important questions. Would not taking 10 minutes to meditate or sit quietly in silence during the workday improve my ability to think more clearly and, perhaps, make more enlightened professional decisions? Shouldn't a 15-minute walk midmorning get me away from my computer, help keep me physically fit, and perhaps positively increase my energy for teaching a class that evening? Would not taking time to emotionally connect with colleagues help engender trust and, perhaps, enhance collaborative initiatives? In examining the spiritual dimension of educational leadership, Riaz and Normore (2008) suggest that leaders can strengthen their "spiritual muscles" (p. 4). Citing Covey (2004), the authors also claimed that "human beings are endowed with four intelligences at birth, including mental, social, emotional, and spiritual" (cited in Riaz & Normore, 2008, p. 4). While perhaps not an "intelligence" as such, the physical realm should be added to these four dimensions of leadership. Informed by my recent deliberations and beliefs about the significance of holism for human growth and development, I am currently engaged in facilitating faculty involvement in departmental visioning and strategic planning through the incorporation of activities that engage mind, body, and spirit. This process is in its preliminary stages and we are all neophytes in terms of how best to approach the holistic development of our professional learning community. However, to some extent we have attended, at least on a superficial level, to addressing the physical realm (e.g., instead of sitting to discuss an educational initiative during a professional learning initiative meeting, we walk with a partner and return to discuss with the whole group). We have also shared quotes and poetry to spark our "spiritual muscles."

Suffice it to say, these experiences I share pertaining to the holistic development of moral leaders are elementary attempts to explore and understand the notion of holism and its implications for creating and sustaining professional learning communities. Furthermore, these deliberations about holistic leadership underscore emerging and still unanswered questions. For example, should we address the challenge of examining current leader preparation programs for ways to integrate holistic approaches to the development of moral leaders? And, if so, how?

## TAMMY'S STORY

Prior to my current position, I worked for 10 years with underserved youth in responsibility-based afterschool physical activity programs. I am now heavily involved in Louisiana Gaining Early Awareness and Readiness for Undergraduate Programs (LA GEAR UP). The mission of LA GEAR UP is to increase the number of low-income students who enter and succeed in postsecondary education (Louisiana Board of Regents, 2005). Accomplishing the program's mission requires a multifaceted approach including summer learning camps (SLCs), professional development (PD) of teachers and counselors, and year-round Explorers Clubs in schools. In addition to directing summer camps, I serve as the leadership coordinator for LA GEAR UP. In this role, I develop leadership and Explorers Club activities each year as options for all SLCs and also conduct PD activities with teachers and school counselors. Therefore, I have had the opportunity to refine my philosophy on the development of youth leadership.

Leadership training for LA GEAR UP is designed to help students learn and practice personal and interpersonal leadership skills within a supportive community of peers and mentors. The leadership style that I espouse is both empowerment and service oriented. We want students to experience leadership as an opportunity for "voice" and "choice" and to consider the importance of raising others up with them as leaders. This is a different philosophy than some of the more authoritarian leadership styles (and ones that our kids have likely been exposed to the most).

The short-term nature of summer camps, and the larger scale of LA GEAR UP, necessitated a much more intensive and strategic approach to leadership development. I incorporated more team-based challenges that would dismantle walls of discrimination, prejudice, and insecurity and compel diverse participants to work cooperatively to achieve success. Some of the activities are associated with Adventure Education. Adventure experiences generally consist of physical team-building challenges that encourage the development of specific leadership skills like trust, communication, and cooperation in a fun environment. The activities elicit different feelings for different individuals, and some participants may initially be uncomfortable participating in certain activities. Participants are encouraged to engage fully in the experience with the understanding that, ultimately, they each can choose their own level of participation and challenge. This concept is called Challenge By Choice (Project Adventure, 1995, p. 9). Another important concept is the Full Value Contract (Project Adventure). This is, essentially, an agreement to respect and value all participants and their contributions.

At the beginning of each leadership session, we discuss our Full Value Contract as the following guidelines or expectations:

1. Be respectful (of yourself, others, equipment, and space).
2. Be safe (physically and emotionally).
3. Be here now (be focused and "in the zone").
4. Let go and move on (persistence; the key is how you respond to challenges).

These guidelines, and the adventure activities, set up an environment ripe for leadership development. However, it is the use of debriefing after the activities and at the end of each session that provides the most powerful opportunities for processing the emergence and display of leadership skills, challenges or barriers to success, and strategies for transfer of leadership skills to other settings.

Across my experiences in promoting youth leadership, a consistent set of beliefs have emerged and been reinforced. These are described below.

### Belief in the Capacity of Young People to Be Leaders

With continued emphasis on disempowering curriculum and standardized testing, and the beat-down of even our most effective teachers, the most critical roles of students may be as educational leaders and active participants in changing the current school culture. After all, teachers often remain in the profession because of the inspiration of their students. In our programs, I have seen numerous youth participants demonstrate surprisingly mature resilience and moral leadership. For me, the challenge continues to be helping all youth participants see in themselves what we see and nurturing motivation to explore that capability. This process cannot be top-down nor can you pour leadership rhetoric on kids and hope it sticks. They need to experience personal meaning in the process and feel that there is some benefit to being courageous enough to step up as leaders.

### Belief in the Use of the Physical Domain as a Medium for Holistic Development

The physical challenges that we use in LA GEAR UP stimulate cognitive development in terms of strategic problem solving. Additionally, physical activity promotes unique opportunities for personal and social development (Hellison, 2011). Participating in physical activities or challenges facilitates body, space, and self-awareness and requires the courage to put your body and physical ability on display. Since we are typically in a gym with a variety of different types of equipment, some participants may initially perceive challenges through the lens of competition. This can elicit a higher level of emotions (e.g., pressure on oneself and others to be first to finish). These situations provide us with powerful teachable moments where we can reinforce the importance of focusing on your group, the positive results of cooperation, and the notion that all of us can be, and are, winners in the challenges. Contrary to popular belief, this is a good thing.

### Belief in Reflection as a Key to Continual Leadership Development

As noted earlier, debriefing is an important component following the team-building challenges. Debriefing provides opportunities to use analogies in reflection. For example, in our Stepping Stones activity, five or six students work together using life support vehicles (wood blocks) to transport their group across the toxic land to another planet that has food, water, and most importantly, available technology use. This is a challenging activity that requires balance and physical support as students must share blocks in order to advance across the toxic land. At the end of this activity, we often consider their destination on the court as students' postsecondary aspirations (i.e., where do you see yourself after high school?). We discuss barriers, or challenges (toxic land), and sources of support (life support vehicles) in achieving their goals.

Deeper reflection about morality and values is also important and occurs at the end of the leadership session. In some years, I have focused on a theme such as "take your place," which was emphasized by Cicely Tyson's character in *Madea's Family Reunion*. In other years, I have been inspired by something I have read. For example, in Wayne Dyer's (1996) book, *Your Sacred Self*, he discusses the three most difficult things in life: (1) return love for hate (positive for negative), (2) include the excluded, and (3) admit when you are wrong. These points are conducive for jump-starting students to consider how these might be put into action in their own lives and for discussing serious issues in schools like bullying and our role as leaders in addressing bullying.

## Belief in the Importance of Empowerment in Leadership Development

For leadership to develop, youth must feel empowered. This requires adults to respect youth and their right to ownership in the process. It also means that we need to be genuine in our empowerment and listen to the voices of youth, even if we do not necessarily agree with their perspective all the time. As Hellison (2011, p. 27) notes, this does not mean "caving in to everything kids want or demand." We must be courageous in standing up for our core values and in confronting kids when warranted. The key is in how we confront them—with respect, and valuing what they can positively contribute and how they respond to the situation.

In other work (Schilling, Martinek, & Tan, 2001), my colleagues and I have articulated principles of empowerment that affect leadership development, including: (1) one size does not fit all; (2) various contexts dictate the type and potential for leadership of youth participants; and (3) leadership development is a dynamic process marked by grand successes, disappointing failures, and, sometimes, average experiences. This process necessitates an understanding of the balance for knowing the best situations and potential for empowerment, and times when empowerment is not effective and could even be detrimental.

As a final discussion point, small and barely recognizable windows of opportunity for empowerment can result in remarkable possibilities for youth leadership. It is important not to discount such windows. The story of Ja'Marcus Goudeau is a notable example. Ja'Marcus (also known as Turbo) attended LA GEAR UP Sports Medicine Camp one week in 2012. The entire group that week was strong and cohesive, but there was something else remarkable under the surface about this group. After the graduation dinner and our awards ceremony, Ja'Marcus was granted his request to share his poem about camp, "Pass the Message." It was an impressive reading and included a very interesting part:

> You guys are unique
> I never met a group that's full of some kind of pain
> Yet smile through the situations and find some calling or distraction even
> to keep you on a straight path

I wasn't sure about the exact meaning but felt it was powerful. Buoyed by the strength of his own words and voice, and by the positive response to his poetry, Ja'Marcus asked if he could share another one about his brother. Here is what he read:

### Understanding

> As I open the doors to hell which you don't see hell
> You see a door because our eyes see two different things
> Meaning me and you have no understanding
> At the moment he was twelve
> All he needed was a ear but I couldn't offer mine because His mouth and my ear were on
>    two different pages of a book
> And what he said I couldn't understand
> Therefore me and him had no understanding

*And at 2:02*
*A phone call to my house telling me the life of my brother that I knew and loved was*
*taken by the front grill of some massive vehicle who seemed to get away because the*
*intoxication of his mind didn't enable him to stop*
*At that point my mind is racing going crazy because over the phone what I hear is differ-*
*ent from what they hear because no one understands what it means to lose a brother*
*Meaning we have no understanding*
*Why drive and drink?*
*See at the moment you don't know the consequences just one sip could mean one life*
*Being that the life isn't yours you will never feel the pain inhabited to one's soul as a mem-*
*ber of their heart is lost*
*But in your behalf maybe it was a long day that needed that one sip but at 2:02 in the*
*morning take yo ass home sober because this young generation creeps at night only to*
*fit in*
*Therefore we have no understanding*
*Society is so confused labeling we people Menaces not realizing the pain of fitting in could*
*Hurt our small fist of a heart*
*So therefore we have no understanding*
*and forced to take hold of a name not needed and treated to ways not deserved but we*
*deal with the after effects of every drunk driver in the world*
*We need understanding*

Opening this small window of opportunity, and trusting in Ja'Marcus, fueled his courage to share his poetry and his pain. In turn, other campers felt empowered to embrace their own pain and fears, which resulted in a tremendous release of deep, pent-up emotions. This experience significantly impacted the high school students, our college student counselors, and the adult staff. The impact on Ja'Marcus contin- ues as he, along with some classmates, have started a poetry club at his school.

### Final Thoughts

For me, promoting self-awareness, confidence, and leadership skills of youth has warranted consideration of the whole person (mind, body, and soul) in leadership development. I am fortunate to have knowledge and experience in the physical realm, which is an undeniably effective and powerful arena for promoting holistic develop- ment. Without a doubt, my own development in multiple dimensions has also been positively impacted by the young people with whom I have been fortunate to work.

## TONY'S STORY

I am a university faculty member and department chair with a background in edu- cational leadership, ethics, and social justice. Among my experiences in facilitat- ing leadership development is my work with helping incarcerated populations to self-rehabilitate through the Education-Based Incarceration (EBI) program at the Los Angeles County Sheriff's Department (LASD). These inmates are generally repeat offenders who made bad decisions around issues such as substance abuse, neglectful parenting, and robbery—to name a few of their crimes that landed them in the county jail. The more hardened criminals end up in the state prison system as opposed to the county jail system.

My current role as a lead facilitator is to facilitate leadership development among the male inmates in the Maximizing Education Reaching Individual Transformation (MERIT) program, who have not only graduated as masters in this EBI program, but also have completed further study so that they can teach their fellow inmates. In the MERIT program, men participate in a series of activities that require them to revisit their value systems, explore their spirituality, and participate in a specific set of courses aimed at preparing them to be successful citizens once they reenter society.

I was first introduced to EBI in 2010 when I received an invitation from LASD personnel to join the EBI steering committee to help develop a program that would reduce the high rate of recidivism in Los Angeles County, with potential impact on the rate of recidivism in the United States. My interest in EBI programs (also known as "correctional education") is based on the following research findings:

- The goal of education-based incarceration and/or correctional education programs is to reduce recidivism rates and aid offenders in adapting to society and becoming productive citizens (Hendricks, Hendricks, & Kauffman, 2001).
- According to Mentor and Wilkinson (2006), "Researchers consistently demonstrate[d] that quality education is one of the most effective forms of crime prevention" (p. 1). Education programs decreased the likelihood that people would return to crime and prison.
- The nationwide recidivism rate of nearly 70% provides strong evidence that the contemporary approaches being used by most correctional agencies throughout the nation are woefully ineffective (Mentor & Williams, 2006).
- Leadership development is a key component for the holistic approach to preparing inmates for their reentry back into communities and into the larger society (Hendricks et al., 2001).

I recognize that the role of leaders in any organization is, at least in part, to advocate on behalf of traditionally marginalized and poorly served citizens. It carries a corollary contention that leaders must increase their awareness of various explicit and implicit forms of oppression, intentionally subvert the dominant paradigm, and act as a committed advocate for circumstances that make a meaningful and positive change in the education and lives of traditionally marginalized populations. EBI and correctional education take a penetrating look at the needs and challenges of society's disenfranchised—the denizens of our streets, the emotionally and physically incarcerated, and our children in juvenile hall and in unsettled homes. Further, it is incumbent to encourage public awareness of the causes that underlie the destructive cycles plaguing these populations, including the abuse and neglect that cycle through generations (Normore & Fitch, 2011).

## Education-Based Incarceration Within the Context of Los Angeles County

For years, inmates have served their sentences in county jails and prisons throughout the nation with little educational or vocational training to prepare them for a successful transition back into our communities. The results of this strategy have been a staggering nationwide recidivism rate of nearly 70% (Mentor & Williams, 2006). Yet, law enforcement agencies throughout the nation continue to repeat the same thing and expect a different result. Fortunately, there is a better way—EBI. EBI, as practiced by the LASD, is a systematic effort to provide educational, vocational, and life skills training to all inmates who qualify. Currently, approximately 32% of inmates housed in the Los Angeles County jail system are exposed to educational and vocational training in all of its nine facilities, using both traditional and nontraditional delivery methods, including conventional classroom meetings, self-study workbooks, and instructive videos. EBI also offers a variety of vocational courses that include commercial printing, sign making, pet grooming, bicycle repair, landscaping, and painting. All of the hours spent in EBI are tracked and reported (Baca, 2010).

The LASD is the nation's "largest sheriff's department, second largest policing agency, and in addition to dozens of patrol stations and the country's largest court security responsibilities, operates the nation's largest jail system" (Baca, 2010, p. 58). In the wake of the current state budget crisis, the LASD isn't giving up, especially when it comes to the housing of the new "state" inmates commonly referred to as AB109ers. With close to 20,000 incarcerated men and women, LA County Sheriff Leroy D. Baca established a set of guiding principles intended to provide a framework on which the LASD's education programs are based (Baca, 2010, pp. 54–58, cited in Choate, Normore, & Bates, 2012, para 1):

Principle 1: Assess and evaluate both the educational and trade skills of all offenders.

Principle 2: Develop a system of educating Los Angeles County prisoners who inevitably will serve time in the state prison system that begins and ends in the Los Angeles County Jail.

Principle 3: Develop and implement an automated case management information system.

Principle 4: Strengthen and systemize the partnership with the California Department of Corrections and Rehabilitation.

Principle 5: Develop curriculum that puts into action learning programs that are both structured and unstructured.

Principle 6: Transform the LASD Custody Operations Division and State Corrections.

One of the premier education programs found within the seven LASD's jail facilities is MERIT. The program is an integral part of the LASD's EBI Bureau—a new bureau in the Sheriff's Department under the command of a captain. To date, over 8,000 men and women have graduated from this 12-week extensive life skills training program that teaches students to make good decisions while obtaining life and work skills. Students attend classes for 30 hours per week until they are released or they graduate with their 12-week certificate. The following is a brief description of the program (see Choate, Normore, & Bates, 2012, paras. 4–6):

MERIT is an incentive-based program in which students begin as "general population" and move toward becoming elite MERIT masters. As students move through the progression, they are awarded more privileges, such as more access to the telephones and longer yard time. An unusual component of the MERIT program is the teachers. Qualified inmates, deputies, and professional facilitators teach MERIT life skills classes.

*MERIT Beginnings* is a program facilitated by MERIT graduates (inmates who are still incarcerated), as well as interested deputies. These facilitators are given a series of 45 different lessons to use for facilitation.

Unless court ordered, students who graduate from the MERIT Beginnings course are given the opportunity to participate in this 12-week program. Parenting, anger management, drug education, relationships, and spiritual growth are the major components of the program. While spiritual growth is a component, only students who volunteer for this portion attend the classes.

*MERIT Graduates.* After 12 weeks or approximately 360 hours of instruction, students are transitioned to a new class and in some cases a new dormitory. This program is designed to cover the primary areas of one's life, such as recovery; employment; financial, legal, and medical issues; family; and recreation. Goals and objectives are determined that will help in the first few months following the students' release from custody.

*MERIT Masters.* Students are chosen for this program based on their desire to teach and enforce the rules and their leadership capabilities or potential. MERIT masters are divided into teams of two: one senior and one junior. Each group of two teaches approximately 30 general population inmates. Prior to teaching and throughout the process, the inmate teachers are trained in adult learning, facilitation skills, basic lesson planning, basic curriculum design, and leadership principles.

*MERIT Continuum* is a support group that provides an opportunity for all MERIT students who have been released from custody to return to a designated meeting place for continued support. These support groups (including families) meet on weekday evenings and are strategically placed throughout Los Angeles County for travel convenience.

### Holistic and Spiritual Growth

The strength of the MERIT program lies in its ability to bring participants to the point where they each recognize the importance of a personal commitment to reaching their goals, accepting responsibility for their actions, and being accountable for their life choices. The participants are challenged to evaluate past abusive behaviors, create goals for recovery, demonstrate the will and motivation to modify behavior, and accept responsibility for future actions. The holistic education and rehabilitation program is framed in a community setting. Students are housed together, eat together, and attend classes together. In addition to the drug education component in place, the students receive classes on parenting and personal relationships. The "spiritual growth" component of MERIT explores the philosophy of substance dualism—the belief that "body" and "soul" are two distinctly different things, as well as the idea that decisions and actions affecting the body also affect the soul. The curriculum includes the concepts of absolute right and absolute wrong and helps participants learn to make better decisions based upon appropriate moral principles.

This focus on spirituality is closely aligned with the need to find meaning within one's work while using the work to serve spirituality (Frankl, 2006). Fairholm (1997) suggests that infusing spirituality within one's leadership is a vital adaptation to the shifting dynamic within today's workforce. Fairholm states, "People are hungry for meaning in their lives. They feel they have lost something and they don't remember what it is they've lost. . . . [I]t has left a gaping hole in their lives" (p. 60). Fairholm believes individuals are integrating spirituality within their everyday work lives to fill the void. For the MERIT masters, this is vital. They have daily chores that include tending to, nurturing, and cultivating a garden in the compound. Routinely, they visit this garden and take pride in seeing it grow.

### Context of the Learning

While teaching my MERIT masters, it is critical to identify the context in which their learning occurs. The following is one example of the context in which my students learn. Immediately inside the entrance of their dormitory is their classroom space, where they learn about value systems, spirituality, and leadership development. The larger space of the dorm facility serves as their living quarters, where all 30 men routinely live, sleep, read, tend to personal hygiene, and engage in learning. Bunk beds line the walls and are surrounded by reading material, including books about spirituality, moral development, and philosophy. Hanging from the ceiling beams are painted banners of clichés, proverbs, and adages that were created by them and reflect how they want to live their lives while incarcerated and once they reenter their communities (see Appendix A). Included are:

> Integrity needs no rules
> There is life in doing what is right
> To know the road ahead ask those coming back
> Well done is better than well said
> Man enters each stage of life as a novice
> Human improvement is from within outward
> Nothing is difficult to those who have the will
> Pride ends in a fall while humility brings honor
> Poor eyes limit your sight; poor vision limits your deeds
> We cannot reach the top unless we start climbing
> Better to be late than never
> Crises refine life; in them you discover who you are

In efforts to document personal testimonies about the impact of the MERIT program, the following testimonies denote voices from MERIT masters who recently graduated from the MERIT program. These graduates share the successes of the program and how their thinking processes and behaviors have transformed as a result of it (Choate et al., 2012).

### Inmates' Perspectives

"Now I think before I act, and act on what I think about. By being mindful of my thoughts, I can control my actions. Now I can evaluate a problem by looking at all aspects."

"I spent two years in a state program and only stayed out 49 days. I hit rock bottom and wanted to get help. This program has transformed me and helped me grow spiritually."

"A mix of drinking and unemployment led to a brush with the law that sent me to jail. The MERIT program may be the thing that keeps me from coming back. The teachers are the role models that I didn't have as a kid. This is my first trip to jail and because of them, it's my last."

"In the seven months of MERIT I've learned more about myself and about life than in the past seven years upstate (in prison). You see, in prison, all I got was a drug habit. But through the MERIT program, I've gotten hope that I'll never have to come back to jail again, that I'll see my family again, and the hope that comes from knowing that I have a future and I have a choice. I heard something I haven't heard in a long time—my father told me how proud he is of me, and the man I've become. I finally see the true essence of who I am, and what I value."

"I no longer doubt or contradict myself. I'm still proceeding in my broken development. MERIT taught me to see who I really am. It allowed me to see what integrity means and does—such as doing the right thing when no one is looking."

### Reflections

EBI is a component of the criminal justice system that "is focused on deterring and mitigating crime by investing in its offenders through education and rehabilitation. By providing substantive and intellectual education in jails, and being supportive rather than punitive in efforts to reduce crime related behavior, the likelihood to recidivate will be lowered while success and stability in the community occurs" (Baca, 2010, p. 54). My colleagues at the LASD and I (see Choate et al., 2012), believe that there is a better option than incarceration. The MERIT program creates a safe and empowering environment conducive to learning and self-retrospection while allowing the offenders to reprioritize their lives and opt for success. Without our community partners, however, it would be a much greater struggle. Our teamwork is a tribute to the thousands of people who have helped build and maintain those partnerships, such as those who help with short- and long-term drug and alcohol rehabilitation; restoring personal dignity and hope to families of arrested gang members, domestic violence victims, and others; finding employment for released offenders; providing shelter for homeless offenders; gateways to a complete spectrum of social services for inmates with issues of homelessness, mental health, and substance use disorders; and veteran services, including housing placement, job training, parenting, managing money, legal and financial assistance, counseling, remedial learning, and life skills training (for more about these services, see Baca, 2010).

Clearly, EBI is not for everyone. Certain inmates will undoubtedly refuse to participate, while others will be precluded from contributing because of their preference for violence or their history of jail discipline. Yet for those who choose to partake, EBI can be a life-altering experience in support of social and restorative justice where education enables people to become productive members of society, both as citizens sharing in democratic processes and as workers in the economy. Hopefully, as more agencies adopt the EBI model, we can finally begin to reduce the devastating effects of recidivism nationwide.

## CROSS-NARRATIVE THEMES

Although the preceding three narratives reflect programmatically and contextually different avenues for addressing holistic development of leaders, several consistencies emerged across them.

### Developing Self-Awareness/Reflection

In each of the narratives, self-awareness and reflection were critical for opening doors for leadership development. Pauline discussed the importance of Branson's (2007) structured reflective process for preservice and inservice teachers as well as faculty. Debriefing following the team-building challenges in Tammy's LA GEAR UP camps enhanced self-awareness and reflective skills of youth leaders. The inmates with whom Tony works were consistently involved in retrospection, gaining insights on whom and where they are, how they arrived there, and where their journey will lead them next. Self-awareness and reflection are also critical for those leading the initiatives. Through critical reflection of our needs, experiences, and behaviors, we grow as people and professionals, develop consistency between what we say and do, and refine strategies for enhancing holistic development.

### Fostering a Safe and Empowering Environment

According to Maslow (cited in van Linden & Fertman, 1998), individuals have *deficiency* needs including survival, safety, self-esteem and belonging, and love. Once these needs are met, individuals can fulfill *being* needs, such as knowing, understanding, and self-actualization. The environment is critical in meeting all needs and also influences behavior, as noted in Bandura's (1986) social cognitive theory. Whether working with inmates, underserved youth, or teacher education students and faculty, a safe, supportive, and empowering environment that values all participants' voices is warranted for leadership development. Participants are only able to let go and experience their full leadership potential if they can fully trust the people and situation. This was particularly evident for marginalized populations, with whom Tony and Tammy work, that reside on the fringe of mainstream society and have limited opportunities for stability, growth, and leadership.

### Providing External Support

As van Linden and Fertman (1998, pp. 47–48) note, "Being a leader involves inter-acting with people; it cannot be done in isolation. Other people are always an essen-tial source of guidance." This was true for the adult and youth participants in all three narratives in terms of the importance of a support system to foster resilience and motivation beyond the actual leadership initiatives. For inmates in the MERIT pro-gram, family support and the MERIT Continuum are essential for transitioning back into their home and work lives. Similarly, the LA GEAR UP program is structured to provide support when students return to their schools through a guidance coun-selor or teacher who serves as a sponsor for the Explorers Club. Finally, in Pauline's situation, faculty members are instrumental in supporting each other, and her, in day-to-day activities that facilitate holistic development. Additionally, support from immediate supervisors allows each of the authors to devote the time and energy required for sustaining the leadership process in their own contexts.

### Subverting the Dominant Paradigm

Each of our stories reflects the need to question the status quo and advocate for change in traditional yet flawed systems. Pauline and Tammy are immersed directly or indirectly in an educational system that is in need of an overhaul. As standard-ized assessment and accountability dominate, teachers and students are devalued and their voices are ignored. Putting forth new ideas that run against the grain in educational policy is necessary for holistic development and requires commitment, persistence, and courage.

In Tony's case, the current structure of our jails and prison systems come into question. They often serve only as "holding places" for those individuals deemed unworthy to remain in society. Consequently, practices do not generally deter inmates from becoming repeat offenders and may even contribute to the current recidivism rates. Purposeful, creative, and perhaps even controversial educational strategies are needed to promote skills to help inmates lead productive lives after their release. The MERIT program is a positive response, which focuses on providing inmates the skills necessary to live productive, crime-free lives outside of custody.

### Reuniting the Mind, Body, and Spirit

Due to the increased emphasis on efficiency, technology, and commercial entertain-ment, development in the physical domain has suffered greatly in our society. Due to her background in physical education and kinesiology, Tammy's utilization of the physical domain in leadership development is a natural undertaking. Her expe-riences have reinforced strong beliefs in the power of physical activity in holistic development. For youth participants, the activities compel them to understand and utilize their bodies strategically and cooperatively with other participants to achieve the team-building challenges. For many participants, it is an introduction to mind, body, and soul in symphony and for others a reunion. It is evident in Pauline's professional life, and in her work with faculty, that she also seeks this reunion.

Also embedded in each narrative, and worthy of note, are references to the spiritual dimension—the soul—of leadership development. For example, Pauline explicitly indicates that she has transitioned to a realization that leadership and leadership development should be a holistic process, which would include a focus on integrating the spiritual dimension. She fully acknowledges that her recent attempts to incorporate holism and spirituality in her approach to leadership fall short of having any real impact. Nevertheless, she believes that the concept warrants attention and study. Tammy's references to spirituality are more implicitly stated. In sharing her beliefs about the importance of reflection and empowerment in cultivating student leadership, she describes the relationships that develop between and among the students and the adults in the LA GEAR UP camps. There is an undercurrent of spirituality that resonates in her storytelling, which is clearly evident when she relates the event of Ja'Marcus reading his poem "Understanding" to the group. The images and concepts he captured in his poem suggest that he was able "to establish a connection with a transcendent source of meaning" (Riaz & Normore, 2008, p. 1), an important feature of spirituality.

Although the concept of transcendence is underplayed within the literature, it represents an integral aspect used to define spiritual leadership, as evidenced by the ceiling banners in the classroom setting for the MERIT masters learning. The ability to establish a connection with something beyond mere physical experiences provides leaders (e.g., MERIT masters) with the inner strength to deal with difficult situations. Tony's narrative addresses the fact that the MERIT program is one where incarcerated men participate in a series of activities that require them to revisit their value systems and explore their spirituality.

## CONCLUSIONS

We contend that the holistic and spiritual component of leadership enables leaders to find deeper meaning in their work by heightening self-awareness and the desire to establish a connection with a transcendent source of meaning. In a narrow sense, "spirituality concerns itself with matters of the spirit that help form an essential part of a leader's holistic health and well-being. . . . By attending to other's needs, these leaders may define the shared values and purposes necessary for revitalizing their community" (Riaz & Normore, 2008, p. 8). As supported in the literature, leadership involves the complex cohesion of inspiration, encouragement, multiple paradigms of ethics, authenticity, morality, relationship building, reflective self-honesty, and the renewal of spirituality (Starratt, 2007). It is within these dimensions that leadership provides integrity and authentic leadership practices that can influence thinking and understanding of individual and collective values, not only in educational settings but also in the greater society. We concur with Riaz and Normore that by incorporating the spiritual dimension into leadership practices, leaders in any discipline and at any level are able "to think more holistically, to act responsibly in judgments, to challenge others, to learn more clearly their own worldview and points of view, and to regard their own professional work as one that builds and enhances not only their own character and identity but those with whom they interact" (p. 7) while simultaneously empowering themselves as agents of transformative change who align everyday practice with core values in ways that will make a significant difference in their professional and personal lives.

The literature supports the notion that spirituality is a "meaning system" (Solomon & Hunter, 2002, p. 38) that has a broad-ranging impact on how leaders think and act in daily life routines. It is a sense of profound internal connection to things beyond and/or within one's self. When leaders have made this connection, in all likelihood they will be able to motivate others. Solomon and Hunter further claim that "approaching work tasks and colleagues with humility and respect not only provides important models for how others should conduct themselves but also establishes a tone, or ethos" (p. 41) that tends to the moral imperative of communities. We shared poignant and relevant experiences that were through the lens of growth and self-reflection about three leadership development projects in the United States (teacher leadership, youth leadership, and inmate leadership within a corrections facility). Engaging learners and leaders in authentic learning experiences (self-reflection, ethics of responsibility, moral literacy, spiritual development and connectedness) signifies critical steps toward a holistic educational approach to moral and leadership development. As initially highlighted by the authors, these projects were intended to engage in critical reflection and to cultivate development of morally literate and responsive leaders in education. Participants ranged from PK–12 teachers, administrators, higher education faculty, and community and youth leaders to inmate master teachers in education-based incarceration programs for an improved society. The process of reflecting critically on shared experiences, as both inquirers and respondents (Lincoln et al., 2011), presents implications for holistic leadership development.

## IMPLICATIONS

Current educational leadership discourse is typically characterized by discussions that serve to broaden our conceptualization of what constitutes effective leadership. One important outcome in relation to what Normore (2010) refers to as "cross-fertilization" is the increasing interest in exploring the multidimensionality of leadership and leadership development. While there may be increasing emphasis on the moral dimension of leadership in education, less attention has been given to other, nontraditional dimensions that characterize holistic leadership, such as the leadership model presented by Quatro and colleagues (2007). Their model focused on analytical, conceptual, spiritual, and emotional components of leadership where significant skills, practices, and behaviors not only embrace moral and ethical values but also serve as catalysts of trust, self-reflection, and meditative thinking. Consequently, organizational and program leaders will need to deliberately and intentionally create an organizational social covenant whereby integrity and trust are built, nurtured, sustained, and honored while simultaneously supporting and fostering a safe and psychologically secure environment for holistic development.

As indicated throughout the literature, there are various definitions and terms embedded in discussions of holistic leadership. However, a growing consensus exists that leadership is more than an activity of the mind. Leadership is a multidimensional activity, which invokes action of the mind, body, and spirit. For example, caring for others proves to be an essential component within an effective ethical framework and within spiritual-based leadership. Holistic leaders focus on the human element—relationships, values, and actions of individuals within the community. When this happens, opportunities to learn about ways in which leaders and learners are developed and prepared to take leadership roles in communities are enormous in scope. Individually and collectively, these same leaders and learners bring knowledge, strategies, skill sets, research understanding, and practical experiences in dimensions that promote and foster moral literacy, social responsibility, self-awareness, and spirituality, thereby embracing holistic educational leadership. Moreover, when education programs encourage learners to explore the spiritual dimension of "who" they are, then in all likelihood they will be better grounded within their inner beings and more likely to flourish. In the words of Fairholm (1997), "Our spirit is what makes us human and individual. It determines who we are at work. It is inseparable from self. We draw on our central values in how we deal with people every day. Our values dictate whether we set a good example, take care of people, or try to live the Golden Rule. Our spirituality helps us think and act according to our values" (p. 77). It is our contention that those who are responsible for creating and delivering leadership development programs need to incorporate the multidimensionality of humanity so that mind, body, and spirit are critical components.

## REFERENCES

Baca, L. (2010, March-April). Education-based incarceration: A reentry plan—changing the way we incarcerate. *Sheriff Magazine*, 54–58. Retrieved from www.lasdhq.org/divisions/correctional/ebi/assets/ebi-6principles-sheriffmag-mar-apr2010.pdf

Bandura, A. (1986). *Social foundations of thought and action: A social cognitive theory.* Englewood Cliffs, NJ: Prentice-Hall.

Begley, P. T. (2003). In pursuit of authentic school leadership practices. In P. T. Begley & O. Johansson (Eds.), *The ethical dimensions of school leadership* (pp. 1–12). Boston: Kluwer Academic Publishers.

Branson, C. (2007). Improving leadership by nurturing moral consciousness through structured self-reflection. *Journal of Educational Leadership, 45*(4), 471–495.

Chase, S. E. (2011). Narrative inquiry. In N. K. Denzin & Y. S. Lincoln (Eds.), *The Sage handbook of qualitative research* (pp. 421–434). Los Angeles: Sage.

Choate, B., Normore, A. H., & Bates, D. (2012, Fall). Maximizing Education Reaching Individual Transformation (MERIT): A groundbreaking leadership development program for inmates in Los Angeles County Sheriff's Department. *Law Enforcement Today.* Retrieved from http://lawenforcementtoday.com

Clandinin, D. J., & Connelly, F. M. (2000). *Narrative inquiry: Experience and story in qualitative research.* San Francisco: Jossey-Bass.

Dyer, W. W. (1996). *Your sacred self: Making the decision to be free.* New York: HarperCollins Publishers.

Fairholm, G. (1997). *Capturing the heart of leadership: Spirituality and community in the new American workplace.* Westport, CT: Praeger.

Frankl, V. E. (2006). *Man's search for meaning.* Boston: Beacon Press.

Hellison, D. (2011). *Teaching personal and social responsibility through physical activity* (3rd ed.). Champaign, IL: Human Kinetics.

Hendricks, C., Hendricks, J. E., & Kauffman, S. (2001). *Literacy, criminal activity, and recidivism*. Retrieved from www.americanreadingforum.org/01_yearbook/html/12_Hendricks.htm

Leonard, P. (2005). The ethics of practice: Navigating the road of authenticity: Journey interrupted. *Values and Ethics in Educational Administration, 3*(4), 1–8.

Leonard, P. (2007). Moral literacy for teacher and school leadership education: A matter of attitude. *Journal of Educational Leadership, 45*(4), 413–426.

Leonard, P., & Basinger, D. (2008). Educating the whole teacher. *The Beacon, 4*(2), 1–8.

Lincoln, Y. S., Lynham, S. A., & Guba, E. G. (2011). Paradigmatic controversies, contradictions, and emerging confluences, revisited. In N. K. Denzin & Y. S. Lincoln (Eds.), *The Sage handbook of qualitative research* (pp. 97–128). Los Angeles: Sage.

Louisiana Board of Regents. (2005). *Request for proposals for Louisiana GEAR UP summer/academic year learning projects*. Baton Rouge: Author.

Mentor, K., & Wilkinson, M. (2006). *Literacy in corrections*. Retrieved from http://kenmentor.com/papers/literacy.htm

Normore, A. H. (2010). Introduction: Global perspectives on educational leadership: The development and preparation of leaders and learners of leadership. In A. H. Normore (Ed.), *Advances in educational administration: The development, preparation, and socialization of leaders of learning and learners of leadership: A global perspective* (pp. xiii–xiv). Bingley, UK: Emerald Group Publishing.

Normore, A. H., & Fitch, B. D. (2011). *Leadership in education, corrections, and law enforcement: A commitment to ethics, equity, and excellence*. Bingley, UK: Emerald Group Publishing.

Orlov, J. (2003). The holistic leader: A developmental systemic approach to leadership. In *The Wisdom of ASTD-LA 2003*. Los Angeles: American Society for Training and Development.

Project Adventure. (1995). *Youth leadership in action*. Dubuque, IA: Kendall/Hunt Publishing.

Quatro, S. A., Waldman, D. A., & Galvin, B. M. (2007). Developing holistic leaders: Four domains for leadership development and practice. *Human Resource Management Review, 17*(4), 427–441.

Riaz, O., & Normore, A. H. (2008). Examining the spiritual dimension of educational leadership. *Values and Ethics in Educational Administration, 6*(4), 1–8.

Schilling, T., Martinek, T., & Tan, C. (2002). Fostering youth development through empowerment. In B. Lombardo, K. Castagno, T. Caravella-Nadeau, & V. Mancini (Eds.), *Sport in the 21st century: Alternatives for the new millennium* (pp. 169–179). Boston: Pearson Custom Publishing.

Shinn, S. (2010, May/June). The holistic leader. *BizEd*, 58–63.

Sinclair, A. (2007). *Leadership for the disillusioned: Moving beyond myths and heroes to leading that liberates* [DX version]. Retrieved from www.amazon.com

Solomon, J., & Hunter, J. (2002). A psychological view of spirituality and leadership: Finding meaning through Howard Gardner's notion of existential intelligence. *School Administrator 59*(8), 38–41.

Starratt, R. J. (2004). *Ethical leadership*. San Francisco: Jossey-Bass.

Starratt, R. (2007). Leading a community of learners: Learning to be moral by engaging the morality of learning. *Educational Management Administration & Leadership 35*(2), 165–183.

Taggart, J. L. C. (2010). *Becoming a holistic leader: Strategies for successful leadership using a principle-based approach* (2nd ed). Retrieved from http://changingwinds.files.wordpress.com/2010/10/becoming-a-holistic-leader-2nd-edition.pdf

Tedlock, B. (2011). Braiding narrative ethnography with memoir and creative nonfiction. In N. K. Denzin & Y. S. Lincoln (Eds.), *The Sage handbook of qualitative research* (pp. 331–339). Los Angeles: Sage.

Tuana, N. (2007). Conceptualizing moral literacy. *Journal of Educational Administration, 45*(4), 364–378.

van Linden, J. A., & Fertman, C. I. (1998). *Youth leadership: A guide to understanding leadership development in adolescents*. San Francisco: Jossey-Bass.

# APPENDIX A

**Table 20.1** Proverbs, clichés, and adages: MERIT Masters Holistic Development

| | |
|---|---|
| Make the most of yourself, for that is all there is to you. | If one can be certain that his principles are right, he need not worry about consequence. |
| The first rule of leadership is that a leader can always do better. | Integrity needs no rules. |
| No achievement is possible without persistent work. | No man becomes wise by chance. |
| When life isn't the way you like it, like it the way it is. | Brotherhood: helping yourself by helping others. |
| What is destructive is impatience, haste, expecting too much too fast. | The difficulty in life is the choice. |
| No man should part with his own individuality and become that of another. | No achievement is possible without persistent work. |
| I am part of all that I have met. | I do not pray for a lighter load, but a stronger back. |
| We reform others unconsciously when we walk uprightly. | The difficulties of life are intended to make us better, not bitter. |
| Rule your mind or it will rule you. | Only I can change my life, no one can do it for me. |
| Unity creates strength. | Attitudes determine our actions for good or bad. |
| Dependability: fulfilling what I agreed to do even though it requires unexpected sacrifices. | Life isn't about finding yourself, life is about creating yourself. |
| To teach is to learn twice. | We walk by faith, not by sight. |
| Practice is the best of all instructors. | Give others a piece of your heart, not a piece of your mind. |
| In the middle of difficulty lies opportunity. | Conduct is an unspoken sermon. |

# 21

## A MEASURE OF ETHICS

### LYSE LANGLOIS AND CLAIRE LAPOINTE

Change experienced by some democracies can be considered as the transformation of their models of governance. In Western societies, legislation serves as the basis for governing social cohabitation. However, financial scandals and corruption have highlighted the limitations of such an approach, raising complex, challenging issues. These situations have led to concern for integrity, ethics, and standards of transparency and leadership. As a result, there is renewed interest in applied ethics. Far from being abstract concepts, organizational context and work culture are integrated into practical ethics to permeate organizational structures. Consequently, ethical leadership has served as leverage to promote proper governance. Based on research projects conducted within a number of public organizations (schools, municipalities, police, hospitals, and community organizations), we have found that ethical leadership is a specific method of governance. It serves as a complementary means to compensate for legislative shortfalls and resolve current issues so as to ensure harmonious cohabitation in current individualistic and pluralistic societies. In this chapter, we discuss ethical leadership as a new method of governance and its relationship with organizational culture. We also present some of our most recent observations.

## TOWARD A NEW WAY OF GOVERNING: ETHICAL LEADERSHIP

Educational administration has not eluded the wave of ethical concern currently sweeping the business world and professional circles. Ethics is omnipresent and garnering increasingly stronger interest. This ethical trend has gained momentum in the wake of scandals of corruption and collusion occurring in the corporate world. Ethics is on the agenda of many organizations, whether public or private. However, in educational administration, interest in ethics did not stem from deviant conduct or corruption, but from reaction to greater state standardization and surveillance that emerged in the

1970s. These disruptions, due to economic conditions, have affected the quality of school administration, and people are speaking up on dehumanizing climates, lack of concern in training, and staff losing motivation. Researchers such as Halpin (1957), Willower (1961), Hodgkinson (1978), Griffiths (1979), Foster (1980, 1985, 1989), and Greenfield (1981, 1987) have alerted the scientific community regarding the shifting—in certain cases, the absence—of values in educational administration. These two movements will drive a new research current on applied ethics in educational leadership.

This chapter highlights factors that are linked to the emergence and development of ethics in educational organizations, particularly in Canada. To do so, we define the main concepts revolving around ethics and its institutionalization within public organizations. More particularly, we address ethical leadership, a concept that has been the greater focus of our research program for more than 15 years. We also look into the characteristics enabling the actualization of ethical leadership in the workplace and the conditions required to better support it. Through studies conducted in the field of educational administration, and our own work undertaken in the field of applied ethics, we have observed the emergence of a different mode of governance in education, a form of management more considerate of current issues and more authentic toward those who are committed to promoting a quality education.

## GOVERNING EDUCATIONAL ORGANIZATIONS IN TODAY'S WORLD

Current conditions in educational administration require capacities that are quite different from those required some 40 years ago. Decision makers work in an unruly world where the single stable element is *turbulence* (Shapiro & Gross, 2012). Reality becomes more complex and different logics create confusion. Pretty much everywhere in the world of education, reforms are conducted at breakneck speed. Those reforms have introduced various measures of decentralization and, in certain regards, a hierarchical deconcentration of power and responsibilities. It is all the more important to act using better judgment in a world in crisis where points of reference are hard to find. Professional associations have played a significant support role regarding these changes in education, but such support has often been more reactive than proactive.

For instance, during the 1990s, the Quebec provincial government introduced a major education reform. From an administrative viewpoint, this reform allowed a new distribution of powers among the minister, school boards, and elementary and secondary schools. From an administrative viewpoint, this reform provided greater autonomy to the schools, as under Quebec's Education Act each school is now required to establish a council that represents the political branch of the educational system. This council, made up mostly of parents, has many prerogatives and defines up to 25% of curricula. As a result of these prerogatives, the political sphere is increasingly present in school principals' work. Several issues and restraints are involved in making strategic decisions, which will affect, in the long term, choices that will be made by schools and school districts.

However, everyone is not always on the same wavelength in terms of ethical consciousness regarding the impact of decisions on students, teachers, and parents.

Everyone does not have the same modus operandi to address sensitive cases, such as school closure and student transfers. Relationships of power arise and deviant conduct and conflicts of interest occur, not always correctly detected by school administrators. Cohabitation of administration, pedagogy, and politics entails acquiring a new outlook on the world involving heightened awareness of ethics.

## THE RISE OF ETHICS

Interest in the ethical aspects of administration is partly justified by a wish to win back the public's trust in people in authority. Maintaining integrity in the workplace and improving conduct become vital objectives for organizations committed to institutionalizing ethics. In Canada, the institutionalization of ethics took place in public administration under the impetus of the OECD (Organisation for Economic Co-operation and Development, 1996). Implemented in federal and provincial public administration, this movement also reached municipalities and universities, as well as other educational organizations. According to Boisvert, "the institutionalization of ethics is a process through which a social setting seeks to standardize, through the implementation of mechanisms, the conduct of stakeholders involved in activities specific to their areas for action" (2011, p. 6; our translation). The purpose of such mechanisms is to counter deviant conduct and improve the public's trust.

### The Positioning and Occurrence of Ethics in Educational Structures

In Quebec, institutionalization primarily occurs through mechanisms such as value statements and codes of conduct intended for school personnel. Some organizations also implement an ethics committee with a role and functions to improve support provided to school staff in complex situations such as ethical dilemmas. Sometimes committees also have to evaluate requests submitted by university faculty in order to conduct research in schools. Within this strong movement involving the formalization and institutionalization of ethics, a major asymmetry can be observed between the implementation of ethics mechanisms and educational leaders' legal perception of ethics. Faced with complex situations and an increasingly restrictive normative framework, these administrators sometimes fail to understand what ethical logic implies. The means to remove such an asymmetry consists in a better understanding of one's ethical reasoning as well as appropriate training, resulting in renewed ways of governing. Before discussing these elements any further, we will clarify how the concepts of ethics, law, and deontology are understood and developed in Canada under the impetus of the OECD's work.

## ETHICS: A MODE OF SOCIAL REGULATION

Several concepts are related to ethics, such as deontology, morality, and mores. All share a common element, as they are all related to conduct, but they do not share the same end. For the purposes of this chapter, we will clarify some of them.

## Deontology

The origin of the term "deontology" is the Greek word *deon*, which means "duty," and *logos*, which means, "reason." Deontology is related to the concepts of duty and responsibility incumbent upon any professional. It stresses the aspects of duty and the obligation to act according to standards of practices, represented by a code of conduct. Respect for the code of conduct is considered in this logic as a command or order, as an imperative, and professional conduct is based on unconditional compliance with duty.

The concept of deontology is often considered as an integral part of ethics. Some people believe that their code of conduct is the same as a code of ethics. However, the comparison is to be nuanced. In a code of conduct, there are certain elements related to ethics, such as respect for professional secrecy. This value is defined in terms of a standard of conduct aimed at heightening professionals' awareness of the importance to preserve the confidentiality of specific information. Deontology is often integrated into the norms of a profession or trade aimed at guiding professionals' conduct. In Canada, for instance, several provincial teachers' associations now have a code identifying professional norms and standards. Social regulation imposed by deontology, through a code, is part of a concept referred to as *hetero-regulation*, where professionals are guided by a code of conduct that commands compliance to norms expected by their profession.

## Hetero-regulation

Hetero-regulation stems from a set of rules imposed by an outside authority. These rules are part of a vision of control and are restrictive in nature. Those who do not abide by these rules are imposed sanctions. The rules are also legal in nature and control the conduct of those who are subjected to them. Boisvert (2003) defines the concept of hetero-regulation in these terms:

> A movement of regulation established and imposed from the outside; in other words, external authority dictates individuals what to decide or how to act. From a heteronomous perspective, the regulation of conduct is defined as the observance of rules enacted by authority and the fear of sanction in cases of non-compliance.
>
> (p. 27, our translation)

For instance, if we fail to respect road signs or stop at a red traffic light, we are liable to a fine. Hence, the fine is the means allowing the outside authority to better regulate the conduct of individuals, with the purpose of ensuring public safety. However, individuals have relative autonomy; in this case, they can choose to respect or not respect road signs, while considering the potential consequences in case of noncompliance. Ward (2007) observed two orientations in the philosophy of codes of conduct: The first philosophy does not involve disciplinary procedures in case of misconduct, while the second philosophy comprises disciplinary measures. However, both philosophies are related to the hetero-regulatory mode.

## Morality or Ethics

The concepts of morality and ethics are sometimes used indistinctly. Etymologically speaking, the two terms mean morals, or mores. The Latin origin of the word "morality" is *mores,* while the word "ethics" comes from the Greek word *ethos.* Some authors consider them as opposed, others consider them as cognates and interdependent (Ricoeur, 1990). In our research work, we adopted the second position, where the concepts of morality and ethics are used without any major distinctions, both referring to individual conduct.

The concept proposed in this chapter defines ethics as a reflective process providing enhanced guidance on the conduct to adopt. This reflection is based on personal, professional, and organizational values as much as rules, norms, and procedures, with the purpose of finding a path to identifying morally acceptable behavior (Paquet, 2011). Hence, ethics will operate a thinking and discernment process based on these elements while raising the following questions: Does this norm or rule still fairly apply in the current context? What value should be promoted? How should I behave in a particular situation? Is it the best decision to make, given the context? What will be the consequences of my decision for me, and others? Through a meticulous examination of conscience, ethical reflection will attempt to identify particular values meaningful to an individual. As ethics is anchored in reality and adapts to given circumstances, it is characterized as flexible in comparison with rights and deontology, which are rather static. Hence, several authors identify ethics as a mode of interrogation and questioning aimed at finding moral certainties, which nonetheless remain uncertain (Bourgeault, 2004; Legault, 2004).

## Self-Regulation: Exercising Free Will

Rules, principles, and values that individuals decide to apply in an autonomous and free manner are part of a mode referred to as self-regulation. This perspective encourages individuals to exhibit responsible conduct without the pressure of sanctions. To do so, individuals use their will to regulate their own conduct in order to take on responsibility toward others. These were Foucault's (2008) words in 1982–83 as reported in his teaching notes *Le Gouvernement de soi et des autres.* For Boisvert, Campeau, and Jutras (2004), ethics has a double nature. "Although fundamentally self-regulatory, which means that ethics fosters self-control and autonomous behaviour, yet, ethics does not lead to radical individualism" (p. 29; our translation). Rather, this self-governance is attached to life in community. Ethics is not expressed in a disembodied world; it is deployed within an organization with all that it entails: ethics is challenged, dismantled, and rebuilt once more through contact with others. Hence, ethics should not be considered as a cutting knife, but rather as a needle that patiently weaves its work with others, like a community working on a collective patchwork (Langlois, 2011).

Fundamentally, ethics is considered from a perspective of autonomy because it requires a certain level of leeway for individuals to exercise their capacity of discernment and judgment. Leeway is one of the essential conditions to exercising ethical

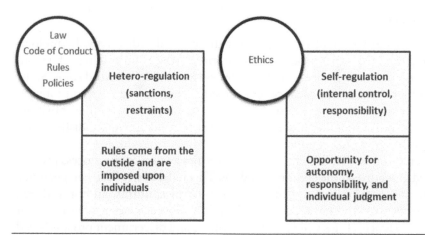

**Figure 21.1** Regulatory modes of conduct.

reflection in a mode of self-regulation. Figure 21.1 shows the two regulatory modes of conduct and serves to better clarify the elements underlying this movement of institutionalization currently being implemented, and the logic targeted.

### Ethical Leadership

In light of our literature review, we can assert that the concept of care, as developed by Gilligan (1982) and later by Noddings (1984), has influenced most scholars interested in the application of ethical leadership in the field of educational administration. The earliest researchers were Kimbrough (1985), Lakomski (1987), Strike, Haller, and Soltis (1988), Crowson (1992), Greenfield (1981), Starratt (1991), Kirby, Paradise, and Protti (1990), Sergiovanni (1992), Beck (1992, 1994), Marshall, Patterson, Rogers, and Steele (1993), Larocque and Coleman (1993), Crogan (1996), Langlois (1997), Bhindi and Duignan (1997), Brunner (1998), and Begley (1999). Moreover, Starratt (1991) and Sergiovanni (1992) initiated a major breakthrough by integrating moral dimensions into the concept of ethical leadership while proposing a new mode of governance. Another wave of researchers, all the more insightful, then contributed to this emerging field (e.g., Fullan, 2003; Maxcy, 2002; Murphy, 2002; Shapiro & Stefkovich, 2005). Their contribution has helped to gain a better understanding of the actualization of ethics in educational administration.

## APPLIED RESEARCH ON ETHICAL LEADERSHIP IN EDUCATION

Although the field of ethics in educational administration is under ongoing development, its understanding is mainly based on qualitative research. Most of the time, samples include fewer than 20 participants, and in certain cases, results are generalized in spite of those small samples. Empirical aspects are limited and remain relatively exploratory.

Furthermore, regarding their epistemological stand, most studies use a mixed perspective of ethics based on social regulation. Some authors identify their concepts more closely with a hetero-regulatory model of conformity, while others tend toward a notion of self-regulation in which ethics is considered as a process aiming at autonomy. Although we are still far from an operational definition of ethics likely to create a consensus among researchers in educational administration, Starratt's three-dimensional model of ethics remains a major reference.

## DEFINING ETHICAL LEADERSHIP

In his book *Leadership*, Burns (1978) states that ethics is a major component of leadership. He came to this conclusion by realizing that some people were considered leaders despite exhibiting questionable conduct. He proposed three types of ethical leadership: (a) ethical leadership anchored in traditional ethical values such temperance, chastity, kindness, and altruism (Judeo-Christian values); (b) ethical leadership based on personal rules of conduct and ethical values such as honesty, integrity, reciprocity, and responsibility; and (c) ethical leadership based on moral values such as freedom, equality, justice, and community solidarity. Adopting the third perspective, Starratt (1991) proposed a concept of ethical leadership deployed in three dimensions: justice, critique, and care. Subsequently, he completed his vision of ethical leadership with a concern for ethics based on presence and authenticity (Starratt, 2004).

Our initial interest in ethical leadership was reinforced after reading Starratt's 1991 paper not long after its publication, as it represented, at the time, the most consistent and innovative theoretical framework. Our intent in our own work and contribution to the field was to gain a better understanding of these dimensions in the study of real-life administrative practices. The first step consisted of defining moral actions associated with each dimension of ethical leadership. Research conducted by Gilligan (1982), Noddings (1984), and Brown, Tappan, Gilligan, and Miller (1988), as well as the work of critique theory philosophers, was very useful. Once the moral actions were identified, hundreds of interviews were conducted with educational leaders (Langlois, 2004, 2011; Langlois & Lapointe, 2007). Based on the qualitative results, a questionnaire was developed to measure Starratt's three dimensions in the exercise of ethical leadership, as well as ethical sensitivity (Langlois & Lapointe, 2010; Langlois, Lapointe, Valois, & de Leeuw, in press). Our current quantitative database for the sector of education contains more than 800 participants.

## THE PARAMETERS OF ETHICAL LEADERSHIP

In light of our empirical data, a definition of ethical leadership emerged:

> Ethical leadership is a social practice that integrates autonomous professional judgement. Ethical leadership is as much a resource based on three ethical dimensions (care, justice, and critique), as a capacity and power to act in a responsible and acceptable manner.
>
> (Langlois, 2013, our translation)

Three major aspects emerge from this definition. The first highlights the fact that the exercise of ethical leadership arises from applied ethics, which in turn facilitates the exercise of professional judgment. Such an affirmation implies that exercising ethical leadership requires autonomy and flexibility in decision making. The second aspect involves the word *resource*. This word is important, as it implies that ethical leadership becomes a resource for individuals who are aware of their own ethical leadership profile. In the absence of such knowledge, exercising ethical leadership becomes difficult. Once this knowledge is acquired, individuals are in a better position to analyze and discern the aspects related to one or all three ethical dimensions. Knowledge is acquired by heightening the awareness of one's ethical sensitivity, which is defined threefold: care, justice, and critique. These resources represent opportunities for ethical analysis. In turn, knowledge leads to the last important aspect: capacity, understood as the power to act (Le Boterf, 2006), which provides leeway and opportunities to choose and act in any political, social, or economic situation, as well as the power to make better decisions.

During one of our research projects conducted in Canada, we met educational leaders who appeared not to have the leeway required to actualize and exercise their ethical leadership. This led to the realization that a key factor in allowing the exercise of ethical leadership was the presence of an organizational culture supporting ethical self-regulation. Therefore, we investigated more in-depth the organizational conditions needed to facilitate the actualization of ethical leadership. The last section of this chapter sheds light on the following question: What kind of support is needed in order for leaders to deploy ethical leadership and what governing practices hinder enacting it?

## HOW DOES ORGANIZATIONAL CULTURE INFLUENCE THE EXERCISE OF ETHICAL LEADERSHIP?

As mentioned earlier, over the last 10 years, we have had the opportunity to engage hundreds of educational leaders throughout Canada in meaningful conversations about ethics at work. Based on these conversations, we realized that the kind of culture permeating organizations in which leaders work has a strong influence on the emergence and actualization of their ethical sensitivity and ethical competency. In fact, we observed that certain organizational cultures nurture leaders' awareness of ethically challenging situations and promote their empowerment as ethical leaders, whereas other cultures hinder educational leaders' capacity to recognize those situations or prevent them from developing their capacity to act ethically. Our most recent exploratory work using the Ethical Leadership Questionnaire confirmed these initial observations and provided insightful preliminary results on the relationship between organizational culture and the enactment of ethical leadership.

In this section of the chapter, we will briefly review the concept of organizational culture and its applications in educational administration and discuss some of the most recent literature on the subject. Afterward, we will reflect on the relationship observed between different kinds of organizational cultures and the exercise of ethical leadership.

*The Concept of Organizational Culture*

The earliest literature defining organizational culture as an area of study was developed in the early 1970s. This literature was primarily based on analyses that compared management models applied in Japanese and American businesses (Martin, Frost, & O'Neil, 2004; Morgan, 1986). These analyses highlighted the fact that human-related characteristics found in Japanese industries best explain Japan's outstanding commercial success, as opposed to structural aspects (Martin et al., 2004; Ouchi, 1981).

Interest in the cultural component of organizations soon emerged among educational administration researchers and practitioners (e.g., Deblois & Corriveau, 1994; Erikson, 1987; Pettigrew, 1979; Sarason, 1971; Steinhoff & Owens, 1989). In fact, Pettigrew was the one to make the first applications in this field. In his article published in 1979, he defined key concepts and methodological processes associated with an organizational culture theory. He reported the results of a study into the impact on their culture and climate of amalgamating a public school with a private school. Interest in studying organizational culture in educational contexts continues to grow today, as shown by an overview of recent publications (Balcı, Özdemir, Apaydın, & Özen, 2012; Fabricio, Labrie, & Lapointe, 2008; Frick, 2009; Höög & Johansson, 2005; Kythreotis, Pashiardis, & Kyriakides, 2010; Somech & Ron, 2007; Sun-Keung Pang, 2006; van der Westhuizen, Mosoge, & Coetsee, 2005).

When defining organizational culture, it is interesting to note that today's key scholars (e.g., Alvesson, 2002; Martin, 2002; Schein, 2004) still refer to definitions provided by founding researchers such as Clegg (1981), Smircich (1983), Schein (1985), and Mills (1988). According to Martin and colleagues (2004), the culture of an organization represents a unique configuration of rule-bound activities, such as procedures and human resource management policies. This way of organizational life is characterized by specific rules of conduct and values, ranging from formal codes of ethics to informal value statements. Martin in 1992 (Martin et al., 2004) also stated that rules are not only applied and followed, they may also be resisted or questioned by individuals or groups. Hence, there are some dimensions of reality that must be taken into account when studying the influence of organizational culture on the school leader's ethical sensitivity and conduct, including: (1) Members of an organization neither follow organizational rules in the same way nor do so to the same extent; and (2) higher authority within an organization may impose a given definition of a situation on its leaders, limiting their capacity to exercise their own professional judgment and impacting on the development of their ethical leadership.

## AN EXPLORATORY TYPOLOGY OF ETHICAL CULTURE

In previous publications, we described how the exercise of ethical leadership is anchored in leaders' decision-making processes when faced with ethical dilemmas (e.g., Langlois, 2004, 2013; Langlois & Lapointe, 2007). During challenging—and often heart-wrenching—situations, the presence of ethical sensitivity is tested. When this sensitivity is awakened and developed, leaders demonstrate a stronger capacity to properly discern issues and values at stake. By using this capacity in an optimal way, they can make ethically fair and responsible decisions. However, in order for this ethical reflection to translate into action, authenticity toward one's declared values as well as moral courage are required (Cooper, 1990).

Over the last 20 years, data collected through our mixed-method research program has shown that most organizations adhere either to a hetero-regulated vision of ethics, where an external form of control is imposed upon leaders, or to a self-regulated vision of ethics, where leaders use their own regulations in their decisions and actions. This characteristic of organizations appears to impact the emergence and actualization of ethical sensitivity and conduct among leaders, whose capacity to exercise ethical judgment depends heavily on the leeway allowed by their superiors (Langlois & Lapointe, 2007).

Our first insight on the significant influence of organizational culture on the emergence and actualization of ethical leadership came about in 2002–2005 during a study for the Social Sciences and Humanities Research Council of the distinctive experience of school leaders in official-language minority settings in Canada. Using an open-ended interview guide on ethical dilemma, 47 school principals from seven different provinces were asked to describe the tensions and possibilities related to ethical leadership in their specific contexts. We were surprised when, in a particular region, participants told us they had never encountered any ethical dilemmas, explaining that rules and policies were clearly defined by the higher authority and that all they had to do was to implement these directives. Examining more closely how superintendents and educational department officials governed in that province, we noticed the presence of a particularly high degree of control over school principals, which left almost no leeway for individual reflection and action.

A few years later, as we were conducting an action-research project with educational administrators and teacher leaders working within the same organization, we gained a deeper understanding of the interactions among ethics, individual transformation, and organizational culture. We noticed that as a result of regular group reflection on action, subcultures present within the organization appeared to shift from an oppositional to an interrelational stand due to participants seeking a common meaning with regard to ethical leadership. Practices were realigned so that managerial modes became less hierarchical and more dialogical, hence initiating a process toward the institutionalization of ethics.

Acknowledging the existence of different kinds of organizational culture with regard to ethics, we created a three-dimensional typology of school culture based on the presence of a hetero-regulatory or an auto-regulatory vision of ethics. The typology comprises three archetypes of conduct that superiors might show when leaders under their responsibility are faced with ethical dilemmas.

- The Supporting Culture, where leaders are encouraged to consult with their superiors, all the while having leeway to exercise their professional judgment and being expected to make their own decisions
- The Controlling Culture, where leaders must defer to their superiors, who will make the decision
- The Indifferent Culture, where leaders are left to fend for themselves

Items predicting the occurrence of each of the three cultures were added to the Ethical Leadership Questionnaire[1] (Lapointe, Langlois, Centeno, & Giasson, 2012). Although still at an exploratory stage, results reveal intriguing links between organizational culture and ethical leadership. First, we observed a statistically significant relationship between a controlling type of organizational culture, where leaders must comply with their superiors' decisions, and the presence of all three ethics (justice, care, and critique), with higher scores for the presence of a controlling culture linked to higher scores for each of the three ethics. These results are in line with our previous observations derived from more than 200 open-ended interviews and an action-research project showing that individual ethical sensitivity can trigger the decision to question normative and controlling rules and standards. This might be more the case when individual conduct is rooted in the ethics of critique. In fact, we believe that individuals whose ethical leadership is more developed also possess a more acute awareness of abuse of power and can experience feelings of disempowerment when pressured to comply with their superiors' norms.

Second, results also indicated a significant relationship between a supporting culture and the ethic of justice, with higher scores for a supporting culture being linked to higher scores for the ethic of justice. These results might be linked to the present trend toward the institutionalization of ethics within organizations, which promotes respect for authority and social order. Organizations sharing this vision often adopt ethics programs, codes of ethics, and other deontological tools, which help frame leaders' ethical reflection. Such a trend might reinforce leaders' propensity and capacity to apply the ethic of justice in their decision-making processes. However, it might also weaken their ability to call upon the ethics of critique and care. Further research is needed in order to shed more light on these results.

## CONCLUSION

Scholars and practitioners from different fields, including education, have stressed the pressing need for a better understanding of ethical leadership and the means to learn and enact this concept (Langlois & Lapointe, 2011). Some have also insisted on the urgency to encourage organizations to become more ethical. The proposed concept of ethical leadership that we defined, and validated through several research projects, possesses a significant ability to rise to current complex challenges. Deviant behavior at work can be enacted through organizational mimesis and permissiveness, as much as ethical conduct can build on an ethical leadership model through mimesis. Research has unquestionably proven that leaders remain models of ethical conduct for employees. Leaders send a message about what is tolerated or unacceptable conduct. Encouraging people to emulate ethical leaders is vital in empowering them to "rise above" and develop responsible conduct and abilities.

Organizational culture is, we believe, a promising pathway toward ethical transformation. Our research shows that ethical cultures will emerge through individuals' commitment to building collective ethical capacity. At the same time, we noticed that different organizational cultures seem to impact on individuals differently, triggering reactions rooted in their personal ethical stands. This seems to be particularly true with the ethics of justice and of critique.

Based on observations from our applied and action research, we strongly believe that individuals and groups of people who engage earnestly and actively in learning about ethics can become strong agents of change in their organizations. In doing so, they help transform organizational culture and modify the ethical principles at the basis of governance models and decision-making mechanisms.

In conclusion, we hope that the development of ethical environments through ethical leadership and culture will influence good practices as much as conduct. For once, we will be in a position to take positive advantage of mimesis, a mechanism so highly valued by society and organizations.

## NOTE

1. The Ethical Leadership Questionnaire is an instrument that predicts the dimensions of ethical leadership proposed by Starratt (1991) and validated by Langlois (1997), as well as ethical sensitivity.

## REFERENCES

Alvesson, M. (2002). *Understanding organizational culture.* London: Sage Publications.

Balcı, A., Özdemir, M., Apaydın, C., & Özen, F. (2012). The relationship of organizational corruption with organizational culture, attitude towards work and work ethics: A search on Turkish high school teachers. *Asia Pacific Education Review, 13*(1), 137–146.

Beck, L. G. (1992). Meeting the challenge of the future: The place of caring ethic in educational administration. *American Journal of Education, 100*(4), 454–496.

Beck, L. G. (1994). *Reclaiming educational administration as a caring profession.* New York: Teacher College Press.

Begley, P. T. (1999). Practitioner and organizational perspectives on values in administration. In P. T. Begley (Ed.), *Values and educational leadership* (pp. 3–8). Albany: State University of New York Press.

Bhindi, N., & Duignan, P. A. (1997). Leadership for a new century: Authenticity, intentionality, spirituality and sensibility. *Educational Management and Administration, 25*(2), 117–132.

Boisvert, Y. (2003). *Petit manuel d'éthique appliquée à la gestion publique.* [Little manual of applied ethics in public management.] Montréal: Liber.

Boisvert, Y. (2011). *Éthique et gouvernance publique: principes, enjeux et défis.* [Ethics and public governance: Principles, issues and challenges.] Montréal: Liber.

Boisvert Y., Campeau, L., & Jutras, M. (2004). *Deux perspectives régulatoires de l'éthique.* [Two ethics regulatory perspectives.] Unpublished working paper. Montréal: ENAP, Laboratoire d'éthique publique.

Bourgeault, G. (2004). *Éthiques, dit et non-dit, contredit, interdit.* Québec: Presses Université du Québec.

Brown, L. M., Tappan, M., Gilligan, C., & Miller, B. (1988). *A guide to narratives of conflict and choice for self and moral voice.* (Unpublished document). Harvard University, Cambridge, MA.

Brunner, C. (1998). Can power support an ethic of care? An examination of professional practices of women superintendents. *Journal for a Just and Caring Education, 4*(2), 160–182.

Burns, J. M. (1978). *Leadership.* New York: HarperCollins.

Clegg, S. R. (1981). Organization and control. *Administration Science Quarterly, 26*(4), 545–562.

Cooper, T. (1990). *The responsible administrator: An approach to ethics for the administrative role* (4th ed.). San Francisco: Jossey-Bass.

Crogan, M. (1996). *Voices of women aspiring to the superintendency.* Albany: State University of New York Press.

Crowson, R. (1992). *School-community relations under reform.* Berkeley, CA: McCutchan.

Deblois, C., & Corriveau, L. (1994). *La culture de l'école secondaire et le cheminement scolaire des élèves.* [High school culture and student progress.] Québec: CRIRES, Université Laval.

Erikson, F. (1987). Conception of school culture: An overview. *Educational Administration Quarterly, 23*(4), 11–24.

Fabricio, C., Labrie, D., & Lapointe, C. (2008). Le Projet Axé, une pratique d'éducation à la citoyenneté qui transforme la communauté. [The Axé Project, an approach to citizenship education which transforms communities.] In R. Deslandes (Ed.), *La collaboration de l'école, de la famille et de la communauté à l'apprentissage.* [School, family and community collaboration in learning.] (pp. 151–168). *Cahiers scientifiques de l'ACFAS, 109.*

Foster, W. (1980). The changing administrator: Developing managerial praxis. *Educational Theory, 30*(1), 11–23.

Foster, W. (1985, April 1–5). *Critical theory and critical practice: A perspective on educational administration.* Paper presented at the annual meeting of the American Educational Research Association, Chicago.

Foster, W. (1989). Toward a critical practice in leadership. In J. Smith (Ed.), *Critical perspectives on educational leadership* (pp. 27–42). New York: Routledge.

Foucault, M. (2008). *Le Gouvernement de soi et des autres. Cours au Collège de France 1982–1983.* [Governing oneself and others: Courses given at the Collège de France 1982–1983.] Paris: Gallimard/Seuil.

Frick, W. C. (2009). Principals' value-informed decision making, intrapersonal moral discord, and pathways to resolution. The complexities of moral leadership praxis. *Journal of Educational Administration, 47*(1), 50–74.

Fullan, M. (2003). *The moral imperative of school leadership.* Thousand Oaks, CA: Corwin Press.

Gilligan, C. (1982). *In a different voice: Psychological theory and women's development.* Cambridge, MA: Harvard University Press.

Greenfield, T. B. (1981). Can science guide the administrator's hand? A critique of the 'new movement' ideology in educational administration. In T. T. Aoki (Ed.), *Re-thinking education modes of inquiry in the human sciences* (pp. 5–15). Edmonton: University of Alberta.

Greenfield, W. (1987, April 20–24). *Moral imagination and value leadership in school.* Paper presented at the annual meeting of the American Educational Research Association, Washington DC.

Griffiths, D. (1979). Intellectual turmoil. *Educational Administration Quarterly, 15*(3), 43–45.

Halpin, A. (1957). A paradigm for research on administrative behaviour. In R. F. Campbell & R. T. Gregg (Eds.), *Administrative behaviour in education* (pp. 55–199). New York: Harper & Brothers.

Hodgkinson, C. (1978). *The philosophy of leadership.* Oxford: Blackwell.

Höög, J., & Johansson, O. (2005). Successful principalship: The Swedish case. *Journal of Educational Administration, 43*(6), 595–606.

Kimbrough, R. B. (1985). *Ethics: A current study for educational leaders.* Arlington, VA: American Association of School Administrators.

Kirby, P. C., Pardise, L. V., & Protti, R. (1990, April 16–20). *The ethical reasoning of school administrators: The principled principal.* Paper presented at the annual meeting of the American Educational Research Association, Boston.

Kythreotis, A., Pashiardis, P., & Kyriakides, L. (2010). The influence of school leadership styles and culture on students' achievement in Cyprus primary schools. *Journal of Educational Administration, 48*(2), 218–240.

Lakomski, G. (1987). Values and decision-making. *Educational Administration Quarterly, 23*(3), 70–82.

Langlois, L. (1997). *Relever les défis de la gestion scolaire d'après un modèle de leadership éthique: une étude de cas.* [Taking on the challenges of school management through ethical leadership: A case study.] (Unpublished dissertation). Université Laval, Québec,.

Langlois, L. (2004). Responding ethically: Complex decision-making by school district superintendents. *International Studies Educational Administration Management, 32*(2), 78–93.

Langlois, L. (2011, April 8–12). *Professionnalisme et éthique au travail.* [Professionalism and ethics at work.] Québec: Presses de l'Université Laval.

Langlois, L. (2013). Ethical sensitivity unfolding in educational settings. In B. J. Irby, G. Brown, R. Lara-Alecio, & S. Jackson (Eds.), *The handbook of educational theories* (pp. 813–819). Charlotte, NC: Information Age Publishing.

Langlois L., & Lapointe, C. (2007). Ethical leadership in Canadian school organizations: Tensions and possibilities. *Educational Management, Administration and Leadership, 35*(2), 247–260.

Langlois, L., & Lapointe, C. (2010). Can ethics be learned? Results from a three-year action-research project. *Journal of Educational Administration, 48*(2), 147–163.

Langlois L., & Lapointe, C. (2011). *Transformative leadership and the creation of ethical and equitable schools*. Paper presented at the annual meeting of the American Educational Research Association, New Orleans.

Langlois, L., Lapointe C., Valois, P., & De Leeuw, A. (in press). Development and validity of the Ethical Leadership Questionnaire. *Journal of Educational Administration*.

Lapointe, C., Langlois, L., Centeno, J., & Giasson, G. (2012, April 13–17). *Social and organizational contexts and ethical leadership: An examination of ethical sensitivity theory*. Paper presented at the annual meeting of the American Educational Research Association, Vancouver.

Larocque, L., & Coleman, P. (1993). The politics of excellence: Trustees leadership and school district ethos. *Alberta Journal of Educational Research, 39*(4), 449–475.

Le Boterf, G. (2006). *Ingénierie et évaluation des compétences*. [Competence design and evaluation.] (6th ed.). Paris: Éditions d'Organisation.

Legault, G. (2004). L'autorégulatoire. [Autoregulation.] In M. Jutras & A. Marchildon (Eds.), *Deux perspectives régulatoires*. [Two regulatory perspectives.] (pp. 51–59). Montréal: Éditions Liber.

Marshall, C., Patterson, J. A., Rogers, D. L., & Steele, J. R. (1993, April 12–16). *Caring as career: An alternative model for educational administration*. Paper presented at the Annual meeting of the American Educational Research Association, Atlanta.

Martin, J. (2002). *Organizational culture: Mapping the terrain*. Thousand Oaks, CA: Sage.

Martin, J., Frost, P. J., & O'Neil, O. A. (2004). *Organizational culture: Beyond struggles for intellectual dominance*. Research Paper No. 1864. Stanford, CA: Stanford Graduate School of Business.

Maxcy, S. J. (2002). *Ethical school leadership*. Lanham, MD: Scarecrow Press.

Mills, A. J. (1988). *Organizational acculturation and gender discrimination*. Athabasca, Alberta: Athabasca University Press.

Morgan, G. (1986). *Images of organization*. Newbury Park, CA: Sage Publications.

Murphy, J. (2002). Reculturing the profession of educational leadership: New blueprints. *Educational Administration Quarterly, 38*(2), 176–191.

Noddings, N. (1984). *Caring: A feminine approach to ethics and moral education*. Berkeley: University of California Press.

Organisation for Economic Co-operation and Development. (1996). *L'éthique dans le secteur public. Questions et pratiques actuelles*. [Ethics in the public sector. Questions and current practices.] Paris: Les éditions de l'OCDE.

Ouchi, W. (1981). *Theory Z: How American business can meet the challenge*. Reading, MA: Addison Wesley.

Paquet, G. (2011). *Gouvernance collaborative: Un antimanuel*. [Collaborative Governance. An Anti-manual.] Montréal: Liber.

Pettigrew, A. W. (1979). On studying organizational cultures. *Administrative Science Quarterly, 24*(3), 570–581.

Ricoeur, P. (1990). *Soi-même comme un autre*. [Oneself as the other.] Paris: Editions du Seuil.

Sarason, S. B. (1971). *The culture of the school and the problem of change*. Boston: Allyn & Bacon.

Schein, E. H. (1985). *Organizational culture and leadership*. San Francisco: Jossey-Bass.

Schein, E. H. (2004). *Organizational culture and leadership* (3rd ed.). San Francisco: Jossey-Bass.

Sergiovanni, T. J. (1992). *Moral leadership: Getting to the heart of school improvement*. San Francisco: Jossey-Bass.

Shapiro, J. P., & Stefkovich, J. A. (2005). *Ethical leadership and decision making in education: Applying theoretical perspectives to complex dilemmas* (2nd ed.). Mahwah, NJ: Lawrence Erlbaum Associates.

Shapiro, J. P., & Gross, S. J. (2012). *Ethical educational leadership in turbulent times: (Re)Solving moral dilemmas* (2nd ed.). New York: Routledge.

Smircich, L. (1983). Concepts of cultures and organizational analysis. *Administrative Science Quarterly, 28*(3), 339–358.

Somech, A., & Ron, I. (2007). Promoting organizational citizenship behavior in schools: The impact of individual and organizational characteristics. *Educational Administration Quarterly, 43*(1), 38–66.

Starratt, J. (1991). Building an ethical school: A theory for practice in educational leadership. *Educational Administration Quarterly, 27*(2), 185–202.

Starratt, J. (2004). *Ethical leadership*. San Francisco: Jossey-Bass.

Steinhoff, C. R., & Owens, R. G. (1989). Toward a theory of organizational culture. *Journal of Educational Administration, 27*(3), 6–16.

Strike, K. A., Haller, E. J., & Soltis, J. F. (1988). *The ethics of school administration*. New York: Teachers College Press.

Sun-Keung Pang, N. (2006). The organizational values of *gimnazija* in Slovenia. *Educational Management, Administration and Leadership, 34*(3), 319–343.

van der Westhuizen, M. J., Mosoge, L. H., & Coetsee, L. D. (2005). Organizational culture and academic achievement in secondary schools. *Education and Urban Society, 38*(1), 89–109.

Ward, A. (2007). Polarization processes. In R. F. Baumeister & K. D. Vohs (Eds.), *Encyclopedia of social psychology* (pp. 675–777). New York: Sage.

Willower, D. J. (1961). Values and educational administration. *Peabody Journal of Education, 39*(3), 157–161.

# 22

## ETHICAL RESPONSES TO EDUCATIONAL POLICIES[1]

### STEVEN JAY GROSS AND JOAN POLINER SHAPIRO

Facing repressive accountability regimes and high-stakes testing in the US and beyond, university and practitioner educators around the world decided to take action. Inspired by the democratic administration movement of the 1930s and 1940s and current scholarship in ethics, we started a movement called the New DEEL (Democratic Ethical Educational Leadership). Our mission is to create an action-oriented partnership dedicated to inquiry into the nature and practice of democratic, ethical educational leadership through sustained processes of open dialogue, right to voice, community inclusion, and responsible participation toward the common good. New DEEL leaders include faculty, students, staff, parents, administrators, and community members.

Since our inception in 2004, we have grown to include colleagues from over 30 universities as well as numerous school districts in the US, Canada, the UK, Hong Kong, Sweden, Australia, New Zealand, Taiwan, and Jamaica. Results from our work include scholarship, new graduate programs, six successful international conferences, and support for emerging leaders in the Pre-K–12 system and in higher education.

Our chapter will illustrate the difference our international movement is making in the lives of students, families, practitioners, and university faculty as we strive to reclaim a democratic ethical alternative in our field of educational administration. We are presenting a descriptive account of our recent history, along with an agenda for future development. We think our example will be useful in an era when creativity and authentic leadership are under direct attack in most of the world's developed economies.

## BACKGROUND

By the dawn of the 21st century, the field of educational administration in the US had turned away from the promise of the 1990s. The days of local innovation and what was called *school restructuring* were largely gone. The new bywords of change were accountability and high-stakes testing, and the vehicle driving this movement was No Child Left Behind (NCLB). For the first time in American history, the federal government seemed bent on evaluating all public schools, based on a single indicator, known as Adequate Yearly Progress (AYP). Nor was this movement limited to North America. As far away as Australia, educators saw their freedom to make local decisions limited by ever more detailed plans created at departments or ministries of education. Few of these plans fit even the loosest definition of hands-on experiential learning.

Equally disturbing was the neoliberal argument that if countries raised test scores and permitted market forces to dominate education policy, income inequalities and high rates of poverty would somehow disappear. These policies were adopted by both Republican and Democratic administrations in the US and were touted as self-evident truths.

Given the punitive nature of NCLB, and the power of the conservative think tanks and media supporting this attack, a hard shift to the right in education policy seemed in full swing. Local democratic decision making seemed out of favor. Yet, there was another narrative emerging from scholars in the field of educational administration calling for more progressive, ethical, and democratic forms of renewal for schools in the US and abroad (Aiken, 2002; Begley, 1999; Begley & Zaretsky, 2004; Boyd, 2000; Davis, 2003; Gross, 2004b; Reitzug & O'Hair, 2002; Sernak, 1998; Shapiro & Purpel, 2004; Shapiro & Stefkovich, 2005; Starratt, 2004; Young, Petersen, & Short, 2002).

These writers were part of a long tradition linking social justice and democracy with education. Jane Addams and Ellen Gates Starr made the same connection at Hull House (Addams, 2002), as did Hilda Worthington Smith at the Bryn Mawr Summer School for Women Workers in Industry (Smith, 1929). At the height of the Great Depression, Franklin D. Roosevelt initiated the Civilian Conservation Corps for unemployed men, also based on much the same logic, while Eleanor Roosevelt made a valiant effort to offer the same kind of program for women (Cook, 1999; Gross, 2004a).

Today's scholars also drew inspiration from the democratic administration movement of the 1930s and 1940s in the US. The parallel between the two eras seemed apt; the US faced harsh economic times in the Depression. At the turn of this century, the technology bubble had burst and our economic future seemed dimmed. The US faced a threat to its democracy from Fascist Italy, Nazi Germany, and Imperial Japan and now faces an era of terror, war, and challenges to civil liberties in the post-9/11 world. Therefore, it is instructive to recall our reaction in school leadership programs in the 1930s and 1940s, which was to emphasize democratic power sharing among administrators, teachers, and parents. The works of Harold Rugg and Alice Miel of Teachers College (Kliebard, 1987; Koopman, Miel, & Misner, 1943) were equally inspired by Counts (1932), as well as by the work of Ella Flagg Young in developing teacher councils when she served as the first woman school superintendent of a major US city (Webb & McCarthy, 1998).

Central to the thinking of this group of 21st century scholars was the philosophy of Young's colleague, John Dewey. In *The School and Society* (1900), Dewey railed against education that sought to mold children like so much raw material:

I may have exaggerated somewhat in order to make plain the typical points of the old education: its passivity of attitude, its mechanical massing of children, its uniformity of curriculum and method. It may be summed up by stating that the center of gravity is outside the child. It is in the teacher, the textbook, anywhere and everywhere you please except in the immediate instincts and activities of the child himself.

(p. 34)

In *Democracy and Education* (1916), Dewey called on educators to rethink the connection between schools and the larger world:

But as civilization advances, the gap between the capacities of the young and the concerns of the adults widens. Learning by direct sharing in the pursuits of grown-ups becomes increasingly difficult except in the case of the less advanced occupations. Much of what adults do is so remote in space and in meaning that playful imitation is less and less adequate to reproduce its spirit. Ability to share effectively in adult activities thus depends upon prior training given with this end in view. Intentional agencies, schools, and explicit material studies are devised.

(pp. 7–8)

The previous year, John and Evelyn Dewey depicted exemplars of what this kind of schooling would look like in their book *Schools of Tomorrow* (1915). Everywhere in that text are scenes of children learning about the world through hands-on activities, including model building, operating small stores, and acting. The connection between experiential learning and preparation for democratic citizenship is clear and intentional. Just as clear is Dewey's contention that the life of children, as children, matters rather than the concept of childhood as merely a preparation for adulthood (Kliebard, 1987).

So, while the external policy world seemed dominated by an accountability movement reminiscent of the "essentialist ideals" of William Bagley (1938) combined with market-forces privatization inspired by Milton Friedman (1962), a counterperspective was emerging. Instead of training educational administrators to manage schools that marched to the beat of accountability and top-down management, a small but growing group began to work in an opposite direction. Raising the next generation of young people capable of running a democratic society was their first priority. A key to achieving this was to immerse future educational leaders in ethical decision making. (Shapiro & Stefkovich, 2001, 2005, 2011; Starratt, 2004).

In *God Has a Dream*, Archbishop Desmond Tutu's (2005) description of *ubuntu* illustrates the potential of democratic-ethical educational leadership:

According to ubuntu, it is not a great good to be successful through being aggressively competitive and succeeding at the expense of others. In the end, our purpose is social and communal harmony and well-being. Ubuntu does not say, 'I think, therefore I am.' It says rather, 'I am human because I belong. I participate. I share.' Harmony, friendliness, community are great goods. Social harmony is for us the *summum bonum*—the greatest good. Anything that subverts, that undermines this sought-after good is to be avoided like the plague. Anger, resentment, lust for revenge, even success through aggressive competitiveness, are corrosive of this good.

(p. 27)

In 2004, two Temple University faculty members, Steven Jay Gross and Joan Poliner Shapiro, decided to take action and moved to organize other like-minded educational administration academics and field administrators. They agreed on the name "New DEEL," as previously described, and challenged themselves with the daunting job of changing the direction of educational administration in the US and abroad.

## EARLY DEVELOPMENT

Almost immediately, Gross and Shapiro shared their vision for a new movement in educational administration with faculty and department leaders from Pennsylvania State University, the University of Vermont, Rowan University, the University of Oklahoma, the University Council of Educational Administration, and the University of North Carolina at Greensboro, as well as US and Canadian practitioner leaders. The group agreed that democratic citizenship and ethical leadership were the top priorities for our educational system in any era, and especially in the new century where violence, economic dislocation, and environmental degradation were daily news events. To develop the New DEEL, two winter strategy sessions were held at Temple University, the first in 2005 and the second in 2006. These resulted in refining the concept of the New DEEL, its implications for educational administration programs, and a mission statement that united the group. The New DEEL's mission statement (Gross & Shapiro, 2005) focuses on these values:

The mission of the New DEEL is to create an action-oriented partnership, dedicated to inquiry into the nature and practice of democratic, ethical educational leadership through sustained processes of open dialogue, right to voice, community inclusion, and responsible participation toward the common good. We strive to create an environment to facilitate democratic ethical decision-making in educational theory and practice which acts in the best interest of all students.

(p. 1)

Gross (2009) described the emerging values of the group in this way:

New DEEL members believe that the first job of the school is to help young people become effective citizens in a democracy. Learning how to earn a living is crucial but it is a close second, in their opinion. Democratic citizenship in any era is a complex task but it seems especially difficult in our era where international conflict and growing economic and social inequality are the rule. New DEEL members consider the either/or choice among school improvement, democracy and social justice . . . to be a false dilemma. They believe, instead,

356 • Gross and Shapiro

that there is no democracy without social justice, no social justice without democracy, and that these mutually inclusive concepts are indispensable ingredients to school improvement worthy of the name.

(p. 262)

The group's concept of educational leadership applied to teachers, students, parents, and community members just as much as the person sitting at the principal's desk. Moreover, to respond to the challenges of our era, educational leaders needed to move beyond their buildings, and their school system's structure, to make alliances with community leaders in areas such as health care and commerce.

All of this was inspiring, but soon people asked just what a New DEEL leader was going to look like, and what difference was there between this person and the typical educational administrator. The mission statement set a general direction aimed at reclaiming a more progressive, socially just, and responsive school system, but now specifics were required. In response, the New DEEL vision for educational leadership was developed (Gross, 2009) (Table 22.1).

Table 22.1 contrasts the five transformational qualities of New DEEL leadership with the corresponding transactional qualities of more traditional leaders. In each of the five areas, the New DEEL leader is someone who sets off in a different, more challenging, and, hopefully, more rewarding direction. The first area, in the quality numbered 1, contrasts the contractual demands of the accountability system with the deeper demands of following one's inner sense of responsibility for students, their

**Table 22.1** Comparison of New DEEL vision for leaders with the behavior of traditional leaders (Gross, 2009)

| New DEEL Vision for Leaders | Behavior of Traditional School Leaders |
|---|---|
| *Transformational* | *Transactional* |
| 1. Guided by inner sense of responsibility to students, families, the community, and social development on a world scale. | Driven by exterior pressure of accountability to those above in the organizational/political hierarchy. |
| 2. Leads from an expansive community-building perspective. A democratic actor who understands when and how to *shield* the school from turbulence and when and how to *use* turbulence to facilitate change. | Bound by the system and the physical building. A small part of a monolithic, more corporate structure. |
| 3. Integrates the concepts of democracy, social justice, and school reform through scholarship, dialogue, and action. | Separates democracy and social justice from guiding vision and accepts school improvement (a subset of school reform) as the dominant perspective. |
| 4. Operates from a deep understanding of ethical decision making in the context of a dynamic, inclusive, democratic vision. | Operates largely from perspective of the ethic of justice wherein obedience to authority and current regulations is largely unquestioned despite one's own misgivings. |
| 5. Sees one's career as a calling and has a well-developed sense of mission toward democratic social improvement that cuts across political, national, class, gender, racial, ethnic, and religious boundaries. | Sees one's career in terms of specific job titles with an aim to move to ever greater positions of perceived power within the current system's structure. |

families, and the wider community. New DEEL leaders cannot focus solely on gaining better scores on standardized tests. Nor can they believe that making AYP is a route to a more just society.

In quality 2, leaders are encouraged to act in democratic ways to help develop young people. This means understanding how turbulence works (Gross, 1998, 2004; Shapiro and Gross, 2008, 2013) and finding ways to protect those they work with from its excesses. In contrast, the traditional leader is a small part of a hierarchy that places constant demands and expects compliance. Members of the New DEEL feel strongly that the former models democracy, while the latter exhibits authoritarian behaviors that undermine the school's attempt to educate for democratic life.

Quality 3 speaks to the need for a coherent vision that connects, rather than atomizes, the values of democracy, social justice, and school reform while encouraging dialogue and high-quality scholarship.

A major element of New DEEL scholarship comes in quality 4, that is, the work of learning and practicing ethical decision making from a multidimensional paradigm. New DEEL leaders understand that the ethic of justice, encompassing laws, rights, rules, and even guidelines, is important because it tells us what statutes and laws have to say on a given matter. But there are other ethics to consider in making important decisions. For example, there is also the ethic of critique that asks: Who made the law? In whose best interest? The ethic of care does not take notice of the law at all. Instead it asks: Who may benefit or be hurt by my decision? What are the likely long-term effects upon different people? Finally, the ethic of the profession takes into account professional ethics from different appropriate organizations as well as one's own code of ethics, both personal and professional. Above all, it asks: What is in the best interests of the student? Stopping with the ethic of justice will not suffice (Shapiro & Stefkovich, 2011; Starratt, 1994).

Finally, quality 5 deepens the discussion of being an educator from merely holding a job to a lifelong calling. Members of the New DEEL believe that this is essential because only that kind of commitment will energize leaders sufficiently to transform our current system. Equally, seeing education as a *calling* honors the energy and sacrifice that these individuals have made.

The group developed a strong conceptual base, and it quickly grew from a handful of academics, mostly in the US, to include educational administration faculty from over 30 universities and practitioner colleagues from Canada, Australia, Taiwan, Sweden, the UK, Hong Kong, New Zealand, and Jamaica, as well as the US. Now, a plan to turn the progressive, democratic ideals of the mission statement and vision for leaders into action was required. Using Furman's (2004) concept of the ethic of the community, the New DEEL was headed for the creation of an alternative way of envisioning and educating school leadership that centered on nurturing a new kind of community. Neither compliant behavior nor shallow heroics that might damage a person's career were deemed acceptable. Instead, development in four interconnected areas was proposed and will be described in the following section of this article.

## COORDINATED APPROACHES TO REALIZE OUR PROGRESSIVE, DEMOCRATIC, *AND ETHICAL* VISION FOR EDUCATIONAL ADMINISTRATION

Organizing our ideas into a coherent form and daring to say that we aimed to change the direction of our field was a start, but then came the task of developing a feasible strategy. Dedicating ourselves to this long-term process challenged each of us to live up to the five elements of the New DEEL vision for educational leaders described in Table 22.1. Above all, quality 5 had a profound effect. The concept of a *calling*, and not a mere *job*, resonated with all of us. We pondered just what it meant to change a field's direction and how this would be accomplished in a way that built an authentically democratic ethical community from P-20.[2]

First, we believed that a new body of scholarship needed to be developed, while existing appropriate scholarship needed to be collected and shared. Second, we needed to bring people together with our own conferences to exchange ideas and perspectives and to enrich everyone's networks. This was both collegial and strategic. We realized that the development of community, with common values, was essential in an era of high-stakes testing and accountability to make certain that educators at all levels did not feel isolated and vulnerable. Since 2007, we have seen our scholarship and conference initiatives grow. More recently, we decided that there was a need to add two additional projects: enhanced technology and a mentoring program for P-20 educators. Below we will examine our experience in each of these.

## BUILDING A FOUNDATION FOR TRANSFORMATIONAL CHANGE: PROMOTING NEW DEEL SCHOLARSHIP

If a progressive movement in educational administration was to be constructed, its foundation needed to rest on a body of scholarship, new research, and the continuing evolution of questions and debates that are the hallmark of any rich field of inquiry. This meant developing new writings and helping our community access existing articles and books. Since the whole question of taking an ethical stand against the accountability movement's excesses was central to our mission, some of our own work in the field of resolving ethical dilemmas became important to share.

Two books, in particular, are notable in this area, both for their content and for the way graduate student practitioners were made central to their development. The first is *Ethical Leadership and Decision Making in Education: Applying Theoretical Perspectives to Complex Dilemmas* (Shapiro & Stefkovich, 2001, 2005, 2011). In this book, Shapiro and Stefkovich expanded upon earlier work of scholars, such as Starratt (2004), to develop the multiple ethical paradigm of the ethics of justice (Sergiovanni, 1992, 2009), critique (Giroux, 1988), care (Gilligan, 1982), and the profession. Their addition of the ethic of the profession asks educators to consider what is in the best interests of the student as they ponder ethical dilemmas. This question looms large for everyone in the New DEEL as we ask: Are high-stakes tests and a lock-step, narrowed curriculum really in the best interests of the student? Just as importantly: Is our social inequality at all compatible with our country's democratic ideals?

Shapiro and Stefkovich provided a theoretical background and then shared ethical problems, developed by their students, thereby making the dilemmas authentic. Using the multiple ethical paradigms, students then explored questions surrounding their dilemma, showing its complexity and ways in which thoughtful solutions might be developed. Again, this process aligned with our New DEEL approach, since it placed heavy responsibility upon individual educators to think through challenging problems rather than simply be willing to accept the dictates of an authority figure. In our view, democratic life demands this kind of skillful reasoning from citizens. This is also an example of our use of progressive education's hands-on approach to learning and connecting school-based learning with conditions in the world beyond the halls of the academy. Shapiro and Stefkovich followed through in community building by creating graduate student panels at national and international conferences, where they not only presented successfully but also made important connections to other P-20 educators facing similar dilemmas.

In a second book, *Ethical Educational Leadership in Turbulent Times: (Re)Solving Moral Dilemmas,* Shapiro and Gross (2008, 2013) connect the multiple ethical paradigms with turbulence theory. Turbulence theory (Gross, 1998, 2004b) helps students of organization to consider the severity of a given dilemma, how that dilemma might be seen by different people, its chances to cascade into a larger problem, and how to gauge the relative stability of an organization facing turbulence. According to this theory, turbulence can be experienced at four levels (light, moderate, severe, and extreme), similar to the levels that pilots are trained to understand and respond to. In addition, the forces of positionality, cascading, and stability act upon turbulence individually and in combination in ways that either raise or lower turbulence. Finally, a turbulence gauge can be constructed that allows students to consider current and possible future levels of turbulence as they weigh their response to the ethical dilemmas they confront. The combination of the two approaches now gives students a powerful way to face, and reason through, the problems confronting conscientious educators in this era. The pattern of using student-authored dilemmas was followed in this book as well as was the habit of bringing practitioners to conferences to present.

While these two books are relevant to the New DEEL and are widely used by our group, they are only an illustration of scholarship supporting our perspective. Other books, book chapters, case studies, dissertations, and journal articles have come from writers associated with us. Some were specifically written about the New DEEL, such as Storey's (2011) *New DEEL: An Ethical Framework for Addressing Common Issues in Florida Schools*. Other cases, such as Normore's (2008) *Leadership for Social Justice: Promoting Equity and Excellence Through Inquiry and Reflective Practice*, included numerous contributions by scholars attempting to confront the core issues of social justice and social responsibility in the context of our current educational policy environment.

Many authors are American, but others consider the issue of democratic life and its implications for school from an international perspective. Woods's (2011) *Transforming Education Policy: Shaping a Democratic Future* is one such example from the UK. Several writers are senior academics, but the list is more than balanced by young scholars at or recently past the tenure stage of their careers. In many instances, they have been successful in finding coauthors among their New DEEL colleagues. Similar to making a point of bringing graduate students to conferences, this collegiality has become an integral part of building a strong, mutually supporting, and progressive community. Publishing together grows our scholarship while it helps the authors establish some career stability. This is an example of what we mean by daring to change our field while not asking people to risk their positions.

If developing and enriching the literature on democratic and ethical educational leadership is a first step, sharing that scholarship is a logical next part of the sequence. Rounding out our commitment to develop and share a body of scholarship is the creation of new courses for masters and doctoral students in educational administration. Since our programs attract future leaders in early childhood, elementary, secondary, and tertiary institutions, new courses offer us an excellent chance to build on our concept of a P-20 continuum of democratic ethical educational leadership in the making.

One course developed just for the New DEEL is called Profiles of Democratic Ethical Leadership. Using a wide cross section of women and men from the US and around the world, both in our own time and from time past, students consider the common qualities these leaders demonstrate as they faced their greatest personal and professional challenge. Some come directly from the field of education, such as Ella Flagg Young. Others are identified with different professions—for example, Desmond Tutu and Aung San Suu Kyi. All have had a major impact on society and have, therefore, shaped education. Students consider the work of these leaders and construct a vibrant and organic definition of democratic ethical leadership that will inform our professional practice. Jerome Bruner's (1966) concept attainment model is used to help in the creation of this definition.[3] His inductive, engaging approach is instrumental in helping students see the complexity of being a democratic ethical leader in any era.

Profiles of Democratic Ethical Leadership is one example of new coursework, but it is not an isolated case. At Temple University, the whole range of principal preparation courses was reworked and now has adopted a consistent New DEEL perspective. Similar work has taken place at other universities affiliated with the New DEEL.

## DEVELOPING A DEMOCRATIC ETHICAL EDUCATIONAL COMMUNITY THROUGH CONFERENCES, TECHNOLOGY, AND MENTORING

At our second winter strategy session, held in 2006, we were at a crossroads. Interest was increasing and pressure was building for us to take the next step and develop a conference of our own. The goal was to bring New DEEL scholars and practitioners together to exchange ideas, debate approaches, and build a sense of common purpose and direction. In February 2007, we held the first of these conferences, with the title "What Do We Mean by Democratic and Ethical Leadership in an Era of Contention?" As the title suggests, the conference helped us to sharpen our common understanding of crucial ideas while it also helped us to broaden our audience. The following year, presidential politics was heating up and we decided that the theme needed to reflect the aspirations and concerns of many in the US and around the world. "Fear Versus Possibility" captured that spirit.

By the spring of 2009, much of the advanced economies in the world faced the worst financial crisis since the Great Depression. We focused on the challenges and potential opportunities of the times by entitling our conference "Reconstructing Our World: Developing Democratic Ethical Communities in Turbulent Times." Yet, by the following year, policy pressures from those emphasizing market forces as the ulti-mate priority in education caused us to refocus our attention in a conference called "Our Children: Economic Warriors or Democratic Ethical Citizens?"

In 2011, we reflected our commitment to social justice and social responsibility by recalling Franklin Roosevelt's appeal to the nation to build upon the first Bill of Rights. "Really Leaving No Child Behind: It's More than Time for FDR's Second Bill of Rights" crystallized this possibility and caused many attendees to broaden their perspective by including Roosevelt's advocacy of progressive legislation (Sunstein, 2004). At this conference, we came to the conclusion that our society faced a cross-road. On the one hand, there was a vision that a laissez-faire, market-based economy would result in an equitable society. On the other hand, there was Roosevelt's conten-tion that democracy required assurances of stability, outlined in his Second Bill of Rights, and that this foundation would create a fair society and inspire generations who would value education. The sixth New DEEL conference was held in May 2013.

Our conferences are designed to be intimate yet large enough to spur dialogue and debate. Typically, this means between 30 and 40 papers presented by scholars, graduate students, or practitioners coming from many universities and school dis-tricts. Typical titles include *We the School: Constitution High's Blueprint for a Demo-cratic School Government, Investigating Developmental Democracy: Early Data from an Academy in England,* and *Connecting with Communities: Small Urban Districts and Democratic Partnerships in Hard Times.*

New DEEL keynote lectures honoring the ideals of scholarship and practice, women's leadership, excellence in teaching, and citizen service to education are a highlight of every conference. Over the years, these have focused on topics meant to challenge and inspire our group. For example, Arizona State University's David Ber-liner's lecture *How the Lack of Caring for America's Children Impacts the Performance of Our Nation's Schools and Damages Our Democracy* underscored our foundational connection between education policy and progressive social policy. Temple Uni-versity's James Earl Davis highlighted a similar concern, this time regarding racial inequalities in his address *Leadership among "The Least of These": African American Males and the Challenge of Schools.* University Council for Educational Administra-tion (UCEA) Executive Director Michelle D. Young reminded us of the weighty deci-sions that groups like ours need to consider in *The Politics and Ethics of Professional Responsibility.*

One of the most important things we do in the New DEEL is to nurture an inter-generational community of scholars. So we started to hold graduate student work-shops at the conclusion of our conferences connecting established academics with the rising generation. At these sessions, senior scholars meet one-on-one with gradu-ate students to help mentor them as they pursue early research projects. Often, these relationships carry on and deepen as graduate students launch their own careers as Pre-K–12 practitioners or higher education faculty.

In July 2010, we added a new kind of conference by holding the first Camp New DEEL in Vermont. Camp New DEEL was designed to build community, share our writing, enjoy a common reading, develop a vision for the schools and universities we would like to see, and plan for the future of the New DEEL around the world. By establishing this community, we followed a long tradition of establishing summer institutes to build cultural and politically focused communities in the United States.[4]

Creating Camp New DEEL was also inspired by the scholarship of Charles Tilly's writing on social movements, in which he claims that successful social movements demonstrate worthiness, unity, numbers, and commitment, or WUNC. Tilly (2004) also describes the conditions needed for social movements to promote democracy:

> In short, social movements promote democratization when—either as explicit programs or as by-products of their actions—they broaden the range of participants in public politics, equalize the weight of participants in public politics, erect barriers to the direct translation of categorical inequalities into public politics, and/or integrate previously segmented trust networks into public politics.
>
> (p. 143)

Along with our conferences and camps, we have made numerous presentations at the American Educational Research Association's (AERA) annual meetings and have created an important niche for ourselves in our learned society, the UCEA. In fact, UCEA, through its executive director and members of its executive committee, have been crucial New DEEL colleagues giving key direction to us since our beginning. UCEA has a wide audience in the US and abroad, and a growing number of UCEA members are affiliated with the New DEEL. We see our work at these conferences as community building as well, and we typically host a special New DEEL dinner for friends and families to socialize and share experiences.

## INTERNATIONAL REACH

The New DEEL orientation has been international from the outset, and that perspective became formalized in 2010 when we joined with like-minded centers at Nipissing University, Canada; Australian Catholic University; Umea University, Sweden; Penn State; and the Hong Kong Institute of Education to become the Center for the Study of Leadership and Ethics (CSLE). As one of UCEA's official centers, CSLE unites scholars and practitioners in the field of educational administration by holding annual conferences and by publishing and sponsoring research opportunities. With colleagues in five countries around the world, we are better able to compare conditions and challenges and establish partnerships.

Research trips by Gross to Australia and Sweden have uncovered similar patterns of a narrowed, teacher-centered curriculum, heavy emphasis on high-stakes testing, and the advance of market forces and privatization. In presentations before hundreds of administrators in both countries, the New DEEL mission and priorities for action have been well received. As one principal from a school near Stockholm recently put it, "I am a progressive educator, but there is pressure to move away from those ideals." It is clear to us that the need for international ties and support is growing.

## ACKNOWLEDGING THE DIFFERENCE WE HAVE MADE TO DATE

We continually ask ourselves: What difference have we made to date and how would we know it? Clearly, the policy world has not been turned around—in fact, the case can be made that things have gotten worse for progressive educators in the years since we started our work. Yet, it would be wrong, in our opinion, to conclude that we have not made a contribution to the creation of an alternative vision for education in an age dominated by neoliberal market forces and high-stakes accountability policies.

First, we have brought together hundreds of scholars and practitioners representing three generations of innovative educators through our conferences. Their shared stories, scholarship, and passion have helped to create an alternative community with its own history and values.

Next, we have helped to nurture numerous young scholars from their doctoral work into their first academic jobs and through to tenure and promotion. While many of these people are at our own university, many more come from across the US and abroad. They represent the next generation of educational leadership and administration professors who, in turn, will teach practitioners and future higher education faculty. Since we believe that our work will require a multigenerational approach, this is a critical role for us to play. We provide publishing opportunities, presentations at national and international conferences, and chances to network with like-minded academics and practitioners.

Finally, we have identified and honored key individuals in the areas of citizen service to education, scholarship that impacts practice, women's leadership in education, mentoring, and graduate teaching. Each of these is reflected in a lecture and award at our conferences. In this way, we believe that we have helped to sustain vital education traditions for our students and colleagues in the US and abroad.

## PREPARING FOR THE WORK AHEAD

The academic year 2013–2014 will mark the end of our first decade, making this a good time to consider the challenges and directions that we see ahead. At times, it feels as though we are in mid-ocean, far away from any shore and facing heavy seas. Still, our community is growing and we have plotted a reasonable, though long, course. While the general conditions that inspired us still pertain, new challenges have emerged.

The first of these is the coming of the Common Core State Standards, now adopted by nearly every US state. This is a historic change from previous experiences in American curriculum history, since the Common Core marks the first attempt at what amounts to a nationalized curriculum (Mathis, 2010). While some consider the Common Core a mere outline of advisable directions for the nation's public schools, the multiplicity of suggested instructional material and the coming of two national tests to measure acquisition of Common Core skills make this a robust project, and to our way of thinking, a dangerous one.

By organizing the broad outlines of the curriculum at the national level, local experiments, often associated with the very hands-on experiential learning, will likely be viewed with suspicion, since they do not directly connect to the larger pattern of top-down mandates. In addition, such a sweeping change in curriculum control threatens to accelerate the pattern of curriculum narrowing witnessed in the implementation of NCLB (Ravitch, 2010). What role can community-related projects possibly play when a nationalized test will determine success or failure for the individual student as well as for her teacher and school? Preparing for such a limited future evaluation seems to us the antithesis of Dewey's contention that learning matters for the child as she or he is now.

The fact that much of the impetus and funding for the Common Core came from the Gates Foundation and is being pushed directly by Bill Gates himself speaks to the role of what is now referred to as venture philanthropists (Saltman, 2010). The power of the venture philanthropists represents the second new challenge. Foundations such as the Bill and Melinda Gates Foundation, the Walton Family Foundation, and the Broad Foundation now appear at the center of this movement, which is dedicated to market-based and high-stakes accountability reforms that challenge the existence of the public schools themselves, since these groups favor charter schools, both privately and publicly managed. Those of us in higher education are not immune from the reach of these foundations, since privatization in such fields as leadership preparation has long been a staple of the Broad Superintendent's Academy. Reading the literature coming from the venture philanthropists, it is clear that their goals for education are more narrowly confined to career preparation rather than raising the next generation capable of sustaining a democratic society (Baltodano, 2012).

Finally, those supporting democratic ethical education must act in a world where threats to physical security, economic dislocation, radical technological transformation, and environmental crisis are taken as part of daily life. Each of these conditions could easily ratchet up tensions for our students, their families, and their communities. Taken together, they raise the potential for serious ethical dilemmas that today's and tomorrow's educators must learn how to resolve. That is why we made these issues the centerpiece of our sixth New DEEL conference.

At this point, perhaps the best we can offer are thoughtful questions: In a dangerous world, how do educators contribute to a sense of realistic security for our society's children? In a world filled with tensions and adversarial relationships, how do we help our young expand the sense of "we" to include "the other"? How shall we advocate for our most needy schoolchildren and their families in a time of budget cutting? What kind of economic security do we envision for our youth and how might we advocate for that vision? How do we encourage technologies that do not exploit fellow educators (the online challenge)? What can we do to help our young *use* technology rather than be *used by* technology (e.g., cyberbullying, hyperconsumerism, hurried lives)? How can we raise awareness of the environmental price we ask the world to pay for our lifestyles in a fair and constructive way? What vision do we want to share with our children for the world they are to inherit from us? What kind of models do we want to be for saving the environment from abuse? How will we infuse the curriculum with these ideas? Questions such as these make the need for ethical decision making more important than ever for tomorrow's educational leaders.

Over the next decade, we will have to find new and more effective ways to respond to all of the challenges raised above, as well as unforeseen ones just over the horizon. In addition to accelerating our work in scholarship and continuing our international community building efforts, we will need to invent new approaches.

One possibility is to further develop our New DEEL curriculum work for aspiring P-20 educational leaders. While our own program has adopted a New DEEL perspective into coursework, this is not sufficiently the case in universities where we have colleagues. We have networked within the UCEA, our learned society, from our earliest days, and it seems likely that this will increase over time as we push for more influence over the direction of our field.

A second project, allied with our curriculum plans, is the development of P-20 mentor/protégé cohorts. As described earlier in this article, mentoring has long been a goal for the New DEEL, since we believe that our work cannot be done well in isolation. At this point we have an intergenerational team working with scholars who specialize in mentoring research. Each team member is currently in a mentoring relationship with a colleague, and the team will comprise the first cohort. From there, they will design a methodical plan to expand the mentoring program for New DEEL colleagues in the US and abroad. The team will submit a proposal to present its work and related research at the 2014 AERA annual conference.

A third aspect of our work is to break out of the current silos we find ourselves in and engage in consistent dialogue with the wider community. Simply put, there are severe limits on what we can achieve if we work only within our own circle of academic and practitioner colleagues in our own programs and schools. Like our plans for the mentoring program, we have started this project first with our own practice.

During his sabbatical year, one of us (Steve Gross) attended state board of education meetings regularly and presented policy papers relevant to board agenda items in his home state of Vermont. He also testified to the state senate, spoke out at county legislative breakfast meetings, and joined a community planning team for local school reform. Joan Shapiro served as Temple University faculty senate president in the 2012–2013 academic year. Her term included the arrival of a new university president and the appointment of a new provost, along with a new budgeting model that held serious implications for every program across all campuses. Joan emphasized shared governance and other New DEEL values in her work with university leaders, faculty, and board members. In both cases, being a consistent presence over time broke down previous barriers and helped to build new alliances. We need to find ways for all of our New DEEL colleagues to break out of their usual confines and start dialogues like these. In our view, not doing so merely concedes the field to those who oppose democratic ethical education and its values.

Fourth, we need to build bridges to like-minded organizations in the US and around the world. Our own network is expanding, but not fast enough, and we know that we are only one small piece of the robust response needed in the coming decade. We have made a start by finding such organizations as the National Education Policy Center (NEPC) at the University of Colorado. Their reviews, publications, and blogs have become an invaluable source for research-based facts on such issues as the efficacy of charter schools and the negative implications for democracy resulting in NCLB. As we speak out more publicly, we will need to transcend our necessarily focused areas of expertise, and organizations such as NEPC can help us broaden our perspective. But we also need to forge reciprocal alliances and find where our work fits that of others. These are early days for that effort, but time is short and the threat to democratic public education is more real than ever, in our view.

Together, these four elements represent our effort to imagine a new level of engagement that combines a greater intensity in teaching our New DEEL approach to rising educational leaders with the support and strategies that will help them to succeed both internally and beyond the confines of their workplace. It is our best strategy so far in helping them become exemplars of the New DEEL vision for leadership in our turbulent era.

## CONCLUSION

Since the founding of our field nearly a century ago, there has been a tension. Cubberly (1916) urged educational administrators to behave like the business leaders of that era. Echoes of that argument have cascaded down to our own time and have picked up momentum in the past 30 years. Yet, there is a different and equally established tradition for educational leaders, that is, emerging from the ideals of Ella Flagg Young and John Dewey, who emphasized progressive education and democratic school leadership.

The accountability movement did not achieve its dominant position overnight but rather evolved over the decades since the *Nation at Risk* report (National Commission on Excellence in Education, 1983). Those of us who desire a very different direction for our field and the children we serve need to have an equally long-range perspective. In the 8 years since our beginning, we have made a small but successful start. We believe that the New DEEL represents one pathway toward the development of a democratic ethical educational community that can nurture the rising generation of scholars and practitioners of educational administration.

Perhaps the words on Dewey's tombstone best describe our need to remember our place in the long line of like-minded educators and our duty to the future:

> The things in civilization we most prize are not of ourselves. They exist by grace of the doings and sufferings of the continuous human community in which we are a link. Ours is the responsibility of conserving, transmitting, rectifying and expanding the heritage of values we have received that those who come after us may receive it more solid and secure, more widely accessible and more generously shared than we have received it.
>
> ("A Common Faith." John Dewey to the
> University of Vermont class of 1879)

## NOTES

1. This chapter is an adaptation of an article appearing in Hogan, M. P., & Bruce, B. C. (Eds.) (2013). Progressive education: What's next?: The future of progressivism as an "infinite succession of presents." *International Journal of Progressive Education, 9*(3) [Special issue]. Available online www.inased.org/v9n2/ijpev9n3.pdf. The authors wish to express their gratitude to the *International Journal of Progressive Education* for allowing us to share our work in this handbook.

2. We were inspired by the democratic administration movement in our field, yet we had to acknowledge that the field of educational administration had a strong conservative tradition often modeled on corporate hierarchies. The foundational work of Cubberly (1916) and the critique of this pattern by Counts (1927) are two prime examples. So we realized that the New DEEL was going to have to swim against strong antiprogressive currents.

3. Our version of Bruner's concept attainment model involved the examination of examples of a given concept, in this case democratic ethical leadership. We would then write down the example's attributes. Then a second example was provided. Attributes from the first example that are found in the second example were kept; those not in evidence were eliminated. We asked about qualities found in the second example that may have also been in the first as a double check. This process was repeated until we had looked carefully at all of the characters in the course. From this, our grounded definition of democratic ethical leadership emerged.

4. These included: the Chautauqua Institution founded in 1874 (Morrison, 1974); the Bryn Mawr Summer School for Women Workers founded in 1921 (Heller, 1984, 1986); the Bread Loaf Writers' Conference established in 1926 (Bain & Duffy, 1993; Morrison, 1976); and the Highlander Research and Education Center, which began its work in 1932 (Adams & Horton, 1975; Horton, Kohl, & Kohl, 1990).

## REFERENCES

Adams, F., & Horton, M. (1975). *Unearthing seeds of fire: The idea of Highlander.* Winston-Salem, NC: John F. Blair.

Addams, J. (2002). *Democracy and social ethics.* Urbana: University of Illinois Press.

Aiken, J. (2002). The socialization of new principals: Another perspective on principal retention. *Educational Leadership Review, 3*(1), 32–40.

Bagley, W. C. (1938, April). An essentialist's platform for the advancement of American education. *Educational Administration and Supervision, 24,* 241–256.

Bain, D. H., & Duffy, M. S. (1993). *Whose woods these are: A history of the Bread Loaf writers' conference, 1926–1990.* Hopewell, NJ: Ecco Press.

Baltodano, M. (2012). Neoliberalism and the demise of public education: The corporatization of schools of education. *International Journal of Qualitative Studies in Education, 25*(4), 487–507.

Begley, P. T. (Ed.). (1999). *Values and educational leadership.* Albany: State University of New York Press.

Begley, P. T., & Zaretsky, L. (2004). Democratic school leadership in Canada's public school systems: Professional value and social ethic. *Journal of Educational Administration, 42*(6), 640–655.

Boyd, W. L. (2000). The r's of school reform and the politics of reforming or replacing public schools. *Journal of Educational Change, 1*(3), 225–252.

Bruner, J. (1966). *Toward a theory of instruction.* Cambridge, MA: Harvard University Press.

Cook, B. W. (1999). *Eleanor Roosevelt. Volume 2: 1933–1938.* New York: Viking.

Counts, G. S. (1927). *The social composition of boards of education: A study in the social control of public education.* Chicago: University of Chicago Press.

Counts, G. S. (1932). *Dare the schools build a new social order?* Carbondale: Southern Illinois University Press.

Cubberly, E. P. (1916). *Public administration.* Boston: Houghton Mifflin.

Davis, J. E. (2003). Early schooling and the achievement of African American males. *Urban Education, 38*(5), 515–537.

Dewey, J. (1900). *The school and society.* Chicago: University of Chicago Press.

Dewey, J. (1916). *Democracy and education.* New York: Free Press.

Dewey, J., & Dewey, E. (1915). *Schools of tomorrow.* New York: E. P. Dutton & Company.

Friedman, M. (1962). *Capitalism and freedom.* Chicago: University of Chicago Press.

Furman, G. C. (2004). The ethic of community. *Journal of Educational Administration, 42*(2), 215–235.

Gilligan, C. (1982). *In a different voice.* Cambridge, MA: Harvard University Press.

Giroux, H. A. (1988). *Schooling and the struggle for public life: Critical pedagogy in the modern age.* Minneapolis: University of Minnesota Press.

Gross, S. J. (1998). *Staying centered: Curriculum leadership in a turbulent era.* Alexandria, VA: Association of Supervision and Curriculum Development.

Gross, S. J. (2004a). Civic hands upon the land: Diverse patterns of social education and curriculum leadership in the Civilian Conservation Corps and its analogues, 1933–1942. In C. Woyshner, J. Watras, & M. Smith Crocco (Eds.), *Social education in the twentieth century: Curriculum and context for citizenship.* New York: Peter Lang Press.

Gross, S. J. (2004b). *Promises kept: Sustaining school and district leadership in a turbulent era.* Alexandria, VA: Association for Supervision and Curriculum Development.

Gross, S. J. (2009). (Re-)Constructing a movement for social justice in our profession. In A. H. Normore (Ed.), *Leadership for social justice: Promoting equity and excellence through inquiry and reflective practice* (pp. 257–266). Charlotte, NC: Information Age Publishing.

Gross, S. J., & Shapiro, J. P. (2005, Fall). Our new era requires a New DEEL: Towards democratic ethical educational leadership. *UCEA Review, 46*(3), 1–4.

Heller, R. R. (1984). *Blue collars and blue stockings: The Bryn Mawr Summer School for Women Workers, 1921–1938.* In J. Kornbluh & M. Fredrickson (Eds.), *Sisterhood and solidarity: Workers education for women, 1914–1984.* Philadelphia: Temple University Press.

Heller, R. R. (1986). *The women of summer: Bryn Mawr Summer School for Women Workers, 1921–1938.* Unpublished doctoral dissertation, Rutgers University, New Brunswick, NJ.

Horton, M., Kohl, H., & Kohl, J. (1990). *The long haul: An autobiography.* New York: Doubleday.

Kliebard, H. M. (1987). *The struggle for the American curriculum: 1893–1958.* Boston: Routledge and Kegan Paul.

Koopman, O., Miel, A., & Misner, P. (1943). *Democracy in school administration.* New York: Appleton-Century.

Mathis, W. J. (2010). *The "Common Core" standards initiative: An effective reform tool?* Boulder, CO and Tempe, AZ: Education and the Public Interest Center & Education Policy Research Unit. Retrieved from http://epicpolicy.org/publication/common-core-standards

Morrison, T. (1974). *Chautauqua: A center for education, religion, and the arts in America.* Chicago: University of Chicago Press.

Morrison, T. (1976). *The first thirty years, 1926–1955.* Middlebury, VT: Middlebury College Press.

National Commission on Excellence in Education. (1983). *A nation at risk: The imperative for educational reform.* Washington, DC: US Government Printing Office.

Normore, A. H. (Ed.). (2008). *Leadership for social justice: Promoting equity and excellence through inquiry and reflective practice.* Charlotte, NC: Information Age Publishing.

Ravitch, D. (2010). *The death and life of the great American school system. How testing and choice are undermining education.* New York: Basic Books.

Reitzug, U. C., & O'Hair, M. J. (2002). Tensions and struggles in moving toward a democratic school community. In G. Furman-Brown (Ed.), *School as community: From promise to practice* (pp. 119–142). Albany: SUNY Press.

Saltman, K. J. (2010). *The gift of education: Public education and venture philanthropy.* New York: Palgrave Macmillan.

Sergiovanni, T. J. (1992). *Moral leadership: Getting to the heart of school improvement.* San Francisco: Jossey-Bass.

Sergiovanni, T. J. (2009). *The principalship: A reflective practice perspective* (6th ed.). Boston: Allyn & Bacon.

Sernak, K. (1998). *School leadership—balancing power with caring.* New York: Teachers College Press.

Shapiro, H. S., & Purpel, D. E. (Eds.). (2004). *Critical social issues in American education: Democracy and meaning in a globalizing world* (3rd ed.). Mahwah, NJ: Lawrence Erlbaum Associates.

Shapiro, J. P., & Gross, S. J. (2008). *Ethical educational leadership in turbulent times: (Re)Solving moral dilemmas.* New York: Lawrence Erlbaum Associates.

Shapiro, J. P., & Gross, S. J. (2013). *Ethical educational leadership in turbulent times: (Re)Solving moral dilemmas* (2nd ed.). New York: Routledge.

Shapiro, J. P., & Stefkovich, J. A. (2001). *Ethical leadership and decision making in education: Applying theoretical perspectives to complex dilemmas.* Mahwah, NJ: Lawrence Erlbaum Associates.

Shapiro, J. P., & Stefkovich, J. A. (2005). *Ethical leadership and decision making in education: Applying theoretical perspectives to complex dilemmas* (2nd ed.). Mahwah, NJ: Erlbaum Associates.

Shapiro, J. P., & Stefkovich, J. A. (2011). *Ethical leadership and decision making in education: Applying theoretical perspective to complex dilemmas* (3rd ed.). New York: Routledge.

Smith, H. W. (1929). *Women workers at the Bryn Mawr Summer School.* New York: Affiliated Summer School for Women Workers in Industry/American Association for Adult Education.

Starratt, R. J. (1994). *Building an ethical school: A practical response to the moral crisis in schools.* Abingdon, Oxon, UK: Routledge Falmer.

Starratt, R. J. (2004). *Ethical leadership.* San Francisco: Jossey-Bass.

Storey, V. A. (2011). *New DEEL: An ethical framework for addressing common issues in Florida schools.* San Jose, CA: JAPSS Press.

Sunstein, C. R. (2004). *The second bill of rights: FDR's unfinished revolution and why we need it more than ever.* New York: Basic Books.

Tilly, C. (2004). *Social movements, 1768–2004.* Boulder, CO: Paradigm Publishers.

Tutu, D. (2005). *God has a dream.* New York: Doubleday.

Webb, L., & McCarthy, M. C. (1998). Ella Flagg Young: Pioneer of democratic school administration. *Educational Administration Quarterly, 34*(2), 223–242.

Woods, P. A. (2011). *Transforming education policy: Shaping a democratic future.* Bristol, UK: Policy Press.

Young, M. D., Petersen, G. J., & Short, P. M. (2002). The complexity of substantive reform: A call for interdependence among stakeholders. *Educational Administration Quarterly, 38*(2), 137–175.

# 23

## THE ETHICAL PERSPECTIVES OF TURKISH SCHOOL LEADERS

### MUALLA AKSU AND GAMZE KASALAK

The main purpose of the study described in this chapter was to quantitatively explore Turkish school leaders' views and understanding of ethical principles. The research population consisted of approximately 600 school principals working in the Antalya province in 2010–2011, and questionnaires were sent out to all of these principals via the Internet. Data collected via the questionnaires included answers to some demographic questions: a 12-item ethical scale for school leaders; a 21-item ethical scale for the school administration process, developed by the researchers for this study; and 5 open-ended questions. As a result, some 310 principals completed the questionnaires. The most important contribution provided by this study is its capacity to present to current and future Turkish school leaders insight into ethical principles, which are highly supported by their peers. This knowledge can then make an important contribution to a school principal's self-reflection process with respect to an understanding of his or her own ethical principles and values.

## A REVIEW OF THE LITERATURE THAT GUIDED THIS STUDY

An "ethic" is defined in dictionaries as a system of moral standards. However, Cohen (2010, p. 73) draws attention to the difference between being ethical and being moral. Being ethical, in the context of leadership, is related to the rules and standards that shape the behaviors of a person or members of a profession. Being moral means complying with the rules of correct behavior. Starratt (2004) indicates the difference between ethics and morality as follow:

> Ethics is the study of what constitutes a moral life; an ethics is a summary, systematic statement of what is necessary to live a moral life. Morality is the living, the acting out of ethical beliefs and commitments. Often, characterizing

leadership activity as moral and characterizing it as ethical mean the same thing: moral leadership involves the moral activity embedded in the conduct of leading; ethical leadership is the attempt to act from the principles, beliefs, assumptions, and values in the leader's espoused system of ethics.

(p. 5)

As quoted by Clark (2005), Walker in 1993 defined ethics as a standard of duty and virtue that indicates how one should behave according to principles of right and wrong. The focus of ethics is on "what one ought to do." Clark also compares ethics and values, and defines values as beliefs leading and motivating attitudes and actions in a broader concept than ethics because it includes a set of beliefs and desires that motivate individual behaviors. Ethics goes beyond the person's belief and focuses on the ability to discriminate "right from wrong" and the responsibility of "doing what's right."

Educators must hold themselves to a higher ethical standard than the average members of society because of the importance of their educational task and the trust students and their families place in them. However, the principals of the schools are the primary architects and promoters of the values and standards that ensure everything and everyone in the school is acting in accord with the expected ethical standards. Therefore, the principals must be leaders who take time routinely to consider their solid ethical principles, primary responsibilities, and core values (Harsh & Casto, n.d.).

But, how can an ethical school be created by a principal? Millett (2002) suggests that help is needed in the following areas: staff agreements, discipline and pastoral care, conformity versus individuality, student empowerment, and student leadership within the whole life of the school. Starratt (1991) affirms that educational administrators need to consider their responsibility to promote an ethical environment in their schools, especially during a period of school restructuring. In order to build such an ethical school, he suggests three ethical themes—critique, justice, and caring—as the pillars of the foundation. Branson (2010) discusses five ethical perspectives—justice, care, critique, the profession, and personal moral integrity—that may impact on others. He suggests a diagram in which the ethic of personal moral integrity is at the center, adapted from Shapiro and Stefkovich (2005, quoted in Branson 2010), and affirms that this perspective will ultimately guide the leader in making the most ethical choice.

Researchers have been very interested in the topic of ethics, especially "ethical leadership." Lashley (2007) suggests the use of an ethical lens for principals as they work to improve educational performance and opportunity for all children. In the study conducted by Engelbrecht, van Aswegen, and Theron (2005), it is found that transformational leaders can make a significant impact on the ethical performance of organizations.

The findings of Valentine, Godkin, Fleischman, and Kidwell (2011) show that group creativity and corporate ethical values are positively related and that both variables are associated with increased job satisfaction. Their results also indicate that corporate ethical values and job satisfaction are associated with decreased turnover intention. Biron (2010) indicates a negative relation between perceived organizational ethical values and organizational deviance. When high levels of abusive supervision and low levels of perceived organizational support took place in the context of low ethical values, the result was the highest level of organizational deviance. Clark (2005) affirms that Illinois superintendents behave in an ethical manner, adhere to some chosen standard of ethics, and respond differently based on their gender, working region, basis of professional ethics, and interpretation of the situation.

According to the findings of Deshpande and Joseph (2010), caring value, perception of ethical conduct, and age had a significant impact on counterproductive behavior of students of a public university in the United States. Narayanasamy and Lama (2008) find no significant effect on the gender, race, or level of education on the ethical values of the lecturers, but rather, the ethical values of the lecturers increased with age, teaching experience, and marriage. However, the ethical values of the male students were found to be significantly higher than those of their female counterparts in the same study. Al-Kahtani (2007) revealed that graduate engineering and business students in three selected Saudi universities were more ethical than their undergraduate counterparts. While there is no apparent consistency in the outcomes from across this array of research, what is clearly evident is that within a particular context, there are such consistencies, which can have meaning and significance for others associated with this context. The context highlighted in this particular chapter is that of schools in the province of Antalya in Turkey.

Aydın (2002) conducted the first study on the topic of ethics in Turkey, which focused on the ethical behaviors of high school principals. The findings of Aydın show that according to the participating principals, high school principals "always" practice 79 ethical principles developed by the researcher, while participating supervisors and teachers think that these principals only ever "generally" or "sometimes" practiced those principles. The findings of Küçükkaraduman (2006) show that school principals mostly act in accordance with ethical principles according to the teachers' views, and there are significant differences in terms of the variables of gender, age, teaching field, and length of service. Kara (2006) found that principals of schools having stronger organizational culture show more ethical behaviors, and principals of private schools are perceived to be more ethical than the principals of public schools. The research of Yılmaz (2007) suggests that beginner academics observe unethical actions in terms of the responsibility toward the profession and colleagues. Kentsu (2007) proclaims that the views of the school administrators on compliance with ethical principles differ only in terms of the variable of gender in favor of males in dimensions of tolerance, fairness, and responsibility. In Akyıldız's (2007) study, it is found that according to 837 teachers' views, educational inspectors were more responsive to veteran teachers than their younger counterparts during the classroom observation process. Döven (2009) identified the principles of professional ethics for educational inspectors. In a qualitative study conducted by Demirtaş (2010), school administrators developed 34 ethical codes, but the most frequently applied ethics were in the codes of justice and honesty.

Hence, it can be seen how research, both abroad and in Turkey, is now reflecting the importance of ethical issues in educational settings. Specific to the Turkish educational system, this importance has been formalized in the 2005 Regulations on the

Principles of Ethical Behavior for Government Officials, and Application Procedures and Essentials, which contain a section pertaining to ethics that must be signed by all government employees. It therefore lacks specificity and needs to be defined further for the school administration process as well as the ethical behavior of school leaders. Schools are the best places for the development of such specific guidelines for knowing how to behave ethically within a school, and school leaders are the most important ethical role models not only for the teachers but also for the students. Therefore, this research study was conducted to examine the current situation in Antalya schools on such ethical issues.

The main purpose of this study was to reveal school leaders' views and understanding of ethical principles. In order to achieve this purpose, the following research questions were developed:

1. According to the school leaders, what is the necessity level of ethical principles? Here, "necessity level" is the mean value obtained from the items developed by the researchers as ethical principles.
2. At what level do school leaders, themselves, practice ethical principles?
3. According to the school leaders, on what level do the other school leaders practice ethical principles?
4. Are there significant correlations among necessity level, school leaders' practice, and other school leaders' practice of ethical principles?
5. Are there significant differences among necessity level, school leaders' practice, and other school leaders' practice when applying ethical principles?
6. What kind of actions do the school leaders choose concerning a specific ethical situation?

## RESEARCH DESIGN

The key to the design of this research was a relational survey. The target population for this study was all of the school leaders working in the province of Antalya in Turkey, as this provided an accessible population. Antalya has more than 600 school leaders either at the elementary or secondary school level. Because the number of the accessible population was not excessive, sampling was not seen as necessary, and the questionnaires developed by the researchers were sent to all of the 600 school leaders via the Internet. After two follow-up procedures, 310 school leaders, providing a 51.66% return rate, voluntarily responded to the questionnaires. This return rate may be seen as statistically very satisfactory because it is relative to the accessible population and not the entire population of Turkish school principals.

## COLLECTING AND ANALYZING DATA

Data from this study were collected from the school principals by means of a questionnaire developed by the researchers through literature review. A pilot version of the questionnaire was sent to a few school leaders from the population, and some changes were made to the questionnaire prior to its full use. The questionnaire consisted of three parts: the first part was a 12-item/10-point scale named the Ethical Scale for School Leaders (ESSL); the second part was a 21-item/10-point scale named the Ethical Scale for the School Administration Process (ESSAP), and the third part contained demographic questions and open-ended items. Both ethical scales were administered on three columns: Necessity level of the chosen principles is placed in the first column, own practice of the school leaders is illustrated in the second column, and the practice of the other leaders is marked in the third column. The questionnaire used a Likert scale from 1 to 10, with 10 being the higher necessity and practice level for a given ethical principle and 1 being the lowest necessity and practice level for a given ethical principle according to the personal opinion of each participant.

The explanatory factor analysis (EFA) was applied on the data obtained from the three columns of scales, and only one factor was determined for each scale. According to the analyses, for the ESSL the factor loadings were between .771 and .952 in the necessity level column, .781 and .936 in the own practice column, and .803 and .882 in the other school leaders' practice column. For the ESSAP, the factor loadings were between .623 and .916 in the necessity level column, .639 and .883 in the own practice column, and .689 and .893 in the other school leaders' practice column. The respective total variances for the ESSL were 80.287%, 75.943%, and 70.303%, and Cronbach's alpha values were .976, .970, and .961. For the ESSAP data, the total variances were 68.180%, 64.168%, and 66.881%, respectively, and Cronbach's alpha values were .974, .969, and .974. The EFA results show that both scales explain at least two thirds of the total variance and are acceptable as one-dimensional research instruments.

In the third part of the questionnaire, an ethical situation quoted from Clark (2005) was presented to the participants, and they were asked to choose from the alternative actions submitted within the scenario. In addition, the participants were asked to share their original solutions with the researchers for this situation if they did not choose one of four alternatives given within the scenario. Furthermore, the participants were asked to share similar ethical situations they had personally experienced and to describe how they resolved each situation. The research questionnaire also had some open-ended and demographic questions. The entire study was conducted through a Web-based survey. Quantitative data were analyzed and interpreted by using the SPSS 13.0 data analysis program, and descriptive data analysis techniques were used for the qualitative data.

## LIMITATIONS

This study has the following limitations:

1. It included only the views of the principals working at the primary or secondary schools, either state or private, in the province of Antalya in Turkey.
2. Data are limited to the questionnaires conducted and collected in the 2011 spring semester.

## DESCRIPTIVE FINDINGS

As shown in Table 23.1, the vast majority of the participants (93.9%) were male principals, which is in line with the gender balance of the overall Turkish school principal population itself. The fields of more than half of the principals (57.1%) were classroom teaching, the overwhelming majority (96.5%) worked at state schools, and nearly three fourths of their schools (74.2%) were at the primary education level.

In addition, 71.0% of the responding principals had worked for 10 years or less as principals, while 54.7% had served within the education system for 20 years and more.

Table 23.2 shows the descriptive data on ESSL within the three columns of necessity levels of the principles, school leader's own practice concerning the related principles, and other school leaders' practice according to the views of the participating principals.

As shown in Table 23.2, the mean values for the necessity level were calculated to be 9.74 at the highest and 9.48 at the lowest, while the means for the school leader's own practice changed from 9.69 to 9.01 and the means for the other school leaders' practice changed from 8.80 to 7.66. The highest means were obtained from item 8: "A school leader does not discriminate among parents based on social class, creed, ethnicity, etc." for the necessity level and principal's own practice columns. The highest mean for the other school leaders' practice column was obtained from item 9: "A school leader does not use school resources for personal gain." The lowest means were obtained from item 6: "A school leader does not divulge private information obtained as a result of the job" for the necessity level column; from item 2: "A school leader fulfills the required responsibility and authority of the position" for the principal's own practice column; and from item 3: "A school leader communicates fairly and objectively with individuals" for the other school leaders' practice column.

As shown in Table 23.3, mean values for the necessity level were calculated 9.69 at the highest level and 9.01 at the lowest level, while the means for the school leader's own practice changed from 9.66 to 8.82 and the means for the other school leaders' practice changed from 9.2 to 7.70. The highest means were obtained from item 14: "Banning teachers and other staff from attending school after consuming

Table 23.1 Demographic data on the participating principals

| Variable | Variable level | *n* | % |
|---|---|---|---|
| Gender of the participants | Female principals | 19 | 6.1 |
| | Male principals | 291 | 93.9 |
| Teaching field of the participants | Branch teacher | 133 | 42.9 |
| | Classroom teacher | 177 | 57.1 |
| School status of the participants | State school | 299 | 96.5 |
| | Private school | 11 | 3.5 |
| School level of the participants | Primary education | 230 | 74.2 |
| | Secondary education | 80 | 25.8 |

**Table 23.2** Means and standard deviations of the items in ESSL*

| No. | A school leader: | Necessity level | | School leader's own practice | | Other school leaders' practice | |
|---|---|---|---|---|---|---|---|
| | | Mean | SD | Mean | SD | Mean | SD |
| 1 | Performs his/her job correctly, honestly, and reliably | 9.72 (2) | 1.26 | 9.27 (10) | 1.39 | 7.68 (11) | 2.02 |
| 2 | Fulfils the required responsibility and authority of the position | 9.50 (11) | 1.30 | 9.01 (12) | 1.49 | 7.80 (10) | 2.02 |
| 3 | Communicates fairly and objectively with individuals | 9.66 (5) | 1.29 | 9.36 (9) | 1.35 | 7.66 (12) | 2.10 |
| 4 | Avoids using the position's authority for personal benefit | 9.64 (8) | 1.45 | 9.60 (3) | 1.46 | 8.38 (6) | 2.01 |
| 5 | Uses mutual affection and respect as bases for human relations | 9.62 (9) | 1.32 | 9.43 (7) | 1.35 | 8.17 (8) | 1.91 |
| 6 | Does not divulge private information obtained as a result of the job | 9.48 (12) | 1.63 | 9.40 (8) | 1.55 | 8.50 (4) | 1.94 |
| 7 | Comes to meetings prepared | 9.54 (10) | 1.35 | 9.09 (11) | 1.48 | 8.17 (9) | 1.92 |
| 8 | Does not discriminate among parents based on social class, creed, ethnicity, etc. | 9.74 (1) | 1.27 | 9.69 (1) | 1.25 | 8.78 (2) | 1.89 |
| 9 | Does not use school resources for personal gain | 9.68 (3) | 1.51 | 9.63 (2) | 1.42 | 8.80 (1) | 1.91 |
| 10 | Distributes tasks fairly among staff | 9.65 (6) | 1.34 | 9.47 (6) | 1.34 | 8.44 (5) | 1.93 |
| 11 | Demonstrates unbiased behavior in the reward/ punishment process | 9.67 (4) | 1.36 | 9.57 (5) | 1.30 | 8.23 (7) | 2.10 |
| 12 | Puts the interest of the school over personal interest | 9.64 (7) | 1.42 | 9.58 (4) | 1.34 | 8.60 (3) | 1.92 |

*Numbers in parentheses show the rank of the means. The lowest number symbolizes the highest mean in the scale, while the highest number stands for the lowest mean.

alcoholic beverages" for the all columns. The lowest mean was obtained from item 7: "Taking precautions to prevent teachers from providing paid tutoring to their own students" for the necessity level and other school leaders' practice columns. The lowest mean for the principal's own practice column was obtained from item 2: "Providing services to not only the school, but also society."

**Table 23.3** Means and standard deviations of the items in ESSAP*

| No. | Ethical principles for the school administration process are: | Necessity level | | School leader's own practice | | Other school leaders' practice | |
|---|---|---|---|---|---|---|---|
| | | Mean | SD | Mean | Mean | SD | Mean |
| 1 | Continuing advantageous projects and implementations initiated by the previous administration | 9.36 (17) | 1.54 | 9.08 (13) | 1.66 | 8.07 (17) | 2.02 |
| 2 | Providing services to not only the school, but also society | 9.30 (18) | 1.48 | 8.82 (21) | 1.61 | 7.83 (20) | 1.99 |
| 3 | Warning colleagues about negative behaviors and attitudes in a constructive manner | 9.42 (13) | 1.41 | 8.88 (19) | 1.55 | 7.87 (18) | 1.90 |
| 4 | Trying to make constructive use of both personal criticism and criticism directed toward the school | 9.21 (20) | 1.74 | 8.94 (17) | 1.67 | 7.87 (19) | 2.03 |
| 5 | Avoiding interference in the private/personal matter of colleagues | 9.40 (15) | 1.65 | 9.36 (7) | 1.50 | 8.49 (9) | 1.84 |
| 6 | Trying to implement an effective administration team with vice principals | 9.60 (4) | 1.37 | 9.24 (10) | 1.41 | 8.21 (16) | 1.80 |
| 7 | Taking precautions to prevent teachers from providing paid tutoring to their own students | 9.01 (21) | 2.11 | 8.85 (20) | 1.98 | 7.70 (21) | 2.28 |
| 8 | Taking precautions to prevent teachers from starting classes late or ending classes early unless they have a valid excuse | 9.55 (7) | 1.42 | 9.12 (12) | 1.52 | 8.45 (10) | 1.91 |
| 9 | Generating ethical rules with stakeholders regarding student absenteeism and tardiness | 9.45 (11) | 1.44 | 9.05 (14) | 1.46 | 8.4 (11) | 1.87 |
| 10 | Preventing the sale of books, periodicals, etc. at school to students for monetary gain | 9.39 (16) | 1.70 | 9.33 (8) | 1.52 | 8.32 (15) | 2.01 |
| 11 | Taking necessary precautions to prevent the use of physical punishment at school | 9.49 (10) | 1.58 | 9.30 (9) | 1.53 | 8.50 (8) | 1.95 |

(*Continued*)

**Table 23.3** (Continued)

| No. | Ethical principles for the school administration process are: | Necessity level | | School leader's own practice | | Other school leaders' practice | |
|---|---|---|---|---|---|---|---|
| | | Mean | SD | Mean | Mean | SD | Mean |
| 12 | Taking the necessary measures to prevent students from cheating | 9.28 (19) | 1.78 | 9.03 (16) | 1.65 | 8.61 (5) | 1.83 |
| 13 | Preventing classes from being impeded due to social, political, and other reasons of a similar nature | 9.60 (5) | 1.26 | 9.44 (3) | 1.39 | 8.82 (3) | 1.74 |
| 14 | Banning teachers and other staff from attending school after consuming alcoholic beverages | 9.69 (1) | 1.42 | 9.66 (1) | 1.40 | 9.20 (1) | 1.80 |
| 15 | Warning staff regarding false health reports | 9.42 (14) | 1.60 | 9.20 (11) | 1.62 | 8.56 (7) | 2.05 |
| 16 | Banning the use of profanity at school | 9.55 (8) | 1.61 | 9.46 (2) | 1.46 | 8.93 (2) | 1.85 |
| 17 | Disallowing staff from smoking in areas that are visible to students | 9.45 (12) | 1.70 | 9.04 (15) | 1.97 | 8.34 (14) | 2.22 |
| 18 | Disallowing the school staff from mobbing each other | 9.58 (6) | 1.41 | 9.40 (6) | 1.35 | 8.35 (13) | 1.99 |
| 19 | Making arrangements at school that meet the requirements of handicapped students and parents | 9.52 (9) | 1.49 | 8.89 (18) | 1.73 | 8.37 (12) | 1.92 |
| 20 | Supporting teachers striving for personal and professional development without impeding their normal tasks at school | 9.65 (2) | 1.32 | 9.43 (4) | 1.42 | 8.58 (6) | 1.84 |
| 21 | Taking the appropriate measures to provide a safe environment within the school for students and teachers | 9.64 (3) | 1.33 | 9.41 (5) | 1.39 | 8.82 (4) | 1.77 |

*Numbers in parentheses show the rank of the means. The lowest number symbolizes the highest mean in the scale, while the highest number stands for the lowest mean.

## RESULTS OF THE STUDY

Table 23.4 shows the differences and correlations between the two columns for both scales. As illustrated in the table, necessity level had the highest means, while others' practice had the lowest means in all of the paired comparisons not only for ESSL but also for ESSAP. All $t$ values show that there were significant differences and correlations between the two means at the alpha level .001. The highest correlation coefficients were

**Table 23.4**  Means, standard deviations, correlation coefficients, and the values for ESSL and ESSAP

| Columns | ESSL | | | | ESSAP | | | |
|---|---|---|---|---|---|---|---|---|
| | Mean | SD | r | t | Mean | SD | r | t |
| Necessity level | 9.63 | 1.22 | .947*** | 9.003*** | 9.45 | 1.26 | .913*** | 9.026*** |
| Own practice | 9.43 | 1.21 | | | 9.19 | 1.24 | | |
| Necessity level | 9.63 | 1.22 | .493*** | 16.021*** | 9.45 | 1.26 | .588*** | 14.184*** |
| Others' practice | 8.27 | 1.65 | | | 8.40 | 1.57 | | |
| Own practice | 9.43 | 1.21 | .576*** | 14.826*** | 9.19 | 1.24 | .676*** | 11.893*** |
| Others' practice | 8.27 | 1.65 | | | 8.40 | 1.57 | | |

***$P < .001$

**Table 23.5**  Mann–Whitney $U$-test results for ESSL

| Name of the variable | Level of the variable | n | Necessity level | Own practice | Others' practice |
|---|---|---|---|---|---|
| Gender | *Female* | 19 | 2,072* | 2,174 | 2,250 |
| | Male | 291 | | | |
| Teaching field | *Subject teacher* | 133 | 10,355* | 11,142 | 11,735 |
| | Classroom teacher | 177 | | | |
| School level | Primary | 230 | 8,895 | 8,965 | 8,998 |
| | Secondary | 80 | | | |
| School status | State | 299 | 1,359 | 1,478 | 1,149 |
| | Private | 11 | | | |

*$P < .05$ (Mean ranks obtained from the level of female and subject teacher are statistically higher than their counterparts.)

calculated between the columns representing necessity level and own practice with the values .947 for ESSL and .913 for ESSAP, while the lowest correlation coefficients were calculated between the columns representing necessity level and others' practice, with the values .493 for ESSL and .588 for ESSAP. However, the lowest correlation coefficients for ESSL and ESSAP were calculated at the medium value as well.

Table 23.5 illustrates the results of the comparisons between two levels of the variables of gender, teaching field, school level, and school status for ESSL. The Mann–Whitney $U$-test was preferred for this analysis because the assumptions of the parametric tests may not be met by the obtained data. As shown in Table 23.5, no significant differences were found in the principal's own practice and other school leaders' practice columns for the variables, although gender and teaching field were significant variables only in the necessity level column, and mean ranks of the participants who were female and subject teachers were higher than their counterparts.

Table 23.6 illustrates the Mann–Whitney $U$-test results concerning the variables of gender, teaching field, school level, and school status for ESSAP. As shown in the table, no significant differences were found in the second and third columns for the variables, although gender, teaching field, and school status were significant variables only in the necessity level column, and mean ranks of the participants who were female, subject teacher, and working at a state school were higher than their counterparts.

**Table 23.6** Mann–Whitney $U$-test results for ESSAP

| Name of the variable | Level of the variable | $n$ | Necessity level | Own practice | Others' practice |
|---|---|---|---|---|---|
| Gender | *Female* | 19 | 1,981* | 2,188 | 2,579 |
|  | Male | 291 |  |  |  |
| Teaching field | *Subject teacher* | 133 | 10,099* | 11,487 | 11,374 |
|  | Classroom teacher | 177 |  |  |  |
| School level | Primary | 230 | 8,630 | 8,292 | 8,526 |
|  | Secondary | 80 |  |  |  |
| School status | *State* | 299 | 1,259 | 1,239 | 1,000* |
|  | Private | 11 |  |  |  |

*$P < .05$ (Mean ranks obtained from the level of female, subject teacher, and state are statistically higher than their counterparts.)

Table 23.7 shows the responses of the participants to the alternatives given by Clark (2005, p. 203) for the following ethical situation:

The parents of a good student and generally responsible youngster have come to you with complaints about the teaching style of a social studies teacher. They claim the teacher is using biased materials and slanted opinions in the classes. Further, they claim that when their son tried to question these approaches, he was greeted with sarcasm and thinly veiled threats to have his grades lowered. The matter is not relieved by the father's active role in town matters, and he demands evidence of action immediately. What action do you take?

In contrast to Clark's (2005) study, in which no participant chose alternatives "a" or "b" and very few selected alternative "e," Table 23.7 indicates that in this Turkish study, 15 participants marked either "a" or "b" and nearly half of them chose alternative "e."

**Table 23.7** Participants' preferences on the ethical scenario

| What action do you take on the above-mentioned ethical situations? | $f$ | % |
|---|---|---|
| a. Agree with the parents that the teacher is in the wrong, and indicate that censure will be applied in some form. | 7 | 2.3 |
| b. Have the boy transferred into another classroom with a teacher whose techniques and methods are well known to you and which you know will placate these irate parents. | 8 | 2.6 |
| c. Call the most immediate supervisor of the teacher and ask for some corroboration of the incidents, then proceed with action. | 4 | 1.3 |
| d. Indicate to the parents that you will take the matter up with the teacher and the teacher's supervisors, but that no direct action will be taken until both sides of the controversy have been aired. | 148 | 47.7 |
| e. None of the above, but rather: | 143 | 46.1 |
| Total | 310 | 100.0 |

The highest frequency responses obtained from the open-ended question for the alternative "e" are categorized in Table 23.8, which shows that nearly 3 of 10 participants preferred meeting with the teacher and listening to him or her. The three most strongly supported alternatives were: "Meets with the student and listen to him/her" (12.2%); "Meets with the parents and listens to them" (11.3%); and "Investigates the issue on the sincerity" (10.4%). The least chosen alternative was the statement "Seeks help from the superior" (3.0%).

In open-ended questions in the research questionnaire, the responding principals were also asked to write down their ethical scenarios if they had experienced any. One principal responded this question and shared the event called a scenario in the study. Only one participant was willing to share his scenario. The source of this scenario is this principal's experience:

A parent working as a teacher comes to the principal's office and tells him angrily that his daughter does not have a passing grade from any course because her teacher gives a poor 44 points. A passing grade must be equal to or higher than 45 points in the evaluation system. The parent is furious and charges the teacher with discrimination. The principal tells the parent his claims are not true because he knows the teacher well, but he cannot convince him. However, the principal promises that he will look into the situation before he leaves the school. Afterward, the principal goes through all of the scores in the mentioned course and observes that the student has got the following scores: 35, 38, and 39 out of 100 from three previous examinations. Later, he meets with the course teacher and discusses the complaint of the parent. The teacher says that he always tries to grade on the high side and give more points to encourage the students, but he did not think the paper earned it.

**Table 23.8** Participants' responses for alternative "e" on the ethical scenario

| Open-ended responses[a] | $f$ | % |
| --- | --- | --- |
| Meets with the teacher and listens to him/her | 97 | 28.9 |
| Meets with the student and listens to him/her | 41 | 12.2 |
| Meets with the parents and listens to them | 38 | 11.3 |
| Investigates the issue on the sincerity | 35 | 10.4 |
| Meets with the other students and listens to them | 24 | 7.2 |
| Warns the teacher about his/her behavior | 22 | 6.6 |
| Convinces the parent that s/he will do what is required | 20 | 6.0 |
| Informs the parents about the real situation | 18 | 5.4 |
| Controls the teacher via either formal or informal procedures | 16 | 4.8 |
| Supports the teacher in all conditions | 14 | 4.2 |
| Seeks help from the superiors | 10 | 3.0 |
| Total | 335 | 100.0 |

[a]Because participants' responses contained more than one category, total number of the frequencies may sum to more than 143, which is the number rated "e" response for the given scenario.

Some questions for discussion of this scenario with school leaders are as follows:

- How can you handle such a complaint?
- Do you need more information? About what?
- What kind of behavior is expected from you as an ethical principal?
- Do you have ethical standards for students, parents, colleagues, and the larger community for being proactive rather than reactive?

How can a school leader be trained to internalize these ethical principles? Answers to this question are summarized in Table 23.9.

As shown in Table 23.9, more than two thirds of the participants wanted in-service education in order to be able to internalize ethical principles. Nearly 1 in 10 respondents suggested pre-service education, while only 1.4% of them recommended graduate education.

Table 23.10 shows pre-service and/or in-service training topics with the frequencies and percentages. "Leadership and administration" was the most suggested topic, with 31.6% support from the participants, while "human relations" followed with 30.6% support. The topics "ethics" and "self-improvement" were chosen by more than one tenth of the participants.

In addition, the participants were asked to state their suggestions for the ways in-service education in ethical principles should be organized. Their recommendations were as follows:

1. In-service courses should be organized every year for all the school leaders.
2. In-service courses should be organized in collaboration with the faculty of education.
3. In-service courses should be conducted within small and interactive groups.
4. Examples of actual school events should be discussed during in-service courses.
5. Important and major problems faced by school principals should be handled at in-service training activities.

**Table 23.9** Ways of internalizing ethical principles according to the participants' views

| How to internalize ethical principles: | $f$ | % |
|---|---|---|
| Through in-service education | 146 | 67.3 |
| Through pre-service education | 20 | 9.2 |
| Through the proper selection of candidates for school principal | 12 | 5.5 |
| Through summer camp | 11 | 5.0 |
| No education is needed because it's related to the personality | 8 | 3.7 |
| Through job training | 6 | 2.8 |
| Through internships with at least 2 years by a school principal | 6 | 2.8 |
| Through continuing education | 5 | 2.3 |
| Through graduate education | 3 | 1.4 |
| Total | 217 | 100.0 |

**Table 23.10** Pre-service and/or in-service training topics

| Training topics recommended by the responding principals | $f$ | % |
|---|---|---|
| Leadership and administration | 62 | 31.6 |
| Human relations | 60 | 30.6 |
| Ethics | 24 | 12.3 |
| Self-improvement | 21 | 10.7 |
| Legislation | 13 | 6.6 |
| Adaptation to change | 8 | 4.1 |
| Economy and accountancy | 6 | 3.1 |
| Information technology | 2 | 1.0 |
| Total | 196 | 100.0 |

## DISCUSSION AND CONCLUSION

This research was conducted in order to reveal the views and understanding of the school leaders in the province of Antalya, Turkey, concerning ethical principles. However, the most important output of this study is the development of two ethical scales, the ESSL and the ESSAP, which complement each other. The results of EFAs applied in the research data show that future researchers can also use them and may explore the reliability and validity of these scales. Admittedly, there is still a need to make an observation on the leaders about these principles while practicing at the school. Nevertheless, the following limitations of this study should not be ignored for the generalization: numbers of the participants (only 310 school leaders), regional study (working in Antalya province), and method chosen for the data collection (questionnaire developed by the researchers).

The main conclusion is that an awareness of ethical principles, not only for school leaders but also within the school administration process, was found to be extremely necessary in the opinion of the participants. Interestingly, though, the participating school leaders see themselves as being much more ethical than their counterparts. As can be seen in the data from this study, the necessity levels obtained from two scales were the highest, while that of the other leaders' practices were the lowest at the alpha level of .001. Indeed, only very few participants reported that they could not know what their colleagues did in regard to complying with ethical principles, whereas a great majority of the participating leaders gave their counterparts a lower rating. How can this result be explained? It implies that the participating school leaders evaluate their own leadership behaviors as being significantly more ethical than how the judge the actions of other school leaders. This result reminds us of Yunus Emre, a Turkish poet living in the 13th–14th centuries, who wrote: "What if you think for yourself / Think about it for others as well."

Another consequence of this study is the finding of significant positive correlations among three columns in both scales at the alpha level of .001. The correlation coefficients between necessity level and own practice for both scales are very high (.947 and .913), while they are moderate for the other binary comparisons. This result shows that the necessity level, own practice, and others' practice are positively interconnected.

Another important result is that the necessity levels are the highest in ethical principles concerning nondiscrimination, honesty, and no personal gain for the ESSL. The leaders also proclaim at the highest levels that they practice nondiscrimination behaviors at the school, and their counterparts do not use school resources for personal gain. However, the mean difference among the three columns—necessity level, own practice, and others' practice—for the ESSL was only 2.08 because the lowest mean obtained from item 3 was 7.66 in the third column, and the highest mean obtained from item 8 was 9.74. This means that even the lowest mean is more than 7 out of 10 points, and this result shows that the chosen principles for the study were accepted and practiced by the participating leaders. On the other hand, the highest means were obtained from the same principles (item 14) expressed in the form "banning teachers and other staff from attending school after consuming alcoholic beverages" in all three columns, and the mean difference among the columns was only 1.99 because the lowest mean obtained from item 7 was 7.70 in the third column for the ESSAP.

It emerged that school leaders participating in this study mostly have similar views and understandings about ethical principles. However, significant differences were found in favor of "female" and "subject teacher" in the variables of gender and teaching field only with regard to the necessity level, while the variable of school status was found statistically different in favor of "state school" in only the ESSAP at the alpha level of .05. Although the alpha level shows that the effect size of the difference may be small, the findings of this research are not consistent with the finding of Kara (2006), which suggested that principals of private schools are perceived to be more ethical than the principals of public schools, or with the finding of Kentsu (2007), where the difference is in favor of males, or with the finding of Küçükkaraduman (2006), who highlighted the differences in terms of the variables of teaching field and length of service. Doubtless, neither populations nor the instruments of the above-mentioned studies are the same as with this current study.

The researchers argue that the most important contribution of this study is to present Turkish school leaders with ethical principles, which are highly supported by the participants. However, only the views of the participants were reflected in this study. Further researchers need not only to focus on observing school leaders' behaviors in an actual school setting but also on a broader population. Admittedly, the limitations of this study should be taken into consideration for generalizing the results. Therefore, further studies are still required for generalization to the whole Turkish educational system. Finally, the following practical suggestions may be given:

1. Turkish school leaders need to empathize with their colleagues and cooperate more with each other.
2. Turkish school leaders should become more explicitly aware of the ethical dimensions and demands of their role.
3. Turkish school leaders need to learn how best to personally model ethical behavior.

# REFERENCES

Akyıldız, S. (2007). *İlköğretim denetmenlerinin etik davranışlarna ilişkin öğretmen görüşlerinin değerlendirilmesi: Diyarbakır ili örneği* [Evaluation of teachers' views on the ethical behaviors of primary education inspectors: Sample of Diyarbakır province]. (Unpublished master's thesis). University of Dicle, Diyarbakır, Turkey.

Al-Kahtani, A. S. (2007). Perceptual ethical values of business and engineering students in Saudi universities. *International Journal of Business Research, 7*(6), 19–27.

Aydın, İ. P. (2002). *Yönetsel mesleki ve örgütsel etik* [Administrative professional and organizational ethics] (3rd ed.). Ankara: Pegem A Yayıncılık.

Biron, M. (2010). Negative reciprocity and the association between perceived organizational ethical values and organizational deviance. *Human Relations, 63*(6), 875–897.

Branson, C. (2010). Ethical decision making: Is personal moral integrity the missing link? *Journal of Authentic Leadership in Education, 1*(1), 1–8. Retrieved from http://csle.nipissingu.ca/JALE/JALE_Num1Vol1.pdf

Clark, S. B. (2005). *A Study to determine the ethical values of school superintendents within the state of Illinois.* (Unpublished doctoral dissertation). Southern Illinois University, Carbondale.

Cohen, W. A. (2010). *Drucker ve Liderlik* [Drucker and leadership]. (Ümit Şensoy, Trans.). İstanbul: Optimist Yayınları.

Demirtaş, Z. (2010). Ethical codes expected of school administrators. *African Journal of Business Management, 4*(6), 1006–1013. Retrieved from www.academicjournals.org/AJBM

Deshpande, S. P., & Joseph, J. (2010). The impact of ethical values and perceptions of ethical conduct on counterproductive behaviour of future managers. *Advances in Competitiveness Research, 18*(1-2), 102–110.

Döven, D. C. (2009). *İlköğretim müfettişlerinin uymaları beklenen mesleki etik ilkelerin iş tatmin düzeyleri bağlamında çok boyutlu incelenmesi: İstanbul ili örneği* [Multidimensional examination of professional ethical principles that primary education inspectors are expected to follow: Sample of İstanbul province]. (Unpublished master's thesis). University of Yeditepe, İstanbul, Turkey.

Engelbrecht, A. S., van Aswegen, A. S., & Theron, C. C. (2005). The effect of ethical values on transformational leadership and ethical climate in organisations. *South African Journal of Business Management, 36*(2), 19–26.

Harsh, S., & Casto, M. (n.d.). *Professional code of ethics: Principles and principals.* Retrieved from http://principalsoffice.osu.edu/files/profreadings.3.08.php

Kara, Y. (2006). *Okullardaki örgütsel kültürün okul yöneticilerinin etik davranişlari üzerindeki etkisi* [The effect of organizational culture at the schools on the ethical behaviors of school administrators]. (Unpublished master's thesis). University of İstanbul, Turkey.

Kentsu, J. (2007). *Okul yöneticilerinin kişilik özelliklerinin örgütsel etik üzerine etkisi* [The effect of personal characteristics of school administrators on organizational ethics]. (Unpublished master's thesis). University of Yeditepe, İstanbul, Turkey.

Küçükkaraduman, E. (2006). *İlköğretim okul müdürlerinin etik davranişlarinin incelenmesi* [Examination of the ethical behavior of elementary school principals]. (Unpublished master's thesis). University of Gazi, Ankara, Turkey.

Lashley, C. (2007). Principal leadership for special education: An ethical framework. *Exceptionality, 15*(3), 177–187.

Millett, S. (2002). *Toward an ethical school.* Retrieved from www.wmich.edu/ethics/pubs/vol_xiv/ethical_school.pdf

Narayanasamy, K., & Lama, J. A. K. (2008). Study of ethical values and practices in academic programmes at a higher learning institution. *Journal of Applied Sciences, 8*(8), 1354–1370.

Starratt, R. J. (1991). Building an ethical school: A theory for practice in educational leadership. *Educational Administration Quarterly, 27*(2), 185–202.

Starratt, R. J. (2004). *Ethical leadership.* San Francisco: Jossey-Bass.

Valentine, S., Godkin, L., Fleischman, G. M., & Kidwell, R. (2011). Corporate ethical values, group creativity, job satisfaction and turnover intention: The impact of work context on work response. *Journal of Business Ethics, 98*(3), 353–372.

Yılmaz, G. (2007). *Akademisyenlik mesleğine yönelik etik kodlarin geliştirilmesine ilişkin görgül bir araştırma* [An empirical research on developing ethical codes for academicians]. (Unpublished master's thesis). University of Celal Bayar, Manisa, Turkey.

# 24

## PREPARATION OF INTEGRITY

### WILLIAM C. FRICK AND JOHN F. COVALESKIE

US preparation standards for advanced programs in educational leadership call for state certification candidates who complete preparation programs to have, among other things, the knowledge and ability to promote the success of all students by acting with integrity, fairly, and in an ethical manner.[1] This higher education preparation standard for principals, superintendents, and other building-level or central office administrative ranks has been with us in the US for some time and is part of a seven-standard program of preparatory study leading to the attainment of most state-level licensure criteria. These standards are for the preparation of the novice and are controlled by professional governing associations, including the Interstate School Leaders Licensure Consortium (ISLLC), the Educational Leadership Constituent Council (ELCC), the National Policy Board for Educational Administration (NPBEA), and the National Council for Accreditation of Teacher Education (NCATE).

Typically referred to as the "ethics standard," the narrative description of the standard covers a range of concerns as it relates to moral school leadership (NPBEA, 2002):

> Standard 5.0 Narrative Explanation: This standard addresses the educational leader's role as the "first citizen" of the school/district community. Educational leaders should set the tone for how employees and students interact with one another and with members of the school, district, and larger community. The leader's contacts with students, parents, and employees must reflect concern for others as well as for the organization and the position. Educational leaders must develop the ability to examine personal and professional values that reflect a code of ethics. They must be able to serve as role models, accepting responsibility for using their position ethically and constructively on behalf of the school/district community. Educational leaders must act as advocates for all children, including those with special needs who may be underserved.

Table 24.1 Standard 5 as it appears in the NPBEA (2002) Standards Document (p. 13)

| Standard 5.0: Candidates who complete the program are educational leaders who have the knowledge and ability to promote the success of all students by acting with integrity, fairly, and in an ethical manner. | | |
|---|---|---|
| **Elements** | **Meets Standards for School Building Leadership** | **Meets Standards for School District Leadership** |
| 5.1 Acts with Integrity | a. Candidates demonstrate a respect for the rights of others with regard to confidentiality and dignity and engage in honest interactions. | a. Candidates demonstrate a respect for the rights of others with regard to confidentiality and dignity and engage in honest interactions. |
| 5.2 Acts Fairly | a. Candidates demonstrate the ability to combine impartiality, sensitivity to student diversity, and ethical considerations in their interactions with others. | a. Candidates demonstrate the ability to combine impartiality, sensitivity to student diversity, and ethical considerations in their interactions with others. |
| 5.3 Acts Ethically | a. Candidates make and explain decisions based upon ethical and legal principles. | a. Candidates make and explain decisions based upon ethical and legal principles. |

In detailing the meaning of the standard, there are three "elements" specified: A leader "acts with integrity," "acts fairly," and "acts ethically" (see Table 24.1). A more detailed examination of the three-pronged standard indicates what *integrity* means: "Candidates demonstrate a respect for the rights of others with regard to confidentiality and dignity and engage in honest interactions" (NPBEA, 2002).

What we argue in this chapter is that the NPBEA is correct in supposing that integrity is important for educational administrators (and educators in general) but that the standard suggests the NPBEA is quite confused about what integrity is. Integrity has nothing, in itself, to do with "respect for the rights of others" or "confidentiality and dignity" in interactions with others, though it is correct in specifying honesty, which is part, but far less than all, of *integrity*.

For example, it can be suggested that members of the Ku Klux Klan are committed, as a significant part of what constitutes their integrity, to not respecting the rights or recognizing the dignity of people of color; the Boy Scouts in the United States are committed, as part of what forms their integrity, to not respecting the rights or recognizing the dignity of gay and bisexual men and boys;[2] many religious traditions are similarly committed to not recognizing the rights or dignity of women. It certainly may be the case that respect for the rights and dignity of others is part of integrity, but only if one's integrity happens to be formed around such commitments. This is related to our other central point: Integrity is not, in and of itself, a virtue or a virtuous achievement, though one cannot properly be said to be virtuous if one lacks integrity. Integrity is a necessary component of virtue, but not a sufficient one. Perhaps it is the intention of the NPBEA to indicate that honesty, recognition of dignity, and respect for others must be part of the integrity around which professional identity is formed, but that is not what they say.

We are going to focus on the meaning of ethics and integrity, their relation to each other, and the role of virtue (implied, though not named, in the standard) in the development of ethical educators. We will approach this inquiry by first considering the nature of integrity and its relation to identity. We will then consider the relationships among integrity, virtue, and virtuous practice.

To begin, consider that integrity is more complicated than the NPBEA standard allows. One could have professional integrity and/or private integrity (civic integrity? familial integrity? community integrity?) independently of each other. For example, the corporate executives described by Robert Jackall (1988) have integrity on the job; they live by and defend an honor code that would be familiar in Homer's warrior culture, but that is not how they live in their churches or families. As a corollary, we will focus on the formation of professional integrity, since we are concerned with the preparation of professional educators generally and school administrators in particular. However, a background assumption, not argued for here, is that in the ideal world one carries integrity from one context to the next; one not only lives undivided within one's various roles, but also carries a *core* integrity across the spaces between one's roles. Another way of putting this is that one's life is better, all things considered, if one does not have to become a totally different person as one commutes to work in the morning, and again as one travels home in the evening.

What, then, is it we consider when we reflect on *integrity*? At root, *integrity* indicates wholeness, one-ness, unity. By derivation, it has come to mean *honesty*, but this is a metaphor: The honest person has *integrity* because there is unity among his or her words, practices, and beliefs. However, integrity is a bit more complex than that.

First, integrity must be about something morally significant. This does not mean that the core of one's integrity has to be morally *correct*, just that it is morally *significant*. So, for example, if one's deepest commitments have to do with being entertained, we would hesitate to grant that person integrity, no matter how deeply and wholeheartedly that commitment were held. Being entertained is just not the sort of thing around which integrity can form: It lacks sufficient moral weight.

On the other hand, the core of integrity can be morally significant but corrupt. Don Corleone is such a compelling figure because he is deeply committed to a consistent set of principles, but they are not morally justifiable. Or, more precisely, the principles themselves are admirable (e.g., loyalty to friends, family, dedication to work), but these goods were unmediated by a properly moral self, resulting in the commission of evil. One definition of evil, we would argue, is the unmediated pursuit of one good such that one is content to perpetrate evil outcomes in the guise of what has been linguistically neutered as "collateral damage."

Finally, we can be committed to a core set of principles that are per se evil—for example, white supremacists who are honestly committed in an identity-conferring way to the subjugation of people of color. National Socialists in Germany were committed to protecting the "purity" of the German people and Aryan race.

These examples indicate three ways in which integrity can (and often does) go horribly wrong. They also suggest another complication in properly understanding integrity: It makes as much sense to talk about the integrity (and the conscience) of the *profession* as of the *professional*. There are serious implications of this fact in the age of simplistic accountability unaddressed in the NPBEA standards.

What integrity means is that the ethical commitments that are part of one's personal identity will also guide one's professional practice. That is not to say that one's actions will be identical in different situations, since the conditions and surrounding circumstances will be different. However, the degrees of difference between the various environments in which one person can act with integrity are limited. It is difficult to imagine, for example, a Roman Catholic bishop serving on the board of directors of Planned Parenthood. If there were a person who served in both roles, we would be justified in wondering how one person could do both: We would be justified, that is, in wondering whether the person had integrity. On the other hand, a parent who is also a teacher will certainly not act identically the same in both roles, but the person of integrity will be able to identify a consistency across domains.

So a person can have integrity and not be a good person. One cannot, however, be a good person if one does not have integrity; that is to say, even if one is a good administrator, acting properly out of prudence or clear bureaucratic guidelines or political common sense, such is not the making of a good *person*. A good person acts virtuously because he or she is virtuous. An important premise for our argument is that a good person is more likely to make a good educator than a person who is not first good: Deficiencies in a person's character are not very easily (or as a matter of fact, likely to be) corrected by even very good professional preparation (education, training, apprenticeship, or the combination thereof). *The individual's character matters.*

We do not have much to say about the standard to act fairly. Reference to *acting fairly* and *acting ethically* as two different elements of the ethics standard, however, indicates that there is some confusion about the meaning of *acting ethically*, at least as applied to educators. One cannot act ethically and unfairly: To act unfairly is to violate the core ethical demands of the profession. Acting fairly is an example of acting ethically, not a complement to doing so.

This suggests a peculiar point about professional ethics: The term *professional ethics* is a redundancy (Green, 1987, p. 105). One cannot be a professional educator (or anything else) if one is not practicing according to the *standards of that profession*. And the standards of a profession, we note, are both of craft and moral norms. It is unremarkable to note that incompetence is a violation of professional norms. What is remarkable, and frequently overlooked, is that the ethical—the moral—norms of a profession are just as much central to membership in the professional community as are the norms of technical craft. This is why we identify violations of the moral norms of a profession as *unprofessional conduct* or *conduct unbecoming the profession*. This sort of failure is not a failure of skill but a failure to understand the point of the profession, or at least a failure to practice according to that understanding. These judgments are quite distinct from a judgment of *incompetence*. What is particularly interesting is how these terms map: *Incompetence* denotes a lack of skill, but to be truly *unprofessional* requires one to misapprehend the very meaning of the practice as evidenced in attitude and conduct. We will discuss briefly some of the implications of this insight for professional preparation in the final section of this article. But one implication we should briefly note here: When the state of the profession is such that we believe we solve the problem of "professional ethics" by offering a course in the subject, the battle appears to be already over. Professional ethics is not an add-on to professional practice; it is at the core. It is, therefore, not a separable part of preparation of ethical professionals (Covaleskie & Howley, 1994).

What appears to be well intentioned with respect to this particular preparation standard is nonetheless inaccurate and misguided. Firstly, the meaning of integrity as defined within the preparation standards framework is insufficient to the intended task; and secondly, how can higher education faculty prepare candidates to act with integrity (even if the definition were correct)? What does it mean to "learn" to act with integrity or to be moral? What does it mean to "teach" such things?

We propose to address these two issues by examining the complicated and nuanced nature of integrity and, ultimately, its relationship to professional preparation when such a focus on dispositional and characterological aspects of candidates appears to pertain more to longer processes of social development and identity formation, either within or outside the profession, than the acquisition of technical educative or administrative knowledge and skills. We will first consider the relationship between virtue and ethics and then consider how they connect to the development (or the existence) of integrity.

## ETHICS, VIRTUE, AND INTEGRITY

To begin with, we should stipulate that there are (at least) two different meanings of the concept of *ethics*. On the one hand, we use the word to describe a personal attribute of an individual: A person is (or is not) said to *be ethical,* by which we mean the person in his or her personal life is generally known to do the right, true, good, and/or praiseworthy thing. On the other hand, we often use the term *ethics* to describe obligations specific to some particular, usually professional, activity. We speak here of what are generally referred to as *professional* or *practical ethics.* Ethical codes such as described in the previous section from the NPBEA are codes of conduct—ethical conduct—specific to the performance of particular professional duties.[3]

One problem with such codes of ethics is that they tend to be minimal—that is, they set the standards below which practice cannot be allowed to fall. In addition, they tend to assume that professional ethics can be considered apart from any question of personal ethics; that is, the model is that what matters is what one does on the job, not the sort of person one is.

Integrity is an attribute of the person's character. Students in formal university-based preparation programs are often surprised when they consider a precise definition of integrity. Their surprise is often manifested in an initial refusal to consider a strict, technical understanding of the word that has no apparent moral flavoring. Strictly defined, integrity means that one is integrated. Being integrated as a person comprises the consistency of assumptions, beliefs, values, espoused ethics, actions and behaviors (morality), commitments, principles, and forms of reasoning. The operative notion is that one is consistent, not that one must "engage in honest interactions or demonstrate respect for the rights of others" as the NPBEA standards would have us believe. In addition to this notion of consistency is the understanding that a person's value system may evolve over time while still retaining integrity if the holder of any given value system accounts for and resolves perceived or internal inconsistencies or frankly adjusts her moral commitments.

Sometimes the word "authentic" is used as a substitute for this notion of consistency. But authenticity has a traditional flavoring, conjuring up notions of a characterological attribute that is socially positive or at least conveying the notion of being true to oneself and "of necessity being in mutually affirming relationships with others" (Starratt, 2004, p. 71). Irrespective, it is doubtful that authenticity really captures what we mean when we consider integrity in precise terms (Taylor, 1991).

In the context of ethical formation, integrity means that one is committed to certain standards of behavior and judgment; standards one does not lightly violate. At its strongest, integrity is simply the commitment that I will do, or not do, certain things; act, or not act, in certain ways. Integrity, then, is a part of what we mean by *identity*.

While integrity is not a virtue, it is a moral achievement, and one cannot be said to have virtue without it. In our postmodern age, it is sometimes suggested that the self is so divided that integrity is unrealistic—that what is moral shifts from context to context according to the different norms of different moral communities. As indicated earlier, Jackall (1988) gives us a clear example of people who lack integrity. He explores the moral universe of corporate managers, mostly men, who act in ways on the job that they would condemn as family men and citizens (and, significantly, vice versa). And it is not that they act immorally on the job and morally off the job; it is that what counts as moral on the job is different from, *and in conflict with,* what counts as moral in the men's families, churches, and communities.

The claim we are making is that the goal in having integrity is to be able to live our different roles without grossly distorting our moral commitments as we move from one role to another. This is not quite the same as saying we do not act differently, taking into account the morally significant different contexts from role to role. It is, on the other hand, to argue that integrity demands that the moral architecture that guides our decision making in one context or role be compatible with the moral architecture that guides us elsewhere. The self who inhabits the role of, say, *parent* should not have to condemn the self who inhabits the role of superintendent of schools or principal, though probably that self will act somewhat differently in these roles. Again, integrity is complex.

## VIRTUE AND VIRTUE'S MERIT

Before engaging directly with the central problem presented in this chapter, an important consideration, made explicit, can further frame our argument and bring clarity to the particular vantage point we are taking with respect to integrity. There are primarily six ethical "paradigms" (moral themes or orientations) commonly referenced within the field of education (and specifically within educational leadership). These ethical perspectives, typically articulated as theories of duty, guidance for individual ethical decision making, expressions of relational morality, or guidance for establishing moral school environments, comprise the basis from which much of the theoretical and empirical literature exists. These six "paradigms" are: (1) justice, (2) care, (3) critique, (4) profession, (5) community, and (6) virtue. Among them, virtue has arguably received the least attention but has relatively recently enjoyed renewed examination within the field of educational leadership. As such, there exists a literature that speaks directly to an aretaic quality of self in view of one's own and other's flourishing. These works articulate specific traits and dispositions necessary to think, and ultimately act, morally as an educator. Starratt (2004) suggests that becoming a moral school leader requires the development of traits of responsibility, authenticity, and presence. Begley (2005), on the other hand, identifies the motivations and dispositions of reflective self-honesty, relational sensitivity, and dialogical openness as indispensable qualities of character that are necessary to lead in diverse democratic school communities.

The significance of virtue is an important moral insight going back to the time of Aristotle's (1989) *Nicomachean Ethics* (c. 334–323 b.c.e.) which instructs us that it is not necessarily what you do, but who you are, that counts morally.[4] Good deeds flow from good character formed through habit, and this basic moral premise finds its relevance in the arenas of both private and public life. A strict ethics of character is limited, though—it does not tell us specifically how to act; virtue is a matter of judgment, not of rule following. In the *Nicomachean Ethics,* Aristotle's description of virtue as the settled disposition to do the right thing, in the right way, at the right time, and for the right reasons (1106b) is probably as accurate a description of virtue as we can give, but it is certainly not action-guiding. Only the application of good judgment (in Aristotle, *phronesis,* usually translated as *wisdom* or *practical wisdom*) can translate a virtuous character into virtuous action and a virtuous life.

Character must be complemented with action. What might be suitably enhancing for this ethical tradition? Possibly a complex understanding of what practical wisdom entails in order to educate and lead for the good—knowing that both characterological disposition and action are required in order to educate and lead morally. In such a case, integrity could be viewed as a special kind of indispensable, executive function of character (e.g., hinting at Aristotelian notions of courage) that informs both the personal and moral dimensions of life (McFall, 1987) connoting both disposition and action.

## A CAVEAT

A distinction can be made between professional ethics and moral professionalism (Higgins, 2003), both signifying important aspects of the moral life of any "professional" doing her work in any given field. Such a claim assumes a differentiation for our enterprise between the latter as *matter,* or particular occupational norms pertaining to the activity of education as initiation, and the former as *manner,* or procedures, modes of conduct, and professional principles of duty incurred through roles and relationships (see Peters, 1966), both of which then must issue through character into performance.

Although occupational norms can be powerful in directing and informing work-related judgment and behavior, and while personal qualities or characterological dispositions of the educator cannot be easily dismissed (Banner & Cannon, 1997), professional ethics are with us, for good or ill. Complete, free-standing courses are often dedicated to a single preparation standard, such as Standard 5. Virtue consciousness may serve as an arena that bridges preparation work for occupational socialization into the normative dimensions of specific kinds of work (school leadership at all levels) and the more explicit educative processes pertaining to the teaching of ethics (Branson, 2006, 2007). Exploring integrity, not as a virtue per se but as an essential aspect of being virtuous, might be a place to start—and that exploration might very well involve a very serious and sustained process of *self-reflection* (to be presented later in this piece) within preparation contexts.

## INTEGRITY, IDENTITY, AND THE POSTMODERN NATURE OF SELF

Possibly the traditional doctrine of mental and moral health that requires a coherent sense of identity (self as realized) is flawed and we are indeed living in a postmodern world where persons carry the potential for many selves realized in different social settings. If "roles" are *merely* constructions (possibly understood as simply social role playing), then perhaps "we are not apt to find a single, basic self to which we can be true" (Gergen, 1995, p. 136). This contested territory is subject to a further and more sustained look at the malleable prospects of social reality as proposed by postmodernist thinking. Here, an examination of integrity as role congruence that simultaneously corresponds with the life of the inner self is most necessary if we are to consider important issues pertaining to professional preparation.

However, this understanding of human life is not really something recently discovered. The realization that we live divided lives not only precedes the postmodern; it also precedes modernity. Shakespeare, for example, in *As You Like It*, tells us: "All the world's a stage / And all the men and women merely players: / They have their exits and their entrances; And one man in his time plays many parts." Earlier than that, Sophocles gave us the conflict between Ismene and Antigone, sisters to Polynices and citizens of Thebes. Ismene gives priority to her identity as a citizen and obeys the prohibition against giving Polynices the burial ritual demanded by tradition; Antigone gives priority to her identity as Polynices's sister, thus earning punishment at the hands of Creon, the ruler of Thebes. Part of Sophocles's message for us is that this sort of irreconcilable conflict between our identities is what can make human life tragic (http://records.viu.ca/~johnstoi/sophocles/antigone.htm).

What is different in our time is that maintaining integrity is a great deal more difficult than it was in past ages, when we lived in small, intimate communities where the multiple roles of the complex self were performed in front of overlapping audiences. Our integrity is complex, with some differences expected between what guides action in different roles, but there still remains an "I" that chooses (1) what roles one will inhabit and (2) how one will inhabit them.[5] Antigone *had to choose* between the demands of her different social roles precisely because, in a small community like Thebes, she could not be a sister *here* and a citizen *there*. The same was true for Ismene. They were forced by circumstances to discover their identity and then to reveal it. In contrast, in the anonymity of today's cities and suburbs, *we live in a world not so much of divided selves as of discrete social settings.* The anonymity of our social world makes a lack of integrity more possible and the attainment and maintenance of integrity more difficult. It is possible to decouple one's roles.

Nevertheless, it remains true that there are limits to the extent to which conflicting roles can be inhabited by the same person if that person has integrity. This is not just a matter of what we would normally call "morality" (which is often organized primarily around sexual behavior), but also what Aristotle more broadly conceived of as the "good life." One of the ideas at the root of the Aristotelian ideal of *eudaemonia* (variously translated as "thriving," "happiness," or the good life) is that the more comfortably the disparate parts of one's life fit together, the better the life. The opposite, the discovery that one's identity-conferring roles are incommensurable, can easily lead to tragedy. This is why integrity is special—it performs a kind of executive function for the virtues, or perhaps is formed recursively by them.

We are forged by our commitments, but we also get to choose at least some of what those commitments are. One is born—thrown into—reality and is situated from the first, but then one must make choices, however constrained those choices are by our starting points. Morally normative communities shape and change us, *but the reverse is also true.* As Viktor Frankl (1984) tells us, "Between stimulus and response there is a space. In that space is our power to choose our response. In our response lay our growth and our freedom" (p. 87).[6] Choice is an important consideration when exploring the notion of identity and integrity because personal volition might be capable of cutting through a provocative analysis made by Gergen (1995):

> I believe we must abandon the assumption that *normal* [italics ours] development equips the individual with a coherent sense of identity. In the richness of human relations, a person receives varied messages about who he is. Parents, friends, lovers, teachers, kin, counselors, acquaintances all behave differently towards us; in each relationship we learn something new about ourselves and, as the relations change, so do the messages. The lessons are seldom connected and they are often inconsistent.
>
> (pp. 142–143)

Is it possible to choose our way through the convoluted and tangled "no big picture" narrative of self-formation, adopt moral commitments, and act upon them consistently? Is there a self that integrates the "messages"? Does the "I" in fact provide a big picture by integrating the different roles one plays? Gergen correctly points to what we observe above: The roles we play in a complex society are often discrete and disconnected. However, that in no way implies there is no "I" negotiating the spaces between these roles. We here have a different way of making the point raised in the discussion of Antigone and Ismene. Our society *allows* a lack of integrity as part of "normal development" in a way that, it seems, traditional societies and small, close-knit communities do not. That is not necessarily a good thing.

A more subtle illustration related by Gergen (1995) points to the very serious and complicated issue we are exploring:

> The behavior and appearance of others inspire self-change, but the setting in which we encounter other persons also exerts an influence. For example, work situations consistently reward serious, steadfast, Calvinistic behavior. But for a

person to act this way in all situations would be unfortunate, especially when the situation demands spontaneity and play. No one wants to live with the Protestant Ethic twenty-four hours a day; in this sense, the office door and the door to one's home serve as signals for self transformation.

(p. 141)

Consensual (co-created) realities of work and home can be ill formed and clearly jeopardize personal integrity, as well as the range of moral dissonance one might experience internally as a result of any number of ascribed moral commitments.

Our position here is that there is an "I" and that the informed self decides which way is proper to act, and where. Integrity, in this instance, can be viewed as the result of balancing and negotiating these different roles without psychological damage and/ or choosing those roles that are not violently opposed to each other. As an illustration to further our point, and harkening back to our earlier reference to the evolving value system of a novice aspirant, Notman (2008, 2010) emphasizes the "interlocking features of value-based self-development" (p. 8), which further elaborates our argument for the promotion of an integrated self (Figure 24.1).

Lynne McFall (1987) explores the nature of integrity by arguing that integrity is expressed in consistency of a certain kind. If I lay claim to commitments I do not in fact have, I am simply a hypocrite. But if I say that I value honesty, and I act accordingly in most areas of my life but routinely cheat in specific circumstances (say, in business), then I lack integrity. I am divided.

In addition, integrity requires more than obedience to a set of rules or conformity with the expectations of others. We must act in accordance with a norm, not merely in compliance to some rule. As McFall puts it: "A *merely* conventional relation to one's principles seems to rule out personal integrity. One must . . . make one's principles . . . one's own" (p. 6). Or, as Thomas Green describes it, "A dog does not lie, but that is not because he is honest" (personal communication). For me to have integrity, my moral commitments and principles must be *mine*. Stephen Carter (1996) adds

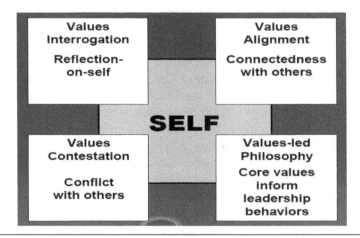

Figure 24.1 Values-based model of self-development (Notman, 2008, p. 8).

another condition: "Integrity grants no credit for being honest about your beliefs unless you have gone through a period of moral reflection, not just to be sure what your beliefs are but to be sure that your beliefs are right" (p. 58).

McFall acknowledges that integrity is not so easy to come by, and considers the possibility that we might better just give up integrity as a goal. However, she rejects this option by saying, "Without integrity, and the identity-conferring commitments it assumes, there would be nothing to fear the loss of, not because we are safe, but because we have nothing to lose" (p. 20).

This point of having nothing to lose without integrity is why we ask our undergraduate pre-service teachers and graduate administrator aspirants to consider: What would they happily and proudly be fired for, or resign over? Asking this question gets at the heart of what it means for them to be educators. If they have no answer to the question, they have no integrity (as an aspiring teacher or administrator), and being a teacher or school leader does not have (morally significant) meaning for them. It may be possible to say that such people know how to teach or how to administer, but *they do not know what it means to be an educator.*

## MORAL JUDGMENT AND INTEGRITY

This brings us to the relationship between personal and public morality, an inevitable question for educators. While public school educators may inhabit what Neuhaus (1986) calls the *naked public square,* that is, a secular public area in which it becomes difficult to make explicitly moral claims, they nonetheless are aware of the responsibility they have for the moral formation of their students (even if that is not always the way we talk about this aspect of the profession).

The educational task is to teach children why the particular rules they face matter.[7] It is not enough that they know what the rules are; it is necessary that they become invested in the norms of the society, that they feel the rules as binding (Durkheim, 1925/1973). The goal is that children will become the sort of people who do the right thing not because they will be rewarded for doing so, nor because they will be punished for not doing so, but *because it is right.* In the preparation of educators, then, the task is to instill an understanding of the moral norms and responsibilities of the profession and to make those norms matter. How do we help educators become the sort of people who live by their highest ideals even when no one is looking?

This all takes place in a social context: Our moral formation is an achievement, but not an entirely individual one. We are members of social groups and public institutions, not just individuals. While the central theme of the Enlightenment has been the development and liberation of the autonomous individual, this is a very incomplete view of what it means to be human: It ignores the extent to which we come to be in community, that we are formed by and with others. We are born into social groups as members and only become individuals over time.

Our individuality is formed in and by a normative community. A society that creates only a "thin" social consensus, while leaving the "thick" normative communities disconnected from each other, forgets the importance of personal integrity maintained across roles and does not help the young to develop it or adults to practice it.

This is the problem that Blacker (2007), Kunzman (2006), and Purpel and McLaurin (2004) all address in different ways, recognizing that schools must not violate the liberty of conscience protected by the First Amendment, but at the same time considering ways that a thick public conversation can take place between people and communities about moral disagreements related to shared civic life.

This points up the educational task: Children need to come early to understand the need for integrity and the importance of forming it around collectively informed commitments and principles. Further, as the child matures and comes into the complexity of social interaction and varied roles to play, developing integrity becomes more difficult to do. A person who enters a professional or career role without integrity already developed is less likely to develop it on the job when faced with conflicts between personal morality and professional morality. Under such circumstances, maintaining integrity is difficult enough; achieving it when it does not already exist strikes us as well-nigh impossible.

## INTEGRITY IN THE LIFE OF THE SCHOOL

Up to this point, we have been discussing questions of integrity in a fairly abstract and general sense. The reader is entitled to be asking what it might be like to work in an institution that takes the task of fostering integrity seriously. Before beginning that description, however, we just note in passing that there are further complications yet to be mentioned, though not explored—a task for another scholarly project.

We have been speaking of integrity as an attribute of individual persons, which it certainly is. On the other hand, it also makes metaphorical sense to talk of institutions, schools specifically but not exclusively included, having (or not having) integrity. When a school has integrity, it is organized and intentionally operated with fidelity to principled commitments mindfully and deliberately chosen. Note that an institution can consist of individuals with integrity and yet not, itself, have that attribute: The members of the school community could well be individuals with integrity whose commitments do not well integrate or jell. Without this shared set of commitments, the institution will not have integrity, though its members do. It probably goes without saying that the institution cannot have integrity if individuals in it do not.

How, then, can a school help foster integrity in both its children and adults? We will explore two examples of educators working on the integrity of their children, their institutions, and themselves. The first example is of Deborah Meier, the legendary principal of the Central Park East Schools in New York City. In *The Power of Their Ideas*, Meier (1995) tells this story, in which she describes her method of addressing discipline problems in her school, or at least one specific example of such a problem. Meier is not interested in manipulating children through rewards and punishments, as the following story makes clear:

> I recently had a conversation that gave me a good deal to think about. Two students had gotten into one of those stupid quarrels. The origins were silly. But what became clear was that one of the kids was a "victim"—over and over he was the subject of teasing and other minor cruelties on the part of his

classmates. Everyone knows about it, including we adults. We worry, feel bad, get angry and end up doing very little good.

I asked the student about it and he agreed that the other student was indeed the target of a lot of peer cruelty, and also that the reasons were silly, petty, and unkind. "Which side are you on?" I asked. "His side or his tormentors?"

We were both startled by my question. He said he wasn't really on any side.

I didn't stop, because I was busy thinking about it myself. So I pushed. "If someone is being cruel to someone else, if someone is the victim and someone the victimizer, rapist and [raped], abused and abuser—can you really be neutral?"

He paused. "No," he said, "I'm never with the abusers."

What we realized was that there were two questions here and they were getting mixed up together. (1) Whose side am I on? And (2) what am I prepared to do about it?

(pp. 86–87)

For our purposes, what is significant about this exchange is that although there is almost certainly a rule in Central Park East Middle School against bullying and hitting other students, the conversation is not about rules. Quite the contrary, she is, in effect, asking the student what sort of person he is. The discussion is less about what the student *did* than who he *is*. This question is the beginning of integrity. Certainly, there is no guarantee that the young man will continue to develop integrity, but Meier has, we suspect, made that more likely, which is probably all we can do.

It is also worth noting that Meier's response to the bullying episode was a function of her own integrity in commitment to the task of education for democratic life. She responded the way she did because she had become the person she was. One of the differences between education for integrity and education for obedience is that the response of the adults cannot be programmed, as is the case with commercial programs of classroom management; we cannot routinize human development, though we can find ways to restrict it. How do we build institutions that not only foster the development of integrity in the young, but also affirm and solidify integrity in adults?

In *The Moral Life of Schools*, Jackson, Boostrom, and Hansen (1993) describe what they call "upward hypocrisy" among the teachers they observed. They do not mean by this what we usually mean when we talk of hypocrisy: pretending to be someone we are not for some sort of gain; either a politician currying favor or anyone seeking to gain the regard and confidence of others by pretending to be what they are not. By *upward* hypocrisy, they mean to describe teachers acting better than their "true selves" when they are in front of the classroom and conscious of being role models for their children. We think Jackson and colleagues are perceptive in their description, yet we would disagree with the notion that this upward hypocrisy does not reflect the teachers' "true" selves. Rather, we would say that this hypocritical state is their aspiration, and is indeed their best true selves, even if they do not always manage to live up to that ideal. This practicing the virtues we do not yet have, but want, is precisely the process of moral development that Aristotle described long ago in the *Nicomachean*

*Ethics*: The exercise of virtues requires skills specific to those virtues. Consequently, we learn to be adept at virtue the same way we learn to be adept at piano playing: We practice. The point here is that the teachers Jackson et al. (1993) describe are practicing virtue they wish they had, or they would not be practicing them. This is quite different from pretending to be patient, for example, because one is being observed by a colleague or a supervisor.

We all know teachers whose behavior with students causes colleagues to cringe and who are themselves oblivious. One of us once worked with a first-grade teacher who spoke loudly and with contempt to her students. We all heard her and we rolled or averted our eyes, but no one confronted her about her behavior, and she herself gave no indication that her colleagues seeing her behavior discomforted her in any way. Our point is that to want to behave well with our students so we will think well of ourselves (as opposed to so that others will think well of us) is an indication of who the teacher really is. Upward hypocrisy tells us something very important about the teacher's moral architecture: It tells us what virtues the teacher holds as important to the meaning of what it means to be a teacher. And we can infer that the reason these teachers work to realize their ideal selves is that these are the moral and ethical commitments they bring into the classroom, and integrity requires them to try to live wholly, to exhibit the virtues in the demanding environment of the classroom that they hold as desirable outside it. Again, by analogy, the same argument can apply to administrators.

## COMING FULL CIRCLE: PREPARATION REVISITED

Most students in professional preparation programs can readily engage in purely cognitive tasks—understanding and communicating the language of well-established ethical paradigms within the field of education: justice, care, critique, community, profession, and an emerging virtue literature. The pedagogical problem is that a purely academic understanding, through associated course exercises, does not sufficiently engage students in deep exercises of self-awareness, reflective practice, and transparency. These kinds of "disruptive" classroom experiences and exercises appear to be necessary in order for educator aspirants to engage the notion of integrity. What kind of preparation pedagogy might lead to the transformative shifts in character that result in a genuine appreciation for integrity and its importance in the modern occupations, and for education in particular? Given the importance of this aspiration, it is important to ask if this pedagogy is possible and what it might look like.

Recent changes in US preparation standards, as limited and deficient as they are, might hold some insight into this problematic and challenging endeavor for education faculty in colleges and universities across the US and elsewhere. The progression of first-draft revisions of Educational Leadership Constituent Council Preparation Standards (NPBEA, 2009), based upon a similar reworking of the standards of the Interstate School Leaders Licensure Consortium (2008), and most recently promulgated by the National Council for Accreditation of Teacher Education as the latest higher education program standards of NPBEA, state the following as it pertains to ELCC Standard 5.0:

ELCC 5.1: Candidates understand and can act with integrity and fairness to ensure a [school/district] system of accountability for every student's academic and social success.

ELCC 5.2: Candidates understand and model principles of self-awareness, reflective practice, transparency, and ethical behavior as related to their roles within the [school/district].

ELCC 5.3: Candidates understand and can safeguard the values of democracy, equity, and diversity within the [school/district].

ELCC 5.4: Candidates understand and can evaluate the potential moral and legal consequences of decision making in the [school/district].

ELCC 5.5: Candidates understand and can promote social justice within the [school/district] to ensure that individual student needs inform all aspects of schooling. (NPBEA, 2011a, pp. 18–19; NPBEA, 2011b, p. 20)

Once again, no attempt is made to define integrity (although, interestingly enough, the age of simplistic accountability mentioned earlier in this article is straightforwardly connected in "element" 5.1). What is encouraging, at some level, are the enumerated "elements" that resemble some of the arguments we have been making in this article, particularly element 5.2.

Structuring and guiding student self-examination in the context of classroom coursework dedicated to Standard element 5.2 appears to be a sensible and responsible pedagogical approach for professors of professional preparation seeking to illuminate the importance of personal and moral integrity as part of professional identity. This work would involve more than asking pointed questions, as we have illustrated earlier. A more accurate conception of curricular and pedagogical approaches for engaging novice aspirants calls for what Derrick Bell (2002) describes as learning how to refuse to compromise one's beliefs through self-examining humility. This kind of intentional classroom endeavor would necessarily call upon pre-service administrators and teachers to demonstrate developing levels of a self-integrative perspective by exploring the relationships between their deep-seated (tacit) assumptions, beliefs, and moral commitments; the various social roles and positions they hold; and the profound professional work they are to perform as educators (most likely in formal public school contexts).[8]

In what in some ways could be seen as a paradoxical experiment, students could be asked to confront both congruity and incongruity between the inner person and role assumption, all requiring some measure of passion, courage, and risk taking. Reflective self-examination might hopefully spark reflective self-honesty—clearly a transformative learning experience (Polizzi & Frick, 2012). To illustrate the centrality of "integrity work," Branson (2010) has offered a reconceptualization of a popular diagrammatic used within the field (see Figure 24.2). And although he addresses the idea of integrity differently than we have here, we see value in integrity's integrative dynamic—integrity is a moral achievement, a fundamental dimension of character

**Figure 24.2** Integrity as central to a multiple ethical framework (Branson, 2010, p. 7).

that is central to the moral life. Branson (2010) illustrates his view this way: "If it is possible to reduce . . . [the] tendency to be influenced by self-deception, impulsiveness and a lack of self-control, then not only is . . . inner freedom reinforced but also . . . moral integrity is consolidated" (p. 5).

How can the discovery of a whole-person kind of integrity (rather than a utilitarian, role-specific kind of "professional" coherence) be encouraged and developed in formal university and college classroom settings? Several approaches come to mind, such as variations of psychodrama and related role-playing activities that require some dimension of impromptu expression (Smith, 1990; Sogunro, 2004) where students might "discover" more about themselves as they move and improvise; or narrative/appreciative inquiry that focuses on incorporating writing and the writing process into experiential learning opportunities (Rapparlie, 2011; Rich, 2012), both possessing the pedagogical *processural* potential for student self-discovery and reassessment. In our effort to improve upon our own practices, Branson (2006, 2007, 2010) offers important insights related to the arguments and pedagogical issues we have tried to enumerate here. He has carefully laid out educative materials and techniques that support what he calls *structured self-reflection*. Through an organized and documented process, students can be encouraged to examine their Self (an "inside-out approach") by attending to the leveled yet fluid dimensions of their person.

As space does not allow for a full review of these works and related teaching practices, we will suggest that experimenting with, and quite possibly fully utilizing, a range of related activities might lead to significant improvements in the way preparation programs deal with stand-alone ethics courses in order to address regulatory agency-driven preparation standards. Needless to say, novice and developing educators of all kinds need our help in understanding the importance of integrity and how one might acquire it—now more than ever.

Nor is it sufficient to allow this focus to be relegated to courses in professional ethics (though this is not to say such courses should not be included in the preparation of educators). If Green (1987, p. 105) is correct and "the term professional ethics is a redundancy," the implication is that *every* course in the preparation of professional educators must be built around a clear ethical vision of the internal meaning of professional practice. As an example of this, one of us recalls his finance professor building the course around the thesis that a school budget is a statement of moral principles and ethical commitments: How a district and building administration allocated limited resources tells, far more powerfully than any "vision statement," what is considered central to the practice of *education* there. Here we see integrity as pedagogically promoted in formal preparation to illustrate that it quite necessarily should be part of the life of the educational community. If this is not the case, if ethics is only a course, that is an indication that the moral life of the enterprise has been given up, and integrity, to the extent that it exists at all, is formed around things that do not matter very much.

## NOTES

1. Similar regulatory specifications are made available for teacher preparation faculty for pre-service teachers as well.
2. In recently reaffirming their policy of discrimination against gay and bisexual scouts and scout leaders, the Boy Scouts of the United States say the following: "After careful consideration of a resolution asking the Boy Scouts of America to reconsider its longstanding membership standards policy, today the organization affirmed its current policy, stating that it remains in the best interest of Scouting and that there will be no further action taken on the resolution."
3. This dual use of "ethics" is probably rooted in the Aristotelian recognition that living well is as much a practice, as much a skill (*techne*), as is building a ship. In these terms the two modern English uses express a single reality: Properly doing some practice requires some skill, not just to do it, but to do it in accordance with the purposes and methods proper to that practice. Thus, the exercise of skill (*techne*) is internal to a practice and is an expression of one's character (*ethos*).
4. Though this distinction may be more of heuristic than practical value; what we do is obviously an indication and expression of who we are. Thus, Aristotle argues that a good man should never experience shame once he is fully matured because good men are men who do not do shameworthy things.
5. We each, as principals, were different than another inhabiting that same role, though there must also be similarities if we are both in the role of *principal*; we each, as principals, acted in some ways differently than we did as fathers, though there was a consistency in the self who performed both those roles.
6. A social and behavioral sciences librarian at a Carnegie-classified "research intensive" university has searched for the legitimacy and source of the quote. The librarian indicates that although there are many ideas that are similar to the quote in Frankl's works, she believes that Stephen Covey's ascription of the quote to Frankl might be misplaced. Alex Pattakos (2010) features Covey in the foreword of his book *Prisoners of Our Thoughts*. Subsequently, Covey writes, "While on a writing sabbatical in Hawaii and in a very reflective state of mind, I was wandering through the stacks of a university library and picked up a book. I read the following, which literally staggered me and again reaffirmed Frankl's essential teachings: *Between stimulus and response, there is a space. In that space lies* [sic] *our freedom and our power to choose our response. In our response lies* [sic] *our growth and our freedom.* I did not note the name of the author, so I've never been able to give proper attribution" (Pattakos, 2010, p. vi). Attributing this quote to *Man's Search for Meaning* probably got started with one of Covey's bestselling books, and the misattribution has taken hold. We offer here a similar statement to the one presented in the article understanding the contextual basis of the statement as referring to Jewish internment in Nazi concentration camps: "Fundamentally, therefore, any man can, under such circumstances, decide what shall become of him—mentally and spiritually" (Frankl, 1984/1946, p. 87).
7. This, in turn, entails that the rules educators establish and enforce do in fact matter—that they are not made merely out of habit or for one's own convenience, but that they connect to serious moral purposes of education and life. Herein lies the difference between teaching children (and teachers!) to be *good* and teaching them to be *obedient*.
8. And quite possibly, as a result of such an exploration, students will adopt newly formed moral commitments. One of us used to teach a course in professional ethics to practicing and aspiring administrators in which he used to tell his students that they would be examining their stated beliefs about education in such a way that by the end of the course they might consider changing either their beliefs or their practices.

# REFERENCES

Aristotle. (1989). *Nicomachean ethics*. (M. Ostwald, Trans.). New York: Macmillan.

Banner, J. M., & Cannon, H. C. (1997). *The elements of teaching*. New Haven, CT: Yale University Press.

Begley, P. T. (2005). *Ethics matters: New expectations for democratic educational leadership in a global community*. University Park, PA: Rock Ethics Institute.

Bell, D. (2002). *Ethical ambition: Living a life of meaning and worth*. New York: Bloomsbury Publishing.

Blacker, D. J. (2007). *Democratic education stretched thin: How complexity challenges a liberal ideal*. Albany: State University of New York Press.

Branson, C. M. (2006). *In search of authentic leadership*. A Learning Links professional development course with Brisbane Catholic Education Primary School principals.

Branson, C. M. (2007). Improving leadership by nurturing moral consciousness through structured self-reflection. *Journal of Educational Administration, 45*(4), 471–495.

Branson, C. M. (2010). Ethical decision making: Is personal moral integrity the missing link? *Journal of Authentic Leadership in Education, 1*(1), 1–8.

Carter , S. (1996). *Integrity*. New York: Harper Perennial.

Covaleskie, J. F., & Howley, A. (1994). Education and the commons: Issues of "professionalization." *Educational Foundations, 8*(4), 59–73.

Durkheim, E. (1973). *Moral education: A study in the theory and application of the sociology of education*. (E. Wilson & H. Schnurer, Trans.). New York: Free Press. (Original work published 1925)

Frankl, V. E. (1984). *Man's search for meaning*. (Revised and updated). New York: Simon & Schuster. (Original work published 1946)

Gergen, K. (1995). The healthy, happy human being wears many masks. In W. T. Anderson (Ed.), *The truth about the Truth: De-confusing and re-constructing the postmodern world* (pp. 136–144). New York: Putnam.

Green, T. F. (1987). The conscience of leadership. In L. T. Sheive & M. B. Schoenheit (Eds.), *Leadership: Examining the elusive* (pp. 105–115). Reston, VA: Association for Supervision and Curriculum Development.

Higgins, C. (2003). Teaching and the good life: A critique of the ascetic ideal in education. *Educational Theory, 53*(2), 131–154.

Interstate School Leaders Licensure Consortium. (2008). *Educational leadership policy standards*. Reston, VA: National Association of Secondary School Principals.

Jackall, R. (1988). *Moral mazes: The world of corporate managers*. New York: Oxford University Press.

Jackson, P. W., Boostrom, R. E., & Hansen, D. T. (1993). *The moral life of schools*. San Francisco: Jossey-Bass.

Kunzman, R. (2006). *Grappling with the good: Talking about religion and morality in the public schools*. Albany: State University of New York Press.

McFall, L. (1987). Integrity. *Ethics, 98*(1), 5–20.

Meier, D. (1995). *The power of their ideas: Lessons for America from a small school in Harlem*. Boston: Beacon Press.

NPBEA [National Policy Board for Educational Administration]. (2002). *Standards for advanced programs in educational leadership for principals, superintendents, curriculum directors, and supervisors*. Washington, DC: National Council for Accreditation of Teacher Education.

NPBEA. (2009). *Educational leadership program standards: ELCC revised standards/for advanced programs that prepare principals, superintendents, curriculum directors, and supervisors*. Washington, DC: National Council for Accreditation of Teacher Education.

NPBEA. (2011a). *Educational leadership program standards: 2011 ELCC building level*. Washington, DC: National Council for Accreditation of Teacher Education.

NPBEA. (2011b). *Educational leadership program standards: 2011 ELCC district level*. Washington, DC: National Council for Accreditation of Teacher Education.

Neuhaus, R. J. (1986). *The naked public square* (2nd ed.). Grand Rapids, MI: Eerdmans Publishing.

Notman, R. (2010, April). *Fire in the heart, ice in the brain! Rekindling the human spirit of educational leaders*. Paper presented at the New Zealand Educational Administration and Leadership Society (NZEALS) Biennial Conference, Christchurch, Canterbury.

Notman, R. (2008). Leading from within: A values-based model for principal self-development. *Leading and Managing, 14*(1), 1–15.

Pattakos, A. (2010). *Prisoners of our thoughts: Viktor Frankl's principles for discovering meaning in life and work* (2nd ed.). San Francisco: Berrett-Koehler Publishers.

Peters, R. S. (1966). *Ethics and education*. London: George Allen & Unwin.

Polizzi, J. A., & Frick, W. C. (2012). Transformative preparation and professional development: Authentic reflective practice for school leadership. *Teaching & Learning: The Journal of Natural Inquiry and Reflective Practice, 26*(1), 20–34.

Purpel, D. E., & McLaurin, W. M. (2004). *Reflections on the moral & spiritual crisis in education*. New York: Peter Lang.

Rapparlie, L. (2011). *Writing and experiential education: Practical activities and lesson plans to enrich learning*. Bethany, OK: Wood 'N' Barnes.

Rich, S. J. (2012, October). *From data to wisdom: Leadership for the 21st century*. Paper presented at the 17th Annual UCEA/CSLE conference "Ethics, Values & Leadership." Brisbane, Queensland, Australia.

Smith, C. (1990). Theatre of spontaneity. *National Forum, 70*(3), 38–39.

Sogunro, O. A. (2004). Efficacy of role-playing pedagogy in training leaders: Some reflections. *Journal of Management Development, 23*(4), 355–371.

Starratt, R. J. (2004). *Ethical leadership*. San Francisco: Jossey-Bass.

Taylor, C. (1991). *The ethics of authenticity*. Cambridge, MA: Harvard University Press.

# 25

## STRIVING FOR MORAL PURPOSE

### CHARLES BURFORD AND MICHAEL BEZZINA

In 2004 a group of Australian educators embarked on an international expedition to Canada, the United States, and the United Kingdom in search of answers to questions about the impact, if any, of leaders on learning in schools and the characteristics of such leadership. The literature was enthusiastic but inconclusive (Hattie, 1999; Leithwood & Reihl, 2003; Marzano, 2003), despite a growing political and popular interest in student outcomes, standards, and the place of leaders in the learning process. The group was deeply influenced by meetings with Professor Jerry Starratt of Boston University, who challenged the group to look to the nature of authentic learning and the leadership processes that seemed to best influence such learning. This challenge led to an ongoing collaboration between Starratt and the authors in a search for a conceptual model of leadership for learning premised on a shared understanding of what constituted authentic learning. The issue that confronted the authors was the debate over learning outcomes and what constituted authentic learning. This question of what outcomes are worth pursuing, and why, is seldom raised by educators as they pursue policy on standard testing regimes, national curriculum, or reform agenda (Bezzina, Starratt, & Burford, 2009). The failure to expose the fundamental values or moral purpose of the educational enterprise, with the same kind of scrutiny as the means by which it is realized, has created an important gap in the discourse. Starratt says of this gap:

> Educators miss this connection because they are accustomed to view the learning agenda of the school as an end in itself, rather than as a means for the moral and intellectual filling out of learners as human beings.
>
> (2007, p. 266)

This missing connection lies in experience of moral purpose in schools—a construct elusive and yet fundamental to the success of schools and the work of their leaders.

This chapter tells the story of the Leaders Transforming Learning and Learners (LTLL) research project that emerged from this collaboration (Bezzina, 2008; Bezzina & Burford, 2010; Burford & Bezzina, 2007; Starratt, 2012) and in particular how this framework for leading for learning with a strong emphasis on moral purpose impacted on teacher perceptions, teaching practices, and leadership within the project schools in Australia from 2005 to the present.

The research reported on the importance of building shared moral purpose but recognized it as a sophisticated enterprise that requires leaders to navigate the complexities of modern schools in times that are ethically ambiguous. The complexity lies often in the challenge for leaders to choose between two "goods" rather than a "good" and a "bad" (Duignan, 2003; Duignan & Burford, 2003). Educational leaders in complex times find themselves constantly engaged in discerning the moral purpose of a community and how best to bring it alive and nurture it in a way that will allow it to shape the educational experience. Australian education is experiencing this ambiguity in the tension between the competing purposes and outcomes of education, with the force for the classical liberal, moral character and civic development approach to education losing out to "learning to earn" reflected in the new national compulsory testing regime (NAPLAN) and the league tabling (MySchool) that ranks schools according to the performance of students. These tensions are engaging teachers, leaders, and communities alike in Australia and elsewhere on the role of morals and ethics in the process of creating authentic learning. This story about the LTLL project is offered as an insight into this tension and one attempt to give leadership and vision to the challenge of leading school communities for authentic learning outcomes.

## THE ETHICAL IMPERATIVE AND MORAL PURPOSE

The fundamental challenge of education is an ethical one, whereby the curriculum should acknowledge the moral character of learning and create a structure within which the learning agenda of the school connects to the central moral agenda of the learners during their 13 or more years in school—that is, the agenda of finding and fashioning themselves as individuals and as a human community (Starratt, 2007). This challenge calls on each school to be clear and explicit about its moral purpose and to build consensus around it.

However described, moral purpose has been consistently identified as one of the fundamental necessities for bringing about the kind of change and improvement that will deliver desirable student learning in schools. For the purposes of this study it can be understood as the commitment to ends that express underlying values and ethics. In the particular context of schools, the commitment is ultimately to the transformation of the learner into a fuller, richer, deeper human being. Klaassen (2012) sees this construct as a form of courage in educators that has three components:

(1) the courage to retain certain professional and moral standards and to promote the development of moral norms and values in one's students; (2) the perseverance to adhere to the goals of well-being of the pupil who is in need

of the daily help and strength of the teacher to reach the cognitive, social and moral goals of the school; and (3) the will and competence to function as a moral example.

(p. 20)

Klassen's approach focuses on the relationship of the characteristics of individual teachers or leaders and how these influence pupils and others in the educational community. While moral purpose has many other expressions, almost all of them include this notion that such purpose should be shared and/or pervasive in some way. Rationally, a purpose that is not shared belongs to the individual rather than the organization and is unlikely to impact on overall performance. The National College of School Leadership (2006) describes shared moral purpose as "a compelling idea or aspirational purpose, a shared belief [a team] can achieve far more for their end users together than they can alone."

Another Australian project, titled IDEAS, focused on school improvement and shared this commitment to shared purpose being grounded in a shared commitment to explicit values (Andrews & Lewis, 2004). In other words, it is not sufficient to have a broad aspiration—there needs to be clarity and detail in the way the purpose is understood, and in particular about the values that underpin it. It has been demonstrated that clear and explicit dialogue about these values has a mutually reinforcing relationship with the emergence of a sense of shared leadership (Bezzina & Burford, 2010).

The most fundamental question—the essence of moral purpose—for educators is this: "What should I do if I am to make a genuine difference in the lives of my students?" It can be argued that educators achieve this when they infuse academic learning with a dimension of personal meaning, and thereby enrich the whole learning process (Starratt, 2004). This authentic learning is more than taking new knowledge and skills for oneself, and broader than the quest for relevance. It is about giving of one's unique humanity to others and to the community. The facilitation of authentic learning is a fundamentally moral activity because it engages students in a deeper understanding of the nature and purpose of their lives and in determining how they can best contribute to the greater good of the community and society (Hodgkinson, 1991). Learning which is not authentic to the needs of the student's life is not only inappropriate but also unethical. In other words, an educator who contributes to practices that are not authentic is engaging in behavior that is morally wrong (Starratt, 2012). This challenge goes to the very heart of what educators do, and was the stimulus for the LTLL project that is described in the next section.

## THE LEADERS TRANSFORMING LEARNING AND LEARNERS PROJECT

The LTLL project aims to explore how leadership and learning practices based on a shared moral purpose might facilitate the work of teachers and leaders in enhancing student learning. It is an initiative that combines dimensions of professional development, school improvement, and research, situated in a sample of schools in New South Wales, Australia. The pilot phase (2005–2006) included 9 primary and secondary schools from four systems; phase 2 (2007–2009) involved 11 primary and secondary schools from five school systems; and phase 3 (2010–2012) involved all 17 primary schools in a rural Catholic school system.

The full project methodology is described elsewhere (Bezzina, 2008; Bezzina & Burford, 2010; Burford & Bezzina, 2007; Starratt, 2012). In brief, schools have been involved, with support from their systems and Australian Catholic University, in a combination of university- and school-based activities, which critically applied a values-based conceptual framework to leadership for learning. Schools reflected on perceptions.

The conceptual framework that is at the heart of the LTLL initiative is an attempt to capitalize on the growing consensus in the literature around leadership and learning behaviors that have been shown to enhance student learning (Leithwood, Bauer, & Riedlinger, 2007; Marzano, Waters, & McNulty, 2005; Robinson, 2007). This consensus extends to such issues as the importance of the quality of the teacher, primacy of assessment for learning, whole-school approaches to planning and implementation of curriculum, shared moral purpose, and the need to link leadership and learner. The set of values and ethics that capture the shared sense of moral purpose and are central to the project were identified through workshops involving an expert group of school and system representatives, which formed the steering group for the pilot study.

The feedback from the pilot phase gave rise to the framework in Figure 25.1.

In this framework, the moral purpose is expressed in the values and ethics espoused by a school, and its sense of a transformed learner. This moral purpose influences the exercise of educational leadership and the approaches taken to authentic learning and gives rise to a strong sense of teacher as leader (Bezzina, 2008; Bezzina & Burford, 2010; Burford & Bezzina, 2007; Starratt, 2012).

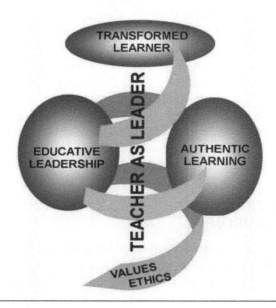

**Figure 25.1** The LTLL conceptual framework.

The elements of the framework are summarized below. In the second and third phases of the study (LTLL 2 and 3), schools worked with these elements, with a detailed set of focuses for each element and indicators for each focus, as a basis for reflection.

## ELEMENTS OF THE LTLL CONCEPTUAL FRAMEWORK

*Values*

Values shape behaviors (Ajzen, 2005) and thus are seen as foundational in the vision of the framework. If a school genuinely holds particular values, these should be visible in both the life and the rhetoric of the school. Different schools may choose to name different values as central to their activities. This perspective follows the position of Begley and Johansson (2003), who in discussing the tendency for scholars in educational administration to adopt the words *ethics* or *moral* as umbrella terms for anything values related, espouse the values definition of Campbell-Evans (1991), Leonard (1999), Begley (2000), and Hodgkinson (1996):

> They reserve the term ethic or principals for a particular and very special category of transactional values and employ the word values as a generic umbrella term for all forms of "conceptions of the desirable."
>
> (Begley & Johansson, 2003, p. 4)

The LTLL model proposed five such values as being basic to Catholic schools involved in the projects. These were developed by an expert group of senior system representatives, school personnel, and Australian Catholic University faculty involved in the study. They were: Catholicity, justice, excellence, the common good, and transformation. Different school communities and different systems would likely choose different sets of values or "conceptions of the desirable." Lopez (2013) highlights a different attempt to capture the generic values of education in her analysis of the Six Pillars of Character developed by the Josephson Institute:

> based on common values applicable to all, regardless of gender, race, age, politics and religion. These values . . . are trustworthiness, respect, responsibility, fairness, caring and citizenship.
>
> (p. 185)

All of these values surfaced to varying degrees in the research into core values for LTLL. In a recent iteration of the model with schools in South Australia that were former Dominican Order schools, a completely different set of values were generated, specific to that particular order; however, like the Six Pillars, respect, caring, and trustworthiness were identified as core to this group as well. The critical issue is not the *nature* of the values but that there is an explicit and owned value platform. This study reports on some of the dimensions of working with such a set of values.

## Ethics

Ethics are the norms and virtues by which members of a community are bound to a way of living out their desirable and preferred values. Starratt (2004) suggests that they are maps that we consult only when the familiar terrain we are traversing becomes a tangle of underbrush. He names three particularly significant ethics, which were adopted for this study: authenticity (calling for integrity in interactions), presence (calling for relationships that are open and engaging), and responsibility (recognizing personal and corporate accountability). Starratt uses the term *virtues* to describe the living out of these three ethics, suggesting that he sees them clearly as a personally preferred priority of values that teachers and leaders can bring to their leadership roles in schools. This model was preferred in the development of the LTLL conceptual model to the more commonly used ethical schema developed by Shapiro and Stefkovich (2001) of justice, care, critique, and the profession.

## The Transformed Learner

The desirable values and ethics that form the basis of the model give rise to a particular set of aspirations for the learner. Transformed learners will take delight in both the subject and the process of learning, for which they take responsibility as part of a lifelong journey, as shown in Fink's (2005) taxonomy, with its emphasis on learning how to learn and become a self-directed learner. Their growing understanding reflects a rigorous, critical, and respectful approach to the subject matter and to their fellow learners. They will be committed to their own growth—physical, intellectual, social, and spiritual. Transformed learners will engage actively with society as citizens seeking to make a difference. The values and ethics already named, and the vision of the transformed learner, give rise to particular approaches to leadership and learning.

The elements of educative leadership, authentic learning, and teacher as leader are the vehicles by means of which the moral purpose is given expression.

## Educative Leadership

Educative leadership is understood as the capacity to influence others in order to enhance student learning. Research identifying key features that distinguish good leadership of learning (Leithwood & Reihl, 2003; Marzano et al., 2005; Robinson, 2007) informs features in this model that embody the values and ethics already discussed. They are: leadership through collegiality, leadership based on evidence, leadership for professional learning, leadership for sustainability, leadership building culture and community, leadership for effective change, leadership through networking, and leadership building capability.

## Authentic Learning

Authentic learning is the very heart of the schooling enterprise. It is the most profound manifestation of the moral purpose, which is captured in its vision of transformed learners. Research has identified a set of features that has been shown to impact positively on learning outcomes (Cuttance et al., 2003; Hattie 1999; Marzano, 2003). These are represented in LTLL as standards for learning, organizing for learning, pedagogy, student engagement, and assessment *for* and *as* learning. In LTLL, each of these is seen as a potential point of influence for the leader, and its implementation needs to be in accord with espoused values and ethics, using the types of leadership behaviors already identified.

### Teacher as Leader

The quest to transform the learning of students challenges teachers to engage in leadership in new and more authentic ways (Duignan & Bezzina, 2006; Harris, 2002). It is through the actions of teachers living out their values and ethics as educative leaders, and in the provision of authentic learning for students, that this transformation will take place. Teachers as leaders have a clear and explicit understanding of the nature of the transformed learner. They are explicit about and committed to the values and ethics underpinning the development of transformed learners. They are skilled in the creation of authentic learning experiences and are contributors to the educative leadership of the school.

## TEACHERS' PERCEPTIONS OF ELEMENTS OF MORAL PURPOSE

### Purpose of the Study

This study tested the significance of the conceptual model that had been reconceptualized after the first LTLL Project (Burford & Bezzina, 2007). The study incorporated a variety of data sources. These sources included a pre-intervention reflective instrument focusing on key elements of the model: moral purpose, authentic learning, educative leadership, teacher leadership and the resultant transformation of the learner, focus group interviews with participating teachers and principals, and journals and Wii-based discussions among participants following an extended engagement with the program. These data were used to chart the success of the model and to enhance it for application in the LTLL 3 phase, which is also reported here.

The conceptual framework described above has informed—and been informed by—the implementation of phases 1, 2, and 3 of the LTLL project. Given the significance of moral purpose, there is comparatively little research data about how teachers understand it and how they see it operating in their schools. One of the objectives of this phase of the LTLL project has been to improve understanding of this aspect of leadership for learning. This chapter shares some of the findings of the second and third research projects.

## METHODOLOGY

*LTLL 2.* The full LTLL 2 sample comprised 11 case study schools, 5 secondary schools, and 6 primary schools, drawn from five Catholic educational systems in New South Wales. The schools were nominated by their systems. Two of these systems are based in country cities and the other three are in metropolitan Sydney. Forty-five teachers made up the 11 project teams that were part of this study. Each project team included the principal, at least one other person in a formal leadership role, and one younger teacher with no formal role. The whole project was designed and managed collaboratively by representatives of the Australian Catholic University, the case study schools, and the systems to which they belonged. The schools were the focus of analysis, and data for the study were gathered through the use of a Reflection Guide built around the conceptual framework, and through in-depth interviews at the conclusion of the second year of the project.

School teams used the LTLL Reflection Guide to rate their school's performance on each focus in each element of the model, using a three-point "traffic light" scale (red = not in evidence, amber = unsure, green = clearly in evidence) and to nominate the sources of evidence for their rating. The Reflection Guide was a refinement of the one used in the pilot (Bezzina, 2008; Burford & Bezzina, 2007). At the conclusion of the workshop, each school had developed a profile of its current performance at the commencement of LTLL. This was then used as a basis on which schools decided on an improvement initiative, and it constitutes a benchmark measure for each school. During 2008 and 2009, schools came together periodically to engage critically with elements of the framework and to refine their school-based initiatives in the light of this experience. They were also supported in an ongoing way by staff of their school systems as they applied their learning to their school improvement initiative. The Reflection Guide was completed again at the conclusion of the LTLL intervention at the end of 2009.

Subsequent to the completion of the developmental element of the LTLL project, a research assistant, who had had no role in the project to date, interviewed each school's project team. There were 11 core questions for these interviews, conducted with each of the 11 school teams. These questions were:

1. How has the LTLL experience impacted on your school in terms of sense of moral purpose?
2. How has the LTLL experience impacted on your school in terms of school leadership?
3. How has the LTLL experience impacted on your school in terms of classroom practice?
4. How has the LTLL experience impacted on your school in terms of staff collaboration?
5. How has the LTLL experience impacted on your school in terms of student engagement in learning?
6. How has the LTLL experience impacted on student outcomes?
7. How has the LTLL experience impacted on your school in terms of the learning culture?
8. How has the LTLL experience impacted on your school in terms of the evidence used by teachers?
9. What has been your most significant learning from LTLL?
10. What were the biggest challenges you faced? How did you address them?
11. What have you achieved through LTLL? What in particular helped you do this?

These interviews were transcribed and then analyzed to identify emerging themes. In LTLL 2, the themes identified were: sense of moral purpose, school leadership practice, classroom practice, staff collaboration, student engagement, student outcomes, learning culture, use of evidence, learnings and challenges. These themes were interrogated through the lenses of the conceptual framework in terms of moral purpose, educative leadership, authentic learning, and the transformed learner.

*LTLL 3.* The LTLL 3 phase (2010–2012) of the study was researched, and the design and methodology varied in some important elements from LTLL 2. This phase included all 17 primary schools from a Catholic system set in rural New South Wales. Some of these schools are amongst the state's most isolated, and some also have high numbers of indigenous students. In addition, unlike LTLL 2, where leadership teams and a young teacher made up the LTLL team of three or four people, LTLL 3 involved all teaching staff. This phase included 269 participating teachers and 17 principals. This variation from the existing practice of the involvement of a leadership team from participating schools was caused by the desire of that system leadership to in-service all teaching staff in the district around the LTLL model and the availability of federal and state government funding for such reform activities. This funding was titled the Partnership Schools Project and was designed to impact on the level of literacy and numeracy in primary schools through the utilization of school improvement models that had a leadership framework within them. The earlier success of the LTLL 2 model made it ideal for the kind of reform required for Partnership Schools. This research also involved the regional leadership team and superintendent.

The number of schools and their isolation necessitated the offering of LTLL 3 in four regional centers of Western New South Wales, with a spacing of 6 months between the programs for each group. The research design for this study replicated that of LTLL 2 except for the elements outlined above concerning numbers and the nature of the staff groups involved.

## RESULTS OF LTLL 2 AND 3 RESEARCH

Analysis of the interview transcriptions for both groups yielded a number of emergent themes under each of the elements of the conceptual framework. These were tallied according to the number of schools in which each theme occurred. Table 25.1 reports those themes that emerged in 5 schools or more, as giving a sense of a significant consensus. The first frequency shown is for the 11 schools of LTLL 2 (2007–2009) and the second is for the 17 schools of LTLL 3 (2011–2012).

An analysis of the emergent themes for each element of the framework gives rise to a pattern that can be described as including four components. While there is no evidence yet for their sequential nature, there is a certain logic to describing them as such, with an implicit movement through each phase as described below.

### Attention

The attention phase involves focusing on a particular issue and giving it some priority.

**Table 25.1** Emergent themes organized under elements of the framework

| Element of the model | Themes | Frequency (number of schools 11/17) |
| --- | --- | --- |
| Moral purpose | Teachers reflected on authenticity and learning | 9/15 |
| | There was a clearer sense of purpose | 8/14 |
| | Moral purpose had a major impact on practice | 7/15 |
| | There was a greater focus on authentic learning | 5/13 |
| Educative leadership/ teacher as leader | Enhanced professional dialogue | 9/15 |
| | Increased focus on teacher leadership | 8/16 |
| | Development of teachers as leaders | 8/14 |
| | Teachers taking greater initiative | 7/14 |
| | More sharing of responsibility | 6/15 |
| | Practice of leadership team has changed | 6/10 |
| | There were increased levels of trust | 6/13 |
| Authentic learning | Teachers work together more | 10/15 |
| | Classroom practice has changed | 10/16 |
| | Evidence of practice was collected | 10/11 |
| | Different ways of thinking about teaching and learning | 9/15 |
| | Changed culture of learning | 9/12 |
| | Teachers used new methodologies | 9/13 |
| | Teachers used evidence to assess student outcomes | 9/12 |
| | Teachers used evidence to reflect on teaching and learning | 8/14 |
| | Greater sharing of resources | 8/14 |
| | Learning tasks are more authentic | 7/14 |
| | Teachers asked deeper questions about teaching and learning | 7/11 |
| | Practice was more student centered | 7/15 |
| Transformed learner | Students were more motivated and engaged | 10/16 |
| | The program was transformational | 8/14 |
| | Students achieved at a higher level | 8/11 |
| | Students took more responsibility for their learning | 8/15 |
| | Students learned at greater depth | 6/12 |

*Reflection*

This is the process of engaging intellectually—and perhaps emotionally—with the ideas and their implications.

*Response*

Taking action as a consequence of having given consideration to some aspect of practice.

*Outcome*

The consequences of having acted in particular ways.

These four phases can be mapped against the responses in Table 25.1.

Turning first of all to moral purpose, responses indicate *attention* in the form of a clearer sense of purpose, and in particular a greater focus on authentic learning as an aspect of this. Teachers *reflected* on authenticity and learning and the *response* took the form of a new sense of moral purpose, which had a major impact on practice. The interview data support this way of understanding the dynamic.

The importance of *attention,* and the extent to which it was part of the LTLL experience, is clear in the words of one interviewee:

> So a lot of people actually stopped and thought, "Why am I here and why am I doing this?"

A young teacher in an LTLL 3 school talked about LTLL as being a "big brush" experience:

> [It] made me actually think about what I was doing because quite often you go into cruise control and do things like old habits. This made me actually think about what I was doing.

One teacher captured the way she reflected on moral purpose and how it impacted on her in these words:

> I was thinking more of me personally as a teacher because when this all started I'd only taught for 2 years and I never once at Uni or I don't know if it was the first year here but I'd never once heard anything about moral purpose. I just knew I wanted to be a teacher, didn't think about why or anything. Learning about this transformational learning, I can't go back. I can't go back and teach any other way. If I go to another school I have no idea what I'm going to do because I now have to teach this way, I've had to change personally.

Once she focused on the question of moral purpose and engaged in reflection on it, it drove a personal response in the way she taught—a change that she argues will go beyond the parameters of her present school.

With respect to educative leadership and teacher leadership, we see *attention* through increased focus on teacher leadership. One participant described this in connection with the way that staff meetings were run:

> And next year we're building on this by changing our whole model of staff meetings and so on so that we have the focus on teacher leadership.

*Reflection* is frequently reported as taking place through enhanced professional dialogue, as in the case of this secondary science department:

> Teaching staff now want to learn more. I mean, I walked into the KLA [Key Learning Area] meetings in the past, in science, for example, and the head of

science was using one of the [LTLL] articles to open professional discussion with the rest of the staff. Now, that's . . . yeah, that's a big change, and it, alright, initially, probably a year ago I kind of said, this needs to be part of your agenda, whereas now it's happening on its own again.

The *response* to this kind of reflection took the form of greater sharing of responsibility, teachers taking greater initiative, and changed practice within the leadership team. In the words of one participant:

There's been a shift from the leadership team doing everything, or the old LTLL team doing everything, to teachers actually taking responsibilities at their own level to do things.

A primary *outcome* of this emerging understanding of leadership has been the development of trust, named explicitly by 6 of the 11 schools in LTLL 2 and 16 of the 17 schools in LTLL 3. This increased response may be due to the presence of the entire staff in the latter program. Trust is given great significance, as captured by this comment:

People trust one another. Not completely everyone but they're getting there. It's that you're not going to judge me; you're going to help me. That's huge, it's really big.

The impact of the LTLL experience in building that trust was identified explicitly by the teacher who said, "The element of trust has grown as a result of the process that we've been through."

With respect to authentic learning, we see attention operating in the form of a changed culture. A typical comment was: "Now we have a culture of questioning and I think that's crucial," and there was widespread recognition (from 9 of the 11 schools in LTLL 2 and 12 of the 17 in LTLL 3) that LTLL had contributed to this. One of the best insights came in this observation of what had occurred, reflecting on the observations of an ex-member of staff who was now an occasional visitor to the school:

Because he comes in occasionally, he really notices the change in culture, and it's a lot easier for him than it is for us, and he said one of the significant things he has seen is a change in educational culture, and pedagogical culture and he said, that's the hardest thing to do. He said, I can really see that shift there. He said, "I was as guilty as anyone around here of thinking, these kids can't achieve very much academically so why bother?" I would have thought he was a fairly conscientious guy, but he said that, you know, there was a culture of saying, well look, these kids are never going to be fantastic, so therefore we just set the mark there. And we've, I think we've moved beyond that, and I get a real sense that, you know, there's a shift there.

This commentary on the renewed culture embodies the idea of having adopted different ways of thinking (*reflection*). The data in Table 25.1 identify a number of *responses* in the form of working together, changed classroom practice and new methodologies, and greater use of evidence, including its use to reflect on outcomes and on teaching and learning practice. For example, in one school they made the following observations about the new approach to the use of evidence:

> I believe what we will see is that the conversation around the evidence about children's learning will become, and I do mean this, more authentic, more responsible. Not that it wasn't in the past, but I have a feeling that some people were doing things because they'd done it for a while and that's how we do it. Now we have a culture of questioning and I think that's crucial.

A system leader in LTLL 3, when commenting on overall outcomes for all the schools, said:

> They now all talk very strongly—and that is at all levels, from the office through to principals and school staff—about the sense of evidence-based learning. It is very clear that they understand what evidence is. They're not just always looking for evidence being a number. They're seeing that evidence has a variety of forms.

Student centeredness, identified by 7 schools in LTLL 2 and 15 in LTLL 3, was a key aspect of the participants' experience and was summed up by one interviewee in these words:

> It isn't about the teachers, it's about the children. Sometimes that can get a bit lost in life.

This refocusing on the centrality of the student led to *outcomes* in the area of changed classroom practice and increased emphasis on authentic tasks, as captured in these observations:

> The children are now really questioning the value of their learning and she [the teacher] says it keeps her on task as well; to make sure what she's doing is truly authentic. So we really do believe, the four of us, that there have been enormous shifts in the classroom that we have data to support.
>
> My observations are that the classrooms are far more active than they were. A comment that one of our students made when we filmed them and got their recordings of the changes was that it's better now because the teachers are doing it with us. And I thought that summed it up, because it's no longer the teacher telling them. They are learning together. . . . It's far more active and engaging and interactive. Far less teacher directed.

The results in the area of the transformed learner understandably emphasized *outcomes*. These were of two types. The first reflected the nature of student dispositions in the form of motivation, engagement, and owned responsibility. The second had to do with learning outcomes, in terms of depth of learning and achievement.

The previous quotation captures the sense of engagement among students well. Another participant emphasized the sense of self-responsibility and shared responsibility in this observation:

> We interviewed children and . . . they spoke very raw but really deep thoughts about how their learning has changed. A lot of students said the responsibility is put onto the students in how they learn and their responsibility as learners. Also the way they use each other to help them with their learning has changed. I think they're really two good points. The responsibility to be responsible for their own learning and also to share their ideas with others.

Turning to learning outcomes, the extent to which these were measurable depended on the focus of each school's initiative. Some lent themselves to quantifiable measures and recorded great success, as was the case in this school, reporting results on an externally set public examination:

> We've seen . . . that we have grown, that we can actually improve. So we don't sort of take it for granted anymore and we look at developing other areas. So particularly because we've done the math, the growth has been unbelievable, we increased by 43 percent and then we're hoping to do that with literacy, so we're putting things in place for literacy. I think it's very exciting because all our little ones in reading have reached the system benchmark—we're very excited about that.

As well as the remarkable growth in student learning here, it is worth noting the shift in perception on the part of teachers—"We can actually improve." There is almost a sense of surprise in the statement.

From another perspective, teachers observed qualitative changes in the learning, and in particular the capacity for meta-cognition:

> I think another clear student outcome lies in the students' ability to talk about their own learning. We've really very much tried to help them to develop really strong meta-cognitive skills and to be able to have those conversations about what helps them to learn better, and what's underpinning what they're being asked to do.

## LEARNINGS AND CHALLENGES

The LTLL project engaged schools in an investigation of the fundamental moral purpose of their work and the relationship between leadership and authentic learning. The processes of participant engagement were shown to follow a fairly consistent pattern of attention, reflection, response, and outcomes in these matters of essence to their learning communities. All the schools involved have viewed the outcomes for staff and students very positively.

Specifically the testing of the elements of the LTLL conceptual model have further supported some positions within the literature and validated the continuation of

LTLL as an appropriate model for meaningful school reform. One of the challenges shown in the LTLL 2 research by 8 of the 11 schools was the challenge of getting the staff to understand and support the conceptual model. The response in LTLL 3 of 14 of 17 schools supporting this suggests that this may have been affected by the whole staff being involved in LTLL rather than just the leadership team.

The linkage of moral purpose and learning has been a recurring theme in the literature in recent years and has again dominated the themes of this research, with 7 of the 11 schools in LTLL 2 and 15 schools in LTLL 3 indicating that moral purpose was now at the center of what they did. According to Sergiovanni (2007), a school built on authentic learning sets out "to transform its students not only by providing them with knowledge and skills but by building character and instilling virtue" (p. 22). Authentic learning, then, is about the transformation of the learner. For this to occur, the nature of learning as we know it needs to change. To show the impact of the model, 10 of the 11 schools importantly said that LTLL helped to transform learning in their school.

Intertwined with this acknowledgment that learning became more authentic was the issue of moral purpose. For this learning to happen in a way that is both effective and sustainable, there needs to be a shared moral purpose in the learning community. This shared moral purpose, which has been the focus of many scholars' writings in recent years (Andrews & Lewis, 2004; Barber & Fullan, 2005; Bezzina, 2008; Cuttance et al., 2003; Fullan, 2001; MacBeath, 2005), again dominated the outcomes of this research, suggesting that unless there is a moral agenda at the heart of the learning community, the learning cannot be authentic (Starratt, 2004).

The conceptual framework that underpins LTLL expresses this moral purpose in the values and ethics espoused by a school, which is inextricably linked to the transformation of the learner. The "moral purpose influences the exercise of educational leadership and the approaches taken to authentic learning, and gives rise to a strong sense of teacher as leader" (Bezzina, 2008, p. 5).

The LTLL research also supports and furthers the findings of Harris (2002), Duignan and Bezzina (2006), Andrews and Lewis (2004), Burford and Bezzina (2007), and Bezzina and Burford (2010) that the construct of teacher as leader is essential to the promotion of learning in the school. This was seen to emerge through the facilitation of sharing leadership and collective responsibility taken for student learning outcomes:

I think the learning and leadership thing is important to me, that everybody is a leader, so therefore accepting that straight away that you're on staff therefore you're a leader.

And again, from an older, experienced teacher:

I found that I saw myself for the first time as a leader. I never really thought that I'd be in a leadership-type position. . . . Being in the school for a long time, I've always thought, well, I'll just be a little worker. But then I was able to see myself as a leader and recognize that I had some things to offer, which, you know but you don't actually do it until something like LTLL comes along.

Eight out of 11 schools in LTLL 2 and 16 out of 17 in LTLL 3 indicated that the LTLL had transformed their approaches to leadership. Other learnings and challenges reported were supported by the literature as enhancing student learning. These components identified in this theme included leadership through collegiality (Novak, 2008; Sergiovanni, 2007), leadership based on evidence (Leithwood et al., 2007), leadership for professional learning (Southworth, 2005), leadership for sustainability (Davies, 2008; Fullan, 2005; Hargreaves, 2005), leadership building culture and community (Caldwell, 2008; Deal, 2007), leadership for effective change (Fink, 2005; Fullan, 2004), leadership through networking (Fullan, 2005; Hopkins, 2007) and leadership building capability (Bezzina, 2008; Robinson, 2007; Sergiovanni, 2007). The research reasserts the position of Busher (2006) that it is the leader's role to build a culture that promotes engaging learning in the context of a learning community where all community members take on leadership for learning while engaging in learning for life (Fink, 2005; Ungunmerr-Baumann, & Wells, 2007). Authentic leaders in schools "not only understand the challenges of their contexts, and commit totally to ensuring such learning for all their students, they possess a philosophy, a mind set, 'a story', 'a 'stance', a value system which guides all of their leadership activities" (Fink, p. 38).

One school principal supported this position when sharing her learning about this as follows:

[W]hen you go through a leadership process as the leader . . . you just have to allow things to grow within themselves. It was pretty messy the first 6 months. You've got to live with it for a while and reflect on it and then say what did we learn from that and what are we going to do next? For me that's been great because at this end of it we can look back and we can see a tremendous amount of things that have happened, but when you're in there it's hard to see how we are going to come out the other end, so that's been very interesting.

The LTLL model provided members of the school communities with a common language with which to address issues of moral purpose, authentic leadership, and authentic learning. This is also a strength of the model, particularly since many people in schools do not "speak the same language" when it comes to such things. A common language supports a common understanding of moral purpose, which in turn fosters a greater sense of ownership and more effective collaboration. The importance of this link was supported by the observation of the superintendent in LTLL 3 when speaking about the impact of LTLL on all the schools of the system:

When you visit schools, they are able to speak a common language and they seem to have gone through a common experience. [One] of the elements of the common language they certainly know about is moral purpose and they speak of moral purpose as the real driver of what they are and who they are. They have a deep understanding of this, whereas it's quite often a concept that is missed by people.

Indeed, the research shows that the LTLL model, which essentially facilitates collaboration among teachers, succeeded in bringing people together in a way that was new and engaging. This collaborative approach, which confronts the isolation of the classroom, has also, for some, made the prospect of facing change less daunting.

One principal identified the importance of dialogue and trust to build this culture:

> But I think we underestimated the power, underestimated the value of professional conversation and actually stopping to listen to people. . . . The beginning teachers had a voice too. So I think as a team the effect of being able to openly and honestly communicate with each other was huge. That was the other thing. It was OK not to get it. It was OK not to be quite there. Despite the vulnerability of this, the trust had to be there.

Despite the challenge of engaging with a new conceptual model of learning, participants saw its utilization as possibly the most important outcome of the project. The model provided participants and members of their school communities with a common language with which to address issues of moral purpose, leadership, and authentic learning. This is also an apparent strength of the model, as many people in schools do not "speak the same language" when it comes to learning and leadership. The common language generated through the use of the model supports a common understanding of moral purpose, which in turn fosters a greater sense of ownership and more effective collaboration. Indeed, the research shows that the LTLL model, which essentially facilitates collaboration among teachers, succeeded in bringing people together in a way that was new and engaging. This collaborative approach, which confronts the isolation of the classroom, has also, for some, made the prospect of facing change less daunting.

Perhaps the interviewee who best summed up the experience of transformation resulting in her school following LTLL was the one who said:

> The transformation has not only been with the students, it's been with the teachers as well. But it's very much a journey. It's far from over. There'll be no end. It's a continuous learning journey because transformation is an ongoing process.

While the research with LTLL 3 schools was conducted, at the same time the schools had varying levels of experience with the LTLL model due to the staggered commencement of the four regional centers over a period of 18 months. While the themes identified corresponded clearly with the LTLL 2 research, other outcomes emerged. Briefly these findings included:

1. Schools are using the LTLL model and the reflection guide to make sense of other initiatives from government and systems.
2. Collaboration is the key—it increases confidence and morale, builds teams, and supports leadership.

3. Younger teachers who were given formal teacher leadership roles continued to exercise this leadership with colleagues despite cessation of targeted partnership funding from the government.
4. LTLL supplied a pool of enthusiastic leaders, both young and experienced, without formal leadership development, mentoring, and/or succession programs in place at the system level.
5. System leaders noted that LTLL had provided a common language and focus that offered potential as an ongoing renewal model for schools.

In an unanticipated outcome, possibly resulting from the compulsory involvement of schools in LTLL 3 as contrasted with the nominated volunteer experience of the earlier iterations of LTLL, a school undergoing cultural upheaval and strong discord among leadership and staff became a participant. The experience indicated that LTLL has the potential to be a circuit breaker for schools with dysfunctional cultures at both the relational and teaching/learning levels. The case in point within this research indicated the required use of the reflective guide in the early LTLL phase and subsequent dialogue, causing relationships, and learning issues at the center of the problems to be surfaced. The toxic level of these issues resulting essentially from leadership and teacher bullying, betrayal of trust, and loss of purpose necessitated both internal and external intervention for change to result; however, the role of the LTLL 3 project in precipitating these events is demonstrated in the following comment:

At the time we were all very angry and bitter and I think having those really clear questions and the traffic lights really set that up for us to talk about what wasn't working and why it wasn't working. I think it was just perfect timing because that wasn't moving. We weren't going to move past it [lack of communication and bullying from the leadership] because we were stuck . . . we were all very cranky, and we were just so angry that we didn't want to move past it because there was nowhere to go.

Acknowledging that LTLL provided the stimulus to break the stalemate, one respondent pointed to the importance of this critical intervention:

Twelve months before LTLL, we probably would have been too afraid and too stuck within ourselves to take on anything like that [change in teaching Information Communication Technology, ICT] due to fear of the wrong reaction or responses coming back to us. Whereas after that [LTLL], we thought, let's give it a go. . . . That wouldn't have happened 12 months ago.

An emotional response from a teacher who now saw meaning in her teaching and felt committed to teaching again after the staff engaged with LTLL emphasized the core issue of moral purpose as essential for authentic learning.

Children aren't silly. They know when their teachers are stressed out and they know when things aren't going right at school. Then, seeing us all being friends and helping each other, and someone jumping into our room whenever something's not right, they realize, wow, that is good. So their learning starts improving because they know that if there's a problem, we're not going to try and work it out on our own. If we can't, we're going to work with the rest, so of course their learning's going to get better.

In addition to this issue, related to the change shock effect of LTLL on a school suffering from a dysfunctional culture, was the impact of LTLL on the leadership understanding and aspirations of many young teachers in LTLL 3 schools. These young teachers were usually given substantial responsibilities for the conduct of the LTLL project, which was a point of contrast to the LTLL 2 and 1 experiences. The evidence from the whole school experience of LTLL 3 was the benefit of the broad-based leadership experiences for staff and the creation of a cadre of young, enthusiastic, and committed teachers who had experienced success in leading peers in an educational renewal experience. Their enthusiasm for further leadership experience despite an absence of formal credentials or professional development in leadership suggests this applied structured experience of leadership for learning may have potential for educational systems experiencing leadership succession problems. The following comment by one young educator, who was involved in LTLL 3 first as a teacher and then in a later group as the new leader of another school, typified this impact on emerging leaders:

It taught me strategic planning . . . so that I'm able to release some responsibility to the other leaders of the school. Not just to the people who hold roles but to everyone. LTLL gave me a good framework to be able to work and embed my learning and leadership into my everyday practice.

The findings of LTLL 2 and 3 yielded a picture of a group of schools undergoing genuine change in leadership, learning practice, and outcomes. The findings showed that teachers and leaders, when focusing on moral purpose, learning outcomes, leadership, and classroom behaviors, all tended to return to the capacity of moral purpose to trigger renewal and improvement.

## CONCLUSION

This chapter told the story of the experience of an innovative Australian education project designed to transform the learning experience of students through the utilization of a conceptual model linking moral purpose, leadership, and authentic learning. The research demonstrated the usefulness of having such a conceptual model that was valued as providing alignment focus and structure as a basis for attention, reflection, response, and outcomes to educational challenges. The schools and systems were impressed and appreciative of the way in which the moral purpose of their work—and in particular the linkage to leading and learning—were made explicit and were challenged. The use of a shared conceptual framework was also seen as giving coherence to the philosophy of sharing and the practices by which this is given expression in leadership in schools. The project has had lasting positive effects on the schools and their learning outcomes, and most participants viewed it as their best career experience of professional learning. The team that set out to discover the link between leadership and learning and found moral purpose shares this experience.

## REFERENCES

Ajzen, I. (2005). *Attitudes, personality, and behavior.* Milton-Keynes, UK: Open University Press/McGraw-Hill.

Andrews, D., & Lewis, M. (2004). Building sustainable futures: Emerging understandings of the significant contribution of the professional learning community. *Improving Schools, 7*(2), 129–150.

Barber, M., & Fullan, M. (2005). *Tri-level development: It's the system.* Retrieved from www.michaelfullan.ca/Articles_05/Tri-Level%20Dev't.htm

Bezzina, M. (2008). We do make a difference: Shared moral purpose and shared leadership in the pursuit of learning. *Leading and Managing, 14*(1), 38–59.

Bezzina, M., Starratt, R. J., & Burford, C. (2009). Pragmatics, politics and moral purpose: The quest for an authentic national curriculum. *Journal of Educational Administration, 47*(5), 545–556.

Begley, P. T. (2000). Values and leadership: Theory development, new research, and an agenda for the future. *Alberta Journal of Educational Research, 46*(3), 233–249.

Begley, P., & Johansson, O. (2003). *The ethical dimensions of school.* London: Kluwer Academic Publishers.

Bezzina, M., & Burford, C. (2010). Leaders Transforming Learning and Learners: An Australian innovation in leadership, learning and moral purpose. In A. Normore (Ed.), *Global perspectives on educational leadership reform: The development and preparation of leaders of learning and learners of leadership* (pp. 265–285). Bingley, UK: Emerald Group.

Burford, C., & Bezzina, M. (2007). *Leaders Transforming Learning and Learners: An Australian experiment in moral purpose and teacher leadership.* Proceedings of the 12th annual conference on Values and Leadership, Pennsylvania State University, University Park.

Busher, H. (2006). *Understanding educational leadership: People, power and culture.* Columbus, OH: Open University Press.

Caldwell, B. J. (2008). Enchanted leadership. In B. Davies & T. Brighouse (Eds.), *Passionate leadership in education* (pp. 175–196). London: Sage Publications.

Campbell-Evans, G. H. (1991). Nature and influence of values in principal decision-making. *Alberta Journal of Educational Research, 37*(2), 167–178.

Cuttance, P., Stokes, S., McGuinness, K., Capponi, N., Corneille, K., Jones, T., & Umoh, C. (2003). *The National Quality Schooling Framework: An interactive professional learning network for schools.* Melbourne: University Press.

Davies, B. (2008). Passionate leadership in action. In B. Davies & T. Brighouse (Eds.), *Passionate leadership in education* (pp. 91–108). London: Sage Publications.

Deal, T. (2007). Sustainability of the status quo. In B. Davies (Ed.), *Developing sustainable leadership* (pp. 87–96). London: Paul Chapman Publishing.

Duignan, P. (2003). *Contemporary challenges and implications for leaders in frontline service organizations.* Sydney: Flagship for Creative and Authentic Leadership, ACU National.

Duignan, P., & Bezzina, M. (2006, October). *Distributed leadership: The theory and practice.* Paper presented at the Commonwealth Council for Educational Administration Conference, Lofkosa, Cyprus.

Duignan. P., & Burford, C. (2003, July). *Preparing educational leaders for the paradoxes and dilemmas of contemporary schooling.* Paper presented at the British Educational Research association annual conference, Exeter, UK.

Fink, D. (2005). *Leadership for mortals: Developing and sustaining leaders of learning.* London: Sage Publications.

Fullan, M., (2001). *Understanding change: Leading in a culture of change.* San Francisco: Jossey-Bass.

Fullan, M. (2004). *Leading in a culture of change.* San Francisco: Jossey-Bass.

Fullan, M. (2005). *Leadership and sustainability.* Thousand Oaks, CA: Corwin Press.

Hargreaves, A. (2005). Sustainable leadership. In B. Davies (Ed.), *The essentials of school leadership* (pp. 173–189). London: Sage Publications.

Harris, A. (2002, July). *Distributed leadership in schools: Leading or misleading.* Paper presented at the BEL-MAS annual conference, Aston University Lakeside Conference Center, Birmingham, UK.

Hattie, J. (1999). *Influences on student learning.* Inaugural lecture, professor of education. University of Auckland.

Hodgkinson, C. (1991). *Educational leadership: The moral art.* Albany: SUNY Press.

Hodgkinson, C. (1996). *Administrative philosophy.* Oxford: Elsevier-Pergamon.

Hopkins, D. (2007). Sustaining leaders for system change. In B. Davies (Ed.), *Developing sustainable leadership* (pp. 175–193). London: Paul Chapman Publishing.

Klaassen, C. (2012). Just a teacher or also a moral example? In D. Alt & R. Reingold (Eds.), *Changes in teachers' moral role: From passive observers to moral and democratic leaders* (pp. 13–31). Rotterdam: Sense Publishers.

Leithwood, K., Bauer, S., & Riedlinger, B. (2007). Developing and sustaining school leaders: Lessons from research. In B. Davies (Ed.), *Developing sustainable leadership* (pp. 97–115). London: Paul Chapman Publishing.

Leithwood, K., & Reihl, C. (2003). *What we know about successful school leadership.* Nottingham, UK: National College for School Leadership.

Leonard, P. (1999). Examining educational purposes and underlying value orientations in schools. In P. T. Begley (Ed.), *Values and educational leadership* (pp. 217–236). Albany: SUNY Press.

Lopez, R. (2013). High-stakes testing, demographic shifts and failing schools. In W. C. Frick (Ed.), *Educational management: Exploring a professional ethic for educational leadership* (pp. 179–195). New York: Peter Lang Publishing.

MacBeath, J. (2005). Leadership as distributed: A matter of practice. *School Leadership and Management, 25*(4), 349–366.

Marzano, R. J. (2003). *What works in schools: Translating research into action.* Alexandria, VA: ASCD.

Marzano, R., Waters, T., & McNulty, B. A. (2005). *School leadership that works.* Alexandria, VA: ASCD.

National College of School Leadership. (2006). *Five pillars of distributed leadership.* Retrieved from www.ncsl.org.uk/distributedleadership

Novak, J. M. (2008). Inviting passionate educational leadership. In B. Davies & T. Brighouse (Eds.), *Passionate leadership in education* (pp. 35–56) London: Sage Publications.

Robinson, V. (2007). *School leadership and student outcomes: Making sense of what works and why.* Sydney: ACEL.

Sergiovanni, T. J. (2007). *Rethinking leadership: A collection of articles.* Thousand Oaks, CA: Corwin Press.

Shapiro, J. P., & Stefkovich, J. A. (2001). *Ethical leadership and decision making in education: Applying theoretical perspectives to complex dilemmas.* Mahwah, NJ: Erlbaum.

Southworth, G. (2005). Learning-centred leadership. In B. Davies (Ed.), *The essentials of school leadership* (pp. 75–92). London: Sage Publications.

Starratt, R. J. (2004). *Ethical leadership.* San Francisco: Jossey-Bass.

Starratt, R. J. (2007). Leading a community of learners: Learning to be moral by engaging the morality of learning. *Educational Management Administration Leadership*, *35*(2), 165–183.

Starratt, R. J. (2012). *Cultivating an ethical school.* New York: Routledge.

Ungunmerr-Baumann, M., & Wells, J. T. (2007). Education is for living and for life. In P. Duignan & D. Gurr (Eds.), *Leading Australia's schools* (pp. 139–149). Winmalee, NSW: Australian Council for Educational Leaders.

# 26

## THE ETHICAL DEMANDS OF MULTICULTURALISM

### KATARINA NORBERG AND OLOF JOHANSSON

The school is an important institution wherein political intentions about what characterizes good civic education and training are expected to be realized. Also, according to Bunar (2001), "It is a place for political aspirations and reforms through which children and young people with different social backgrounds should be given opportunities to transcend the social background constraints" (p. 18). The Swedish School Act, and curricula[1] based on its principles, has a long history of underscoring these purposes of schooling, as they have emphasized the schools' democratic mission. However, a discrepancy exists between the intention formulated at the central level and its realization at the local level, as differences between overall school performance and the performance of groups of students have increased. This chapter discusses this inconsistency with a focus on school leadership in ethnic multicultural schools. It opens with a brief account of the Swedish school's democratic mission to promote equal schooling for all students, followed by a description of student performances from a multicultural perspective and school leaders' experiences of leadership for diversity. The chapter ends by highlighting intercultural leadership and providing some examples of how Sweden's principal training program is intended to educate school leaders for diversity.

### THE SWEDISH SCHOOL'S DEMOCRATIC MISSION

The Swedish school's democratic mission began with the commission for elementary school education in 1914, emphasizing the importance of learning to be an active member of society (Folkskolekommittén, 1914). The 1946 School Commission followed Dewey's (1916/1966) argument that "a democratic society can only be created by education" (p. 87) and affirmed that the school's primary task was to foster democratic human beings. The commission asserted that citizens in a democratic society must have open and critical minds that resist undemocratic ideas. As democratic states have no use for selfish masses of people, the democratic school's primary task is to develop free people for whom cooperation is a need and creates happiness. From this text, developed during the Second World War and published just after peace came to Europe, it is obvious that schooling was treated as a moral project. These formulations in the School Commission's report remain valid today, in that school politics are always up for debate in Swedish society (Johansson & Svedberg, 2013).

The ideas of the School Commission were widely accepted in the parliament, but at the time, Sweden had a school system that sorted children in relation to their maturity and theoretical skills regarding different school subjects. Radical changes would not emerge in the school system for another 15 years. In the early 1960s, school classes became uniformly grouped by age for all schoolchildren between years 1 and 9, and 9 years of compulsory schooling became mandatory for all children. In this system, children were still divided in some subjects in relation to their maturity and theoretical skills. In the revised School Act and the new curricula, we can identify some of the thinking promoted by the school commission. However, the biggest change took effect when a new governing system was introduced in the public sector during the 1990s. The old regulating system, with its many laws and rules, was abolished and replaced with goals and objectives defined by the political level for each public sector. The new governing system came into the education sector in 1994, when the government issued curricula that were adjusted to goals and objectives. The 1994 curricula clearly explained that schools should work both with academic and social goals. The curriculum for the Swedish compulsory school (in which students usually begin at age 6 or 7 and finish at age 15 or 16) is divided into three sections: *basic school values and the school mission; general educational goals and guidelines;* and *syllabuses and knowledge demands.* The government, except for the knowledge demands, which are injunctions set by the National Agency for Education (Skolverket), determines these.

During the closing decades of the 20th century, internationalization through immigration became evident and it was generally accepted that students should be prepared for a life with people of other cultures, emphasizing equality, solidarity, and joint responsibility (Nilsson, 1997). The current curricula and the School Act stipulate that the school must impart such a worldview and shape pupils to these fundamental values upon which their society is based. The key reference points are the inviolability of human life, individual freedom and integrity, the equal value of all people, equality between women and men, and solidarity with the weak and vulnerable (Skollagen, 2010: 800 [Education Act]; Skolverket [National Agency of Education], 2010, 2011a, 2011b). This prescription applies to all staff employed in schools as well as pupils. These values are meant to saturate all school activities and constitute a common frame of reference. All who work in schools should uphold the stated values and should, as the curricula explains, "very clearly disassociate themselves from anything that conflicts with these values" (Skolverket, 2011a, p. 10).

Curricula based on these principles also promote an equivalent and equitable education for all, with the understanding that education should be adapted to each pupil's circumstances and needs, based on the pupil's background, earlier experiences, language, and knowledge, irrespective of where in the country it is provided. How this should be realized is up to the principal and teachers to interpret, based on the local school context, wherein school leaders, teachers, children, adolescents, and their guardians each have unique experiences and qualities that characterize their perceptions of what is right and wrong; what is good education, knowledge, and learning; what causes learning disabilities; and what is needed to overcome learning difficulties.

## AN EQUIVALENT AND EQUITABLE SCHOOL FOR ALL?

A substantial task for the school's leader is to develop the school's culture, structure, and organization to promote diversity from a number of aspects, such as ethnicity, gender, social class, religion, and sexual orientation. This task is not unique to Sweden. Schools are in general viewed as important social institutions, and education in particular is viewed as "a primary means of facilitating the harmonious development of a diverse society" (Lumby & Heystek, 2011, p. 5). Promoting diversity in schools is not an easy task, however, since school leaders, teachers, students, and guardians come together with different gender, socioeconomic, and ethnic backgrounds, all of which influence their respective values concerning teaching and foster a context in which these differences should not negatively affect students' education. However, schools are in general characterized as monocultural, with assimilation as an underpinning goal, whereas students with migrant backgrounds are described from a deficit perspective as "different" compared with the "ordinary" or "normal" Swedish student (Bouakaz, 2007; Gruber, 2007; Sawyer & Kamali, 2006; Runfors, 2007). This assertion is supported by Johansson, Davis, and Geijer (2007), who report an example of a monocultural organization in an ethnic multicultural school that welcomes diversity in its rhetoric while, in practice, it demonstrates a desire for assimilation. As Lahdenperä (2006) puts it, "Swedishness is the starting point for norms, ideals or goals for remedial measures and teaching" (p. 92).

This viewpoint is reflected in periodic reports from the Swedish National Agency, which demonstrates problematic statistics of students' scores from a multicultural perspective (Skolverket, 2004, 2005, 2009a, 2009b, 2009d, 2013). Despite a gradual increase in students' academic achievement since 1998, the following figures show that the distribution in performance among pupils has increased and there is still a strong correlation between socioeconomic background and how students succeed in schools. Students from a migrant background, as a group, have lower grades compared with ethnic Swedes and are overrepresented in the group that is not eligible to apply for higher education.

It is doubtful, however, whether the relationship between low achievement and the percentage of pupils from a migrant background in schools presents a true picture of the problem (Gunter, 2006). The composition of the immigrant students can vary at different times; the school's finances affect what resources the school can offer; and language-teaching arrangements can affect student performance. An immigrant background is important if the student has recently arrived in Sweden when grades are assessed—the student who arrives in Sweden at the age of 12 will have had very few years of experience, in either the Swedish school system or the Swedish language, when assessed in year 9.

Thus, it is not the migrant background itself that contributes to more students in this group leaving school with incomplete grades. Socioeconomic factors largely affect the students' school achievement, and taking this into account removes the differences in the ratings results between ethnic Swedish pupils and those with an immigrant background (Skolverket, 2004, 2005, 2009b). Students whose parents have a low education level generally have lower grades than those with highly educated parents. This tendency becomes particularly evident at the school level when increased residential segregation is implemented, which in turn might have an impact on the family's integration into Swedish society. Also, there are examples of successful schools in very challenging circumstances due to their inner structure and work culture. Thus, an explanation for school results should also be related to the school's inner work, not only to surrounding circumstances (Gu & Johansson, 2012). The opportunity for parents to choose a school has contributed to increased school segregation, which in turn has resulted in segregation when it comes to students' motivation for learning, since highly motivated students tend to use the option to choose a particular school. When students with special needs are gathered in schools and classrooms, there is a risk that they will influence each other negatively and that teachers have low expectations of their opportunities for learning and development (Bouakaz, 2007; Skolverket, 2009d, 2013).

Furthermore, regarding gender, girls earn higher average grades than boys, except in physical education, and the gap is continuing to increase. One explanation for the rating differences may be that for boys, masculine identity is important and this can be illustrated by performing well in physical education (Hedin, 2004; Skolverket, 2009d; SOU, 2009[2]). Meanwhile, it may be seen as "girlish" for boys to study and earn high scores on the other, more academic tests.

The above statistics illustrate Swedish school performance trends and show how the student's background is one significant variable. The remainder of this chapter illustrates school leaders' experiences within diverse school settings, how intercultural leadership could prevent variation in school performances, and what efforts are made in this area through national-level regulations and in-service training for principals.

## DIVERSITY AND SCHOOL LEADERSHIP

The following quotes exemplify how school leaders perceive what they have to deal with in an ethnically diverse school, where increased immigration from outside Europe has sharply raised the multicultural issue (Norberg, 2009, p. 4):

> I have to map out my school from a cultural perspective; I have to examine how we treat our pupils; How do we prepare a parental meeting and how do we know the parents understand us?; I have to elucidate the school's values and their concrete signification

Ethnic and religious diversity, and the increasing percentage of students with traditions and languages originating from outside Sweden, have combined to challenge a traditional presumption of homogeneity in Swedish society and have evoked the need for educational changes. Nonetheless, there is a lack of studies of educational leadership in ethnic multicultural schools in Sweden. Findings by Bunar (2009) provide an overview of some of the problems and opportunities in this field.

School leaders in Bunar's (2009) study[3] do not consider students' multicultural composition as problematic per se; they see housing segregation, unemployment, low education, and exclusion of many immigrant families as important factors that affect the school's inner workings. In segregated school districts, there is a sense of vulnerability among school leaders when parents have the option to move their children to schools with a better reputation and more ethnic Swedish students. Bad reputations and bias toward ethnic multiculturalism contribute to departure from the local school, based on the idea that the more Swedish students, the better. The simultaneous never-ending stream of new students with different backgrounds and special needs into a multicultural school leads to difficulties for the principal in planning for staff recruitment, school improvement strategies, and spending, which negatively influences the school's capacity for change (Bunar). There is a sort of "resigned logic" among school leaders, who on the one hand are convinced of their school's excellence and believe that the students who change schools will surely not receive a better situation in their new schools, while on the other hand the school leaders have difficulty in keeping up with the competition due to prejudice and negative perceptions of schools in multicultural districts, no matter what improvements are made.

The school leaders, in Bunar's (2009) study, believe that their schools meet the demands due to competent teachers, without ignoring the problems that exist both within the school and in the school district. Still, they find themselves caught up in an array of migration and integration policies, the structure of housing, labor market conditions, "individuals' aspirations, the different groups' demands for cultural recognition and the society's symbolic hierarchies" (p. 110), and an image presented by the media, politicians, and other citizens who present the school and the district in negative terms. In the midst of these heavy demands stands the school leader with a mission to create an inclusive school. Such leaders express a feeling that they have reached the "tipping point" when it comes to students with immigrant backgrounds, saying, "Now enough is enough," meaning they should offer a high-quality education but also be able to face the competition and not prevent students from leaving the school because of the high proportion of migrant students. Bunar raises the critical question of what percentage of immigrant students is enough, and in relation to what? The school leader who does not count the percentage of pupils with a migration background and instead works from the current reality has, according to Bunar, encountered an important barrier in handling the school's conditions. Also, Lahdenperä (2008) finds that school staff do not understand how the student body has changed in recent years, which has caused serious problems in adapting staff work to new conditions. She found a nostalgic longing for the days of a student body that teachers recognized, and a "the sooner the better" attitude regarding a return to such conditions (p. 76).

Several of the principals in Bunar's study were not quite clear about the school's role in inclusivity regarding what and how the school could work to promote inclusion.

In practice, inclusion usually meant internal strategies that focused on language issues (i.e., teachers were trained in teaching Swedish as a second language as well as the language's linguistic dimension, with the aim of promoting students' language development in Swedish and integrating their mother tongues into the curricula). However, the principals also highlighted another strategy that they regarded as successful: increased and improved interaction with parents. In addition to information about students' school performance, including their difficulties and opportunities as well as the school's inner workings, Bunar (2009) argues that enhanced and open cooperation with parents has an impact on students as well as the local community. A school to be proud of is an important symbol that spills over to the entire district. By inviting parents to participate in genuine collaboration, parents can be encouraged to take a greater responsibility for their children's education, which in turn has a democratic value. Moreover, the school then has the potential to strengthen the parents with both parenting advice and providing important community information they have difficulty getting from anywhere else. This assertion is supported by international research showing that good and respectful relations with students' guardians are important for students' learning (Day & Leithwood, 2007; Leithwood, Harris, & Hopkins, 2008; Pashiardis, Savvides, Lytra, & Angelidou, 2011). However, Bunar is dubious that the aforementioned strategies are enough to promote students' learning. The reinforced learning strategies must be used in collaboration among schools and provide students and parents with what they want: more Swedes. This is not to reject their school's activities but to increase the school's symbolic capital and strengthen their credibility.

The principal has ultimate responsibility for how learning is organized and has individual values, knowledge, and experiences that coincide with school leadership task significance. Decisions can be carefully designed based on cultural, pedagogical, and didactic skills or influenced by bias, subjective feelings, and beliefs. Disagreements may occur regarding which professional qualifications the school staff need, how a class is designed based on students' needs, how schedules that support learning are designed, which types of training teachers need, and what characterizes a professional approach toward students and guardians. A pedagogy that supports diversity and prevents the reproduction of stereotypes of "the Other" (i.e., one who is different from members of the majority culture, challenging traditional and stereotypical notions of what is "good" and "right"), as well as gender stereotypes, is encouraged by school leaders who believe that diversity is an important issue and who have knowledge of, and dedication to, the subject, while school leaders who regard acknowledgment of diversity and gender equity as irrelevant to student learning and development pay such pedagogy less or no attention.

## LEADERSHIP FOR DIVERSITY

Lahdenperä (2006, 2008) advocates an intercultural perspective based on democratic values such as equality and respect for all humans and their different needs and life values. This perspective focuses on challenging an ethnocentric attitude wherein the majority's values and experiences take precedence and on recognizing diversity in all its forms: gender identity, social origin, disability, creed, religion, sexual orientation, and ethnicity. In this way, diversity becomes a central part of education.

Through an intercultural education, individual values are challenged and reviewed in relation to the professional mandate and the various implications and conflicting perspectives that exist in the organization. A difficulty arises when the majority of the school's teachers and leaders represent the Swedish majority culture from an ethnic and class perspective. Curricula, policy documents, timetables, textbooks, teaching aids, rules, staff recruitment, in-service training, and other elements of a school then build on and reinforce the mainstream culture's assumptions of learning and socialization. The school leader must therefore "walk the diversity walk" and welcome different perspectives and voices into the organization (Grobler, Moloi, Loock, Bisschoff, & Mestry, 2006). If diversity is not recognized and welcomed into the rooms in which negotiations and decision making take place, established hierarchies and normative assumptions of learning will remain (Gunter, 2006; Lahdenperä, 2006). Recognition implies not only using diversity as a basis for learning, but also "using its structures, cultures and systems to think beyond its structures, cultures and systems" (Leo & Barton, 2006, p. 178). Or, as Lahdenperä (2008) suggests, "to actively lead the multicultural school development requires both an understanding beyond the ethnocentrism and some 'multicultural' maturity in the staff group" (p. 22).

A significant manifestation of how different value systems, beliefs, and perceptions create different dilemmas for school leaders and educators is how honor-related problems are interpreted and handled in schools (Darvishour, Lahdenperä, & Lorentz, 2010). Above all, girls are subjected to more control and restrictions in their daily lives at or outside school compared with boys, who in turn also undergo restrictions (Alizadeh, Hylander, Kocturk, & Törnkvist, 2010). These problems must be handled carefully to avoid a situation in which xenophobic actors are able to argue for restrictive migration policies. The recognition of the problem must be discussed in a way that does not create or strengthen an us-versus-them attitude with careless generalizations about immigrants and their traditions. Rather, these dilemmas should be understood as illustrating how various core values can collide in schools and therefore should be discussed seriously. The life conditions for those who live in honor cultures must be recognized to ensure that these students have access to the same legal protections as other young men and women. In schools, the principals have the utmost responsibility for ensuring this protection with support from governing documents. A significant question is whether the school's organization and culture contribute to marginalization of families with immigrant backgrounds, which in turn might lead to a repudiation of the school's values and assignments by these families in order to protect traditions.

If a homogeneous group of school leaders and educators define problems and solutions and make assessments of performance, there is a risk that some questions will never be asked. The organization must therefore invite various perspectives and voices to challenge ingrained ways of thinking (Arvastson & Ehn, 2007; Grobler et al., 2006). In addition to service programs in intercultural education, a recruitment of teachers from different social classes and ethnicities, with disabilities and different sexual orientations, might be of importance in reflecting and representing the student body more accurately. Representing a variety of experience and knowledge in teacher teams can avoid a monocultural education that positions Swedish, white, heterosexual, and middle class as the norm. The underpinning idea of how teaching teams are composed and how the representatives of various working groups are appointed is therefore important to how pedagogical issues are addressed. A multicultural representation might increase the opportunities to meet students with an understanding of their social, cultural, and individual differences.

Given the statistics above, and the challenges school leaders are facing in their mission to support equity in teaching and education in a school saturated by democratic values, how is principal training in Sweden linked to this assignment?

## PRINCIPAL TRAINING IN SWEDEN

Principal leadership has been a frequent topic of attention in the Swedish school development arena for at least 4 decades. Leadership training is often described as a key solution to educational shortcomings and is expected to provide a legitimate basis for new leadership approaches and new forms for governing and regulating schools in a late modern society. Hence, this part of the chapter focuses on the design and experiences of leadership training in relation to equity and social justice, with a concentration on the background of the new National School Leadership Training Program for principals that was launched in late 2009.

In 1986, the Swedish parliament decided on a broader integrated program of school principal training, with the state and municipalities assuming responsibility for different parts of the training. The municipalities were tasked with providing a recruitment training program and an introductory training program; the state was tasked with providing a National Principals Training Program; and universities were tasked with providing continuing school leader training and master programs. The purpose of this entire initiative was to give principals a thorough understanding of the national goals of the school and equip them with leadership skills that would stimulate the development of school activities.

The third program mentioned above—the National Principals Training Program did function very well, in part because the state, through the National Agency for Schools, assumed responsibility for organizing the principals' training and was given sufficient resources to run the program at selected universities. The fourth program, which provided academic master-level courses, has also been delivered at different universities. Unfortunately, these courses have not been able to attract a large number of principals for continued school leader education (Johansson, 2001).

In 2007, a new program was outlined in a committee report, *Clearer Leadership in Schools and Preschools—A Proposal for a New Training Program for Principals* (Ds 2007:34, 2007[4]). The committee identified the following issues from reflecting on the previous initiative:

- Legal aspects of managing and leading schools have not been paid enough attention.
- Issues about how the national goals can be followed up and evaluated as a basis for school improvement have not been prioritized enough.

- The differences among the various universities delivering the initiative are too great.
- The capacity is too small—principals must wait too long before entering the programs in the initiative.

On behalf of the ministry of education, the National Agency for Education commissioned six universities in 2009 to run the National Principals Training Program. This primarily residential program runs for over 3 years, over 36 meeting days, and is open to principals, preschool principals, and deputy principals who are already in service. Principals appointed after March 2010 must complete the program within 4 years. All participants are expected to use 20% of their time studying. The course itself is free of charge, but the participants' organizations pay residential, travel, and literature expenses.

New cohorts enter the program twice annually. By May 2013, about 5,700 principals and deputy principals had enrolled, and of these, about 1,900 had finished the program. This represents approximately 60% of all 8,000 principals and deputy principals in Sweden.

The intentions of the new National Principals Training Program are described by the National Agency for Education (Skolverket, 2009c):

Principals need to understand both their own role and that of the school, share the fundamental values governing how the school works, and be able to transform these values into concrete actions.

The National School Leadership Training Program aims to provide support for head teachers in carrying out their functions. The training program covers three areas of knowledge:

- Legislation on schools and the role of exercising the functions of an authority
- Management by goals and objectives
- School leadership

These areas of knowledge are crucial for the practical implementation of school leadership. They are closely linked to each other, and head teachers must be able to manage them simultaneously, since they form parts of a complex interacting system.

The topic of *legislation on schools and the role of exercising the functions of an authority* covers the provisions laid down in laws and ordinances, with emphasis on how a school's assignment is formulated in the national goals. The knowledge area of *management by objectives and results* covers measures for promoting quality that is required for the school to achieve the national goals for education. The knowledge area of *school leadership* covers how the work should be managed based on the national tasks of the head teacher and the principals set out in the steering system for bringing about development in line with greater attainment of goals.

The above knowledge goals are formulated in relation to each of these areas, but in this context, it is more important that goals are also formulated in relation to the following.

## Skills and Abilities

On completion of the training, the head teacher shall demonstrate the ability to:

- Apply knowledge of applicable legislation in the school district, as well as make assessments
- Communicate and apply knowledge of existing legislation in the school district
- Explain the goals of the school, make them clear, and transform them into concrete actions
- Communicate the national goals
- Use different tools and methods to follow up and evaluate results of the school
- Compile, analyze, and interpret the school's results
- Manage and delegate work to other teaching staff to maximize the learning and development of pupils
- Motivate, initiate, and manage the school's development processes in a strategic way in order to encourage the interest of school personnel in learning and development
- Manage and resolve conflicts
- Communicate future plans and visions
- Communicate goals and results to pupils in the school, to personnel, and to parents
- Apply the principle of the equal value of all people

## Assessment Ability and Approaches

On completion of the training, the head teacher shall demonstrate the ability to:

- Make assessments in the area of school legislation with respect to the legal security of pupils and relevant scientific, societal, and ethical aspects
- Exhibit good leadership abilities for integrating the school's daily work with pupils' results and development of quality in the school
- Evaluate and communicate the school's results as a basis for further development
- Provide explicit focus on the national assignment of the school
- Provide a democratic model to pupils and personnel by creating an open, communicative climate
- Clearly emphasize the importance of cooperation
- Involve the participation of pupils and parents in the work of the school
- Give appropriate prominence to the values laid down in the school's steering documents

To introduce *skills and abilities* as well as *assessment ability and approaches* as clear goals of the program is a challenge for the educators in the principal training centers at universities, as it requires a strong message from the political level that the principal's function and role will be evaluated in relation to performance with the schoolchildren.

In Sweden, it is becoming increasingly obvious how education is negotiated and conditioned in and among three dimensions: politics/profession, national intentions/

local conditions, and public education/private education. The governing of schools has drifted from government toward governance, meaning that more interactive processes are being introduced with a new focus on performance measures. These radical changes of the educational scene call for another approach to train principals (Johansson & Svedberg, 2013).

## CONCLUSION

We conclude by mentioning three examples of special training for principals that will prepare them to handle ethical matters better, all financed by the National Agency for Education. Our first example dates back about 10 years, when the principal training centers at universities were asked to plan and conduct courses in relation to the basic democratic values in the curriculum. These courses were given over a period of 4 years, with the purpose of integrating this subject focus into the regular principal training programs. The second example of special training courses is principal development in relation to how different value systems, beliefs, and perceptions can create different dilemmas for school leaders and educators concerning how honor-related problems are interpreted and handled in schools. Our third example relates to an old phenomenon that has changed in character: During the last 50 years, Sweden has always had immigrant children in its schools, but the number has increased substantially in recent years, and school administrations and the government have also identified a new and growing group of young immigrants who still are schoolchildren and are coming without their parents, mostly as refugees. Again, the principal centers are asked to provide education that is appropriate for this new situation.

The goals for the principal training program and the last three examples of additional in-service programs all build on the administrative and political belief that informed and effective school leadership is part of the solution for the different challenges to our democratic system. While the goals and guidelines in the principal training program do not explicitly emphasize the multicultural school context and its challenges, against this background we can argue that there is a strong awareness in Swedish society to link school actions to the pedagogical ideas formulated after the Second World War. Again, as citizens in a democratic society, we must help our students to develop open and critical minds that resist undemocratic ideas. Democratic states have no use for selfish masses of people; therefore, the democratic school's primary task is to develop free people for which cooperation is a need and creates happiness.

## NOTES

1. The Swedish curricula for the school system are regarded as documents that contain educational goals and guidelines for preschool, preschool class, compulsory school, leisure time center, and upper secondary school.
2. SOU is an abbreviation for Swedish Government Official Report (Statens offentliga utredning).
3. Bunar's (2009) findings come from a study in two school districts with socioeconomic and ethnic diversity. This chapter presents some of his findings from interviews with 14 school leaders of interest.
4. Ds is an abbreviation for Ministry publications series (Departementsserien).

# REFERENCES

Alizadeh, V., Hylander, I., Kocturk, T., & Törnkvist, L. (2010). Counselling young immigrant women worried about problems related to the protection of 'family honour'—from the perspective of midwives and counsellors at youth health clinics. *Scandinavian Journal of Caring Sciences, 24*, 32–40.

Arvastson, G., & Ehn, B. (Eds.). (2007). *Kulturnavigering i skolan.* [Cultural navigation within school.] Malmö: Gleerups.

Bouakaz, L. (2007). *Parental involvement in school. What hinders and what promotes parental involvement in an urban school.* Malmö: Malmö University.

Bunar, N. (2001). *Skolan mitt i förorten—fyra studier om skola, segregation, integration och multikulturalism.* [Urban schools—four studies on schooling, segregation, integration and multiculturalism.] Stockholm: Brutus Östlings Bokförlag Symposion.

Bunar, N. (2009). *När marknaden kom till förorten—valfrihet, konkurrens och symboliskt kapital i mångkulturella områdens skolor.* [When the market arrived to the surburb—freedom of choice, competition and symbolic capital in multicultural schools.] Lund: Studentlitteratur.

Darvishour, M., Lahdenperä, P., & Lorentz, H. (2010). *Hedersrelaterad problematik i skolan—en kunskaps— och forskningsöversikt.* [Honor related problems in school—a research overview]. Stockholm: Fritzes.

Day, C., & Leithwood, K. (Eds.). (2007). *Successful principal leadership in times of change. An international perspective.* Dordrecht, Netherlands: Springer.

Dewey, J. (1966). *Democracy and education. An introduction to the philosophy.* New York: Free Press. (Original work published 1916)

Ds2007:34. (2007). *Tydligare ledarskap i skolan och förskolan—förslag till en ny rektorsutbildning.* [Department series 2007:34. A more explicit leadership in school and preschool—suggestions for a new principal training program.] Stockholm: Utbildningsdepartementet.

Folkskolekommittén. (1914). *Folkundervisningskommitténs betänkande IV angående folkskolan.* [Public school committee report 4 regarding compulsory school.] Stockholm: Norstedt & Söner.

Grobler, B. R., Moloi, K. C., Loock, C. F., Bisschoff, T. C., & Mestry, R. J. (2006). Creating a school environment for the effective management of cultural diversity. *Educational Management, Administration & Leadership, 34*(4), 449–472.

Gruber, S. (2007). *Skolan gör skillnad. Etnicitet och institutionell praktik.* [School makes difference. Ethnicity and institutional practice.] Linköping: Linköpings Universitet.

Gu, Q., & Johansson, O. (2012). Sustaining school performance: School contexts matter. *International Journal of Leadership in Education: Theory and Practice, 1*, 1–26 iFirst Article.

Gunter, H. M. (2006). Educational leadership and the challenge of diversity. *Educational Management Administration & Leadership, 34*(2), 257–268.

Hedin, M. (2004). Lilla genushäftet. Om genus och skolans jämställdhetsmål. [Gender and the school's goals for equality.] Högskolan i Kalmar: Institutionen för Hälso- och Beteendevetenskap.

Johansson, O. (2001). School leadership training in Sweden—perspectives for tomorrow. *Journal of In-Service Education, 27*(2), 185–202.

Johansson, O., Davis, A., & Geijer, L. (2007). A perspective on diversity, equality and equity in Swedish schools. *School Leadership and Management, 27*(1), 21–33.

Johansson, O., & Svedberg, L. (2013). *Att leda mot skolans mål.* [Lead toward the school's goals.] Malmö: Gleerups.

Lahdenperä, P. (2006). Interkulturellt lärande i ledarskap—hur rektorer kan bli interkulturella ledare. [Leadership and intercultural learning—how principals can become intercultural leaders.] In H. Lorentz & B. Bergstedt (Eds.), *Interkulturella perspektiv. Pedagogik i mångkulturella lärandemiljöer.* [Intercultural perspectives. Education in multicultural schools.] (pp. 87–107). Lund: Studentlitteratur.

Lahdenperä, P. (2008). *Interkulturellt ledarskap—förändring i mångfald.* [Intercultural leadership—change in diversity.] Lund: Studentlitteratur.

Leithwood, K., Harris, A., & Hopkins, D. (2008). Seven strong claims about successful school leadership. *School Leadership and Management, 28*(1), 27–42.

Leo, E., & Barton, L. (2006). Inclusion, diversity and leadership: Perspectives, possibilities and contradictions. *Educational Management Administration & Leadership, 34*(2), 167–180.

Lumby, J., & Heystek, J. (2011). Leadership identity in ethnically diverse schools in South Africa and England. *Educational Management Administration & Leadership, 40*(1), 4–20.

Nilsson, I. (1997). Swedish school policy in transition. In I. Nilsson & L. Lundahl (Eds.), *Teacher, curriculum and policy. Critical perspectives in educational research*. Umeå: Umeå Universitet.

Norberg, K. (2009). School leadership for diversity and inclusion—meeting the multicultural challenge in Sweden. *Values and Ethics in Educational Administration, 8*(1), 1–8.

Pashiardis, P., Savvides, V., Lytra, E., & Angelidou, K. (2011). Successful school leadership in rural contexts: The case of Cyprus. *Educational Management Administration & Leadership, 39*(5), 536–553.

Runfors, A. (2007). Lära sig sin plats. Hur "svenskar" och "icke-svenskar" skapas i skolan. [How "Swedes" and "non-Swedes" are constructed in schools.] In G. Arvastson & B. Ehn (Eds.), *Kulturnavigering i skolan.* [Cultural navigation within school.] (pp. 76–84). Malmö: Gleerups.

Sawyer, L., & Kamali, M.(2006). Skolböcker och kognitiv andrafiering. Utbildningens dilemma. [Text books and cognitive construction of "the other." The dilemma of education.] Stockholm: Fritzes.

Skollagen 2010:800 [Education Act 2010:800]. (2010). Stockholm: Utbildningsdepartementet.

Skolverket [National Agency of Education.]. (2004). *Sociala skillnader är avgörande för elevers resultat.* [Social class differences are crucial for students' result.] Retrieved from www.skolverket.se/sb/d/205/a/357

Skolverket. (2005). *Elever med utländsk bakgrund.* [Students with immigrant background.] Stockholm: Fritzes.

Skolverket. (2009a). *En beskrivning av slutbetygen i grundskolan 2008.* [A description of final grades in compulsory school.] Retrieved from www.skolverket.se/publikationer

Skolverket. (2009b). *Föräldrars utbildning påverkar elevers slutbetyg allt mer.* [Parents' education affects students' final grades increasingly.] Retrieved from www.skolverket.se/sb/d/2573/a/18069

Skolverket. (2009c). *Goals of the National School Leadership Training Programme.* Stockholm: Fritzes.

Skolverket. (2009d). *Vad påverkar resultaten i svensk grundskola? En kunskapsöversikt om betydelsen av olika faktorer.* [What affects the results in Swedish compulsory school? A review of the importance of various factors.] Stockholm: Fritzes.

Skolverket. (2010). *Curriculum for the preschool.* Retrieved from www.skolverket.se/om-skolverket/in_english/publications

Skolverket. (2011a). *Curriculum for the compulsory school preschool class and leisure time centre.* Retrieved from www.skolverket.se/om-skolverket/in_english/publications

Skolverket. (2011b). *Curriculum for the upper secondary school.* Retrieved from www.skolverket.se/om-skolverket/in_english/publications

Skolverket. (2013). *Skolverkets lägesbedömning 2013.* [The National Agency of Education's assessment of the situation in schools.] Stockholm: Fritzes.

SOU 2009:64. Flickor och pojkar i skolan—hur jämställt är det? Delbetänkande av DEJA-delegationen för jämställdhet i skolan. [Swedish Government Official Report 2009:64. Girls and boys in school—what about equality? Report from the delegation for equality in school.]

# 27

## CONCLUSION

### *If It Isn't Ethical, It Isn't Leadership*

#### CHRISTOPHER M. BRANSON

A succinct overview of this handbook would propose that it has described the why, how, and what of ethical educational leadership. Part I, "Issues and Perspectives," provides a diverse array of reasons as to *why* educational leadership must, at its very core, be ethical. Here, various international authors provide compelling reasons for accepting that educational leadership must embrace and address professionalism, multiculturalism, sociopolitical awareness, sustainability, social justice, empathy, contextual awareness, and caring. Moreover, these chapters illustrate how the sincere attention to these essential outcomes is inextricably linked to the actions of an ethical leader. Then, Part II, "Developing Ethical Educational Leadership," provides a very coherent and comprehensive explanation and description of a holistic program for the development of ethical leadership. In other words, this section describes *how* ethical educational leadership can be deconstructed and thereby developed by a willing and committed leader. While Nancy Tuana's chapter (see also Tuana, 2007) describes this holistic program in great detail, the subsequent chapters sequentially describe and extend each of the components of this program. Part III provides "Examples From the Field" so that the reader can more easily appreciate *what* an application of ethical educational leadership might look like in reality. By means of descriptions from both qualitative and quantitative research, as well as personal and situational narratives, this section provides a very rich description of the beneficial potentialities and possibilities to be gained through a dedicated commitment to ethical educational leadership.

While it can be argued that this handbook provides a comprehensive, coherent, and compelling case for the preparation and adoption of ethical practices by educational leaders, maybe it is only so for those leaders already committed to wanting to be ethical. Perhaps a more cogent argument for ethical educational leadership is still required—especially for those leaders who still cling to the view that just because they are leaders, they have the sole right to choose how they will lead. In the opinion of such individuals, leadership is the activity performed by a person called a leader. It is time that such a superficial, erroneous, and potentially harmful opinion is challenged. Hence, the question that needs to be closely examined is, "What is leadership?" However, given that in the past 100 years the nature and practice of leadership have been among the most researched and written about fields, is not the question of "What is leadership?" absurd or illogical? Certainly this would be the case if we were confident in the knowledge that all of our leadership research, and all of our leadership theorizing that has resulted from this research, is able to provide an accurate, definitive, and coherent description of what constitutes 'leadership.'

This concluding chapter will challenge the accuracy and comprehensiveness of our existing understanding of leadership. It will show how our research and theorizing has concentrated far too heavily on describing the actions of the leader to the detriment of considering what it means to be leading. Simply, such a lopsided perspective promotes the assumption that whatever a person does, in a designated leader's role, is automatically considered to be leadership behavior of some kind. This assumption must be confronted. We must reverse this perspective so that it becomes: Whoever engages in authentically leading others is a leader. To this end, insights from fields beyond leadership will be used to more accurately describe the nature of authentic leading in a contemporary society. Then, this knowledge will be used to more comprehensively illustrate the nature and practice of leadership.

As a result, this chapter will advance the argument that a leader's actions are not leadership behaviors if they are not ethical. Simply put, a leader who is not deliberately and sincerely striving to be ethical is only simulating, if not fabricating, leadership. The actions of a leader who is not deliberately and sincerely striving to be ethical is management at best, or something far more sinister and deceptive at worst, but it is not leadership. Thus, leading ethically is not optional for anyone wishing to be acknowledged as a leader and to gain the social, financial, and resource benefits from being a leader. In answer to the question "What is leadership?" this chapter will argue that it is fundamentally about being ethical. Only ethical leadership is actual leadership.

## SOME CONCERNS WITH OUR CURRENT LEADERSHIP THEORY

While the claim that only ethical leadership is actual leadership may initially seem improbable and disconcerting, its foundational precept that leadership and ethics are inextricably entwined should come as no surprise. Indeed, the genesis of this precept first came to prominence in James Macgregor Burns's seminal and Pulitzer Prize–winning text, *Leadership*, first published in 1978 and reprinted completely unaltered in 2010. Here, in his second chapter, Burns argues that "leaders must accommodate followers' wants and needs without sacrificing basic principles" (p. 77) so that they can "help transform followers' needs into positive hopes and aspirations" (p. 117). It is not the organization's values or needs or, indeed, the leader's values and needs that Burns is talking about here but rather the values and needs of each person in the group being led.

In this way, Burns is describing how leadership needs to be ethical, whereby it is critically important for leaders to be working in the best interests, for the needs, of those they are leading. Burns describes how important it is for leaders to not only take the time to learn and appreciate the foremost values, needs, motives, and beliefs of those they are leading but, most importantly, that these are embedded in some significant way into their leadership vision and action. For instance, Burns suggests that

> most importantly by far, leaders address themselves to followers' wants, needs, and other motivations, as well as their own, and thus they serve as an *independent force in changing the makeup of the followers' motive base through gratifying their motives.*
>
> (p. 20, italics in original text)

Finally, in a very powerful manner, Burns warns that the

> test of leadership in all its forms is the realization of purpose measured by popular needs manifested in social and human values. Leaders can operate off the "skin" of public opinion—off surges of trending opinion, the applause of idolizing spectators, the bubbling up of passing social and political fads, trumped up foreign crises, and exaggerated dangers to national security—without recognizing the persisting, widespread, and intensive needs and goals that motivate followers and are there for the evoking by leaders.
>
> (p. 251)

The challenge for leaders, according to Burns, is not to be moved and influenced by the superficial, generalist, presumed values and needs of the followers but those that are at the very core of their thoughts, feelings, and actions. Simply stated, this is a view of leadership whereby the needs of those being led, and not the leader's or the organization's interests, is the primary departure point for the leader's actions. Is this not the cornerstone of ethical leadership, as it has been described in this handbook?

Unfortunately, the gravity of Burns's belief in the inseparability of ethics and leadership was overshadowed by his radical division of leadership into what he described as being either transactional or transformational in nature. Arguably, we have been so consumed by the innovative nature of the transactional/transformational dichotomy established by Burns that we have overlooked the very principles upon which he devised the distinctions between these two approaches to leadership. Moreover, this oversight has resulted in a serious imbalance, if not restriction, in how we have understood leadership as a consequence. This is not to suggest that the concepts of transactional and transformational leadership are not of paramount importance. Rather, it is to argue that in themselves, they are deficient for providing a holistic insight into the nature of leadership.

It is not surprising then that despite the initial positive impact of Burns's somewhat radical leadership theory, the limited application of its foundational principles created a continuing perceived need to add clarity to its ultimate purpose. Essentially, Burns's leadership theory promoted the view that the primary purpose of leadership should be to transform those being led. As described by Burns, "the transforming leader taps the needs and raises the aspirations and helps shape the values—and hence mobilizes the potential—of followers" (p. 455). But without a commitment to leadership that "is moral but not moralistic" (ibid.), uncertainty soon arose as to how leaders are able to transform their followers.

Consequently, a plethora of subsequent theories, metaphors, or images were promulgated in an attempt to delineate the means by which leaders should strive toward transforming their followers. A list of such theories, metaphors, images, or approaches would include, but not be limited to, servant leadership (Greenleaf, 1977; Sendjaya & Sarros, 2002), moral leadership (Greenfield, 2004; Sergiovanni, 1992), stewardship (Block, 1993), collaborative leadership (Sofield & Kuhn, 1995), transcendent leadership (Aldon, 2004; Larkin, 1995), intelligent leadership (Kibby, Härtel, & Hsu 2004; Mant, 1997), values-led leadership (Day, 2000), distributed leadership (Gronn, 2000; Harris, 2003), primal leadership (Goleman, Boyatzis, & McKee, 2002), and authentic leadership (Begley, 2003, 2006; Duignan, 2006; Terry, 1993).

Unfortunately, although seeking to overcome the uncertainty about how leaders are able to transform their followers, these approaches to leadership conveyed a tacit acceptance of the primacy of the leader over that of leading. Through the provision of a particular theoretical interpretation with an accompanying practical means, these approaches inadvertently promoted the view that it is the prerogative of leaders to choose the form by which they will lead. It is their choice as to how they will transform their followers. This issue was formally acknowledged by Leithwood, Jantzi, and Steinbach's (1999) meta-analysis of six different approaches to school leadership: instructional, transformational, moral, participative, managerial, and contingent. Based on their analysis, these authors claim that in each of these approaches to school leadership, it is the school leader who makes the fundamental choices. Regardless of the approach used by the school leader, how the approach is interpreted and applied resides with the leader. In other words, the role of the leader takes primacy and the nature of the leading is consequential. Even though this meta-analysis was published prior to the establishment of more recent approaches to leadership, such as distributed leadership, I would claim that the same criticism could be applied. Who determines what is to be distributed? Who determines how responsibilities are to be distributed? Who judges the perceived level of benefit that is being gained through distributed leadership? As Duignan (2012) laments,

> too frequently in education systems and schools, we get the rhetoric of distributed leadership but, essentially, it is simply a variation on an old theme, new wine in old bottles. It is still the principal who 'giveth' and who can just as easily 'taketh away.'
>
> (p. 130)

## A NEW PERSPECTIVE OF LEADERSHIP

A more recent examination of our current leadership theorizing by Haslam, Reicher, and Platow (2011) complements but extends this position. These authors posit (p. 94) that our leadership theory has placed far too much emphasis on the "stereotypicality" of leadership at the expense of its more important "prototypicality" feature. According to these authors, a leader's stereotypicality refers to how closely his or her behaviors mirror those described in the leadership literature. This is about how typically, in terms of traits and actions, leaders represent a particular approach to leadership as described in literature—whereas, leaders' prototypicality refers to the degree to which they are an integral part of the group they are leading. This is about how well leaders represent the group they are leading. Stereotypicality places the focus on the leader but prototypicality places the focus on leading. Moreover, in the minds of Haslam and his colleagues, knowing what is meant by the term " lead-ʾing" is the most important part of leadership. In other words, if we wish to gain a more accurate and comprehensive understanding of leadership, then it is vital that we explore its prototypicality in order to better appreciate what is essential knowledge for leading others.

## EXPLORING THE PROTOTYPICALITY OF LEADERSHIP

Haslam et al. (2011) suggest that prototypicality of leadership is about how well the leader is "one of us" (p. 82). This is about the leader displaying all the attitudes, traits, dispositions, and behaviors that clearly show that s/he is a "fellow in-group member" (ibid.). The use of the phrase "in-group" is meant to highlight that the leader must be *in* the group and not apart from it. Also, the use of "in-group" removes the inherent but tacit dichotomous power and authority linguistic messages automatically conveyed in other common classifications, such as 'followers,' which reinforces the primacy of the leader at the expense of leading.

Specifically, then, what does the prototypicality of leadership entail? Returning to the research of Haslam and colleagues (2011), a protypical leader needs to display two essential characteristics. First, the leader must act in a way that is readily accepted by the in-group as being compliant with its expectations. Second, and even more importantly, the leader must represent all that the in-group stands for. This means that the leader has to have a thorough understanding of the in-group and be able to naturally and genuinely model its ways and means. It is here that insights from other disciplines can make an invaluable contribution toward knowing what these expectations require of the leader, especially in today's organizations.

## LEADERSHIP AS A POSITION

From the field of psychology and, in particular, "positioning theory" (see, for example, Harré & Moghaddam, 2003; Harré & Slocum, 2003; Harré & Van Langenhove, 1999), we are made aware that people do not wish to live scripted lives. People are not robots and so resist being externally programmed. People do not like being told how to live their lives but rather they gain meaning, purpose, and fulfillment by creating their own ways of living their lives. Even on a stage, where the reality is supposedly completely scripted, ad-libbing amongst the actors is a regular occurrence. However, in life this creative process is not an isolated and individualistic process. The way in which a person chooses to live his or her life is co-created or negotiated with those others whose lives interacts with their own.

Hence it is argued that people occupy positions, and not roles, in their lives. Performing a position is co-created or negotiated action, whereas performing a role is predefined or scripted action. Positions are socially formed behaviors around patterns of mutually accepted beliefs, needs, and expectations (Harré & Van Langenhove, 1999). Roles, on the other hand, are prescribed behaviors that are more explicit, precise, individualistic, and practical in formation and nature and often reflect an ideal rather than the reality. To successfully fulfill a particular position, the person needs to first negotiate with those they have to work with in order to build a mutually understood and accepted view of the inherent responsibilities of that position and how it is best to be performed (Harré & Moghaddam, 2003). Clearly, the more interdependent the people are, the more persuasive are the performance negotiating processes for each individual.

Returning to our discussion of leadership, it must be accepted that there is no leadership without interdependence regardless of one's theoretical perspective. In order to lead, a person needs followers who will follow. Thus, positioning theory has relevance for exploring leadership. Simply stated, positioning theory suggests that we should see leadership as a position and not as a role. It questions the inherent assumptions implied in the frequent use of phrases like "the leader's role" and our overestimation of the influence of formally documented role statements or descriptions for guiding or predicting leadership behaviors. Leadership, as a position, acknowledges that it evolves through largely unconscious and unacknowledged negotiations within the in-group in response to the perceived outcomes generated by interactions with these others, and is not formed through the comprehensive implementation of a role description often supplied by others in higher authority but outside of the in-group.

Thus, as described by Harré and Slocum (2003), the leader is enacting a position rather than performing a role. This does not imply that the others impose their image of leadership upon the leader. As a negotiated position, the ultimate image of leadership is co-constructed through the realization and consolidation of mutually accepted values, beliefs, and expectations. Understanding leadership as a position in this way helps focus attention on Burns's (1978, 2010) belief in the dynamic relational aspects of leadership being the true source of the leader's power to bring about change in people and organizations. Davies and Harré (1999) posit that the concept of position readily embraces the dynamic aspects of externally structured and imposed human engagements "in contrast to the way in which the use of 'role' serves to highlight static, formal and ritualistic aspects" (p. 32). Seeing the responsibility of leadership as a role gives the impression that the nature of its enactment, and how others experience it, is the prerogative of role holders and their line managers. In this sense, a role has the potential to be imposed. However, the reality of imposed roles rarely equates with the ideal, as the natural tendency of those being led is to use whatever subtle or explicit means they can to cause leaders to modify their style of leadership to that of a more acceptable form. In this way, there are no true leadership roles, only negotiated positions. Moreover, seeing leadership as a position places the focus on leading, whereas seeing it as a role places the focus on the leader. Dedication to a role promotes stereotypical leadership, while the enactment of a position promotes prototypical leadership.

Hence, positioning theory underscores the importance of considering the prototypicality of leadership. Moreover, it highlights that the elemental nature of leadership is contextual and not generic, because it first emerges out of the sincere interpersonal engagement of the leader with the members of the in-group (Postmes & Branscombe, 2010; Reicher, Spears, & Haslam, 2010). If people sincerely wish to become leaders, then they must see their selves as being, first and foremost, full and active members of the groups they wish to lead. Secondly, they must see the leading of these groups as being a very important part of their lives. Thirdly, they must accept that how they choose to lead is significantly influenced by the needs and expectations of those they are leading.

## THE POWER OF TRUTH

However, acknowledging the reality that leaders occupy a negotiated position rather than a definitive role may raise a concern about how this impacts on their power and authority, which is often simply understood as their capacity to get others to achieve desired outcomes. Inherent within this concern is the assumption that such power and authority is simultaneously conveyed to the leader on appointment—that this power and authority resides solely within the leader. However, literature across the fields of sociology, social psychology, and cultural studies now consistently describe the limitations of this view of a leader's power. For example, these disciplines propose that no matter the political rhetoric, unexpected external forces including global economics, international affairs, natural disasters, cross-cultural conflicts, and socioreligious upheavals are regularly altering the actions of national governments. Ultimately, such forces upon governments influence the quality, flow, and direction of each person's life. Today, people's work lives can be as easily affected by international events as by national, local, or company interests, and their line managers or company executives seem at a loss to prevent this from happening. According to research (Bauman, 1999; Browning, Halcli, & Webster, 2000; Castells, 2000a; Lewis, 2008), this awareness of the limitations of leadership to create personal security for workers has led to a "consumer" mentality in the workplace. This means that people now see themselves as workplace consumers rather than workplace producers. Rather than concentrating on what they are producing, workers are more concerned about creating the best workplace environment that is within their means to create. As explained by Castells (2000c), the person as a workplace consumer embraces the view that

> the growing inability of the state to control capital flows and ensure social security diminishes its relevance for the average citizen. . . . The voiding of the social contract between capital, labor, and the state, sends everybody home to fight for their individual interests, counting exclusively on their own forces.
>
> (p. 309)

What this concept of the worker as a workplace consumer means is that workers will do what they choose to do because that is what is important to them. Rather than valuing themselves based upon beliefs about how line managers might be judging what they are producing, workers now value their own ability to create a feeling of increased personal security, certainty, predictability, and control. In a seemingly unpredictable and ever-changing world, in which there is a perceived lack of any credible or acceptable external authority that can offer ongoing security, workers concentrate on creating their own stable working environments to the extent that they are able to.

Leaders who fully understand and are authentically aligned with their group accept the truth of this reality—they accept the limitations of their control over the workplace environment caused by external forces beyond their influence. In this workplace context, it is far more important for the leader to be seen as being *of and for* the group, that is, being prototypical, than being an ideal leader according to some prescribed, stereotypical format to maintain the pretense and façade of having total control. However, accepting this reality raises questions having to do with the leader's perceived power and authority.

The previously accepted sources of a leader's power—position, coercion, and knowledge—now have limited credibility and traction. Consequently, in more recent times, a leader's power has been described in terms of it being a form of influence or persuasion (Etzioni, 1978; Hersey, Blanchard, & Johnson, 2001; McClelland & Burnham, 1976; Rogers, 1973). For Kreisberg (1992), leaders' capacity to influence or persuade reflects a "power with" their workers. A leader's power, emanating from *power with* others, accepts that people must be free of domination to develop to their full capacity and that it is only within the context of relationships with others that the leader can realize authentic power. *Power over* is exploitative power, while *power with* is integrative power. *Power with* in leadership argues that the greater the leader is able to develop each individual, the more able both will become, the more effective will be the leadership, and the less need there is for the leader to feel that he or she has to limit or restrict others.

What this brief discussion highlights is that our theory has largely moved away from viewing leaders' power being understood in terms of their capacity to impose their will upon the behavior of another to where it is now seen as their ability, through interpersonal influence, to cause their group members to attain specific personal, as well as organizational, goals. In other words, leaders' power is an outcome of the interpersonal relationships they have developed with their followers. This is an understanding aligned with that of Verderber and Verderber (1992) as they describe the leader's influence in terms of a social power and argue that this "social power is a potential for changing attitudes, beliefs, and behaviors of others" (p. 280). Similarly, Cangemi (1992) believes that successful leaders move and influence people through their power toward greater accomplishments for themselves and their organizations by asserting that "power is the individual's capacity to move others, to entice others, to persuade and encourage others to attain specific goals or to engage in specific behavior; it is the capacity to influence and motivate others" (p. 499).

To this end, the philosophy of Michel Foucault provides a deeper appreciation of the manner by which a leader can develop this social or relational power with others (Abel, 2005; Bălan, 2010; Braynion, 2004; Lynch, 1998; Widder, 2004). According to Foucault (Lynch), power is the outcome generated by the interactions between people who occupy unequal positions in an organization. Moreover, Foucault argues that our incomplete understanding, and therefore erroneous interpretation, of a leader's power has been influenced by our attention to the visible macro level of interaction.

These are only the easily observable outcomes or end products of the power relationship and not the actual source of the power. This might include actions that appear as rewards or punishments, or the declaration of decisions, or the implementation of new policies, all of which may present as seats of power and authority but actually are the end result of many other less conspicuous, politically rich interpersonal interactions. For Foucault, a leader's power is constituted within the many particular instances at the micro level of interaction within the relationship the leader has with group members. For example, group members' personal estimation of their leader's level of power over them will be constituted from judgments about their leader's influence over such things as when they can and can't speak during formal and informal meetings, if they can or can't contribute to meeting agendas, if or when they get affirmed or acknowledged, and whether or not the work they do is publicly appreciated and resourced. Hence, Lynch argues that a leader's power should not be discussed as some discrete entity but, rather, as "power relations," where power not only is produced in the dispersions of the social interaction of the group but also produces some of these dispersions. How group members interpret the level of the leaders' power will influence the degree to which the members interact with leaders and engage with their vision and expectations. The closer the relationship group members have with their leader, the more power they assign to their leader and the more engaged they become in the group's activities.

Furthermore, this interplay between power and the group's social interactions with their leader supports the view that any resistance formed by a group member does not oppose the leader as such but, rather, reflects the nature and quality of their interactions, whether in formal or informal situations. More specifically, this judgment about the nature and quality of their interaction with their leader is said to be founded upon the development of a personal perspective or regime of knowledge as to whether or not the leader tends to place unnecessary restrictions or limitations on their thoughts and behaviors (Widder, 2004). This means that resistance does not automatically exist in opposition to power but has its genesis in any perceived differences in perspective or knowledge between the leader and a group member in relation to that particular person's organizational role and how it is to be performed.

Thus, the interplay between power and resistance circles around what Foucault described as the "will to truth": each person's desire to know what is considered to be the truth, at that point in time and in that circumstance, with respect to their capacity to complete their organizational responsibilities in the way that they wish to do so. Hence, where such knowledge is willingly and openly shared between leaders and those they lead, the will to truth is uniformly understood, and the experience of a power differential is minimized (Abel, 2005). This outcome results in the presence of very limited resistance amongst those being led and, thereby, a heightened sense of power in the leadership. On the other hand, where there are tangible differences in perceptions of the truth about the current organizational reality, the experience of a power differential is maximized. Here, resistance is maximized and the sense of leadership power is minimized. Thus, the power relations within a group can be explored through all of the contextual factors impacting upon how each individual interprets the truth about the current organizational reality. In other words, the power of the leader, which is conversely indicated by the level of resistance felt within those being led, is dependent upon how open, transparent, and inclusive the leader is in how the organizational reality is described, understood, addressed, and communicated.

What this means is that the power of leaders emanates from their willingness and capacity to generate organizational knowledge and truth in an open, honest, and inclusive manner (Braynion, 2004; Handy, 1993; Kreisberg, 1992; Shackleton, 1995). It is through their interpretation of the myriad of discourses experienced within their organization that group members construct a belief about the degree of comprehensiveness and completeness of the shared knowledge created by the leader and, thereby, the level of truth within the organization. It is upon this personal judgment that the leader's degree of power is assessed and the measure of required resistance is determined.

## ACHIEVING QUALITY CONTROL

What, then, in regard to the need for quality control? How does the previously described view of "power through truth" impact on the leader's capacity to achieve quality control? In recent decades, the achievement of quality control has become a key function of organizational leadership regardless of the context. Such quality control measures are often manifested in explicit accountability processes in the form of performance reviews. Simply described, the performance review in some way analyzes the quality of the person's worker performance and measures it against a prescribed desired level, thereby determining whether or not the person's performance is meeting the expected level of quality. Also, given that such performance reviews are anticipated, it is assumed that this process encourages people to take more responsibility for their workplace performance in order that they will readily maintain this expected level of quality. However, there is a third, but unacknowledged, aspect of such measures of quality control—trustworthiness. The hidden message inherent within this process is that the people cannot be trusted to achieve the expected work quality on their own accord. The following sections will describe a different approach to achieving quality control by examining the issues of workplace accountability, responsibility, and trustworthiness in a more contemporary, socially informed way.

### Accountability

In order to create their own stable working environments to the level possible, consumer workers must fully embrace their personal strengths and limitations and seek to create workplace networks, which will allow them to fully utilize their strengths and talents while enabling others to cover their perceived weaknesses and limitations (Allan, 2011; Castells, 2000a, 2000b, 2004). Such workplace networks are created so that "we avoid those interactions where we will spend more [benefit] than we gain, and we will pursue those interactions where we have a good chance of increasing our level of [benefit]. We also tend to avoid those interactions where our lack of [capacity] will be apparent" (Allan, p. 317). As a result, it is argued that in today's workplace, people now tend to want to separate themselves into symbolic or status groups or networks around other workers who are seen as having mutually beneficial knowledge, skills, and expertise. It is through a tangible sense of solidarity with others, whose knowledge, skills, and expertise are seen to be mutually complementary and beneficial that the consumer worker gains the deepest sense of workplace purpose and security.

Within a workplace culture influenced by networks formed through selective solidarity, people highly value self-determination (Bauman, 1992). Selective solidarity creates a working environment in which individuals have to strive to do their very best in order to be seen as worthy enough for others to join with them. Hence, if left unimpeded, or even encouraged, this natural process of selective solidarity will cause each person to strive to do his or her best and to keep improving. Quality work emerges out of the individual's need to be seen as worthy by his or her coworkers. When consumer workers are trusted to attend to their workplace responsibilities to the best of their ability and are given the freedom and resources to achieve their desires, then all they need is a clear understanding of meaning to become accountable. "When highly motivated and eminently capable people share a common vision," says Hamel (2007, p. 111), "they do not need to be micromanaged."

Real accountability comes from self-reference and self-organization, which automatically flow from a clear understanding of meaning. Compliance comes from regulations and policies; accountability comes from a conscious commitment to what is meaningful. Accountability results from workers willingly committing to something meaningful to them and being free to adjust their own behavior according to what this meaning mandates. This is the natural, and powerful, process of self-determination. Workers monitor themselves according to the fundamental meaning, the identity, the principles, and values of the workplace. As explained by Wheatley (2006), this self-monitoring conjures up different possibilities for how people can be together because it explains how life creates order without control, and stable identities that are open to change. It describes systems of relationships where both interdependence and individual autonomy are necessary conditions because it illustrates how, if individuals together reference a shared identity, a coherent system can emerge. Ultimately, it illuminates the necessity for meaning making in a world that often feels meaningless.

When workers are helped by their leader to create clarity of meaning around their workplace performance, they discover a common interest or passion, they organize themselves and figure out how to make things happen. Such self-organizing evokes creativity and produces results, creating a strong, adaptive workplace. Moreover, it creates an environment that uses the natural need for self-determination in each worker to achieve the most efficient and effective workplace rather than relying upon the data generated by externally imposed, intrusive, limited, and essentially technical-rational processes to appear to achieve this outcome. In this way, accountability is readily personalized and internalized by each worker, thereby rendering any externally imposed form of accountability unnecessary and meaningless.

### Responsibility

Also, it is essential to recognize that at the very heart of the workplace selective solidarity process is personal moral integrity (Allan, 2011; Barkus & James, 2010; Bauman, 1992, 1993, 1999; Browning et al., 2000; Castells, 2000a). As Browning and colleagues posit, for the consumer worker seeking selective solidarity in today's workplace, "being *for* the other before one can be *with* the other is the first reality of the self" (p. 229). Selective solidarity is founded upon personal moral integrity because others must be able to trust you, and you must be able to trust them. People must get what they see; they must be able to judge others accurately. People will not fully commit to working with others whom they believe they cannot trust. This means that consumer workers must be truly authentic in all that they do and say. This is about showing to others who you really are and not trying to be anything other than the best that you can be so that you can readily act with consistency and predictability and others can accurately assess the worthiness of associating with you in order to gain some preconceived mutual benefit.

Simply stated, the consumer worker must take full personal responsibility for his or her own moral reputation. As described by Bauman (1992), the surprising outcome of becoming a consumer worker "is that it restores to [individuals] the fullness of moral choice and responsibility while simultaneously depriving them of the comfort of the universal guidance that modern self-confidence once promised. Ethical tasks of individuals grow while the socially produced resources to fulfill them shrink. Moral responsibility comes together with the loneliness of moral choice" (p. xxii). Workers have to accept total responsibility for their own organizational performance.

### Trustworthiness

It is in this way that being trustworthy becomes a non-negotiable character trait for workers. They have to be trustworthy, but at the same time they will not commit themselves fully to working with anyone else who is not similarly trustworthy. Hence, perhaps more so than for any other person, the leader must be trustworthy; the leader must have personal moral integrity. The critical importance of the leader being able to achieve moral integrity is echoed in the words of Storr (2004), who writes that "leadership is a complex, paradoxical and moral relationship between people, which can cause harm between some groups, accompanied by benefits to others . . . and is based on trust, obligation, commitment, emotion and a shared vision of the good—no one can be a leader without willing followers" (p. 415).

Although it is a concern for trust that resonates most with people's expectations of leaders, Haslam and colleagues (2011) claim that any estimation of a leader's level of trust is founded upon a judgment of the leader's fairness. According to these authors, the perceived level of the leader's fairness is the foundation upon which trust in that person's leadership is built. More simply stated, "group members expect fairness to underpin their leader's behaviours" (p. 112). Furthermore, the group members judge the leader's level of fairness in two ways. First, the group members judge the way in which their leader rewards themselves compared with the rest of the group. Essentially, leaders are deemed to be fair if they do not treat themselves better than any other group members. "Anything that distinguishes leaders from followers and that suggests that they are removed from the group is liable to limit and compromise their leadership" (p. 113). The second way in which group members judge the level of a leader's fairness is in how the leader treats different members, or different subsections, of the group. Here it is important that leaders do not treat some members (or subgroups) better than others. If they do, their standing as leaders will be diminished. Through a commitment to fairness, not only do leaders gain the willing engagement of their group members in the desired activities of the group, but also it helps to hold the group together. It is the perceived level of leadership fairness that is the basis for the group's cohesiveness, which is a highly desired outcome for most leaders.

But what is "fairness"? In promoting fairness as the foundation of trust, and thereby effective leadership, Haslam et al. (2011) argue that "it is too simple to conclude that leaders will always thrive by displaying intragroup fairness. . . . It is more accurate to say that leaders thrive by acting in line with group values and norms" (p. 132). They go on to say that the leader's fairness is formed from a capacity to promote the group's interests in the terms specified by the group's own norms and values. "It is when the group members can see that their leader is attuned to their sense of what counts in the world, where they have evidence that he or she is committed to advancing 'our cause,' where the leader can be seen to act for the group rather than for [himself/ herself], that they will embrace the leader's vision as their own" (p. 134). This is commensurate with the view proposed by Burns (1978, 2010), who argued that first and foremost, the influential authority and power of leadership is essentially relational because it is made manifest through the quality of the interpersonal relationship that the leader is able to instigate with each of his or her followers. Then, secondly, Burns adds that the starting point for a leader wishing to move his or her followers beyond where they are currently at is to come to truly know and appreciate the followers' core values, beliefs, and needs. Then the leader can begin to refine the meaning of these core values, beliefs, and needs and, thereby, inspire the followers to transcend their current position through largely self-determined actions.

But, what Haslam and colleagues (2011) describe as being fair, and what Burns argues as being the essence of good leadership, is identical to that of being an ethical leader. An ethical leader strives to create a school culture based upon the shared values of trust, openness, transparency, honesty, integrity, collegiality, and fairness (Branson, 2009, 2011). This is a culture in which all in-group members have a sense of safety and security because they each feel that they can rely on each other, but especially their leader, in order to achieve their best. Working together becomes more meaningful and purposeful because each person's strengths are recognized and utilized for the benefit of all. Moreover, individual weaknesses are accepted as either opportunities for future personal growth or opportunities for networking with the strengths of another in-group member in order to overcome it. Thus, being ethical is about being fair, which is the most fundamental element of prototypical leadership and, more likely, leadership in general.

## CONCLUSION

A sincere commitment to being ethical has to be at the very heart of leadership. In times of unpredictability and insecurity, people want their leaders to bring some form of certainty and order to their world. While leaders cannot offer control over the seemingly chaotic external world that is affecting their organization, they can fill the need of their followers for stability by having moral integrity and building a workplace culture based upon fairness and ethical behavior. An ethical leader enables a person to feel that there is order in her relationship with the leader and with others. It provides a kind of internal security even when there is no external security. People want to know and trust their leaders, rather than be dazzled by their charisma. They want their leaders to have moral integrity and to be ethical.

Hence, having a commitment to being ethical is now an inviolable expectation of leaders. It is expected that our leaders will act morally whereby they will not produce harm but rather will show the virtues of doing good, of honoring others, of taking positive stands, and of behaving in ways that clearly show that their own self-interests are not the driving motivation behind their actions (Branson, 2009, 2010). People want to know that their leaders are there for them; that the leader is one of them (Haslam et al., 2011). People will only fully support leaders who act fairly and justly and promote good rather than harm. They want their leaders to be accountable to them in what they do just as they accept that they will be accountable to their leaders and others in what they do. In the words of Normore and Doscher (2007), people will only respect leaders who are ethical whereby they are guided by "an internal moral compass that directs them to take on tasks, assume styles, and behave commensurate with organisational beliefs regarding right and wrong, virtue and vice, and social responsibility" (p. 2). It is not surprising, therefore, for Wheatley (2006) to urge: "We need leaders . . . we do not need bosses. We need leaders to help us develop a clear identity that lights the dark moments of confusion. We need leaders to support us as we learn how to live by our values. We need leaders to understand that we are best controlled by concepts that invite participation, not policies and procedures that curtail our contribution" (p. 131).

While it is true that the past 100 years has witnessed an intense amount of research focused on leadership and has enabled us to better understand its nature and perform it far more effectively, there is still much that we need to know and acknowledge. Despite this lengthy period of study, the core task remains incomplete; there is still much more to learn about leadership. Arguably, to date, the research and subsequent theorizing has placed the spotlight on the stereotypical elements of leadership, and this has brought immense benefit. Simply stated, it has moved us from an overdependency on transactional leadership techniques to a more informed and balanced perspective in which various transformational techniques are at play. As a result, all have benefited—followers, organizations, leaders, and society at large. Yet, this level of understanding, knowledge, and skill remains deficient. More needs to be known about the prototypicality of leadership and, by inference, ethical leadership. If, as has been argued in this concluding chapter, a more informed theoretical perspective of "what is leadership" unequivocally mandates a weaving together of our existing, largely stereotypical, leadership knowledge with new and deeper knowledge associated with the prototypicality dimension of leadership, then ethicalness is the cornerstone of leadership. Indeed, if it isn't ethical, it isn't leadership. Leadership for the future depends on the universal application of ethical leadership, which has been informed through specific research and modified through practice. This handbook provides an important step toward achieving this outcome.

## REFERENCES

Abel, C. F. (2005). Beyond the mainstream: Foucault, power and organization theory. *International Journal of Orgnaization Theory and Behavior, 8*(4), 495–519.

Aldon, L. J. (2004). *Transcendent leadership and the evolution of consciousness.* London: Lightning Source UK.

Allan, K. (2011). *The social lens: An invitation to social and sociological theory* (2nd ed.). Thousand Oaks, CA: Sage.

Bălan, S. (2010). M. Foucault's view on power relations. *Cagito—Multidisciplinary Research Journal, 2*(2), 55–61.

Bartkus, V. O., & James, J. H. (2010). Introduction: The yet undiscovered value of social capital. In V. O. Bartkus & J. H. Davis (Eds.), *Social capital: Reaching out, reaching in* (pp. 1–14). Cheltenham, UK: Edward Elgar Publishing.

Bauman, Z. (1992). *Intimations of postmodernity.* London: Routledge.

Bauman, Z. (1993). *Postmodern ethics.* Oxford: Blackwell.

Bauman, Z. (1999). *In search of politics.* Cambridge: Polity Press.

Begley, P. T. (2003). In Pursuit of authentic school leadership practices. In P. T. Begley & O. Johansson (Eds.), *The ethical dimensions of school leadership* (pp. 1–12). Dordrecht, Netherlands: Kluwer Academic Publishers.

Begley, P. T. (2006). Self-knowledge, capacity and sensitivity: Prerequisities to authentic leadership by school principles. *Journal of Educational Administration, 44*(6), 570–589.

Block, P. (1993). *Stewardship: Choosing service over self interest.* San Francisco: Berrett-Koehler Publishers.

Branson, C. M. (2009). *Leadership for an age of wisdom.* Dordrecht, Netherlands: Springer Educational Publishing.

Branson, C. M. (2010). *Leading educational change wisely.* Rotterdam, Netherlands: Sense Publishers.

Branson, C. M. (2011, September 25–27). *Exploring the relational side of authentic leadership.* Paper presented at the 16th annual Values and Leadership Conference, Victoria, BC, Canada.

Braynion, P. (2004). Power and leadership. *Journal of Health organization and Management, 18*(6), 447–463.

Browning, G., Halcli, A., & Webster, F. (2000). *Understanding contemporary society: Theories of the present.* London: Sage.

Burns, J. M. (1978). *Leadership.* New York: HarperCollins.

Burns, J. M. (2010). *Leadership.* New York: HarperCollins.

Cangemi, J. (1992). Some observations of successful leaders, and their use of power and authority. *Education, 112,* 499–505.

Castells, M. (2000a). *The rise of the network society* (2nd ed.). Oxford: Blackwell Publishers.

Castells, M. (2000b). *End of millennium* (2nd ed.). Oxford: Blackwell.

Castells, M. (2000c). *The power of identity.* Oxford: Blackwell.

Castells, M. (2004). Informationalism, networks, and the network society: A theoretical blueprint. In M. Castells (Ed.), *The network society: A cross-cultural perspective* (pp. 3–45). Cheltenham, UK: Edward Elgar Publishing.

Davies, B., & Harré, R. (1999). Positioning and personhood. In R. Harré & L. Van Langenhove (Eds.), *Positioning theory* (pp. 32–52). Oxford: Blackwell Publishers.

Day, C. (2000). Beyond transformational leadership. *Educational Leadership, 57*(7), 56–59.

Duignan, P. (2006). *Educational leadership: Key challenges and ethical tensions.* New York: Cambridge University Press.

Duignan, P. (2012). *Educational leadership: Together creating ethical learning environments* (2nd ed.). Melbourne: Cambridge University Press.

Etzioni, A. (1978). Comparative analysis of complex organizations. In D. Hampton, C. Summer, & R. Weber (Eds.), *Organizational behavior and the practice of management.* Glenview, IL: Scott Foresman & Co.

Goleman, D., Boyatzis, R., & McKee, A. (2002). *Primal leadership: Learning to lead with emotional intelligence.* Boston: Harvard Business School Press.

Greenfield, W. D. (2004). Moral leadership in schools. *Journal of Educational Administration, 42*(2), 174–196.

Greenleaf, R. K. (1977). *Servant leadership.* New York: Paulist Press.

Gronn, P. (2000). Distributed properties: A new architecture for leadership. *Educational Management and Administration, 28*(3), 317–338.

Hamel, G. (2007). *The future of management.* Boston: Harvard Business School Press.

Handy, C. (1993). *Understanding organizations* (4th ed.). Harmondsworth, UK: Penguin.

Harré, R., & Moghaddam, F. (2003). Introduction: The self and others in traditional psychology and in positioning theory. In R. Harré & F. Moghaddam (Eds.), *The self and others: Positioning individuals and groups in personal, political, and cultural contexts* (pp. 1–11). Westport, CT: Praeger Publishers.

Harré, R., & Slocum, N. (2003). N. Disputes as complex social events: On the uses of positioning theory. In R. Harré & F. Moghaddam (Eds.), *The self and others: Positioning individuals and groups in personal, political, and cultural contexts* (pp. 123–136). Westport, CT: Praeger Publishers.

Harré, R., & Van Langenhove, L. (1999). The dynamics of social episodes. In R. Harré & L. Van Langenhove (Eds.), *Positioning theory* (pp. 1–13). Oxford: Blackwell Publishers.

Harris, A. (2003). Teacher leadership as distributed leadership: Heresy, fantasy or possibility? *School Leadership & Management, 23*(3), 313–324.

Haslam, S. A., Reicher, S. D., & Platow, M. J. (2011). *The new psychology of leadership: Identity, influence and power.* New York: Psychology Press.

Hersey, P., Blanchard, K. H., & Johnson, D. E. (2001). *Management of organisational behaviour* (8th ed.). London: Prentice-Hall.

Kibby, L., Härtel, C., & Hsu, A. (2004, June). Noetic leadership: Leadership skills that manage the existential dilemma. Presentation at the 2004 Gallup Leadership Institute Summit, University of Nebraska-Lincoln.

Kreisberg, S. (1992). *Transforming power: Domination, empowerment and education.* Albany: SUNY Press.

Larkin, D. (1995). *Beyond self to compassionate healer: Transcendent leadership.* (Doctoral dissertation). Seattle University, WA.

Leithwood, K., Jantzi, D., & Steinbach, R. (1999). *Changing leadership for changing times.* Buckingham, UK: Open University Press.

Lewis, J. (2008). *Cultural studies: The basics.* London: Sage.

Lynch, R. A. (1998). Is power all there is? Michel Foucault and the "omnipresence of power relations." *Philosophy Today, 42*(1), 65–70.

Mant, A. (1997). *Intelligent leadership.* Sydney: Allen & Unwin.

McClelland, D. C., & Burnham, D. H. (1976, March–April). Power is the motivator. *Harvard Business Review,* 100–110.

Normore, A. H., & Doscher, S. P. (2007). Using media as the basis for a social issues approach to promoting moral literacy in university teaching. *Journal of Educational Administration, 45*(4), 427–450.

Postmes, T., & Branscombe, N. R. (Eds.). (2010). *Rediscovering social identity: Core sources.* New York: Psychology Press.

Reicher, S. D., Spears, R., & Haslam, S. A. (2010). The social identity approach in social psychology. In M. S. Wetherell & C. T. Mohanty (Eds.), *The Sage identities handbook* (pp. 45–62). London: Sage.

Rogers, M. F. (1973). Instrumental and infra-resources: The bases of power. *American Journal of Sociology, 79*(1), 1418–1425.

Sendjaya, S., & Sarros, J. C. (2002). Servant leadership: Its origins, development and application in organizations. *Journal of Leadership and Organizational Studies, 9*(2), 57–64.

Sergiovanni, T. (1992). *Moral leadership: Getting to the heart of school improvement.* San Francisco: Jossey-Bass.

Shackleton, V. (1995). *Business leadership.* London: Routledge.

Sofield, L., & Kuhn, D. H. (1995). *The collaborative leader: Listening to the wisdom of God's people.* Notre Dame, IN: Ave Maria Press.

Storr, L. (2004). Leading with integrity: A qualitative research study. *Journal of Health Organisation and Management, 18*(6), 415–434.

Terry, R. W. (1993). *Authentic leadership: Courage in action.* San Francisco: Jossey-Bass.

Tuana, N. (2007). Conceptualizing moral literacy. *Journal of Educational Administration, 45*(4), 364–378.

Verderber, R. F., & Verderber, K. S. (1992). *Inter-act using interpersonal communication skills.* Belmont, CA: Wadsworth.

Wheatley, M. J. (2006). *Leadership and the new science: Discovering order in a chaotic world* (3rd ed.). San Francisco: Berrett-Koehler Publishers.

Widder, N. (2004). Foucault and power revisited. *European Journal of Political Theory, 3*(4), 411–432.

# CONTRIBUTING AUTHORS

**Christopher M. Branson** PhD (Editor) is Professor of Educational Leadership in the Faculty of Education at the University of Waikato in Hamilton, New Zealand, as well as the Executive Director of the UCEA Center for the Study of Leadership and Ethics and the editor of the *Values and Ethics in Educational Administration* journal. His research interests include the nature and practice of leadership, ethical leadership, educational leadership, personal and organizational values, and organizational change. He is the author of two books, *Leadership for an Age of Wisdom* and *Leading Educational Change Wisely*.

**Steven Jay Gross** (Editor) is Professor of Educational Administration at Temple University and Founding Director of the New DEEL Community Network. His research interests include initiating and sustaining deep, democratic reform in schools, leadership mentoring, and turbulence theory. His books include: *Ethical Educational Leadership in Turbulent Times* (with Joan Shapiro) (2013, 2nd ed.), *Leadership Mentoring: Maintaining School Improvement in Turbulent Times* (2006), *Staying Centered: Curriculum Leadership in a Turbulent Era* (1998), and *Promises Kept: Sustaining School and District Leadership in a Turbulent Era* (2004). Gross has been Distinguished Visiting Research Scholar (Australian Catholic University) and is on the roster of the Fulbright Specialist Program.

**Mualla Aksu** PhD is Professor of Educational Sciences in the Faculty of Education, as well as the Head of Educational Administration and Supervision Program for the Graduate Institute of Educational Sciences at the University of Akdeniz in Antalya, Turkey. Her prior work experience includes twelve years in the primary schools as a teacher and six years in the Ministry of National Education as an educational expert. Her research interests include job stress, clinical supervision, peer coaching, strategic planning and total quality management, teacher leadership, ethical leadership, educational leadership and policies, novice teachers, and theory–practice relations.

**Michael Bezzina** PhD is the Director of Teaching and Learning at the Catholic Education Office, Archdiocese of Sydney, Australia. He is an Adjunct Professor at Australian Catholic University, and previously held the posts of Director of the Centre for Creative and Authentic Leadership and Head of School, Educational Leadership at that university. His research interests are centered on the capacity of moral purpose to impact on leadership and learning in schools. He has published in the fields of curriculum, religious education, and educational leadership.

**Mike Bottery** is Professor of Education, Policy, and Values and Director of Research for the Faculty of Education at the University of Hull in England. He is also a member of the National Council of the British Educational Leadership Management and Administration Society (BELMAS). His research interests center around the values and policies influencing leadership decisions, and he is currently writing a book on the effects that issues of sustainability will have upon school leadership.

**Charles Burford** PhD is an Associate Professor in educational leadership and the Director of the Centre for the Study of Creative and Authentic Leadership at The Australian Catholic University in Sydney, Australia. Over 35 years, his research, writing, and work in the development of programs for educational leaders have received international recognition. Dr. Burford's research interests include moral literacy, ethical leadership, and linkages between leadership and learning. He is a fellow of the Australian Council for Educational Leadership and was awarded the 2008 Willower Award for Excellence for his contribution to the study of values and ethics in educational leadership by the UCEA Center for the Study of Leadership and Ethics.

**John F. Covaleskie** is Associate Professor of Educational Studies in the department of Educational Leadership and Policy Studies at the University of Oklahoma and Professor Emeritus of the School of Education at Northern Michigan University. Research interests include moral formation, schools as public institutions, and the place for religious belief in public discourse. He has taught at all levels of public schools from kindergarten to advising doctoral students, and has been a principal and curriculum coordinator. He is the author of *Membership and Moral Formation: Shame as an Educational and Social Emotion* from Information Age Press.

**Neil Cranston** is Professor of Educational Leadership and Curriculum in the Faculty of Education, University of Tasmania, and Honorary Professor, The University of Queensland. He is a Life Member and Fellow of the Australian College of Educators, Fellow of the Australian Council for Educational Leaders and received the Nganakarrawa Award in 2009 for contributions to educational leadership. He has co-authored two books with Lisa Ehrich, *What Is This Thing Called Leadership? Prominent Australians Tell Their Stories* and *Australian School Leadership Today*.

**Lisa C. Ehrich** is an Associate Professor in the School of Cultural and Professional Learning, Faculty of Education, at Queensland University of Technology in Australia. Her substantive research interests include ethical leadership, mentoring for school leaders and professionals, and leadership as artistic practice. With Neil Cranston, she has published two books on leadership: *What Is This Thing Called Leadership? Prominent Australians Tell Their Stories* and *Australian School Leadership Today*.

**William C. Frick** is an Associate Professor in the Department of Educational Leadership and Policy Studies, Jeannine Rainbolt College of Education, University of Oklahoma. He holds a PhD in educational theory and policy from Pennsylvania State University. His prior work experience includes fourteen years in the public schools as a teacher, school counselor, principal, and director of curriculum and instruction. Dr. Frick's current research activity includes both theoretical and empirical work related to (1) ethics in educational administration; (2) linkages between school system reform and broader community revitalization efforts; and (3) cultural studies in education addressing the intersection of identity and schooling.

**Kathrine J. Gutierrez** is an Assistant Professor in the Department of Educational Leadership and Policy Studies, Jeannine Rainbolt College of Education, University of Oklahoma. She holds a PhD in educational leadership from Pennsylvania State University. Her research centers on issues germane to the field of educational leadership to include: instructional leadership, ethical and democratic leadership, curricular and instructional considerations for educational leadership preparation, administrative/organizational theory, and policy implications of legal school case decisions. Her recent research and scholarly activities investigate and discuss school leaders' perceptions of being "effective" leaders, "leaders of learning," and "authentic leaders."

**Qian Haiyan** is Assistant Professor of the Department of Education Policy and Leadership, Hong Kong Institute of Education. Her major research interest is school leadership and education change in the Chinese societies.

**Kjersti Lien Holte** received her PhD degree in Working Life Science at Karlstads University in Sweden in 2009. She now works as an Associate Professor at the Faculty for Teacher Education at Østfold University College in Norway. Dr. Holte's research concerns ethics, communication, professionalism, leadership, and social justice in education. She is a member of the European Network for Improving Research and Development in Educational Leadership and Management (ENIRDELM) and the Justice through Education (JustEd) program supported by the Nordic Centre of Excellence.

**Olof Johansson** is Professor of Political Science and Chair of the Centre for Principal Development at Umeå University in Sweden, and a member of the board of governors for the UCEA Centre for the Study of Leadership and Ethics. His research interests are school leadership, values and ethics in relation to school leadership, school governance, school effectiveness and improvement, and policymaking and democratic processes. Currently he is working on four large international research projects: the International Successful School Principalship Project; Structure, Culture, and Leadership; Prerequisites for Successful Schools; and the National Policy meets Local Implementation Structures and European Policy Network on School Leadership. He and his center are a partner of the International Superintendents Research Network (ISRN).

**Gamze Kasalak** is a PhD student in Educational Administration and Supervision Graduate Program, Faculty of Education, Department of Educational Sciences, at Akdeniz University in Turkey. Her research interests include organizational cynicism, ethics, and higher education policy.

**Megan Kimber** is a Senior Researcher in the School of Cultural and Professional Learning, Faculty of Education, at Queensland University of Technology in Australia. Her research traverses ethics, education policy and management, public sector reform, and democratic theory. With Neil Cranston and Lisa Ehrich, she has published several articles on the ethical dilemmas experienced by leaders.

**Sigurður Kristinsson** received his PhD in philosophy from Cornell University in 1996. He is Professor of Philosophy and former Dean of the School of Humanities and Social Sciences, University of Akureyri, Iceland. Most of his published research concerns ethics, moral psychology, and applied ethics. It includes work on the nature and value of individual autonomy as well as related concepts such as individuality and authenticity. It also includes work on informed consent, research ethics, professional codes of ethics, and the public role of universities.

**Lea Kuusilehto-Awale** is the Program Director of an international master's degree program of educational leadership and a PhD candidate at the University of Jyväskylä, Finland. Prior to her university career she had a long career in teaching, principalship (including an International Baccalaureate Diploma School), and principal training. She has also been a CEO in the NGO sector and a local politician. She lectures internationally on the reasons behind the success of Finnish basic education, and the ethos of equity and equality of the Finnish education system. Her research interests include administrative change, leading diversity, and responsible and caring leadership.

**Lyse Langlois** (PhD in Educational Administration and Policy Studies, Laval University, 1997) is a Full Professor at Laval University's Department of Industrial Relations, where she teaches human resources management. She has worked on the implementation of managerial ethics in a variety of organizations including school districts, health agencies, and municipal police. Her current research focuses on the institutionalization of ethics, moral and amoral leadership, and the impact ethical training programs have on organizational change initiatives. She recently published a book entitled *Anatomy of Ethical Leadership*. She is a member and leader at Laval University Institute of Applied Ethics.

**Claire Lapointe** (PhD in Educational Administration and Policy Studies, Laval University, 1995) is a Full Professor and Chair of the Department of Educational Administration and Foundations at Laval University, Canada. She is a member of the Centre de Recherche et d'Intervention sur la Réussite Scolaire, one of the most active international French-language research groups in the field. Her research interest for the cultural and ethical aspects of education stems from her 20-year-long experience as an educator and project manager in different parts of Canada as well as in Germany, New Zealand, French Polynesia, and Gabon.

**Pauline E. Leonard** is a Professor and Chair in the Department of Curriculum, Instruction, and Leadership in the College of Education at Louisiana Tech University. She holds a PhD in educational administration from the University of Toronto. Pauline has authored and co-authored numerous journal articles and book chapters on topics such as school culture, professional learning communities, moral literacy teaching competencies, and holistic development of educational leaders. She spent 16 years as a public school teacher in rural and remote regions of Atlantic Canada before transitioning into higher education in Canada and the United States.

**Rachel McNae** PhD is a senior lecturer of educational leadership and pre-service teacher education at the University of Waikato, Hamilton, New Zealand. Dr. McNae's research agenda is founded on a firm belief for social justice and utilizes strength-based approaches to assist school leaders to enhance their leadership practices. Generating research that spans the fields of women and leadership, student voice, youth leadership, and leadership curriculum development in schools and communities, she advocates for reshaping leadership learning in order to seek out and interrogate the relational aspects of leadership, so that these experiences are culturally responsive, relevant and meaningful. Dr. McNae was the recipient of the 2011 Emerald Publishing/European Foundation for Management Development (EFMD) Research Award for Leadership and Strategy and was also awarded the New Zealand Educational Administration and Leadership Society President's Research Award.

**Katarina Norberg** is an Associate Professor of Education at the Centre for Principal Development, Umeå University, Sweden. Her research interest is the ethical dimension of schooling linked to schools' democratic assignments with focus on issues concerning ethics and values in multicultural schools and school leadership for social justice. Dr. Norberg is also on the board of governors for the UCEA Centre for the Study of Leadership and Ethics and serves on the editorial board for the journal *Values and Ethics in Educational Administration*.

**Anthony H. Normore** (Tony) holds a PhD from the University of Toronto. He is currently professor of educational leadership in the Graduate Education Division, California State University Dominguez Hills in the Los Angeles area, where he also serves as Department Chair of Special Education in the Teacher Education Division. His research focuses on leadership development, preparation, and training in the context of ethics and social justice. His extensive outreach activity includes the facilitation of inmate learning at the Los Angeles County Sheriff's Department, where he works with law enforcement personnel in the Education-Based Incarceration Bureau. Dr. Normore has authored more than 100 scholarly publications and presented more than 150 conference papers.

**Ross Notman** is an Associate Professor in Education at the University of Otago in Dunedin, New Zealand, and director of the Centre for Educational Leadership and Administration at this university. He has worked extensively in principal appraisal and in principal support groups through activities such as coaching and group support networks. His major research interests focus on teacher and school principal development, particularly in the field of the personal dimensions of principalship. He is the New Zealand director for both the International Successful School Principalship Project and the International School Leadership Development Network Project. He is a member of the editorial board for the *Journal of Educational Leadership, Policy and Practice* and recipient of a Fulbright Travel Scholarship in 2011.

**Tammy Schilling** is an associate professor in the Department of Kinesiology at Louisiana Tech University. Her professional experience includes teaching and coaching in public schools. She worked in responsibility-based afterschool physical activity programs at University of North Carolina–Greensboro for 9 years before moving to Louisiana Tech. For the past 7 years, she has utilized adventure education and team building in leadership training for middle and high school participants in Louisiana GEAR UP summer programs. Her scholarly activities are focused on the use of physical activity as a powerful avenue for holistic development and youth leadership.

**Joan Poliner Shapiro** is a Professor of Educational Administration at Temple University, who has served as Associate Dean and as Chair of her department. Recently, she was elected President of Temple University's Faculty Senate. She holds a doctorate in Educational Administration from the University of Pennsylvania. She has received numerous awards, among them the Lindback Teaching Award, the Great Teacher's Award, and UCEA's Master Professor Award. She has published seven books, including *Ethical Leadership and Decision Making in Education*, co-authored with Jacqueline Stefkovich, in its third edition, and *Ethical Educational Leadership in Turbulent Times*, with Steven Jay Gross, in its second edition.

**Carolyn Shields** PhD is professor and dean of the College of Education at Wayne State University in Detroit, Michigan. She is past president of the Canadian Association for Studies in Educational Administration and a former Canadian representative to the Board of the Commonwealth Council for Educational Administration and Management. Her teaching is in the area of transformative leadership and ethics, deep democracy, equitable policy, social justice, and research methodology. Her research focuses on how educational leaders can create learning environments that are deeply democratic, socially just, inclusive of all students' lived experiences, and that prepare students for excellence and citizenship in our global society. These interests are reflected in her presentations and publications—over 100 articles and 9 books—the most recent of which is *Transformative Leadership in Education: Equitable Change in an Uncertain and Complex World*. She has received recognition for both her teaching and her career contributions to the field of educational leadership.

**Robert J. Starratt** has been a member of the faculties at the Graduate School of Education at Fordham University and the Lynch School of Education at Boston College, serving as department chair of Educational Leadership at both universities and participating in the redesign of their Masters and Doctoral programs in Educational Leadership. His scholarly publications have led to invitations to speak with educators in Asia, India, Australia, Europe, and Canada, as well as in the United States. Besides book chapters and essays in scholarly journals, he has published, with Thomas Sergiovanni, nine editions of a popular text in instructional supervision, *Supervision: A Redefinition*. His other publications include, *The Drama of Schooling, the Schooling of Drama; The Drama of Leadership; Building an Ethical School; Centering Educational Administration: Meaning, Community and Responsibility; Ethical Leadership; Refocusing School Leadership: Foregrounding Human Development Throughout the Work of the School*; and most recently, *Cultivating an Ethical school*. He has been awarded the Donald Willower Award for Lifetime Achievement in Educational Leadership, the UCEA Roald Campbell Award for Lifetime achievement in Educational Leadership, and the University of Illinois Alumni Award for Lifetime Achievement in Education.

**Jacqueline A. Stefkovich** is a Professor of Ethics at Pennsylvania State University, where she has served as Associate Dean and as Head of the Department of Education Policy Studies. She holds a doctoral degree in Administration, Planning, and Social Policy from Harvard University's Graduate School of Education and a J.D. from the University of Pennsylvania. She has published five books, including *Ethical Leadership and Decision Making in Education,* co-authored with Joan Shapiro, which is now in its third edition. The second edition of her latest book, *Best Interests of the Student,* is due for release early in 2014.

**Nancy Tuana** is the founding director of Penn State's Rock Ethics Institute and DuPont/Class of 1949 Professor of Philosophy and Women's Studies. The Rock Ethics Institute, under her direction, has as its central focus moral literacy at all levels of education and has been involved in integrating ethics education into technical classes in all fields including the sciences and education. The Institute has also taken the lead nationally and internationally in developing innovative and deeply interdisciplinary modes of engaging in socially relevant ethics research.

**Allan Walker** is Joseph Lau Chair Professor of International Educational Leadership and Dean of Faculty of Education and Human Development, Hong Kong Institute of Education.

# INDEX

Note: Page numbers in *italics* indicate figures or tables.